From Industrial Organization to Entrepreneurship

Erik E. Lehmann • Max Keilbach
Editors

From Industrial Organization to Entrepreneurship

A Tribute to David B. Audretsch

Editors
Erik E. Lehmann
Business and Economics
Augsburg University
Augsburg, Bayern, Germany

Max Keilbach
Wedgebrook Music Productions
Berlin, Germany

ISBN 978-3-030-25239-7   ISBN 978-3-030-25237-3   (eBook)
https://doi.org/10.1007/978-3-030-25237-3

© Springer Nature Switzerland AG 2019
This work is subject to copyright. All rights are reserved by the Publisher, whether the whole or part of the material is concerned, specifically the rights of translation, reprinting, reuse of illustrations, recitation, broadcasting, reproduction on microfilms or in any other physical way, and transmission or information storage and retrieval, electronic adaptation, computer software, or by similar or dissimilar methodology now known or hereafter developed.
The use of general descriptive names, registered names, trademarks, service marks, etc. in this publication does not imply, even in the absence of a specific statement, that such names are exempt from the relevant protective laws and regulations and therefore free for general use.
The publisher, the authors, and the editors are safe to assume that the advice and information in this book are believed to be true and accurate at the date of publication. Neither the publisher nor the authors or the editors give a warranty, express or implied, with respect to the material contained herein or for any errors or omissions that may have been made. The publisher remains neutral with regard to jurisdictional claims in published maps and institutional affiliations.

This Springer imprint is published by the registered company Springer Nature Switzerland AG
The registered company address is: Gewerbestrasse 11, 6330 Cham, Switzerland

Preface

A Festschrift to David B. Audretsch

The Festschrift may be an idea whose time has passed, but it is still a lovely idea. There is still room for the human touch in scientific writing.

Justine Cullinan

Dear David,

It's been a long journey that we've been travelling together until now. And when we issued the call for papers to attract contributors to this Festschrift, we realized that we're part of a much bigger Morgenland Ride and a lot of mates participate in this journey with us. We were overwhelmed about the number and excitement of reactions we received to our call for papers, and when reading through the contributions, we realized how big the community has grown around you and how large of a body of research has emerged. How did that happen? What's your trick?

1. We believe that the first ingredient is curiosity. We have rarely met someone who is so curious and open to new ideas. When people come into your office with questions and new ideas, you are never judging or negative or ignoring them with a "know-it-all" attitude. You would rather help put their ideas into perspective and therefore giving them (and the people that came with them) value. Very often, we saw people leaving the office with a smile and eagerness to work on their ideas.
2. You also have trust and belief. You have an unconditional trust in your mates which creates a strong base for letting ideas flow freely. We exchanged an uncountable number of crazy ideas. Maybe in the end, a few of them were just that—crazy ideas, but every idea is taken seriously by you and in the end, this creates that "anything is possible" spirit which can drive a field. But this holds vice versa: people can trust you in that you will never make them look silly or foolish. A very important ingredient to create a strong team.

3. Then there is your enthusiasm and energy. The energy that emerges from you is legendary. Where do you gain all of this energy from? This enthusiasm can be intoxicating and the energy that comes with it inspires the people around you. It simply makes anybody around you more energetic. Combine this with trust and belief and there is no better way to thrive a team.
4. Finally, there is your brilliant spirit that channels all this. Maybe it is rather a broad vision than a narrow research program. You carry at the same time a vision that is open enough to allow new ideas to unfold but focused enough to create an identifiable body of research. It is a knowledge or an intuition about what is scientifically sound which made your research field grow bigger and bigger. We also know that you can be mercilessly sharp in the details, in your arguments, and in the conclusions. That is of course the key to scientific advancement without which the other ingredients would be baseless and without cohesion.

These ingredients, and the way you put them together, make it a recipe for a magic potion.

We know that a scientist often wears several hats – friend, teacher, mentor, administrator, and researcher, among others. And while many prominent awards honor the research role, like the Schumpeter School Award from the University of Wuppertal, or the prestigious Global Award for Entrepreneurship Research by the Swedish Foundation for Small Business Research, a Festschrift volume uniquely recognizes the many facets of an outstanding and influential scientist, an exceptional scholar, a creator of a research field and a community, a mentor, and a friend. "The idea behind a Festschrift is to honor the teacher, mentor and friend, not only the researcher," says Justine Cullinan, the Managing Editor of the *Annals of the New York Academy of Sciences*, "a book of essays and papers contributed by the honoree's students and colleagues, where even family members and close friends contribute."[1]

And so, this Festschrift aims to provide a short snapshot to highlight all of your hats: starting in Part I with your family—Joanne and your kids—followed by close friends staying side-by-side with you in all phases of your life and career. An outstanding researcher is one that creates a research topic that stimulates the world of academia. Part II is dedicated to you David, as a true pioneer in the fields of small business and entrepreneurship research. However, a true scientist does not work in isolation, but brings in other scholars to collaborate with and push the limits of the field. The essays in Part III are dedicated to you as a creator of a community. While the first three parts mostly express the roots of your work, the future of your legacy, the wings, are laid down in Part IV.

---

[1] Cited in: Ricki Lewis (2006), Festschriften Honor Exceptional Scientific Careers, Scholarly Influences, The Scientist, download, https://www.the-scientist.com/profession/festschriften-honor-exceptional-scientific-careers-scholarly-influences-57891, Accessed 15 October 2018.

Preface vii

We see from the contributions in this Festschrift that the fields of small business and entrepreneurship research are thriving and we enjoy being a part of it. So we're glad to be able to present to you this Festschrift; a personal gift from your community to you. We feel honored to be able to put these contributions together for you as a symbol of our gratitude, to celebrate your incredible body of work and the immense impact that you have had on all of our lives.

Happy Birthday David, from all of us. Thanks for great years we spent together. The journey is not over, we keep travelling together, and we look forward to it.

Always Yours
Erik and Max

Augsburg, Bayern, Germany
Berlin, Germany

Erik E. Lehmann
Max Keilbach

Contents

Part I Family

Scenes from a Marriage 3
Joanne Audretsch

I Will Always Be Proud to Call Him My Father 11
James Audretsch

**My Dad, the Athlete, Entertainer, Phrase Philosopher, Conformist
and Analogist** 17
Christopher Audretsch

Perhaps David Audretsch Is Not a Good Man 21
Jack Harding

Henry David Bruce Audretsch: A Retrospective ... Perhaps 27
Albert N. Link

**Distinguished Professor Dr. David B. Audretsch: World Renowned
Researcher – Legendary Icon in Entrepreneurship** 31
Donald F. Kuratko

A Journey Through Entrepreneurship 39
Mary Lindenstein Walshok

Part II Creating a Research Topic and a Field

**The Symmetry of Acs and Audretsch: How We Met,
Why We Stuck and How We Succeeded** 59
Zoltan J. Acs

Visions of the Past: David was Always There 71
Roy Thurik

ix

Contents

Structural Change, Knowledge Spillovers and the Role of SMEs and Entrepreneurship. 77
Pontus Braunerhjelm

David B. Audretsch: Spilling Knowledge All Over the World 95
Per Davidsson

The Shape of Things to Come 99
Martin Prause and Jürgen Weigand

David Audretsch: A Source of Inspiration, a Co-author, and a Friend. 121
Enrico Santarelli

David: A Cultural Entrepreneur 125
Marco Vivarelli

David Audretsch and International Business: Bringing It All Back Home. 129
Saul Estrin and Daniel Shapiro

Regional Trajectories of Entrepreneurship and Growth 149
Michael Fritsch and Michael Wyrwich

David Audretsch and New Directions in Spillover Academic Entrepreneurship 163
Mike Wright

David Audretsch – A Bibliometric Portrait of a Distinguished Entrepreneurship Scholar 169
Charlie Karlsson and Björn Hammarfelt

David Audretsch: The Capacity to Design and to Influence a Research Agenda 193
Maria Callejón

Education, Human Capital Spillovers and Productivity: Evidence from Swedish Firm Level Production Functions. 203
Johan E. Eklund and Lars Pettersson

Part III Creating a Community

Productivity Slowdown, Innovation and Industry Dynamics 229
Johannes Bersch, Josefine Diekhof, Bastian Krieger, Georg Licht, and Simona Murmann

Dr. Audretsch: or How I Learned to Stop Worrying and Love Doing Small Business Research 243
Julie Ann Elston

Contents xi

"I Want to, But I Also Need to": Start-Ups Resulting from Opportunity and Necessity 247
Marco Caliendo and Alexander S. Kritikos

Working with David on Both Sides of the Atlantic 267
Adam Lederer

Festschrift to David B. Audretsch 271
J. L. González-Pernía and Iñaki Peña-Legazkue

An Overview of the Economics of Entrepreneurship and Small Business: The Legacy of David Audretsch 279
David Urbano and Sebastian Aparicio

Location and Firm Performance 307
Dirk Dohse and Johanna Schnier

The Inclusive Vision 319
Maria Minniti

You Made it the Best of Times 323
Sharon Alvarez

On Regional Innovator Networks as Hubs for Innovative Ventures 325
Uwe Cantner and Tina Wolf

The Emergence of Parental Entrepreneurship: Some Thoughts About Family Life, Professional Careers and Entrepreneurship 349
Iris Kunadt

Financial and Institutional Reforms for an Entrepreneurial Society 359
Mark Sanders

Entrepreneurship in Public Policy Education: The Willy Brandt School as a Case 369
Heike M. Grimm

Connecting People and Knowledge: Knowledge Spillovers, Cognitive Biases, and Entrepreneurship 385
Werner Bönte and Diemo Urbig

Where Would I Be If My 25 Year-Old Self Was Aware of the Gravitas of Dr. David Audretsch? 399
Brett Anitra Gilbert

The Multidisciplinary Entrepreneurship Scholar 403
Erik Stam

Thoughts About David 407
Sameeksha Desai

xii   Contents

Part IV   Creating the Future

Building Stronger Research Communities and Collaboration Between Established and Young Scholars 413
Maksim Belitski

"Lessons from David Audretsch" in Festschrift for David Audretsch 421
Siri Terjesen

Off to New Shores: Knowledge Spillovers Between Economics and Psychology or How I Published with David Audretsch in PLOS One 425
Martin Obschonka

A Brief Case Study of the Audretsch Form of Davidial Entrepreneurship Research Ecosystems 431
Allan O'Connor

David Audretsch Has Impacted My Academic Life in Many Ways and I Would Like to Use This Opportunity to Thank Him for His Tremendous Support 437
Kathrin Bischoff

David Audretsch: A Great Mind, An Outstanding Researcher, and A Humble Individual 439
Mehmet Akif Demircioglu

Happy Birthday, David Audretsch: And All That Jazz 443
Monika Herzig

A Simple Behavioral Model of Stochastic Knowledge Accumulation 447
Torben Klarl and Matthias Menter

David Audretsch: A Literary Steckbrief 453
Sandra Schillo

Wings to Escape the Roots 459
Alexander Starnecker

Professor David Audretsch: My Doktorvater 465
Jagannadha Pawan Tamvada

Building Entrepreneurial Societies Through Entrepreneurial Ecosystems and Business Incubators 467
Christina Theodoraki

David B. Audretsch, a Gatekeeper and Globetrotter 479
Silvio Vismara, Katharine Wirsching, and Jonah Otto

Part I
Family

Part I
Family

Scenes from a Marriage

Joanne Audretsch

> *"Happy is the person who finds a true friend, and far happier is that person who finds the true friend in their spouse."*
> *(paraphrased from Franz Schubert)*

Abstract David Audretsch is a renowned scholar, teacher, mentor and friend to many in the world. But he is also a husband, partner and father. He and I have experienced many years of adventures, ups and downs, joy and sadness, struggles and achievements, births and deaths, all of which have served to enrich our lives on so many levels. Life as a team has taken us to many places where we have shared meaningful moments with colleagues and acquaintances but most importantly with our boys and dear friends – cherished memories for which we are forever grateful. My life's adventure with this extraordinary and talented man with an over-sized passport, a CV that runs seemingly forever, and a penchant for casual attire (aka "the man in the robe") started back in the '80's. Let me take you with me on our remarkable life's journey.

The Courtship

May 1984. Back alley of 2723 Woodley Place, Washington, DC.

"Mel, what's up? Can I help?" I asked my neighbor, who stood in the back alley, seemingly at odds about something.

"Well, I can't seem to get into my car... we have a friend of a friend staying with us, and he parked his MG here but forgot to leave the keys. And I can't seem to open the door of my car enough to squeeze in!"

J. Audretsch (✉)
Bloomington, IN, USA

© Springer Nature Switzerland AG 2019
E. E. Lehmann, M. Keilbach (eds.), *From Industrial Organization to Entrepreneurship*, https://doi.org/10.1007/978-3-030-25237-3_1

"Let me drop you off at work then. It's right on the way. Hop in!" As we drove off, Mel added, "You should probably meet him. He's looking for a place to stay, and I know you have friends looking as well. He's very nice."

"Have him drop by then," I replied, "and I'll get in touch with the other guys."

A day later, the doorbell rings. There stands a bearded man a bit over 6 feet tall, late 20's, slightly disheveled, with nice brown eyes and a friendly smile. "Hi! I'm David," he says, "a friend of the Rosenbergs. Mel said I should drop by and meet you." "Oh! You're the guy with the sports car! Come in – would you like a drink? We make pretty good frozen daiquiris here!"

And that's how it began. Later that week, we went on a real date to a Vietnamese restaurant in Georgetown, bopping around the city and cruising past the monuments in that little white MG David cruised around in back then. At dinner, we discovered many unusual commonalities in our lives; conversation flowed easily and a connection was made. So date #2 was set for the weekend: a trip to Assateague Island. Despite the bright sunshine, our brains were a big foggy from previously-arranged dates with other people the night before. The drive to Assateague passes through lovely countryside, and sooner than we realized, several hours had passed and we had arrived at this beautiful island populated by wild ponies. Soon we found a picture-perfect beach set below a ridge. We parked and took our beach things to the high dunes. My bathing suit was under my sundress, so as I undressed and set out the towels, David arrived with the picnic basket. As he got undressed and turned, I noticed that his bathing suit was inside out: the webbing, the pockets, the drawstring were all simply hanging out. The wind suddenly whipped up and I said, "David, look-- your bathing suit!" He looked at me and said, "Gee, you guys wear your suits funny down here in Virginia!"

And so began our crazy, fun, and unexpected journey through life! (You can't say I wasn't warned!)

The rest of the summer of 1984 passed with increasing speed. Although David had come to DC to work for the International Trade Commission, he had also been in pursuit of a girl (isn't that always the story?!). I, too, was coming off a serious relationship... and although our relationship was deepening with each passing day, each home-cooked meal, each daiquiri party or G&T cocktail afternoon, I strongly encouraged him to figure it out. Knowing this could simply be "a summer love," I personally tried to keep things as light as I could, despite the tell-tale feeling that I was falling in love more and more with each passing day. As June rolled over to July, we ended up spending more time together until it was everyday. When August rolled around and it was time for David to return to Middlebury College, he invited me along for the drive back. From there, our relationship entailed daily conversations on the work WATS lines, monthly visits, and Thanksgiving and Christmas holidays spent together. The relationship was deepening as the months flew past.

Scenes from a Marriage

The Man Without a Passport

Argentina, Australia, Austria, the Bahamas, Belgium, Brazil, Canada, Columbia, Costa Rica, Denmark, England, Estonia, Finland, France, Germany, Greece, India, Indonesia, Ireland, Israel, Italy, Japan, Korea, Lithuania, Mexico, The Netherlands, New Zealand, Norway, Poland, Portugal, Puerto Rico, Russia, Saudi Arabia, Scotland, Singapore, Spain, Thailand, Turkey, Tunisia... When we think of David, we think of the man on the move, traveling from city to city, country to country, continent to continent, in the pursuit of meaningful personal connections and contributions to the world of ideas and science as he simultaneously shrugs off the mantle of jet lag! But when I met David in 1984, he did not possess a passport. In fact, he had only done a small amount of local travel as a child; his greatest travel adventure was his post-college hiking trip to the California Sierra mountains. David was a "stay-cation" kind of guy who really did not like change (Who knew?!). The summer of 1984, when presented with an opportunity to work at the Wissenschaftszentrum Berlin (WZB) for his upcoming sabbatical, he was a bit hesitant: no passport, no living-abroad experience, no knowledge of the language ... But with enthusiastic support and much encouragement on my part, he applied for a passport and accepted a 2-year position at the WZB. Our life's adventure was about to begin in earnest!

The Proposal

In March, prior to his impending departure for Berlin in May, David and I rendezvoused in the Bay area, where he was visiting his mother and I had just terminated a cross-country trip with my roommate. We were staying with my friend's parents in the wine country near Santa Rosa. As we were preparing to go to dinner our first night, David casually said, "You know, I was thinking... I'd like you to come to Berlin with me. I thought maybe we could get married." WHAT???!!! "What did you just say?" I asked, a bit incredulously. "I said, I thought maybe we could get married." "Oh my God...!!! Well, I'm going to give you 24 hours to think about it, and if you still want me to, then YES, I will! But after 24 hours, there's no backing out!" A day later, we sealed the deal – we agreed to a marriage but there were no other details to report at that time.

And such was "the proposal" – nothing in today's terms of young lovers staging grand, romantic events on hot air balloons, underwater diving reefs or mountain tops. No...this proposal was simple, honest, and from the heart. Although there was no tangible evidence (i.e. a ring), I trusted in love and sold my car, moved my belongings back to Rhode Island, packed two suitcases and left for a divided city still in the throes of the Cold War where neither of us spoke the language or knew the culture. This would be a deal breaker... or a deal maker. Only time would tell.

The Ring

The first months in Berlin were spent getting to know the city, the culture, and the language. We both attended intensive Goethe Institute classes after which David would then go off to the WZB to work and I would head back to do homework and engage in the everyday tasks of life in a German city in the mid-1980's, when stores closed daily at 6 pm (promptly!) and were only opened until 1 or 2 pm on Saturdays – nothing open on Sundays! Slowly, we acquired usable language skills which we inflicted upon friends and strangers alike. We began to acclimate to our new culture and were happy to embrace the habits and mores of our new home country. We both greatly appreciated the different ways of life, the customs, and the social system of our new "home" – for that was where our hearts were.

In December, David recognized the need for a token of his appreciation for our upcoming marriage. We went "window shopping" in the Schloss Strasse near our Schmiljanstrasse apartment. At a local jeweler, we found a modest, lovely, understated sapphire ring that I thought would do a fine job representing our engagement on an official level. Not being absolutely certain, we continued to shop but I still hadn't found anything I liked better as the holidays approached. I thought that perhaps, maybe, I might find something under our very first Christmas tree on Christmas day. I went down to the jeweler just before the holiday to see if the ring was still there (we had asked them to hold it for us) but when I asked about it, our young saleswoman just shook her head and said, "I'm so sorry... it's been sold!" I was extremely disappointed and truthfully, a bit sad. So I wasn't surprised that Santa did not leave an engagement ring under the tree or dangling from an ornament. Nor was there one forthcoming on New Year's Eve or New Year's Day... I just thought we would have to start looking again once the holidays were past.

One cold work-day afternoon in early January, I was home ironing when David came home unexpectedly early. "Here," he said, as he gingerly placed a small black velvet box down on the ironing board. "What is it?" I asked, somewhat puzzled as I gently opened the box. What did I find inside but "my" sapphire ring! "I bought it before Christmas... that's why it wasn't there when you went back to ask. But I wanted to surprise you so I didn't give it to you for Christmas." LOL... I must say, I was indeed surprised! And I don't think there are too many women who have received their engagement rings while engaged in domestic labor... so David gets point in the area of originality! (And for the record, I still iron his shirts to this day! Could that have been the economist in him, not only considering division of labor but also economies of scale? LOL! Who knows?)

The Marriage

Short, sweet, simple. We did try to romanticize the act by organizing a very small "destination wedding" in Paris before it was trendy to do such a thing. But thanks to French bureaucracy, life's best-laid plans went awry so our planned May 1985 wedding turned into a lesser battle with German bureaucracy – with greater success. On July 25th, 1986, David and I stood side by side in the Standesamt of the Rathaus Schoeneberg and said, "Ich bin ein Berliner!" Actually, we both said, "Ja!" and exchanged rings and meaningful yet questioning glances, as neither of us completely understood German at the time and weren't exactly sure what we'd committed to, except that we knew it was to a future, in sickness and in health, in good times and in bad... And on that note, after we signed papers and received our Stammbuch and its first official entry – our wedding certificate – we headed down the stairs and out the front door to the same place JFK stood in November 1963. To our surprise, we were personally heralded by the sounds of a lively brass band headed up by David's secretary and her hobby band, as we descended into the weekly Friday market on the platz in front of the Rathaus. Our married life had officially begun!

The Wall

As David's two-year stint at the WZB was nearing a close, the decision needed to be made: do we stay or do we go now? David's work was starting to get published, and he was discovering that he was as good at research as he was at teaching. After much soul-searching and discussion, the decision was made: we would remain in Berlin. David received a multi-year extension on his contract. Berlin had really now become our home.

Since I would now be living in the city for an undetermined amount of time, I realized I had only one real choice for a job: the occupying US Army, Berlin Brigade. After a brief stint of 4 months commuting to my friend's art gallery in Paris, I finally received word that my security clearance was approved, so in January 1988 I began work for the Commander of Berlin's Combat Support Battalion at the old Prussian Army barracks in Lichterfelde. In January 1989, I began working for the General Staff's G-3 at Clay Allee Headquarters, learning an entire new lexicon, lots of history and a very different kind of social order that affected our adopted city of Berlin.

The Fall of the Wall

The winter of '89 was a fierce one, with early snow, wind that bit your cheeks, and temperatures cold enough to start putting the area's lakes into a deep freeze. The evening of November 9th, we were out with WZB colleagues at the (original) Cafe Einstein, discussing the weather as well as the recent events and unrest in Hungary and East Germany. The Berliners in the group mused that despite the stirrings coming out of the East Block and Gorbachev's policy of *glasnost*, nothing was going to happen. Life would certainly continue as it had since the Wall went up in August 1961. There was no way we would ever in our lifetimes see a solution to "the German question." After dinner, we all headed home through the icy streets. Upon returning to our apartment in the Wiesbadenerstrasse, David hopped into the bath to relieve the chill and I turned on the evening news. It was about 11 pm, more of less, and I prepared for bed, I half-listened to the newscaster. Suddenly, an image caught my eye and I turned up the volume, listening intently. My German was good but not perfect, and I sometimes had trouble with "trennbar" verbs. Pictures of crowds gathered at the Wall filled the screen, and I thought I understood: "The Wall has fallen." WHAT?! I listened again but I wasn't certain, so I ran to the bathroom and implored David to get out. After some grumbling, he did and standing in the doorway, dripping, with a towel wrapped around him, he confirmed," That's what he said: the Wall has fallen!" The utterly unthinkable had happened! The entire world changed in those few short hours – all without a shot being fired or a life being lost. We were living at the crossroads of history as an almost indescribable feeling of exhilaration filled the city. The excitement of those heady first days slowly settled down as the city – and the world – realized that this was real and the old world order as we knew it was truly gone. But it was an extraordinary moment to have witnessed first-hand.

The Family

Summer of 1990 I discovered I was pregnant. On April 25th, 1991 our dear firstborn son, Alex, entered this world. We were overjoyed to be the parents of a healthy boy who brought such joy to us as we stumbled through first-time parenthood in a foreign country with no family support. But we took advantage of all Berlin had to offer: walks through the Tiergarten and along the Spree, play times in the multitude of lovely city parks, frequent visits to the Zoo, hours observing the cranes and worksites that peppered the center of the city as it prepared to resume its place as Germany's capital.

David continued his work, traveling, publishing, lecturing, mentoring. Time passed and our wonderful son number two was born: James graced us with his company on a gray overcast Berlin day on February 26th, 1991. We now had two official Berliners! Life continued much as it had when Alex was a baby except now it was double the fun.

The Return of the Prodigal Academic

In 1996, opportunity presented itself in the form of a job offer from Georgia State University. We had always said we would know when the time was right to return to the US. And despite the politics of the time, we both felt that "the right time" had come to leave our beloved Berlin. So in July 1996, we picked up and left our changing Berlin for a new life back in our home country.

Less than 2 years after landing in Atlanta and buying our first house, David received an exceptional offer for an endowed chair at Indiana University. So the summer of 1998 had us packed up once again and moving yet further west into the country's heartland. Shortly after our arrival in Bloomington, we were blessed with the addition of another amazing son, Christopher, who came into the world on September 5, 1998. Two Berliners and a Hoosier... our family was now complete!

David's career continued its upward trajectory as we continued to juggle his travel and our family life. In the year 2001, David was awarded the Global Award for Entrepreneurship Research by the Swedish Foundation for Small Business Research. – a great honor which he accepted with his usual combination of gratitude, humility and grace. A lecture circuit was part of the award, so Christopher and I accompanied David on his speaking tour during a bout of unusually warm, sunny and glorious spring weather.

In 2003, opportunity knocked once again. David was able to work out a plan to retain his position at IU but still become Director at Max-Planck in Jena. It was an ideal time for the family, so we rented a lovely apartment in Weimar and decamped for 9 months. We continued to enjoy summers in Weimar throughout David's tenure there, as well as the company of a multitude of young doctoral and post-doc students as well as new career academics who have since become dear friends. It was an exciting chapter in our lives, and brought us back to Germany, which will always hold a special place in our hearts.

As the decade of the naughts merged into the teens, David's resume continued to grow: more articles, more books, more interviews, more accolades. He was greatly honored to receive an honorary doctorate from the *University of Augsburg* as well as one from the *University of Jonkoping*. Other awards include the Schumpeter Prize from the University of Wuppertal as well as a Distinguished Professor title awarded by Indiana University. Associations with other institutions such as the WHU, the Friedrich-Schiller-University of Jena, or the King Saud University, continued to add to his world influence. Summers were spent enjoying the Max-Planck Institute, its people and numerous conferences and events. The boys were privileged to be part of European culture that included much travel as well as immersion into everyday German life. We were fortunate that we were able to include the boys' friends in these visits as many of the boys' 12life lessons stem from these shared adventures. There is a family-written volume aptly entitled, *"The Book of Transitions,"* excerpts of which are shared by the boys elsewhere in this volume. Some of the more famous quotes include: "Do not EVER EVER cross over the white line!" "Boys, focus! We are in transition." "Do you see anybody else doing it? No... so don't do it!"

David Audretsch, International Man of Mystery

Academics who know of David are aware of his storied academic credentials, and rightfully in awe of his accomplishments. But those who really know David know that this globe-trotting man with the ready grin and low-key nature, the backpack holding the ever-present computer and passport, and his ubiquitous black carry-on suitcase, is one of the most humble and unassuming people on the planet. He never takes himself too seriously, doesn't really like people who do, and is always ready with a goofy joke: "Never let truth stand in the way of a good story!" is one of his mantras. He is a ready mentor to anyone who asks. He is beyond generous with his time and talents, always ready to help, assist, guide and mentor. His intellectual largess spills over to his colleagues as well, always offered without pretension and in the true spirit of academe: exchange of ideas and the pursuit of knowledge. Some have speculated that David might actually be a spy... but those "in the know" realize this cannot possibly be true. This is a man who has worn two different shoes to work (without even noticing), who mixes plaids with stripes, who's lost wallets (but never keys!), whose favorite outfit is a "dressing gown," and who wears his bathing suit inside out. It's probably not likely that he is a spy (but you never know – this just might be the best disguise ever!)

Transitions

As time continues to fly by, we have seen our boys grow into amazing, funny, talented, loyal, kind and generous young men, much like their father. Once dark hair (yes – there is still some!) now shows some gray. Amazingly, there aren't too many wrinkles. And the mind seems to still come up with new ideas and contributions. Attitudes are definitely youthful yet mellowed by age and wisdom. After more than three decades, I am fortunate enough that my adventures with this extraordinary, humble, talented and generous man continue as we transition into a different phase of life, back to just the two of us again, as it began back in the '80's. If I could do it all over again... I absolutely would! I consider myself one of the luckiest people I know, being married to such a wonderful man who has remained my partner, my best friend, my guide and support through life's uneven terrain, and whose constant love and generosity has been the anchor of our family. It has been an honor and a privilege to call this man my husband. Who knew a simple "Ja" would have resulted in such a magnificent, exciting roller coaster ride of life? No one knows what life has in store for this next phase of life now that we are "empty-nesters." But whatever it is, I'm buckling my seat belt, holding on tight, and enjoying the ride into our autumn years, knowing we will continue to travel the world and spend as much time possible with our boys and those who are near and dear to us!

I Will Always Be Proud to Call Him My Father

James Audretsch

Abstract Undoubtedly many know David Audretsch the prolific scholar, teacher and administrator, but a few are even luckier to know a deeper facet of his life – David Audretsch the father. This chapter, penned by one of his sons, provides an in-depth and humorous look at the unique manner in which David has imparted wisdom to his children and helped to mold them into the men that they have become. Often humorous and light-hearted, but always sincere, the following pages illuminate David as the caring father that those close to him and his family know him to be.

"If you don't like it, you can just quit," he tells me. "You often feel like you're trapped, but it is an illusion. You can always just walk away." This piece of advice as I contend as perhaps the best he has preached, spoken to me the day before I leave to Saudi Arabia as my father nears 64 years of age. Dad has always supported me, ever since I can remember. Genuine, sincere, unconditional love and support. What more could you ask for from a father?

I'll outline this with an issue that affects every parent/child relationship – what should the child do with his/her life? As one grows older, the question so fondly asked to children, "What do you want to be when you grow up?", morphs from dreamlike childhood romanticism to existentially terrifying, leading one to manufacture responses to ward off whomever may ask the question. You have no idea what you want to be when you grow up. You have no idea, and you're sick of being asked.

I think a lot of people might assume there was pressure to follow in my dad's footsteps in the scientific community, especially related to economics. Astoundingly, I truly don't know if it affects my father that none of his children pursued the same interest that he did. I'd be surprised to know if it dismays him at all – there was not even a hint of pressure growing up to fulfill this preordained trajectory. I very much expect he wants us to live as he did – blazing our own trails as we navigate our uncertain lives.

J. Audretsch (✉)
Bloomington, IN, USA

© Springer Nature Switzerland AG 2019
E. E. Lehmann, M. Keilbach (eds.), *From Industrial Organization to Entrepreneurship*, https://doi.org/10.1007/978-3-030-25237-3_2

Dealing much with this concept of life's uncertainty is a book my Dad holds most dear; it is a book he gifted to me on my 23rd birthday, *"Zen and the Art of Motorcycle Maintenance"*. In this book a father embarks on a motorcycle road trip with his son, navigating through the United States as they travel West from Minnesota to California. Together the father and son voyage on a journey that is as much emotional and spiritual as it is physical, symbolically climbing mountains and traversing precarious terrain as their abstruse relationship unfolds. One of the meaningful messages of this book is that you should find joy in whatever you may be doing, especially the mundane. If you are repairing a motorcycle, a zen state should be achieved during the repairing process itself, not only from the joy in the final product. Particular striking is that Robert Pirsig, a man who wrote computer manuals for a living, authored Zen and the Art of Motorcycle Maintenance. I'm sure Pirsig never thought that a profession of authoring computer manuals would be succeeded by becoming a multi-million bestselling book author. When I'm unsure of my career choices, my father often advises something like, "Where you are now, the decisions you make, it never seems like the destination you'll end up at... in a roundabout way it will lead you there".

This book substantially influenced my father's ideals and beliefs. The reason he considers himself a successful person is not necessarily because of his accomplishments in academia (which he is very proud of though); it is because he enjoys the processes of his career, from writing papers, to giving talks, to teaching students. When one considers the fleeting evanescence of life and legacy, awards and achievements pale in comparison to the real honest-to-good enjoyment of the zen of living.

In the Summer of 2017, my final summer after undergraduate, I climbed Mt. Kilimanjaro in Tanzania to conclude a 6-week adventure in the heart of the Serengeti. It was a profound trip in many regards, but none so much as the random chain of events would lead me to Saudi Arabia 3 months later. Another one of my father's conversations resonates with me: It's little moments that can have the most influential and far reaching impact on your life. Instead of rigidly pursuing a specific goal, you must be flexible and willing to reorient yourself.

Coincidentally in parallel, my father also embarked on a mountaineering trip in the final summer of his undergraduate degree. He climbed Mt. Whitney, a several week journey that culminated in the 14,505-foot ascent. His accidental death wish came from drinking treacherous river water during one of the stops. Later, he would be throwing up uncontrollably all night, draining the little energy that remained from nearly 2 weeks of trekking. The only thing that saved his life, he says, is a fire that his friend built that kept him on a warm lifeline through the night. Certainly an apt metaphor for the uncertainty and unpredictability of life.

My father knew where he was going after this; he would begin a master's degree in Madison, Wisconsin. Yet, Mt. Whitney was still an ephemeral, epiphanius transition in his life. He remembers it vividly like the waking moments upon a dream, yet recalls it with surreal blurriness as if spilling liquid on a watercolor painting. One man left, and another returned from the mountain. It was a gradual metamorphosis, the kind that one can only retrospectively look back upon and realize: *yes, this moment changed me.*

I Will Always Be Proud to Call Him My Father

The fact that he even tells stories about this experience bespeaks it's significance. When it comes to his personal life, my father is oddly quiet, seeking comfort in solitude. The man who so eagerly outbursts theatrical stories and witty jokes with his family suddenly suppresses his tongue when discussing his childhood. As a man of few words when it comes to his own history, his indulgence in telling a personal story means that you should listen carefully, as you might not hear it again for years. I think that he is proud of how he has shaped his own life, so he lives in the present more than in the past. Things are very peaceful and routine in regards to his career and family now; this structured happiness is desirable.

Things weren't always this stable and happy. I remember some years when my father wasn't around that much. Overseas business was such a commonality that at one point he only rented cars when he was home because it made more financial sense than actually owning a car. I liked this side effect at the time because he rented a convertible for my 12th birthday, and relayed my friends to laser tag back and forth in it.

His most difficult sacrifices came from these overseas trips during my youth. It wasn't any particular large occasions; in fact, I know he valued the everyday moments more than the overblown events. None hurt more-so than missing my soccer games. It's impossible to understand as a kid how nostalgically you'll reminisce these moments when you're older. Especially as a parent, there's an undeniable allure of watching your kid participate in sports. These are moments where you can watch your child grow in real time right before your eyes; you see them struggle and undergo hardships, overcome challenges, compete, showcase their talents, practice humility, experience passion and joy. Every time he missed one of my soccer games, I could feel the regret in his voice from across the world, reconciling, "*I really wish I could have been there. I'll be at the next one.*" For me, that was always enough, to hear the sincerity in his voice. For him, he would have done anything to be there.

My father taught me a great deal about being a man, in traditional "father-to-son" manner. He taught me how to drive a car, throw a baseball, catch a football, and grill a steak; how to shave a beard, tie a tie, and drink a beer. He would drive me to school before I was 16, take me to soccer practice, and cheer for me at soccer and ultimate frisbee tournaments. Our family would often have dinner together at the dining room, discussing events that occurred in the day. In many ways, we are the traditional twenty first century American family.

I vicariously feel nostalgia from remembering my Dad teach my younger brother how to ride a bike in Weimar, and vaguely recall a memory of riding around our cul de sac in Bloomington on training wheels. Many earlier childhood memories, like competing with my brothers in algebra problems on the car-rides to school, reflect our edified upbringing.

Most importantly, my father taught me about perspective. Why is perspective valuable? When you lose perspective, you begin to lose the truth. You begin to force yourself to do things that you don't want to do and become unhappy. When my dad considered job offers from different cities around the US, some paying substantially more, he decided to stay in Bloomington. When he decided to stop working at Max

Planck in Jena, Germany (which sourced many of his overseas flights), it was because he wanted to be in Bloomington more with his family. This is perspective; he realized what would make him and his family happiest.

In my life, my father, best described using chremamorphism, is a compass. He is a compass that provides me perspective. When I feel like I've lost my way, especially career related, I simply look to the compass to guide me in the right direction. It is not perfect; the hands waver, uncertain of the right path. Sometimes they change dramatically, sweeping in an arc around the circumference to point in an entirely new direction. Even the cardinal labels "NESW" aren't evenly spaced apart, dynamically shifting around. "What good is a compass like this?" you might ask. Well, what the compass does convey remarkably well is what directions not to take. My father always seems to help orient me into avoiding the wrong directions; his advice in completing an undergraduate education helped me keep as many doors open as possible. My father taught me: perhaps most importantly in life is not making the *right* choice, for it's likely in the absence of foresight there are indistinguishably many; it is avoiding the wrong ones.

The merit of this approach is in fact employed by companies engaged in recruiting. The most valuable recruiting system is one that avoids bad employees, rather than one that acquires the cream of the crop along with a few bad ones. The reason being that the characteristic of bad (as an employee or a decision in a person's life) erodes the future substantially more than the difference between good and great. I guess the reverberations of my father's economics work do echo through me a little bit.

Imagine you're (potentially trapped) on a road trip with my dad and mom. You can ask them to do complete tasks for the trip. If you know my dad, you surely wouldn't want him to navigate the directions (ironically he's not much of a real compass) or pack the essential items (you might end up with shorts and a t-shirt on a ski trip, or a fur coat on the beach). Only my mother can pack right! To book the accommodation, get snacks for the road, or remember to fill the car with gas – that's best left up to my Mom for your own safety and comfort. If you want to play a game to pass the time in the car, my mom would think of one much better than my dad. You might ask him to pick the destination. It will almost certainly involve nature, hiking, probably on a mountain in a cabin, certainly remote. "The less people the better," I can almost hear him say. You ask to engage him in conversation during the long ride up, because this is where he really excels – contemplative, insightful, and interesting conversation.

The discrepancy between my father and mother's personalities is unequivocally humorous. Their success comes from the unlikely way they complement one another, like the unsuspecting way a mouthful of peanut butter is washed down with a glass of milk. Their personalities are comically different; any member of our family can recall with a perplexed grin how my dad would host elaborate dinner parties and mysteriously disappear halfway through the night – meanwhile, my mom enthusiastically entertain the entire party.

My father is big idea oriented and my mother small detail oriented. It is why, against odds, they manage to have a successful marriage – that and the fact that I set up Netflix on their TV.

I readily believe that my mother is a primary factor in how my father has been so successful. You wouldn't be able to write a complete biography on my father without discussing their relationship in great depth. As an incredibly emotionally introverted person, having my mother to talk to openly with must mean a great deal to him. Through difficult times for both of them, like my mother's grandmother passing away, they are always there for each other. They do get the small things wrong sometimes, but every relationship has hills and valleys. It is incredibly admirable to know, and really know for certain, in a time of need they would drop their current activity in a heartbeat to be at each other's side.

With their children, my parents witnessed different manifestations of themselves. Different aspects of my father's and mother's personalities are more pronounced in my brothers and me. My younger brother with a mix of softer and rigid aspects of their personalities: pensive, mathematical, independent, composed, creative and extremely gifted. Christopher definitely contains my dad's mysteriousness. Myself balanced: humorous, social, adaptable, patient, spontaneous, and creative. I thank my mother for bestowing her socialness and my father for his insight. My older brother with the most extreme aspects of both of my parents' personalities: hyper intense intelligence, curiosity, stubbornness and passion. Alex is blessed with brilliant traits and mildly cursed with others. Through their parenting, my father and mother managed to raise us all to excel in whatever walk of life we find ourselves in – and trust me, raising us was no easy task (wholly due to Alex and Christopher no doubt). My father taught me lessons in philosophy, ideals, and morals that I will pass onto my children. My brothers uniquely learned their own life altering lessons.

Presently, when we talk these days, I notice a glossy translucence hovering over my father's eyes. He gets this way when he ponders, which, I might say, happens somewhat often. There's a sort of hazy mirror when he looks at me, like watching your own reflection morph from ripples in a pond. Often I wonder what he is thinking about, but I don't ask. I theorize it may be this:

Your lasting imprint on the world, beyond and exceeding the legacy of your work, is in the nascent impressions of your children and generations to follow. My father's legacy will last far beyond his lifetime.

He is going to be 65 in a year. And what a remarkable life he's had. Yes, he has his share of faults. But what makes a man is not a collection of individual moments; it's something indescribably greater than the sum of his moments. From the academic intellectual community, to our local community, to our own friends and family, David has forged lasting impressions and created meaningful impact in our lives. I will always be proud to call him my father.

My Dad, the Athlete, Entertainer, Phrase Philosopher, Conformist and Analogist

Christopher Audretsch

Abstract This chapter, authored by his son Christopher, portrays many of the different sides to David. Giving insight behind the easy-going and mild-mannered professor, Christopher details the complexity and multi-dimensional aspects of his father that most do not know. From his wit to his disciplined nature and everything in between, this chapter gives the reader a into the different areas of David's personality.

When I was a child, I harbored the idea that my dad was not a single person, but rather some sort of amalgamation of thirteen different people in one body. My diagnoses of multiple-personality-disorder may not have been completely spot-on, but there is more than a kernel of truth to what I was thinking. My dad who calmly takes his blood-pressure in the morning really can seem like a different person that my dad who panics if he only gets to the airport 2 hours early. At the end of the day, my dad's quirky moods are what makes him unique, and I'm happy to say that they are more endearing than annoying.

The Athlete

It is Sunday morning, and the athlete wakes up at 5:45 am and puts on his robe (which, until his 64th birthday, was about 20 years old, and contained many holes and other imperfections). He moves downstairs, makes a cup of green tea and brings it to the living room, which houses the designated blood-pressure couch and monitor. David sits on the couch, carefully placing his right leg over his left knee, while his left leg rests comfortably on the carpet. This position has been anecdotally shown to reduce blood pressure by up to 2%, so it is imperative that it mustn't vary. The athlete picks up his tea and leans back, resting for a bit; minutes away from the performance, it is crucial that his pulse remains low and his blood well-oxygenated.

C. Audretsch (✉)
Bloomington, IN, USA

© Springer Nature Switzerland AG 2019
E. E. Lehmann, M. Keilbach (eds.), *From Industrial Organization to Entrepreneurship*, https://doi.org/10.1007/978-3-030-25237-3_3

Now, it is time to don the equipment. The competitor rolls up the sleeve on his robe and gently cuffs his right bicep with the monitoring band, taking care to move slowly throughout the process – a jerky movement at this point could render his entire relaxation routine useless. Content with the cuffing (firm and without play or excessive pressure), the sportsman reaches down with his non-dominant hand to press the "Start" button.

A gentle hum, and it begins. A pleasant buzzing in the upper arm – a feeling the contestant has associated with intense concentration and excitement. Seconds pass, and a twinge of anxiety attacks his mind – what if I don't score well today? Though startled for an instant, David regains his composure; years of eating flax seeds and taking fish oil have given him a deep confidence in his ability. Clear in the mind, the contestant focuses on breathing, inhaling for precisely 8 counts and exhaling for 4 — a method that has been taught to him by some of the most cutting-edge internet articles on the planet. Omega-3 s circulate his bloodstream, providing a healthy fat ratio in the man's cells. Finally, the buzzing stops, and two numbers appear on the monitor: 92 over 65. Extremely healthy by all metrics. A score that medical professionals praise, health-nuts aspire to, and the average joe would kill for. But David's record is 90 over 64.

Unsatisfied, the sportsman reaches down with his non-dominant hand to press the "Start" button.

The Entertainer

It is impossible to be in the presence of both a bottle of Budweiser and my dad without hearing: "How is American beer like making love in a canoe? They're both fucking close to water."

If you're lucky enough to be around him and his wife, you'll inevitably be told his favorite (fictional) story about her. "Do you know what Joanne said before we saw the movie Lincoln? 'Don't tell me how it ends!'"

Like many fathers, mine believes that jokes and humorous quips get funnier the more times they are told. When Joanne complains of a mess in the kitchen, David will be the first to yell "It was Alex!" – despite (or rather precisely because of) Alex being 2000 miles away and James and I being right there. In fact, my dad has a whole genre of "blame-the-brother-who-isn't-here" jokes; on a good night, he can pump out over a dozen during a single dinner.

The Phrase Philosopher

Early on in my life, I was taught the importance of "knowing when to hold 'em and when to fold 'em." Any instance of a young person taking a risk is a fitting example of how "the difference between old people and young people is that old people assume the null hypothesis is true; young people reject it." By squinting your eyes a little, my dad's view on IU ("it's all about the parking") can be abstracted and applied to whatever he deems fit. "Not good enough!" – a Davidism with long-forgotten origins – now both applies to an unsatisfactory meal and verbally embodies the idea of the invisible hand.

Success in life – be it finding love, a job, or a place to live – is simply a matter of "choosing a large n." As a frequent traveler, David has realized that a person's identity depends on what country they are currently in; Joanne is correspondingly referred to as "little", "klein", or "pequeña". And if you ask my dad what freedom is, he'll give you an answer straight from a classic rock song: "Freedom's just another word for nothing left to lose".

Transition David

Transition David materializes during or slightly before periods of extended travel (particularly travel on public transportation with his family). Contrary to his usual self, Transition David is high-strung, impatient, and, quite frankly, a bitch to be around. Transition David can often be spotted at airport terminals, standing seriously by his baggage and keeping precise track of both the minute hand on his watch and the arrival status of his flight. What Transition David lacks in agreeability and overall pleasantness, he makes up in his outstanding walking pace (over 7 miles an hour!) and excellent flight-attendance record.

The Conformist

Spending 10 years abroad will change you. For my dad, it's clear that that the German spirit of ordentlichkeit rubbed off on him.

Perhaps the most ashamed of me my dad has ever been was at a train station in Berlin, circa 2009. A foot or so before the platform stopped and the track began, there was a yellow line signifying the limits of where one could stand. In fact, David had drilled me for years about the importance of keeping my distance and specifically not crossing the yellow line at train stations.

So here I was, standing absentmindedly by the tracks (perhaps half a foot from the yellow line), when I heard my dad tell me to move away from the line. In an act of impulsion, undoubtably inspired by teenage rebellion and angst, I stepped forward instead of backward, crossing the yellow line and my father's boundaries. One small step for me, but a complete destruction of the Weltanschauung that David had tried to impart on my young mind.

Upon further reflection, many of David's iconic comments from my childhood echo the symbolism of not crossing the yellow line. For instance, he would scold me for eccentric behavior on the U-Bahn by saying, "Do you see anybody else doing

[that]?" Or, upon not finishing my dessert, being told to eat my damn rote grütze. In quintessential David style, these phrases were repeated constantly. And, to his credit, I still remember them (and the idea of social ordentlichkeit) today.

The Analogist

Here are a few things that I've learned are like the Hunger Games:

Deciding which restaurant to eat at
Bidding No Trump in the game of Bridge
Applying to college
Flying with Delta
JFK Airport
Going to a gay bar in Berlin
Finding love
Being a professor
Grading students
Applying for jobs
Being married to Joanne

Perhaps David Audretsch Is Not a Good Man

Jack Harding

Abstract Chapter author Jack Harding is a nearly life-long friend of David's, stemming back from their days together in college. Although they took different career paths, their strong friendship and common professional interests have always kept them close to one another. The stories that Jack tells paint a picture of the thoughtful and kind friend that David has been to so many, always giving of himself in just the exact way that it's needed, when it's needed.

Is David Audretsch a Good Man?

Is David Audretsch a good man? His colleagues in the field of economics admire him globally as a deep thinker, scholar, superb communicator and innovator of economic thought. Also, I am blessed to know him in many more ways; friend, confidante and family man. David brings his lifetime enthusiasm for ideas and fresh perspective to every member of his world. I have witnessed and benefited from my fair share of those interactions. But, how does one answer the question of whether David is a good man? Let's consider the point.

My tale of a lifetime of friendship with David begins in September, 1973. It was my first day at Drew University. It was the beginning of that phase of life where, fundamentally, mistakes are efficiently converted into life lessons and one emerges afterwards as a yet feeble, but legitimate, member of society. That said, day one had all the attributes of the mistake phase of the process. For me, the first mistake I wanted to avoid was getting lost on campus as I realized it was time for my first campus meal. In other words, how would I find the cafeteria in time to get some lunch?

As the prep for my culinary expedition was just underway, this tall, bearded guy stuck his head into my doorway and said, "Hi, I'm Dave. I live across the hall. Would you like me to show you where the cafeteria is?" My first thought, even back

---

J. Harding (✉)
eSilicon, San Jose, CA, USA
e-mail: jharding@esilicon.com

© Springer Nature Switzerland AG 2019
E. E. Lehmann, M. Keilbach (eds.), *From Industrial Organization to Entrepreneurship*, https://doi.org/10.1007/978-3-030-25237-3_4

then, was, "He didn't ask me if I was hungry. He didn't ask me if I wanted lunch." Instead, David simply perceived the deeper, more relevant point about which this first day freshman was fundamentally worried – finding the cafeteria. Intuitively, David already knew what I was thinking, "I have some food my parents left with me when they dropped me off at the dorm. I won't starve." Certainly, I was onto the much larger point – could I predictably find the building that provided the basic fuel needed for every other task that laid before me? Could I meet the very first challenge of university life without making my very first mistake? David Audretsch knew the real issue. He knew my real fear, and it wasn't starving to death my first day.

In those first few moments I experienced and appreciated the insight and special intelligence of a college kid, now an internationally recognized scholar, who saw instantly beyond the opaque yet shallow surface of even the most basic human need; getting some lunch. I observed a depth of thought and perception that gave me the durable confidence of simply walking around my new campus home. And in time, I gratefully recognized that just across the hall I had a willing resource to whom I could ask not, simply, "What do you think of Dr. Jones?" But, rather, I could ask, "Do you think Dr. Jones can help me meet my academic goals?" The difference in 1973 between those two questions could have seemed small. But multiply that small difference by thousands of similar exchanges between me and David over a 45-year span, and you may begin to understand the immeasurable value David has brought to my life; academics, life choices, fatherhood, career decisions, glowing in victory, reeling from failure. David is and has been on a very short list of friends that enables me to say with appreciation and profound simplicity, "He gets me."

That lunch may have been the most important one of my life. As a warm and affable person, David was very popular on our campus. I discovered this minutes after the first bite of my nearly missed meal. Two very attractive sophomore women ran over to greet him after the summer break. The first to speak, Wendy, was definitely smitten with Dave and made it perfectly clear. After her initial burst of exuberance, she paused briefly and David seized the conversation long enough to introduce this new freshman lost puppy to the vastly more mature and sophisticated young women in front of me. I already mentioned Wendy. The other was Lois, Lois Schultes for my German friends. Lois and I married in January of 1977 while I was still a student. We've been happily married since then.

Now, that introduction alone is enough to think the world of David Audretsch. But, there's much more. However, I'm going to take full credit for winning the hand as my bride of the beautiful and brilliant Lois. But, try to imagine the rich retrospective I treasure to this day, which amounts to, "Hi, I'm Dave, would you like me to show you where the cafeteria is so you can meet your future wife?" This is how I think about David Audretsch.

Even as a freshman in college David's influence drafted me into an appreciation for the study of economics. While I primarily studied chemistry as an undergraduate, I clung to Dave's econ coattails, so much so that as I entered my senior year I was told that with the completion of only two more classes I could earn a double major in economics. How could this happen? Well, recall the fictitious Dr. Jones example from above. In the economics department David was regarded as among the very top students, if not the top student. This provided him easy access to any and all of the professors in that department, including the Chairman, H. Jerome Cramner. Dr. Cramner was a thoughtful and warm person. Also brilliant. Dave admired him deeply and suggested I try to study with Dr. Cramner as much as possible. After David introduced me to Dr. Cranmer, I took every course with him I could schedule given an already full course load. But, in the process, Dave and I had yet more and more to discuss or, should I say, it gave him more and more to explain to me. To this day, David will reference Dr. Cranmer, his teachings and why I should already understand something we're discussing four decades later. Thorstein Veblen is still a favorite.

Somewhere along the way David and I recognized our worlds were converging. He, of course, enjoyed a career filled with early recognition about the fundamental economics of small business. This evolved gracefully into the study of entrepreneurship, which earned him even more public recognition for his work. With some similarity, out of my 40-year career, I have spent all but six years in start-ups seeking exits that have included IPO and M&A. But the point is that while we were sharing thoughts about marriage, kids, and the ways of the world, our conversations became deeper and more richly founded in discussions of public policy decisions that drove small business growth and innovation. His views were and are based upon years of study and research. Mine are rooted in inventing products and services and making the monthly payroll with other peoples' money, or venture capital. In a way, I became a one-man laboratory for David to ask the, "What do you guys really think about [fill in the blank]? " question.

My interest in the field of economics and business landed me, eventually, onto the Steering Committee of the U.S. Council of Competitiveness, many public boards and industry leadership roles and as Vice Chairman of our alma mater. I've also enjoyed a long-term relationship with David's institution, the School of Public and Environmental Affairs at Indiana University. But my outside bona fides are neither the point nor the foundation of our relationship. Frankly, they are largely the result of our relationship. My policy roles and experience are materially due to my decades of dialogue with David and his influence throughout my adult life. I am thoughtful about the global macroeconomic issues because David Audretsch has been my instigator, provocateur and teacher. As an entrepreneur trying to lift his head out of the daily survival challenges, who could ask for a better thought partner than David?

David and I have shared the podium at events all over Europe and the U.S. Each one has been different but they have in common the in-person juxtaposition of the researcher and the practitioner. David's reputation precedes him and he is typically among the keynote speakers. I, on the other hand, have been unknown to other than a few economists with whom I've had the sheer delight to become reacquainted at several events. They know that, from me, they will hear a story of the real issues, priorities and challenges of the entrepreneur. That dialogue has gone well beyond business models, preferences and outcomes. Thanks to the situations in to which David has inserted me, we have enabled truly thoughtful discussion that touches upon even the psyche of the entrepreneur. Over the years, David has taken the time to understand what drives us innovators, risk takers and adrenaline addicts and that we define the success of our ventures in terms of altering entire industries. (One need only look from Amazon to Uber to understand the phenomena.) But, to understand what is in the heart and soul of those of us willing to "bet everything" with the low likelihood that our idea will be among the next great ones is the margin of victory in David's contribution to his field. Of course he knows the economic science but, more importantly, he also empathizes with the relentless drive entrepreneurs must feel to be willing to have one chance in 10,000 of achieving an IPO, or the one in 1,000 chance of surviving at all. David can see entrepreneurship through both lenses of statistical outcome and individual, heartfelt commitment. In my experience, very few in the academic community can make that claim.

No event better captures the dynamic of the Dave-Jack Show than the one hosted by David at the Max Planck Schloss Ringberg Conference Site. David was still on the faculty of Max Planck Institute. He had invited me to give a presentation to approximately 50 economists, three of whom today have received the Nobel Prize in Economics. My talk was entitled Vision, Nerve and Other People's Money. My intention was to provide a light-hearted, ground-up entrepreneurial view of the field. When I arrived at the castle and checked in, I was dumbfounded to see my photograph on the cover of the event brochure. I was listed as the "Keynote Speaker". Do you recall my first day of university when I was afraid I couldn't find the cafeteria? Well, multiply that horror by 10 and you'll be 1/10th of the way to understanding how I felt at that exact moment. When I saw David, I said, "You must be out of your mind. You invited me as the keynote speaker for the most prominent economists studying the field of entrepreneurship and you didn't bother to tell me [explicative(s) deleted]." David smiled and said, "Oh, you'll be fine. Just tell them the truth." I ranted to myself, "Hmmm, I can do that. If nothing else, I'm direct. I'll just get up there and tell these folks what I think. What's a few Nobel Prizes anyway? Have they ever started a company? Besides, it will be just opinion. No facts. No statistics. It will be just one man telling this friendly audience his view on choosing to live this life." I was cool, calm and ready. That is until David introduced me.

David took the podium and made the usual welcoming comments and introduced my background. After a pause, he then said, "You know, I've been thinking about Jack's talk tonight, and it occurred to me that we are all kind of like Masters and Johnson, except we study entrepreneurship instead of sex. Jack, on the other hand, is like the porn star. He gets to do it. [Big laugh]. Jack, it's all yours…"

Porn star? Nobel Prize club! Only my opinion? Wow! But, if there was ever a, "You've got nothing to lose moment", this was it. I took a breath, produced my first slide and told my story of why we do it, how we do it, and what we measure. I offered no pretense of any real understanding of economics. I was my passionate self. I took David's advice and simply told the truth. The truth, by the why, that had me nose to nose with one of the Nobel laureates who decided my claim of not prioritizing financial return was disingenuous. In a two-minute "Less filling, Tastes great" melee, the floor erupted into one half who believed me and one half who thought I was, in fact, downplaying the greedy side of the entrepreneur. It was spectacular. The talk had met every goal; controversy, engagement, debate and entertainment.

The next day I couldn't help but reflect on my debut as a guest of this elite club. Once again, as had happened many times in the past, I concluded David had led me to this moment; just like the cafeteria, economics, and my wife. Instead of trying to argue that my inadvertent bachelor degree in economics somehow qualified me to address this audience, he went the other way. Not only was I absolutely unqualified academically, I was the porn star equivalent of someone perceived to be dabbling in academia. He had ensured my success by prioritizing truth, and he had inoculated me from criticism by eliminating any hope of the audience deriding my qualifications. What were they to do, call me a porn star?

The years since my inaugural knock at the front door of policy debate have left me and, I believe, David with many fond memories. Whether it's sharing our harmonious views in front of an already opinionated audience, interviewing each other for broadcast or simply jumping onto the phone to discuss his latest research or publication, the content of our time together becomes richer and more relevant. Further, the output from our many exchanges becomes more actionable in my real world deployment of our conclusions. Most importantly, our relationship continues to become deeper and for me is a go-to source of personal satisfaction and power. I believe few friendships achieve these potent heights.

Finally, I'd like to close with a tribute to the most important facet of my friend's world, his family. David is the father of three fine young men, Alex, James and Christopher. I've known all three sons their entire lives. I know them to be gifted, curious, virtuous and bold, and dedicated to their family. They have fantastic senses of humor, they are scholars and skilled musicians. One need only to know David to believe you know from where such outstanding offspring hail. But if you also know David's wonderful wife, Joanne, then any remaining doubt as to what an Audretsch child can grow up to be will disappear from your mind permanently. They are a powerful couple in all the best senses of the praise.

I mention this sometimes unappreciated facet because many accomplished men and women achieve at the expense of something else; a marriage, friendships or, worst case, wonderful relationships with one's children. But David, among everything else and perhaps primarily, is a world-class family man. If there were an international prize for greatness in this category, beyond all his other accomplishments, David would be a recipient.

It's for this reason and a lifetime friendship I can definitively respond to my opening question: I conclude David Audretsch is not a good man.

Husband, father, friend and scholar: Indeed, David Audretsch is a great man.

And it's the full measure of his lifetime contributions that have earned him this historic and well-deserved recognition from his friends and colleagues.

Henry David Bruce Audretsch: A Retrospective ... Perhaps

Albert N. Link

Abstract Professor Albert Link is a longtime friend and collaborator of David's. Drawing upon decades of humorous anecdotes from their friendship, Al reveals little-known parts of David's history, allowing the reader to grasp some of his complexity. Al's chapter shows that no matter the setting or the company, David will always unapologetically be his authentic self.

Henry David Bruce Audretsch: A Retrospective ... Perhaps

I first met Henry David Bruce Audretsch on a freezing cold Saturday morning in 1981. We were at a conference hosted by the Middlebury College, which is near Burlington, Vermont. David and I were a few of the young upstarts who were invited to sit at the feet of the masters in attendance. Actually, meeting David at this event was a rather uneventful experience.

However, our paths crossed again in the summer of 1986 at a conference at INSEAD, in Fontainebleau, France. Again, if memory serves me well, that encounter was as memorable as the first.

But then, we both were invited to be involved in a 1998–1999 study on the U.S. Small Business Innovation Research Fast Track program at the Department of Defense sponsored by the National Research Council, which is part of the National Academies. A bond began to develop between us, and that bond led to our first collaborative research project, which appeared in *Research Policy* in 2002. During the committee meetings, we frequently reminisced about our decade plus old meetings and, quite honestly, neither of us could remember very much. Perhaps we both impressed each other to the same degree.

Over the intervening years, we have shared a number of experiences, written together many articles and books, and traveled together from here to there. "Here" is Greensboro, North Carolina, and "there" is many places ranging from La Jolla,

---

A. N. Link (✉)
University of North Carolina at Greensboro, Greensboro, NC, USA
e-mail: anlink@uncg.edu

© Springer Nature Switzerland AG 2019
E. E. Lehmann, M. Keilbach (eds.), *From Industrial Organization to Entrepreneurship*, https://doi.org/10.1007/978-3-030-25237-3_5

California, on the Pacific coast; to the Champs-Élysées in Paris while at the OECD; to the hills near Nottingham University in Nottingham, UK; to the beaches in San Sabastian, Spain. I have learned quite a lot about David over the intervening years, and in this chapter I would like to share a few gems about his life as I recall them.

David was born Henry David Bruce Audretsch, but later he legally changed his first two names to simply David, dropping the Henry part. I learned that as a child he would often ride his tricycle inside of the house, and on more than one occasion his cycling journeys would propel him straight down the stairs into the basement. In fact, David tells of one of those downhill occasions in his 2007 book, *The Entrepreneurial Society*; and if it is in print it must be true. Whenever these joy rides would occur, and we know how they all ended up, his mother would yell at him in repeated sarcastic disgust, "Oh, Henry." As David tells the story, his mom's bellowing "Oh, Henry" day after day left an indelible impression, one that he wanted to forget so much that he legally dropped the name "Henry" and stuck with the name "David."

In 2001 David came to a National Science Foundation sponsored conference at my University of North Carolina at Greensboro (UNCG). All in attendance stayed at the O. Henry Hotel ... yes, William Sydney Porter, known by his pen name O. Henry, was born in Greensboro in 1862. Unbeknownst to me at the time, staying at this hotel caused David a great deal of consternation because it brought back memories and perhaps old body aches.

David and I worked though his Henry issues together on his first evening in the hotel. Surprisingly, what seemed to help David the most was that at the front desk of the hotel was a jar full of miniature Oh Henry candy bars. I send David a box of Oh Henry candy bars about once a year. He asks that I send them to his office rather than to his home because he hoard them from Joanne. To this day, not only is David tolerant of being called "Henry," but truth be known he actually becomes endeared to anyone who slyly slips an Oh Henry candy bar into his pocket and takes revenge on anyone who sneaks into his desk (second drawer on the left!).

A few years ago, David came back to UNCG to give a seminar on new advances in entrepreneurship. At his insistence, we booked a suite for him at the O. Henry Hotel, and we made sure that the candy jar was full on his arrival. After the seminar, my wife and I hosted a dinner in David's honor at our home, and he spent his second night with us.

We have two cats. The next morning we—my wife Carol, our daughter Jamie, David, and myself—were having coffee on the deck. Not being fully awake, and quite by accident, David left the sliding door from the porch to the deck open a bit too long and one of our cats, who was named Equilibrium, tried to scurry out. Quick-minded David slid the door closed just in time to take off part of Equilibrium's tail. Well, chaos ensued. Carol spared few words aimed at David, our daughter was crying, and our other cat, who was name Disequilibrium, was under the couch. I had Equilibrium in my arms trying to figure out what to do. David, who himself was upset, simply said to me "Take Equilibrium to Walmart." "Walmart," I gasped. "Yes, of course Walmart," David said, "it is after all the largest *re-tailer* in Greensboro."

One more story, and this one came directly from David during one of our recent weekly Skypes. As he tells the story, his parents pressured him, even as a young child, to be an over achiever. As the story goes, his parents completed an application for him to attend the Young Einstein Academy, an elite preschool in the town of Lake Wobegon, Wisconsin, where David was born. His parents honestly believed that attending this Academy would catapult David to academic heights.

An interview was involved as part of the admission process to the Academy, and David's parents, or anyone's parents for that matter, were not allowed to be present during the interview. Well, apparently, the required personal interview was the brainstorm of the Headmaster of the Academy. The Headmaster wanted a one-on-one discussion with each child. Presumably, and this is the best spin that I can offer, the Headmaster was interested in learning how in touch with reality each of the youngsters were at age 4.

One of the questions that he asked to David was for him to name 2 days of the week that start with the letter "T." That question could indeed be a puzzler to many a 4-year old, and in fact many who are 4 years old likely do not even know what the word "week" means. But, as David tells the story, he told the Headmaster that the 2 days of the week that start with the letter "T" are "today" and "tomorrow." Out of the mouths of babes ... and out of the Academy he went.

Now, for those who are reading this chapter, if you believe anything that I have written above about David, in honor of this auspicious occasion of his well-deserved Festschrift, then you might also believe that as a youth he had aspirations of being a ballet dancer.[1] Now where might those tights be?

In all seriousness, my professional and social interactions with David have enriched my career and many aspects of my life. Our most recent scholarly endeavor, with our friend John Scott, was to assemble papers from eminent scholars for a special issue of *Review of Industrial Organization* in honor of the academic career and intellectual achievements of Professor F.M. (Mike) Scherer. David's mastery of the discipline that was known as industrial organization in our day, including the subtleties of the fields of antitrust, imperfect competition, and history of economic thought, was something to behold. The breadth of David's knowledge and insight was nothing short of amazing.

I pondered long and hard about how to end this retrospective, and I decided to end it on a note of advice to all who have continued to read. Perhaps the next time, and forevermore, when you see David at a conference, or wherever, it might be nice if you say: "Oh, Henry, how are you doing!."

Regardless of his age, and regardless of any factual or fictitious episodes about his life that you might have read, Henry ... I mean David ... is clearly a giant in the profession upon whose shoulders anyone would be privileged to stand.

By the way, this chapter was approved by Joanne by voice mail from her car as she was on the way to the second drawer on the left of David's office desk.

---

[1] Actually, the above dates are approximately correct, the story about David riding his tricycle down the stairs is true, and David's favorite candy bar is in fact an Oh Henry.

Distinguished Professor Dr. David B. Audretsch: World Renowned Researcher – Legendary Icon in Entrepreneurship

Donald F. Kuratko

Abstract Written by close friend and co-author Professor Donald F. Kuratko (Dr. K), this chapter portrays David's work and life in a snapshot. This viewpoint from a colleague and friend gives an overview of David's career, highlighting his positions, awards, travels and achievements. Most importantly, it serves as an example of how highly admired David is by those that know him best.

Background

Dr. David B. Audretsch is a University Distinguished Professor and the Ameritech Chair of Economic Development at Indiana University-Bloomington. He is also the Director of the Institute for Development Strategies, as well as Director of the School of Public & Environmental Affairs Overseas Education Programs. Distinguished Professor David B. Audretsch has produced wide-ranging, sustained, and deeply influential work in entrepreneurship and international economics. These research efforts have had a profound impact on both the academic and policy components of the entrepreneurship field.

Professor Audretsch came to Indiana University in 1998 as the Ameritech Chair in Economic Development, with nearly two decades of experience teaching and researching in international settings. This included his roles as the Acting Director of the Wissenschaftszentrum Berlin für Sozialforschung (Berlin Social Science Center), a Research Fellow at the Centre for Economic Policy Research in London, and a Visiting Research Professor at the Tinbergen Institute in the Netherlands. He had also served as a consultant to the U.S. International Trade Commission, the Dutch Ministry of Economic Affairs, the Organisation for Economic Co-operation and Development (OECD), the United Nations, and the European Parliament.

D. F. Kuratko (✉)
Indiana University – Bloomington, Kelley School of Business, Bloomington, IN, USA

© Springer Nature Switzerland AG 2019
E. E. Lehmann, M. Keilbach (eds.), *From Industrial Organization to Entrepreneurship*, https://doi.org/10.1007/978-3-030-25237-3_6

International Impact

Professor Audretsch's zeal for working in the international arena has been apparent at Indiana University as he has organized annual conferences in Germany, the Netherlands, Spain, Sweden, and Bloomington. In his role as Director of the Institute for Development Strategies at Indiana University he expanded it from a state/regional enterprise to one of international scope. Leveraging his broad network of scholars and practitioners, he brought a series of visitors to the university from organizations like the Bank of the Netherlands, Erasmus University, and the Wissenschaftliche Hochschule für Unternehmensführung (WHU) Otto-Beisheim School of Management, many of whom spent a full year with the university. Several enduring collaborations emerged from these visits, such as the Bloomington-Rotterdam International Development Exchange (BRIDGE) program, a joint course in "Globalization, Entrepreneurship, and Public Policy" offered at IU and Erasmus University in which international teams of students worked together on policy projects. Professor Audretsch and his colleague Professor Roy Thurik at Erasmus University obtained funding from a research institute in the Netherlands to bring the Dutch students to Bloomington for 2 weeks to complete the course together. The student teams' papers were so accomplished that they were published as chapters in Springer Publishers' *Entrepreneurship: Determinants and Policy in a European--U.S. Comparison* (2002). SPEA continues to offer a course modeled on the BRIDGE program with the University of Augsburg in Germany and the University of Bergamo in Italy, now with IU students traveling to Europe to meet and interact with their counterparts. Again, this work made such a valuable contribution to the discipline that it was published in another Springer volume, *Globalization and Public Policy: A European Perspective* (2015b).

In addition Professor Audretsch has actively recruited faculty participants from Indiana University to develop and lead overseas programs. Notably, he also sought out Lilly Family School of Philanthropy Professor Gregory Witkowski to participate in the overseas study program that Professor Audretsch personally developed with the Hertie School of Governance in Berlin. The Hertie School is one of four international institutions with which Professor Audretsch has personally initiated cooperative agreements on behalf of Indiana University. The University of Erfurt and Augsburg University in Germany and Jönköping University in Sweden have also become international IU partner institutions thanks to Professor Audretsch's contributions.

Max Planck Institute of Economics in Jena, Germany

In 2003, Professor Audretsch accepted an appointment as Director of the Max Planck Institute of Economics in Germany. There he created the first institute devoted to entrepreneurship research providing him the opportunity to establish entrepreneurship as a major scholarly activity throughout Europe. Numerous faculty and doctoral students from all over the globe serving as Research Fellows at Max Planck. Many of the faculty at IUs Kelley School of Business such as myself, Jeff McMullen, Patricia MacDougall, and Dean Shepherd also became involved with Max Planck through Professor Audretsch's efforts. The result has been enduring internationally oriented research collaborations between Kelley and SPEA faculty, most recently the partnership of the Augsburg University's Center for Entrepreneurship with IU's Johnson Center for Entrepreneurship and Innovation.

I had the pleasure of working with Dr. Audretsch on a special conference at Max Plank Institute where we brought together some of the world's leading scholars on entrepreneurship to present their research on Strategic Entrepreneurship. This work became the genesis of a special issue of the top journal, *Entrepreneurship Theory & Practice*, published in 2009. In addition, Dr. Audretsch's efforts with Max Planck paved the way for numerous international scholars to visit Indiana University and share global knowledge from their research. This has benefitted our professors and graduate students at the Kelley School of Business. Please know that throughout Europe Dr. Audretsch is a revered scholar and leader. This has brought tremendous prestige to Indiana University. I believe that his efforts have positioned IU to be viewed as a global research force.

Research Impact

Despite these demanding teaching and administrative roles, Professor Audtretsch had consistently made highly influential contributions to the entrepreneurship and international economics literatures. His prolific studies of entrepreneurship and "the strategic management of place," a German economic concept he introduced to the U.S., led to his ranking as the 21st most-cited scholar in economics and business during the decade from 1996 to 2006 (Thompson Essential Science Indicators). Among his many notable books are The Entrepreneurial Society (Oxford University Press, 2007), *Everything in its Place: Entrepreneurship and the Strategic Management of Cities, Regions, and States* (Oxford University Press, 2015), and *The Seven Secrets of Germany: Economic Resilience in an Era of Global Turbulence* (Oxford University Press, 2016). In all, Professor Audretsch has authored over 15 books and edited another 34 books, he has published almost 300 articles in refereed journals and 150 chapters in edited books. This work has made such a significant impact on the entrepreneurship field that, as of this writing, he stand as the 2nd most cited scholar in entrepreneurship more than 80,800 citations according to Google Scholar. He has also been profiled as one of the sixty most important scientific thinkers in the world since the time of Aristotle (Linß 2007).

Professor Audretsch has served as an editor or editorial board member for numerous prestigious journals. Dr. Audretsch is a founding co-editor of *Small Business Economics: An Entrepreneurship Journal*. Founded in 1989, the journal has risen to be one of the highest quality journals in the entrepreneurship realm and

Dr. Audretsch has remained a co-editor to this day! His involvement with this journal has brought great attention and prestige to it across the globe with some of the world's leading scholars having published their work there. Professor Audretsch also chaired the Entrepreneurship Division of the Academy of Management. His leadership helped to increase the size and impact of that division into one of the largest divisions in the Academy of Management.

Policy Impact

From a policy impact perspective, Professor Audretsch has consulted for the World Bank, the European Union, OECD, and testified before the U.S. House of Representatives on spurring innovation and job creation, along with serving on a great many international boards and committees. Professor Audretsch continues to serve as a consultant for the Science, Technology, and Economic Policy Board of the National Research Council at the National Academy of Sciences and for the joint research institute of the Rotterdam School of Management and the Erasmus School of Economics in the Netherlands.

Special Honors

Indiana University recognized Professor Audretsch's research impact across the world by awarding him the prestigious title of *University Distinguished Professor*, the highest honor for a scholar/professor at IU. In 2016 the university awarded him the *John W. Ryan Award for International Programs* in honor of his incredible contributions to the international field and his comprehensive internationalization of Indiana University.

Other notable global honors include recipient of the prestigious *Global Award for Entrepreneurship Research* (with Zolton Acs) in 2001 by the Swedish Entrepreneurship Forum, which each year recognizes the worlds' leading researchers in entrepreneurship. This award has been nicknamed the "Nobel Prize for Entrepreneurship Research." He has also been named one of the 60 Most Influential Economists of all Time, in the 2007 book, *Die Wichtigsten Wirtschaftsdenker by Verla Linß* (Frankfurter Rundschau). Dr. Audrestch received Honorary Doctorates from Jönköping University in Sweden in 2010 and the University of Augsburg, in Germany in 2008. He was named a *twenty-first Century Entrepreneurship Research Fellow* by the Global Consortium of Entrepreneurship Centers in 2011 and was recipient of the *Technology Innovation Management Research Award* in 2013. In addition, he was recipient of the *Highly Commended Paper Award* by the Emerald Literati Network, in 2012, 2013, and 2015. These awards definitely reflect the incredible impact that Dr. Audretsch has made in the research realm. Without question, he stands as one of the world's leading minds in entrepreneurship.

Personal Research Collaborations

It was important to me to also provide some perspective on research that I was able to collaborate on with him. The first article that I had the privilege to co-author with Professor Audretsch was based on a special research conference that he and I organized as part of the Max Planck Institute in Germany in 2007. We worked together to conduct a specialized international conference on the topic of "Strategic Entrepreneurship." The partnership was created between the Kelley School of Business and the Max Planck Institute of Economics in Germany, of which David B. Audretsch is the director. Thirty-six of the world's most renowned scholars in the field of entrepreneurship and economic development were in attendance at the Schloss-Ringberg Castle in Bavaria just south of Munich. The castle was owned by the Max Planck Institute in Germany. It was a special experience for all the scholars who attended.

Research papers were presented and discussed as part of an intense research retreat format where all scholars contributed to every topic being presented. The research included both empirical and theoretical aspects of entrepreneurial development focusing within a framework of "strategic entrepreneurship."

We had discussed the concept with Professor Ray Bagby from Baylor University, who was the editor of *Entrepreneurship, Theory & Practice* (one of the leading academic journals in the field of entrepreneurship) and he agreed that we could serve as guest editors of a special issue on Strategic Entrepreneurship to feature the very best articles developed from this conference. After a double – blind review process and assessments of the co-editors the best articles were selected for inclusion in this special issue. The manuscripts went through two and three rounds of revisions before any final decisions were made so this issue represented the very best scholarly work. Some of the many scholars who participated in the conference included: Professors Patricia P. McDougall, Dean A. Shepherd, G. Thomas Lumpkin, R. Duane Ireland, Johan Wiklund, Per Davidsson. Erik Lehman, Michael H. Morris, Andrew Zacharakis, Holger Patzelt, and G. Dale Meyer.

The opening article of that 2009 special issue authored by me and Professor Audretsch was entitled, "Strategic Entrepreneurship: Exploring Different Perspectives of an Emerging Concept" (Kuratko and Audretsch 2009). In that article we explored the different perspectives that had been portrayed in the literature up to that point. We explained that within the entrepreneurship and strategic management domains there had been a movement by scholars to combine certain aspects of both areas to create a new concept of strategic entrepreneurship. To that point, there remained much to know about what constituted this concept. The special issue that we edited was the result of the unique research conference in Tegernsee, Germany where, as just explained, some of the world's most renowned scholars gathered to explore this concept in depth. The set of articles in that special issue examined different perspectives that relate to strategic entrepreneurship and we believed each article contributed to the growing body of knowledge on this concept by examining diverse scholarly topics. Our introduction provided an overview of the perspectives contained in *strategic entrepreneurship* and argued for the importance of embracing diverse views rather than attempting to restrict the analysis of the emerging topic.

In 2011, the *International Entrepreneurship & Management Journal (IEMJ)* published a special issue on Corporate Entrepreneurship. Professor Audretsch and I collaborated again in an article entitled, "Clarifying the Domains of Corporate Entrepreneurship" (Kuratko and Audretsch 2013). We explained while there was a broadly held belief in the need for and inherent value of entrepreneurial action on the part of established organizations, much remained to be revealed about how corporate entrepreneurship (CE) was defined in organizational settings. Fortunately, knowledge accumulation on the topic had been occurring at a rapid rate and many of the elements essential to constructing a theoretically grounded understanding of CE could be readily identified from the extant literature. We argued that corporate entrepreneurship possessed the critical components needed for the future productivity of global organizations. However, it was a far reaching concept that encompassed differing aspects and as research continued to increase in this field, a stronger perspective of what constituted corporate entrepreneurship needed to be examined. Our purpose in this article was to outline the various domains that currently existed in the research arena of corporate entrepreneurship. We believed that our exploration of these domains would help researchers gain a sharper focus on the corporate entrepreneurship process. Our article was intended to layout the groundwork as an important step for scholars interested in moving the field forward.

After some interesting discussions about the various definitions of entrepreneurship with Professor Audretsch and Professor Albert Link of the University of North Carolina-Greensboro in 2014, we decide to collaborate on a research article that would explore the entire field of entrepreneurship and how it was portrayed as a discipline. In 2015, the article entitled, "Making Sense of the Elusive Paradigm of Entrepreneurship" was published in *Small Business Economics Journal (SBEJ)*. (Audretsch et al. 2015a). In this article we discussed how the term "entrepreneurship" apparently meant different things to different people including scholars and thought leaders. Because entrepreneurship is multifaceted, it was studied from many different perspectives, yet, that had fostered a multitude of definitions. Even the scholarly literature (where normally the deepest understanding would be found) was rife with disparities and even contradictions about what is and is not entrepreneurship. Some had suggested a narrower and more defined focus on entrepreneurship where only bona fide entrepreneurship research theories would explain entrepreneurial phenomena. We believed that constricting the field may be the wrong approach. Our purpose in the article then was to try and make sense of the disparate meanings and views of entrepreneurship prevalent in both the scholarly literature as well as among thought leaders in business and policy. We reconciled the seemingly chaotic and contradictory literature by proposing a coherent approach to structure the disparate ways that entrepreneurship was used and referred to in the scholarly literature. We examined three coherent strands of the entrepreneurship literature and identified an emerging eclectic view of entrepreneurship, which combined several of the views prevalent in the main approaches discussed.

In 2016, both Professor Audretsch and I again collaborated with Professor Albert Link of the University of North Carolina-Greensboro in an article distinguishing between the constructs of "dynamic entrepreneurship" and "static entrepreneurship." The final article entitled, "Dynamic Entrepreneurship and Technology-based Innovation," was published in the *Journal of Evolutionary Economics* (Audretsch et al. 2016). In that article we distinguished between dynamic and static entrepreneurship by defining the construct of dynamic entrepreneurship in terms of Schumpeterian innovativeness and then developed a hypothesis suggesting that human capital is conducive to such action. In contrast, a paucity of human capital is more conducive to static entrepreneurship (defined in terms of organizational or ownership status). Based on a rich data set of entrepreneurs receiving research funding through the U.S. Small Business Innovation Research (SBIR) program, our empirical evidence suggested that academic-based human capital was positively correlated with dynamic behavior, whereas business-based human capital and prior business experience was not.

Our latest collaboration came in 2019 (Audretsch et al. 2019) when we teamed up with Matthias Menter, Erik Lehmann, and James Cunningham, to publish an article in the Journal of Technology Transfer entitled, "Entrepreneurial Ecosystems: Economic, Technological, and Societal Impacts." It was the openinig article of a special issue that focused on focus on the key elements that characterize an ecosystem, and hence, sought to untangle under what conditions entrepreneurial firms shape and influence economic, technological, and societal thinking within their ecosystem. Working again with David, and with the outstanding leadership efforts of Matthias Menter, this article and special issue were a great success.

Personnel Reflections

Amidst all of Professor Audretsch's huge number of research publications, academic books, profound research impact, and global influence, he always found time to guide and mentor so many young scholars that have now gone on to become excellent researchers themselves. His willingness to provide such impactful guidance to the next generation of entrepreneurship scholars was deservedly recognized by the Academy of Management in 2015 when he was awarded the prestigious *Entrepreneurship Mentor Award*. This award is not an annual award but presented only when a professor has demonstrated outstanding guidance to the next generation of scholars on a continued basis. Professor Audretsch's long history of developing scholars both in the United States and abroad internationally was a shining example of what this award encapsulates. He was most deserving.

From a personal perspective, I have found David Audretsch to be one of the most kind and welcoming professors in my entire career. He and I have become dear friends and I am most grateful to him for his warmth, his knowledge, his perspectives, and his dedication to the field of entrepreneurship. David, along with his wife,

Joanne have joined my wife, Debbie and I on many occasions for various social events and we have all spent time together at each other's homes. Needless to say, we have always enjoyed each other's company with evenings spent on conversation, humor, sharing of family issues and successes. For my wife and me, the friendship with David and Joanne is one of our true blessings and we cherish it immensely.

Professor David B. Audretsch will always be recognized as a world renowned researcher as well as a legendary icon in entrepreneurship. But more deeply to me, he will always be one of my greatest friends!

References

Audretsch, D. B. (2007). *The entrepreneurial society*. Oxford: Oxford University Press.
Audretsch, D. B. (2015). *Everything in its place: Entrepreneurship and the strategic Management of cities, regions and states*. Oxford: Oxford University Press.
Audretsch, D. B., & Lehmann, E. E. (2016). *The seven secrets of Germany: Economic resilience in an era of global turbulence*. Oxford: Oxford University Press.
Audretsch, D. B., & Thurik, R. (2002). In I. Verheul & S. Wenneker (Eds.), *Entrepreneurship: determinants and policy in a European-U.S. comparison*. Boston: Kluwer Academic Publishers.
Audretsch, D. B., Kuratko, D. F., & Link, A. N. (2015a). Making sense of the elusive paradigm of entrepreneurship. *Small Business Economics, 45*(4), 703–712.
Audretsch, D. B., Lehman, E., Richardson, A., & Vismara, S. (2015b). *Globalization and public policy: A European perspective*. Heidelberg/New York: Springer.
Audretsch, D. B., Kuratko, D. F., & Link, A. N. (2016). Dynamic entrepreneurship and technology-based innovation. *Journal of Evolutionary Economics, 26*(3), 603–620.
Audretsch, D. B., Cunningham, J. A., Kuratko, D. F., Lehmann, E. E., & Menter, M. (2019). Entrepreneurial ecosystems: Economic, technological and societal impacts. *Journal of Technology Transfer, 44*(2), 313–325.
Kuratko, D. F., & Audretsch, D. B. (2009). Strategic entrepreneurship: exploring different perspectives of an emerging concept. *Entrepreneurship Theory and Practice, 33*(1), 1–17.
Kuratko, D. F., & Audretsch, D. B. (2013). Clarifying the domains of corporate entrepreneurship. *International Entrepreneurship and Management Journal, 9*(3), 323–335.
Linß, V. (2007). *Die Wichtigsten Wirtschaftsdenker*. Wiesbaden: Marix Verlag.

A Journey Through Entrepreneurship

Mary Lindenstein Walshok

Abstract After 9 years of post-secondary education in sociology and a decade of studying workforce trends, chapter author Mary Walshok began her journey of integrating the fields of innovation and entrepreneurship into her discipline. As a young dean at a new, aggressive research university, Walshok already had much on her plate when she began to interact with David and his body of research. In this chapter the author describes how David's work gave her a framework that not only has shaped her research career but has allowed her to be a resource to civic leaders and policy influencers as they try to renew regional economies.

Introduction

I have been a lifelong student of innovation and entrepreneurship. This may be partly because my father was an entrepreneur in California in the post-World War II era. I grew up with the struggles and joys, the ups and downs of a small family business having good times and bad times. My parents were from Sweden and we spoke Swedish at home while living amidst the movie industry in Palm Springs, California 100 miles from Hollywood in the 1940's, 50's, and 60's. This fact is important because my distinctive family culture did not always match the glamorous Southern California movie culture in which we lived. I also traveled multiple times abroad, before many other American children did. I think these experiences contributed as I went off to Pomona College, a small liberal arts college in the Los Angeles area in 1960 to my fascination with the Social Sciences as a lens for understanding a complicated world.

After 9 years of post-secondary education and a decade of studying workforce trends, I began my journey of attempting to understand the dynamics of innovation and entrepreneurship through the lens of a sociologist as a young dean at a very new, aggressive research university, UC San Diego. It has become the anchor institution

M. L. Walshok (✉)
University of California, San Diego, La Jolla, CA, USA
e-mail: mwalshok@ucsd.edu

© Springer Nature Switzerland AG 2019
E. E. Lehmann, M. Keilbach (eds.), *From Industrial Organization to Entrepreneurship*, https://doi.org/10.1007/978-3-030-25237-3_7

in what was a dynamic military focused R&D region that eventually pivoted to a more active technology transfer, commercialization, and business creation focus. I interacted with entrepreneurs in the region starting in the 1980's and immersed myself in the academic and policy literatures. Most of that literature was about individual entrepreneurs and companies. Rarely, did one find work that captured the full dynamics and nuances of an integrated economy that was entrepreneurial, of a community or a region that engaged innovation as a strategy for economic growth as was San Diego. Most regions at that time were focused on company attraction or scaling large vertically integrated companies so that they could serve larger national and international markets.

Among those who were studying regional dynamics or economic issues in the 1980's there was a tendency to reduce the dynamics of innovative regions to specific ingredients, essential attributes, assets, and components which together could yield more innovative and entrepreneurial behaviors and outcomes with the ultimate goal, of course, being to grow new economy companies, high wage jobs, and regional prosperity. I was struck by all these various approaches. Bodies of literature began to develop around the importance of R&D institutions. Other bodies of literature focused on technology transfer and commercialization. Still others addressed the power of social networks to assure high quality and accelerating rates of research commercialization and business formation and eventually, others focused on talent and the need to attract or grow scientists, engineers, and business people with entrepreneurial know-how.

More recently a whole literature on eco-systems has emerged focused on integrating all these ingredients so that there are opportunities for interdisciplinary, cross functional communication and initiatives. All this literature has been rich in helping us understand specific ingredients, but very little has yet helped us understand why a city like San Diego has exceeded a great industrial city like St. Louis for example, in growing its innovation economy. Understanding all of these ingredients and ecosystems has yet to elucidate why one of the most innovative hubs in America beginning with the building of the Erie Canal and continuing well into the 1940's and 50's, Rochester, New York, flat lined as of the 1980's with the demise of large companies such as Kodak and Corning and Bausch and Lomb.

The point of this paper is to elucidate the value of the work of Audretsch and Thurik (2001) and in particular their seminal essay "What's new about the new economy" in helping to make sense of these unlikely differences. As a person who stands at the intersection of academic knowledge and practical, behavioral initiatives to affect economic change in a region, their work provided more value than practically anything else I was reading at the time; more clues to the dynamics shaping the innovation differences between regions and that was in understanding entrepreneurial versus managerial economies.

Much of what at the time was core to the research, scholarship, and policy analysis in the innovation/entrepreneurship space read like a recipe of ingredients for baking a cake. My father's Palm Springs restaurant served a fabulous dessert which was originated by a company founded by a German woman, Frieda Shroeder. It was a Lemon Crunch Cake that was spectacularly tasty after enjoying a smorgasbord of herrings, gravad lax, pickles, beets, Swedish meatballs and all manner of salty and pickled delicacies. The ingredients of the cake were fairly straight forward; flour, butter, sugar, baking powder, fresh lemons, and an incredible vanilla frosting sprinkled with roasted, sugared almonds. Multiple resort customers would ask for the recipe for the cake which was gladly shared. All would report they just weren't able to bake it so that it tasted the way our cake tasted.

What was our secret to success they would ask? Academics ask the same question about disparate entrepreneurial outcomes. How is it that a place like St. Louis which has apparently similar or even better ingredients for baking an innovation cake than a place like San Diego, yet doesn't. What's missed in all discussions of essential "ingredients" is the proportionality of those ingredients, the quality of those ingredients, and the interaction effects that come from that. By proportionality, I mean flour, sugar, and baking soda but in the exact right amounts. If you put as much baking powder as flour in a cake, it will fry. If you put more sugar than flour in the cake, it will not rise. And so the good chef understands and takes care to assure the right proportional use of the very different ingredients.

The quality of the ingredients is also not to be missed. Finely sifted flour versus coarse flour versus whole wheat flour will make a difference. Whether the lemons are freshly picked, Meyer lemons or lemons that have been delivered from 2000 miles away on the back of the truck can affect the flavor. Even sugar comes in different qualities, brown sugar versus granulated sugar versus fine sugar. And so the quality of the ingredients and clarity about quality is important to making that cake work. And of course there are the interaction effects where you can have high-quality ingredients. You can plan to use the right proportions but if you inadvertently miss one component or over use another you can ruin the cake. I did this many times as a child learning to bake; using a tablespoon of baking powder rather than a teaspoon. Using four tablespoons of butter rather than eight. The interaction effects give rise to very different outcomes.

And finally, as any cook or chef knows, where you cook or bake makes a difference. When you try to bake a Frieda Shroeder cake in Los Angeles or Palm Springs which are basically at sea level, a certain temperature and time work. But when you move to 5000 feet or 8000 feet at a ski resort or a place where you do mountain climbing, both the temperature and time needed to bake the cake change. It turns out that there's also a difference whether you're baking in an electric or a gas stove because that in turn can affect how the heat develops and the ingredients work together, what it takes for everything to cohere to produce that gorgeous cake, that tasty cake everyone longs for can be complicated. My point is simply that a great deal of literature (even today) on innovation and entrepreneurship is made up of recipes which identify critical components of any ecosystem. But very few of them delve into the proportional value of the different components; the ways in which you mix and blend so the whole thing works much less the ways in which the local context, the regional dynamics within which this new cake is being baked affect how long it will take to rise and even how tasty it will be at the end.

In the next few sections, I would like to suggest that one of the greatest contributions of our good friend and colleague, David Audretsch, to the study of innovation and entrepreneurship is that he understood and articulated superbly the deeper issues and dynamics that enable regional transformation. This is in part because he resisted the temptation to simply list the five critical elements or ingredients needed to grow an entrepreneurial economy. Rather he offered a very nuanced understanding of how innovation and entrepreneurship emerge from a community; a culture; a way of solving problems; a way of thinking and communicating, and getting things done. This contrast between what drives industrial economies, characterized by a managerial and corporate mindset, strategies, problem solving techniques, and social dynamics compared to the more nimble, open, entrepreneurial economy mindset, strategies, problem solving techniques and social dynamics, is brilliant.

Audretsch's Distinction: Entrepreneurial vs Managerial Economies

In an age of increasing globalization, technological revolutions and unpredictable geo-political developments, uncertainty is a permanent, not an episodic, characteristic of life. Successfully coping with, even managing, uncertainty, thus becomes the sine qua non of personal and organizational success, as well as regional economic prosperity. In spite of the extreme volatility of social, economic and political developments over the last decade, many enterprises and regions in the United States have evolved and prospered, while others have remained "stuck." Those that have demonstrated a capacity for change and reinvention, in other words, innovation and entrepreneurship provide valuable insights and lessons for others. They demonstrate that to effectively engage the forces of change, integrate unplanned for opportunities and challenges, as well as develop new capabilities, communities capable of engaging entirely new ways of thinking and doing can prosper.

Most of the corporate approaches to innovation and growth, as well as the economic development policies of governments, are built on a model of change anchored in the Industrial Age. As such they are not well suited to the challenges of the twenty-first Century. The Industrial Age was characterized by the gradual application of new technologies to traditional human functions and industries, as well as a gradual adaptation to new markets for products and new skill requirements among workers. Such attenuated timeframes gave rise to a model of change that was linear. A new technology or creative idea was introduced, incubated, then tested in a few settings and eventually was integrated into professional and institutional practice, perhaps over a 20 year period. Such a model also gave rise to the expectation that certainty and stability would ultimately be achieved, were just around the corner. The "fits and starts" introduced by new technologies or ideas were perceived as mere "transition costs" as described by Audretsch (1991) in an otherwise stable universe. Metaphors and tools, such as management by objectives, technology transfer, career ladders and business attraction, have imbedded in them assumptions that the universe is essentially orderly and predictable.

A Journey Through Entrepreneurship 43

In the disorderly, unstable universe in which we live today, what many refer to as the "new global economy," these sorts of ideas and tools are less useful. Part of the reason people, companies and even regions are "stuck" is that they are trying to apply old models, industrial models, when addressing what factors impel change and what strategies are needed to deal with it. Regrettably, these are no longer relevant or useful. Audretsch's work described this "new economy" and introduced new ways of thinking, strategizing and acting, appropriate to the new dynamics of change confronting individuals and communities who must continuously adapt to unplanned-for opportunities and challenges in two-to-four year time frames.

At its' heart innovation is a social enterprise, not just a technical process. A sustainable quality of economic and social life depends upon continuing economic prosperity and competitiveness, and that in turn depends on reinvention enabled by innovation and entrepreneurship. There is no better way to get it right than by dissecting its essential components and understanding the critical dynamics of entrepreneurship which was what Audretsch's work did.

In my observation of multiple regions, over multiple decades there has been a failure to factor in the less easily quantifiable aspects of regional capacity, such as culture, confidence, mutual trust, ability to share risks and accept failure, a commitment to place, a willingness to collaborate. Thus there has been a critical gap in our understanding of innovation/entrepreneurship and ultimately of how to enable it. These qualitative dimensions of a place emerge from observable social processes which can be described and understood. And for me, as a researcher of comparative regional competitiveness, Audretsch's framing of entrepreneurial economies vs managerial economies has been fundamental to understanding why some succeed and others do not.

So What Is the New Economy?

David Audretsch and Roy Thurik (2001), in their seminal piece published at the beginning of the new millennium, focused on a question that was on everyone's mind when the dot-com bubble burst leaving thousands unemployed and equal numbers holding worthless stock, "What's New about the New Economy?" They provided a highly evocative characterization of the distinctive features of what they described as the "new economy," which they argued is a shift between "two polar worlds," old and new. Through a detailed analysis of what it means to move from a "managed" (by which they meant corporate and rational) to an "entrepreneurial" economy (open and nimble) their analysis provided useful insights into what is problematic about many traditional models of social and economic change as well as what is promising about new emerging models of the economy. It offered a major intellectual shift in how to think about growth and competitiveness.

To understand what is different about the new, it was important to examine some of the traditional assumptions about the forces shaping economic opportunity and growth. In competitive environments, the data used, the assets and gaps identified to inform strategy, are affected by the assumptions one begins with. The work of Audretsch and Thurik, as well as that of Paul Krugman, Richard Florida and others, provided concepts, categories and potential metrics that were different from what, until recently, had been commonly used. They offered new and essential ideas critical to any reliable discussion of innovation and its role in competitiveness in the twenty-first Century (Audretsch and Thurik 2001) Audretsch, a business economist at Indiana University, had been writing all his life about the incredible shift advanced economies have been making as they move from what he characterized as managed, by which he meant corporate and rational approaches to growth and entrepreneurial, by which he meant nimble and experimental approaches. The former are highly influenced by traditional factors such as land, labor, capital and complex equipment and facilities needs, all of which have traditionally benefited from economies of scale, corporate management regimes and command and control forms of organization. He argued that while these factors still play a role in the entrepreneurial economy, knowledge has emerged as the most important factor of production today (Audretsch and Thurik 2001, p. 273).

This knowledge is both formal and explicit (theory, information and data), as well as embedded and tacit (in practice, memory and history). Knowledge also is shared and enlarged upon in public and private contexts, in local and global settings and at faster and faster rates. Thus it cannot be controlled – organized and managed – in the way natural resources, labor and facilities can. In fact, as Audretsch pointed out, the new growth theorists argue that knowledge differs inherently from the traditional factors of production in that it cannot be costlessly transferred across geographic space. In fact, it is best developed and exploited in the context of localized production networks embedded in innovative clusters (p. 273). This is because knowledge is in the people and organizational practices embedded in specific geographic regions and can be shared more quickly and accurately through continuous face-to-face interactions. As Michael Porter at Harvard observed, "The paradox of globalization is that location still matters" (Walshok and Shragge 2014, p. 184). Audretsch would argue it actually matters more.

A key differentiating characteristic of organized and entrepreneurial economies is the extent to which geography in the former is merely a platform on which to combine capital and labor for mass production and distribution. In the entrepreneurial economy geography (characterized by the agglomeration of intellectual capital and related knowledge resources) is the critical incubator of the types of activities which can take place, drive innovation and entrepreneurial economic growth (Audretsch 2007) Geography represents a critical innovation platform in the new economy.

This juxtaposition of "innovation" and "place" as the economic drivers of twenty first century advanced societies is still not universally understood, either in terms of its defining characteristics or in terms of its implications. Policymakers, corporate strategists and everyday citizens concerned about the future, Audretsch would argue, need to rethink the myriad of everyday practices (still anchored in traditional economic assumptions about innovation, growth and prosperity) in order to integrate these new realities. Audretsch's work (2007) did a superb job of beginning to elucidate this phenomenon and to identify the "trade-offs," one might even call them paradoxes, of this "new economy."

He pointed out that localization becomes more important because of the spillovers and synergies that come with high concentrations of knowledge in spite of the standardization of processes and speed of communication that globalization represents. In the old economy, large firms innovated within the boundaries of their core technologies and markets to sustain and grow their markets, as Porter and others have so well described. In the entrepreneurial economy there are many more firms with a greater diversity of technology and approaches to decision-making which benefit overall innovation and technical breakthroughs for regions and citizens though not necessarily for individual firms (Audretsch 2007). Concentrations of large numbers of small R&D firms in a geographic region can also drive more overall innovation than does R&D in large firms locked into specific technologies. The result, Audretsch notes, is that in the new economy, more and more regional jobs and wealth grow as a function of the clustering of many new companies rather than because of growth in a single, multinational company. In fact, 90% of all new jobs in the United States, over the last decade, have been created by small firms (Audretsch 2007).

Traditional economies are based on a model of stability for firms and long-term employment for workers, according to Audretsch. In fact, recent decades have demonstrated time and again that large firms are not stable and cannot guarantee lifetime employment. He provided a convincing view of how in entrepreneurial economies specific firms rise and fall, jobs come and go, but overall employment and wealth increase because of the density of related small firms and skill sets aggregated in a region across large numbers of smaller firms.

The old economy is also based on homogeneity, uniformity and standardization whereas the new entrepreneurial economy thrives and grows on diversity, be it in technical solutions, organizational cultures, or social and managerial practices. Permeable boundaries, inter-firm mobility and alliances, cross professional associations and social relationships as well as formal collaborations and strategic alliances characterize entrepreneurial economies. Audretsch also noted how in more managed economies "trade secrets," competitive anxieties, routines and procedures, as well as isolated and specialized functions and divisions dominate. Entrepreneurial economies in contrast are characterized by open systems through which lots of potentially proprietary knowledge is shared (Audretsch and Thurik 2001).

The "new economy," so aptly characterized by Audretsch, depends upon "flexibility" as the organizing principle for economic growth, as opposed to "scalability," the engine for growth in the traditional economy (Audretsch and Thurik 2001; p. 200). Thus, freedom and incentives rather than regulation; outputs rather than inputs; local control versus national policy; a system of finance based on risk, access and multiple forms of return on investment versus domination by a few national financial institutions also differentiate entrepreneurial from managed economies. As he noted, the industrial economies are all about picking winners, whereas entrepreneurial economies are all about market makers. (Audretsch and Thurik 2001)

Audretsch concluded his discussion of entrepreneurial versus managed economies with the point that it is not possible to exploit knowledge or assure continuous innovation building upon the outputs of knowledge clusters using a traditional economy paradigm. His main argument was that "knowledge as an input into economic activity is inherently different from land, labor and capital. It is characterized by high uncertainty, high asymmetries across people and is costly to transact (Audretsch and Thurik 2001; p. 306)." This means that communities and workers need a high tolerance for change and for failure and a capacity to learn new skills and adapt to new circumstances.

"An externality of failure is learning. In the entrepreneurial economy, failure accompanies the process of searching for new ideas. It similarly follows that the positive virtues of long-term relationships, stability, continuity under the managed economy give way to flexibility, change and turbulence in the entrepreneurial economy. What is a liability in the managed economy is, in some cases, a virtue in the entrepreneurial economy."

Audretsch's characterization of the "new economy" presented three core ideas which have profound implications for how communities think about, plan for and embrace change (Audretsch 2007). The following traits are fundamental to effectiveness in the "new economy:"

The expansion of science and global economic forces means that change and uncertainty are fundamental aspects of everyday life and occur at an ever increasing rate. As a consequence …

Knowledge Matters In the context of continuous change and uncertainty, where ideas and inventions matter most, the discovery, development and deployment of knowledge represent a community's key asset/resource and drives economic growth and prosperity.

Talent Matters A diverse pool of talent, enabled by collective social processes is critical because of the importance of knowledge flows to invention and the organizational dynamics critical to turning knowledge into globally competitive value-added products and services in environments characterized by uncertainty.

Place Matters Geographic regions become the platform for embracing change and uncertainty and exploiting knowledge-based growth opportunities, because geographic proximity and frequent social interaction in a congenial place to live, enables knowledge flows, builds interpersonal confidence and trust and, with that, the ability to mobilize the competent teams needed to turn opportunities into new value-added products and services.

The emergence of previously second tier economic regions such as Austin, Texas, San Diego, California and Raleigh Durham in North Carolina into global leaders in R&D and entrepreneurial science-based companies represents a strong affirmation of the three main principles captured by Audretsch's work. Regions such as these have deliberately cultivated and enabled growth in knowledge creation (research); talent (highly educated, creative people); "know-how" (professionals and managers who understand technology and can work with uncertainty); and investors (diverse forms of seed, venture and longer term capital resources). They have also developed through a diverse range of boundary spanning institutional mechanisms and social networks, integrative mechanisms which enable (a) the nimble and astute evaluation of new opportunities, (b) the mobilization of appropriate teams to help translate ideas into viable enterprises and (c) knowledgeable sources of coaching, manufacturing, setting milestones and evaluation of performance. All of these regionally anchored capabilities are critical to building sustainable and profitable growth companies. All were anticipated by Audretsch's seminal work.

Many places are very good at basic research and discovery because they possess superb centers of research. Many places are good at licensing their science and technology research outputs worldwide. Many places are good at early stage spin-outs and start-ups, thanks to government programs and incubators. HOWEVER, only a few places in the post-industrial world – places such as San Diego, Austin and Raleigh Durham, for example, have demonstrated the ability to not only do these things, but do them in a manner which: (a) additionally retains and grows innovative enterprises regionally; (b) retains and attracts diverse forms of talent, investment and "know-how" to the region; (c) grows significant clusters of science-based companies which are contributing new high wage jobs and new forms of wealth to the region; and (d) enable the community learning which coalesces the new values and new business practices which allow for a sustainable innovation system to take hold. In other words, to become entrepreneurial economies.

Understanding the critical components of these successful regions AND the dynamic interplay among them, as a result of (a) the social processes and networks which (b) support collaboration and continuous learning as well as (c) the development of a collective sense of purpose and confidence, supported by (d) a wide range of explicit and tacit "ways of doing things," is the secret to unraveling the innovation equation. Audretsch's work helped us move beyond lists to an understanding of the dynamic processes which mix, blend and give "rise" to positive entrepreneurial outcomes.

Implications for My Own Work

My encounter with the nuanced distinctions between entrepreneurial and managerial economies articulated by Audretsch and Thurik shaped my thinking and approach to the study of regional innovation outcomes in diverse and complex ways. Over the last 20 years in particular I have researched, authored, and published a number of papers, book chapters and books that have been informed by this important framework. I have also had the privilege of co-editing books with David Audretsch over that period (Audretsch et al. 2015; Audretsch and Walshok 2013).

The regionally anchored, attitudinally and behaviorally distinct dimensions of entrepreneurial economies resonated with my own experience in San Diego and in other dynamic locales. As a consequence it became a framework that informed the sorts of variables, interaction affects, regional personality characteristics and social dynamics I have sought to understand through a variety of funded research projects (U.S. Department of Labor, NSF, Pew Charitable Trust, Lilly Foundation, Kaufmann Foundation).

The often overlooked social and cultural dimensions of place which had always captured my imagination, moved center stage in my research and writing. Thanks to the inspiration of Audretsch's work and my evolving friendship with him, I developed a new self confidence in my work. The importance of teasing out cultural norms and values which are often shaped by industrial legacies and demographic trends that have characterized a region or a city moved center stage as did the need to understand the social dynamics that characterize a place. The formal and informal mechanisms that allow continuous and diverse knowledge flows across traditional jurisdictional, organizational and social boundaries became a focus. And finally, it affirmed for me my long term conviction that **regions** matter because each has unique industrial and demographic legacies, distinctive cultural norms and values, and embedded social dynamics.

The multiple ingredients needed to assure innovation and entrepreneurship are filtered through or interpreted through the lenses of these characteristics of place. They become more or less embedded based on how they are understood and acted upon. Cultural norms and values, as we have learned in contemporary American politics today, can frame in very different ways how the same facts, the same issues are understood and appropriated. One region can behave in a very different manner than another even though operating from similar data bases and following parallel "recipes".

At the end of this paper, I have a complete listing of the work colleagues and I have produced emboldened by the distinction Audretsch and Thurik offered 20 years ago. However I would like to share two examples that I think drive home the utility of these distinctions to the academic work of students and peers who have been inspired by it. In the late 1990's a colleague of mine, Carolyn Lee and I had funding to look at the extent to which an academic entrepreneurial science culture was as significant to San Diego's entrepreneurial economy as a nimble entrepreneurial business culture (see Walshok and Lee 2014). We based this on a close assessment of the regional implications of the expanding public investment in basic science in the 1950's across the United States and in the Health Sciences in the 1970's across the United States, California and in San Diego. What we identified was that campuses that had been built in the post-World War II era with a focus on building exceptional scientific infrastructure from day one turned out to be much more successful in securing large grants from the federal government and foundations than many campuses that were older in more traditional cities.

Of particular interest to us were campuses such as the New York State University campus in Stony Brook and UC San Diego in California. What was clear from our analysis was that the increase in investment in higher education generally and the growth of research universities and state colleges across America from the 1950's onward enabled a few places, but only a few to build globally competitive research institutions from the ground up. This seemed to be tied to differing social expectations and institution building strategies in different regions of America. Many, like the University of Wisconsin, Indiana, and Pennsylvania built regional campuses that were feeders to a flagship institution which provided lower division and in most cases bachelor degrees with a minimum emphasis on post baccalaureate education much less building a research profile. Others like the State University of New York established independent undergraduate colleges across the state with the expectation that some would evolve into graduate research institutions.

UC San Diego, in contrast, once approved by the Regents of the California in 1958 was built on the back bone of Scripps Institution of Oceanography which had been a venerable research partner to the U.S. Department of the Navy, as well as the Southern California home for the UC Division of War Research in the late 1930's and 40's. The defense contracting companies in San Diego recognized that the development of future technology after the war, given the impact of the Atomic bomb, required them to pivot in the direction of basic science. And, civic leaders who earlier had actively recruited the Navy, the defense contractors and the supportive R&D institutions for the defense establishment, recognized that future economic development as well as retaining the military presence in San Diego would be tied to building more powerful basic science capabilities.

To this end in 1955, the mayor and city council launched a series of promotional efforts to attract science companies to the region as well as lobbied for zoning decisions to assure that large plots of land, particularly in La Jolla, were zoned for R&D institutions and light, clean industries. This became the geographic platform for the new University of California San Diego, the Salk Institute and a multitude of R&D institutions. Eventually, the entrepreneurial "new economy" companies proliferated. This civic commitment to "clean" zoning decisions and efforts to build an advanced research university in the region were based on retaining the military as well as attracting new talent to the region. As early as the 1950's leadership believed that would contribute to the growth of high wage jobs and overall regional prosperity (Walshok and Lee 2014; Walshok and Shragge 2014). And, it did!

In contrast to most U.S. universities, older as well newly established ones, UC San Diego started life in the 1960's as a graduate school of science and technology focused on research in the new Physics and Biology. Undergraduates arrived later, as did the growth of UC San Diego as a general university encompassing Arts, Humanities, Social Sciences and Medicine. The founding science faculty recruited by prominent members for the World War II research effort included two Nobel laureates and 13 National Academy of Science members, all risk takers, intellectual mavericks and leaders in their field. These academic stars were the entrepreneurial "nerds" of that era before the term nerd existed. And, in the words of the man who led this effort, Roger Revelle, "Starting a new physics department, in a nonexistent university, in a remote resort town, where one would be surrounded by oceanographers, was the just kind of far out gamble that these sorts of researchers would be completely unable to resist." (Walshok and Lee 2014, p. 133).

The sorts of founding faculty who accepted research positions at UC San Diego brought with them funded grants, graduate students and lab equipment. Since they were all world class researchers with proven ability to win extramural funding for their work, UC San Diego shot up rapidly in the university rankings and indeed as Revelle later said "Attracting superstars is the cheapest way to start a university."

These facts about the culture of the research university begun in San Diego in the 1960's, a hundred years after the establishment of such venerable institutions as the

University Wisconsin, Washington University in St Louis, or the University of Rochester in upstate New York may have a lot to do with how quickly San Diego, in contrast to other cities with great universities, was able to more rapidly achieve entrepreneurial outcomes and build new technology clusters that created enormous wealth and new jobs for the region. The other cities did not experience a similar growth in new economy companies and jobs especially from the 1980's onward. Each region had great research universities but the culture, the norms, the aspirations and social dynamics of the campuses gave rise to a different kind of science and a different orientation to the value and utility of that science in the economy and especially in the region.

Audretsch's work suggests that it is these subtler dimensions of place, the culture and social dynamics which allow us to better understand how organizations and or regions move from an old economy to a new economy model. My work lifelong on the role of research universities in regional economic development has confirmed such assumptions.

A second example of how social and cultural dynamics are pivotal to how an entrepreneurial economy emerges and becomes central to regional strategies is a paper colleagues and I published in the Journal of Technology Transfer in 2012, "Transnational Innovation Networks Aren't All Created Equal: Towards a Classification System" (Walshok et al. 2012). We attempted to look at the way in which new forms of social networking intended to span academic fields and functional competencies such as investment, marketing and management operated. What we discovered was that social networking took different forms in different places and was often organized around different forces. Our paper offered a preliminary classificatory system of four distinct kinds of forces which give rise to social networks that facilitate knowledge flows, relationship building, and collaborative initiatives important to accessing global markets. Based on this close observation of multiple networks we suggested that networks form around at least four distinct factors. Networks can be formed around a technology sector such as the life sciences or computer science, they can be identity based in organizations such as TIES or an Association of Women Entrepreneurs. They can also emerge from government led initiatives which is quite common across the European Union and in the particular initiative we studied supported by the Mexican central government, the Tech-BA network. Finally a fourth kind of networking which seemed to be more common in highly entrepreneurial innovative regions was stimulated from the ground up by civic leadership or philanthropic organizations enabling new forms of social interaction. The paper goes on further to point out that each of these types of networks has a different mode of organizing, financing, and meeting objectives. It was also clear that each of these forms of networks measured outcomes and success in distinctive ways.

At the time we did a literature search on networks there was a tendency to address social networking as though it was a single phenomenon rather than one that could be influenced by different stakeholder interests and values which shape in different ways how they go about creating their purpose and organization. These can also influence how they are financed and often measured according to different performance metrics. The implication is that networks in and of themselves are not enough to explain why some regions develop significant entrepreneurial capacity and others do not. There is very little literature that elucidates the cultural and social underpinnings of different kinds of network groups and the specific issues that bind them.

The knowledge flows between basic research, application and integration into practice are actually only beginning to be understood particularly at the regional level (Bercovitz and Feldman 2006; Charles 2006; Agrawal and Rosell 2009). Research has been done on networks of science, networks of entrepreneurs. Local networks clearly can have an international or transnational focus. The insights we gained from this transnational network analysis helped us understand the uneven pace of different economies in achieving new economy outcomes. The work of Coe, Yeung, Dicken, Hess and Henderson in 2001 reinforced our insights.

Our classification system was organized around the four types of networks identified above and our research spelled out the organizational and financing characteristics of each of the four, the purpose/focus of each of the four, as well as their performance metrics. In the article we provided a detailed description of each of these dimensions. We concluded the paper suggesting that when communities, researchers and civic activists talk about social networks, particularly networks that will enable global connectivity in the service of new economy enterprises, they need to think long and hard about how they are organized, funded and measured. Early indications suggest that self-organizing networks play a valuable role related to helping create a more entrepreneurial mindset along with strategies and tactics that are supported broadly in a community. It appeared that the more top down initiatives were able to engage elites but did not result in the sorts of innovation outcomes that require deeply embedded ecosystems. We suggested that a region's innovation horizons are based on unique regional economic histories, industrial legacies, and cultural patterns based on differing demographics. These in turn shape what drives the character of social networks. As science and technology become more important to a region, as regions seek to build new economy capabilities new forms of social networking are likely to emerge in order to enhance this new form of economic development. Echoing back to Audretsch, new kinds of knowledge flows, new forms of trust building, new forms of partnering are essential to growing strong entrepreneurial economies and communities wishing to create new economy capabilities. And thus, we all need to assess more thoughtfully the character of the social networks that exist as well as need to be cultivated in order to achieve new economy goals.

In Conclusion

As a researcher and an activist, I am animated by understanding the aspects of collective life which enable clusters of new economy industries combined with networks of services and entrepreneurial leaders to emerge. They all are embedded in an ecosystem which, if integrated by a set of social relationships can result in the shared values and aspirations, a sense of common cause, and ultimately the trust so essential to dealing with uncertainty and innovative risk taking. They are the platforms for the mutual trust and respect essential to integrative communities of creative people and experimental ventures, in other words, an entrepreneurial economy. It has been ever so whether in the art world of turn-of-the-century Paris; the scientific societies of nineteenth Century Europe; the post World War I industrial districts of Tuscany; the World War II community of researchers around the Manhattan Project, or the contemporary innovators anchored in "places" such as the Silicon Valley. Each has been enabled by a shared culture and web of social relationships, which enables and supports creativity and innovation, rather than inhibits it. These social dynamics are critically important to success in uncharted territories and for "breakthrough innovations," characterized by high degrees of uncertainty and risk.

Ultimately it is the community milieu that matters and to understand that milieu, one must identify those forms and qualities of social interaction which take place in and between the "clusters" and "networks." It is in the interstices where the sense of excitement and possibility are created, the shared identity and community confidence built and, ultimately, the innovative breakthroughs made. It is the collective life of a place that creates the sense that one has to be "in" such a place in order to be part of something big and important, that one needs to be proximate to all that "talent" which gathers every evening in the cafes of Montparnasse or the wine bars in the Silicon Valley.

Previous economic eras were profoundly shaped by specific natural resources, infrastructure and well organized concentrations of human capital and effort. However, as intellectual capital (knowledge) has become the driver of economic growth through innovation, geographic place matters in new and different ways. Place is where creative people can be assured: (1) useful colleagues, (2) alternative employment opportunities, (3) intellectually nurturing opportunities for learning, (4) connectivity to peers globally, (5) quality of work life characteristics, (6) lifestyle/amenity preferences and (7) acceptance and tolerance. Today the Silicon Valley, Atlanta, Seattle, Austin, San Diego are the places where economic growth is happening. These are the places where the types of talent, competency and resources, which drive the new economy agglomerate and develop overlapping webs of social relationships. More than we realize, it is these social relationships and the competence, trust and resource sharing they enable, which are the drivers of the new economy.

"What's New About the New Economy" helped me and many of us to dig deeper into these factors, to move beyond bounded lists of ingredients and superbly presented social network analyses. It stimulated us to ask what is the content – the mindset, the values, the norms, the social dynamics – that enable pivoting from a managerial platform to an entrepreneurial one. David Audretsch's work gave me a framework that not only has shaped my research career but has allowed me to be a resource to civic leaders and policy influencers as they try to renew regional economies. For this, and so much more, I am grateful to my friend and colleague David Audretsch.

References

Agrawal, A., & Rosell, C. (2009). Have university knowledge flows narrowed? Evidence from patent data. *Research Policy, 38*, 1–13.

Audretsch, D. B. (1991). New-Firm Survival and the Technological Regime. *Review of Economics and Statistics, 73*(3), 441–450.

Audretsch, D. B. (2007). *The Entrepreneurial University*. New York: Oxford University Press.

Audretsch, D. B., & Thurik, R. (2001). What's new about the new economy? Sources of growth in the managed and entrepreneurial economies. *Industrial and Corporate Change, 10*(1), 267–315.

Audretsch, D. B., & Walshok, M. L. (Eds.). (2013). *Creating competitiveness: Entrepreneurship and innovation policies for growth*. Cheltenham: Edward Elgar Publishing.

Audretsch, D. B., Link, A., & Walshok, M. (Eds.). (2015). *The Oxford handbook of local competitiveness*. New York: Oxford University Press.

Bercovitz, J., & Feldman, M. (2006). Entrepreneurial universities and technology transfer: A conceptual framework for understanding knowledge-based economic development. *The Journal of Technology Transfer, 31*(1), 175–188.

Charles, D. (2006). Universities as key knowledge infrastructures in regional innovation systems. *The European Journal of Social Science Research Innovation, 19*, 117–130.

Walshok, M. L., & Lee, C. (2014). The partnership between entrepreneurial science and entrepreneurial business: A study of integrated development at UCSD and San Diego's high-tech economy. In T. J. Allen & R. O'Shea (Eds.), *Building technology transfer within research universities: An entrepreneurial approach* (pp. 129–155). Cambridge: Cambridge University Press.

Walshok, M. L., & Shragge, A. J. (2014). *Invention and reinvention: The evolution of San Diego's innovation economy*. Stanford: Stanford University Press.

Walshok, M. L., Shapiro, J. D., & Owens, N. (2012). Transitional innovation networks aren't all created equal: Towards a classification system. *The Journal of Technology Transfer, 39*(3), 345–357.

Part II
Creating a Research Topic and a Field

David was appointed in 1985 as a Research Fellow in the research unit, *Industriepolitik und Strukturwandel*, or Industrial Policy and Structural Change at the Institute for International Management (now the *Wissenschaftszentrum* Berlin fuer Sozialforschung or Social Science Center Berlin), to undertake research analyzing the impact of large corporations on international competitiveness. He dutifully began a research project with his colleague, Hideki Yamawaki, that generated interested papers such as "R&D, Industrial Policy and U.S.-Japanese Trade," which was published in the *Review of Economics and Statistics* in 1988, and "Import Share Under International Oligopoly with Differential Products: Japanese Imports in US Manufacturing," also published in the Review of Economics and Statistics in 1988.

However, when he looked back across the Atlantic in the mid-1980s, what David realized was unique, interesting and important about the American industry – but remained under the radar of analysis in economics and management – were the emerging high-technology and small companies that no one had heard of just a few years earlier. David's major field in economics, industrial organization, had an almost exclusive emphasis on the largest corporations and their impact on the economy. This was generally true of most of the fields in economics and management. Companies such as Apple Computer, Intel and Microsoft were thriving in an economy that was increasingly populated by the stalwarts of the manufacturing era, such as U.S. Steel and Bethlehem Steel, that were rapidly facing extinction.

Building on the seminal ideas of scholars such as Josef Schumpeter, he set off to understand the one bright spot of American industry at that time – small innovative firms. However, to do that, he needed new data sources. At that time, most of the data bases and measurement reflected the presumed source of economic growth, prosperity and competitiveness – the large corporation. Together with Zoltan Acs, and thanks to the generous support of first the Institute of International Management and later the *Wissenschaftszentrum Berlin fuer Sozialforschung*. David undertook at large-scale research project to explicitly identify the contributions of small companies to innovation, as well as to the overall economy more broadly. The result was a number of his most important and certainly breakthrough publications, such as "Innovation in Large and Small Firms: An Empirical Analysis," published in the

American Economic Review in 1988 and "Innovation, Market Structure and Firm Size," published in the *Review of Economics and Statistics* in 1987, and *Innovation and Small Firms*, published with MIT Press in 1990, all together with Zoltan. These studies unequivocally showed that not only were small companies innovative but they were actually more innovative than their larger counterparts in many industries.

The answer to this question of how small and young companies could exhibit such a strong innovative performance, even with a paucity of knowledge resources such as human capital and research and development (R&D), was provided in what is no doubt David's most important book – *Innovation and Industry Evolution*, published by MIT Press in 1995. In particular, David posited and found compelling empirical evidence for what subsequently became known *as the knowledge spillover theory of entrepreneurship*, which suggests that entrepreneurs endogenously respond to knowledge and ideas created in one organizational context, such as an existing company or university, but create a new company in order to actually pursue and commercialize those ideas.

It was Maryann Feldman who got David interested in the role of geography and place. When she asked whether the innovation data base also included the location of the innovating firm, the sheepish answer was that the geographic indicators had simply been discarded along with other extraneous records. Going back to include the actual location of innovating companies, resulted in a new dimension of research – the geography of innovation, as Maryann famously titled her book on the subject. Maryann co-authored David's most highly cited work, "R&D Spillovers and the Geography of Innovation and Production," published in the *American Economic Review* in 1996, as well as "Real Effects of Academic Research", also published in the *American Economic Review* in 1992 (together with Zoltan) and "R&D Spillovers and Recipient Firm Size," published in the *Review of Economics and Statistics* in 1994 (together with Zoltan). The most salient finding in their papers was not only are knowledge spillovers spatially bounded within close geographic proximity to the source of that knowledge, such as company research and development (R&D) or university research, but that knowledge spillovers are particularly important for small and new firm innovative activityIt became clear to David that no particular field in economics was dedicated to, let alone had the bandwidth, to prioritize and focus on the economic and societal contributions of what had long been the neglected portion of the firm-size distribution – small firms. In response, David and Zoltan sought not just to create a journal, *Small Business Economics*, but ultimately a new field of research. The topic simply did not seem to fit well in to any of the existing fields of either economics or management and strategy. The inaugural issue of *Small Business Economics* was launched in 1989, and still contains some of the best articles ever published not just in the journal itself, but what would ultimately evolve into the now vibrant field of entrepreneurship and small business economics.

However, back in the early days of the journal, that a *bona fide* research field would ultimately coalesce was anything other than obvious. Rather, it took the sustained resources and commitment of a serious research institute, such as the

Wissenschaftszentrum Berlin fuer Sozialforschung, to sponsor a series of conferences, workshops, meetings and seminar speakers that provided key articles which were published from leading scholars in economics, finance and management for the new journal. It also took a substantial amount of travel and networking to forge linkages with the emerging group of scholars and researchers who felt isolated in their traditional fields of research but were quick to embrace the opportunity for publishing in a new journal in a new field. Thanks again to the WZB in Berlin, all of these crucial steps to creating the new field were possible. That the journal was fueling an emerging field of research was evident by 2001, when David was awarded, along with Zoltan, The Global Award for Entrepreneurship by the Swedish Entrepreneurship Forum. Not only was their research on small firm innovation explicitly recognized in the award but also the contribution that *Small Business Economics* made in helping to launch the new field of research.

Zoltan Acs, David's congenial partner and co-author and always a critical companion surveys the past four decades with David in his essay: *The symmetry of Acs and Audretsch: How we meet, why we stuck and how we succeeded.*

Key colleagues, such *Roy Thurik* at the Erasmus University in Rotterdam, *Al Link* at the University of North Carolina in Greensboro, U.S., *Enrico Santarelli* at Bolognia University in Italy, *Marco Vivarelli* at the University of Piacenza in Italy, and *Rui Baptista* in Portugal, quickly became key linchpins not just in the journal but in the emerging field.

The Symmetry of Acs and Audretsch: How We Met, Why We Stuck and How We Succeeded

Zoltan J. Acs

Abstract The author of this chapter, Zoltan Acs, is one of the people who has known David the longest and knows him well. Although they had very different backgrounds and took very different paths, their career arcs led them to meet and become colleagues in Berlin in the 80's and they have been close friends ever since, with Acs even serving as the best man in David's wedding. This essay tells their story.

The Symmetry of Acs and Audretsch: How We Meet, Why We Stuck and How We Succeeded

Like trying to recall a party 40 years ago where people were drinking I can't quite remember when or how we first met. It's a bit of a fog. I know the broad outlines. We were at a conference on industrial organization at Middlebury College in Vermont in May of 1980. But exactly how this happened is not clear. I have no memory. But we did participate in the conference. I do not remember any discussions, drinks or other social interactions. I suspect we attended the conference dinner and at some point someone mentioned in the introductions that David was hired by the department. I guess I would have introduced myself and said that I looked forward to meeting him in September. David had a girlfriend and that they were both moving to Middlebury. I was married living in New York City and I was going to leave my wife in New York (she had a job) and I rented a house with another new hire named Michael Krauss, a political scientist from Princeton. He also had a girlfriend that lived in New York City. But that is another story. So David and I met at Middlebury College in Vermont in 1980 as we were both finishing up our Ph.D.'s and were hired as assistant professors in the economics department.

I arrived in late August in Middlebury, Vermont with my 1971 Cadillac Sedan De Ville, a four door black monster that got about 8 miles to a gallon of gas on a good

---

Z. J. Acs (✉)
George Mason University, Fairfax, VA, USA
e-mail: zacs@gmu.edu

© Springer Nature Switzerland AG 2019
E. E. Lehmann, M. Keilbach (eds.), *From Industrial Organization to Entrepreneurship*, https://doi.org/10.1007/978-3-030-25237-3_8

day. I also bought my motorcycle along with some furniture, pictures and a trailer full of books. Michael and I moved into a huge white house on the same street where Steven Clark Rockefeller lived who was in the religion department. We started to decide who will cook and what. I would make Hungarian chicken paprika and Michael would make Czech mashed potatoes. Rumors spread quickly that some professor has shown up with a huge Cadillac. David moved into a faculty apartment with his girlfriend on campus about three blocks from my house. Our next meeting would have been the new faculty orientation before school started. This took place at the Bread Loaf Campus up in the green mountains. Here David and I would have been in the same seminars on teaching and new faculty orientation. I believe we were going to both teach introductory economics to freshmen. Still no strong recollection of how we actually met.

The fall was beautiful. If you have never spent a fall in Vermont you have not lived. It is beyond spectacular. The air becomes crisp, the sky is bright blue, the sun is a brilliant yellow and the leaves turn every shade of red against a backdrop of the green mountains where the snow has started to fall. We were there with the students that were not much older than David who was just 25. I was 33. He was a little young and I was a little old. While I was a lot older I was just as youthful if not more so than David. These early months were full of the adventures of being young new professors thinking about the world. Middlebury was beautiful, challenging and seductive. The early years were taken up with teaching, hiking, biking and swimming. I guess at first we had department gatherings especially for the younger faculty. But my immediate contact was Michael Krauss since we shared a house. This provided a great opportunity to gossip about college life.

Like a relationship with a woman my relationship with David developed slowly. Not the big bang. I suspect we talked about teaching, the students and our wives and girlfriends. My wife would come up on a few weekends and I would go to New York at times. David was preoccupied with his girlfriend and so did not socialize too much. On thanksgiving weekend, when everyone came to Middlebury College, my wife took me for a walk around the town square and informed me she was going to have a baby. I was in shock. For the next few months I tried to figure out what my life was going to be like. In the spring semester David's girlfriend got up and left one morning like a puff of smoke. I think all of a sudden David and I had something in common to talk about—women. How they fit into our lives, what role they played etc. I remember we started going to the gym together and playing basketball with the students after class. We were in great shape and had lots of fun beating the students. It was during these times that we also started using the swimming pool and taking long hot showers and just talking about everything. One thing that was on everyone's mind was the energy crisis and the cost of oil as OPEC raised prices. How were we going to fix energy, inflation, unemployment etc.? Nice macroeconomic questions for class discussion. However, what had focused my attention and also some of our discussions with David were the election of Ronald Reagan as president of the United States. Why did this happen? I will return to this below.

As the snow melted and the spring flowers bloomed David decided to buy a car—an MGB. I remember going with him to look at the car, thinking about it and finally deciding to buy it. All of a sudden David was a professor driving around campus in a beautiful white MG. I am a car guy so this gave us something to do, driving around the most beautiful place in New England. We now started to expand our activities, we went hiking up the green mountains (4000 feet) biking miles in the valleys and socializing. I liked David and I think he liked me. We were not your average boring stuffy academics like in the religion department. We were exciting, engaging and had a passion for life. We started to bond socially.

In the summer of 1981 I returned to New York City. On June 18, my son Ashley was born in Manhattan. It was actually pretty exciting. We traveled to England during that summer for 2 months and returned to Middlebury College in the fall of 1981. The three of us rented a farm outside of town and started life with my son Ashley who now has a PhD from Princeton and is an assistant professor at the Ohio State University. The fall was amazing with lots of activity at the college including the visit of Charles Kindleberger from MIT for a year and the hiring of David Colander. I spent the fall working on a book Free Market Conservatism: A critique of theory and practice with Edward Nell my advisor and I think David was working on some statistical paper and trying to get his thesis published.

Jane and I returned to New York City for the spring semester and I accepted a visiting position at Columbia University. The real bonding between David and I came during the summer of 1981. I went up to Middlebury with my son Ashley and moved in with David. We sent my son to day care on a dairy farm, and spent the summer riding our bikes, climbing mountains, driving around in the MG and playing with my son. We also might have done some work but I do not recall. Jane would come up on weekends and we just had a lot of fun. We also kept up our discussions about the economy. The Reagan economic policy was starting to take shape and it was rather interesting: tight macroeconomic policy, loose fiscal policy, tax cuts, spending cuts and deregulation. It was deregulation that gave us a way to connect since it was a part of industrial organization. During that summer David and I bonded for life. We developed an affinity for each other that is rare in today's world. It was an ideal world that would not last.

Why did the relationship stick? It's an interesting question (Acs 2017). We talked a lot about it. We enjoyed a lot of the same things; we were youthful, adventurous, curious and competitive. I suspect that our backgrounds also played a role. I never had a brother, David had a brother but they were not close. We both had somewhat difficult family situations and both had two sisters but neither of us was close to them. We wanted to forge a path forward in our lives both personal and professional and we found a sympathetic ear in our friendship.

In the fall of 1982 I took a position at Manhattan College in New York City teaching Money and Banking. Jane went back to work at a consulting firm and my son went to a fancy daycare on the upper west side of Manhattan. It was the modern world. I now started to work on my book that was an outgrowth of my dissertation. The changing structure of the U. S. economy would be about explaining how technology was reshaping both macroeconomics and microeconomics and offered a clear justification for the Reagan economic program. The next 2 years went by with both of us working more and having less fun. While at Manhattan College working on my book I had gotten to know Michael Piore at MIT and invited him to give a talk. We actually became rather close as his book was also very important in identifying the changing structure of the economy. I was starting to build up a network of people with intellectual firepower. I kept in close contact with my colleagues at Columbia too.

In the summer of 1984 two things happened. I went to Italy for a vacation with Jane and Ashley and David went to Washington D.C. for the summer to work at the U.S. Federal Trade Commission. At that moment our lives both changed forever. My wife got pregnant and David met Joanne. David also ran into Leonard Weiss again who was worried that David might be tempted by those big government salaries and leave academia. Later that summer Jane and I went up to Middlebury College and while having drinks at Mr. Ups, a beautiful pub on the Otter River, David explained how he met this great woman. Joanne came up to Middlebury College and was sold on the lifestyle immediately. The discussions also shifted to Berlin as Leonard Weiss had secured a visiting position for David at the world famous WZB in West Berlin. The WZB Berlin Social Science Center, is an internationally renowned research institute for the social sciences, the largest such institution in Europe not affiliated with a university. It was founded in 1969 through an all-party initiative of the German Bundestag. All of a sudden our focus started to shift from teaching and fun to research and the unknown. This event is as vivid as if I happened yesterday.

The fall of 1984 bought major changes to our lives and set the stage for a much closer bonding between us that would last a lifetime. First, David secured a 2 year leave from the economics department to go to Berlin. This was a very hard choice to make going from an ideal certainty to an uncertain future. Will the Russians invade? I found out that I was going to have another baby and had a midlife crisis. It just came out of left field. My book was published and it created an instant conversation piece. Here was a graduate of the New School for Social Research defending a market based economic policy driven by a conservative president.

Joanne decided to follow David to Europe one way or another. These were all steps into the unknown, the abyss of life and life changing events. The friendship was set but there was nothing as of that moment to bond us together professionally. In the spring of 1984 my daughter Annabel was born, I was fired from Manhattan College and went into therapy. Jane and I could not make things work so she left for England right after Annabel was born with the two kids. Why was I fired from Manhattan College, it's a long story, but basically I was not publishing in scholarly journals. The one article that I was pushing did not go anywhere. Supporting Reagan did not help either. This was a low point of sorts, a professional and personal crisis of immense proportions. I had to find another job, David was leaving for Berlin and my personal life came apart. So I bought David's MGB and rented a summer house in the Hamptons, the second most beautiful place on earth. During that summer I visited Jane in England and went over to Berlin to see David. Neither one was very pretty. Jane and I went to Paris with the kids, met Joanne there and had a pretty good time but it was tense. After the visit I went to Berlin. There I found David crying on the couch clutching a picture of Middlebury College in his one bedroom apartment on the edge of the city. But it was great to see David and we had a great visit talking about our women, family, communism, the communist, East West tensions and a little about research. Finally, we had the possibility to perhaps get on the research track.

I returned to New York City and started looking for a job. I had a book, a degree from the New School, some teaching experience but not much more. The prospects looked bleak. I had a fight with my dissertation advisor over the future direction of the economy and our book and was left alone looking for a job. As luck would have it I found a job in Springfield, Illinois at a small state college called Sangamon State University. Just the thought of going to the Midwest made my blood curdle. I went for a job interview to look around and met a man named John Munkers. John was a great person. An ex-Marine! He was an institutional economist and had also just written a book arguing the large firms jointly maximized profits. He had developed a table that showed their interlocking directorships. I liked John so much that I took the job. Jane and I moved to Springfield Illinois in the fall of 1985, rented an apartment near campus and started raising the kids.

David and I were now in different worlds. He was starting to do research in Berlin and I was adjusting to a new and very difficult job. I had to tech graduate mathematical economics and graduate microeconomics and statistics neither subject that I was very familiar with. I spent hours into the wee morning preparing lectures. However, my research interests and David's were starting to come together that year. The catalyst was the institutional economics of American history and the Birch database on firm size as well as my friendship with John Munkers. I secured some funding from the University and leased the USEEM data base from the U.S. Small Business Administration (SBA) and came across a database on innovation. This started a long and fruitful relationship with the SBA and Bruce Phillips. I used this resource to write a proposal to the WZB based on Michael Piore's work about the second industrial divide and the proposal was accepted—I got a 3 month visiting scholar's position. I was ecstatic. Jane and the kids went off to the English country side in Devon and I went to Berlin for the summer to research small business and entrepreneurship. David found me an apartment near the WZB. The research agenda was conceived.

I arrived in Berlin in early June of 1986 and went over to David's apartment where Joanne had now settled in. This was the start of a routine. I arrived, we had a few beers and nuts and Joanne would make dinner. I believe that first evening as we are finishing up dinner and drinks we sat down and I took out the draft of the innovation database and showed David. I still have it! He started to look at it and immediately went into a trance. He picked up a magic marker and started marking up the hard copy of the innovation database. And he would be mumbling four-digit SIC, four-digit SIC, four-digit SIC. I just kept drinking beer not quite sure what four-digit SIC was—standard industrial classification. But the hook was that David had a huge database with hundreds of variables by four-digit SIC. But of course what did not exist was innovation by four-digit SIC at the time and David knew this. We had just discovered gold.

The next day we go to the office at Platz der Luftbrücke and David had the data entered into the computer. The USEEM data proved to be more difficult. The Germany could not read the four data tapes. The data was massive. But we had innovation data by four-digit SIC and by firm size, large vs small firms. So it was the start of our joint research project trying to figure out and untangle this idea of mine that small firms could be innovative like in the steel industry and perhaps more innovative than large firms. So in the summer of 1986 over beers, long walks, late nights David and I bonded professionally as we had personally in the summer of 1982 in Vermont. It was an incredible summer living and working in Berlin, being at a world class research institute with world class scholars. What an adventure, we merged Vermont with Berlin and we had a research project to test the restructuring thesis I had cobbled together over the previous few years. Our guide now was the text book of F. M. Scherer on industrial organization and the edited volume of Z. Grilliches on Patents, Innovation and Productivity. His is one of the best books ever written on the subject.

We were now bonded but, "Why did we succeed?" To answer this question takes a much longer narrative. We could not have been any more different professionally. David graduated from the University of Wisconsin a top ten school where he studies industrial organization with the late Leonard Weiss. He was a student of the structure-conduct-performance school of industrial organization just as game theory was taking off. I remember having just read Stiglitz that perhaps market structure was endogenous, and David replied, "That is the kiss of death for our business."

I received my Ph.D. from the Graduate Faculty of the (the university in exile) New School for Social Research in New York City. It had been said that there were only three places to study economics in the 1970s, The University of Chicago (monetary economics), MIT (mathematical economics) and the New School for Social Research (Marxian economics). My advisor was Edward J. Nell a growth theorist in the neo Ricardian tradition and an Oxford Don. I wrote an old fashion dissertation on price behavior in competitive and corporate markets using the steel industry as a case study to understand inflation. If one recalls the 1970s this was one of the most vexing problems facing western democracies.

I became interested in entrepreneurship by accident and like most important discoveries it was part preparation and part luck, part inspiration part perspiration. I wanted to be a scientist but did not have the proper math training. I also wanted to be an engineer, dabbled a bit but found it not satisfying. I found economics fascinating and satisfying. While I was interested in both macroeconomics and microeconomics entrepreneurship did not fit into either branch of economics. But the subject was so fascinating that it has occupied most of my professional life.

"My education at the New School for Social Research taught me two things about the world. First, that industrial capitalism was about large firms and mass production on both sides of the Atlantic, and second, that the world was likely heading toward socialism, where state planning and nationalization would be the norm. It appeared that it was only a matter of time until capitalism would fail, as predicted by Marx (1867) and Schumpeter (1942). Put simply, over–investment in industry would lead to a falling rate of profit, and without profit the Capitalist world as we know it would cease to exist. My education included nothing about entrepreneurship or small firms.

And then fate stepped in. In my dissertation—by today's standards probably not a very good one—there was a small but important discovery. I had attempted to understand the evolution of capitalism through price theory and the study of industry. My discovery, the "two steels," showed that technical change can come from small firms, even in industries that have been dominated by large firms for a century or more. This curiosity was my first foray into the study of small firms and entrepreneurship, and it put me on the path to becoming a scholar of entrepreneurship.

I knew I had discovered something potentially significant, but was not sure what its relevance was at the time or what its full impact would be. However, I was not alone in my discovery: David Birch and Michael Piore, both at MIT, had independently and simultaneously found the same thing: that the capitalist model we had been studying no longer fit the facts, at least not as well as it should. Birch (1979) found that large enterprises in almost all metropolitan areas in the United States were no longer the main engines of job creation. Michael Piore and Charles Sable (1984) suggested in their book, The Second Industrial Divide, that after two hundred years the organization of industry was again changing, this time away from mass production to flexible production."

At the time most economist were still wedded to the belief that large firm were the engine of the economy. These behemoths like IBM, ATT, U.S. Steel, Exxon, General Motors and many more were both technologically superior to other firms and that monopoly power was important for innovation. No one saw that technological change would come from the universities and not the industrial laboratories.

"My contribution, in The Changing Structure of the U.S. Economy (Acs 1984), centered on technology, markets, and democracy, such as how small firms were both able to and allowed to innovate in industry after industry. And then, with the election of then President Ronald Reagan in 1980, a set of institutional and social changes were unleased upon the economy.

What did I know in 1980? Well, I put several issues on the table that would stand the test of time: If Schumpeter was wrong about the future of capitalism, who was right? If this new capitalism prevails, what might it look like? I also knew that economic growth had to be a piece of the puzzle, that we had to measure what was happening at the industry level, and that it had to be done in the tradition of existing studies on industrial organization.

At the policy level, I knew Keynesian economics was finished. As I wrote: Keynesian anticyclical policies cannot restore growth and eliminate unemployment. Planning would only make it worse. The conservative programs relying on small firms and markets, while going through a learning curve, appear to be moving in the "right" direction. The conclusion of this book is that the market today is a guiding light through the maze of economic uncertainty created by technological evolution.

These discoveries occurred from about 1976 to 1982. To understand what was happening, one only needed to read "The Coming Entrepreneurial Revolution: A Survey," an article by Norman Macrae that appeared in The Economist (1976, p. 41). The Economist had understood already that the world was going to change and that it was not moving toward more top–down management, central planning, and state ownership. The magazine's view was that we were approaching the end of big business, that state capitalism would not prevail, that it was the end of the "organization man," and that educated people would become more entrepreneurial. If any of this did prove true, then the field of small business and entrepreneurship were surely born out of a crisis in economics and the economic crisis of the 1970s.

Calling on a bit of economic theory at this point will be helpful in understanding a world in transition. For one thing, there are no entrepreneurs in general equilibrium theory. This means that, in a static world where all markets clear, the quantity supplied equals the quantity demanded, there is no role for the entrepreneur. General equilibrium theory had thus put the brakes on our understanding of the economy and on the development of economic theory in general.

One of the greatest developments in the field of economics was the Solow residual [Solow 1957]. Appearing in 1957, the concept had been years in the making. It shed light on where economic growth comes from and on what causes it—that is, technical change. Solow pointed out that technical change was a term used for any kind of shift in the production function, and this calculation of his data was seen as an indication of where we needed to concentrate our attention—which was not on capital accumulated or hours worked. In fact, much economic growth (87%) remained unexplained, so it was now the turn of the explainers. What was in the residual?

A second discovery that shed light on development appeared in an essay by Harvey Leibenstein (1968). Leibenstein argued that entrepreneurs were needed to shift the production function and suggested that there are two kinds of entrepreneurs. The first is the replicative entrepreneur, who practices a kind of management that does not shift the production function but instead replicates an existing one, such as by opening another restaurant. The other is the novel or innovative entrepreneur, who shifts to a new production function, such as the cell phone. This creative destruction is what propels the capitalist system forward.

We now have the background for understanding the rebirth of entrepreneurship. The simultaneous discoveries made by Acs, Birch, and Piore and Sabel all revealed an empirical observation that did not fit with existing views of capitalism. In fact, their analyses predicted the entrepreneurial revolution, the fall of communism, and the rebirth of capitalism.

Now let's put some meat on the bones of this analytical skeleton. It was easy to study capitalism and socialism from an industrial perspective, as both systems had relatively few firms active in each industry. The West had more diversity in firm size, but not much more, than the Soviets in terms of what counts—innovative small firms. In the industrial organization literature, economists have at best studied a few hundred industries and the Fortune 500 firms. Small firms have long been thought to play a minimal role in job creation, innovation, and technical progress. Moreover, there was no perceived need for new firms, as the existing ones could do whatever was needed—even get man to the moon!

So this raises an obvious question: Why study small business? It may be helpful to start this discussion about the evolution of entrepreneurship with a story about small business. Small firms, which are smaller than big businesses no matter how measured, are at a disadvantage relative to larger firms—they have less money, less talent, etc.—which is common knowledge. However, we know very little about the history of small firms and, without an understanding of them vis–à–vis industry dynamics, it is almost impossible to understand entrepreneurship."

We found common ground between David's empirical training and my radical views about where the economy was headed: inflation, oil crisis, slow growth and unemployment. But we were more journalistic in our approach then scholars. Neither one of us published much in the first few years. We both ended up with a book in the early 1980s in with Charles Kindleberger played a key role. We had a conference at Middlebury College organized by Kindleberger on the multinational organization and David ended up with an edited volume with Kindleberger as coauthor. I turned my dissertation into a book on the changing structure of the U.S. economy and Charles wrote the introduction. We both benefited from this association.

So the first symmetry in our relationship was that I had a framework about the economy shifting from large firms to smaller entrepreneurial firms. However, my training did not really teach me how to do research and certainly did not teach me how to write high level academic articles. So David and I teamed up that summer and wrote three papers. It was a real learning experience especially for me. Of course they were not published immediately but were interesting papers on innovation in large and small firms. This break of merging different databases and looking at issue in the size distribution of firms influenced by technological change was a hot topic and of wide interest to a range of scholars.

The promise of this research led to another contract for me at the WZB and David was also contemplating staying for two more years after his original leave. My concern was that if David did not return could I finish this work on my own. David said I was right to be concerned. It turns out that I came to Berlin, David Stayed and I was the best man at their wedding. The year was a very hard one. I had to produce some serious research and get a few articles published or I would not have a job and might end up driving a taxi cab.

The research ended up being extremely successful. We in rapid succession published one article in Economica, one in RESTAT and one in the American Economic Review (Acs and Audretsch 1988). We also got and MIT Press book and a contract to start Small Business Economics. This symmetry continued with the fall of the Berlin Wall that pointed out the importance of small firms in the economy. In the meantime David and Joanne got married at the Rathaus Schoenefeld in Berlin, I was the best man and we all went on a honeymoon to Budapest.

At this point it is important to try and explain how this rock solid relationship got such a stable footing. There were other players. Not in any order of importance they were Frederick Scherer who was visiting the WZB and had a keen interest in the

Schumpeterian issue of firm size and innovation. Then there was David S. Evans who had just finished breaking up bell with his Chicago friends and was also using the Dunn and Bradstreet data. His partner Boyan Jovanovic had just published a seminal article on the passive learning model in Econometrica and their joint article in the Journal of Political Economy (JPE) on liquidity constraints was path breaking. Evans other two articles one on firm growth in the JPE and one on Entrepreneurship in the AER were also path breaking. The other persons that played an important role were Bo Carlsson and Gerhard Mensch at Case Western Reserve University. By this time we had also met David Story, Roy Rothwell and Mark Dodson, Bruce Kirchhoff, William Dunkelberg, Danny Blanchflower, Richard Nelson and a host of other scholars. We might not have been world class, neither of us went to MIT, but we surrounded ourselves with world class scholars at every opportunity.

The symmetry of our visions and the networks that we forged at the WZB would stand the test of time. David and I often thought of this foundation as a tripod upon which we would build and change the world. The tripod was the AER article, the MIT Press book and the Small Business Economics Journal. I believe I had suggested the idea for the journal on a visit of Kluwer to the institute. David was very enthusiastic and we put together a proposal with the small network of people we had around us. You have to keep in mind that at this time there were no journals of entrepreneurship or small business per say. Richard Caves at Harvard thought it was a terrible ides. The American Journal of Small Business, a rag of 50 pages published four times a year at the University of Baltimore was the closest to a scholarly publication. The journal was moved by Ray Bagby to Baylor University and renamed Entrepreneurship Theory and Practice. Ironically, I went to the University of Baltimore as Ray left and took Small Business Economics.

What is interesting in hindsight is that as this technological revolution was starting to sweep the country a score of academic journals came into being around this time. In addition to Small Business Economics and Entrepreneurship Theory and Practice you had, Journal of Business Venturing, Technovation, Research Policy, Regional Studies, Entrepreneurship and Regional Development, Journal of Small Business Management, Industrial and Corporate Change, Journal of Technology Transfer, International Small Business Journal among others. In one way or another, these journals all focused on innovation and entrepreneurship. While the topic of innovation was well research the topic of entrepreneurship was not and creating forums to study this interaction proved to be of lasting value. However, the experiment is far from successful or finished. These are some of the best ranked journals in the business and economics areas.

The inaugural issue of Small Business Economics in 1989 laid out our symmetric vision for the field. The lead article was written by David S. Evans and William S. Brock, followed by Bo Carlsson, Roy Rothwell, Bruce Kirchhoff, Felix R. Fitzroy, Robert Hebert and Al Link presented our vision for the integration of innovation and entrepreneurship in a fast changing technologically driven world. The journal was now backed with solid research in the leading economics journals and a cadre of young scholars that was attracting an ever larger and larger group of followers.

We returned to the U. S. and my family and I (Ashley and Annabel) moved to Baltimore, Maryland. The University of Baltimore proved to be a very useful place where I could continue to do research and work with David and Baltimore proved to be a great place to raise children. It was here that I met Richard Florida and Maryann Feldman and introduced them to David. This resulted was another stream of research on the geography of innovation with articles in the American Economic Review and RESTAT again. A few years later I met Attila Varga and the Jaffe-Feldman-Varga thesis on knowledge spillovers fell into place.

As in all good relationships things got very rocky after a few mistakes on my part around 1995 and we did not talk for years. Time has a way of healing most things. If you put time into any regression it is always significant. I had spent the 1990 working on entrepreneurship and cities, working at the U. S. Small Business Administration and the Census Bureau. David and I made up like most partners and we started another large research project this time with Bo Carlsson and Pontus Braunerhjelm on entrepreneurship and growth. Influenced by endogenous growth theory we were going to join the growth crowd.

Out of this came the second symmetry the Knowledge Spillover Theory of Entrepreneurship and scores of papers. Well it is really difficult to sort out who actually gets credit for this invention. Everything is symmetric. Our original work on large and small firm innovation should be interpreted in light of the second paper on 'The Knowledge Spillover Theory of Entrepreneurship,' (Acs et al. 2009), Small Business Economics, with over 1000 Google citations and several review articles. Knowledge spillover entrepreneurship put the former research into context. Indeed, it was not small firms per say that were innovative but it was young firms that took advantage of knowledge spillovers in an entrepreneurial ecosystem—place mattered.

We were now also gearing up the Max Planck Institute in Jena where David was director and we had all converged to push entrepreneurship research. By all measures it was a great success except we could no longer get articles into the best journals. We settled into entrepreneurship research identified by a large and growing group of scholars and the new set of journals of which Small Business Economics was one of the leading players.

Given this background three things are very interesting. First, While David and I started out working together on innovation and firm size that was a rather short period of time perhaps 7–10 years. Second, while after that we both moved on to work with different scholars we stuck to similar topics in our respected research, cities, regions, nations, growth, entrepreneurship and today ecosystems. This is rather interesting and shows that the crucible that we forged out intellectual interests in early 1980 survived the test of time. Thirdly, I had three forays over the years, one into obesity, one into philanthropy and one into systems. The much larger one was National Systems of Entrepreneurship (NSE) and the Global Entrepreneurship Index (GEI). Finally, the trilogy is complete with the publication of 'National Systems of Entrepreneurship', (Acs et al. 2014), Research Policy, with over 400 Google citations, that measures the health of the entrepreneurial ecosystem, where entrepreneurs flourish and offers policies for improving ecosystem performance.

What drove us during these 40 years is also interesting. In the beginning it was just learning how to publish good articles in order to get tenure. This was no easy task in the early years as the topic of small firms and entrepreneurship was not on anyone's radar screen. However, as we became more and more successful what kept us going I believe is not only being able to come up with new and more interesting research topics but an intense symmetric competition to succeed. David, if we measure by convention is a better scholar, able to slice the "baloney" very thin. I however, have had very good insights and vision. How to parse this is also an exercise in slicing the baloney.

So the symmetry of our working relationship is now clear. However, one part of it is not symmetric. We come from very different social backgrounds. I was born in a refugee camp in Austria, moved to a working class ghetto in Cleveland, Ohio and quit school to support our family at age 15. David grew up in an upper middle class family in upstate New York his father an engineer for IBM. He attended good schools and lived in nice communities. What I learned from David is how to treat people with respect. This is the asymmetry in our relationship. This is a hard lesson to learn or unlearn and I am still working on it. That is the symmetry and asymmetry in our professional and personal relationship.

The story would not be complete without a mention of our families. We married great women, raised good and successful children and had wonderful families. Congratulations on a life well lived!

References

Acs, Z. J. (1984). *The changing structure of the U.S. economy*. New York: Praeger Publishers.

Acs, Z. J. (2017). The godfather of entrepreneurship. In D. B. Audretsch & E. E. Lehmann (Eds.), *The Routledge companion to the makers of modern entrepreneurship* (pp. 3–9). London: Routledge.

Acs, Z. J. D., & Audretsch, B. (1988). Innovation in large and small firms. *The American Economic Review, 78*, 678–690.

Acs, Z. J., Braunerhjelm, P., Audretsch, D. B., & Carlsson, B. (2009). The knowledge spillover theory of entrepreneurship. *Small Business Economics, 32*(1), 15–30.

Acs, A. J., Autio, E., & Szerb, L. (2014). National systems of entrepreneurship: Measurement and policy implications. *Research Policy, 43*(3), 476–494.

Birch, D. (1979). *The job generation process*. Cambridge, MA: M.I.T. Program on Neighborhood and Regional Change.

Leibenstein, H. (1968). Entrepreneurship and development. *American Economic Review, 58*, 72–83.

Macrae, N. (1976). The coming entrepreneurial revolution: A survey, The Economist p. 41.

Marx, K. [1867] (1977). *Capital* (Vol. 1). New York: International Publishers.

Piore, M., & Sable, C. (1984). *The second industrial divide*. New York: Basic Books.

Schumpeter, J. (1942). *Capitalism, socialism and democracy*. New York: Harper and Row.

Solow, R. (1957). Technical change and the aggregate production function. *Review of Economics and Statistics, 39*(3), 312–320.

Visions of the Past: David was Always There

Roy Thurik

Abstract Longtime close friend and colleague Roy Thurik uses this chapter to detail his relationship with David, both in and out of Academia. He tells of David being there for him during difficult times and providing invaluable advice when he needed it most. He also tells of his admiration for the man and scholar, the friend and confidante. Thurik's writing gives the reader a glimpse behind the curtain, so that one can see how highly esteemed David is as a pioneer in small business economics.

Visions of the Past: David was Always There

At conferences, coffee is a critical lubricant, bringing people together as they wait for it to be served, while drinking it, and waiting for the caffeine to kick in. For me, the most important coffee I've ever waited for was on September 1, 1988, in Rotterdam, at the 15th EARIE (European Association for Research in Industrial Organization) conference. Next to me was this man, who mentioned that he had just come from Dordrecht, where he'd made a deal with Kluwer Publishers to establish a new journal entitled *Small Business Economics Journal*. Oddly, I had just made a deal with my dean at the Erasmus School of Economics to name my chair as "small business economics." David Audretsch was the man and it was commonalities between our deals that brought us together.

Although we had independently coined the term, "small business economics," jointly, it was the start of a long friendship that has taken many surprising twists, taking on many different affinities and identities. Since then, David and I have co-authored almost forty articles. At the same time, I have co-authored nearly thirty articles in *Small Business Economics Journal* and refereed at least a hundred articles. Most importantly, I have slept many nights in the "famous economist guest room" at Audretsch residences on both sides of the Atlantic.

R. Thurik (✉)
Erasmus School of Economics and Montpellier Business School, Rotterdam, The Netherlands
e-mail: thurik@ese.eur.nl

© Springer Nature Switzerland AG 2019
E. E. Lehmann, M. Keilbach (eds.), *From Industrial Organization to Entrepreneurship*, https://doi.org/10.1007/978-3-030-25237-3_9

EARIE conference organizers were quick to understand the role of small businesses for the organization of industries. In 1985, my submission to the 12th EARIE conference in Cambridge was rejected because, in the words of the referees, "it was about small business and we were meant to know that small businesses were no part of the scholarly field of industrial organization." With that in mind, David and I only whispered the words "small business economics" conspiratorially at the 15th edition in Rotterdam. There were a dozen or so small business papers at the 16th edition in Budapest, all well quarantined in separate sessions. Finally, at the 17th edition in Lisbon in 1990, empirical small business papers were an integral part of the entire program, despite the fact that the promising future of industrial organization lay in the theoretical game theory papers addressing the struggles of large businesses.

David and I did not just observed this kink in the then important scholarly field of industrial organization, we also assisted in crafting it. For most, this would probably have been enough to develop a lifetime bond, but for us, it was a harbinger of things to come.

The 1990s witnessed the first signs of 'small business economics' as a recognized subfield of economics. This coincided with a series of stimulating and productive visits to the Institute of Development Strategies (IDS) at the School of Public and Environmental Affairs (SPEA) at Indiana University Bloomington (IUB). The IDS director was the young man I first met in 1988: David Audretsch. As a research fellow, I contributed to investigations of how geographical places perform, how to identify what needs to be done to make them better, and what the role of entrepreneurship may be.

A few years later, David Audretsch re-appeared in Europe, this time as Director of the Entrepreneurship, Growth and Public Policy group at the Max Planck Institute of Economics in Jena, Germany, from 2004 through 2010. There I served as a visiting research professor, participating in the three Kauffman-Max Planck-Ringberg conferences, in 2006, 2007, and 2008. These were clear highpoints for scholars of entrepreneurship, economic development, and public policy, defining markers of an era.

More importantly, I arrived at what would become a main theme for at least 50 years: the interplay between small firms – and what was later termed as entrepreneurship – and the macro economy. It started off with a series of empirical publications in obscure journals and in edited book volumes. Showing with simple means that smallness can positively affect economic performance at aggregate levels, these studies provided the roots for four approaches. The *first* approach was a conceptual one about the role of small firms – which was more and more frequently referred to as entrepreneurship – in the macro economy and, in particular, for economic growth. My 1999 publication, with Sander Wennekers, in *Small Business Economics Journal*, called "Linking Entrepreneurship and Economic Growth" would prove to be my best cited, with more than 2500 Google Scholar hits in 2018. It remains among the most highly cited articles ever published in *Small Business Economics Journal*.

The *second* approach consisted of a series of empirical single equation studies, often based on aggregate panel data, on the role of small firms for economic growth and development. In particular, the two 2005 *Small Business Economic Journal* publications in volume 42, nr 3, using material from the Global Entrepreneurship Monitor received many citations.

The *third* approach was again conceptual and coupled the changing role of small business and entrepreneurship with a larger change in the economic system, which was coined "the switch from the managed to the entrepreneurial economy." David Audretsch played a crucial role in helping me understand this switch and writing up the analyses. These analyses also helped to better understand the role that the second ICT (information and communication technology) revolution played in both modern developed and developing economies. It provided important material for the foundation of courses in small business economics for both students and entrepreneurs with a distinct societal flavor that I gave at the Free University of Amsterdam and at Erasmus University Rotterdam. Without David's brilliant style of associating different literatures and schools of thought and then gluing it together in a compelling fashion, I would never have been able to teach these courses and to pursue the next approach.

The *fourth* approach was based upon a stylized fact: in many OECD countries, U-shaped entrepreneurship rates (business owners per workforce) can be observed over time as well as over the level of economic development. This U-shape results from the fact that the entrepreneurship rate has declined since there is economic life, but this decline stopped in the early 1990s and a reversal has even set in. The resulting trough marks the beginning of the entrepreneurial economy. I never managed to theoretically derive this U-shape from the many interplays between entrepreneurship and macroeconomic phenomena, such as unemployment or economic growth, which separately have all been well documented. However, David showed me how deviations from this U-shape consequently lead to growth penalties.

The studies David and I performed on the changing role of small business and entrepreneurship in the economy and society inevitably led to policy contemplations. The so-called "eclectic theory of entrepreneurship," published in a 2002 Kluwer Academic Publishers book, provided a basis with many offshoots. This model is not based on real theory because it is highly eclectic in that it borrows many stylized facts from diverse fields showing the complex effects different policies may have on entrepreneurship and how entrepreneurship then influences the structure of the economy. It should have provided the basis for a contemplation that entrepreneurship policy does not exist, *per se*, but that policies in general have entrepreneurship effects. Sadly, David and I never wrote this up. My "entreprenomics" paper, a combination of the "from the managed to the entrepreneurial economy" view and the eclectic theory never caught much attention, while I kept struggling with whether entrepreneurship policy existed in an Edward Elgar Handbook of Research on Entrepreneurship Policy in 2007.

Like many fellow researchers I learn more from my students than they do from me. I learned a lot from having had a part-time chair at the Econometrics Institute of the Erasmus School of Economics (ESE); a chair to which I was appointed at a far too young an age. I learned a lot from having a full-time chair in the Department of Applied Economics of ESE and then setting up a Bachelor's major program for third year economics students, a Bachelor's minor program for third year students of all backgrounds and a Master's program for economics students. I learned a lot from setting up and directing the Centre for Advanced Small Business Economics (CASBEC), which was a joint effort between Panteia BV (a commercial research firm where I worked for 40 years) and ESE. It is a platform coupling societal relevance and scientific rigor. I learned a lot from the gigantic exercise of trying to set up the Erasmus Centre for Entrepreneurship (ECE), which was such a struggle that I gave up at the precise moment that anybody of any importance started to support the initiative. Currently, I am scientific director of ECE, which is mainly ornamental. I learned a lot from my own ESE, which has always been tolerant and even generous with my field and with me. My field, my research small group, and I have survived three reorganizations. I learned a lot from my activities for public bodies such as the Dutch Ministry of Economic Affairs, "Brussels", the OECD, the Dutch Retail Trade Board, and many others. I learned a lot from my 30 or so PhD students who are, on average, far more clever than me. I also learned from setting up and directing the "Erasmus University Rotterdam Institute of Behavior and Biology" (EURIBEB).

Regardless of the lessons I've learned from all my resume-visible activities, ultimately, the principle teacher in my life is David Audretsch, my friend and co-author. He discouraged me from moving out of the field, although we seldom talked about the field. He discouraged me from doing stupid things in my personal life. He did so in hundreds of transatlantic telephone calls and hundreds of meetings that we had in dozens of countries at countless conferences, workshops, and other meetings. Good meals, enjoyable drinks, and fine views inevitably accompanied our encounters.

How great can life be! It has given me countless presents and David is easily one of its most precious ones.

This long friendship helped me stay in the field at times when I was desperate because what I saw as a field, others did not. It helped me explain what I was doing in the first place. It connected me to many people who are now my closest friends.

Observing David is also an inherent joy. He has a 'bee function' that is based upon friendliness, a keen eye on a helping hand, avoidance of any stress, and the aim to connect people. Like the insect, he flies around, but unlike the insect, he is simultaneously everywhere. He shares everything he knows with everybody he meets. Like bees, David has his limitations. In 2008, David crossed the Atlantic some forty times – that's 40 round trip flights. "But I mostly travel business class." Sure! "But I sleep a lot." I don't think so. "But I write books." Yes, you do! Nobody doubts this given his intimidating production of books.

Every small industry or group has its black sheep: colleagues you would rather avoid. The "small business economics" industry has no black sheep. This is due to the culture in our field, a culture that reflects our leader's style. As our unchallenged leader, David's style renders it impossible for any sheep to turn black or for a black one to avoid bleaching if they are serious about making an impact in the field of "small business economics." The atmosphere found when researchers in the field meet is rare in academia. It is the positive atmosphere created by David that makes it possible. Although including the words "charismatic" and "altruistic" in a Festschrift is entirely predictable, I include them here because they fit exceptionally well. It can be seen in how his personality, the pervasiveness of his influence, and the distinctiveness of his character permeate the chapters of the present Festschrift.

In many ways, David is an extraordinary human: as an American, he is the most European American, I know. Comfortable in a Biergarten or in an all-night diner, David needs a new challenge. So I want to, for a change, offer an idea to David: as he turns 65, he ought to write the next Great American Novel. Although he might need to take on a pseudonym to protect the innocent, his wealth of experience and his exceptional writing skills provide the necessary foundation. Surely, I, and everybody else who has contributed to this Festschrift, will each appear as a minor character. The unforgettable adventure that was the invention of 'small business economics' cannot be captured in scholarly texts. It deserves so much better.

Comments

See A.R Thurik (2016), Visions of the past: wish you had been there, in D.B. Audretsch and E. Lehmann (eds.), *Routledge Companion to Makers in Modern Entrepreneurship*, (Routledge Publishing, London), 181–201 for some references. I would like to thank Adam Lederer for his invaluable advice.

Structural Change, Knowledge Spillovers and the Role of SMEs and Entrepreneurship

Pontus Braunerhjelm

Abstract In this essay, Pontus Braunerhjelm surveys David's impact in the field of small business economics and entrepreneurship. By giving in-depth analysis into one of David's interest areas, Braunerhjelm grants the reader the opportunity to more fully understand the scope of David's research. The following chapter therefore helps to clarify the underlying nature of David's scholarly work.

Introduction

David Audretsch contributions in the field of small business and entrepreneurship are unique, his achievements have been referred to previously in this volume. Basically, Audretsch's research has focused on the links between entrepreneurship, innovation, economic development and policy. I like to think of David Audretsch as a great knowledge transmission mechanism, an influencer and an enabler when it comes to small business research. In fact, David has himself become a conduit for knowledge spillover, an area he has written extensively about. He is one of the most networked and connected people that I know of.

My first encounter with David was sometime 1991/92 when Professor Bo Carlsson involved me in an EU project (then EC) called Industrial Dynamics and Small Firms. I was about to conclude my thesis at The Graduate Institute for International Studies (University of Geneva), dealing with international trade theory and foreign direct investment. After a few more project meetings with David and his colleagues, all being renowned scholars in the field of small businesses and to some extent entrepreneurship, I gradually re-directed my research focus towards these areas. Since at least 15 years back the overwhelming part of my works relates to entrepreneurship, innovation and economic growth. David was of course one main inspiration to why that happened.

P. Braunerhjelm (✉)
KTH Royal Institute of Technology, Department of Industrial Economics and Management, Stockholm, Sweden
e-mail: pontus.braunerhjelm@indek.kth.se

© Springer Nature Switzerland AG 2019
E. E. Lehmann, M. Keilbach (eds.), *From Industrial Organization to Entrepreneurship*, https://doi.org/10.1007/978-3-030-25237-3_10

Around 2001/2002 I received at generous research funding from Marcus and Marianne Wallenberg's Research Foundation for a project named Entrepreneurship and Society. That became the departure point for a number of years of intensive cooperation with David, where also Zoltan Acs and Bo Carlsson participated. During highly constructive meetings (one in Bretton Woods in a room just adjacent to the Golden Room), characterized by very open discussions, juggling and testing different arguments and thoughts, a couple of new ideas emerged where the ambition was to link contemporary growth models to a more rigorous micro-economic foundation. The discussions were, to say the least, vivid. I was often accompanied by one of my PhD students who at one time confided to me that he thought we were going to start a fight. Still, this is one of the most constructive and fruitful project I have been involved in throughout my career and resulted in the so called Knowledge Spillover Theory of Entrepreneurship (KSTE, Acs et al. 2009), together with a number of other papers linking entrepreneurship to endogenous growth (e.g. Carlsson et al. 2009; Braunerhjelm et al. 2010; Audretsch et al. 2012).

The prevailing theories of entrepreneurship traditionally revolved around institutions, the ability of individuals to recognize opportunities and how that generated new ventures. This sparked a literature asking why entrepreneurial behavior varies across individuals with different characteristics while disregarding where the opportunities stem from. Thus, the source of entrepreneurial opportunities was implicitly taken as given.

The KSTE provided a framework showing how individual entrepreneurial ability, together with opportunities generated by incumbents' knowledge investments, led to the creation of new ventures. Hence, by exploiting knowledge (new and old and their combinations) entrepreneurs themselves became a mechanism for knowledge spillovers. Consequently, endogenous growth is not only about knowledge investment but also about efficient transformation of knowledge into societal use. That in turn requires a different policy setup as compared to the traditional mix of tax incentives and subsidies that the endogenous growth models advocated. Hence, mainstream growth models suffer from a missing link – the genuine entrepreneur.

I will start this essay with a brief account on David's role to firmly anchor and establish the research field of small businesses and entrepreneurship. This will be followed by some observations on the role of start-ups in times of recession, i.e. how they perform and whether they may, at least partially, mitigate an economic down-turn thereby acting as a kind of automatic stabilizers. In my view this particular issue deserves more attention.

The Role of Small Businesses and Entrepreneurship 2.0

Together with particularly Zoltan Acs, but also others, David has made a tremendous effort to establish entrepreneurship and small business research as a fully acknowledged academic discipline. This started with organizing conferences, articles, editing of numerous books, etc., focusing on small and medium sized enterprises (SMEs). Still, the single most important contribution is probably establishing the Small Business Economics Journal and serving as editor since the very beginning 20 years back. Under their joint leadership this journal has developed into a high-quality outlet for small business and entrepreneurship research, theoretical as well as empirical.

Hence, David was one of the main causes as to why research on small business and entrepreneurship recurred after being absent for almost half a century. Few paid any attention to what small businesses may contribute with in terms of employment, innovation and economic development. That drastically changed sometime around the late 1980s, early 1990s. One of the reasons was research by David Audretsch, often jointly with Zoltan Acs. The holy grail of large businesses became increasingly questioned, Audretsch claimed that the managed economy had been replaced by the entrepreneurial economy. Previously mass production, big business and strong labor unions was regarded as the key to prosperity and social welfare (Galbraith 1956). However, increasingly these gains were questioned and challenged by an emerging new literature which nuanced and upset some of the previously alleged truths.

In 2001 David Audretsch, together with Zoltan Acs, received The Global Award for Entrepreneurship Research for their outstanding research achievements, and for their contributions to establish small business and entrepreneurship as a research field. In their prize lecture they posed three questions:

What are the gains to size and large-scale production?
What are the economic welfare implications of having an oligopolistic market structure, i.e. is economic performance promoted or reduced in an industry with just a handful of large-scale firms?
Given the overwhelming evidence that large-scale production resulting in economic concentration is associated with increased efficiency, what are the public policy implications?

This is almost 20 years ago, and for some time research seemed to generate answers to at least some of the suggested issues. Yet, today we can witness a new trend towards concentration, i.e. oligopolistic market structures (if not monopolistic) and increased concentration. There seems to be a revival of the Schumpeter II prediction, "What we have got to accept is that the large-scale enterprise has come to be the most powerful engine of progress." (Schumpeter 1942, p. 106). As Acs and Audretsch, (2001) put it in their prize lecture (p. 2):

> The fundamental issue confronting western societies at that time was how to live with this apparent trade-off between concentration and efficiency on the one hand, and decentralization and democracy on the other. The public policy question of the day was: How can society reap the benefits of the large corporation in an oligopolistic setting while avoiding or at least minimizing the costs imposed by a concentration of economic power?

These questions are obviously on the agenda also today. Acs and Audretsch's answer in 2001 was that policies to counteract concentration, entry barriers and political influence of large firms, typically was related to public ownership, regulation and competition policy or antitrust. Today digitization, network externalities and globalization puts these questions in a somewhat different perspective. What are the implications for competitions policies of technology driven network effects? How do you regulate price collusion that happens through interacting algorithms? How can the concentration of market power be reduced and how is reliable information secured? What are the long-term consequences of increased concentration on innovation, prices and entry? Can the present market structure be attributed long Schumpeterian waves, and are dynamic forces at work that will result in functioning competition over time?

The picture is further complicated by changing structures due to the gig-economy and technologies like additive production (3-D printing), which tend to challenge some old "truths". The combination of almost zero marginal cost of transmitting information across geographic space and new production technologies (3D-pronting, robotization, digitization, etc.), could imply that the disadvantages of high labor costs in industrialized countries may vanish or disappear over time. Adidas new Speed factory, located in Germany, is one example. Thus, the substitution of capital and technology for labor, the location of production and the optimal scale/downsizing, are all influenced by new technology.

Even though Acs and Audretsch's original questions are still highly relevant, the reasons – and probably the answers – differs as compared to the situation 20 years back. The bottom line is that today there is ample room, and also an urgent need, for more research along the lines suggested two decades ago. Still, there are also new issues on the research agenda. One refers to the role of SMEs as moderators in times of cyclical swings in the economic activity.[1] Do they serve as automatic stabilizers by being less inclined to quickly lay off workers? Or do entrepreneurs identify new opportunities as performance by incumbents dwindle? Below I will discuss how SMEs and entrepreneurs may cushion a downturn in the economy.

Crises, Structural Change and Entrepreneurship[2]

The global economy has recently experienced one of its worst recession in modern times. What originally seemed to be a crisis limited to the U.S. financial markets was quickly diffused to other financial markets at a pace that surprised private sector agents as well as policy-makers. The subsequent phase of the crisis hit the real economy: demand dwindled, trade shrunk, wealth evaporated, subsequently followed by increasing unemployment as well as personal and firm bankruptcies.

The dynamics of the crisis clearly illustrates the deeper integration of the global economy where shocks become transmitted not only through financial but also real economy linkages such as trade and cross-border investments. Now the recovery

---

[1] Koellinger and Thurik (2012) and Fritsch and Kritikos (2016) are a few notable exception even though they address a somewhat different issue.

[2] Partly based on a speech to the European Parliament "CRIS" Committee some years ago.

seems quite robust and globally synchronized, albeit there are obvious geopolitical, protectionistic and climate related threats to a continued and sustainable growth trajectory. Moreover, when the next crisis appears much of the instruments in the traditional toolbox – i.e. monetary and fiscal policies – may more or less be exhausted due to continuously low interest rates, increased debt burden and shaky internal balances in a number of countries.

The question is what the implications have been – and will be in the near future – for entrepreneurs and SMEs, and if there are reasons to redesign policies to alleviate the conditions for young and small firms. In the following I will briefly discuss the structural future changes that can be expected, the importance of small firms in that context, how smaller firms have been affected by the crisis, the role of new start-ups for employment and, finally, present some policy suggestions in order to propel dynamism and growth that are based in a sound microeconomic setting. I will use a few examples from Sweden.

Looking Ahead – What to Expect?

Presently there are political forces that aims at isolating national markets from structural changes triggered by globalization and technological breakthroughs. Yet, such measures are likely to have miniscule effects in a medium- to long-term perspective. In the short-run the most likely effect is to postpone necessary structural adjustments which may be difficult to catch up with later. Overall, continued global restructuring and technological progress can be expected to influence productions structures and the role played by entrepreneurs and SMEs. To exploit such opportunities, institutions should be designed to encourage entrepreneurship, experimentation and competition. Measures that hamper economic dynamism is very likely counterproductive in the somewhat longer run.

The ongoing interaction between old and new industrialized countries, i.e. the traditional north-south model may be slowed down due to protectionist measures mentioned above, but is likely to gain momentum in the somewhat longer run. Simultaneously, competition between already industrialized countries can also be expected to become fiercer, where agglomeration forces together with the microeconomic prerequisites for production will be critically important in order to attract investments, talent and capital. New technological breakthroughs are likely to influence this pattern. Competitors, be it in production or demand for labor, is increasingly just one click away.

That will however not deteriorate the role of knowledge. If anything, knowledge – albeit probably different as compared to today's needs – will become an increasingly critical component for enhanced growth and prosperity. Note that knowledge does not simply refer to investments in research and development (R&D) and education, but also competencies like handling global, or at least international, sales and procurements structures, marketing and branding, new technology and the interaction between man and machine. Such competencies are among those that supposedly will become more strategically important in a globalized economy. This will require expertise of a different kind. Furthermore, to adapt and integrate such knowledge, a new organizational architecture may be required within and between firms.

Yet, economies that can provide an institutional framework that enable and stimulate an entrepreneurially driven economy, where knowledge is converted into economically useful purposes, will be well positioned for a continued vibrant and welfare enhancing economic development. Where rapid technological and implementation take place, SMEs and entrepreneurship can be expected to become increasingly important for innovation, employment, dynamism and growth (Acs et al. 2009; Braunerhjelm et al. 2010).

Global Structural Change

On an aggregate level the expected economic global restructuring is depicted in Fig. 1. Based on a standard computable general equilibrium model, conceivable future paths of the world economy as well as the Swedish economy have been simulated. According to these simulation exercises there will be a continuous shift of more labor intensive production towards less developed and emerging economies here represented by China and India, which is expected to culminate 2025–30. These simulations, having 2000 as their base year, captures the actual development of the world economy fairly well.[3]

Sweden, being a small open economy highly dependent on trade, will have to adjust to these changes. Given the assumptions underlying CGE-models, i.e. perfect flexibility in terms of prices, wages and mobility, labor would remain roughly constant in the non-tradable sector while there would considerable shifts between sectors in the tradable sectors (Fig. 2). In particular, labor would flow from the less knowledge intensive sectors to those more dependent on knowledge, whereas capital –intensive sectors would become even more dependent on capital.

As shown in Fig. 2, a considerable down-sizing of the labor-intensive tradable sector is expected, accompanied by an increase in particularly knowledge intensive production (goods and services).[4] The simulation result corroborates the actual development in the Swedish economy quite closely, having experienced an expansion in employment in predominantly in more knowledge intensive service sectors. Yet, such real sectors adjustments are far from trivial since it implies substituting declining manufacturing sectors with expanding service sectors.

When we simulate the corresponding effects on relative wages, we find a downward pressure on wages in low skill sectors whereas wages tend to increase in more

---

[3] About 10 years ago the Swedish government set up a Globalization Council which provided a number of simulations to illustrate conceivable effects of globalization and technology on the Swedish economy (see Braunerhjelm et al. 2009).

[4] See Braunerhjelm (2016).

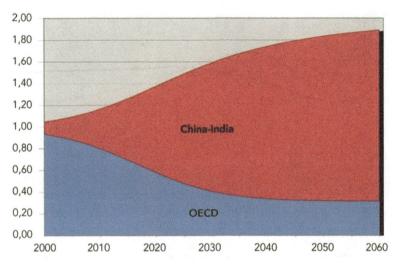

Fig. 1 Global restructuring 2000–2060. Shifts in labor intensive production. (Source: Braunerhjelm et al. (2009))

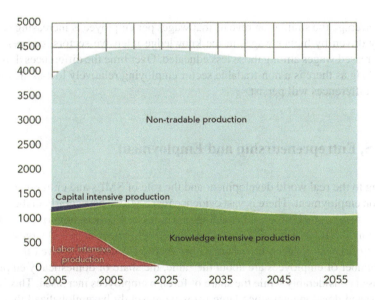

Fig. 2 Expected restructuring in the Swedish private sector, 2000–2060. Employment levels. (Source: Braunerhjelm et al. (2009))

advanced production (Fig. 3). The difference across sectors will, according to the simulations, peak around 2020–2025. As measured by for instance the Gini-coefficient, income distribution has also widened in Sweden in the last decade, a development that can be expected to continue for at least some time ahead.

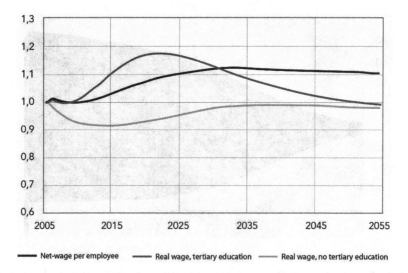

Fig. 3 Wage dispersion among highly educated (tertiary education) and less educated, 2005–2060. (Source: Braunerhjelm et al. (2009))

On average the simulation reveals that wages per employee is increasing but that is fully driven by higher wages in the knowledge intensive sectors, compensating for decreased wages among those less educated. Over time the differences diminish, but as long as there is a non-tradable sector employing relatively low-skilled workers the differences will persist.

SMES, Entrepreneurship and Employment

Turning to the real world development and the role of SMEs and entrepreneurs, we focus on employment. There is vast evidence that SMEs – particularly in the service sector – play a crucial role in providing new net employment opportunities. First, examining the large firms, Fig. 4 display how employment in the 30 largest manufacturing firms in Sweden has changed between 1975 and 2006. Even though the total number of employees are about the same, the share of domestically employed decreased considerably while the share of foreign employees increased. This is also an expected development since large firms increasingly have globalized their production and are also taking advantage of new technologies that enables replacing labor with capital and new technology. Looking at all firm (service and manufacturing) this development has basically continued up until at least 2015 (Fig. 4), albeit the expanding large service sector firms make up for the decline in the Swedish units of the manufacturing firms (Fig. 5).

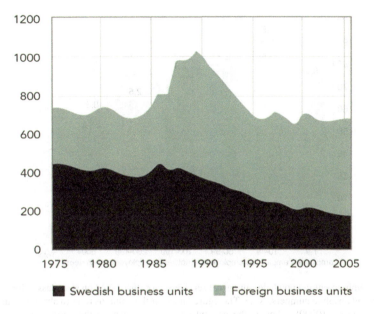

Fig. 4 The distribution of employment in the 30 largest Swedish manufacturing firms between foreign and domestic units 1975–2006. (Source: Braunerhjelm and Halldin (2008))

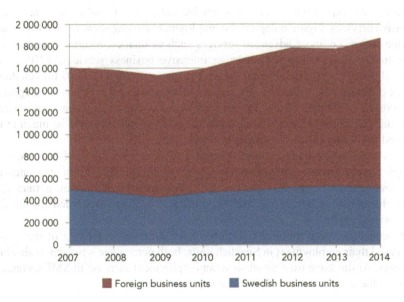

Fig. 5 The distribution of employment in the 30 largest Swedish firms between foreign and domestic units 2007–2014, all industries. (Source: Braunerhjelm et al. (2009))

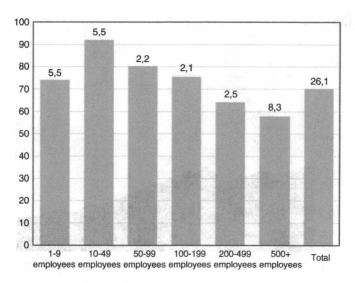

Fig. 6 Employment in knowledge-intensive service sector distributed on size classes 1993–2007, changes and absolute numbers. Note: The figure on top of the columns refer to absolute number of new employees (10000), whereas the percent change is shown on the vertical axis. (Source: Braunerhjelm et al. (2009))

As regards expanding sectors, those are basically to be found among knowledge intensive services. Figure 6 depicts the employment development in the "high-end" service sector, i.e. more advanced services such as finance, insurance, real estate, consultancy, etc. (basically knowledge intensive business services, KIBS). The figure illustrates net employment changes over the period 1993–2007 broken down on six different size categories. Employment has increased for all size categories, and mostly so in smaller firms. For services in the "low-end" segment (not shown), a similar picture would emerge, however, the positive effects would be much more focused to smaller firms (Braunerhjelm et al. 2009).

This development has continued up until 2015 (Fig. 7) in the KIBS-sectors, even though the percentage change is much less pronounced. The largest size category contribution to employment is also considerably more modest. Looking at manufacturing firms for the period 2007–2014, a distinct decline is recorded for all size categories (Fig. 8).

To conclude, large multinational firms have since the beginning of the 1990s decreased their employment in Swedish units, both percentage wise and in absolute numbers. At the same time we observe an employment increase in SMEs, concentrated to the more advanced service sectors.

Structural Change, Knowledge Spillovers and the Role of SMEs and Entrepreneurship 87

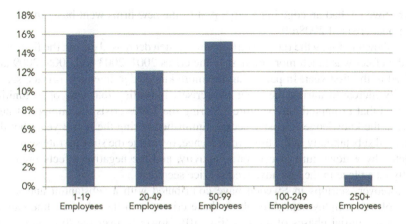

Fig. 7 Employment changes in the knowledge-intensive service sector distributed on size classes, 2007–2014. (Source: Braunerhjelm (2016))

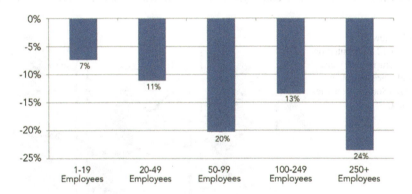

Fig. 8 Employment changes in manufacturing sector distributed on size classes 2007–2014. (Source: Braunerhjelm (2016))

Start-ups, Crises and Employment

Structural changes originating in technology breakthroughs, or because of other reasons such as changing relative costs or even crises, implies new business opportunities. Since incumbents frequently are tied to their existing technologies, capital structure and product assortment, there are good reasons to expect that SMEs and entrepreneurial start-ups will attempt to exploit these opportunities. They may consequently also contribute to, and speed up, structural adjustment.

Since the early 1990s Sweden has experienced three severe crises: the real estate and financial market crisis 1991–1993, when 500,000 workers lost their jobs and the budget deficit peaked at 13% of GDP, the dotcom bubble that burst 2000–2003 where Sweden had an edge but a large part of the new firms went bust, and finally the global crisis of 2008/09.

As shown in Fig. 9 the rate of start-ups in Sweden decreased during the first crisis but the effect was much more modest in the crises 2001–2003 and 2008–2009 and limited to the first year. In particular, the more knowledge-intensive service sector actually increased during the latter two crises, indicating that new opportunities emerged that prompted new ventures. During the 1990s crisis the number of new firms in the knowledge-intensive sector diminished during the first 2 years but the increased substantially in the third year. Hence, over time the start-up rate seem less affected by a down-turn in economic activity, and the negative effects predominantly take place in the less advanced service sectors.

Moreover, startups in Sweden have contributed with a substantial and stable share of new employment throughout these crises, even though a decline can be seen in the initial phases of a crisis (Fig. 10). However, over the three crises the reduction in employment has become smaller and almost negligible for the knowledge intensive service sector in the last crisis. Altogether new firms contributes with approximately 80,000 new employment opportunities annually, whereof the over-

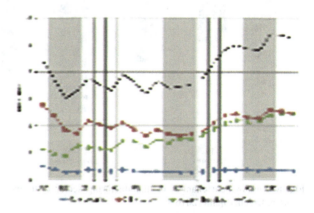

Fig. 9 New firms 1990–2012 distributed on manufacturing, services and advanced services (1000). (Source: Statistics Sweden)

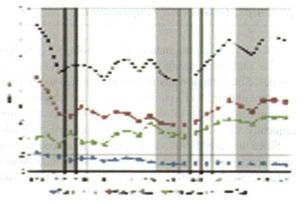

Fig. 10 Employees in new firms 1990–2012, distributed on manufacturing, services and advanced services (1000). (Source: Statistics Sweden)

whelming part in the service sectors. This is an impressive figure in a country with roughly 3–3, three million employees in the private sector. That indicates that new firms tend to cushion economic downturns and to some extent acts as automatic stabilizers that mitigates decreases in aggregate demand.

In addition to an increasing start-up rate, in Sweden new and young firms' growth expectation in terms of employment has been steadily increasing between 2007 and 2014, but since then decreased substantially (GEM 2018). At the same time fear of failure is also reported to have increased, which of course is likely to hamper expansion in SMEs as well as start-ups. The diminished growth ambitions in the last years are most likely associated with uncertainty linked to policies regarding the prerequisites for entrepreneurship in certain industries which relatively recently has opened up for private firms (services traditional provided by the public sector in Sweden, e.g. schooling and health care). Also signals about an increased future tax burden may have stifled potential entrepreneurs to enter or to grow their firms. It highlights the importance of a transparent and trustworthy business climate.

Policy Implications

We conclude with a brief policy discussion, concentrating on a few areas of particular importance. It is essential to understand that entrepreneurship policies stretches over a large number of policy areas, from housing to venture capital. Hence, there is no single policy area that can be addressed which is likely to improve the conditions for SMEs and entrepreneurs in the short run. Given a proper macroeconomic setting, the four following areas are however deemed as critically important to propel and escalate entrepreneurial activities: Taxes, knowledge provision, labor market and dynamic markets.

Taxes

Taxes have the dual tasks of redistributing incomes and promoting an environment conducive to growth, implying that conflicts of interest may appear in attaining those objectives. In welfare states like Sweden the former tax function has been emphasized. Hence, a tax system targeting both growth and redistribution must be carefully balanced for both objectives to be attained, making sure that the structure and level of taxes does not deter incentives for entrepreneurial activities.

In the last couple of decades, institutional competition between countries has been on the rise, a trend that can be expected accelerate in the future as competition for talent, entrepreneurs and investments are likely to increase. As regards taxes this is most obvious for corporate – and to some extent – capital taxes, i.e. the more mobile tax bases. However, entrepreneurship also seems negatively correlated with the overall tax burden as illustrated in Fig. 11.

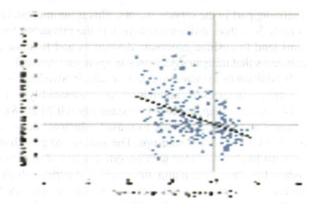

Fig. 11 Tax pressure (total taxes in relation to GDP) and entrepreneurship (TEA), 2014. (Source: Braunerhjelm (2016))

It illustrates one of the challenges in designing a tax system incorporating both an incentive structure and redistribution policies. The difficulties relate to the risks between different types of economic activities, i.e. being a wage earner or becoming an entrepreneur. The relationship between calculated risks and expected future remuneration, must be proportional in order for individuals to undertake an entrepreneurial endeavor. In addition, the structure of taxes is probably as important as the overall tax pressure. For example, stock options is an important instrument to incentivize scaling up of new and small businesses. A considerable number of European countries have shifted towards becoming start-up nations, there is however a long way before they can call themselves scale-up nations. As discussed above, scaling up is important since large firms tend to reduce their employment in their original home countries.

Knowledge Provision: Institutional Setup and Knowledge Investments

As mentioned above, knowledge is one of the corner pillars to achieve growth and augmented prosperity. But it has to be combined with policies that foster the diffusion of knowledge and its implementation in economically meaningful ways.

The share of EU-investments in R&D still falls way below the target outlined for 2020. Presently it is around 2%, but the objective is to reach 3% by 2020. Compared to the US the share is almost 1% lower and about 1.5% lower than the corresponding share for Japan (about the similar difference to Sweden). Hence, there seems to be room for increased governmental R&D-expenditure, simultaneously as measures are introduced to further facilitate commercialization of new knowledge, for instance through R&D tax credits and R&D-vouchers combined with improved links to universities and research institutes.

Another area of importance for knowledge transfers has to do with the universities' legal environment. Europe has witnessed a shift towards a more US like system (Bayh-Dole) where the university owns the intellectual property rights. Yet, the evidence showing an increase in innovation are basically non-existent. That indicates the need for complementary reforms related to diffusion and commercialization of knowledge. Increased competition between universities, better governance and an allocation of research funds based on universities and research institutes global excellence are probably some of the measures that have to be undertaken in order to maintain and advance the knowledge base and to attract talent. Universities should also be encouraged to specialize, thereby enabling excellence simultaneously as the possibilities of complementing industrial specialization of the universities' host regions are ameliorated.

Labor Market Policies and Innovation

Measures that tend to lock in employees in existing industries and firms are likely to have a detrimental effect on long-term growth and prosperity. In the U.S. non-compete contracts, implying that employees agree not to move to a competitor or to set up a potentially competing new firm, has increased and has also been forwarded as an explanation to the faltering productivity performance. What is needed is more of flexibility on labor markets, not less, combined with institutions that allows upgrading and retraining of unemployed. That should be a key concern for policy makers.

A number of studies have provided empirical evidence for a causal relationship between labor mobility and higher productivity (Scarpetta and Tressel 2004. Similarly, more recent studies find a strong positive relationship between labor mobility and innovation, the explanations being better matching and improved networks (Kaiser et al. 2015; Braunerhjelm et al. 2017). In addition, less strict labor market regulation seems to promote more of entrepreneurship and to enhance growth expectations of young firms (Fig. 12). The latter, often referred to as gazelles, have been shown to have an un-proportionate large effect on employment Henrekson and Johansson (2010).

Dynamic Markets: Angels, Exit and Competition

Other building blocks to support dynamic markets and facilitating restructuring refer to well-functioning venture and angel capital markets, focusing at the earlier stages of firms' development. The UK experience with tax incentives for private investments in small or newly started firms deserves to be carefully studied and implemented, it could be seen as a role model for other advanced economies. More

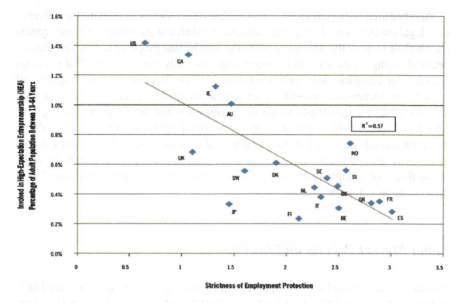

Fig. 12 Relationship between number of gazelles and strictness of employment protection. (Source: GEM 2009)

generally, to promote a dynamic and entrepreneurial micro-economic setting, it seems important to develop financial markets which are based on equity- rather than loan-financing.

To exploit the potential benefits from rapid technological development entrepreneurial experiments are necessary. Since the economic outcomes of implementing new technology, or of setting up new technology-based firms, is hard to assess there will be failures. As shown by Eberhardt et al. (2017), the quality of institutions governing exit will also influence the quality of new ventures. Presently the exit institutions are functioning less well in a number of countries, leading to long-term stigma for individuals who fails with their entrepreneurial endeavors, while in other cases hindering the release of resources from failing industries and firms thereby blocking an efficient allocation of factors of production. Exit policies are thus as important as policies aimed to foster more of entry into markets.

A particular entry barrier related is the lack of competition and the presence of public operators in certain the service sectors. The health care sector is one example, construction and transports are others. The remaining obstacles to competition have to be removed if productivity, product variety and quality are to increase.

Concluding Remarks

As I have tried to demonstrate above there are a number of reasons why we can expect the role of SMEs and entrepreneurs to be increasingly important in times of continuing restructuring. Yet, the emergence of large and cost-efficient firms due to first-mover advantages and network effects are likely to obstruct competitive markets and raise the costs for entry and innovation. Hence, policy-makers face a number of thorny and complex issues in order to secure a dynamic and growth-oriented continued economic development. The combination of rapid technological development and deployment requires experiment and search in order to reap the benefit of those advances. An economic environment lacking entrepreneurs will be less prepared to address such challenges. In addition, new and young firms may, to some extent, play an important role as automatic stabilizers as future crises appear. Particularly when traditional fiscal and monetary policy measures are exhausted.

References

Acs, Z., & Audretsch, D. (2001). Prize Lecture: The Emergence of the Entrepreneurial Society. The Global Award for Entrepreneurship Research, www.e-award.org/wp-content/uploads/Acs-and-Audretsch-Prize-Lecture.pdf

Acs, Z., Braunerhjelm, P., Audretsch, D., & Carlsson, B. (2009). The knowledge spill-over theory of entrepreneurship. *Small Business Economics, 32*, 15–30.

Audretsch, D., Acs, Z., Braunerhjelm, P., & Carlsson, B. (2012). Growth and entrepreneurship. *Small Business Economics, 39*, 289–300.

Braunerhjelm, P., & Halldin, T. (2008). *Globalization and the large nordic MNC*. Stockholm: Royal Institute of Technology.

Braunerhjelm, P. (2016). Entreprenörskap i det tjugoförsta århundradet, Governmental Report 2016:72, Stockholm.

Braunerhjelm, P., von Greiff, C., & Svaleryd, H. (2009). Utvecklingskraft och omställningsförmåga, Final report from the Secretariat to the Swedish Government's Globalisation Council, Ministry of Education, www.regeringen.se/globaliseringsradet (co-authors).

Braunerhjelm, P., Acs, Z., Audretsch, D., & Carlsson, B. (2010). The missing link. Knowledge diffusion and entrepreneurship in endogenous growth. *Small Business Economics, 34*, 105–125.

Braunerhjelm, P., Ding, D. and Thulin, P. (2017), Labor Mobility, Knowledge Flows and Innovation, Working Paper 54, Swedish Entrepreneurship Forum, Stockholm.

Carlsson, B., Braunerhjelm, P., Acs, Z., & Audretsch, D. (2009). The knowledge filter, entrepreneurship and economic growth. *Industrial and Corporate Change, 18*, 1193–1229.

Eberhardt, R., Eesley, C., & Eisenhardt, K. (2017). Failure is an option: Institutional change, entrepreneurial risk and new firm growth. *Organization Science, 28*, 93–112.

Fritsch, M., & Kritikos, A. (2016). Entrepreneurship and the business cycle, CESifo DICE Report, http://hdl.handle.net/10419/167270

Galbraith, J. (1956). *American capitalism: The concept of countervailing power*. Boston: Houghton Mifflin.

GEM. 2009. Global Report, http://www.gemconsortium.org/

GEM. 2018. Global Report, http://www.gemconsortium.org/

Henrekson, M., & Johansson, D. (2010). Gazelles as job creators: a survey and interpretation of the evidence. *Small Business Economics, 35*, 227–244.

Kaiser, U., Kongsted, H.C., and Rønde, T. (2015), "Does the Mobility of R&D Labor Increase Innovation?" Journal of Economic Behavior & Organization, 110, 91–105.

Koellinger, P., & Thurik, R. (2012). Entrepreneurship and the business cycle. *Review of Economics and Statistics, 94*, 1143–1156.

Schumpeter, J. (1942). *Capitalism, socialism and democracy*. New York: Harper and Row.

Scarpetta, S., & Tressel, T. (2004). Boosting productivity via innovation and adoption of new technologies: any role for labor market institutions?, World Bank Discussion Paper, 2004.

David B. Audretsch: Spilling Knowledge All Over the World

Per Davidsson

Abstract Per Davidsson discusses in the following chapter how he and David met and how they became close friends and collaborators. Using the economic analogy of knowledge spillovers, Davidsson creates a narrative of how David has built friendships across the world while also becoming one of the most prolific scholars in his field. These insights show how well-respected and connected David became by way of his open and honest demeanor.

David B. Audretsch: Spilling Knowledge All Over the World

According to my memory, I first met David Audretsch in person at the RENT conference in Durham in late 1990. David had then just published his landmark piece "Innovation and Small Firms" (Acs and Audretsch 1990a) of which I may or may not yet have been aware at that time. It was a very different, pre-Internet world back then, and knowledge sometimes spilled over at very low viscosity. On the other hand, "SME/entrepreneurship research" was still a small business (albeit innovative and growing; cf. Acs and Audretsch 1988, 1990b), so one would not miss a major contribution due to information overload.

Anyway, the image I have in memory is one where David is sitting in the audience a few rows in front of me. I have posed a question or made a suggestion to the presenter, whereupon David turns around, looks at me and delivers an example of his lifetime scholarly journey of creating knowledge spillover (Acs et al. 2013; Audretsch and Keilbach 2007) by sharing some sharp observation. Although the psychologist in me realizes that my memory is probably partly false (as a case in point, before I checked it up I was convinced this happened in 1989, and my recollection of my first encounter with Michael Frese some 10 years later is suspiciously similar) I think it is safe to say David impressed me the first time we met. Since then

P. Davidsson (✉)
Australian Centre for Entrepreneurship Research, Queensland University of Technology and Jönköping International Business School, Brisbane, QLD, Australia
e-mail: per.davidsson@qut.edu.au

© Springer Nature Switzerland AG 2019
E. E. Lehmann, M. Keilbach (eds.), *From Industrial Organization to Entrepreneurship*, https://doi.org/10.1007/978-3-030-25237-3_11

our paths have crossed at many junctures all over the world, and I have had the privilege of being at the receiving end of his spilling over of knowledge, wisdom and inspiration – and hopefully been able to produce a trickle in return.

A few years after Durham, in 1994, the Jönköping International Business School (JIBS) was formed. My 10 years as full time professor there were an incredibly enjoyable journey shared with a fantastic team that built a strong research environment that gained great international recognition. David was with us on that journey as a regular visitor, advisor and door-opener through his extensive network, spilling his sparkles of knowledge so skilfully that it eventually earned him an honorary doctorate at JIBS, helping that institution to spill over in its own right, e.g., to Stockholm School of Economics and Syracuse University, which absorbed some of our best PhD graduates. During this time his knowledge spillovers to the world at large had grown sufficiently large to spawn another lingering connection to Sweden when he and Zoltan Acs received what is now the Global Award for Entrepreneurship Research. As to myself, I merely served on the award committee.

When I left Jönköping for Australia in 2004, I stayed in David's knowledge spillover shower as associate editor for *Small Business Economics* where he was one of the founders and main editors. We also worked together in the leadership of the Entrepreneurship Division of the Academy of Management, (ENT), one of the rare contexts in which I was above and ahead of David (as Division Chair and by entering the 5-year leadership cycle 2 years earlier than him, respectively). But only temporally and temporarily. One of the daunting first-year tasks not revealed when they asked one to run for office was to raise funds to support the pre-conference activities. I was pretty chuffed when I topped earlier efforts by raising USD 30,000. Two years later, David tripled the amount, and when he later ascended to Division Chair it was as leader of a 3000-member community rather than the 2500 heads that I had handed over. No evidence of detrimental impact of ENT's elevation to the league of large divisions on its capacity for innovation has emerged (cf. Acs and Audretsch 1988).

In 2010 I got the opportunity to start and lead the Australian Centre for Entrepreneurship Research (ACE) at QUT, Brisbane. Again, David enters the scene. Having realized that one continent and one full-time job weren't quite enough for him, he assumed leadership of the Max Planck Institute of Economics in Jena (Germany) without relinquishing his professorship at Indiana University. Despite seemingly spending half his working week crossing the Atlantic en route to frequent flyer mile multi-millionaire status, he established in Jena a process of creative construction (Agarwal et al. 2008) resulting in a veritable pyrotechnic display of flames and sparks around the institute. Events, working papers, newsletters, presentations, journal articles, etc., created very high visibility that inspired us at ACE to try to achieve something similar. Eventually we imported direct knowledge spillover from Jena in the form of two rounds of Michael Stuetzer – first as visiting PhD student and then as Post Doctoral Fellow – and later Martin Obschonka, both with their research training in Jena and at least some role for the Max Planck Institute. We also had the benefit of David visiting as ACERE Conference keynote speaker and for the ENT Division midwinter meeting (in February, with temperatures over 30C/90F and 100% humidity).

These knowledge spillovers also enhanced ACE/QUT's own ability to spill over knowledge – notably to the University of Adelaide, which is the current affiliation of former ACE Deputy Director, Paul Steffens, and former ACE Post Docs, Scott Gordon and Chengli Chu. As it were, UoA is also David's most recently added "affiliated position"; one of six in five countries on three continents that he currently holds apart from his professorship, editorships, etc.[1] Age does not seem to slow him down!

The second most remarkable thing about all the above is that it is just one colleague's incomplete account of the many ways in which David has affected their academic life and the institutions they have represented. How many other colleagues, disciples, institutions – and more – has he affected to a similar extent – or more? The thought is mind-boggling. However, the most remarkable thing is that amidst all these contributions to the evolution of our industry (Audretsch 1995) and the geography of its innovation and production (Audretsch and Feldman 1996) and despite his authoring of several hundred works that have amassed 85,316 citations and a H-index of 125 (and counting) I cannot remember ever having seen David visibly stressed or lacking time for social events. I wish we could have some more of that spilling over as well, but it might be the absorptive capacity (Audretsch and Lehmann 2006) at the receiving end that is lacking!

References

Acs, Z. J., & Audretsch, D. B. (1988). Innovation in large and small firms: An empirical analysis. *The American Economic Review*, 678–690.
Acs, Z. J., & Audretsch, D. B. (1990a). *Innovation and small firms*. Cambridge, MA: MIT Press.
Acs, Z. J., & Audretsch, D. B. (1990b). The determinants of small-firm growth in US manufacturing. *Applied Economics, 22*(2), 143–153.
Acs, Z. J., Audretsch, D. B., & Lehmann, E. E. (2013). The knowledge spillover theory of entrepreneurship. *Small Business Economics, 41*(4), 757–774.
Agarwal, R., Audretsch, D. B., & Sarkar, M. (2008). The process of creative construction: Knowledge spillovers, entrepreneurship, and economic growth. *Strategic Entrepreneurship Journal, 1*(3–4), 263–286.
Audretsch, D. B. (1995). *Innovation and industry evolution*. MIT Press: Cambridge, MA.
Audretsch, D. B., & Feldman, M. P. (1996). R&D spillovers and the geography of innovation and production. *The American Economic Review, 86*(3), 630–640.

---

[1]After all the flying across the Atlantic one can only wonder what might attract David Bruce Audretsch to an adjunct affiliation in Australia. It can't be that he needs the frequent flyer miles and I know for certain it is not for the joy of 20-hour spells of coach class intimacy. It could be the climate like in my case, but my research underlying this Festschrift note suggests it is instead the irresistible lure bestowed upon him the moment his parents gave him his middle name, which (according to the Monty Python skit) he shares with all Australian males and in particular the country's somewhat unsophisticated male academics (see http://www.montypython.net/scripts/bruceskit.php for a printout of the Oxbridge-Australian vernacular. The video has unfortunately been pulled from Youtube due to copyright reasons).

Audretsch, D. B., & Keilbach, M. (2007). The theory of knowledge spillover entrepreneurship. *Journal of Management Studies, 44*(7), 1242–1254.
Audretsch, D. B., & Lehmann, E. (2006). Entrepreneurial access and absorption of knowledge spillovers: Strategic board and managerial composition for competitive advantage. *Journal of Small Business Management, 44*(2), 155–166.

The Shape of Things to Come

Martin Prause and Jürgen Weigand

Abstract In the summer of 1999 two economists, David and Jürgen, were strolling along the lakeshore promenade of Lake Mendota, Madison, Wisconsin. It was a beautiful, serene summer evening. That past afternoon they had presented a paper at the Econometric Society Summer Meetings on the influence of industry knowledge conditions, firm size and ownership structures on innovation and investment. The topic had attracted some prominent scholars in the field who vividly discussed the paper and provided valuable comments. Walking at a leisurely place David and Jürgen were reflecting on the session and how to utilize the received feedback to improve their paper for submission (After many revisions this ESSM paper was published as Audretsch and Weigand (2005)).

The Meeting

Quickly, their conversation broadened beyond the paper. Ten years after the fall of the Berlin wall globalization was picking up steam. With the opening up of China and India new opportunities for trade, capital investments and profitable international expansion were emerging. The global economic outlook was bright and promising. How would globalization affect industries and the conditions for innovation? As David's previous research had shown, small entrepreneurial firms contributed significantly to innovation and technological progress. How much would firm size matter for innovation in the future? How much scale and scope would firms need to do well in globalizing markets? The boom of dotcoms had drawn investors in droves to the stock markets. Prospects for profitable capital investments and wealth creation seemed unlimited. Would financing constraints for innovative start-ups and small firms be alleviated in the knowledge-centered "new economy"? What

---

M. Prause (✉) · J. Weigand
WHU–Otto Beisheim School of Management, Vallendar and Düsseldorf,
Düsseldorf, Germany
e-mail: martin.prause@whu.edu

© Springer Nature Switzerland AG 2019
E. E. Lehmann, M. Keilbach (eds.), *From Industrial Organization to Entrepreneurship*, https://doi.org/10.1007/978-3-030-25237-3_12

kind of technologies would emerge in the future? Would these be conducive for entrepreneurship and start-ups or would they favor large firms?

While pondering the shape of things to come David and Jürgen arrived at a lakeside open air venue where crowds of cheerful people had gathered to listen to the music of a cover band. The sun was setting in an amazing glow of colors. Now it was time to relax and enjoy the splendid summer night over a pitcher of beer. When the band started playing ABBA's "Dancing Queen", the mood of our two economists became nostalgic. They got into reminiscing their lives, about Madison where David had earned his doctorate, how they first met at Manfred Neumann's industrial organization research seminar at the University of Erlangen-Nuernberg where David gave a talk, about Berlin where David had spent many years at the WZB and Jürgen had interned at the Federal Cartel Office some years before the wall came down, how David hosted Jürgen as a post-doc researcher at Georgia State University in Atlanta before Jürgen followed David to Bloomington, Indiana. As the beer unfolded its spiritual effects, life presented itself as a wonderful fountain of opportunities to learn and develop. A cab helped them to find their way back to the hotel. Neither David nor Jürgen would have guessed that night how much different the world would look 20 years later, that the end of capitalism would be proclaimed by missionaries of a new world order.

Capitalism is what Joseph Schumpeter succinctly called "that form of private property economy in which innovations are carried out by means of borrowed money" (1939, 223). Since its origins in thirteenth century Florentine capitalism has created tremendous wealth for nations and well-being for individuals. As it seems now, its time has come. Today we are facing huge transformations of economy and society resulting from technological progress (e.g. information technologies, artificial intelligence), demographics (ageing, migration), climate change as well as depletion of nature and natural resources.

When David and Jürgen studied economics in their time at the university economists were concerned with the optimal allocation of scarce resources, how capital accumulation and technological progress influenced economic growth and wealth creation, and what the nature and intensity of competition should be to facilitate innovation. Now with the innovations in information technologies is not so much about dealing with scarce resources anymore but dealing with the abundance of information. Information is the new "capital", the "oil" of the 4th industrial revolution as some say. Due to this enormous impact of information our economies are arguably transforming into "zero marginal cost economies" (Rifkin 2014) where sharing seems to be economically more productive than owning (Sundajararan 2016), where the functioning of the market mechanism obviously is either defunct or following new rules, and where most traditional jobs may vanish soon due to automation or the use of robots (Economist 2018).

Are we in the middle of a fundamental paradigm shift? Is this indeed the end of capitalism, as predicted by Schumpeter? Are we already in "post-capitalism" (Mason 2016)? If information abundance is becoming economically more relevant than scarcity, will those who monopolize and control information, such as Google, Amazon or Alibaba, dominate the future of our economies? What is the shape of things to come?

Whatever it may be. At least, this new era is providing plenty of new opportunities for innovation and entrepreneurship. Looking at the latest numbers venture capitalist investments are at an all-time high with $46bn in the fourth quarter of 2017 (KPMG 2017). Under the umbrella of digitalization aggressive start-ups are disrupting major established industry sectors such as banking, transportation, healthcare or education. Private banks are being challenged by Fintechs, the closed tier-based value chain of car manufacturers is transforming into a transportation hub-and-spoke systems of IT suppliers, device manufacturers and service providers, with car manufacturing playing just a minor role (Cometlabs 2017). Are we in for a fundamental leap in technology that will change our thinking and way of living in such a profound way as electrification and computers have changed us?

Economic Growth and Wealth Creation:
Through the Macro Lens

The Scottish moral philosopher Adam Smith (1776) was the first to seriously look into the determinants of economic growth and the creation of wealth of nations. He argued that a nation's economic surplus, that is, its gross output minus the necessary inputs, was produced by the use and combination of three input factors: capital, labor, and land. Capital played the key role in Smith's production function. Continuous capital accumulation by saving and investing in tangible and intangible capital was the essential prerequisite for expanding production to feed a growing population. Free markets, undisturbed by the government, would guarantee the allocation of scarce resources to their most productive uses. Pursuing their self-interest consumers and producers would be coordinated by the invisible hand of the market. Competition would enforce the efficient allocation of resources and yield maximum welfare for all. Economic prosperity resulted from the division of labor within and across firms which allowed for cost advantages through specialization and led to increases in (labor) productivity.

From Smith's reasoning one may conclude that the potential for economic growth seemed to be limited only by the division of labor, and the latter, by the extent of the market (cf. Stigler 1951). However, as pointed out by David Ricardo (1817), scarcity of natural resources such as land could restrict the beneficial effects of capital accumulation due to diminishing marginal returns. As specialization as a consequence of the division of labor gives rise to economies of scale and learning, firms seek to grow bigger in order to exploit these economies and create competitive advantage. If firm size matters that much for growth, larger or faster growing firms can conquer more market space than smaller or slower growing firms and push them aside. Taking this argument to its logical conclusion means that in the longer run every market should eventually become dominated by a single large supplier who will be able to exploit her size-related cost advantage to eliminate competition. That outcome doesn't reconcile easily with Smith's model of competitive markets which rests on the idea of competition among many market participants. The creation and strengthening of individual market power, and as a consequence of it, the potential monopolization of markets may impede the functioning of the invisible hand and the realization of maximum welfare, begging for state intervention to curb welfare reducing behaviors. State intervention however may turn out to be a curse rather than a blessing.

The conjectured limits to economic growth due to diminishing returns to scale or the detrimental effects of market power could be overcome by technological progress. Although Adam Smith gave some thought to it, his notion of technical progress didn't go further than seeing it as "division of labor dynamics" (Aspromourgos 2010, 1180). Despite the importance of technological progress for the unfolding industrialization and the associated tidal shifts in the economies and societies of the late 18th and nineteenth century economists of that period largely ignored technological progress and its sources.[1]

The wake-up call for neo-classical economics came in the shape of Robert Solow. In a seminal paper Solow (1957) integrated technical progress as a time (t) dependent shift factor, A(t), into a neoclassical aggregate production function which relates the economy's output, Q, to the employed input factors capital, K, and labor, L:

$$Q(t) = A(t)K^{\wedge}(\omega\_K)L^{\wedge}(\omega\_L) \tag{1}$$

where ωK and ωL are the relative shares of capital and labor.[2] Total differentiation of (1) with respect to time t yields

$$Q/Q = A/A + \omega\_K K/K + \omega\_L L/L \tag{2}$$

The change in output is attributed to changes in capital and labor as well as to technical progress. From the perspective of production theory technical progress materializes if with given factor inputs the economy can produce more than before or if it can realize the same output with a smaller volume of factor inputs than before.

The beauty of Solow's path breaking contribution can easily be seen from (2). It lies in its simplicity of turning theory into an empirical model. Using time series data for the change in the economy's output (typically measured by a country's gross national product), for the changes in capital stock and labor employed and adding a stochastic noise parameter μ the growth Eq. (2) can be examined by regression analysis to estimate ωK and ωL. The economy's rate of technical progress is picked up by the regression constant. Assuming constant returns to scale which implies $\omega K + \omega L = 1$ and neutral technical change Eq. (2) can be formulated as

---

[1] See e.g. Kurz and Salvadori (2003) for discussion.

[2] Formally, $\omega\_x = \partial Q/\partial x \; x/Q$ is the output elasticity of the respective input factor, $x = K, L$.

$$A/A = (Q/Q \quad L/L) \quad \omega_{-}K(K/K \quad L/L) + \mu \tag{3}$$

Technical progress thus is the difference between the change in labor productivity, Q/L, and the change in capital intensity, K/L, while the remainder is stochastic noise. With data for the USA this so-called Solow residual accounted for almost 90% of the change in labor productivity in the estimation period of 1909–1949.

Solow's finding spurred an entirely new area of empirical research, commonly known as "growth accounting". Subsequent studies refined the measurement, e.g. by including new inputs such as education, capital quality, R&D, and human capital, and thus downsized the residual to some extent but it did not really enhance our understanding of what was left.[3] The Solow growth model failed to explain long-run economic growth or technical progress. Rather it described how technical progress triggered an economy's continuous adjustments to a conjectured long-run growth equilibrium. However it could not explain for instance the empirically observed acceleration of economic growth for industrializing economies.

In Solow's conception technical progress improves the productivity of the employed input factors and increases the quantity of the goods produced. By doing so it offsets the tendency for the rate of capital returns to decline upon progressing capital accumulation. However technical progress was just an exogenous "something" that fell like manna from heaven, incessantly providing new investments opportunities. Growth in this neoclassical approach implied an increase in the quantity of goods produced in the economy or in the size of the economy. After growth, i.e. after the transition from the previous to the new equilibrium, there would be more or bigger firms that have employed more of the same labor and capital to produce more of the same goods.

In sum, the neoclassical growth theory a lá Solow relied on technological progress to explain long-run economic growth but technological progress itself remained a "terra incognita of modern economics" (Schmookler 1966, 3).

It was Paul Romer (1986, 1990) who explored this uncharted territory. Romer introduced knowledge as a new input factor to the production function. He argued that technological progress was the endogenous outcome of knowledge creation. In his model profit-maximizing firms make intentional investments into the conventional factors of production, capital and labor, as well as into the creation of new knowledge through R&D. At the firm level, these investments are subjected to diminishing returns to scale. However, firms can't keep newly created knowledge secret forever. Ultimately, it will spill over and spread, to the benefit of other agents in the economy. Individual knowledge creation leads to positive external effects so that the economy's knowledge stock grows as well. Thus at the economy level knowledge accumulation engenders increasing returns to scale. All firms benefit from this externality. The marginal productivity of their input factors increases through no fault of their own. The increasing returns are the consequence of the

---

[3] See for overviews and discussions e.g. Maddison (1987), Griliches (1996), Barro (1999), or the contributions in Boianovsky and Hoover (2009).

special nature of the input factor knowledge: it is neither a conventional nor a public good, but a non-rival, and only partially excludable one. Knowledge once created can be used over and again by an unlimited number of users without being used up or worn off. This feature is very different from capital goods or consumption goods. And Romer's characterization of knowledge is congruent with what we say about information today.

In Romer's theory knowledge derives from investments in ideas, and knowledge creation is subject to economic incentives to be exploited for gain. The main incentive for firms to invest in R&D is the prospect of economic profits resulting from innovation. These profits are necessary to cover the high fixed costs of investment and development. They need to be secured by intellectual property rights to appropriate them in due time. Market size matters. The bigger the market for a new product, the lower will be its unit costs and the higher will be economic profits from innovation. These profits offer an incentive for competitors to develop similar products and steal away some share of the market. With the diffusion and imitation of the new product the knowledge and know-how of its production will spread. The economy's knowledge base expands and so reduces the costs for future R&D and innovation activities. One important result of Romer's theory is that the firms can't be price takers as suggested by the neoclassical model of perfect competition but must have price-setting power to cope with the peculiarities of knowledge creation and innovation. Romer's insights derived from a formal model but they had been derived earlier, without formal theory, by one of Economics' greatest thinkers: Joseph Schumpeter.

Growth, Innovation and Entrepreneurship

Schumpeter pioneered the analysis of the sources of technological progress. He linked the macro level consideration of economic growth and wealth creation to the micro level of firms and individuals.

In Theorie der wirtschaftlichen Entwicklung (1912, as Theory of Economic Development, 1934) he argued that economic growth and development resulted from the endeavors of firms and individuals to find and carry out "new combinations" (1912/1949, 66). For him innovative and entrepreneurial activities constituted the micro source of technological progress. He defined five types of new combinations: product innovation, process innovation, market innovation, sourcing innovation, and organizational innovation (1942, 66). For him, innovation was "[t]he fundamental impulse that sets and keeps the capitalist engine in motion" (1942, 82). More so, it is "the outstanding fact in the economic history of capitalist society" (Schumpeter 1939, 86).

The Theory of Economic Development rests on two intertwined micro theories, a theory of innovation and a theory of entrepreneurship. Innovations were carried out by resourceful and aspiring entrepreneurs who identified opportunities for profitably doing things differently and who had the will to succeed. There were quite a number of examples in Schumpeter's lifetime such as Edison, Rockefeller, Ford, or Siemens to inspire his theory.

Schumpeterian entrepreneurs are not necessarily the inventors or originators of innovation but rather they are the "doers" who break the status quo:

> [T]he function of entrepreneurs is to reform or revolutionize the pattern of production by exploiting an invention or, more generally, an untried technological possibility for producing a new commodity or producing an old one in a new way, by opening up a new source of supply of material or a new outlet for products, by reorganizing an industry and so on. This [entrepreneurial] function does not essentially consist in either inventing anything or otherwise creating the condition which the enterprise exploits. It consists in getting things done. (Schumpeter 1942, 132)

By carrying out innovation entrepreneurial firms disrupt the tranquility of existing product markets by challenging incumbent firms, outpacing them and even displacing them in a process of competitive elimination. In a "perennial gale of creative destruction" the new replaces the old (Schumpeter 1942, 83). It is an organic "process of industrial mutation ... that incessantly revolutionizes the economic structure from within, incessantly destroying the old one, incessantly creating a new one." (Schumpeter 1942, 83) However, this gale of change is not constantly blowing but develops in a cycle:

> Those revolutions are not strictly incessant; they occur in discrete rushes which are separated from each other by spans of comparative quiet. The process as a whole works incessantly however, in the sense that there always is either revolution or absorption of the results of revolution, both together forming what are known as business cycles.

Further, economic development is "evolutionary" (Schumpeter 1942, 82). Not quantitative changes matter but qualitative ones:

> Obviously, the face of the earth would look very different if people ... had done nothing else except multiply and save ... This historic and irreversible change in the way of doing things we call 'innovation' and we define: innovations are changes in production functions which cannot be decomposed into infinitesimal steps. Add as many coaches as you please, you will never get a railroad by so doing. (Schumpeter 1947, 152)
> As a consequence of these qualitative changes economic development pushes living standards up and the economy moves to a state of higher welfare but also of greater complexity.

In the Theory of Economic Development innovation emerged from firms of undefined size led by dynamic entrepreneurs. Innovation was a leadership topic rather than one of industrial or firm organization. Later, with the rise of the modern corporation, Schumpeter diagnosed a transition of capitalism from "competitive" to "trustified". He saw big corporations ("trusts") rather than start-ups or small firms as the agents of technological change:

> Innovation is ... not any more embodied typically in new firms, but goes on, within the big units now existing, largely independently of individual persons. ... Progress becomes 'automatized', increasingly impersonal and decreasingly a matter of leadership and individual initiative. (Schumpeter 1928, 361)

The leading actors in Schumpeter's dynamic competition had now become the large manager-controlled corporations with their institutionalized R&D departments which were able to churn out new combinations in a systematic way. They operated in concentrated markets and enjoyed oligopolistic market power which they exploited in terms of price setting and restricting output. In Schumpeter's view these dominant players were ...

> ... the most powerful engine ... of the long-run expansion of total output not only in spite of, but to a considerable extent through, this strategy [of monopolistic practices, added by MP/JW] which looks so restrictive when viewed in the individual case and from the individual point of time. (Schumpeter 1942, 106)

As innovation seemed to thrive well in what Fellner (1949) later described as "competition among the few", Schumpeter's answer to the question of what kind of market competition would be conducive for innovation was very different from Smith and the neoclassic growth model. The notion of competition he championed was not about price competition in established markets like in the neoclassical model of perfect competition but about competition for new markets. Schumpeter thus dismissed perfect competition as a basic condition for economic growth and development because its implementation was "not only impossible" in his view but it was also "inferior ... as a model of ideal efficiency" (Schumpeter 1942, 106). Static price competition, the core message of the perfect competition model, was irrelevant to Schumpeter. What really counted was ...

> ... the competition from the new commodity, the new technology, the new source of supply, the new type of organization (the largest-scale unit of control for instance)—competition which commands a decisive cost or quality advantage and which strikes not at the margins of the profits and the outputs of the existing firms but at their foundations and their very lives. (Schumpeter 1942, 84)

This "competition from the new" would rein in incumbent dominant firms and force them to continue innovating, "not only when in being but also when it is merely an ever present threat" (Schumpeter 1942, 85).

The incentive to innovate arises from the prospect of economic profits. When economic profits of existing products are being eroded because of intense competition and declining prices established firms need to be creative and find new ways of generating income. If they don't do it someone else will. The threat of innovation "disciplines before it attacks" (ibid.). In Schumpeter's eyes, potential competition was as effective in curbing market dominance as actual competition. The threat of elimination forces every firm to innovate in order to remain competitive and to avoid extinction. Innovators are only save for some time. Their pioneering profits attract competitors who will try to imitate the innovator and appropriate a share in the economic profits.

In a nutshell, Schumpeterian competition is about "doing something new" rather than "doing more of the same". It is a continuous sequence of innovation and imitation, of running ahead of rivals while enjoying innovation profits, and eventually being caught and commoditized by "more of the same". From this perspective, Schumpeter argued that market power and monopolistic practices should not be judged by their short-term effects but from a long-run perspective:

In analyzing such business strategy ex visu of a given point of time, the investigating economist or government agent sees price policies that seem to him predatory and restrictions of output that seem to him synonymous with loss of opportunities to produce. He does not see that restrictions of this type are, in the conditions of the perennial gale, incidents, often unavoidable incidents, of a long-run process of expansion which they protect rather than impede. (Schumpeter 1942, 88)

The growth and welfare implications of Schumpeterian competition are dynamic and thus quite different from the neoclassical comparative-static implications:

A system – any system, economic or other – that at every given point of time fully utilizes its possibilities to the best advantage may yet in the long run be inferior to a system that does so at no given point of time, because the latter's failure to do so may be a condition for the level or speed of long-run performance. (Schumpeter 1942, 83)

Therefore, Schumpeter argued that ...

[i]t is a mistake to base the theory of government regulation of industry on the principle that big business should be made to work as the respective industry would work in perfect competition. (Schumpeter 1942, 106)

Governmental competition and industry policies should rather be shaped by a long-run, systemic view.

Schumpeter's theories of innovation and entrepreneurship sparked a huge bulk of academic literature over the following decades with innumerable critical assessments, theoretical models and refinements as well as empirical testing. David Audretsch, together with his congenial partner Zoltan Acs, made very significant contributions to answering the empirical question of which firm sizes foster innovation. Most of the then existing empirical evidence was derived from industry-level studies overrepresented by data of large firms or it was based on case studies. Almost nothing was known about the importance of small firms for innovation.[4]

In a series of contributions, Acs and Audretsch (1987, 1988, 1990, 1991) could utilize a new data set collected by the US Small Business Administration. This data set allowed a representative view on small firms. In sum, Acs and Audretsch found that small firms were as innovative as large ones, and also at least as efficient as their large counterparts. However small firm contribution to total innovation activities was determined by industry-specific and market-specific factors. Small firms seemed to be disadvantaged in capital-intensive industries as well as in concentrated markets and in markets with a high advertising ratio. Acs and Audretsch (1988) presented supportive arguments for Winter's (1984) hypothesis that innovation activities of small and large firms respond to distinct technological and economic regimes. Specifically, Acs and Audretsch highlighted that concentrated industries inhibit higher levels of innovation activity because (1) the increase of innovation activities is subject to diminishing returns and (2) innovation activities tend to originate from small firms rather than large ones.

---

[4]It is not the place to review this literature. However, we at least want to mention some pathbreaking work, such as Nelson and Winter (1982) in theory, Jewkes et al. (1969) in case study research, and Mansfield (1962, 1963) and Scherer (1965) in empirical testing.

The research of Acs and Audretsch showed that small firms were indeed very important for the process of innovation. Their empirical work inspired many other researchers to go the extra mile of collecting and exploring new data sets with a better representation of small firms. Eventually, a coherent picture of firm size and innovation won wide-spread recognition, namely that real world innovation processes are characterized by a division of labor between large and small firms, as was already suggested by Mansfield et al. (1977, 16) almost 20 years earlier:

There is often a division of labor, smaller firms focusing on areas requiring sophistication and flexibility and catering to specialized needs, bigger firms focusing on areas requiring larger production, marketing, or technological resources.

Small firms are typically characterized by creativity and flexibility which give them specific advantages for venturing into new untested technology areas and developing disruptive products or processes. Large firms possess the means to embark on and pursue risky or cost-intensive innovation projects. However they typically will do so only if they have developed a culture which embraces "creative self-destruction" and if the profitability of their existing products is not at risk. The strength of being large lies in the financial and man power to find, acquire and commercialize "rough" innovations, coming from small firms or independent inventors. Large firms have a clear edge over small firms to systematically exploit existing technology areas. Under the prevailing technology and management paradigm they can reap cost efficiencies from scale, scope and experience and so lead product improvement and process innovation. In the overall economic process of innovation they have the important role of driving incremental or automated technological change (Malerba 1992).

With the relationship of innovation to firm size and industry structure clarified David Audretsch (1995a, b) set out to analyze empirically how the dynamic process of innovation and industry evolution worked. Using a large longitudinal data set provided by the US Small Business Administration he could study the start-up of new firms in different industries and track their performance over time. His research showed that start-up activities as well as firm survival varied widely across industries depending on industry characteristics. However he also found that, overall, industry structures were surprisingly fluid for entry and exit and that industry evolution was accompanied by quite some turbulence. He concluded that three fundamental factors determine how the dynamic process by which firms and industries evolve over time takes shape: demand, technology and the presence of scale economies.

Next David became interested in geography. Where does innovation take place? And why there and not anywhere else? Together with Maryann Feldman, David Audretsch (1996) looked at the role of location and locational knowledge spillovers for innovation and entrepreneurship. Audretsch and Feldman provided practical answers to the pressing questions, why small firms matter. They examined to which extent industrial activity clusters spatially and how this is linked to the geographic concentration of knowledge externalities, such as universities or industries with white collar workers. By controlling for the implicit concentration effects of production, Audretsch and Feldman were able to show that knowledge spillovers and

The Shape of Things to Come

innovation activities are not just a result of industry concentration but also a matter of geographic location: The proximity to knowledge externalities matters.

Audretsch and Feldman's research laid the foundation for a theory of entrepreneurship based on knowledge spillovers as proposed in Audretsch and Keilbach (2007). Its core essence can be described as:

> Entrepreneurship is an endogenous response to an opportunity created but not exploited by incumbent firms. (Audretsch 2009, 251)

The more knowledge spills over, the more opportunities arise for entrepreneurship. Therefore, the new hypothesis for economic growth accounts for the so-called knowledge filter, which impedes investments in knowledge from spilling over and being commercialized:

> Given a level of knowledge investment and severity of the knowledge filter, higher levels of economic growth should result from greater entrepreneurial activity, since entrepreneurship serves as a mechanism facilitating the spillover and commercialization of knowledge. (Audretsch et al. 2006, 57)

The main message of a large body of literature in the late 1990s and early 2000s on innovation and entrepreneurship as drivers of economic growth was that knowledge-based economies and industries would be conducive for innovative activities and start-ups. The fourth industrial revolution has shifted the focus in recent years from "knowledge" to "information", from the "knowledge production function" to the "internet of things" and "big data".

The competition for new markets is very much relying on "information-based" digital business models. Access to, control over and exploitation of information is essential for their success. Some players, such as Google, Amazon or Alibaba, have created "information monopolies". They not only dominate their respective markets but their data empires allow them to penetrate deep into our lives and observe our personal behavioral patterns and habits. They shape our preferences, our likes and dislikes. How should we think about these information monopolies? Will they impede or rather invite innovation and entrepreneurship?

The Rise of Information Monopolies

In Schumpeterian competition, the chances of a temporary monopoly position are necessary to provide sufficient incentives for innovation. While monopolies have the resources to innovate, they also have the incentive to not innovate but pursue a calm life and enjoy monopoly profits. As Hicks (1935, 3) once wrote, "The best of all monopoly profits is a quiet life." But precisely these monopoly profits are an incentive for people to challenge the market incumbents, take risks and develop new kinds of products and services with the means to make the existing obsolete and forcing the monopolist to adapt. Market dominance is broken when innovative newcomers leap-frog dominant players who are locked into their existing technologies and business models. There are many examples of large dominant firms who ignored the signs of time and the shape of things to come, such as Kodak, sunken by digital photography (their own invention) or Nokia, their linear business model defeated by the platform business models of smart phone firms like Apple and Samsung.

Digitalization is a disruptive megatrend fuelled by ubiquitous computing, cost-less data generation, and intelligent information extraction for decision-making. Various commentators have claimed that "data is the new oil" (Economist 2017a). The economic impact of data has been compared to the role oil as a natural resource played in the second industrial revolution. The widespread utilization of oil and electricity stimulated enormous economic growth in industrializing countries and elevated their economic welfare to ever new heights. Not only did it change the manufacturing landscape forever. Also, society was deeply and irreversibly affected by the novel forms of manufacturing (mass production), transportation (automobile), communication (telephony and media) and living (suburbanization) (Rifkin 2011).

The main source of economic growth during the second industrial revolution was still manufacturing. Under the prevailing technological paradigm the application of a stringent well-honed linear process of turning inputs into outputs was driven by pure efficiency considerations. Business models were built around optimizing production by exploiting scale and scope economies and decentralizing the supply chain (Chandler 1990). In the course of this evolutionary process industry clusters emerged, capturing agglomeration effects (Marshall 1920; Jacobs 1969). The business mantra for firm growth was shaped by the idea that competition for customers was about value and price. Firms flourished by focusing on either operational excellence (cost leadership) to offer low prices or innovation (differentiation) to provide high value. However, scarce resources and competition forced firms to excel not only in providing a compelling value-price proposition but also in developing a winning strategy, to attract more customers, instead of just beating the competition on price or value (Pietersen 2002).

The linear nature of these business models has economic limitations: (1) the price for a product or service is bound by its marginal cost of production, and (2) linear growth models give rise to diseconomies of scale and scope. First, the production of every good or service is subject to the use of input factors and the utilization of production processes, all of which set a minimum non-zero cost level to every unit of output produced. Second, the presence and exploitation of economies of scale and scope lead to bigger organizations. Every new customer creates a new one-to-one relationship that must be managed. Therefore, increasing numbers of customers raise the number of one-to-one connections and induce diseconomies of scale in managing the organization (McAfee and McMillian 1995).

These two limitations, a non-zero minimum marginal cost of production and diseconomies of scale and scope, are mitigated in the age of digitalization. Data is supposed to be the new source of economic growth and social welfare. Whether this really holds true, is an empirical question to be examined (Lim et al. 2013; Larson and Chang 2016). What has become real though is the rise of a new sort of dominant market players, such as Google, Facebook or Amazon, whose key asset is control over big data. Competition authorities are rising to this challenge of existing competition laws (Just 2018). True, in any of the commonly depicted waves of industrialization there have been dominant market players, be it giants of their time like US Steel, AT&T, now reloaded after its breakup in the 1970s, and most recently Microsoft. Should we therefore be concerned?

In the era of data hegemony dominant market players evolve naturally due to the characteristics of data and its consequences for creating and capturing value. First, unlike oil, data is not a scarce resource. Rather it is generated, can be reproduced and analyzed at zero marginal cost. Second, data is (almost) not bound by trade barriers. It is typically instantly available everywhere, because it doesn't need to be shipped physically. And third, data exhibits individual and personal information and therefore is non-fungible. Thus, the characteristics of data, as the economic driver in the third and fourth industrial revolution, are entirely different from those of oil in the second industrial revolution.

The necessity to account for these data characteristics became clear a decade ago. With the increasing automation of manufacturing firms generated more and more structured and transactional data internally to optimize production processes and to guide research and development. With the advent of digitalization, valuable consumer and competitor data became available outside of firm boundaries, not only structured but also unstructured data, as images, videos, audios, and sensor data in real-time across numerous devices (Internet of Things). This data explosion paved the way for new non-linear business models, which established digital platforms to serve as trustees for any kind of digital transaction. Typical examples of such digital platform models are online auctions, social networks (for communication, images, videos, etc.) and search engines (general web search engines or specific ones for hotels, flights, products, etc.).

Instead of creating value internally, these digital platform models aim at external value creation by enabling transactions between different stakeholder groups (e.g., consumers, producers, and advertisers). In its essence, the platform model represents a two- or multi-sided market that facilitates transactions by charging one of the stakeholder groups more than the other groups (Rochet and Tirole 2006). Actually, two-sided markets have existed long before digitalization. A classic example is the traditional newspaper which brings together two distinct customer groups: advertisers and readers. The value creation of digital platforms however differs from conventional multi-sided markets. A traditional newspaper company creates value primarily in-house by creating content (i.e. writing articles). A digital platform company facilitates transactions between consumers and producers and provides tools for one or both sides to create content.

Social media platforms may serve as a good example. They usually have three distinct user groups: content consumers, content producers, and advertisers. On such a platform, users can upload their videos, images or messages and consume uploaded content of other users. Thus users can belong to different groups simultaneously. The platform suggests the content shown to the consumer by analyzing the preferences and needs of the consumer and the credibility of the producers. By conducting more and more transactions consumers and producers reveal their preferences, which in turn can be used by advertisers to customize their marketing campaigns.

The primary task of a platform company is to initiate and facilitate connections between different stakeholder groups, to empower their participation in the network, to establish trust among them and to extract economic value from the transactions. Therefore, the size of the network is critical. Every new customer does not only interact with the company, like in the linear business model, but with everyone else in the network. Each additional individual on the platform adds more value to the platform because of direct and indirect network effects. By joining one of the platform groups, each customer directly increases the attractiveness and importance of the respective group. Indirectly, each new customer attracts also new ones to the other platform groups. These reciprocal network effects lead to non-linear network growth. For example, it took approximately 13 years for the TV to reach 50 million consumers, while social media companies achieve this number in less than 1 year (Dobbs et al. 2015).

Typically, the technical development of a platform is "asset light" so barriers for newcomers to enter are comparatively low. The marginal cost of adding one more customer is zero, leading to negligible variable cost. However, the initial investment to solve the so-called "chicken-and-egg-problem" – how to get a critical mass of content consumers and producers in the first place – can be significant. Thus, successful platform models foster indirect network effects and scale the model (following power law) as fast and as big as possible (Zang et al. 2016). This exponentiality creates a "winner-takes-it-all" situation (Moazed and Johnson 2016) with two consequences: First, in a market where price is not a differentiator and where digital assets can be replicated at zero cost, there is no need for a competing, slightly inferior digital product or service, like in the physical or service world. Second, by adjusting to consumer preferences and providing reputation incentives within the network, these models create high switching costs for consumers due to the risk of losing full network access, reputation, and network trust. As shown by Doganoglu and Wright (2006), "multihoming", that is, being active as a consumer in multiple social networks, is costly. Unsurprisingly, platform firms have little incentive to facilitate any transition.

Digital platform models tend to create information monopolies such that they lock in their stakeholder groups while making direct competition obsolete. In one way these information monopolies are similar to natural monopolies because economically search costs for the consumer are minimized, while market reach for the producer is maximized. Unlike natural monopolies however, information monopolies are not bound by geography. Therefore, they are difficult to control by local jurisdictions and competition laws. More specifically, the question arises whether in the face of lacking competition regulations should be implemented. Do platform models and the subsequent market evolution reduce economic welfare and impede innovation? The academic literature does not provide a clear-cut answer yet. Some authors are in favor of general regulations (Von Blanckenburg and Michaelis 2008), some prefer specific regulations, focusing on non-price competition (Just 2018), while others argue for less regulation (Haucap and Heimeshoff 2014). A holistic assessment is called for and should be the focus of future research. One conclusion can already be drawn: the competition landscape will be changing according to where competition will take place and how it will be played out.

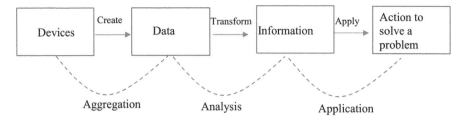

Fig. 1 The horizontal value chain of turning data into economic value. The straight lines highlight the data process flow and the dotted lines the related business cases

Two arguments are brought up on the shape of things to come in terms of the nature and intensity of competition. First, when looking at the horizontal value chain of transforming data into economic value (Fig. 1), we learn that digital platforms are data-driven organizations who are primarily concerned with data aggregation and data analysis (Latzer et al. 2016), while solving a specific problem (e.g., connecting users, booking hotels, providing or sharing music, videos or images). The heterogeneity of customer needs fosters competition, not only in the market for data aggregation and analysis but more so in the downstream market of applications. According to the Information Technology and Innovation Foundation (ITIF 2017), the number of technology start-ups grew at a rate of 47% in the last decade. Start-ups focusing on the application area of data analysis are currently booming in the main entrepreneurial hubs around the world (Shoham et al. 2017). Although they tend to inhibit some form of market competition, information monopolies also create incentives for new players to engage and thrive in the downstream market of the data analysis.

Second, while competition in traditional markets revolves around exploiting value-price trade-offs, digital platforms compete on innovation, quality, and data privacy (Just 2018). As stated by Haucap and Heimeshoff (2014, 60): "In fact, many online markets have been characterized by a large degree of Schumpeterian competition where one dominant player follows the other." Digital platforms risk obsolescence in the face of cross-domain competition and commoditization of data analysis. Today any firm, be it a start-up, a SME or a large corporate, in any industry has access to data analytics and can solve problems across domains, even unrelated to their original market. This accessibility from inside or outside puts industry incumbents under pressure. Countermeasures of the incumbents are vertical integration of the data value chain (Fig. 2), such as providing IaaS, PaaS or SaaS services, research investments or software development (Economist 2017b).

Industry disruption is not only the result of competition but it also comes from technology itself. Let's stick to the example of social networks and online market platforms where information monopolies act as trusted intermediaries to facilitate transactions. One potential threat arises from the advent of mature blockchain technology and smart contracts (Konstantinos and Devetsikiotis 2016). The blockchain is a distributed ledger to facilitate transactions in markets subjected to asymmetric information. It is inherently built as a distributed network to connect every partici-

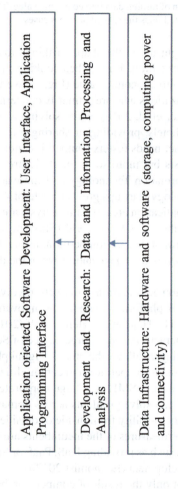

Fig. 2 The vertical value chain of data aggregation, analysis, and application

pant with everyone else and to guarantee trustworthy transactions by providing full transparency through smart contracts. By utilizing this technology, any intermediary becomes redundant, putting the business model of those information monopolies at risk.

Summing up, platform-based information monopolies emerge due to the inherent characteristics of data. Exploiting data is an economic driver for growth and the creation of wealth. It depends on the heterogeneity of customer needs and creates incentives to compete, specifically in downstream markets. Given that innovation in the digital world has primarily happened in a disruptive way, platform monopolies are under pressure at any time to become obsolete through cross-domain competitors and technological advancements. Therefore, in addressing the issue of data dominance competition authorities should be cautious and selective in applying the instruments of competition policy. Currently at least, it seems that these information monopolies stimulate innovation rather than impeding it.

Conclusion

What is the shape of things to come? Digitalization is a transformational megatrend that affects developed and developing economies alike. Currently, we are still assessing its potential and challenges. We understand that data is the driver, and data analytics is its refinery for extracting information, taking decisions and automating tasks which were previously reserved for humans. We are standing on the brink of a future which, in many respects, can be expected to be very different from the past and the present.

The cost of information extraction and automation has dropped significantly. This encourages profound democratization of advanced technologies to tackle the Sustainable Development Goals of the United Nations at a large scale (UN 2016) on the one hand, but is also fosters complementary tasks to be more valuable, on the other hand. Nevertheless, the commoditization of data and its refinery as an economic driver is a double-edged sword for business and society.

As envisioned by the late Peter Drucker (2001), data and knowledge extraction have become crucial business resources (Davenport 2006). Firms without a digital mindset and culture will experience competitive disadvantages (Brynjolfsson and McAfee 2014). While information monopolies arise as a new form of market power due to the particularities of data and digitalization, their longevity could be significantly shorter compared to monopolies during the first and second industrial revolution. The commoditization of data aggregation and analysis helps SMEs to execute innovation activities. The incentive for cross-domain competition may lead to more disruptive rather than incremental innovation. Therefore, a firm's business model may have to be changed more rapidly and frequently than today, requiring higher organizational flexibility and avoiding strong path dependencies. While large corporates may be able to safeguard themselves by vertical and horizontal integration, SMEs have to creative to protect their intellectual property. Moreover, information monopolies increasingly invest in fundamental research, hiring the best researchers from universities and paying them dearly (Economist 2017b). Will universities remain the primary source for fundamental research? Further, they acquire innovative firms in lateral areas, thus absorbing newly generated knowledge first and fast.

The effects of market volatility and uncertainty require firms and individuals to be agile. They demand a new set of skills for both blue- and white-collar workers, while putting certain jobs at risk. Automated information extraction by so-called predictive machines (e.g. machine learning) and robotics will replace humans in narrow tasks in production, retail, service, finance, transportation with well-defined inputs and outputs (Brynjolfsson and Mitchell 2017). But a machine that takes care of the customer service of a company is (currently) not able to drive a car or vice versa, meaning their application field is very limited. This limitation increases the value for tasks that involve mobility, rapid change over time, common sense making, creativity and artistic capabilities. Therefore, one can expect a higher value of labor in craftsmanship and research and development. The challenge will be to master the transition for the existing generations and those to come.

All of this puts the educational system under pressure because the current technological advances are following an exponential growth curve (Brynjolfsson and McAfee 2014). The educational system, which is responsible to prepare the society for the new skills, however, typically evolves only at a slow pace. As noted by Aoun (2017), new literacies, such as data literacy, technological literacy and human literacy, are needed in the very near future to establish a fruitful co-existence with intelligent software and hardware systems. Creativity and innovation need strong cognitive capabilities in system thinking, entrepreneurship, cultural agility and critical thinking (Aoun 2017). Will we be able to align the educational systems to the speed of technological change? Given the pace of digital change life-long learning might become the new rule and norm. Are individuals prepared to continuously learn and advance while pursuing their daily work?

As Friedrich A. Hayek (1945, p. 525) already noted: "[…The] economic problem of society is mainly one of rapid adaption to change […]". Technological advances, goods markets and educational systems, are just some elements in the larger system of our economies and societies. The fourth industrial revolution reminds us that every part of a system is connected to everything else. If individual elements of the system change at different paces and in an unsynchronized way, the interaction and network effects will become unbalanced and unpredictable. So far, human nature has proven to be adaptable.

References

Acs, Z. J., & Audretsch, D. B. (1987). Innovation, market structure and firm size. *Review of Economics and Statistics, 69*, 567–574.

Acs, Z. J., & Audretsch, D. B. (1988). Innovation in large and small firms: An empirical analysis. *American Economic Review, 78*, 678–690.

The Shape of Things to Come 117

Acs, Z. J., & Audretsch, D. B. (1990). *Innovation and small firms*. Cambridge: MIT Press.

Acs, Z. J., & Audretsch, D. B. (1991). R&D, firm size, and innovative activity. In Z. J. Acs & D. B. Audretsch (Eds.), *Innovation and technological change: An international comparison*. Ann Arbor: University of Michigan Press.

Aspromourgos, T. (2010). Universal opulence: Adam Smith on technical progress and real wages. *The European Journal of the History of Economic Thought, 17*, 1169–1182.

Audretsch, D. B. (1995a). Innovation, growth and survival. *International Journal of Industrial Organization, 13*, 441–457.

Audretsch, D. B. (1995b). *Innovation and industry evolution*. Cambridge: MIT Press.

Audretsch, D. B. (2009). The entrepreneurial society. *Journal of Technology Transfer, 34*, 245–254.

Audretsch, D. B., & Feldman, M. (1996). R&D spillovers and the geography of innovation and production. *American Economic Review, 86*, 630–640.

Audretsch, D. B., & Keilbach, M. (2007). The theory of knowledge spillover entrepreneurship. *Journal of Management Studies, 44*, 1242–1254.

Audretsch, D. B., Keilbach, M., & Lehmann, E. (2006). *Entrepreneurship and economic growth*. Oxford: Oxford University Press.

Audretsch, D. B., & Weigand, J. (2005). Do knowledge conditions make a difference? Investment, finance and ownership in German industries. *Research Policy, 34*, 595–630.

Aoun, J. (2017). *Robot-proof, higher education in the age of artificial intelligence*. Cambridge: The MIT Press.

Barro, R. J. (1999). Notes on growth accounting. *Journal of Economic Growth, 4*, 119–137.

Boianovsky, M., & Hoover, K. D. (2009). *Robert Solow and the development of growth economics*. History of Political Economy 41, Annual Supplement.

Brynjolfsson, E., & McAfee, A. (2014). *The second machine age*. New York: W. W. Norton & Company.

Brynjolfsson, E., & Mitchell, T. (2017). What can machine learning do? Workforce implications. *Science Magazine, 358*(6370), 1530–1534.

Chandler, A. (1990). *Scale and scope: The dynamics of industrial capitalism*. Cambridge: The Belknap Press of the Harvard University Press.

Cometlabs. (2017). Available online at: https://blog.cometlabs. io/263-self-driving-car-startups-to-watch-8a9976dc62b0

Davenport, T. (2006). Competing on Analytics. *Harvard Business Review, 84*, 98.

Dobbs, R., Manyika, J., & Woetzel, J. (2015). *No ordinary disruption. The four global forces breaking all the trends*. New York: Public Affairs.

Doganoglu, T., & Wright, J. (2006). Multihoming and compatibility. *International Journal of Industrial Organization, 24*, 45–67.

Drucker, P. (2001) *The next society*, The Economist, 1st November.

Economist. (2017a). Available online at: https://www.economist.com/news/leaders/21721656-data-economy-demands-new-approach-antitrust-rules-worlds-most-valuable-resource

Economist. (2017b). Available online at: https://www.economist.com/business/2017/12/07/google-leads-in-the-race-to-dominate-artificial-intelligence

Economist. (2018). Available online at: https://www.economist.com/bartleby/2018/07/12/the-robots-coming-for-your-job

Fellner, W. (1949). *Competition among the few*. New York: Alfred Knopf.

Griliches, Z. (1996). The discovery of the residual: A historical note. *Journal of Economic Literature, 34*, 1324–1330.

Haucap, J., & Heimeshoff, U. (2014). Google, Facebook, Amazon, eBay: Is the Internet driving competition or market monopolization? *International Economics and Economic Policy, 11*, 49–61.

Hayek, F. V. (1945). The use of knowledge in society. *American Economic Review, 35*, 519–530.

Hicks, J. R. (1935). Annual survey of economic theory: The theory of monopoly. *Econometrica, 3*, 1–20.

ITIF. (2017). *How technology-based start-ups support U.S. Economic Growth*. Online available at: https://itif.org/publications/2017/11/28/how-technology-based-start-ups-support-us-economic-growth

Jacobs, J. (1969). *The economy of cities*. New York: Random House.

Jewkes, J., Sawers, D., & Stillerman, R. (1969). *The sources of invention* (2nd ed.). London: Macmillan.

Just, N. (2018). Governing online platforms: Competition policy in times of Platformization. *Telecommunications Policy, 42*, 386–394.

Konstantinos, C., & Devetsikiotis, M. (2016). Blockchains and smart contracts for the internet of things. *IEEE Access, 4*, 2292–2303.

KPMG. (2017). Available online at: https://home.kpmg.com/sg/en/home/media/press-releases/2018/01/kpmg-venture-pulse-q4-2017.html

Kurz, H. D., & Salvadori, N. (2003). Theories of economic growth – old and new, Ch. 1. In N. Salvadori (Ed.), *The theory of economic growth – a 'classical' perspective*. Cheltenham: Edward Elgar.

Latzer, M., Hollnbuchner, K., Just, N., & Saurwein, F. (2016). The economics of algorithmic selection on the Internet. In J. M. Bauer & M. Latzer (Eds.), *Handbook on the economics of the internet*. Cheltenham: Elgar.

Larson, D., & Chang, V. (2016). A review and future direction of agile, business intelligence, analytics and data science. *International Journal of Information Management, 36*, 700–710.

Lim, E.-P., Chen, H., & Chen, G. (2013). Business intelligence and analytics. *ACM Transactions on Management Information Systems, 3*, 1–10.

Maddison, A. (1987). Growth and slowdown in advanced capitalist economies: Techniques of quantitative assessment. *Journal of Economic Literature, 25*, 649–698.

Malerba, F. (1992). Learning by firms and incremental technical change. *Economic Journal, 102*, 845–859.

Mansfield, E. (1962). Entry, gibrat's law, innovation and growth of firms. *American Economic Review, 55*, 1023–1051.

Mansfield, E. (1963). Size of firms, market structure and innovation. *Journal of Political Economy, 71*, 556–576.

Mansfield, E., John, R., Anthony, R., Edmond, V., Samuel, W., & Frank, H. (1977). *The production and application of new industrial technology*. New York: W.W. Norton & Company Inc.

Marshall, A. (1920). *Principles of economics: An introductory*. London: Macmillan.

Mason, P. (2016). *PostCapitalism: A guide to our future*. London: Penguin.

McAfee, R. P., & McMillian, J. (1995). Organizational diseconomies of scale. *Journal of Economics and Management Strategy, 4*, 399–426.

Moazed, A., & Johnson, N. L. (2016). *Modern monopolies: What it takes to dominate the 21st century*. New York: St. Martin's Press.

Nelson, R., & Winter, S. (1982). *An evolutionary theory of economic change*. Cambridge: Harvard University Press.

Pietersen, W. (2002). *Reinventing strategy*. New York: Wiley.

Ricardo, D. (1817). *On the principles of political economy and taxation*. London: John Murray.

Rifkin, J. (2011). *The third industrial revolution*. New York: St. Martin's Press.

Rifkin, J. (2014). *The zero marginal cost society*. New York: St. Martin's Press.

Rochet, J.-C., & Tirole, J. (2006). Two-sided markets: A progress report. *RAND Journal of Economics, 37*, 645–667.

Romer, P. (1986). Increasing returns and long-run growth. *Journal of Political Economy, 94*, 1002–1037.

Romer, P. (1990). Endogenous technological change. *Journal of Political Economy, 98*, 71–102.

Scherer, F. M. (1965). Firm size, market structure, opportunity, and the output of patented innovation. *American Economic Review, 55*, 1097–1125.

Schmookler, J. (1966). *Invention and economic growth*. Cambridge: Harvard University Press.

Schumpeter, J. (1912). *Theorie der wirtschaftlichen Entwicklung, München/Leipzig: Dunker & Humblot, as Theory of Economic Development.* Cambridge: Harvard University Press, 1934, 3rd printing 1949.

Schumpeter, J. (1939). *Business cycles. A theoretical, historical and statistical analysis of the capitalist process.* New York: Harper & Brothers.

Schumpeter, J. (1942). *Capitalism, socialism and democracy.* New York: Harper & Brothers.

Schumpeter, J. (1928). The instability of capitalism. *Economic Journal, 38,* 361–386.

Schumpeter, J. (1947). The creative response in economic history. *Journal of Economic History, 7,* 149–159.

Shoham, Y., Perrault, R., Brynjolfsson, E., Clark, J., & LeGassick, C. (2017). *Artificial intelligence index – 2017 annual report,* https://aiindex.org/2017-report.pdf

Smith, A. (1776). *An inquiry into the nature and causes of the wealth of nations.* Oxford: Oxford University Press. (Reprint 2008).

Solow, R. (1957). Technical Change and the Aggregate Production Function. *The Review of Economics and Statistics, 39*(3), 312–320.

Stigler, G. (1951). The division of labor is limited by the extent of the market. *Journal of Political Economy, 59,* 185–193.

Sundajararan, A. (2016). *The sharing economy: The end of employment and the rise of crowd-based capitalism.* Cambridge: MIT.

United Nations. (2016). *Sustainable development goals.* Online available at: https://www.un.org/sustainabledevelopment/sustainable-development-goals/

Von Blanckenburg, K., & Michaelis, M. (2008). Regulierungsmöglichkeiten auf dem Markt für Online-Auktionen. *Wirtschaftsdienst, 88,* 415–420.

Winter, S. (1984). Schumpeterian competition in alternative technological regimes. *Journal of Economic Behaviour and Organization, 5,* 287–320.

Zang, C., Cui, P., & Faloutsos, C. (2016). *Beyond sigmoids: The NetTide model for social network growth, and its applications.* Proceedings of the 22nd ACM SIGKDD international conference on knowledge discovery and data mining, 2015–24.

Martin Prause is Assistant Professor of Computational Economics and Business Analytics at WHU Otto Beisheim School of Management, Vallendar and Düsseldorf, Germany.

Jürgen Weigand is Professor of Economics and Chair of the Institute of Industrial Organization at the same institution.

David Audretsch: A Source of Inspiration, a Co-author, and a Friend

Enrico Santarelli

Abstract In this chapter, Enrico Santarelli discusses the profound impact that David had on his career. Beginning with a conference in Budapest, Santarelli and David became close friends and colleagues. They went on to collaborate on many papers and projects, several of which Santarelli highlights below.

Beginning

I have known David Audretsch for nearly 30 years. We first met in 1989, towards the end of August at the 16th Annual Conference of the European Association for Research in Industrial Economics (E.A.R.I.E.) that was hosted by the Karl Marx University in Budapest.[1] A general feeling of excitement characterized the conference and the city: transition from a centrally planned economy to a market economy was already under way in Eastern Europe, with Hungary leading the pack. Representatives of Western multinationals attended the conference and arranged meetings in town in search of useful hints from academic researchers and solid investment opportunities in the country.

At that time, I was starting the research program that would have characterized the rest of my academic career. I would define myself as a Schumpeterian economist (neither neo-, nor post-) who, by reading Schumpeter's early writings learned a lot about the interplay of entrepreneurship and innovation as joint drivers of economic change. In fact, my first publication on these topics (Santarelli and Pesciarelli 1990) deals with the original, German editions of two of Schumpeter's books: *Das Wesen und der Hauptinhalt der Theoretischen Nationalökonomie* (1908) and *Theorie der Wirtschaftlichen Entwicklung* (1911). In such books, Schumpeter gives

---

[1] The name of the university was changed the next year into Budapest University of Economic Sciences.

E. Santarelli (✉)
University of Bologna – Department of Economics, Bologna, Italy
e-mail: enrico.santarelli@unibo.it

© Springer Nature Switzerland AG 2019
E. E. Lehmann, M. Keilbach (eds.), *From Industrial Organization to Entrepreneurship*, https://doi.org/10.1007/978-3-030-25237-3_13

a clear definition of the entrepreneur as the engine of development whose distinctive psychological and behavioral traits are energy of action and the ability to introduce the new by breaking with established routines.

A few years before, David Audretsch had started, together with Zoltan Acs his own research program on firm size, firm growth, innovation, and eventually entrepreneurship which makes him one of the most influential economists of our time. In fact, while Eastern Europe was opening up to the free market economy, David and Zoltan were among the promoters of a major breakthrough in economics: by giving new stamina to the study of entrepreneurship and innovation with the foundation of *Small Business Economics* and the publication of some of their seminal contributions they paved the way for the emergence of an entirely new field in economics.

Following that first encounter in Hungary, David and I became good friends. Keeping constantly in touch through the years, working at joint projects, and seeing each other so many times in occasion of conferences and workshops held here and there in Europe, America, and Asia. The opportunity to conduct joint research was caught thanks to Marco Vivarelli, who shared with us the belief that before making any recommendations for entrepreneurship policy action it is worth to study in depth the mechanism linking firm initial size to firm post-entry growth and survival. The importance of this relationship had already been pointed out by Paul Geroski (1995), and has attracted the curiosity of dozens of scholars since then. In our paper "Start-up size and industrial dynamics: some evidence from Italian manufacturing" published in 1999 in the *International Journal of Industrial Organization* (Audretsch et al. 1999a; see also Audretsch et al. 1999b), we present empirical evidence on some previously unnoticed features of the firm size/firm growth/firm survival relationship. Consistent with Jovanovic's (1982) model of *competitive selection*, we show that the issue in studying such a relationship may not be why Gibrat's Law fails to hold among new and small enterprises, with smaller ones growing faster than their larger counterparts, but rather why the likelihood of survival does not appear to be significantly related to firm *start-up* size. Our conclusion is that this statistical relationship is weaker when smaller firms in any cohort of new entries are able to grow very fast, in this way enhancing their likelihood of survival.

A few years later, David, Roy Thurik, Luuk Klomp, and I broadened the analysis of the firm size/firm growth relationship to include the case of the service industries (Audretsch et al. 2004; see also Piergiovanni et al. 2003). Examining whether the basic tenet underlying Gibrat's Law – namely, that growth rates are independent of firm size – can be rejected for the services, we find evidence for a large sample of Dutch firms in the hospitality industries that in most cases growth rates are independent of firm size. Validation of Gibrat's Law in some sub-sectors of the small-scale services shows that the dynamics of firm demographics may be more complex than suggested by most previous studies that had rejected it for manufacturing.

I continued and concluded this line of research in the next years in collaboration with Francesca Lotti and Marco Vivarelli. Two of our several joint papers are worth a mention. The first one, "Does Gibrat's Law hold among young, small firms?", was published in the *Journal of Evolutionary Economics* (Lotti et al. 2003). This is to my knowledge the first study showing that the overall rejection of Gibrat's Law over a given period of time may in fact conceal a possible convergence in favor of the

Law through time. Using quantile regression techniques to test whether Gibrat's Law holds for new entrants, we find that for some selected industries in Italian manufacturing it fails to hold in the years immediately following start-up, when smaller firms have to rush in order to achieve a size large enough to enhance their likelihood of survival. Conversely, in subsequent years the patterns of growth of smaller ones among the new firms in the same cohort of entries do not differ significantly from those of larger entrants, and the Law therefore cannot be rejected. Encouraged by David Audretsch to continue with this line of investigation, in the second paper, "Defending Gibrat's Law as a long-run regularity", published in *Small Business Economics* (Lotti et al. 2009), we strengthen our conclusions. On the one side, consistently with previous studies, we find that Gibrat's Law has to be rejected *ex ante*, provided that smaller firms tend to grow faster than larger ones. On the other side, we find that a significant convergence toward Gibrat-like patterns of growth can be detected *ex post*. These results are found testing the empirical specification of Gibrat's equation over the entire period of analysis (1987–1994) and year-by-year. From a methodological viewpoint, we use the two-step Heckman's (1979) estimator and perform robustness checks by augmenting the main equation with a firm age variable, squared and interaction terms. Our conclusion is that the processes of firm learning and market selection originate a fringe of surviving firms which behave according to Gibrat's Law, therefore reconciling the diverging results emerged from the previous empirical literature and corroborating theoretical models of market selection á la Jovanovic (1982).

Analysis of the relationship between structural characteristics of new entries and their post-entry performance leaves room open for policy discussion. We have extensively debated this issue with David Audretsch, reaching substantially similar conclusions about policy action in support of entrepreneurship. In a paper with Zoltan Acs, Thomas Åstebro, and David Robinson published in *Small Business Economics* (Acs et al. 2017), David Audretsch observes that most entrepreneurship policies end up in a waste of taxpayers' money by either encouraging individuals already intent on becoming entrepreneurs or primarily addressing other market failures. This view is fully consistent with the ideas that I developed with Marco Vivarelli in a paper, "Entrepreneurship and the process of firm's entry, survival and growth", published in *Industrial and Corporate Change* (Santarelli and Vivarelli 2007). Building upon a huge theoretical and empirical literature, we submit that entry of new firms is heterogeneous with successful and innovative entrepreneurs being found together with passive followers, over-optimist gamblers, and escapees from unemployment. Accordingly, policy action should be selective, identifying among nascent entrepreneurs those endowed with progressive motivation and characterized by a higher likelihood of post-entry growth and profitability. Such entrepreneurs represent the 'efficient' fringe of new entries in Jovanovic's market selection mechanism and they should be the only ones to receive public subsidies in all those circumstances in which a market failures impede them to complete their initial investment and enter into the stable portion of the market. Thus, we conclude that *erga-omnes* policies supporting new firm formation in general should be replaced by post-entry subsidies in favor of young firms which have already proved themselves able to cope with market selection.

References

Acs, Z. J., Åstebro, T., Audretsch, D. B., & Robinson, D. T. (2017). Public policy to promote entrepreneurship: A call to arms. *Small Business Economics, 47*, 35–51.

Audretsch, D. B., Santarelli, E., & Vivarelli, M. (1999a). Start-up size and industrial dynamics: Some evidence from Italian manufacturing. *International Journal of Industrial Organization, 17*, 965–983.

Audretsch, D. B., Santarelli, E., & Vivarelli, M. (1999b). Does start-up size influence the likelihood of survival? In D. B. Audretsch & A. R. Thurik (Eds.), *Innovation, industry evolution and employment* (pp. 280–296). Cambridge: Cambridge University Press.

Audretsch, D. B., Klomp, L., Santarelli, E., & Thurik, A. R. (2004). Gibrat's law: Are the services different? *Review of Industrial Organization, 24*, 301–324.

Geroski, P. A. (1995). What do we know about entry? *International Journal of Industrial Organization, 13*, 421–440.

Heckman, J. J. (1979). Sample selection bias as a specification error. *Econometrica, 50*, 153–161.

Jovanovic, B. (1982). Selection and evolution of industry. *Econometrica, 50*, 649–670.

Lotti, F., Santarelli, E., & Vivarelli, M. (2003). Does Gibrat's law hold among young, small firms? *Journal of Evolutionary Economics, 13*, 213–235.

Lotti, F., Santarelli, E., & Vivarelli, M. (2009). Defending Gibrat's law as a long-run regularity. *Small Business Economics, 32*, 31–44.

Piergiovanni, R., Santarelli, E., Klomp, L., & Thurik, A. R. (2003). Gibrat's Law and the Firm Size/Firm Growth Relationship in Italian Small Scale Services. *Revue D'Economie Industrielle, 102*, 69–82.

Santarelli, E., & Pesciarelli, E. (1990). The emergence of a vision: The development of Schumpeter's theory of entrepreneurship. *History of Political Economy, 22*, 677–696.

Santarelli, E., & Vivarelli, M. (2007). Entrepreneurship and the process of firms' entry, survival and growth. *Industrial and Corporate Change, 16*, 455–488.

David: A Cultural Entrepreneur

Marco Vivarelli

Abstract In this essay Marco Vivarelli, a longtime collaborator with David, discusses David's impact on his career as well as on the field of entrepreneurship research in total. Touching on David's influence in economic and social science research, Vivarelli posits that David has been a key figure in the advancement of entrepreneurial research and think. This chapter emphasizes David's position as a leader in the field.

David: A Cultural Entrepreneur

"Marco, we have to stand on the giants' shoulders and move research forward": this was said by David to a young post-doc in 1993… The giants were scholars such as Scherer, Griliches, Geroski: the fathers of empirical IO able to provide the general frameworks and key results we are still referring to nowadays. David is today the most prominent continuator of that rich tradition and still a mentor for many of us.

More specifically, David was able to transmit to me his enthusiasm for research and an ambition to aspire to high quality results ("Marco, we have to go to the best journals, starting from the very best ones"), without forgetting the intrinsic nature of our work and the general meaning of our research purposes. Unfortunately, nowadays and particularly within mainstream economics, form has prevailed over content: what is important is just the journal in which one publishes, while the longer-term targets of our research mission are neglected. What are these targets? Here again David teaches: a strong link with reality, social impact, policy implications.

In contrast with a common trend in mainstream economics, David has maintained, and transmitted to a community of scholars, his concern for policy-relevant issues and general research questions fundamental for society as a whole. Within this context, David is a leading world scholar, recognized not only by economists but

---

M. Vivarelli (✉)
Università Cattolica del Sacro Cuore, Milan, Italy
e-mail: marco.vivarelli@unicatt.it

© Springer Nature Switzerland AG 2019
E. E. Lehmann, M. Keilbach (eds.), *From Industrial Organization to Entrepreneurship*, https://doi.org/10.1007/978-3-030-25237-3_14

also by social scientists in general. Another lesson from David: what is important is not belonging to a narrowly defined discipline, but rather investigating a relevant issue; in doing this, an interdisciplinary and open-minded research program is often much more useful than an economic model based on apodictic (and often absurd) ad-hoc hypotheses.

Obviously, David was a master in applying this methodological approach to "Entrepreneurship" as a social phenomenon, to be investigated from different angles and perspectives. Referring to his huge cultural contribution, here below I will try to isolate and discuss the possible answers to a fundamental question which is still on the table: "What is entrepreneurship?"

Answering this question is not an easy task, and the lesson we can learn from David is to avoid both an apologetic view of the phenomenon, i.e. that every self-employed person and every start-up is 'entrepreneurial', and a restrictive definition, according to which the Schumpeterian entrepreneur is just the innovative superstar. Indeed, since the seminal contribution by Baumol and David we have become aware that 'Schumpeterian innovative entrepreneurs' coexist with 'defensive and necessity entrepreneurs', the latter being those who enter a new business not because of market opportunities and innovative ideas, but merely because they need an income to survive.

On the one hand, new firm formation may play a crucial role in fostering competition, inducing innovation and fostering the emergence of new sectors; within this framework, the entrepreneurs at the head of new small firms may compensate the restructuring of mature sectors and the downsizing of larger incumbent firms. In this context, while endogenous growth theorists have highlighted the importance of human capital and R&D as additional explanations for increasing returns in the aggregate production function, more recently, some scholars – including David – have proposed entrepreneurship as a third driver of economic growth and employment generation. More specifically, through their new companies entrepreneurs would be able to exploit the opportunities provided by new knowledge and ideas which are not fully understood and commercialized by the mature incumbent firms. Thus, entrepreneurship represents the missing link between investment in new knowledge and economic development, serving as a conduit for both entirely new knowledge and knowledge spillovers.

On the other hand, if we turn our attention from the macroeconomic to the sectoral and microeconomic levels, the empirical evidence on industrial dynamics casts some doubt on the progressive potentialities of business start-ups. Indeed, survival rates for new firms are strikingly low; the available (and vast) econometric evidence at the sectoral and microeconomic levels is largely consistent with this outcome: studies on different countries and different sectors reveal that more than 50% of new firms exit the market within the first 5 years of activity. Moreover, entry and exit rates are significantly correlated; this is one of the uncontroversial 'stylized facts' of the entry process according to the afore-mentioned Paul Geroski; therefore, if entry and exit rates are positively and significantly correlated, market 'churning' emerges as a common feature of industrial dynamics across different sectors and different countries. This means that economic sectors are characterized by a fringe of firms operating at a suboptimal scale where the likelihood of survival is particularly low and where 'revolving door' firms are continuously entering and exiting the market.

Obviously, David's books and articles convey the message that industry-specific characteristics such as scale economies and an endowment of innovative capabilities exert a significant impact on entry, exit, and the likelihood of survival of newborn firms. For example, in industries characterized by a higher minimum efficient scale (MES), small newborn firms face higher risks, which are likely to push them out of the market within a short period after start-up. As a consequence, in many sectors new firm start-ups may simply originate what has correctly been called 'turbulence'. Conversely, larger start-ups characterized by an initial size close to the MES should result into higher survival rates.

By the same token, new firm formation may be more or less conducive to technological upgrading and industry growth, according to the different sectors in which it occurs. For instance, 'new technology-based firms' in advanced manufacturing and service sectors certainly play a different role compared with small-sized start-ups in traditional sectors. Thus, in some sectors the 'creative destruction' role of new firm formation may be dominant compared with simple 'turbulence', while the opposite may hold in other sectors.

To summarize, as David continues to teach us, 'Entrepreneurship' is an extremely complex, and somewhat controversial phenomenon. Far from being solely the result of the entrepreneurial 'creative destruction' process proposed by Schumpeterian advocates, any set of entrepreneurial ventures can be seen as a somewhat heterogeneous aggregate where real and innovative entrepreneurs are found together with passive followers, over-optimistic gamblers and even escapees from unemployment.

In this context, policy makers should bear in mind that the aggregate "entrepreneurship" covers a very wide range of "animals". Indeed, as discussed above, founders are heterogeneous and may make 'entry mistakes', many new firms are doomed to early failure, and market churning and turbulence are very common across economic sectors. Thus, policy makers should be able to disentangle these different components of the entrepreneurial aggregate, and encourage a selected subsample of potential/actual entrepreneurs; for instance, those characterized by a larger start-up size, higher education, longer previous job experience, better innovative capabilities, and so forth.

In contrast, as rightly pointed out by Scott Shane and by David himself, the widespread diffusion of general, 'erga-omnes' entry subsidies as policy instruments is particularly unfortunate. Indeed, 'umbrella' subsidies should be discarded in favor of selective and targeted measures addressed to the more promising potential entrepreneurs, such as those characterized by superior human capital or by challenging, but feasible, innovative ideas.

The considerations above show how entrepreneurship is still a fascinating research issue and how much David has contributed to shape and address entrepreneurial studies. As a scholar community, we have to thank him for this, confident that he will continue in his role of providing challenging stimuli and wise advice to all of us for many years to come.

David Audretsch and International Business: Bringing It All Back Home

Saul Estrin and Daniel Shapiro

Abstract In this essay, the authors tell the tale of David's research journey, ebbing and weaving throughout his academic career. While the subject of David's focus has drifted over time from Industrial Organization, to Multinational Firms, to Small and Medium-sized Enterprises, the interplay between public policy, entrepreneurship, and innovation has been ever-present. The authors discuss how many of the ideas that he has developed over the years have relevance and insight for new issues now emerging in the International Business literature.

Introduction

David Audretsch is known primarily for his economic research on innovation (Acs and Audretsch 1988), knowledge spillovers (Acs et al. 1994), and their relation to entrepreneurial activity (Audretsch and Keilbach 2007a), the growth of small firms (Acs and Audretsch 1990) and firm location (Audretsch and Feldman 1996). This body of work is primarily about new ventures and small-scale organizations; indeed, this interest is highlighted by the fact that he has co-edited for 29 years a journal that he jointly founded, *Small Business Economics*. Rather less well-known is that David, early in his career, also looked at large, multinational firms (Kindleberger and Audretsch 1983). However, subsequent to that, he moved in an entirely different intellectual direction and did not publish a single paper on multinationals and not a single paper in international business journals until 2018 (Audretsch et al. 2018).

David began his academic life as an industrial organization (IO) economist at the University of Madison- Wisconsin. In the late 1970's, when he was a PhD student, the literature on multinational enterprises (MNEs) and foreign direct investment (FDI) was in some flux, and there was "no unique theory of direct investment"

S. Estrin
London School of Economics, London, UK

D. Shapiro (✉)
Beedie School of Business, Simon Fraser University, Burnaby, BC, Canada
e-mail: dshapiro@sfu.ca

© Springer Nature Switzerland AG 2019
E. E. Lehmann, M. Keilbach (eds.), *From Industrial Organization to Entrepreneurship*, https://doi.org/10.1007/978-3-030-25237-3_15

(McClain 1983: 291). If there was a dominant framework at that time, it was attributable to Hymer (1960), Kindleberger (1969) and Caves (1976), who developed theories built on ideas from IO, focused on market imperfections that allow monopoly advantages developed at home to be exploited abroad. The papers in the Kindleberger and Audretsch 1983 volume reflect the significance of this approach, as well as the degree of heterogeneity of alternatives.

It is important to note that at this time, international business did not really exist as a unique area of study. That changed during the 1980's, as the influence of the authors listed above created a separate body of literature, summarized by Dunning's (1988) eclectic paradigm organized around studying the MNE. A separate and distinct area of study, International Business (IB), was thus formed, and is now an established field of research and teaching (see for example the textbook by Peng and Meyer (2016)). It was in this time period that David chose not to follow the literature down that path. Rather, in the 1980's he first followed a relatively standard IO agenda, though one that was focused on small firms (Acs and Audretsch 1987, 1988). This in turn led him to focus on the importance of knowledge spillovers to these firms (Acs et al. 1994) and finally to the knowledge spillover theory of entrepreneurship (Audretsch and Keilbach 2007a).

In this paper, we elaborate on the direction that David took, and discuss how many of the ideas that he has developed over the years have relevance and insight for the new issues now emerging in the IB literature. Our arguments are summarized in Fig. 1. We focus on three critical junctures in David's career that led him away from what we now call the IB literature, and on recent developments in IB that make David's body of work relevant to that literature.

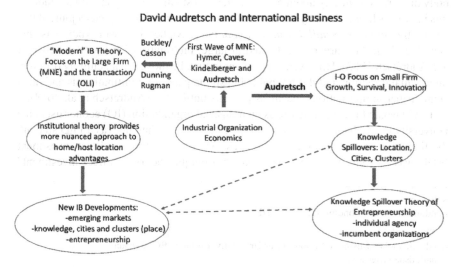

Fig. 1 David Audretsch and International Business

From MNEs to Small Firms

The idea that there was something distinctive and interesting to study about FDI goes back to Hymer (1960). Before then, investments overseas were viewed as cross-border capital flows driven by differences in national interest rates. Hymer identified a distinct class of such investments, which were not financial (portfolio) and gave the investor control over the entity that they purchased, which he termed foreign direct investments. The theme was picked up by Hymer's doctoral supervisor, Charles Kindleberger, who viewed FDI as a way for large firms to reduce the competition that they face in domestic markets. Of course, David enters the story a few years later as the co-editor with Kindleberger of *The Multinational Corporation in the 1980's* (Kindleberger and Audretsch 1983). The most commonly cited authors in that volume are in fact Hymer, Kindleberger and Caves, and many of the other papers also reflect their influence. However, at the same time the volume also encompasses international trade and finance theory (Krugman 1983; Aliber 1983), empirical IO (Shapiro 1983), and some newly emerging ideas focusing on the firm-specific advantages of MNEs and the transfer of these advantages via internal markets (Kogut 1983; McClain 1983). These latter ideas are linked to the work of Buckley and Casson (1976) and Dunning (1979) whose approach came to dominate the IB literature.

Kindleberger and Audretsch 1983 is now out of print, but the point is that David was editing it as an IB scholar, but after that he chose to go in another direction. The book did not fully anticipate the directions IB would subsequently take, first defined around that time by the work of Buckley and Casson (1976), Dunning (1979, 1988), and Rugman (1981). These authors collectively moved the direction of the field toward a focus on the large multinational enterprise (MNE) and its internationalization choices. Although IB was a nascent field, its dimensions were beginning to take shape and were coalescing around the *Journal of International Business Studies* – then relatively unknown and now the premier journal in IB.

Thus, IB moved away from its IO-trade roots to more fully embrace an "eclectic" view summarized in the work of Dunning (1979, 1988) as the OLI perspective. This was centered more around the firm, the MNE, and the firm-specific resources and capabilities that provided it with a competitive advantage (O), the transaction cost factors that led to the internal transfer of these advantages (I) and the locations to which they were most effectively transferred (L). Country context became increasingly important in determining the choice of host location (Bevan et al. 2004) and in explaining the characteristics of MNEs themselves, especially as the share of FDI from emerging economies began to rise (Cuervo-Cazurra and Ramamurti 2014). There was also increasing interest in the differences between host countries, in which FDI was located, and home countries from which it was sourced, referred to as "distance" (Ghemawat 2007). Moreover, the IB literature subsequently expanded to include a strong emphasis on institutions, both in host and home countries (Globerman and Shapiro 2002; Peng et al. 2008, 2009). Many economists, including the authors, migrated from pure economics to embrace this new IB.

However, David did not follow suit. He stayed within the bounds of traditional IO economics, but his work migrated to a focus on small firms; a direction exactly the opposite of that towards large MNEs taken by the IB literature. Thus, much of his research in the 1980's and early 1990's focused on entry and exit of small firms (Audretsch 1991, 1995; Acs and Audretsch 1987; Audretsch and Acs 1994; Audretsch and Mahmood 1995); and innovation in small firms (Acs and Audretsch 1987, 1988, 1991).

If the analysis of the MNE is about the entrenchment of monopoly power by large firms and across borders, David remained true to the competitive tradition within IO, in which new firm entry would erode strong market positions. Thus, his work makes a persuasive case for the importance of small firms as drivers of industrial dynamism and employment within countries, as sources of innovation and as essential ingredients in the emerging new (at the time) knowledge economy (Audretsch and Thurik 2001). Audretsch and Thurik (2001) in particular contrast this with an economy (and economic policy) focused on large, oligopolistic firms. Thus, while the IB literature focused on large firms operating across borders, David focused on small firms usually operating within a single country.

In recent years, the IB literature has focused on country characteristics as *exogenous determinants* of firm performance and location choices (Tihanyi et al. 2005; Chacar et al. 2010; Banalieva et al. 2018). David's work did not ignore the country context, but he was interested primarily in the role of small firms in *determining* country performance, notably growth at country and regional levels (Audretsch and Keilbach 2004; Audretsch et al. 2006; Audretsch 2007a, b; Carlsson et al. 2009). Indeed, David had begun to draw inspiration not from the IO literature but from the literature on economic growth, which links growth and entrepreneurship together via innovation (Audretsch et al. 2011), and more recently endogenous growth, which allows for the role of policy to influence growth outcomes (Aghion and Howitt 1992; Braunerhjelm et al. 2010). In this work, Audretsch' s ideas ran in parallel with another IO economist who became increasingly interested in entrepreneurship, William Baumol (Baumol 2011; Baumol and Strom 2007), though Baumol was perhaps more interested in the impact of institutions per se (Baumol 1990).

From Small Firms to Localized Knowledge Spillovers and Cities

In the course of studying small firms, David asked a critical question. His results suggested that small firms could be more innovative than large firms, despite lower investments in R&D, so the question was, from where do they get their knowledge (Audretsch 1995, 1998, 2007a, b)? The answer, which had already been suggested in various contexts (Jaffe 1989; Jaffe et al. 1993; Glaeser et al. 1992) was localized spillovers of knowledge coming from both universities and other firms (clusters). David argued, with various co-authors, that knowledge spillovers are not only localized but that they are not homogeneous across firms. Thus, small firms may benefit disproportionately from knowledge spillovers, (Acs et al. 1992, 1994), particularly from university research in specific sectors (Audretsch and Stephan 1996). Moreover, while innovative activity tends to cluster geographically (Audretsch and Feldman 1996), the impact is greater for knowledge-intensive industries at earlier stages of the life cycle, which suggests that knowledge spillovers are higher in such industries in earlier stages of the life cycle. The apparent conclusion is that innovative activity is promoted by knowledge spillovers that occur within a distinct geographic region, particularly in the early stages of the industry life-cycle, but as the industry evolves toward maturity and decline, innovation may become more dispersed. This may be the result of "congestion".

One question that emerges from this literature is to specify the exact mechanism by which knowledge spillovers occur in localized contexts. In various contributions, summarized in Audretsch (1998) and Feldman and Audretsch (1999) David studies and compares two different mechanisms. The first, referred to as the Marshall—Arrow—Romer model (Glaeser et al. 1992) focuses on localized knowledge spillovers between firms in a given industry. The assumption is that knowledge externalities with respect to firms exist, but only for firms within the same industry, and therefore that knowledge spillovers across industries are less important. In contrast, the second mechanism focuses on inter-industry spillovers, and is therefore related to diversity. This view is associated with Jane Jacobs (1969) who argues that knowledge spillovers are external to the industry in which the firm operates and that cities are the most important source of innovation because of their diverse knowledge sources. Thus, so-called Jacobian externalities arise from the increased variety of industries within a geographic area. Feldman and Audretsch (1999) provide evidence supporting the view that diversity is important to the growth of cities, supporting the idea that cities are a major source of innovation because of the diversity of knowledge sources (Audretsch and Feldman 1996).

Knowledge spillovers are a well-studied phenomenon in the IB literature (Meyer and Sinani 2009). However, in Audretsch's work, the externality is generated by the local cluster, be it within an industry or in the city, and it is reaped by firms, especially new and small ones. In the IB literature, the externality is generated by the MNE and the gains go to domestic firms. Thus, the crucial distinction is that in Audretsch' s work, the beneficiary is the firm being analyzed, and in IB the source of the spillover is the firm being analyzed, while the beneficiaries are the host economy enterprises. The IB literature does make the distinction between horizontal spillovers, which operate within an industry, and vertical spillovers, which operate up and down a supply chain (Bruno et al. 2019) but there is rarely a focus on the potentially localized nature of spillover benefits, nor on the particular benefits for small firms. Moreover, the role of cities in both generating innovation and supporting economic growth has received very little attention. We discuss this further below.

There has also been a small amount of recent IB work on an IO theme of potential interest to a young Audretsch, considering whether FDI raises the barriers to entry for domestic firms. Caves (1976) saw FDI as a mechanism for large firms from one country to transmit their monopoly power across borders, raising the possibility that innovation and new firm entry by domestic enterprises would be crowded out in the host economy. There is some empirical work on this question, mainly single industry or country studies which provide contradictory results. Thus, De Backer and Sleuwaegen (2003) show that FDI crowds out new firm entry in Belgium while Görg and Strobl (2002) find that FDI presence has a positive effect on domestic entry in the Irish manufacturing sector. Danakol et al. (2017) address the issue across countries and find strong evidence for the crowding out view across seventy countries, 2000–2009. Spillovers from both the host and home economies to domestic entrepreneurs and firms therefore remain firmly on the research agenda, with large new cross country datasets opening up the possibilities for fruitful empirical research (Reynolds et al. 2005).

From Knowledge Spillovers to Entrepreneurship and Agency

David's work on small firm formation and innovation was for the most part conducted within a traditional IO framework (Acs and Audretsch 1990). However, inspired in part by a 1989 conference in Berlin on new firm entry which provided numerous international comparisons (Geroski and Schwalbach 1991),[1] he decided that the focus on industries and firms was less important than a focus on individuals and individual agency. The IO approach saw entry as an equilibrating mechanism in a market – entry is seen as an error correction mechanism whereby entrants respond to excess profits and eliminate them via entry. The problem was that the empirical evidence did not fully support this idea because much entry was simply churning (Geroski 1995). This led David in another direction, one that rejects the notion that entry is a simple equilibrating device. He came to conclude that successful entry requires both innovation (to overcome entry barriers) and individual agency (people making decision regarding entry opportunities). Thus, he set out on a different path, into the field of entrepreneurship.

In his book laying out frameworks for research on entrepreneurship, Davidsson (2016) argues that this literature has two broad streams. The first focuses on the entrepreneurs themselves: their traits, experience and human capital. The second views entrepreneurship as the creation of new economic activity. Thus, the entrepreneur is a conceptual construct or abstraction: the "underlying theme here is that the development and renewal of any society, economy or organization requires micro-level actors who show the initiative and persistence to make change happen" (Davidsson 2016, p.4). Thus, as in Schumpeter (1934), entrepreneurship is seen as playing an economic role as well as comprising the actions of a person. David's approach to entrepreneurship and his view that the role of new firms in bringing technological innovations to market and in job creation was disproportionate (Parker 2009), fits directly into this way of thinking. Thus, entrepreneurs are the

---

[1] Also attended by both authors of this paper.

agents who transfer scientific and process innovations from the laboratory and the workshop to the marketplace; their role is one of commercialization of new ideas, products and systems. In so doing, they provide the forces of competition to improve the efficiency and performance of incumbents, as argued by IO economists, and they are potential drivers of economic growth (Audretsch et al. 2006; Carree and Thurik 2003).

In his book, *Innovation and Industry Evolution*, Audretsch (1995) proposes changing the focus of analysis away from exogenously given firms to individual agents who bring with them endowments of new economic knowledge. Thus, he proposed "shifting the unit of observation away from exogenously assumed firms to individuals—agents confronted with new knowledge and the decision whether and how to act upon that new knowledge." (Audretsch 1995, p. 48). In turn, this shift also raised another important question, which is how these economic agents can best appropriate the returns from their knowledge?

This question became the basis for the knowledge spillover theory of entrepreneurship (KSTE), which in one way or another has occupied much of David's intellectual work since that time (Audretsch et al. 2006; Audretsch and Keilbach 2007a, b, 2008; Acs et al. 2009; Agarwal et al. 2010; Acs et al. 2013; Aparicio et al. 2016). The basic argument is that high impact and knowledge-based entry is created through the decisions of individual agents, often scientists and engineers employed in a private or public institution, who create new ventures in order to appropriate the expected value of their knowledge. Firm creation is therefore an endogenous process arising from an individual's effort to appropriate the value of his or her knowledge through innovative activity.

In formalizing the KSTE, it becomes apparent that there are two key mechanisms. First, the focus on potential founders who are employees with strong knowledge capital makes entrepreneurial opportunities, rather than being exogenously available, actions that are endogenously created through knowledge investments. Second, because current employees are co-creators of knowledge with the organizations for which they work, the potential entrepreneur balances the value of exploiting their knowledge within their organization against the benefits of starting a new firm. Thus, the degree to which existing organizations can mobilize internally to commercialize knowledge is an important factor limiting entrepreneurship.

We have noted a strong theme linking entrepreneurship research to both economic growth and to policy and this is especially true in the KSTE framework. KSTE was originally conceived not entirely as a theory of entrepreneurship, but also as component of the theory of economic growth. It does this by first distinguishing between economic knowledge and commercialized economic knowledge, with only the latter contributing to growth. Second, the theory underscores the possibility that not all knowledge spills over; incumbent organizations and institutions that create and possess knowledge may, if they utilize it internally, limit the degree to which knowledge is disseminated.

Thus, the KSTE sees new firms as being created endogenously through individual agent's efforts to appropriate the value of his/her knowledge via their own innovative activity. The probability of becoming an entrepreneur depends on the individual's estimate of the potential returns to commercializing their knowledge, and this in turn depends on the degree to which incumbents act to commercialize that knowledge. In other words, the expected profit opportunities from entrepreneurship are dependent on knowledge not commercialized by the incumbent firms, and thus on their commercialization capabilities. Successful entrepreneurship in the KSTE depends on the interaction between incumbent firms and potential entrepreneurs. We emphasize this point because it is relevant to our subsequent discussion of emerging economies.

If, for example, scientists or engineers can pursue a new idea within the organizational structure of the firm developing the knowledge and appropriate the expected value of that knowledge, they have no reason to leave. On the other hand, if he or she places a greater value on his ideas than does the incumbent firm, the decision may be to leave the incumbent firm and form one's own organization. Thus, the KSTE emphasizes the importance of individual agency, albeit in an interactive relationship with incumbent institutions.

As the KSTE was being developed, the IB literature began to focus intensively on the importance of institutions. It became (and remains) a central tenet of the IB literature that context matters, especially with reference to FDI to and from emerging markets, and that institutions are the critical source of contextual differences across countries. Thus, institutional differences have become more important in the IB discourse as emerging markets add heterogeneity to the institutional spectrum (Hoskisson et al. 2013; Peng et al. 2008), a point we take up below. In particular, institutional differences across countries can help explain the existence of "country effects" as determinants of differential firm performance (Bhaumik et al. 2016; Carney et al. 2019).

However, it is important to recognize that while context is important in both, the institutional approach taken in the KSTE is quite different from that taken in the IB literature. For David, institutions refer to incumbent firms, public institutions and indeed levels of human and financial capital and infrastructures driving innovation and entrepreneurship. Many of the ideas have been more recently captured in the idea of entrepreneurial ecosystems (Acs et al. 2017). There are certain parallels in the IB literature, which also places considerable stress on domestic resources as an attractor of foreign investors, notably financial institutions and human capital. However, much of the tradition in IB has been to analyze institutional differences between host and home economies in terms of so called "institutional voids" (Khanna and Palepu 1999); deficiencies in terms of resource and capability availability in the host economies that MNEs have to make up for from their own resources. Because KSTE is usually framed within a single jurisdiction, it does not need to address these consequences of cross border differences. Thus, if anything, as David moved to consider the individual, the IB literature moved to focus more intensely on the country.

Bringing It All Back Home: New Directions in IB

Despite starting from a similar place, David's work and the IB literature have developed in rather different directions. Moreover, even given the considerable commonality in research themes, there has been surprisingly little cross fertilization of ideas between the two. We regard this as a lost opportunity because David's work has many important ideas and concepts that could deepen and enrich the IB literature. In this final section we therefore consider three broad recent trends in the IB literature that we believe have the potential to bring David's thinking back into the mainstream of IB. The three areas we consider are emerging markets and in particular emerging market multinationals (EMNEs); the increased recognition of the importance of international and comparative entrepreneurship; and the rise of the knowledge economy and the associated importance of global cities and clusters.

Emerging Markets

As we have seen, the increased importance of emerging markets has been widely recognized and studied in the IB literature (Estrin et al. 2018a; Carney et al, 2019). From the perspective of this paper, we focus on only two things: the challenge to the received theory of the MNE created by EMNEs; and the challenge to understanding entrepreneurship in those countries, which are often dominated by large, conglomerate, family-controlled business groups (BGs).

There is some debate over whether the existing theory of the MNE is relevant to EMNEs (Ramamurti 2012; Hennart 2012; Cuervo-Cazurra and Ramamurti 2014). There are (at least) three schools of thought, all rooted in one of David's original questions: where do EMNEs get the knowledge required to create the firm-specific advantages necessary to be globally successful? The first argues that EMNEs possess no particular firm-specific advantages, and their success abroad is typically linked to advantages associated with their home countries (e.g. low wages or state policies). The second argues that EMNEs do have firm-specific advantages, but they are different from those normally found in developed country MNEs because they are rooted in non-market advantages relevant to operating in countries with less developed institutions. The third argues that EMNEs are not very different from developed economy MNEs in that they acquire knowledge and capabilities through knowledge spillovers.

The third argument requires a precise understanding of the nature of knowledge acquisition and spillovers that permit EMNEs to acquire the capabilities to compete abroad. These may differ from those analyzed for developed economies because institutional voids may include labor and capital market deficiencies and the inability to enforce intellectual property rights. There have been a few studies that look at this question. For example, Filatotchev et al. (2011), Li et al. (2010), and Li et al. (2012) have all examined various spillover mechanisms that allow Chinese firms to access foreign knowledge. These include migration and location near foreign knowledge clusters at home and abroad. There is considerably more work to be done to enhance our understanding of whether these knowledge spillovers are significant, how long they take to materialize, and whether they exist in emerging markets outside of China. In short, there is considerable room for research on the nature of knowledge spillovers across borders and in particular to emerging markets, something David has recognized in recent work (Audretsch et al. 2014; Audretsch and Caiazza 2015). A related issue arising from emerging markets is the observation that the structure of firm ownership and governance is different from that in developing countries. In particular, emerging markets are often characterized by the prevalence of large, diversified business groups (Carney et al. 2017, 2018) many of which are family-owned (Carney et al. 2017). The existence of these organizations provides an opportunity to test the boundary conditions surrounding KTSE.

While there is some controversy surrounding the nature of business groups (Carney et al. 2018), it is generally accepted that they provide members with access to internal markets, including financial markets, and with access to relevant political networks. Thus, business groups can be effective in mobilizing resources to support and launch new firms within the group. The research question, related to the more general spillover one above, is therefore whether the prevalence of business groups stifles entrepreneurial activity, and in particular entrepreneurial activity associated with knowledge spillovers. While there is some research on entrepreneurial activity across countries (discussed below) there is almost no research on the relationship between business group prevalence and entrepreneurial activity, although Mahmood and Mitchell (2004) and Cantwell and Zhang (2011) do analyze how different types of business groups affect innovation. This is close to one of Audretsch's central themes: the issue of whether new small firms or existing large incumbent ones are likely to be the most fruitful source of innovation and ultimately growth. While David's prior would likely be in support of the former, the current very preliminary evidence suggests the latter. If true, it would be extremely interesting to understand why, perhaps because in emerging markets there is a generic shortage of resources relevant to innovation and these tend to be concentrated in business groups. Thus, the degree to which the KTSE is relevant in emerging economies with strong business groups is a fertile area for future research.

International and Comparative Entrepreneurship

Interestingly, the entrepreneurship and IB literature have recently come much closer together because they each have a research strand focused towards the internationalization of entrepreneurial businesses. However, to date the bulk of work in each field has operated in isolation from the other, though there are strong areas of overlap.

An important development in IB research about entrepreneurship concerns returnee entrepreneurs. We will focus on only two strands of this literature. The first concerns the return of migrant workers who have worked in developed economies and then gone back to their home emerging economy, often to become entrepreneurs. Such returnee entrepreneurs are often scientists and engineers who transfer back home to create an entrepreneurial venture after obtaining business experience and/or education in OECD countries (Saxenian 2006). This is an interesting internationalization of Audretsch' s original KTSE insights; entrepreneurs gain their skills and knowledge via spillovers in developed economy contexts and then commercialize them in their home economies. For example, consider the case of the Indian software industry, which was built to a considerable extent by returnees from the US (Arora and Gambardella 2006). Indeed, there is some evidence that the KTSE concept applies in both the home and host economy; returnee entrepreneurs with academic knowledge in the form of patents have been found to seek complementary assets by locating in science parks (Wright et al. 2008).

Returnee entrepreneurs from developing economies are therefore viewed as bringing the benefits of commercial, academic, scientific and technical knowledge, as well as sometimes access to financial resources, from developed economies to entrepreneurship-deficient emerging economies. Returnees understand the culture, speak the language and can operate in the system and therefore, while they are often bringing commercial opportunities and ideas from their former country, they are able to implement them in the country of their birth without facing the "liability of foreignness" (Zaheer 1995). In terms of the OLI framework discussed above, returnees are able to operate in their emerging home economies drawing on the technological and innovative skills of their adopted countries while facing lower costs of distance than other developed economy firms. There is a further cross-border twist in that entreprencurial ventures founded by returnees appear to be especially likely to internationalize themselves, allowing their founders to combine their knowledge of new technologies in creating the venture with their experience of living in international environments (Yamakawa et al. 2008). However, there remains much work to be done in this area, especially associated with David's concerns with entrepreneurial performance, in this case perhaps focusing on the relationship between returnee entrepreneurship, company performance and economic development. There is already some preliminary evidence that returnee ventures outperform non-returnee firms with respect to innovation and exporting, but the theoretical arguments are underdeveloped, and stronger evidence is needed. There are also rich veins of research to be mined concerning the possibilities for economic policy to encourage and facilitate returnee entrepreneurship.

A second strand of IB research has focused on Diasporas; groups of migrants who have moved in a cluster to a new location, often but not exclusively in a developed economy. The IB literature has tended to focus on these diaspora as a potential resource that might facilitate the entry of MNE's, providing a basis of information and a source of knowledgeable labor recruitment. Once again, the diaspora could provide a mechanism to reduce the liability of foreignness for MNEs entering distant or poorly understood locations (Estrin et al. 2018b). However, it also possible to view these diaspora through lens closer to Audretsch's research agenda. It has long been argued that immigrant groups are more likely to be entrepreneurial than the indigenous population, perhaps because discrimination alters the balance of advantage between paid employment and entrepreneurship in favor of the latter (Parker 2009). Immigrant entrepreneurs utilize their ethnic and cultural social capital to establish new ventures often initially within those local enclaves with the same religion, cultural and language (Estrin et al. 2018b). But they quickly spread out to become major players in their home countries, and are often likely to internationalize, once again because their ethnic and national linkages provide them with important international business contacts, thereby reducing the liability of foreignness that typically restricts internationalization, especially for smaller companies.

At the same time, the entrepreneurship literature has begun to focus on international entrepreneurship, though once again Audretsch' s work is not receiving due credit. Thus, in the most recent review of research on comparative international entrepreneurship (Terjeson et al. 2016), Audretsch is hardly cited. Terjeson et al. (2016) summarize the findings from 259 papers from 1989 to 2010. They note that this literature is highly fragmented and with few clear universal theories or messages. For example, findings concerning the characteristics of international entrepreneurs remain highly context specific, and the results with respect to various measures of performance, including innovation, are inconsistent across studies. Their call for the development of integrative approaches which combine the development of theories with rigorous empirical work highlights the need for a rediscovery of Audretsch' s work by this literature.

Knowledge Economy, Cities And Clusters

David and various co-authors had by the late 1990s recognized that the creation and diffusion of knowledge was associated with urban agglomerations (cities) and clusters; see Audretsch (1998) and Feldman and Audretsch (1999). While a few IB scholars had also begun to acknowledge these issues (Cantwell and Santangelo 2002; Cantwell and Mudambi 2005), for the most part the "L" (location) in the OLI model remained the country.

However, this has rapidly changed over the last few years, with an increasing recognition by IB scholars of the role of cities and clusters, as essential components of the process of knowledge creation and diffusion across borders (Cano-Kollmann et al. 2016; Santangelo 2018; Mudambi et al. 2018; Iammarino et al. 2018). These have been accompanied by an increasing number of empirical studies focused on the role of cites and clusters.

Cantwell (2017) provides a useful summary of the new IB interest and the direction it is taking. In the IB tradition, the focus is on the MNE, and in particular their role in building and exploiting international knowledge networks. Thus "the two processes of innovation and internationalization have become ever more interconnected as central drivers of development" (Cantwell 2017: 41). In essence, the increased importance of knowledge-based activities to the MNE and the global sourcing of knowledge accompanying the emergence of global value chains (GVCs) have "linked localized innovation systems to IB and to international knowledge exchange" (Cantwell 2017: 42). Thus, it is argued that IB must encompass the nature of innovation, and its role is to understand their global implications. The MNE is reconceived as a global creator, organizer, and connector of knowledge networks across locations, rather than a simple vehicle for technology transfer from a given location, as was the case in the original theory. The MNE is now seen as a connector of spatially dispersed knowledge sources (Cano-Kollmann et al. 2016), so that innovation becomes both firm- and location-specific.

The importance of location in the creation and diffusion of knowledge leads naturally to the importance of cities and clusters, as David had previously recognized. What the IB literature proposes to add to the discussion is the international connectivity of these locations, and in particular the bi-directional flows between them. That is, knowledge spillovers are seen as flowing in both directions across national borders, with the MNE being a possible orchestrator of the flows via its global subsidiaries. Cities and clusters may be localized producers of knowledge, but their success depends on the degree to which they are globally connected. This IB research has turned to the importance of global cities (Goerzen et al. 2013; Belderbos et al. 2017), and the international connectivity of clusters (Turkina and Van Assche 2018). Importantly, these finer-grained approaches to location have resulted in IB scholars paying more attention to related literatures in innovation and economic geography (Mudambi et al. 2018).

Thus, we see many opportunities to continue this line of research linking the literature on innovation and spillovers in localized locations with the IB literature and its new emphasis on MNEs as orchestrators and facilitators of the diffusion of knowledge across borders. Specific opportunities could involve enhanced analysis of the nature of global cities, and their role as creators of knowledge and a preferred location for the knowledge-based activities of MNEs; how MNEs contribute to innovation and growth; and how movements of people both within and outside MNEs contribute to knowledge diffusions and spillovers. We also need to know more about the ways in which firm-specific and location-specific advantages are matched across borders, and their possible co-evolution. It is clear that David's work on the localized nature of innovations and knowledge spillovers can be helpful in this regard.

Finally, we note that David has continued to explore the role of cities, in particular in relation to entrepreneurial activity (Audretsch et al. 2015; Audretsch and Belitski 2017). The relation between entrepreneurship and cities has not yet been addressed in the IB literature in the context of cities and in particular with respect to the phenomenon of the "born global" MNE (Knight and Liesch 2016). Nor have cities and clusters figured in the literature on international and comparative entrepreneurship discussed above.

Conclusions

We have traced the parallel but divergent evolution of both David Audretsch's work and the IB literature from their common origins in industrial organization theory. In our telling, the IB literature moved away from a focus on market power and industries to a focus on the large, multinational firm, and the nature of the resources and capabilities that makes them successful abroad. David Audretsch moved from a consideration of large firms and market power to consider the innovative capabilities of small firms, the localized sources of knowledge that contribute to the capabilities of existing firms, and the way that knowledge spills over to create new firms. At the same time, it has always been clear that the ultimate purpose of David's academic journey is understanding the nature of economic growth, and the public policies that might contribute to it. The IB literature has focused on the performance of MNEs, not countries, and until very recently has not paid a lot of attention to public policy except as it affected MNEs. Finally, in IB, the institutions that create country effects are for the most part exogenous, whereas for David, country outcomes can be endogenously determined by choices regarding entrepreneurial regimes.

We have argued that the prospects for cross fertilization between David's ideas and the IB literature are as high now as at the point when the two strands first diverged in the 1980s. This is because the IB literature has begun to consider more carefully the mechanisms whereby economic policies at the national level as well as the local ecosystem within major cities and clusters affect the attractiveness of locations for FDI and influence the performance of firms based within these jurisdictions. This research direction has become increasingly significant with the rise of emerging markets, in which institutions are changing very rapidly and thus cannot so easily be treated as exogenous in the manner traditional to the IB literature. Moreover, the increasing significance in global FDI of EMNEs highlights the importance of reversing the causality from a focus on (host country) exogenous institutions leading to FDI location choice to one in which institutional arrangements, driven in part by policies and clusters in the home economy help to generate the availability of resources for MNEs to internationalize. This could be considered, for example, from the perspective of ubiquitous emerging economy firms such as business groups, or by considering the role and performance of returnee entrepreneurs. This new framing of research questions makes David's work much more central to the development of the IB literature.

Finally, IB scholars could also benefit from reflecting on David' s notion of institutions, with particular reference to the drivers of innovation. The IB literature has a natural tendency to gravitate towards institutions whenever drawing comparisons across countries, and these institutions are mostly national, as can be seen in Fig. 1. However, David has sought to understand what elements of the environment make some local areas more entrepreneurial than others, and this he links to the generation of innovative ideas and technologies available for entrepreneurs to exploit. Thus, from his perspective entrepreneurship and innovation are localized phenomena, not national ones, and for the most part, his analysis is subnational and at a micro level. Perhaps, a way to square the circle here is by using the concept of embedded systems. For the IB literature, institutions represent the environment in which firms operate, though they have recently accepted that this may be changing, and in ways influenced by policies and firms' choices. Such institutions may be a necessary condition for the emergence of innovation, but for David Audretsch perhaps they are not sufficient, unless they also lead to localized entrepreneurial ecosystems, the knowledge clusters at the heart of his contribution.

Acknowledgments The authors gratefully acknowledge conversations on the themes of this paper with Maryann Feldman, Bruce Kogut, Tomasz Mickiewicz, Mark Sanders and David Audretsch himself. We have benefitted from outstanding research assistance from Angelina Borovinskaya. None of them bear any responsibility for our arguments and interpretations.

References

Acs, Z. J., & Audretsch, D. B. (1987). Innovation, Market structure, and firm size. *The Review of Economics and Statistics, 69*(4), 567–574.
Acs, Z. J., & Audretsch, D. B. (1988). Innovation in large and small firms: An empirical analysis. *American Economic Review, 78*(4), 678–690.
Acs, Z., & Audretsch, D. (1990). *Innovation and small firms*. Cambridge: MIT Press.
Acs, Z., & Audretsch, D. (1991). *Innovation and technological change: An international comparison*. London: Harvester Wheatsheaf.
Acs, Z. J., Audretsch, D. B., & Feldman, M. (1994). R&D spillovers and recipient firm size. *Review of Economics and Statistics, 76*(2), 336–340.
Acs, Z. J., Audretsch, D. B., & Lehmann, E. E. (2013). The knowledge spillover theory of entrepreneurship. *Small Business Economics, 41*, 757–774.
Acs, Z. J., Braunerhjelm, P., Audretsch, D. B., & Carlsson, B. (2009). The knowledge spillover theory of entrepreneurship. *Small Business Economics, 32*(1), 15–30.
Acs, Z., Stam, E., Audretsch, D., & O'Connor, A. (2017). The lineages of the entrepreneurial ecosystem approach. *Small Business Economics, 49*(1), 1–10.
Acs, Z. J., Audretsch, D. B., & Feldman, M. P. (1992). Real effects of academic research: Comment. *American Economic Review, 82*(1), 363–367.
Agarwal, R., Audretsch, D., & Sarkar, M. (2010). Knowledge spillovers and strategic entrepreneurship. *Strategic Entrepreneurship Journal, 4*, 271–283.
Aghion, P., & Howitt, P. (1992). A model of growth through creative destruction. *Econometrica, 60*(2), 323–351.
Aliber, R. (1983). Money, multinationals and sovereigns, Ch. 11. In C. Kindleberger & D. B. Audretsch (Eds.), *The Multinational Corporation in the 1980s*. Cambridge: MIT Press.
Aparicio, S., Urbano, D., & Audretsch, D. (2016). Institutional factors, opportunity entrepreneurship and economic growth: panel data evidence. *Technological Forecasting and Social Change, 102*, 45–61. https://doi.org/10.1016/j.techfore.2015.04.006. CrossRefGoogle Scholar.
Arora, A., & Gambardella, A. (Eds.). (2006). *From underdogs to tigers: The rise and growth of the software industry in Brazil, China, India, Ireland, and Israel*. Oxford: Oxford University Press.
Audretsch, D. (1991). New-firm survival and the technological regime. *Review of Economics and Statistics, 73*(3), 441–450. https://doi.org/10.2307/2109568.
Audretsch, D. (1995). *Innovation and industry evolution*. Cambridge: MIT Press.
Audretsch, D. B. (1998). Agglomeration and the location of innovative activity. *Oxford Review of Economic Policy, 14*(2), 18–29.

Audretsch, D. B. (2007a). Entrepreneurship capital and economic growth. *Oxford Review of Economic Policy, 23*(1), 63–78. https://doi.org/10.1093/oxrep/grm001. CrossRefGoogle Scholar.

Audretsch, D. B. (2007b). *The entrepreneurial society*. Oxford: Oxford University Press.

Audretsch, D., & Acs, Z. (1994). New-firm startups, technology, and macroeconomic fluctuations. *Small Business Economics, 6*(6), 439–449.

Audretsch, D. B., & Belitski, M. (2017). Entrepreneurial ecosystems in cities: establishing the framework conditions. *Journal of Technology Transfer, 42*(5), 10301051.

Audretsch, D. B., Belitski, M., & Desai, S. (2015). Entrepreneurship and economic development in cities. *The Annals of Regional Science, 55*(1), 33–60. https://doi.org/10.1007/s00168-015-0685-x. CrossRefGoogle Scholar.

Audretsch, D. B., & Caiazza, R. (2015). Technology transfer and entrepreneurship: Cross-national analysis. *Journal of Technology Transfer, 41*(6), 1247–1259.

Audretsch, D., Falck, O., Heblich, S., & Lederer, A. (2011). *Handbook of research on innovation and entrepreneurship*. London: Edward Elgar.

Audretsch, D. B., & Feldman, M. P. (1996). R&D spillovers and the geography of innovation and production. *American Economic Review, 86*(4), 253–273.

Audretsch, D., & Keilbach, M. (2004). Entrepreneurship and regional growth: an evolutionary interpretation. *Journal of Evolutionary Interpretation, 14*(5), 606–616.

Audretsch, D., & Keilbach, M. (2007a). The theory of knowledge spillover entrepreneurship. *Journal of Management Studies, 44*(7), 1242–1254.

Audretsch, D. B., & Keilbach, M. (2007b). The localisation of entrepreneurship capital: Evidence from Germany. *Papers in Regional Science, 86*(3), 351–365.

Audretsch, D. B., & Keilbach, M. (2008). Resolving the knowledge paradox: Knowledge-spillover entrepreneurship and economic growth. *Research Policy, 37*(10), 1697–1705.

Audretsch, D., Keilbach, M., & Lehmann, E. (2006). *Entrepreneurship and economic growth*. New York: Oxford University Press.

Audretsch, D., Lehmann, E., & Wright, M. (2014). Technology transfer in a global economy. *Journal of Technology Transfer, 39*(3), 301–312.

Audretsch, D., Lehmann, E., & Schenkenhofer, J. (2018). Internationalization strategies of hidden champions: Lessons from Germany. *Multinational Business Review, 26*(1), 2–24.

Audretsch, D., & Mahmood, T. (1995). New firm survival: New results using a hazard function. *The Review of Economics and Statistics, 77*(1), 97–103. https://doi.org/10.2307/2109995.

Audretsch, D. B., & Stephan, P. E. (1996). Company-scientist locational links: The case of bio-technology. *American Economic Review, 86*, 641–652.

Audretsch, D. B., & Thurik, A. R. (2001). What's new about the new economy? From the managed to the entrepreneurial economy. *Industrial and Corporate Change, 10*(1), 267–315.

Banalieva, E., Cuervo-Cazurra, A., & Sarathy, R. (2018). Dynamics of pro-market institutions and firm performance. *Journal of International Business Studies, 49*, 858–880.

Baumol, W. (2011). Invention and social entrepreneurship: Social good and social evil. In D. B. Audretsch et al. (Eds.), *Handbook of research on innovation and entrepreneurship*. Cheltenham/Northampton: Edward Elgar.

Baumol, W. J. (1990). Entrepreneurship: Productive, unproductive and destructive. *Journal of Political Economy, 98*(5), 893–921.

Baumol, W. J., & Strom, R. J. (2007). Entrepreneurship and economic growth. *Strategic Entrepreneurship Journal, 1*(3–4), 233–237.

Belderbos, R., Du, H. S., & Goerzen, A. (2017). Global cities, connectivity, and the location choice of MNC regional headquarters. *Journal of Management Studies, 54*(8), 1271–1302.

Bevan, A., Estrin, S., & Meyer, K. (2004). Foreign investment location and institutional development in transition economies. *International Business Review, 13*(1), 43–64.

Bhaumik, S. K., Driffield, N., & Zhou, Y. (2016). Country specific advantage, firm specific advantage and multinationality –sources of competitive advantage in emerging markets: Evidence from the electronics industry in China. *International Business Review, 25*(1), 165–176.

Braunerhjelm, P., Acs, Z., Audretsch, D. B., & Carlsson, B. (2010). The missing link: Knowledge diffusion and entrepreneurship in endogenous growth. *Small Business Economics, 34*(2), 105–125.

Buckley, P. J., & Casson, M. C. (1976). *The future of the multinational enterprise.* London: Macmillan.

Bruno, R., Campos, N., Estrin, S., & Tian, M. (2019). The effects of European union membership on foreign direct investment and international trade, LSE mimeo.

Cano-Kollmann, M., Cantwell, J., Hannigan, T. J., Mudambi, R., & Song, J. (2016). Knowledge connectivity: An agenda for innovation research in international business. *Journal of International Business Studies, 47*(3), 255–262.

Cantwell, J. A., & Santangelo, G. D. (2002). The new geography of corporate research in information and communications technology (ICT). *Journal of Evolutionary Economics, 12*(1–2), 163–197.

Cantwell, J. A., & Mudambi, R. (2005). MNE competence-creating subsidiary mandates. *Strategic Management Journal, 26*(12), 1109–1128.

Cantwell, J. A., & Zhang, Y. (2011). Exploration and exploitation: The different impacts of two types of Japanese business group networks on firm innovation and global learning. *Asian Business and Management, 10*(2), 151–181.

Cantwell, J. (2017). Innovation and international business. *Industry and Innovation, 24*(1), 41–60.

Carlsson, B., Acs, Z., Audretsch, D. B., & Braunerhjelm, P. (2009). Knowledge creation, entrepreneurship, and economic growth: A historical review. *Industrial and Corporate Change, 18*(6), 1193–1229.

Carney, M., Estrin, S., van Essen, M., & Shapiro, D. (2017). Business group prevalence and impact across countries and over time: What can we learn from the literature? *Multinational Business Review, 25*(1), 52–76.

Carney, M., Estrin, S., van Essen, M., & Shapiro, D. (2018). Business groups reconsidered: beyond paragons and parasites. *Academy of Management Perspectives 32*(4), 493–516.

Carney, M., Estrin, S., Liang, Z., & Shapiro, D. (2019). National institutional systems, foreign ownership and firm performance: the case of understudied countries. *Journal of World Business: 54*(4), 244–257.

Carree, M. A., & Thurik, R. (2003). The impact of entrepreneurship on economic growth. In D. Audretsch & Z. Acs (Eds.), *The handbook of entrepreneurship research* (pp. 425–486). Boston: Kluwer.

Caves, R. E. (1976). *Multinational enterprise and economic analysis.* Cambridge: Cambridge University Press.

Chacar, A., Newburry, W., & Vissa, B. (2010). Bringing institutions into performance persistence research: Exploring the impact of product, financial, and labor market institutions. *Journal of International Business Studies, 41*(7), 1119–1140.

Cuervo-Cazurra, A., & Ramamurti, R. (2014). *Understanding multinationals from emerging markets.* Cambridge: Cambridge University Press.

Danakol, S., Estrin, S., Reynolds, P., & Weitzel, U. (2017). Foreign direct investment via M&A and domestic entrepreneurship: Blessing or curse? *Small Business Economics, 48*(3), 599–612.

Davidsson, P. (2016). *Researching entrepreneurship.* Cham: Springer.

De Backer, K., & Sleuwaegen, L. (2003). Does foreign direct investment crowd out domestic entrepreneurship? *Review of Industrial Organization, 22*(1), 67–84.

Dunning, J. H. (1979). Explaining patterns of international production: In defense of the eclectic theory. *Oxford Bulletin of Economics and Statistics, 41*, 269–295.

Dunning, J. H. (1988). The eclectic paradigm of international production: A restatement and some possible extensions. *Journal of International Business Studies, 19*, 1–29.

Estrin, S., Meyer, K. E., & Pelletier, A. (2018a). Emerging economy MNEs: How does home country munificence matter? *Journal of World Business, 53*(4), 514–528.

Estrin, S., Mickiewicz, T., Stephan, U., & Wright, M. (2018b). Entrepreneurship in emerging economies. In R. Grosse & K. Meyer (Eds.), *Oxford handbook on management in emerging markets*. Oxford: Oxford University Press.

Feldman, M. P., & Audretsch, D. (1999). Innovation in cities: Science-based diversity, specialization and localized competition. *European Economic Review, 43*(2), 409–429.

Filatotchev, I., Xiaohui, L., Jiangyong, L., & Wright, M. (2011). Knowledge spillovers through human mobility across national borders: Evidence from Zhongguancun Science Park in China. *Research Policy, 40*(3), 453–462.

Geroski, P. A. (1995). What do we know about entry? *International Journal of Industrial Organization, 13*, 421–440.

Geroski, P., & Schwalbach, J. (Eds.). (1991). *Entry and market contestability: An international comparison*. Oxford: Basil Blackwell.

Ghemawat, P. (2007). *Redefining global strategy: Crossing borders in a world where differences still matter*. Cambridge: Harvard Business School Press.

Glaeser, E., Kallal, H., Sheinkman, J., & Schleifer, A. (1992). Growth in cities. *Journal of Political Economy, 100*, 1126–1152.

Globerman, S., & Shapiro, D. (2002). Global foreign direct investment flows: The role of governance infrastructure. *World Development, 30*(11), 1899–1919.

Goerzen, A., Asmussen, C. G., & Nielsen, B. B. (2013). Global cities and multinational enterprise location strategy. *Journal of International Business Studies, 44*(5), 427–450.

Görg, H., & Strobl, E. (2002). Multinational companies and indigenous development: An empirical analysis. *European Economic Review, 46*(7), 1305–1322.

Hennart, J.-F. (2012). Emerging market multinationals and the theory of the multinational enterprise. *Global Strategy Journal, 2*(3), 168–187.

Hoskisson, R. E., Wright, M., Filatotchev, I., & Peng, M. W. (2013). Emerging multi- nationals from mid-range economies: The influence of institutions and factor markets. *Journal of Management Studies, 50*(7), 1295–1321.

Hymer, S. (1960, 1976). *The international operations of national firms: A study of direct foreign investment*. Cambridge: MIT Press.

Iammarino, S., McCann, P., & Ortega-Argilés, R. (2018). International business, cities and competitiveness: Recent trends and future challenges. *Competitiveness Review: An International Business Journal, 28*(3), 236–251.

Jacobs, J. (1969). *The economy of cities*. New York: Vintage Books.

Jaffe, A. (1989). Real effects of academic research. *The American Economic Review, 79*(5), 957–970. Retrieved from http://www.jstor.org/stable/1831431.

Jaffe, A., Trajtenberg, M., & Henderson, R. (1993). Geographic localization of knowledge spillovers as evidenced by patent citations. *Quarterly Journal of Economics, 63*, 577–598.

Khanna, T., & Palepu, K. (1999). The right way to restructure conglomerates in emerging markets. Harvard Business Review, 77, 125–134.

Kindleberger, C., & Audretsch, D. B. (1983). *The multinational corporation in the 1980s*. Cambridge: MIT Press.

Kindleberger, C. P. (1969). The theory of direct investment. In C. Kindleberger (Ed.), *American business abroad*. New Haven: Yale University Press.

Knight, G. A., & Liesch, P. (2016). Internationalization: From incremental to born global. *Journal of World Business, 51*(1), 93–102.

Kogut, B. (1983). Foreign direct investment as a sequential process, Ch. 2. In C. Kindleberger & D. B. Audretsch (Eds.), *The multinational corporation in the 1980s*. Cambridge: MIT Press.

Krugman, P. (1983). The "new theories" of international trade and the multinational enterprise, Ch. 3. In C. Kindleberger & D. B. Audretsch (Eds.), *The multinational corporation in the 1980s*. Cambridge: MIT Press.

Li, J., Li, Y., & Shapiro, D. (2012). Knowledge seeking and OFDI of emerging market firms. *Global Strategy Journal, 2*, 277–295.

Li, J., Chen, D., & Shapiro, D. (2010). Product innovations in emerging economies: The role of foreign knowledge access channels and internal efforts in Chinese firms. *Management and Organization Review, 6*(2), 243–266.

Mahmood, I., & Mitchell, W. (2004). Two faces: Effects of business groups on innovation in emerging economies. *Management Science, 50*(10), 1348–1365.

Meyer, K., & Sinani, E. (2009). When and where does foreign direct investment generate positive spillovers? A meta-analysis. *Journal of International Business Studies, 40*, 1075–1094.

McClain, D. (1983). Foreign direct investment in the United States: Old currents, "new waves" and the theory of direct investment, Chapter 13. In C. Kindleberger & D. B. Audretsch (Eds.), *The multinational corporation in the 1980s*. Cambridge: MIT Press.

Mudambi, R., Narula, R., & Santangelo, G. D. (2018). Location, collocation and innovation by multinational enterprises: A research agenda. *Industry & Innovation, 25*(3), 229–241.

Parker, S. C. (2009). *The economics of entrepreneurship*. Cambridge: Cambridge University press.

Peng, M., & Meyer, K. M. (2016). *International business* (2nd ed). Cengage Learning, Andover UK: South-Western.

Peng, M. W., Sun, S. L., Pinkham, B., & Chen, H. (2009). The institution-based view as a third leg for a strategy tripod. *Academy of Management Perspectives, 23*(3), 63–81.

Peng, M. W., Wang, D. Y., & Jiang, Y. (2008). An institution-based view of international business strategy: A focus on emerging economies. *Journal of International Business Studies, 39*(5), 920–936.

Ramamurti, R. (2012). What is really different about emerging market multinationals? *Global Strategy Journal, 2*(1), 41–47.

Reynolds, P. D., Bosma, N., Autio, E., Hunt, S., De Bono, N., Servais, A., Lopez-Garcia, P., & Chin, N. (2005). Global entrepreneurship monitor: Data collection design and implementation 1998–2003. *Small Business Economics, 24*, 205–231.

Rugman, A. M. (1981). *Inside the multinationals*. New York: Columbia University Press.

Santangelo, G. D. (2018). Multinational enterprises and global cities: A contribution to set the research agenda. *Competitiveness Review: An International Business Journal, 28*(3), 230–235.

Saxenian, A. (2006). *The new argonauts: Regional advantage in a global economy*. Cambridge: Harvard University Press.

Schumpeter, J. (1934 [2008]). *The theory of economic development*. Brunswick: Transaction Publishers.

Shapiro, D. M. (1983). Entry, exit and the theory of the multinational corporation, Ch. 5. In C. Kindleberger & D. B. Audretsch (Eds.), *The multinational corporation in the 1980s*. Cambridge: MIT Press.

Terjeson, S., Hessels, J., & Li, D. (2016). Comparative international entrepreneurship: A review and research agenda. *Journal of Management, 42*(1), 299–344.

Tihanyi, L., Griffiths, D., & Russell, C. (2005). The effect of cultural distance on entry mode choice, international diversification, and MNE performance: a meta-analysis. *Journal of International Business Studies, 36*, 270–283.

Turkina, E., & Van Assche, A. (2018). Global connectedness and local innovation in industrial clusters. *Journal of International Business Studies, 49*(6), 706–728.

Wright, M., Liu, X., Buck, T., & Filatotchev, I. (2008). Returnee entrepreneur characteristics, science park location choice and performance: An analysis of high technology SMEs in China. *Entrepreneurship Theory and Practice, 32*(1), 131–156.

Yamakawa, Y., Peng, M., & Deeds, D. (2008). What drives new ventures to internationalize from emerging to developed economies? *Entrepreneurship Theory and Practice, 32*(1), 59–82.

Zaheer, S. (1995). Overcoming the liability of foreignness. *Academy of Management Journal, 38*(2), 341–363.

Regional Trajectories of Entrepreneurship and Growth

Michael Fritsch and Michael Wyrwich

Abstract The development of regions is considerably shaped by their history. We review research that finds significant persistence of regional levels of entrepreneurship over longer periods of time. It is argued that the long term persistence of regional entrepreneurship indicates the presence and effect of a culture of entrepreneurship that is conducive to new business formation and regional growth. Hence, regional development is characterized by long term trajectories of entrepreneurship. We derive a number of policy implications and propose avenues for further research.

The Important Role of Entrepreneurship for Innovation and Growth

The effect of entrepreneurship on innovation and growth is a key topic on David Audretsch's research agenda. In our contribution to this Festschrift for David we reflect on our related work on regional trajectories of entrepreneurship, knowledge, and growth (Fritsch and Wyrwich 2019). Specifically, this includes the roles of history and culture in regional development. We review empirical work that shows the long-lasting effects of historical levels of self-employment and innovation on new business formation, innovation, and growth many decades later. It is argued that historical developments can cultivate certain cultural traits and personal attitudes in the local population that shape developments today.

In what follows we first review the empirical evidence on persistence of regional levels of entrepreneurship and growth (section "The Long-Term Persistence of Regional Levels of Entrepreneurship"). We then show how historical levels of

M. Fritsch (✉)
Friedrich Schiller University Jena, Jena, Germany

Halle Institute for Economic Research (IWH), Halle, Germany
e-mail: m.fritsch@uni-jena.de

M. Wyrwich
University of Groningen, Groningen, The Netherlands
e-mail: m.wyrwich@rug.nl

© Springer Nature Switzerland AG 2019
E. E. Lehmann, M. Keilbach (eds.), *From Industrial Organization to Entrepreneurship*, https://doi.org/10.1007/978-3-030-25237-3_16

entrepreneurship are related to the entrepreneurial attitudes of the regional population (section "What Is a Regional Culture of Entrepreneurship?"). This empirical assessment is linked to a conceptual distinction of different layers of entrepreneurship culture (section "The Two Layers of Entrepreneurship Culture: Systemizing a Multifaceted Phenomenon"). Section "Persistence of Regional Innovation Activities" reviews some recent empirical evidence of persistence of innovation activity across space. Finally, we draw policy implications (section "Policy Implications"), and discuss avenues for future research (section "Avenues for Further Research").

The Long-Term Persistence of Regional Levels of Entrepreneurship

A key recognition of research about the role of entrepreneurship, innovation, and growth is that there is a rather pronounced variation of the relationship between these factors across regions (Audretsch and Fritsch 2002; Audretsch, Keilbach and Lehmann 2006; Fritsch and Wyrwich 2019). Clearly, region-specific factors play an important role and need to be accounted for in empirical analyses.

Region-specific determinants of entrepreneurship also remain relatively constant over time, or, as stated by Alfred Marshall (1920), *natura non facit saltum* (nature does not make jumps). Indeed, variables that have been shown to be conducive to the emergence of new firms, such as qualification of the regional workforce or employment share in small firms (Sternberg 2009), do tend to remain fairly constant over successive years (Fotopoulos 2013; Fritsch and Kublina 2019). This pattern is one reason for the pronounced persistence of regional differences in entrepreneurship rates that was found in prior research.[1] Even if the overall level of new business formation in a country is increasing or decreasing, the rank order of regions tends to remain rather constant (Fotopoulos and Storey 2017; Fritsch and Kublina 2019).

An alternative explanation for the persistence of entrepreneurship is the presence of an entrepreneurial culture. Such a culture may emerge due to a self-perpetuation process where past entrepreneurial activity induces further start-up activity in the future. Key elements of this type of self-perpetuation is demonstration and the peer effects of successful founders who act as role models (Andersson and Koster 2011; Fornahl 2003; Minniti 2005). The main idea behind this conjecture is that an individual's perception of entrepreneurship, the cognitive representation, is shaped by observing entrepreneurial role models in the social environment. The presence of entrepreneurial role models in the social environment, particularly among one's peers, reduces ambiguity for potential entrepreneurs and may help them acquire entrepreneurial skills and necessary information (Bosma et al. 2012). Observing successful entrepreneurs provides potential entrepreneurs with examples of how to

---

[1] Fritsch and Mueller (2007), van Stel and Suddle (2008), Andersson and Koster (2011), Mueller, van Stel and Storey (2008), Fotopoulos (2013), Fotopolous and Storey (2017).

organize resources and activities, and increases self-confidence in the sense of 'if they can do it, I can, too' (Sorenson and Audia 2000, 443; see also e.g., Minniti 2005; Nanda and Sørenson 2010).

Based on these arguments one can assume that a high number of entrepreneurial role models in a region leads to widespread social acceptance or legitimacy (Etzioni 1987; Kibler et al. 2014) of self-employment in the local population. Figure 1 illustrates the self-perpetuation of entrepreneurship through demonstration and peer effects, as well as social acceptance of entrepreneurship.

An empirical challenge is to disentangle the effect of entrepreneurial culture on entrepreneurship levels from the influence of persistent structural determinants of entrepreneurship. The case of Germany that we analyzed in our previous work provides an appropriate "natural laboratory" to cope with this empirical challenge (see Fritsch and Wyrwich 2019). The basic premise is based on the reality that the development of Germany over the course of the twentieth century was marked by several disruptive changes to framework conditions: two lost World Wars, destruction of economic infrastructure, housing, and production facilities, occupation by Allied Powers, as well as several switches of the political regime, particularly in Eastern Germany. Thus, there is no persistence of structural determinants of entrepreneurship in Germany. Hence, if we find the persistence of entrepreneurship despite these devastating shocks, then the driving force behind the persistence pattern is probably a culture of entrepreneurship.

Our empirical analyses for Germany have shown that regional levels of entrepreneurship are indeed persistent despite disruptive changes to framework conditions (Fritsch and Wyrwich 2014, 2019). The case of East Germany is particularly interesting in this respect. After World War II a socialist state—the German Democratic Republic (GDR)—was founded in the eastern part of the country that implemented a rigorous anti-entrepreneurship policy that included massive socialization of private enterprises and the suppression of any remaining private-sector activity (for details, see Brezinski 1987; Pickel 1992). The socialist East German state collapsed in late 1989, and East and West Germany were reunified in 1990. The subsequent transformation process of the East German economy to a market economic system

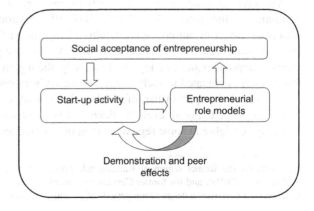

Fig. 1 Self-perpetuation of regional levels of entrepreneurship

was a "shock treatment" where the ready-made formal institutional framework of the West German market economic system was adopted practically overnight (e.g., Brezinski and Fritsch 1995; Hall and Ludwig 1995).

Our empirical analyses for East Germany show that——despite these massive path-breaking shocks——those regions with high levels of self-employment at the outset of the twentieth century had relatively high start-up rates after the collapse of the socialist regime and seem to have managed the transformation to a market economic system relatively well.[2] For West Germany, we also find that places with relatively high levels of self-employment in the early twentieth century had high levels of self-employment and new business formation about 100 years later (Fritsch and Wyrwich 2014, 2019). The analyses showed an effect of today's new business formation on employment growth that is explained by the historical pre-war level of entrepreneurship (Fritsch and Wyrwich 2017). Our main explanation for persistence of regional entrepreneurship, despite massive changes of the social and economic environment, is that regions with high levels of entrepreneurial activity in the past tend to be characterized by an entrepreneurial culture.

What Is a Regional Culture of Entrepreneurship?

An entrepreneurial culture can be thought of as an informal institution that is 'in the air', i.e., reflected in norms, values, and codes of conduct in a society (North 1994) that are in favor of entrepreneurship. An entrepreneurial culture should, at least to some degree, be independent of the factual socio-economic conditions and may, therefore, even survive considerable shocks to the socio-economic environment, such as serious economic crises, devastating wars, and drastic changes of political regimes (North 1994; Williamson 2000). According to Williamson (2000), culture belongs to the level of social structure that is deeply embedded in a population and that tends to change only very slowly. Research has indeed shown that informal institutions tend to change much more slowly than formal institutions, and only over rather long periods of time (North 1994; Nunn 2009; Williamson 2000).

An entrepreneurial culture is typically understood "as a positive collective programming of the mind" (Beugelsdijk 2007, 190). Etzioni (1987) argues that one important aspect of entrepreneurial culture is spatial variation in the social legitimacy of entrepreneurs and their activities. As a consequence, the more society views entrepreneurship as a legitimate activity, the higher its demand and the more resources are dedicated to such activity. A society's acceptance of entrepreneurship can be regarded as part of the informal institutions of a community. Applying this argument to the regional level, the degree of societal legitimacy for entrepreneurship may be higher in some regions than in others (Kibler et al. 2014).

---

[2]Analyses for the former region of Kaliningrad, which now belongs to the Russian Republic (Fritsch et al. 2019a), and for former German regions of Poland (Fritsch et al. 2019c) also show high levels of persistence despite long periods of an anti-entrepreneurial socialist regime.

Taking the conceptualization of an entrepreneurial culture a step further is to characterize it as an "aggregate psychological trait" (Freytag and Thurik 2007, 123) in the regional population that favors core entrepreneurial values such as individualism, independence, and motivation for achievement. A way of capturing such a conceptualization of entrepreneurship culture is to assess what share of people in the regional population have an entrepreneurship-prone personality profile. Applying the Big Five concept of personality measurement, entrepreneurial people score high on extraversion, conscientiousness, and openness, but have low scores in agreeableness and neuroticism (Obschonka and Stuetzer 2017). According to Rentfrow, Gosling and Potter (2008), regional differences in the share of people with an entrepreneurial mindset today may be explained by social influences within the region as people respond, adapt to, or become socialized according to regional norms, attitudes, and beliefs. Another phenomenon that could reinforce an entrepreneurial culture is that people with an entrepreneurial mindset may tend to migrate to places where the local population has similar personality characteristics (see also Obschonka et al. 2013, 2015).

Empirical analyses for Germany (Fritsch et al. 2019b), the UK (Stuetzer et al. 2016), and the US (Rentfrow et al. 2008) have revealed significant differences in the entrepreneurial personality profile of regional populations. In the case of Germany, we have shown that an entrepreneurial personality profile is particularly pronounced in the population of those regions that had historically high levels of self-employment at the outset of the twentieth century (Fritsch et al. 2019b). This may reflect an effect of long periods of high levels of regional self-employment.[3]

There is considerable overlap between the idea of an entrepreneurship culture and the concept of social capital that has been put forward by Coleman (1988), Putnam (2000) and others (Fritsch and Wyrwich 2016). In essence, social capital refers to the social acceptance of certain values and respective behaviors, as well as trust and particularly the networks of social relationships between actors, both public and private (for an overview, see Westlund and Bolton 2003). It includes information channels such as role models that can have a considerable effect on individual behavior. An important element of an entrepreneurship culture may be the acceptance of not only the founding of new businesses but also of business failure. A low stigma of failure in a region may encourage people to give entrepreneurship a try because the psychological costs of failure are lower than elsewhere (e.g., Wyrwich et al. 2016). In short, there are many aspects of the regional environment that may be, to different degrees, conducive to new business formation (Dubini 1989).

---

[3] Quite interestingly, we also find a rather pronounced entrepreneurial personality structure of the regional population in some regions that had high levels of historical self-employment but are characterized by low levels of self-employment and new business formation today (e.g., the region of Stuttgart). This finding suggests that the relationship between entrepreneurial tradition and current entrepreneurial culture is rather complex. One explanation in the case of the Stuttgart region may be that a number of regional enterprises have grown into rather large firms, and that employment opportunities in these firms make self-employment relatively unattractive. Quite remarkably, the regional entrepreneurial culture, in terms of the local population's personality structure, still prevails.

The Two Layers of Entrepreneurship Culture: Systemizing a Multifaceted Phenomenon

A regional culture of entrepreneurship may need more than societal legitimacy of entrepreneurial behavior, individuals able and willing to become entrepreneurs, entrepreneurial role models, networks, and peer effects. An infrastructure of supporting services may also be necessary, particularly the availability of competent consulting as well as appropriate financial institutions. It is not farfetched to expect that regions characterized by high levels of new business formation and a pronounced entrepreneurship culture may develop such a supporting infrastructure over time.

In earlier work, we developed a framework that is helpful in understanding the interplay between different elements of an entrepreneurial culture (Fritsch and Wyrwich 2016). The basic idea is to distinguish between a political and a *normative-cognitive* layer of a regional culture of entrepreneurship (Fig. 2). The normative-cognitive layer of an entrepreneurship culture is a largely informal institution that represents the social acceptance of self-employment and a widespread positive attitude toward entrepreneurial activity among the population. Specifically, this includes:

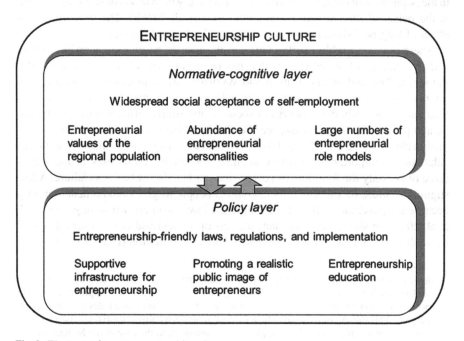

Fig. 2 Elements of an entrepreneurship culture

- *Entrepreneurial values of the regional population* such as individualism, autonomy, achievement, and mastery are widespread.
- *Abundance of entrepreneurial personalities*, i.e., a high share of persons with an entrepreneurial personality profile, which is characterized by traits such as extraversion, openness to experience, conscientiousness, and the ability to bear risk.
- *Large numbers of entrepreneurial role models who generate demonstration and peer effects*: high levels of self-employment in the region.

The *political layer* consists of formal institutions and mechanisms to create and support a regional culture of entrepreneurship. This may include:

- *Entrepreneurship-friendly laws and regulations* such as low barriers to entry and exit, high freedom of establishment and trade, a competition policy that controls for abuse of market power, low tax levels, an appropriate social security system, and, last but not least, a low level of corruption (Elert, Henrekson and Stenkula 2017).
- *A supportive infrastructure for entrepreneurship* such as training and consulting services for business founders, as well as good access to financial resources for start-ups and small businesses.
- *Promoting a realistic public image of entrepreneurs*: awareness campaigns, programs for encouraging contact with entrepreneurial role models.
- *Entrepreneurship education* particularly at universities, but also at lower levels of the education system.

The two layers are, of course, interdependent. Policy can and does influence the beliefs and experiences of the regional population, and the preexisting culture can and does influence the design and implementation of policy. Empirical evidence, however, clearly suggests that the normative-cognitive layer of a regional entrepreneurship culture plays the dominate role. The survival of regional pockets of entrepreneurial activity that endured the anti-entrepreneurial policies of the socialist regime of East Germany (Fritsch and Wyrwich 2014, 2019) demonstrates that these entrepreneurial norms and values are able to withstand even severe policies aimed at their elimination.

It is quite debatable as to how far policy may be able to 'create' a culture of entrepreneurship. Perhaps it is more realistic to delegate policy to the role of supporting the preconditions for self-employment and promoting an awareness of successful entrepreneurial role models. Nevertheless, given the merits of an entrepreneurial culture, other policy measures in the form of a strategic management of places (Audretsch 2015) that attempt to promote such a culture may be a significant step toward creating fertile conditions for the cultivation of an entrepreneurial society (Audretsch 2007).

Persistence of Regional Innovation Activities

Entrepreneurship in its very core includes behaviors such as creativity, recognition of opportunities, taking initiative, readiness to assume risk, and introducing new ideas, products, and services to the market. These behavioral elements are not only conducive to setting up one's own business, but should also be relevant for innovation activity——the process of transforming new ideas and knowledge into concrete products and services.

The transformation of ideas and knowledge into commercial application is at the core of the knowledge spillover theory of entrepreneurship (Acs et al. 2009, 2013). This theory regards the regionally available knowledge, particularly new knowledge, as an important source of entrepreneurial opportunities. Accordingly, a large and dynamically growing knowledge base should have the potential to provide rich opportunities for start-ups. This should be especially true for innovative new businesses as they are critically dependent on knowledge inputs. Consistent with these considerations, research has documented a pronounced relationship between indicators of regional knowledge and new business formation (particularly with start-ups in innovative and knowledge-intensive industries), such as the presence of academic institutions and the level of R&D activities (Audretsch et al. 2006; Fritsch and Aamoucke 2013, 2017).

It follows that an analysis of the persistence of entrepreneurship should be complemented by investigating the persistence of regional innovation activity. This necessarily starts with an assessment of the determinants of innovation activity. Accordingly, Audretsch and Feldman (1996), in their seminal contribution to the discussion of knowledge spillover and the geography of innovation, stress that innovation and technical change depend upon new knowledge much more than other kinds of economic activities. Theory and evidence suggest that spatially limited knowledge spillovers are of crucial importance for innovation and economic growth (e.g., Romer 1986). In particular, tacit knowledge, which is bound to specific people and only transmitted via face-to-face contacts, makes knowledge and parts of the regional knowledge base "sticky."

Due to this stickiness of tacit knowledge, it tends to remain in the local population and may be transferred across generations. This characteristic, as well as the continuity of well-established institutions of higher education and research (such as universities), shapes the persistence and scope of regional knowledge levels and knowledge profiles over longer periods of time. Hence, there are significant differences in the amount and the character of the available knowledge across regions.

In our own analyses we measured the historical knowledge of a region by a high employment share in science-based industries at the outset of the twentieth century, or by the local presence and geographic proximity to a technical or classical university founded before the year 1900. We find that these indicators of the historical knowledge base are positively related to the levels of R&D inputs and patenting more than 100 years later (Fritsch and Wyrwich 2018, 2019). In particular, German regions with a technical university in the year 1900 have high levels of start-ups in technology-intensive industries today. These results clearly indicate the persistence of regional knowledge that constitutes an important source of entrepreneurial opportunities. This persistence of regional innovation activity is currently only incompletely understood.

Policy Implications

Regions do not only differ in their current levels of entrepreneurship and innovation, but also with regard to the role of entrepreneurship and innovation in their history. These differences clearly confirm the recognition that a 'one size fits all' policy approach that might be appropriate for all regions does not exist. Hence, different policy measures and strategies may be needed to account for regional histories, cultures, and the psychological dispositions of the regional population.

The recognition that regional levels of self-employment and new business formation tend to be rather persistent over time means that regions with high levels of entrepreneurship today are likely to have also relatively high levels of entrepreneurship in the future, while regions with currently low levels of entrepreneurship may expect correspondingly low levels in the coming decades. Hence, policies that aim at raising the level of regional entrepreneurship and stimulating an entrepreneurial culture may require rather long periods of time before significant changes can be noticed. Clearly, creating an entrepreneurship culture is a long-term strategy. However, once such a culture is created it may generate long-lasting positive effects.

In regions that already have a pronounced culture of entrepreneurship, policy might play the distinctive role of preserving this culture and opening avenues to overcome development bottlenecks. Regions where a culture of entrepreneurship is more or less lacking may require considerably more attention and effort by policymakers to build such a culture. As a first step, any policy approach should try to identify the reasons for the relatively low levels of regional entrepreneurship. In a second step, the results of such an analysis can then serve as a basis for the development of a region-specific strategy to improve the level of entrepreneurial activity.

It has been shown that entrepreneurship in innovative industries (a type of entrepreneurship that can be regarded as particularly important for regional growth) is closely related to the regional knowledge base (Fritsch and Wyrwich 2018, 2019). Hence, strengthening the regional knowledge base may be an important way of raising especially the number of innovative new businesses. This pertains to all levels of education, as well as to research. Our own research shows that a historically grown knowledge base is likely to imply a long-lasting impact on the spatial distribution of patenting activity and the regional employment share in R&D-related activities. Thus, there is a long-term dividend of investing in this regional resource that endures. Altogether, it is important to keep in mind that any place-based policy that aims at fostering entrepreneurship and innovation activities as a conduit for regional growth needs a long-term orientation.

Avenues for Further Research

Although we have shown that there is a persistence of regional entrepreneurship and innovation activity, we still know very little about the reasons for the pronounced regional differences of historical self-employment rates and innovation activity. An important avenue for further research is, therefore, to investigate those factors that contributed to the emergence of a regional culture of entrepreneurship in the past. What explains these regional differences? What is the role of natural conditions such as location and a region's accessibility, of climate conditions, of quality of the soil and soil resources in the emergence of an entrepreneurial culture? Do social practices such as the prevailing modes of inheritance play a role here? What is the specific effect of formal institutions, such as region-specific barriers to entry, or a legal framework that allowed for a relatively high level of economic freedom?

The question about the legal framework conditions points to the relationship between formal and informal institutions. Although the diverse studies that show persistence of regional levels of entrepreneurship confirm the common conjecture that informal rules tend to be much more persistent than formal ones (Williamson 2000), there is also solid empirical evidence that certain formal rules can stimulate the level of entrepreneurship, and hence, the emergence of an entrepreneurial culture. It is, therefore, important to inquire more deeply into the effect that formal institutions have on informal ones, such as a regional entrepreneurial culture. It would also be important to know more about possible effects in the opposite direction, i.e., how an informal institution like an entrepreneurial culture might impact the design and formation of formal institutions? Do high levels of entrepreneurship and a positive attitude of the regional population towards entrepreneurship lead to the implementation of more entrepreneurship-friendly formal rules?

Another key issue that requires further investigation is how a regional culture of entrepreneurship is able to be transferred across generations despite severe disruptive shocks of the social, political, and economic framework conditions. A primary mechanism for the transmission of an entrepreneurial spirit over time that has been well investigated is the transfer from parents to their offspring (e.g., Chlosta et al. 2012; Lindquist et al. 2015). Much less is known about the potential contribution of spatial mobility of people to the persistence of a regional entrepreneurial culture. If, for example, people with an entrepreneurial mindset are particularly attracted to regions that are already characterized by high levels of entrepreneurship, this would support the persistence of a regional culture of entrepreneurship. A further mechanism——already mentioned above——that may contribute to persistence of an entrepreneurial culture is the effect of such a culture on the formal institutions. There may also be an effect of collective memory about the historical success of entrepreneurship that leads to persistence of entrepreneurship, e.g., the knowledge that entrepreneurship has been successful in former times (Fritsch et al. 2019a, 2019c).

A further point that deserves attention is the design of appropriate political strategies. What policies can be recommended for regions that have a pronounced culture of entrepreneurship? What policy measures are appropriate if such a culture is missing? How can policy support the emergence and the development of an entrepreneurial culture? Do regions with a strong entrepreneurial culture respond differently to certain policy measures than regions lacking, or with a weaker, entrepreneurial culture? Little is by known about such questions.

Since entrepreneurship has a close relationship with innovation activity, we also need to understand the historical sources of persistent regional differences with respect to regional knowledge bases and how they remain a source for innovation activity and for the recognition of entrepreneurial opportunities. This also provokes the question of how to stimulate regional innovation and its exploitation via entrepreneurship. Is a regional culture of entrepreneurship important, if not required, to commercialize regional knowledge?

Analyses of long-term regional development trajectories requires historical data. This may particularly include indicators for historical entrepreneurship, a detailed assessment of the regional knowledge base, information about government policies towards entrepreneurship and the supporting infrastructure for entrepreneurs such as the local banking system, information on social practices (e.g., modes of inheritance), as well as information about social values and attitudes of the regional population. This type of more comprehensive data would not only lead to a better description of historical entrepreneurship and related issues, but could also allow researchers to identify those elements of the historical entrepreneurship system that are of key relevance for persistence over longer periods of time.

References

Acs, Z. J., Zoltan, J., Braunerhjelm, P., Audretsch, D. B., & Carlsson, B. (2009). The knowledge spillover theory of entrepreneurship. *Small Business Economics, 32*, 15–30. https://doi.org/10.1007/s11187-008-9157-3.

Acs, Z. J., Zoltan, J., Audretsch, D. B., & Lehmann, E. E. (2013). The knowledge spillover theory of entrepreneurship. *Small Business Economics, 41*, 767–774. https://doi.org/10.1007/s11187-013-9505-9.

Andersson, M., & Koster, S. (2011). Sources of persistence in regional start-up rates—evidence from Sweden. *Journal of Economic Geography, 11*, 179–201. https://doi.org/10.1093/jeg/lbp069.

Audretsch, D. B., & Feldman, M. P. (1996). R&D spillovers and the geography of innovation and production. *American Economic Review, 86*, 630–640. https://www.jstor.org/stable/2118216.

Audretsch, D. B., & Fritsch, M. (2002). Growth regimes over time and space. *Regional Studies, 36*, 113–124. 10.1080/00343400220121909.

Audretsch, D. B., Keilbach, M., & Lehmann, E. E. (2006). *Entrepreneurship and economic growth*. Oxford: Oxford University Press.

Audretsch, D. B. (2007). *The entrepreneurial society*. Oxford: Oxford University Press.

Audretsch, D. B. (2015). *Everything in its place——entrepreneurship and the strategic management of cities, regions, and states*. Oxford: Oxford University Press.

Beugelsdijk, S. (2007). Entrepreneurial culture, regional innovativeness and economic growth. *Journal of Evolutionary Economics, 17*, 187–210. https://doi.org/10.1007/s00191-006-0048-y.

Bosma, N., Hessels, J., Schutjens, V., Van Praag, M., & Verheul, I. (2012). Entrepreneurship and role models. *Journal of Economic Psychology, 33*, 410–424. https://doi.org/10.1016/j.joep.2011.03.004.

Brezinski, H. (1987). The second economy in the GDR—Pragmatism is gaining ground. *Studies in Comparative Communism, 20*, 85–101. https://doi.org/10.1016/0039-3592(87)90017-2.

Brezinski, H., & Fritsch, M. (1995). Transformation: The shocking German way. *MOCT-MOST: Economic Policy in Transitional Economies, 5*, 1–25.

Chlosta, S., Patzelt, H., Klein, S. B., & Dormann, C. (2012). Parental role models and the decision to become self-employed: The moderating effect of personality. *Small Business Economics, 38*, 121–138. https://doi.org/10.1007/s11187-010-9270-y.

Coleman, J. S. (1988). Social capital in the creation of human capital. *American Journal of Sociology (Supplement), 94*, 95–120. https://www.jstor.org/stable/2780243.

Dubini, P. (1989). The influence of motivations and environment on business start-ups: Some hints for public policies. *Journal of Business Venturing, 4*, 11–26. https://doi.org/10.1016/0883-9026(89)90031-1.

Elert, N., Henrekson, M., & Stenkula, M. (2017). *Institutional reform for innovation and entrepreneurship——an agenda for Europe.* Cham: Springer Nature. https://doi.org/10.1007/978-3-319-55092-3.

Etzioni, A. (1987). Entrepreneurship, adaptation and legitimation. *Journal of Economic Behavior and Organization, 8*, 175–199. https://doi.org/10.1016/0167-2681(87)90002-3.

Fornahl, D. (2003). Entrepreneurial activities in a regional context. In D. Fornahl & T. Brenner (Eds.), *Cooperation, networks, and institutions in regional innovation systems* (pp. 38–57). Cheltenham: Elgar.

Fotopoulos, G. (2013). On the spatial stickiness of UK new firm formation rates. *Journal of Economic Geography, 14*, 651–679. https://doi.org/10.1093/jeg/lbt011.

Fotopoulos, G., & Storey, D. J. (2017). Persistence and change in interregional differences in entrepreneurship: England and Wales 1921–2011. *Environment and Planning A, 49*, 70–702. https://doi.org/10.1177/0308518X16674336.

Freytag, A., & Thurik, R. (2007). Entrepreneurship and its determinants in a cross-country setting. *Journal of Evolutionary Economics, 17*, 117–131. https://doi.org/10.1007/s00191-006-0044-2.

Fritsch, M., & Mueller, P. (2007). The persistence of regional new business formation-activity over time – assessing the potential of policy promotion programs. *Journal of Evolutionary Economics, 17*, 299–315. https://doi.org/10.1007/s00191-007-0056-6.

Fritsch, M., & Aamoucke, R. (2013). Regional public research, higher education, and innovative start-ups – an empirical investigation. *Small Business Economics, 41*(4), 865–885. https://doi.org/10.1007/s11187-013-9510-z.

Fritsch, M., & Wyrwich, M. (2014). The long persistence of regional levels of entrepreneurship: Germany 1925 to 2005. *Regional Studies, 48*, 955–973. https://doi.org/10.1080/00343404.2013.816414.

Fritsch, M., & Wyrwich, M. (2016). Does persistence in start-up activity reflect persistence in social capital? In H. Westlund & J. P. Larsson (Eds.), *Edward Elgar handbook on social capital and regional development* (pp. 82–107). Cheltenham: Elgar. https://doi.org/10.4337/9781783476831.00009.

Fritsch, M., & Aamoucke, R. (2017). Fields of knowledge in higher education institutions, and innovative start-ups – an empirical investigation. *Papers in Regional Science, 96*(S1), 1–27. https://doi.org/10.1111/pirs.12175.

Fritsch, M., & Wyrwich, M. (2017). The effect of entrepreneurship for economic development – an empirical analysis using regional entrepreneurship culture. *Journal of Economic Geography, 17*, 157–189. https://doi.org/10.1093/jeg/lbv049.

Fritsch, M., Sorgner, A., Wyrwich, M., & Zazdravnykh, E. (2019a). Historical shocks and persistence of economic activity: Evidence on self-employment from a unique natural experiment. *Regional Studies, 53*, 790–802. https://doi.org/10.1080/00343404.2018.1492112.

Fritsch, M., & Wyrwich, M. (2018). Regional knowledge, entrepreneurial culture and innovative start-ups over time and space——an empirical investigation. *Small Business Economics, 51*, 337–353. https://doi.org/10.1007/s11187-018-0016-6.

Fritsch, M., & Kublina, S. (2019). Persistence and change of regional new business formation in the national league table. *Journal of Evolutionary Economics*. https://doi.org/10.1007/s00191-019-00610-5

Fritsch, M., & Wyrwich, M. (2019). *Regional trajectories of entrepreneurship, knowledge, and growth——the role of history and culture*. Cham: Springer. https://doi.org/10.1007/978-3-319-97782-9.

Fritsch, M., Pylak, K., & Wyrwich, M. (2019c). *Persistence of entrepreneurship in different historical context*. Jena Economic Research Paper #2019-003, Friedrich Schiller Universtiy Jena, Germany. https://zs.thulb.uni-jena.de/receive/jportal_jparticle_00684973

Fritsch, M., Obschonka, M., & Wyrwich, M. (2019b): Historical roots of entrepreneurial culture and innovation activity– An analysis for German regions. *Regional Studies*. https://doi.org/10.1080/00343404.2019.1580357

Hall, J., & Ludwig, U. (1995). German unification and the "market adoption" hypothesis. *Cambridge Journal of Economics, 19*, 491–507. https://doi.org/10.1093/oxfordjournals.cje.a035327.

Kibler, E., Kautonen, T., & Fink, M. (2014). Regional social legitimacy of entrepreneurship: Implications for entrepreneurial intention and start-up behaviour. *Regional Studies, 48*, 995–1015. https://doi.org/10.1080/00343404.2013.851373.

Lindquist, M. J., Sol, J., & Van Praag, M. (2015). Why do entrepreneurial parents have entrepreneurial children? *Journal of Labour Economics, 33*, 269–296. https://doi.org/10.1086/678493.

Marshall, A. (1920). *Principles of economics* (8th ed.). London: MacMillan.

Minniti, M. (2005). Entrepreneurship and network externalities. *Journal of Economic Behavior and Organization, 57*, 1–27. https://doi.org/10.1016/j.jebo.2004.10.002.

Mueller, P., van Stel, A., & Storey, D. J. (2008). The effect of new firm formation on regional development over time: The case of Great Britain. *Small Business Economics, 30*, 59–71. https://doi.org/10.1007/s11187-007-9056-z.

Nanda, R., & Sorenson, O. (2010). Workplace peer effects and entrepreneurship. *Management Science, 56*, 1116–1126. https://doi.org/10.1287/mnsc.1100.1179.

North, D. (1994). Economic performance through time. *American Economic Review, 84*, 359–368. https://www.jstor.org/stable/2118057.

Nunn, N. (2009). The importance of history for economic development. *Annual Review of Economics, 1*, 65–92. https://doi.org/10.1146/annurev.economics.050708.143336.

Obschonka, M., Schmitt-Rodermund, E., Gosling, S. D., & Silbereisen, R. (2013). The regional distribution and correlates of an entrepreneurship-prone personality profile in the United States, Germany, and the United Kingdom: A socioecological perspective. *Journal of Personality and Social Psychology, 105*, 104–122. https://doi.org/10.1037/a0032275.

Obschonka, M., Stuetzer, M., Gosling, S. D., Rentfrow, P. J., Lamb, M. E., Potter, J., & Audretsch, D. B. (2015). Entrepreneurial regions: Do macro-psychological cultural characteristics of regions help solve the "knowledge paradox" of economics? *PLoS One, 10*, e0129332. https://doi.org/10.1371/journal.pone.0129332.

Obschonka, M., & Stuetzer, M. (2017). Integrating psychological approaches to entrepreneurship: The entrepreneurial personality system (EPS). *Small Business Economics, 49*, 203–231. https://doi.org/10.1007/s11187-016-9821-y.

Pickel, A. (1992). *Radical transitions: The survival and revival of entrepreneurship in the GDR*. Boulder: Westview Press.

Putnam, R. D. (2000). *Bowling alone: The collapse and revival of American community*. New York: Simon & Schuster.

Rentfrow, J. P., Gosling, S. D., & Potter, J. (2008). A theory of the emergence, persistence, and expression of geographic variation in psychological characteristics. *Perspectives on Psychological Science, 3*, 339–369. https://doi.org/10.1111/j.1745-6924.2008.00084.x.

Romer, P. (1986). Increasing returns and long-run growth. *Journal of Political Economy, 94*, 1002–1037. https://www.jstor.org/stable/1833190.

Sorenson, O., & Audia, P. G. (2000). The social structure of entrepreneurial activity: Geographic concentration of footwear production in the United States, 1940–1989. *American Journal of Sociology, 106*, 424–462. https://doi.org/10.1086/316962.

Sternberg, R. (2009). Regional dimensions of entrepreneurship. *Foundations and Trends in Entrepreneurship, 5*, 211–340. https://doi.org/10.1561/0300000024.

Stuetzer, M., Obschonka, M., Audretsch, D. B., Wyrwich, M., Rentfrow, P. J., Coombes, M., Shaw-Taylor, L., & Satchell, M. (2016). Industry structure, entrepreneurship, and culture: An empirical analysis using historical coalfields. *European Economic Review, 86*, 52–72. https://doi.org/10.1016/j.euroecorev.2015.08.012.

van Stel, A., & Suddle, K. (2008). The impact of new firm formation on regional development in the Netherlands. *Small Business Economics, 30*, 31–47. https://doi.org/10.1007/s11187-007-9054-1.

Westlund, H., & Bolton, R. (2003). Local social capital and entrepreneurship. *Small Business Economics, 21*, 77–113. https://doi.org/10.1023/A:1025024009072.

Williamson, O. E. (2000). The new institutional economics: Taking stock, looking ahead. *Journal of Economic Literature, 38*, 595–613. https://www.jstor.org/stable/2565421.

Wyrwich, M., Stuetzer, M., & Sternberg, R. (2016). Entrepreneurial role models, fear of failure, and institutional approval of entrepreneurship: A tale of two regions. *Small Business Economics, 46*, 467–492. https://doi.org/10.1007/s11187-015-9695-4.

David Audretsch and New Directions in Spillover Academic Entrepreneurship

Mike Wright

Abstract David Audretsch's work emphasizes the importance of context for knowledge spillover entrepreneurship. His work helps explain why innovative activity is not evenly distributed geo-graphically. Instead, it has a tendency to cluster spatially within close geographic proximity to the knowledge source. Further, hi s work shows that con-texts with rich investments in knowledge generally exhibit greater entrepreneurial activity. This is in contrast with contexts lacking in knowledge investments since these generally show less entrepreneurial activity.

Introduction

Among his extensive research publications, David Audretsch has made a major contribution to the understanding of the role of knowledge spillovers in developing entrepreneurship and its impact on regional growth (Audretsch 2018). Knowledge spillover entrepreneurship involves entrepreneurship that occurs from an incentive and opportunity created in the context of an incumbent organization but realized and actualized in the context of a new organization (Audretsch et al. 2006). The knowledge spills over from the organization where it was originally created, but also the entrepreneurial startup serves as the conduit facilitating the spillover of that knowledge to the new company where the idea is actually commercialized and actualized. Knowledge spillover entrepreneurship is important because that knowledge and ideas not actually commercialized and pursued in the context of the organization investing in their creation can generate the incentives and opportunities for entrepreneurship.

David's work emphasizes the importance of context for knowledge spillover entrepreneurship. His work helps explain why innovative activity is not evenly distributed geographically. Instead, it has a tendency to cluster spatially within close geographic proximity to the knowledge source (Audretsch and Feldman 1996).

M. Wright (✉)
Center for Management Buyout Research, Imperial College Business School, London, UK
e-mail: mike.wright@imperial.ac.uk

© Springer Nature Switzerland AG 2019
E. E. Lehmann, M. Keilbach (eds.), *From Industrial Organization to Entrepreneurship*, https://doi.org/10.1007/978-3-030-25237-3_17

Further, his work shows that contexts with rich investments in knowledge generally exhibit greater entrepreneurial activity. This is in contrast with contexts lacking in knowledge investments since these generally show less entrepreneurial activity (Audretsch et al. 2006).

An important insight from David's work is that the organization in receipt of the knowledge spillover tends to be located geographically close to the organization that creates the knowledge. Hence, new-firm startups tend to be found close to the knowledge source (Audretsch et al. 2006).

Spillovers and Universities

David's work has obvious implications for the spilling over of knowledge from universities. These spillover effects may involve both firms created by external entrepreneurs that draw on the knowledge created at the university as well as spin-off firms started by faculty at the university based on knowledge developed at the university. However, the spillover effects are, it seems, quite nuanced.

We know from David's work that university spillovers in terms of their impact on the location of high technology firms are heterogeneous. Audretsch and Lehmann (2005b) show that the number of firms located close to a university is positively influenced by the knowledge capacity of the region and the knowledge output of a university. Using German data on IPOs of high tech firms Audretsch et al. (2005) show that new knowledge and technology based firms have a high propensity to locate close to universities but is dependent on spillover mechanisms relating to the type of research knowledge and human capital that can be accessed from universities. In a related study, Audretsch and Lehmann (2005a) compare the impact of technical and general universities, finding that performance is not influenced by the type of university the firm is located near.

An extensive body of research has also developed on the impact of university knowledge spillovers from the university perspective. Much of this work has focused on direct academic entrepreneurship which typically includes patenting, licensing and consulting provided to both established and new high tech firms, and most recently the creation of spin-offs involving academic faculty (see Siegel and Wright 2015a, b for a detailed review). Although such activities are extensive, studies raise questions about the actual impact in terms of economic, financial and social value creation (Grimaldi et al. 2011).

New Directions

In the limited space available, I highlight three broad directions that I see as key for future research on knowledge spillovers in academic entrepreneurship that build on David's work.

University Heterogeneity

University contexts are not homogeneous. Universities vary in terms of scale, scope, research quality, history and culture, location and local networks, as well as in resources and capabilities. These differences may impact the nature of knowledge spillovers in terms of the influence of world class science, medical and engineering, and computer science faculties on different types of student entrepreneurship than those focused on arts and social sciences. Apparently similar universities, such as leading research universities, technical universities, liberal arts universities or newly designated universities, may vary significantly in how they view their role in promoting the development of knowledge spillover entrepreneurship. This role may be path dependent based on how universities have evolved over the past. It may be quite difficult to change even if governmental policies toward the stimulation of spillovers change. For example, Holstein et al. (2018) show how the different approaches to the development of entrepreneurial activities by two research intensive universities in the UK were influenced by differences in their relationship with the local region.

While some elite universities have worldwide reputations, they may be less connected to their locality than other mid-range universities who have built local connections over many years. Hence, there are some new potential challenges for elite universities in seeking to face both ways, locally and internationally, that need to be addressed. Research is needed to explore these challenges.

Student and Alumni Entrepreneurship

While much attention has been devoted to high tech start-ups by external entrepreneurs and to faculty spin-offs, less attention has been paid to knowledge spillovers by students, notably undergraduates and masters students, as well as alumni. This is unfortunate as these start-ups are considerably more numerous than those created by faculty (Astebro et al. 2012). University education and research experience may lead indirectly to entrepreneurial actions through corporate spin-offs and start-ups by alumni. The spillover impact of university efforts to promote entrepreneurship, through formal entrepreneurship courses or experiential learning through entrepreneurship 'labs', may not occur until sometime after graduation (Nabi et al. 2017).

Wennberg et al. (2011) explore the indirect spillover of knowledge from universities to entrepreneurship by individuals with university degrees who engage in start-ups after gaining industrial experience compared with those who move directly from university to start-up and show that the performance of the former is significantly greater than that of the latter group. This has important policy implications given that startups by graduates with industry experience substantially outnumber those created by individuals going directly from university to start-up.

There are large variations across universities in terms of graduates' intentions and propensities to enter entrepreneurship (Daghbashyan and Hårsman 2014). Weak cultures of entrepreneurship at particular universities may adversely impact start-up activity (Nabi et al. 2017). However, geographical location of the university is important. Swedish data shows that students graduating in a metropolitan area, and in a region with a strong presence of university peer entrepreneurs and family members, are much more likely than other graduates to locate their business in the region of graduation (Larsson et al. 2017). The metropolitan effects are consistent with the importance of local opportunities, while the presence of peer entrepreneurs and family highlight the importance of social embeddedness. This indicates that elements of the entrepreneurial ecosystem have an important effect on the extent and nature of student entrepreneurship. At present, we have only a fragmentary picture of the relationships between different contexts and their ecosystems that facilitate knowledge spillover entrepreneurship related to universities. Further research is needed on this topic.

Knowledge Spillover Entrepreneurship Processes

The notion of knowledge spillover entrepreneurship raises a major question concerning how the spillovers are to be effected. While much work has focused on examining quantitatively the relationship between different measures of university quality, types of firms and types of spillovers, as well as the human and social capital resources needed we know relatively little about the processes through which the spillover occurs. The role of intermediaries has been highlighted by Wright et al. (2008). Rasmussen et al. (2011) for example emphasize the importance of recruiting external members with commercial experience to enable faculty spin-offs to establish a market presence. Recent work has begun to focus on the need to understand the elements in the emergence and development of an entrepreneurial ecosystem surrounding particular universities that will enable knowledge spillovers. These include the links between the impact of specific policies, instruments and institutions on entrepreneurial activity at the local and regional levels (Autio et al. 2018), as well as the elements of an ecosystem to facilitate student entrepreneurship (Wright et al. 2017). However, much of this work is theoretical or schematic and there is a need for further detailed empirical work that identifies the different configurations of ecosystems that may be effective under different university contexts (Mayer et al. 2018).

Conclusion

In sum, the academic entrepreneurship research program stimulated by David's knowledge spillover work demonstrates significant longevity. Given the importance attached to knowledge spillover entrepreneurship by universities and governments, a major challenge, and an important further opportunity for future research remains how to measure the direct and indirect knowledge spillovers from universities relating to student and alumni entrepreneurship. Numbers of spin-offs created, or number of interactions with universities tell us little about the economic and social benefits. Tracking alumni for many years after graduation is important but will involve a major data gathering exercise. As the contribution of universities to society is exposed to increasing scrutiny from local and national governments, business, and other interested parties the continuing relevance of this research program cannot be overstated. Scholars shouldn't hesitate to pursue this research program. Or, as David is wont to say, quoting a real Nobel Prize winner, "Don't Think Twice It's Alright".

References

Astebro, T., Bazzazian, N., & Braguinsky, S. (2012). Startups by recent university graduates and their faculty: Implications for university entrepreneurship policy. *Research Policy, 41*(4), 663–677.

Audretsch, D. (2018). Entrepreneurship, economic growth and geography. *Oxford Review of Economic Policy, 34*, 637–651.

Audretsch, D., & Feldman, M. (1996). R&D spillovers and the geography of innovation and production. *American Economic Review, 86*(3), 630–640.

Audretsch, D., & Lehmann, E. (2005a). Do University policies make a difference? *Research Policy, 34*, 343–348.

Audretsch, D., & Lehmann, E. (2005b). Does the knowledge spillover theory of entrepreneurship hold for regions? *Research Policy, 34*(8), 1191–1202.

Audretsch, D., Lehmann, E., & Warning, S. (2005). University spillovers and new firm location. *Research Policy, 34*, 1113–1122.

Audretsch, D., Keilbach, M., & Lehmann, E. (2006). *Entrepreneurship and economic growth.* Oxford: Oxford University Press.

Autio, E., Nambisan, S., Thomas, L., & Wright, M. (2018). Digital affordances, spatial affordances, and the genesis of entrepreneurial ecosystems. *Strategic Entrepreneurship Journal, 12*, 72–95.

Daghbashyan, Z., & Hårsman, B. (2014). University choice and entrepreneurship. *Small Business Economics, 42*, 729–746.

Grimaldi, R., Kenney, M., Siegel, D., & Wright, M. (2011). 30 years after Bayh–Dole: Reassessing academic entrepreneurship. *Research Policy, 40*(8), 1045–1057.

Holstein, J., Starkey, K., & Wright, M. (2018). Strategy and narrative in higher education. *Strategic Organization, 16*(1), 61–91.

Larsson, J., Wennberg, K., Wiklund, J., & Wright, M. (2017). Location choices of graduate entrepreneurs. *Research Policy, 46*(8), 1490–1504.

Mayer, C., Siegel, D., & Wright, M. (2018). Entrepreneurship: An assessment. *Oxford Review of Economic Policy, 46*(8), 1490–1504.

Nabi, G., Liñán, F., Fayolle, A., Krueger, N., & Walmsley, A. (2017). The impact of entrepreneurship education in higher education: A systematic review and research agenda. *Academy of Management Learning & Education, 16*(2), 277–299.

Rasmussen, E., Mosey, S., & Wright, M. (2011). The evolution of entrepreneurial competencies: A longitudinal study of university spin-off venture emergence. *Journal of Management Studies, 48*(6), 1314–1345.

Siegel, D. S., & Wright, M. (2015a). Academic entrepreneurship: Time for a rethink? *British Journal of Management, 26*(4), 582–595.

Siegel, D. S., & Wright, M. (2015b). University technology transfer offices, licensing, and start-ups. In A. N. Link, D. Siegel, & M. Wright (Eds.), *Chicago Handbook of University Technology Transfer and Academic Entrepreneurship* (pp. 1–40). Chicago: University of Chicago Press.

Wennberg, K., Wiklund, J., & Wright, M. (2011). The effectiveness of university knowledge spillovers: Performance differences between university spinoffs and corporate spinoffs. *Research Policy, 40*, 1128–1143.

Wright, M., Clarysse, B., Lockett, A., & Knockert, M. (2008). Mid-range universities in Europe linkages with industry: Knowledge types and the role of intermediaries. *Research Policy, 37*(8), 1205–1223.

Wright, M., Siegel, D., & Mustar, P. (2017). An emerging ecosystem for student start-ups. *Journal of Technology Transfer, 42*, 909–922.

David Audretsch – A Bibliometric Portrait of a Distinguished Entrepreneurship Scholar

Charlie Karlsson and Björn Hammarfelt

Abstract The purpose of this paper is to highlight David Audretsch's exceptional career and contextualize his influence on the field of entrepreneurship research. Firstly, we will highlight his most important works and the central common themes in these publications to provide insights on his contribution to the entrepreneurship field. Secondly, we will by applying bibliometric methods illustrate David Audretsch's scholarly networks by showing his most common co-authors, i.e. the authors that together with him have contributed to develop the field of entrepreneurship research, and thirdly, we illustrate David Audretsch's scientific influence by presenting information on the countries and scientific institutions which most frequently has cited his research.

Introduction

David Audretsch is an outstanding and very productive entrepreneurship scholar. Whatever measure we use, his achievements are magnificent. In early April 2018, *Google Scholar* identifies about 1000 publications and more than 75,000 citations. If we instead turn to *Web of Science* core collection, we get almost 200 publications and more than 12,500 citations.[1] When we study his CV, we find that he during his career until 2018 has authored 16 books, edited 33 books and 13 special issues of journals, and authored 276 journal articles and 158 book chapters, of which a high share can be classified as falling within the entrepreneurship research field. His contributions to the entrepreneurship field has been acknowledged in

---

[1] Almost 63 citations per paper.

C. Karlsson (✉)
Jönköping University, Jönköping, Sweden
e-mail: charlie.karlsson@ju.se

B. Hammarfelt
Swedish School of Library and Information Science, Borås, Sweden

© Springer Nature Switzerland AG 2019
E. E. Lehmann, M. Keilbach (eds.), *From Industrial Organization to Entrepreneurship*, https://doi.org/10.1007/978-3-030-25237-3_18

several ways.[2] He received (together with Zoltan Acs) the Global Award for Entrepreneurship Research in 2001 and has also received three Honorary Doctorates, one from the University of Augsburg, Germany in 2008, one form Jönköping University, Sweden in 2010 and one from the University of Siegen, Germany in 2018.

The purpose of this paper is to highlight David Audretsch's exceptional career and contextualize his influence on the field of entrepreneurship research. Firstly, we will highlight his most important works and the central common themes in these publications to provide insights on his contribution to the entrepreneurship field. Secondly, we will by applying bibliometric methods illustrate David Audretsch's scholarly networks by showing his most common co-authors, i.e. the authors that together with him have contributed to develop the field of entrepreneurship research, his scientific peers in terms of which authors he has cited most often, i.e. the authors that have inspired his research,

- his scientific peers in terms of which authors he has cited most often, i.e. the authors that have inspired his research,
- the authors for which David Audretsch has been a peer in the sense that they frequently cite his contributions, i.e. the authors that over the years have been inspired by him, and
- how these relations and networks have developed over time.

Thirdly, we illustrate David Audretsch's scientific influence by presenting information on the countries and scientific institutions which most frequently has cited his research.

The paper is organized as follows: In section "The Most Highly Appreciated Scientific Contributions by David Audretsch", we present the most highly appreciated scientific contributions by David Audretsch. David Audretsch's key publication channels during four different periods are presented in section "Key Publications Channels Used by Audretsch and their Frequency Over Time". We analyse the most central analytical concepts in David Audretsch's scientific publications in section "The Central Analytical Concepts in David Audretsch's Scientific Publications". In section "David Audretsch's Network of Co-Authors", we illustrate David Audretsch's network of co-authors during two different periods. David Audretsch's scientific peers and predecessors are presented in section "David Audretsch's Scientific Peers and Predecessors", while authors that frequently have cited David Audretsch's scientific works are exhibited in section "Authors that Frequently Has Cited David Audretsch". The geographic reach of David Audretsch's scientific influence is the theme for section "The Geographical Reach of David Audretsch's Scientific Influence". Section "Conclusions" concludes.

---

[2] According to a bibliometric study by Cancino, et al. (2017), David Audretsch is the most influential innovation researcher during the period 1989–2013.

The Most Highly Appreciated Scientific Contributions by David Audretsch

In this section, we briefly present those of David Audretsch's scientific contributions that other scientists seem to have acknowledged most in terms of citations. The number of citations cannot directly be equated with the quality of research, yet citations are a useful shorthand for studying the visibility and influence of a scholar. For most of the analyses in this paper we use data from *Web of Science*, and the reason for this is the superior quality and consistency of bibliographic records in this database compared to *Google Scholar*. However, when evaluating the scientific contributions of an individual scientist *Web of Science* has some severe limitations since not all scientific publications are listed there. For this reason, we here in Table 1 also include data from *Google Scholar*.[3] We find that 17 of the 51 publications listed in *Google Scholar* and included here are not listed by *Web of Science*. This clearly illustrates that the degree to which David Audretsch has influenced and inspired other scientists would be severely underestimated by only using data from Web of Science. Indeed, *Web of Science* is limited to a distinct set of internationally oriented journals in the English language, while more nationally oriented as well as non-English journals are excluded. We can observe that the ranking by *Web of Science* differs substantially from the ranking by *Google Scholar* (see Table 2), which is mainly due to the fact that some of the highly cited books, such as *Innovation and Small Firms* (1990), are not indexed in *Web of Science*.[4]

Key Publications Channels Used by Audretsch and Their Frequency Over Time

Another approach for discerning changes in topics and research interest is to review the journals in which Audretsch has published. We use *Web of Science*, which means that publications in journals not indexed by the database are omitted. To make it possible to make comparisons over time, we present the most frequently published in journals and book series in four time periods, 1983–1991, 1992–2000, 2001–2010 and 2011–2018 (Tables 3, 4, 5, and 6).

Two notable trends are visible when studying the journals Audretsch publish in: first, we see a increasing concentration of publications in a smaller set of journals over time, and in the later period (2011–2018) more than half of the papers are found in two journals, *Small Business Economics* (SBE) and *Journal of Technology Transfer*. Partly this can be explained by direct engagement in these journals – Audretsch is the editor of SBE – and we suggest that this could be an indication of

---

[3] The data from Google Scholar was collected on April 4th, 2018.

[4] However, it should be noted that citations to books can be retrieved from *Web of Science* using the cited reference search, but they are not indexed as 'source items' in the database.

Table 1 David Audretsch's most highly cited works

Title	Google Scholar citations	Web of Science citations
R&D Spillovers and the Geography of Innovation and Production (1996a)	6292	1688 (1)
Innovation and Small Firms (1990)	2777	–
Innovation and Industry Evolution (1995b)	2625	–
Innovation in Large and Small Firms: An Empirical Analysis (1988)	2650	707 (2)
Innovation in Cities: Science-Based Diversity, Specialization and Localized Competition (1999)	2314	583 (3)
Agglomeration and the Location of Innovative Activity (1998)	1569	349 (5)
Company-Scientist Locational Links: The Case of Biotechnology (1996)	1511	474 (4)
Innovation, Market Structure, and Firm Size (1987)	1400	314 (8)
Entrepreneurship and Economic Growth (2006)	1303	–
Knowledge Spillovers and the Geography of Innovation (2004)	1217	–
R&D Spillovers and Recipient Firm Size (1994)	1169	326 (7)
What's New about the New Economy? Sources of Growth in the Managed and Entrepreneurial Economies (2001a)	1128	–
The Knowledge Spillover Theory of Entrepreneurship (2009)	1119	332 (6)
New Firm Survival: New Results Using a Hazard Function (1995)	1103	304 (9)
Real Effects of Academic Research: Comment (1992)	1094	264 (13)
New-Firm Survival and the Technological Regime (1991)	1066	277 (11)
Innovation, Growth and Survival (1995a)	957	266 (12)
Innovative Clusters and the Industry Life Cycle (1996b)	890	247 (14)
Entrepreneurship Capital and Economic Performance (2004a)	867	280 (10)
Capitalism and Democracy in the 21st Century: From the Managed to the Entrepreneurial Economy (2010)	733	181 (18)
The Entrepreneurial Society (2007a)	672	–
Growth Regimes over Time and Space (2002)	639	191 (17)
Entrepreneurship: A Survey of the Literature (2003)	634	–
Does Entry Size Matter? The Impact of the Life Cycle and Technology on Survival (2001)	599	151 (22)
Does the Knowledge Spillover Theory of Entrepreneurship Hold for Regions? (2005)	589	212 (15)
New Venture Growth: A Review and Extension (2006)	567	195 (16)
Linking Entrepreneurship to Growth (2001b)	553	–
Does Self-Employment Reduce Unemployment? (2008)	537	154 (22)
The Geography of Firm Births in Germany (1994)	523	165 (19)
Patents as a Measure of Innovative Activity (1989a)	522	164 (20)
University Spillovers and New Firm Location (2005)	483	162 (21)
Innovation and Technological Change (2003)	463	–

(continued)

David Audretsch – A Bibliometric Portrait of a Distinguished Entrepreneurship Scholar   173

Table 1 (continued)

Title	Google Scholar citations	Web of Science citations
Small Firms and Entrepreneurship: An East-West Perspective (1993)	447	–
Start-Up Size and Industrial Dynamics: Some Evidence from Italian Manufacturing (1999)	443	139 (23)
An Eclectic Theory of Entrepreneurship: Policies, Institutions and Culture (2002)	442	–
Entrepreneurship: Determinants and Policy a European-US Comparison (2002)	416	–
Entrepreneurship Capital and Economic Growth (2007b)	419	100 (29)
The Missing Link: The Knowledge Filter and Entrepreneurship in Endogenous Growth (2004)	409	–
A Model of the Entrepreneurial Economy (2004)	414	–
Strategic Entrepreneurship: Exploring Different Perspectives of an Emerging Concept (2009)	402	91 (30)
The Dynamic Role of Small Firms: Evidence from the US (2002)	394	104 (28)
The Missing Link: Knowledge Diffusion and Entrepreneurship in Endogenous Growth (2010)	381	109 (26)
Gibrat's Law: Are the Services Different? (2004)	374	109 (26)
Knowledge Spillovers and Strategic Entrepreneurship (2010)	382	47 (34)
Clusters, Knowledge Spillovers and New Venture Performance (2008)	351	112 (25)
The Theory of Knowledge Spillover Entrepreneurship (2007)	347	123 (24)
Handbook of Entrepreneurship Research: An Interdisciplinary Survey and Introduction (2006)	342	–
Does Firm Size Matter? Evidence on the impact of Liquidity Constraints on Firm Investment Behaviour in Germany (2002)	338	81 (33)
Small-Firm Entry in US Manufacturing (1989b)	328	100 (29)
Entrepreneurship and Regional Growth: An Evolutionary Interpretation (2004c)	311	90 (31)
The Role of Small Firms in US Biotechnology Clusters (2001)	297	83 (32)
Sustaining Innovation and Growth: Public Policy Support for Entrepreneurship (2004)	296	–
R&D, Firm Size and Innovative Activity (1991)	294	–

an on-going specialisation. This specialisation is a general trend – encompassing many research fields – and a trend in the works of Audretsch. The second trend, which is partly related to the first, is the tendency to towards publishing in more specialised journals in the later period, whereas more general economic journals (*Economic Letters and Review of Economics and Statistics*) dominated in the early period (1983–1991). Notable here is that several journals, such as *Entrepreneurship Theory and Practice* (2009), have been founded during the period under study.

Table 2 The scientific publications by David Audretsch with the highest citation frequency (citations/year)

Title	Web of Science citations
R&D Spillovers and the Geography of Innovation and Production (1996a)	73.4
The Knowledge Spillover Theory of Entrepreneurship (2009)	33.5
Innovation in Cities: Science-Based Diversity, Specialization and Localized Competition (1999)	29.2
Innovation in Large and Small Firms: An Empirical Analysis (1988)	22.8
Company-Scientist Locational Links: The Case of Biotechnology (1996)	20.6
Entrepreneurship Capital and Economic Performance (2004a)	18.7
Agglomeration and the Location of Innovative Activity (1998)	16.7
New Venture Growth: A Review and Extension (2006)	15.2
Does the Knowledge Spillover Theory of Entrepreneurship Hold for Regions? (2005)	15.1
Does Self-Employment Reduce Unemployment? (2008)	14.1
R&D Spillovers and Recipient Firm Size (1994)	13.1
New Firm Survival: New Results Using a Hazard Function (1995)	12.7
The Missing Link: Knowledge Diffusion and Entrepreneurship in Endogenous Growth (2010)	12.2
University Spillovers and New Firm Location (2005)	11.6
Growth Regimes over Time and Space (2002)	11.5
The Future of Entrepreneurship Research (2011)	11.4
Innovation, Growth and Survival (1995a)	11.1
Innovative Clusters and the Industry Life Cycle (1996b)	10.7
The Knowledge Spillover Theory of Entrepreneurship (2013)	10.7
From the Entrepreneurial University to the University in the Entrepreneurial Society (2014)	10.4
The Theory of Knowledge Spillover Entrepreneurship (2007)	10.3
Clusters, Knowledge Spillovers and New Venture Performance (2008)	10.2
Innovation, Market Structure, and Firm Size (1987)	9.9
New-Firm Survival and the Technological Regime (1991)	9.9
Real Effects of Academic Research: Comment (1992)	9.8
Capitalism and Democracy in the 21st Century: From the Managed to the Entrepreneurial Economy (2010)	9.5
Strategic Entrepreneurship: Exploring Different Perspectives of an Emerging Concept (2009)	9.1
Emotions and Opportunities: The Interplay of Opportunity Evaluation, Fear, Joy, and Anger as Antecedent of Entrepreneurial Exploitation (2012)	8.9
Does Entry Size Matter? The Impact of the Life Cycle and Technology on Survival (2001)	8.4
Entrepreneurship Capital and Economic Growth (2007b)	8.4
Gibrat's Law: Are the Services Different? (2004)	7.7
Entrepreneurship Capital and Its Impact on Knowledge Diffusion and Economic Performance (2008)	7.1

(continued)

Table 2 (continued)

Title	Web of Science citations
Start-Up Size and Industrial Dynamics: Some Evidence from Italian Manufacturing (1999)	7.0
Growth and Entrepreneurship (2012)	7.0
Entrepreneurial Finance and Technology Transfer (2016)	6.7
The Geography of Firm Births in Germany (1994)	6.6
Entrepreneurship and Regional Growth: An Evolutionary Interpretation (2004c)	6.4
Knowledge Creation, Entrepreneurship, and Economic Growth: A Historical Review (2009)	6.3
Regional Competitiveness, University Spillovers and Entrepreneurial Activity (2012)	6.3
The Dynamic Role of Small Firms: Evidence from the US (2002)	6.1
Entrepreneurship and Regional Growth: An Evolutionary Interpretation (2004c)	6.1
The Emergence of Entrepreneurship Policy (2004)	5.7
Industry Structure, Entrepreneurship, and Culture: An Empirical Analysis Using Historical Coalfields (2016)	5.7
Does Entrepreneurship Capital Matter? (2004b)	5.5
Patents as a Measure of Innovative Activity (1989a)	5.5
Location: A Neglected Determinant of Firm Growth (2007)	4.9
Does Firm Size Matter? Evidence on the impact of Liquidity Constraints on Firm Investment Behaviour in Germany (2002)	4.8
The Role of Small Firms in US Biotechnology Clusters (2001)	4.6
Small-Firm Entry in US Manufacturing (1989b)	3.3

Table 3 The journals that Audretsch most frequently publish in 1983–1991

Journal	No. of papers
Economics Letters	6
Review of Economics and Statistics	4
Business History Review	3
Economics of Small Firms	3
Kyklos	3
Southern Economic Journal	3
Studies in Industrial Organization	3
Innovation and Technological Change	2
International Journal of Industrial Organization	2
Journal of Institutional and Theoretical Economics	2
Zeitschrift für die Gesamte Staatswissenschaft	2

Table 4 Journals/book series that Audretsch most frequently publish in 1992–2000

Journal/book series	No. of papers
Review of Industrial Organization	7
Small Business Economics (first issue 1989)	5
International Journal of Industrial Organization	4
Journal of Institutional and Theoretical Economics	4
Zeitschrift für die Gesamte Staatswissenschaft	4
American Economic Review	3
Journal of Economic Literature	3
Kyklos	3
Comrades Go Private	2
Economics Letters	2
Geonomics Institute for International Economic Advancement Series	2

Table 5 Journals/book series that Audretsch most frequently publish in 2001–2010

Journal/book series	No. of papers
Small Business Economics	8
Research Policy	7
International Journal of Industrial Organization	4
International Studies in Entrepreneurship (first issue 2004)	4
Journal of Economic Literature	4
Annals of Regional Science	3
Entrepreneurship Theory and Practice (first issue 2009)	3
Journal of Business Venturing	3
Journal of Technology Transfer	3
European Planning Studies	2

Table 6 Journals that Audretsch most frequently publish in 2011–2018

Journal	No. of papers
Small Business Economics (Editors-in-chief: Audretsch & Acs)	16
Journal of Technology Transfer	15
International Entrepreneurship and Management Journal (first issue 2005)	4
Research Policy	4
Entrepreneurship Theory and Practice	3
Annals of Regional Science	2
Economic Development Quarterly	2
Eurasian Business Review	2
European Economic Review	2
Journal of Evolutionary Economics	2

The Central Analytical Concepts in David Audretsch's Scientific Publications

Research, especially in the social sciences, largely evolves around concepts and terms. Highly influential concepts may even evolve into whole fields of research (for example 'entrepreneurship'), and scholars being able to influence the 'conceptual' toolbox is likely to become leaders in their respective fields. Therefore, it is highly rewarding to study how concepts are use, and how they evolve over time. In this case we focus on the large and influential oeuvre of David Audretsch, but we also suggest that conceptual trends discovered here might be indicative of broader trends.

In this section, we highlight central analytical concepts in David Audretsch's scientific publications. We start in Table 7 with an overview of the most common analytical concepts in the titles of the scientific publications included in Tables 1 and 2. It should be no surprise to anyone that the most frequent concept is "entre-preneurship/entrepreneurial". The frequency rate is on average double that than for any other central analytical concept. This is what one should expect when analysing the publications of an entrepreneurship researcher. As one also can understand, all the main analytical concepts in Table 1 have a clear relationship to "entrepreneurship/entrepreneurial". "Innovation/innovate" is a fundamental input in entrepreneurial processes and "knowledge/R&D" is an input in innovation pro-cesses, where "spillover/spillovers" function as the transfer mechanism between "knowledge/R&D" and the innovation process. That analytical spatial concepts such as "geography", "location" and "clusters" are rather common is expected given the fact that knowledge production processes, innovation processes and entrepreneurial processes are all localized processes. That the concepts "small" and "size" are frequently present is natural since entrepreneurship research to a substantial degree did grow out of small business research. That the concept "growth" is quite frequent is also typical, since a major motivation for studying entrepreneurship is to understand its importance for economic growth.

In sequel, we leave the static picture to study how the central analytical concepts in David Audretsch's publication have changed over time. The data we use here come from *Web of Science* and the analytical concepts used have been distilled from the abstracts and titles of 196 items (articles, reviews and letters in the *Web of Science*). We start in Fig. 1 with the period 1983–2000, when David Audretsch was

Table 7 Central analytical concepts in the titles of the scientific publications by David Audretsch included in Tables 1 and 2

Concept frequency	Table 1	Table 2
Entrepreneurship/Entrepreneurial	22	23
Innovation/Innovative	14	8
Small/Size	12	9
Growth	11	10
Knowledge/R&D	11	10
Geography/Regions/Location/Agglomeration/Clusters/Cities/Space	10	9
Spillover/Spillovers	9	9

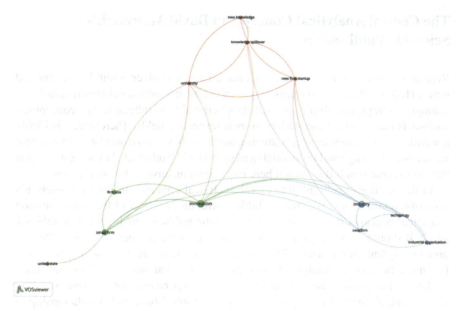

Fig. 1 Central analytical concepts in David Audretsch's research during the period 1983–2000

a young researcher. What immediately struck us was the analytical concept pair "entrepreneurship/entrepreneurial" is missing and yet we know that David Audretsch in 2001 together with Zoltan Acs got the international prize known as "The Global Award for Entrepreneurship Research". This is intriguing. However, when we study the short prize motivation we see that even there the concept of "entrepreneurship" is missing. The short prize motivation was the following: "For their research on the role of small firms in the economy, especially the role of small firms in innovation". The focus in the motivation is on small firms and innovation, and indeed, in 2001 the name of the prize was "The International Award for Entrepreneurship and Small Business Research".

If we now return to Fig. 1, we see that Audretsch in his early research in particular used the analytical concepts "small firms", "firm size" and "innovation". Later in the period, he did broaden his research and now four new analytical concepts take centre stage: "industry", "technology", "industrial organization" and "new firm". With the concept "new firm" we can suspect an emerging interest in research questions which are central in the entrepreneurship field. Towards the end of the period, four new analytical concepts are coming into focus in his research: "university", "new knowledge", "knowledge spillover" and "new firm startup". We clearly see strong couplings to entrepreneurship research but as we remarked above the concept of "entrepreneurship" is missing. A search April 13 2018 using Google Scholar for the period 1983–2000 combining "David Audretsch" and "small business" gave 121 hits, while a combination with "entrepreneurship" only gave 71 hits indicating that in relative terms David Audretsch in his research was more focused on small businesses than on entrepreneurship during this period. This is by no means exceptional. On the contrary, during this period research on small business dominated

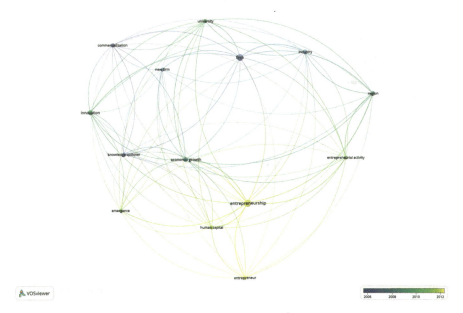

Fig. 2 Central analytical concepts in David Audretsch's research during the period 2001–2018

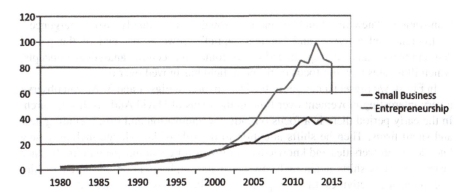

Fig. 3 The competition between "small business" and "entrepreneurship" according to Google Scholar 1980–2018. No. of hits in thousands April 13, 2018

over entrepreneurship research as illustrated in Table 2. It is only from 2001, that we can register more hits for "entrepreneurship" than for "small business" (Fig. 2).[5]

Turning now in Fig. 3 to period 2001–2018, we see that at the beginning of the period four analytical concepts are in the centre of attention of his research: "industry", "firm", "knowledge spillover" and "commercialization". Towards the middle of the period, a new set of analytical concepts take the centre stage: "university",

---
[5] Interestingly, the number of hits for "small business" has a peak in 2012 and the number of hits for "entrepreneurship" has a peak in 2013. Thereafter the number of hits is lower. The authors have no explanation for this new trend.

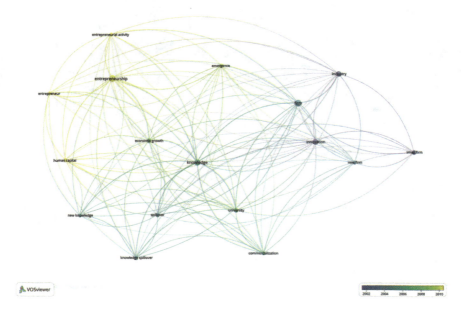

Fig. 4 Central analytical concepts in David Audretsch's research during the period 1983–2018

"innovation", "new firm" and "economic growth" but gradually also "emergence", "entrepreneurial activity" and "human capital". Towards the end of the period "entrepreneur" and "entrepreneurship" becomes the central analytical concepts, which illustrates how the focus of research field has moved over time.

In Fig. 4, we present a merger of the information in Figs. 1 and 3. We can observe a very interesting movement over time in the focus of David Audretsch's research. In the early period there is a focus on industry, innovation and firm including new and small firms. Then he shifts attention to the role of knowledge including new knowledge, universities and knowledge spillovers for economic growth. In the later years, his focus shifts again and now the main emphasis is on entrepreneurship, entrepreneurial activities, the entrepreneur and the role of human capital.

David Audretsch's Network of Co-authors

This section is devoted to a survey of the structure and development of David Audretsch's scientific co-operation and collaboration network as it is mirrored by his network of co-authors. In line with what we did in section "The Central Analytical Concepts in David Audretsch's Scientific Publications", we first study the period 1983–2000 and then the period 2001–2018. As in section "The Central Analytical Concepts in David Audretsch's Scientific Publications", the data does come from Web of Science and visualizations are made using the VosViewer software (Van Eck and Waltman 2010).

Figure 1 illustrates how David Audretsch's network developed during the period 1983–2000. What is striking here is the very strong co-author link with Zoltan Acs. We have reason to believe that this very productive scientific collaboration was the result of a lucky chance. In 1980, both became assistant professors at Middlebury College in Vermont but not only that, they also became friends and found out that they shared interest in the same economic issues. And even if Zoltan Acs left already in 1982, these 2 years were a long enough period for them to build a long-term scientific co-operation relationship. Besides the many co-authored articles in the period discussed here, Audretsch and Acs also co-authored highly cited and influential books, such as "Innovation and Small Firms" (1990) and "Small Firms and Entrepreneurship: An East-West Perspective" (1993) as well as co-edited books, such as "Innovation and Technological Change: An International Comparison" (1991).

Figure 5 identifies 18 of Audretsch's co-authorship relations in the period 1983–2000. In the late 1980's he starts publishing together with Hideki Yamawaki and in the early 1990's he also publishes together with Bo Carlsson, J-M. Graf von der Schulenburg and Talat Mahmood. In 1992, the first article co-authored with Maryann Feldman (and Zoltan Acs) is published. This is the beginning of a very productive co-operation during the 1990's, which among other things generates his most highly cited article "R&D Spillovers and the Geography of Innovation and Production" (1996a). Some of the articles co-authored with Maryann Feldman also includes Zoltan Acs as the third author. In the mid-1990's his co-authorship network is extended to include

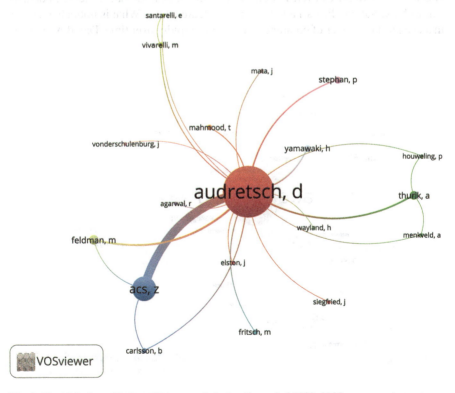

Fig. 5 David Audretsch's co-author network during the period 1983–2000

among others Marco Vivarelli, Michael Fritsch, José Mata, Julie-Ann Elston, Paula Stephan and Roy Thurik. Towards the end of the period 1983–2000 researchers such as Enrico Santarelli and Rajshree Agarwala are added to his co-authorship network. The above collaboration links generally resulted in several co-authorships but of course the link with Zoltan Acs is outstanding in terms of productivity.

We now turn to David Audretsch's co-authorship relations in the period 2001–2018, which are illustrated in Fig. 6. When comparing Fig. 6 with Fig. 5, tree things are striking: (i) the number of relationships is much larger in Fig. 6 and is equal to 32 compared with 18 in Fig. 5, (ii) the relationship with Zoltan Acs is no longer dominating even if it is still there and (iii) only four names from Fig. 5 – Zoltan Acs, Bo Carlsson, Roy Thurik and Julie-Ann Elston – remain in Fig. 6.

This last observation illustrates that David Audretsch during the second period almost totally renewed his co-authorship network. During the first third of the period 2001–2018, we can register co-authorship relations with among others Adrian Van Stel, Albert Link, Jürgen Weigand, Pontus Brunerhjelm, Max Keilbach, Erik Lehmann, Patricia McDougall, Taylor Aldrige and Dirk Dohse. It is worth stressing that four of these researchers are Germans, which illustrates David Audetsch's strong links with the research community in Germany. During the second third of the period, his co-authorship network is now extended by among others Werner Bönte, Erik Stam, Donald Kuratko, Marcel Hülsbek and Maksim Belitski. Towards the end of the period new co-authors, such as Sameeksha Desai, Samuel Gosling, Peter Rentfrow, Jeff Potter, Martin Obschanka, Michael Stuetzer, Forzana Chowdhury, Stefano Paleari and George Licht, are added. What is noticable here is that even if the number of co-authors has grown rapidly over time, David Audretsch

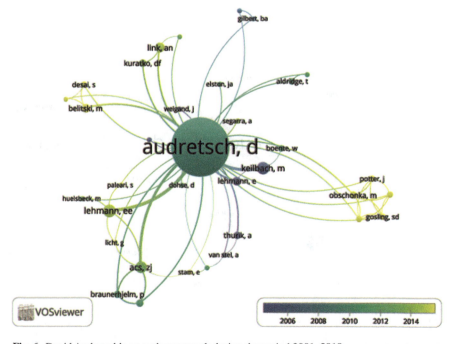

Fig. 6 David Audretsch's co-author network during the period 2001–2018

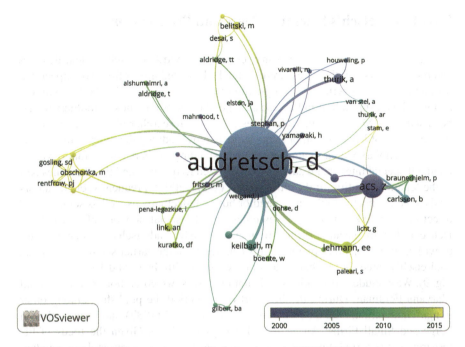

Fig. 7 David Audretsch's co-author network during the period 1983–2018

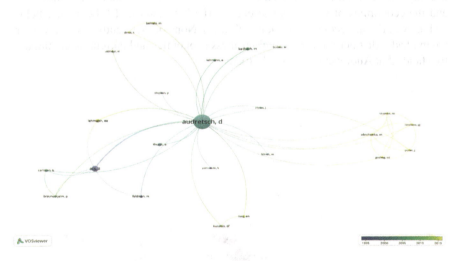

Fig. 8 David Audretsch's co-author network during the period 1983–2018

continues to publish together with his since long established co-authors. The result is nothing less than a very impressive and productive scientific co-operation network. In Fig. 7, we present David Audretsch's co-author network for the whole period 1983–2018. What is striking in this summary network is the very strong link to Zoltan Acs. Strong co-author links also exist with Roy Thurik, Max Keilbach, Erik Lehmann and Maryann Feldman Fig. 8.

David Audretsch's Scientific Peers and Predecessors

The purpose of this section is give an overview of David Audretsch's scientific peers and predecessors, i.e. those researchers that he has cited most often. We expect that his citation patterns will give as a picture of those researchers that he has admired and who has inspired him in his research, i.e. the giants on whose shoulders he has been standing. Moreover, the references used by a researcher gives us clues to the intellectual profile of the author in question, and by studying the referencing behaviour of a scholars we can gain further understanding of their intellectual development. Of special interest are authors that are cited frequently, and thus becomes part of the 'citation identity' of the citing author (White 2001). Frequently, cited authors tends to be connected to the citing author both intellectually as well as socially, and direct citation links therefore gives clues into the social network of researchers. Hence, following the authors most frequently cited by Audretsch over time provides us with a complementary picture of his oeuvre. As in the earlier sections we divide Audretsch's career in two halves and first we start with the period 1983–2000 (See Fig. 9). We exclude self-citations and citations to his two co-authors Zoltan Acs and Maryann Feldman. During the first part of the period, he published among other things "Innovation, Market Structure, and Firm Size" (1987) and "Innovation in Large and Small Firms: An Empirical Analysis" (1988). Given the focus of his research in this period it is natural that he has been inspired by researchers in industrial organization (F.M. Scherer, Ariel Pakes and William Comoner), in innovation and the economics of technological change (F.M. Scherer and Edwin Mansfield) and in evolutionary economics (Sidney Winter). None of these authors is known for having had a distinct focus on small business economics and entrepreneurship, the two fields that Audretsch later would focus.

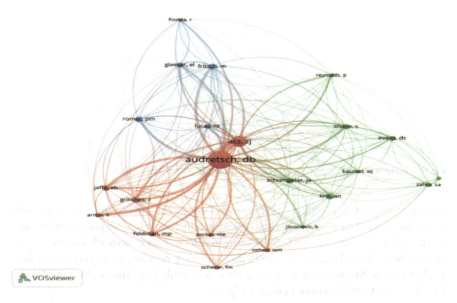

Fig. 9 David Audretsch's scientific peers during the period 1983–2000

During the middle of the period 1983–2000, David Audretsch published among other things "Small-Firm Entry in US Manufacturing" (1989b), "Patents as a Measure of Innovative Activity" (1989a), "Real Effects of Academic Research: Comment" (1992), "R&D Spillovers and Recipient Firm Size" (1994) and "The Geography of Frim Births in Germany" (1994). In this period, his citation network is expanded to include more researchers in industrial organization, but it is now also widened to also include entrepreneurship researchers. The expanded citation network includes Leonard Weiss (industrial organization), Richard Caves (industrial organization and multinational firms), Timothy Dunne (industrial organization/industrial economics), Paul Geroski (industrial organization, innovation, technical change and corporate performance), David Evans (entrepreneurship and small business economics) and Boyan Janovic (entrepreneurship and evolutionary economics).

During the third part of the period 1983–2000 David Audretsch's publications include "New Firm Survival: New Results Using a Hazard Function" (1995), "Innovative Clusters and the Industry Life Cycle" (1996b), "R&D Spillovers and the Geography of Innovation and Production" (1996a), "Company-Scientist Locational Links: The Case of Biotechnology" (1996), "Agglomeration and the Location of Innovative Activity" (1998), "Innovation in Cities: Science-Based Diversity, Specialization and Localized Competition" (1999), "Start-Up Size and Industrial Dynamics: Some Evidence from Italian Manufacturing" (1999) and "Capitalism and Democracy in the 21st Century: From the Managed to the Entrepreneurial Economy" (2010). In this period, his research is inspired by scientific giants such as Zvi Griliches (economics of technological change, innovation diffusion, and the role of R&D, patents and education), Paul Krugman (new trade theory, new economic geography, agglomeration and scale economies) and Kenneth Arrow (endogenous growth theory and the economics of information) but also other leading economists, such as Adam Jaffe (innovation, the economics of R&D and knowledge spillovers) and Wesley Cohen (innovation, absorptive capacity and the economics of R&D).

Turning now to David Audretsch's scientific peers during the period 2001–2018, we find in Fig. 10 a pattern that is significantly different from that for the period 1983–2000 illustrated in Fig. 9. The most distinct difference is that Audretsch in this period frequently cites leading entrepreneurship researchers. Besides Zoltan Acs, we find the names Joseph Schumpeter, Paul Reynolds, Scott Shane, David Evans, William Baumol, Shaker Zahra, Albert Link and Boyan Janovic. This new citation pattern is the result of that it is in this second period that David Audretsch establish himself as a leading entrepreneurship researcher in the world, with publications such as "An Eclectic Theory of Entrepreneurship: Policies, Institutions and Culture" (2002), "The Emergence of Entrepreneurship Policy" (2004), "A model of the Entrepreneurial Economy" (2004), "Handbook of Entrepreneurship Research: An Interdisciplinary Survey and Introduction" (2006), "New Venture Growth: A Review and Extension" (2006), "The Theory of Knowledge Spillover Entrepreneurship" (2007), "Strategic Entrepreneurship: Exploring Different Perspectives of an Emerging Concept" (2009), "The Knowledge Spillover Theory of Entrepreneurship" (2009, 2013), "The Future of Entrepreneurship Research" (2011), "Emotions and Opportunities: The Interplay of Opportunity Evaluation, Fear, Joy and Anger as Antecedent of Entrepreneurial Exploitation" (2012), "From the Entrepreneurial University to the University in the Entrepreneurial Society" (2014), and "Entrepreneurial Finance and Technology Transfer" (2016).

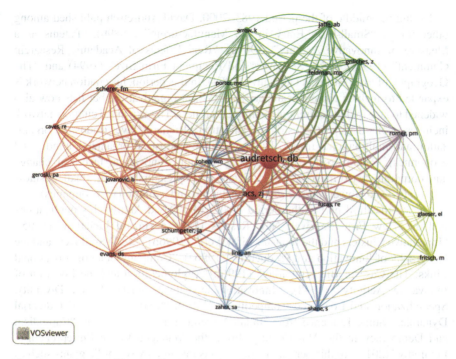

Fig. 10 David Audetsch's scientific peers for the whole period 1983–2018

Among his peers in this period, we also find growth economists, such as Robert Lucas, Kenneth Arrow and Paul Romer. This is an indication of Audretsch's interest in this period in the importance of entrepreneurship for economic growth, which is illustrated by publications such as "What's New About the New Economy? Sources of Growth in the Managed and Entrepreneurial Economies" (2001a), "Linking Entrepreneurship to Growth" (2001b), "Growth Regimes over Time and Space" (2002), "Sustaining Innovation and Growth: Public Policy Support for Entrepreneurship" (2004). "Entrepreneurship and Economic Growth" (2006), "Knowledge Creation, Entrepreneurship and Economic Growth: A Historical Review" (2009), "The Missing Link: Knowledge Diffusion and Entrepreneurship in Endogenous Growth" (2010), and "Growth and Entrepreneurship" (2012).

A third important aspect of Audretsch's citation pattern during this period is that it includes researchers with an interest in regional and urban economics and economic geography such as Edward Glaeser, Michael Fritsch, Maryann Feldman, Michael Porter, Zoltan Acs and Adam Jaffe. Many of David Audretsch's contributions in this second period deals with spatial aspects of innovation and entrepreneurship, including "Entrepreneurship and Regional Growth: An Evolutionary Interpretation" (2004c), "Does the Knowledge Spillover Theory of Entrepreneurship Hold for Regions?" (2005), "University Spillovers and New Firm Location" (2005), "Location: A Neglected Determinant of Firm Growth" (2007), "Clusters, Knowledge Spillovers and New Venture Performance" (2008), "Entrepreneurship Capital and Its Impact on Knowledge Diffusion and Economic Performance" (2008), and "Regional Competitiveness, University Spillovers and Entrepreneurial Activity" (2012).

We see that David Audretsch's research during this period is highly focused on entrepreneurship research. What is notable is that he doesn't have the narrow definition of entrepreneurship that is so common among entrepreneurship researchers. On the contrary, he exhibits a very wide definition of the entrepreneurship research field (Fig. 10).

As indicated above Audretsch has a broad and dynamic 'citation identity' which develops over time, and one explanation for his long and successful career is probably his ability to incorporate new literatures (and new co-authors). In fact, a characteristic of innovative researchers is their ability to move (with) the field, and stay at the forefront of research over long periods of time.

Authors That Frequently Has Cited David Audretsch

In this section, we in Table 8 present information about those authors for which David Audretsch has been a peer in the sense that they have frequently cited his scientific contributions and most probably been inspired by him. Interestingly, we recognize many leading entrepreneurship researchers in the table.

Table 8 Authors the frequently has cited David Audretsch's scientific contributions

Author	No. of citations
Z. J. Acs	64
M. Fritsch	48
H.W. Yu	43
R. Thurik	41
P. Nijkamp	37
S. Roper	34
C. Lammerzahl	33
D. Urbano	33
M. Wright	33
A.N. Link	32
E. Santarelli	32
Rodriguez-Pose	31
V.B. Bezerra	29
Van Stel	29
R. Huggins	28
R. Agarval	26
M. Obschonka	26
M. Vivarelli	26
A.R. Thurik	25
M.G. Colombo	24
K.P. Marzlin	24
T. Konrad	23
P. McCann	23
R. Capello	22
E.E. Lehmann	22
M.P. Feldman	20

The Geographical Reach of David Audretsch's Scientific Influence

As a leading entrepreneurship researcher, David Audretsch has been cited by researchers in many countries. In Fig. 1, we illustrated the geographical distribution of the citations of Audretsch's scientific contributions. We see three geographical clusters: North America (USA and Canada), Asia (China, Taiwan and South Korea) and Western, Southern and Northern Europe. Perhaps the most striking observation is the missing countries. One could, for example, had expected that Japan and Australia should be present in the figure. This probably tells us something about the uneven distribution of entrepreneurship research globally (Fig. 11).

In Fig. 12, we present information about those institutions from where most of the citations of David Audretsch's scientific contributions originate. We see clearly

Fig. 11 The geographical distribution of the citations of David Audretsch's scientific contributions

Fig. 12 The institutions from where most of the citations of David Audretsch's scientific contributions originate

how institutions in the US dominate but there are also four institutions from the UK, two from Italy and one from Canada, Germany, the Netherlands and Sweden. Thus, there is a substantial clustering of these citations indicating a clustering also of entrepreneurship research.

Conclusions

This chapter confirms Audretsch position as a leading researcher in the entrepreneurship field, and his accomplishments in terms of papers and citations are outstanding. Moreover, Audretsch has been able to maintain a high productivity over a long period of time combined with a steady increase in citations. While the increase in citations should be interpreted with some caution – the number of possible citers has increased substantially over the years – it is clearly so that Audretsch's work is heavily used by other scholars. Undoubtedly the impact of Audretsch's contributions, as measured by citations, is mainly due to the sheer intellectual quality of the research done. However, based on the bibliometric overview presented here we can also draw some conclusion to how he has achieved this prominent position. For example, the early, highly successful and long-lasting collaboration with Zoltan Acs is clearly an important factor in the career of both these scholars. Yet, while strong and durable collaborations are important we also find that Audretsch has been able to extend and widen his network of co-authors over time, and this is probably crucial for developing novel ideas, and to enter new fields of interest. When analysing the concepts used by Audretsch it is evident that 'entrepreneurship', which in the early periods rarely was used, take centre stage in his later works. This clearly demonstrates his ability to 'move with the field' and the keep up-to-date with trends and novel areas of research. However, given the influence that Audretsch's research has had we suggest that he not only has been able to quickly pick up on new approaches and perspectives, but that he been highly active in 'moving the field' forward and thus forming research agendas for colleagues and predecessor. This, the ability to have direct influence over the formation of research fields and specialties, is a key characteristic of a great scholar.

References[6]

Acs, Z. J., & Audretsch, D. B. (1987). Innovation, market structure, and firm size. *The Review of Economics and Statistics, 69*, 567–574.

Acs, Z. J., & Audretsch, D. B. (1988). Innovation in large and small firms: An empirical analysis. *American Economic Review, 78*, 678–690.

Acs, Z. J., & Audretsch, D. B. (1989a). Patents as a measure of innovative activity. *Kyklos, 42*, 171–180.

Acs, Z. J., & Audretsch, D. B. (1989b). Small-firm entry in US manufacturing. *Economica, 56*, 255–265.

---

[6] Only includes publications mentioned in the text.

Acs, Z. J., & Audretsch, D. B. (1991). R&D, firm size and innovative activity. In Z. J. Acs & D. B. Audretsch (Eds.), *Innovation and technological change: An international comparison* (pp. 39–59). Ann Arbor: University of Michigan Press.

Acs, Z. J., & Audretsch, D. B. (Eds.). (1993). *Small firms and entrepreneurship: An east-west perspective.* Cambridge: Cambridge University Press.

Acs, Z. J., & Audretsch, D. B. (2003). Innovation and technological change. In Z. J. Acs & D. B. Audretsch (Eds.), *Handbook of entrepreneurship research* (pp. 55–79). Boston: Kluwer Academic Publishers.

Acs, Z. J., & Audretsch, D. B. (Eds.). (2006). *Handbook of entrepreneurship research: An interdisciplinary survey and introduction.* Boston: Kluwer Academic Publishers.

Acs, Z. J., Audretsch, D. B., & Feldman, M. P. (1992). Real effects of academic research: Comment. *The American Economic Review, 82,* 363–367.

Acs, Z. J., Audretsch, D. B., & Feldman, M. P. (1994). R&D spillovers and recipient firm size. *Review of Economics and Statistics, 100,* 336–367.

Acs, Z. J., Audretsch, D. B., Braunerhjelm, P., & Carlsson, B. (2004). The missing link. The knowledge filter and entrepreneurship in economic growth. In *Discussion papers on entrepreneurship, growth and public policy.* Jena: Max Planck Institute.

Acs, Z. J., Braunerhjelm, P., Audretsch, D. B., & Carlsson, B. (2009). The knowledge spillover theory of entrepreneurship. *Small Business Economics, 32,* 15–30.

Acs, Z. J., Audretsch, D. B., Braunerhjelm, P., & Carlsson, B. (2012). Growth and entrepreneurship. *Small Business Economics, 39,* 289–300.

Acs, Z. J., Audretsch, D. B., & Lehmann, E. E. (2013). The knowledge spillover theory of entrepreneurship. *Small Business Economics, 41,* 757–774.

Agarwal, R., & Audretsch, D. B. (2001). Does entry size matter? The impact of the life cycle and technology on survival. *The Journal of Industrial Economics, 49,* 21–43.

Agarwal, R., Audretsch, D. B., & Sarkar, M. B. (2010). Knowledge spillovers and strategic entrepreneurship. *Strategic Entrepreneurship Journal, 4,* 271–283.

Audretsch, D. B. (1991). New-firm survival and technological regime. *The Review of Economics and Statistics, 73,* 441–450.

Audretsch, D. B. (1995a). Innovation, growth and survival. *International Journal of Industrial Organization, 13,* 441–457.

Audretsch, D. B. (1995b). *Innovation and industry evolution.* Cambridge: MIT Press.

Audretsch, D. B. (1998). Agglomeration and the location of innovative activity. *Oxford Review of Economic Policy, 14,* 18–29.

Audretsch, D. B. (2001). The role of small firms in US biotechnology clusters. *Small Business Economics, 17,* 3–15.

Audretsch, D. B. (2002). The dynamic role of small firms: Evidence from the US. *Small Business Economics, 18,* 13–40.

Audretsch, D.B. (2003), Entrepreneurship: A survey of the literature, Enterprise Papers No 14, Enterprise Directorate General, European Commission, Brussels.

Audretsch, D. B. (2004). Sustaining innovation and growth: Public policy support for entrepreneurship. *Industry and Innovation, 11,* 167–191.

Audretsch, D. B. (2007a). *The entrepreneurial society.* Oxford: Oxford University Press.

Audretsch, D. B. (2007b). Entrepreneurship capital and economic growth. *Oxford Review of Economic Policy, 23,* 63–78.

Audretsch, D. B. (2014). From the entrepreneurial university to the university in the entrepreneurial society. *Journal of Technology Transfer, 39,* 313–321.

Audretsch, D. B., & Acs, Z. J. (1990). *Innovation and small firms.* Cambridge: MIT Press.

Audretsch, D. B., & Dohse, D. (2007). Location: A neglected determinant of firm growth. *Review of World Economics, 143,* 79–107.

Audretsch, D. B., & Elston, J. A. (2002). Does firm size matter? Evidence on the impact of liquidity constraints on firm investment behaviour in Germany. *International Journal of Industrial Organization, 20,* 1–17.

Audretsch, D. B., & Feldman, M. P. (1996a). R&D spillovers and the geography of innovation and production. *American Economic Review, 86,* 630–640.

Audretsch, D. B., & Feldman, M. P. (1996b). Innovative clusters and the life cycle. *Review of Industrial Organization, 11*, 253–273.

Audretsch, D. B., & Fritsch, M. (1994). The geography of firm births in Germany. *Regional Studies, 28*, 359–365.

Audretsch, D. B., & Fritsch, M. (2002). Growth regimes over time and space. *Regional Studies, 36*, 113–124.

Audretsch, D. B., & Keilbach, M. (2004a). Entrepreneurship capital and economic performance. *Regional Studies, 38*, 949–959.

Audretsch, D. B., & Keilbach, M. (2004b). Does entrepreneurship capital matter? *Entrepreneurship Theory and Practice, 28*, 419–430.

Audretsch, D. B., & Keilbach, M. (2004c). Entrepreneurship and regional growth: An evolutionary interpretation. *Journal of Evolutionary Economics, 14*, 605–616.

Audretsch, D. B., & Keilbach, M. (2007). The theory of knowledge spillover entrepreneurship. *Journal of Management Studies, 44*, 1242–1254.

Audretsch, D. B., & Lehmann, E. E. (2005). Does the knowledge spillover theory of entrepreneurship hold for regions? *Research Policy, 34*, 1191–1202.

Audretsch, D. B., & Mahmood, T. (1995). New firm survival: New results using a hazard function. *The Review of Economics and Statistics, 77*, 97–103.

Audretsch, D. B., & Stephan, P. E. (1996). Company-scientist locational links: The case of biotechnology. *American Economic Review, 86*, 641–652.

Audretsch, D. B., & Thurik, A. R. (2001a). What's new about the new economy? Sources of growth in the managed and entrepreneurial economies. *Industrial and Corporate Change, 10*, 267–315.

Audretsch, D. B., & Thurik, A. R. (2001b). *Linking entrepreneurship to growth, OECD science, technology and industry Working Papers, No. 2001/02*. Paris: OECD Publishing.

Audretsch, D. B., & Thurik, A. R. (2004). *A model of the entrepreneurial economy, discussion papers on entrepreneurship, growth and public policy*. Jena: Max Planck Institute.

Audretsch, D. B., & Thurik, A. R. (2010). Capitalism and democracy in the 21st century: From the managed to the entrepreneurial economy. *Journal of Evolutionary Economics, 10*, 17–34.

Audretsch, D. B., Santarelli, E., & Vivarelli, M. (1999). Start-up size and industrial dynamics: Some evidence from Italian manufacturing. *International Journal of Industrial Organization, 17*, 965–983.

Audretsch, D. B., et al. (Eds.). (2002). *Entrepreneurship: Determinants and policies in a European--U.S. comparison*. Boston: Kluwer Academic Publishers.

Audretsch, D. B., Klomp, L., Santarelli, E., & Thurik, A. R. (2004). Gibrat's law: Are the services different? *Review of Industrial Organization, 24*, 301–324.

Audretsch, D. B., Lehmann, E. E., & Warning, S. (2005). University spillovers and new firm location. *Research Policy, 34*, 1113–1122.

Audretsch, D. B., Keilbach, M., & Lehmann, E. E. (2006). *Entrepreneurship and economic growth*. Oxford: Oxford University Press.

Audretsch, D. B., Bönte, W., & Keilbach, M. (2008). Entrepreneurship capital and its impact on knowledge diffusion and economic performance. *Journal of Business Venturing, 23*, 687–698.

Audretsch, D. D., Hülsbeck, M., & Lehmann, E. E. (2012). Regional competitiveness, university spillovers and entrepreneurial activity. *Small Business Economics, 39*, 587–601.

Audretsch, D. B., Lehmann, E. E., Paleari, S., & Vismara, S. (2016). Entrepreneurial finance and technology transfer. *Journal of Technology Transfer, 41*, 1–9.

Braunerhjelm, P., Acs, Z. J., Audretsch, D. B., & Carlsson, B. (2010). The missing link: Knowledge diffusion and entrepreneurship in endogenous growth. *Small Business Economics, 34*, 105–125.

Cancino, C. A., Merigó, J. M., & Coronado, F. C. (2017). Big names in innovation research: A bibliometric overview. *Current Science, 113*, 1507–1518.

Carlsson, B., Acs, Z. J., Audretsch, D. B., & Braunerhjelm, P. (2009). Knowledge creation, entrepreneurship and economic growth: A historical review. *Industrial and Corporate Change, 18*, 1193–1229.

Feldman, M. P., & Audretsch, D. B. (1999). Innovation in cities: Science-based diversity, specialization and localized competition. *European Economic Review, 43*, 409–429.

Gilbert, B. A., Audretsch, D. B., & McDougall, P. P. (2004). The emergence of entrepreneurship policy. *Small Business Economics, 22*, 313–323.

Gilbert, B. A., McDougall, P. P., & Audretsch, D. B. (2006). New venture growth: A review and extension. *Journal of Management, 32*, 926–950.

Gilbert, B. A., McDougall, P. P., & Audretsch, D. B. (2008). Clusters, knowledge spillovers and new venture performance: An empirical examination. *Journal of Business Venturing, 23*, 405–422.

Kuratko, D. F., & Audretsch, D. B. (2009). Strategic entrepreneurship: Exploring different perspectives of an emerging concept. *Entrepreneurship Theory and Practice, 33*, 1–17.

Stuetzer, M., Obschonka, M., Audretsch, D. B., Wyrwich, M., Rentfrow, P. J., Coobes, M., Shaw-Taylor, L., & Satchell, M. (2016). Industry structure, entrepreneurship and culture: An empirical analysis using historical coalfields. *European Economic Review, 86*, 52–72.

Thurik, A. R., Carree, M. A., van Stel, A., & Audretsch, D. B. (2008). Does self-employment reduce unemployment? *Journal of Business Venturing, 23*, 673–686.

Van Eck, N. J., & Waltman, L. (2010). Software survey: VOSviewer, a computer program for bibliometric mapping. *Scientometrics, 84*, 523–538.

Verheul, I., Wennekers, S., Audretsch, D. B., & Thurik, A. R. (2002). An eclectic theory of entrepreneurship: Policies, institutions and cultures. In D. B. Audretsch et al. (Eds.), *Entrepreneurship: determinants and policies in a European-U.S. comparison* (pp. 11–81). Boston: Kluwer Academic Publishers.

Welpe, I. M., Spörrle, M., Grichnik, D., Michl, T., & Audretsch, D. B. (2012). Emotions and opportunities: The interplay of opportunity evaluation, fear, joy, and anger as antecedent of entrepreneurial exploitation. *Entrepreneurship Theory and Practice, 36*, 69–96.

White, H. D. (2001). Authors as citers over time. *Journal of the Association for Information Science and Technology, 52*, 87–108.

Wiklund, J., Davidsson, P., Audretsch, D. B., & Karlsson, C. (2011). The future of entrepreneurship research. *Entrepreneurship Theory and Practice, 35*, 1–9.

David Audretsch: The Capacity to Design and to Influence a Research Agenda

Maria Callejón

Abstract David Audretsch outstanding production has a pervasive influence in Industrial Dynamics analysis as we all know. The present text discus some lines of his research that have spurred particular interest and influenced many academic works inside the wider group of international scholars active in the field of business dynamics. The aspects of David Audretsch extensive works that are mentioned below are: the impact of small firms' dynamics on economic efficiency; firms' start up role in economic growth; turbulence and regularities in industrial structure evolution and the Gibrat approach; interfirm heterogeneity and survival; and policy rationales and its evolution.

Introduction

Few economists have the deep and extensive influence of David Audretsch academic work in the fields of industrial dynamics and entrepreneurship analysis. For at least two decades Audretsch work has been an inspiration and a source of powerful new ideas for junior and senior scholars. Moreover, it is a remarkable characteristic of David Audretsch, his generous disposition to collaborate with other researchers, as his long list of prestigious co-authors demonstrate.

In Audretsch (1995a, b) we find his influential approach to the heterogeneity of new firms. Two clear groups are identified that present high heterogeneity inside each group. On one side it can be found the relatively small group of Schumpeterian innovators that give way to the economic process of "creative destruction" by disruption of previous production ways. On the other side we find the large group of "imitating" or followers new firms seeking to establish themselves in the market (Schumpeter, 1942). The second group corresponds to Audretsch's successful model of the "revolving door" where most exiting business are recent entrants that could not find accommodation due to market barriers or own limitations. The first

---

M. Callejón (✉)
University of Barcelona, Barcelona, Spain
e-mail: maria.callejon@ub.edu

© Springer Nature Switzerland AG 2019
E. E. Lehmann, M. Keilbach (eds.), *From Industrial Organization to Entrepreneurship*, https://doi.org/10.1007/978-3-030-25237-3_19

group fits in the metaphor of "the forest", where incumbent establishments tend to be displaced by new innovative entrants (Audretsch 1995b).

Both the "revolving door" and the "forest" models present conceptual links to the Schumpeter's concept of "creative destruction" in industrial evolution. Both have caught the interest of researchers in the field. Audretsch has opened a window to very fundamental aspects of industrial organization. It is precisely the variety of new entrants and the objectives and incentives propelling them, that constitute a magnet and a research challenge to scholars that feel intellectually intrigued about the consequences of that sheer turbulence in economic behavior. The impact of both kinds of entrepreneurs on economic efficiency and growth are likely very different, even opposed, according to the type of entrants. This crucial fact has given way to a good quantity of high-quality research on the heterogeneity of star-up and exiting firms and, consequently, on the policy rationale of public programs.

In parallel to the divide "innovators" and "followers", Schumpeter observed that innovations may be generated by independent genuine innovators (Mark I), or, be the result of systematic, planned, innovation projects carried out by large companies (Mark II). The dominance of one or another technological regime would depend on the specific industry and, or, the phase of the industry product cycle.

After a long period in the last quarter of the 20th C where young small firms took the lead, it seems that the dominant business model might change again. At present one interesting question would be: is the pattern of industry structure switching again away from the dominance of independent innovative entrepreneurs? Is industry dynamics switching again from a Schumpeter Mark I model to a period of growing concentration better represented by the Schumpeter Mark II model? The huge global market power of the high-tech companies popularly known as FANG (Facebook, Amazon, Netflix and Google) points toward a highly concentrated organization of industry in the years to come. A recent impressive paper by David Audretsch (2018) describes the evolution of the theoretical approach of the Industrial Organization field and also highlights the significant capacity of IO models to capture incipient structural changes and, also, its capacity to analyze the changes of technological trends and the "life cycle" of specific industries.

We are now witnessing a technological phase dominated by the unleashing of strong deep forces that push toward global business concentration and domination. A transition that is not based on the exploitation of scale economies of production and hard investment, like in the past, but based on global disembodied knowledge, unlimited information, and global consumption. The material production is being effectively carried out by automated equipment, and even the management can partially rely on Artificial Intelligence. International commitment to free trade is weakening and this may have an impact on the international division of labor. The Industrial Organization field of analysis has started to consider the new situation and, consequently, we might expect changes in research approaches to firm behavior and to the dynamics of labor reallocation. And, very likely, we can expect new policy approaches.

The "life cycle" model so richly built and documented by Klepper (1996) describes how industries evolve over time. It constitutes another complementary and compatible approach to the "revolving door" model and the "forest" model of industrial structural change: the initial phase of industries is characterized by high entry and exit in a process "trial and error" of the young entrants. With time passing, and the stabilization and standardization of technologies and markets, the industry "matures" and enters in a process of concentration of activity with a smaller number of firms of larger size. If the present big global high-tech companies will reach soon a mature stage, or not, is also a new and interesting area of research for Industrial Organization.

The transition towards concentration taking place at the right side of the size distribution does not imply that entry stops, or even slows down sharply. A significant degree of turbulence is always present at the left side of the size distribution. What probably differs with time is the kind of barriers and "frictions" that affect new ventures (Haltiwanger 2017) mostly in terms of public policy priorities, funding opportunities, recruiting of specialized labor, and the gathering a customer base. All changes are expected to affect the markets, the technological and industry environment for both new and established agents.

Impact

In the European Union, each year between 2008 and 2016, a number of firms equivalent to 20% of all existing firms, were new or had abandoned the markets (Eurostat 2018). The five-year survival rate of firms born in 2010 and still active in 2015 is about 50% in average (Eurostat 2017). A percentage fairly stable through time and space (OECD Stat, 2018).

In United States the rate of business churning is slightly smaller than in Europe (Bartelsman et al. 2005). Other differences observed are that: the rate of mortality of new firms in US is a little lower than in Europe; the surviving new firms in United States experiment higher employment growth than in Europe, and reach a larger average size. One possible reason of the differences might be that entry frictions of regulatory origin are lower in United States, but the most important reason can be the larger United States market size. Even considering those, not so critical, differences, it seems clear that the structural conditions of new firm dynamics is quite similar among developed economies, and this empirical fact leads to hypothesize the presence of some underground forces affecting production structure that are common to most countries with similar degree of development. The discovery of regularities in economic structure and behavior help researchers to feel better grounded, and reinforce the confidence of being in the right track. But this would be true only under the condition that some kind of reliable explanations for the regularities could be hypothesized.

The rates of employment reallocation in US are also notable. Calculations made for the period 1977–2005 (Haltiwanger et al. 2008) report that the mean annual rate of new job creation stands at 18%, while the equivalent rate for job destruction reaches 16%. It means a reassignment of 34% of labor force to achieve a net increase in employment of less than 2%. Of the new jobs created each year, 7% correspond to jobs generated by new start-ups, and the rest is employment originated by the growth of incumbents. And the destruction of employment is equally high. Of the 16% of jobs lost on average each year, around 6% are due to exiting firms while the rest is attributable to the reduction of employment in incumbents.

Economic prosperity has been related with entrepreneurship not only in many studies but and also among public opinion. Governments in Europe and US have listened to expert advice and to reports of economic organizations and have adopted a fair number of public programs. The existing literature mentions various reasons why the rate of new business creation is positively associated to economic growth. It is often argued that a dynamic society is less averse to risk and presents a greater proportion of individuals that prefer self-employment to dependent work (European Commission 2015). In Schumpeter view the new "innovative" entrepreneurs keep the capitalist engine in motion by discovering new products, new production processes, new markets, new methods of transportation and new forms of industrial organization. And, as we saw earlier, Schumpeter also mentioned the high numbers of "followers" that try to reproduce what they observe and learn, so they disseminate and generalize innovations to the wider economy.

The expected important effects derived of the, non-trivial, amount of business reallocation translates into enhanced academic interest in the theoretical analysis and the policy formulations of this intriguing reality. One discussion relates to the quantity of reallocation the economies have to accept in order to generate enough innovation. Or if it would be possible to obtain the benefits of innovation and productivity improvements with less churning and less social costs.

The amount of reallocation is not the only item of discussion. There is not agreement about the main source of innovation. Most accepted literature argues that new firms are among the main sources of innovation, employment and economic growth (Audretsch 2001, Acs & Audretsch 1988, and Audretsch and Thurik 2001). Other scholars (Hsieh and Klenow 2018) interpret that most innovation and productivity growth is originated by incumbents. This discussion, based on empirical analysis, reminds us of the Schumpeter Mark I and Mark II models.

Local governments, in many instances, have also taken a side in the discussion. They view self-employment initiatives as a "steam valve" when the market does not absorb a part of the labor supply. If some potential job-seekers try to create their own business, this is positively viewed by policymakers. As it has been mentioned earlier, in the last two or three decades, governments and institutions have been adopting programs, or disseminated policy advice reports, to spur the creation of start-ups. Among them the European Commission, OECD, and World Bank. It is not clear if those institutional efforts have accomplished significant results. At least in Spain it would be convenient to obtain more data and information from the public agencies concerned that have been running entrepreneurial programs.

The formalization of a neoclassical model that links entrepreneurship and growth has been done by Audretsch and Keilbach (2004). Their paper includes an empirical model where entrepreneurship capital – measured as the rate of start-ups relative to existing firms – appears as an input factor, together with labor and physical capital, within a neoclassical production function linking factors to output. They estimate the empirical model the for German regions, and find that entrepreneurial capital is a significant and important variable to explain the growth of output and productivity. In another work by Audretsch et al. (2006) it is demonstrated that entrepreneurs in advanced economies contribute to productivity with the generation of knowledge spillovers. Under this spillovers approach, the crucial role of new entrepreneurs is not to generate "creative destruction". To the contrary, they are significant contributors to "creative construction", that is, their activity improves the economic environment.

Callejon and Segarra (1999) and Segarra and Callejon (2002) have estimated a production function, with data from Spanish regions, allowing for entrepreneurship as an argument. The results show that both firm entry and exit rates appear positively related with productivity. Empirical analysis in the field is not easy. Some research works reach more ambiguous results, and do not show a clear positive association between firm start-up and output or productivity, and some others even find negative relationship between entry and growth. Given that each empirical test uses a different data set, there is also a diversity in findings and comparisons are not straightforward. But, as it is continuously remembered, new firms are highly heterogenous. Studies that segment entrants in different categories by size or activity or growth usually find a diversity of results.

Entrepreneurial Intensity and Economic Development

Business incubators and technological parks have been first line programs in many local and regional public agencies. The problem, as already mentioned, is that it is not clear enough if policy makers can base their programs on a sound numerical or qualitative target for business creation and, eventually, which should be the benchmark. How much entry and churning are optimal, or simply good? There has been some good research in this area.

A pioneering estimation by Carree et al. (2002) tried to discover the connection between the rate of business ownership and income levels over time in an OECD group of developed countries. Two different fits of a relationship in L shape and U shape were estimated. The results showed that, with a long-term tendency represented by a L shape, the proportion of business owners would not grow with rising income levels but rather would tend to become flat towards an asymptote at around 7%. The U-shaped fit, in its growing segment, showed that in 25 years the proportion of business owners would reach 12%, in average, in de group de developed countries. For United States specifically the point of stabilization would be reached at around 10%.

Wennekers et al. (2005) have estimated the relationship between entrepreneurship and the level of economic development. They use the rate of nascent entrepreneurship calculated in the Global Entrepreneurship Monitor (GEM 2002) for 36 countries, and the level of income per capita, to estimate a quadratic fit (U shape).

Not surprisingly they find that nascent opportunity entrepreneurship is positively related to income, and that necessity entrepreneurship is negatively related to the level of income. The result is, again, compatible with the Schumpeterian notion of innovative entrepreneurs that improve productivity and replicative entrepreneurs that do not.

In their empirical paper, Wennekers et al. suggest that there is some kind of "natural rate" of nascent entrepreneurship that is determined by the level of economic development. In addition, they argue that, for advanced countries, the exploitation of scientific findings is a good policy, and for developing economies it can be better to exploit scale economies and to promote management skills and education.

In a complementary direction with Wennekers et al., further research (van Praag and van Stel 2013) finds that the top performing business owners are responsible for most of the value creation of business owners. It is found that better educated people usually run larger firms. This would be a certain evidence in favor of policy programs targeting skilled entrepreneurs, or providing better skills to entrepreneurs. Additional research has been devoted at the formation of "clusters" of small business and its exploitation of external economies (Audretsch et al. 2008).

Turbulence and Regularities in the Size Distribution of Firms: Gibrat Law

Researchers and academicians in industry dynamics have been quite puzzled by the permanent coexistence between turbulence at the individual level, and stability of the size distribution of firms in industry structures. One the possible mathematical explanations to this regularity is Gibrat's Law. Robert Gibrat (1931) rule of proportionate growth states that the highly asymmetric distribution observed in firm sizes – a multitude of small firms and just a few large ones – can be explained if the growth of each firm in each time period is proportional to its size. The result would be identical if the growth of each firm follows a random pattern. However, as Caves (1998) aptly observes "…although the importance of these facts for economic behavior is manifest, their development has not been theory-driven". And Gibrat's Law is still an empirical regularity in search of sound theoretical justification (Gabaix 2009).

Several good surveys about the intra-industry dynamics of firms, Ericson and Pakes (1995), Geroski (1995), Sutton (1997) and Caves (1998) have concluded that the empirical evidence does not support Gibrat's Law. But as David Audretsch has pointed out, most of the empirical estimations are based on the manufacturing sector. Different studies find that in the services sector Gibrat's Law holds Audretsch et al. (2004) and Lotti et al. (2009). As in other analysis on the highly complex behavior of firms and industries, it is difficult to reach unambiguous results. And as in other blurred problems we may not expect that researchers will give up of finding a better explanation of the coexistence of turbulence and stability of the distribution of firm sizes, and consequently we can expect that research in this field will continue.

Interfirm Heterogeneity and Survival

The concept of turbulence and the concept of the "revolving door" imply that exit and mortality is extremely high among new business (Bartelsman et al. 2013). We should remind that less than 50% firms survive more than 5 years (EC 201). Even if exiting firms are very small in terms of employment and sunk capital, a doubt remains about the social cost of such a "waste" of efforts and resources, if it is assumed that exiting firms make losses.

One of the firsts studies in mortality based in a hazard function was due to Audretsch and Mahmood (1995). An application of the hazard function estimation to Spain can be found in Segarra and Callejon (2002) and in Callejon and Ortun (2009). Both pieces of research find that capital investment, employment numbers and innovation effort impact favorably on survival. But, surprisingly, R+D expenditures do not. One possible explanation might be that, because the benefits of R+D efforts confront internal and external frictions and takes time to mature, many firms do not survive the "death valley" crossing. It is a frequent observation that the first innovative entrant in a given business does not survive or thrive, but the second one finds better opportunities probably because they count with better information. From the social point of view, the early mortality of new tech business is less damaging if the commercial knowledge passes to other agents are able to exploit it.

Competition in the market, and institutional frictions, may form temporary barriers to the survival and accommodation of new entrants (Haltiwanger 2017). It takes some time for a new firm to master its market conditions, and to find its customer group. To the findings of Hisieh and Klenow (2018) that incumbents contribute to innovation and productivity in a larger degree than new entrants, Haltiwanger highlights the effect of frictions that new entrants have to learn to master before they can operate efficiently.

Heterogeneity is most prevalent in the case of young high growth firms or "gazelles". According to Decker et al. (2016) "...it is the very high growth of a relatively small number of young firms that accounts for the high mean net growth rate of young, surviving firms and the long-lasting contribution of startups and young firms to job creation". Decker et al. (2017) also argue that the pace of business dynamism and entrepreneurship in the United States has declined in the last two decades, and that this slow down affects particularly the growth of young firms. If there is a relationship, and what kind of relationship, between the apparent lower dynamism of high-tech young firms in US and the trends toward concentration has still to be seen.

The fact that knowledge intensive startups confront significant hurdles means that the economic system configuration is important. Biotechnological start-ups use the notion of "time to the market" to describe how advanced are their lab tests, and when they expect to start to commercialize its innovation. In the meantime, before commercialization they can secure some money from public or private venture capital funds. In those business activities like biotechnology where research becomes innovation immediately, or like in pharmaceuticals, or internet-based projects, sometimes it is sufficient a "proof of concept" from the would-be high technology entrepreneur to obtain some initial funding. In this context Haltiwanger objections to Hsieh and Klenow would make sense. The different institutional and market receptivity to innovations can make a difference in survival and, hence, on the innovation and productivity addition of new entrants to the economy.

Policy Rationales and Its Evolution

Inside the academic world the discussion continues about the consequences of firm churning and the rationale for industrial policy programs for new firms (Asturias et al. 2018; Bartelsman et al. 2013; Hsieh-Klenow 2018; Acemoglu et al. 2017; Antony et al. 2017; Haltiwanger 2017, Audretsch and Callejon 2007).

Most policy recommendations related to incentives to new entrants point to the highly heterogenous profiles of agents, and the need to establish selective programs that target high quality, knowledge based new firms, and do not stimulate low quality startups. In this last case, pure market selection can optimal for the economy (Santarelli and Vivarelli 2002).

David Audretsch (2018) has analyzed how policy programs have changed from antitrust – or nationalizations in Europe – to regulation of natural monopolies and big corporations in the years previous to the 70's. And how, in the following decades, policymakers turned their focus towards innovation and knowledge dissemination, operated by new entrants. Preferred schemes were the Bayh–Dole Act, science or research parks, universities spin-off programs, incubators, and local development policies. David Audretsch own words:

> Perhaps one reason why a New Industrial Organization keeps emerging with remarkable temporal regularity is because the policy issues of the day continue to evolve over time. That the field of industrial organization from just a few years earlier typically seems antiquated to the next generation of scholars, may less reflect the repudiation of incorrect knowledge and methods by correct ones and more reflect a discipline whose inherent value is based on the evolution of public policy issues.

In agreement with David Audretsh thoughts it is reasonable to think at industrial policy, and entrepreneurship policy, and even to any other economic policy, not as a given recipe but as a set of recommendations based on the analysis of a changing reality. Policy recommendations will be as good as the underlying analysis be correct. In this aspect Audretsch opinion is positive towards the capacity of Industrial Organization to understand the changing reality.

The next step in policy development would be to discuss Political Economy considerations to evaluate the capacity and autonomy of governments and influential institutions to design technically solvent policy programs (Acemoglu et al. 2017), and to implement them. This is a very problematic issue that affect with different degrees of severity to each country, although the global environment has tremendous impact on all country's decisions.

References

Acemoglu, D., Akcigit, U., Alp, H., Bloom, N., & Kerr, W. R. (2017). *Innovation, reallocation and growth.* NBER working paper 18993. Available at http://www.nber.org/papers/w18993

Acs, Z., & Audretsh, D. B. (1988). Innovation in large and small firms. An empirical analysis. *American Economic Review, 78*(4), 678–690.

Antony, J., Torben, K., & Lehmann, E. (2017). Productive and harmful entrepreneurship in a knowledge economy. *Small Business Economics, 49,* 189–202.

Asturias, J., Hur, S., Kehoe, T., Ruhl, K. (2018). *Firm entry and exit and aggregate growth.* Federal Reserve Bank of Minneapolis, Research Department Staff Report 544.

Audretsch, D. (1995a). The propensity to exit and innovation. *Review of Industrial Organization, 10*(5), 589–605.

Audretsch, D. (1995b). *Innovation and industry evolution.* Cambridge: The MIT Press.

Audretsch, D. (2001). Research Issues Relating to Structure, Competition, and Performance of Small Technology-Based Firms, Small Business Economics, 16(1), 37–51.

Audretsch, D. (2018). Industrial organization and the organization of industries: Linking industry structure to economic performance. *Review of Industrial Organization, 52,* 603–620.

Audretsch, D., & Callejon, M. (2007). La política industrial actual. *Revista de Economía Industrial, 363,* 33–46.

Audretsch, D., & Keilbach, M. (2004). Entrepreneurship capital and economic performance. *Regional Studies, 38,* 949–959.

Audretsch, D., & Mahmood, T. (1995). New firm survival: New results using a hazard function. *The Review of Economics and Statistics, 77,* 97–103.

Audretsch, D. & Thurik, R. (2001). *Linking entrepreneurship and growth.* OECD STI working paper 2001/2. Available at https://www.oecd-ilibrary.org/science-and-technology/linking-entrepreneurship-to-growth_736170038056, https://doi.org/10.1787/736170038056

Audretsch, D., Callejon, M., & Aranguren, M. J. (2008). Chapter 5, Entrepreneurship, small firms and selfemployment. In D. Parrilli, P. Bianchi, & R. Sugden (Eds.), *High technology, productivity and networks. A systemic approach to SME development* (pp. 117–137). New York: Palgrave Macmillan.

Audretsch, D., Keilbach, M., & Lehmann, E. (2006). *Entrepreneurship and economic growth.* Oxford: Oxford University Press.

Audretsch, D., Klomp, L., Santarelli, E., & Thurik, A. R. (2004). Gibrat's law: Are services different? *Review of Industrial Organization, 24,* 301–324.

Bartelsman, E., Scarpetta, S., & Schivardi, F. (2005). Comparative analysis of firm demographics and survival: Evidence from micro-level sources in OECD countries. *Industrial and Corporate Change, 14*(3), 365–391.

Bartelsman, E., Scarpetta, S., & Schivardi, F. (2013). Cross-country differences in productivity: The role of allocation and selection. *American Economic Review, 103*(1), 306–334.

Callejon, M. & Ortun, V. (2009). *The black box of business dynamics.* XREAP working papers, no. 2009–7. University of Barcelona. Available at SSRN: https://ssrn.com/abstract=1480235 https://doi.org/10.2139/ssr.1480235

Callejon, M., & Segarra, A. (1999). Business dynamics and efficiency in industries and regions, the case of Spain. *Small Business Economics, 13,* 253–271.

Carree, M., van Steel, A.,Thurik, R. & Wennekers, S. (2002). Economic development and business ownership: an analysis using data of 23 countries in the period 1976-1996, Small Business Economics, 19 (3), 271–290.

Caves, R. E. (1998). Industrial organization and new findings on the turnover and mobility of firms. *Journal of Economic Literature, 36*(4), 1947–1982.

Decker, R. A., Haltiwanger, J., Jarmin, R. S., & Miranda, J. (2016). Where has all the skewness gone. The decline of high-growth young firms in the US. *European Economic Review, 86,* 4–23.

Decker, R. A., Haltiwanger, J., Jarmin, R. S., & Miranda, J. (2017). Declining dynamism, allocative efficiency, and the productivity slowdown. *American Economic Review, 107*(5), 322–326.

Ericson, R., & Pakes, A. (1995). Markov perfect industry dynamics: A framework for empirical work. *The Review of Economic Studies, 62*(1), 1–17.

European Commission, (2015), Flash Eurobarometer 283, EU Open Data Portal. Available at http://data.europa.eu/88u/dataset/S765_283.

Eurostat. (2017). *Business demography statistics, 2017* https://ec.europa.eu/eurostat/web/structural-business-statistics/entrepreneurship/business-demography

Eurostat. (2018). Business demography statistics. Statistics Explained https://ec.europa.eu/eurostat/statistics-explained/index.php?title=Business_demography_statistics

Gabaix, X. (2009). Power laws in economics and finance. *Annual Review of Economics, 1*, 255–249.

Geroski, P. A. (1995). What do we know about entry? *International Journal of Industrial Organization, 13*(4), 421–440.

Gibrat, R. (1931). Les inegalités économiques. Paris: Librairie du Recueil Sirey.

Global Entrepreneurship Monitor, GEM. (2002). Available at https://www.gemconsortium.org

Haltiwanger, J. (2017). *Comments on "The Reallocation Myth" by Hsieh and Klenow (2017)*. Mimeo. Available at http://econweb.umd.edu/~haltiwan/Comments_on_Hsieh_Klenow_Aug_22_2017.pdf. Accessed in 30 Aug 2018.

Haltiwanger, J., Jarmin, R., Miranda, J. (2008). Business Formation and Dynamics by Business Age. US Census Bureau. Available at: http://www.census.gov/library/publications/2008/adrm/Business-Formation-and-Dynamics-by-Business-Age.html.

Hsieh, C-T., & Klenow, P. J. (2018). *The reallocation myth*. CES 18–19. Discussion papers, EU Census Bureau.

Klenow, P. (2018). *Reply to Haltiwanger remarks on reallocation myth*. Available at http://klenow.com/Reply_to_Haltiwanger_Remarks_on_Reallocation_Myth.pdf

Klepper, S. (1996). Entry, exit, growth, and innovation over the product life cycle. *American Economic Review, 86*(3), 562–583.

Lotti, F., Santarelli, E., & Vicarelli, M. (2009). Defending Gibrat's law as a long-run regularity. *Small Business Economics, 32*(1), 31–44.

OECD Stat. (2018). *SDBS business demography indicators* (ISIC Rev. 4). Available at https://stats.oecd.org/Index.aspx?DataSetCode=SDBS_BDI_ISIC4

Santarelli, E., & Vivarelli, M. (2002). Is subsidizing entry an optimal policy? *Industrial and Corporate Change, 11*(1), 39–52.

Schumpeter, J. A. (1994). *[1942]. Capitalism, socialism and democracy*. London: Routledge.

Segarra, A., & Callejon, M. (2002). New firms survival and market turbulence: New evidence from Spain. *Review of Industrial Organization, 20*, 1–14.

Sutton, J. (1997). Gibrat's legacy. *Journal of Economic Literature, 35*, 40–59.

Van Praag, M., & van Stel, A. (2013). The more business owners, the merrier? The role of tertiary education. *Small Business Economics, 41*(2), 335–357.

Wennekers, S., van Wennekers, A., Thurik, R., & Reynolds, P. (2005). Nascent entrepreneurship and the level of economic development. *Small Business Economics, 24*(3), 293–309.

Education, Human Capital Spillovers and Productivity: Evidence from Swedish Firm Level Production Functions

Johan E. Eklund and Lars Pettersson

Abstract David Audretsch has made significant contributions to our understanding of the role of knowledge spillovers for innovations and growth. This paper follows this line of research in examining the link between education, human capital spillovers and productivity. Human capital spillovers arise when the presence of individuals with high levels of human capital makes other workers more productive. If higher education is associated with human capital spillovers, a social return to education is generated. We use firm-level production functions to estimate the social returns to higher education in Sweden. The data include more than 50,000 Swedish firms and cover the period from 2001 to 2010. This was a period when Sweden experienced a rapid regional expansion of higher education, and the share of Swedish workforce with higher education has increased dramatically over the past decades. We find economically significant spillover effects from highly educated workers and that a 1 % increase in the share of educated workers is associated with a 0.4–1.0% increase in productivity. When controlling for university-based R&D and business services, the spillover effect is significantly reduced. We also find an economically significant decline in the spillover effect over the 10 year period. According to our estimations, the spillover is positive at the beginning of the period and gradually diminishes by the end of the period, such that we no longer find any significant spillover effect. We interpret this as marginally diminishing social returns to education. The results have policy implications for higher education (We gratefully acknowledge financial support from the Marianne and Marcus Wallenberg foundation and the Kamprad family foundation. We also grateful for the valuable comments provided by Pontus Braunerhjelm, Gunnar Eliasson and Hulya Ulku. Peter S. Karlsson has provided valuable statistical assistance).

J. E. Eklund (✉)
Swedish Entrepreneurship Forum, Jönköping International Business School and Blekinge Institute of Technology, Jönköping, Sweden
e-mail: johan.eklund@entreprenorskapsforum.se

L. Pettersson
Jönköping International Business School, Jönköping, Sweden
e-mail: lars.pettersson@ju.se

© Springer Nature Switzerland AG 2019
E. E. Lehmann, M. Keilbach (eds.), *From Industrial Organization to Entrepreneurship*, https://doi.org/10.1007/978-3-030-25237-3_20

Introduction

David Audretsch has made significant contributions to our understanding of the role of knowledge spillovers for innovation and growth, particularly regarding the entrepreneurial process entailed in knowledge spillovers. Audretsch and Feldman (1996) examine the link between industrial clusters, geographical concentration and knowledge externalities. For a review of knowledge spillovers and the geography of innovation, see Audretsch and Feldman (2004). This paper follows this line of research by examining the link between regional levels of educational attainment, human capital spillovers and firm-level productivity. In particular, we use this approach in an attempt to estimate the social return to education, which has important implications for educational policy.

Education is also frequently assumed to increase human capital (e.g., Becker 1964). Human capital and education are therefore important for economic outcomes and have often been highlighted as important determinants of economic growth (see, e.g., Nelson and Phelps (1966)). Mankiw et al. (1992) argue that cross-country differences in human capital may explain income disparities. In endogenous growth models, human capital is an important component. Lucas (1988), for example, argued that productivity depends on skills and that human capital is associated with external returns, while Romer (1990) argued that societies with more skilled workforces generate more ideas and therefore grow faster. Jacobs (1970) argued that citizens drive growth because they enable the exchange of ideas, which suggests that human capital is likely to be associated with positive external effects (social returns to education). If being around and interacting with educated people makes other people more productive, this leads to positive human capital externalities or human capital spillover effects (see, e.g., Moretti 2004a; Acemoglu and Angrist 2000, Audretsch and Feldman 2004).

This paper estimates the human capital spillover effects, i.e., social returns to education, in Sweden for the period from 2001–2010.[1] This is a period when the Swedish labor market experienced dramatic changes, as did the labor markets of most developed nations. During the last two decades, the number of employed and highly educated workers has risen sharply, and during the period from 2001–2010, the share of educated workers in Sweden increased from approximately 30% to approximately 39%. Part of the explanation for this expansion is an increase in the number of regional universities and university colleges, which has been viewed as an important contributing factor to regional development. In 1977, Sweden had 6 institutions for higher education. In 2010, this had increased to over 20 institutions of higher education. Much of the expansion has taken place outside the metropolitan regions of Sweden and has been part of a regional economic development policy (for a review of the expansion of higher education in Sweden, see Anderson et al. 2004). However, the economic effects of this expansion are uncertain. By international standards, Sweden has low private returns on education (among the

---

[1] The time period is also characterized by a boom in the economy that ended in the last half of 2008, with a share recession in 2009. This has influenced our choice of stochastic frontier model and not using a regular panel model.

lowest in the OECD areas), which makes the potential human capital spillover effects and external returns to higher education important from a policy perspective. Social returns to education may justify public subsidies for education.

During the past decades, the capacity of the Swedish system for higher education has expanded dramatically. From the early 1990s until 2012, student enrollment increased by more than 100%. See Table 1 for the levels of education in the Swedish workforce (Eklund and Petersson 2019) (Fig. 1).

The number of degrees awarded followed a similar pattern, and a number of new universities and university colleges were established during this period. The expansion of the system for higher education followed a deep economic crisis that Sweden experienced in the early 1990s. One of the responses to the crisis and the high unemployment numbers that immediately followed the crisis was to expand the educational system. This strategy came from insights in economics that human capital and knowledge are central to economic growth and important for employment opportunities. Education has been thought to influence productivity in two distinct ways: first, in a direct manner by making workers more productive, increasing marginal productivity and wages and second, in an indirect manner by generating knowledge spillovers. The argument behind knowledge spillovers is that firms in regions (or cities) with a high level of educational attainment are more productive because of spillovers between firms. In the literature, there are, in principle, two types of spillovers between firms: spillovers between firms in the same industry (Marshall-Arrow-Romer spillovers) and spillovers between firms in different industries (so-called Jacobs spillovers) (Glaeser et al. 1992). We estimate the latter type. Given the strong expansion of higher education in Sweden, we are also interested in how these effects evolved over time? In order to allow technology and technological efficiency to vary over time, we also use stochastic frontier models. We find significant external returns to education in the beginning of the period, but marginally diminishing and insignificant returns by the end of period.

Human Capital Externalities and Social Return to Education

A number of studies have tried to estimate the economic effects of spillovers generated by education by looking at the wages of individuals that share the same characteristics, but work in different cities or regions. See, for example: Rauch (1993), Acemoglu and Angrist (2000), Ciccone and Peri (2002) and Moretti (2004b). Rauch (1993) finds that a one-year increase in average education leads to a 3% wage-increase. An alternative approach is to look at productivity effects arising at the firm or plant level (see Moretti 2004a). This paper follows the second approach and estimates human capital spillovers by estimating the effect on firm productivity.[2]

---

[2]There are a large number of agglomeration studies that look at spatial concentration and its economic effects on productivity. The core idea is that agglomerations of production factors (people or human capital) enhance productivity. For evidence using the estimates of productivity effects, see Ciccone and Hall (1996), Henderson (2003) and Moretti (2004a).

Table 1 Human capital spillovers in local labor market regions

	Cobb-Douglas, Sij per local labor market region									
	2001	2002	2003	2004	2005	2006	2007	2008	2009	2010
Sij	0.767	0.616	0.478	0.444	0.502	0.451	0.404	0.432	0.413	0.378
	(0.056)	(0.055)	(0.098)	(0.080)	(0.058)	(0.070)	(0.051)	(0.476)	(0.053)	(0.040)
L_low	0.579	0.586	0.587	0.596	0.603	0.593	0.593	0.590	0.601	0.608
	(0.017)	(0.012)	(0.013)	(0.013)	(0.013)	(0.018)	(0.014)	(0.015)	(0.016)	(0.015)
L_high	0.395	0.389	0.402	0.420	0.423	0.437	0.449	0.455	0.465	0.462
	(0.025)	(0.023)	(0.029)	(0.031)	(0.029)	(0.032)	(0.031)	(0.034)	(0.031)	(0.028)
K	0.151	0.140	0.135	0.139	0.130	0.127	0.118	0.110	0.102	0.095
	(0.003)	(0.003)	(0.004)	(0.004)	(0.003)	(0.003)	(0.004)	(0.005)	(0.003)	(0.003)
Industry dummy	Yes	Yes	Yes	Yes	Yes	Yes	Yes	Yes	Yes	Yes
No. obs.	44630	46802	47639	51338	53245	55150	56763	56365	54770	57453
R2	0.79	0.79	0.76	0.77	0.78	0.77	0.77	0.77	0.76	0.76
Restriction $(\beta_L + \beta_H + \beta_K = 1)$	No	No	No	No	No	No	No	No	No	No

Robust standard errors clustered over labor market regions in brackets

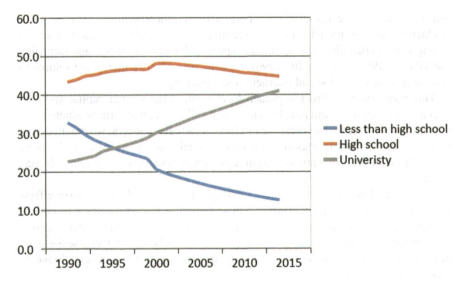

Fig. 1 Educational attainment of individuals aged 25–64 years old 1990–2014. (Source: Statistics Sweden (17))

Our approach is similar to Moretti (2004a), but we use a more extensive dataset that allows for more detailed analysis, particularly the analysis of the evolution over time, and that still allows comparison of the results for Sweden with Moretti's results for the US.

Studies have also found that educated workers tend to migrate to areas with relatively educated workforces, which also are the areas with higher returns (e.g., Borjas et al. (1992). Bhagwati and Rodriguez (1975) have suggested that this migration of educated workers away from areas with low levels of human capital constitute an important barrier for development in many countries). As Acemoglu (1996) points out, the underlying argument is that low levels of human capital may create a vicious circle trough socially increasing returns and vice versa.[3] A number of empirical studies have also shown that human capital variables explain cross-country variation in growth rates and investment (e.g., Barro 1991, Benhabib and Spiegel 1994).

Alfred Marshal (1890) recognized that workers might learn from each other through social interaction and thereby become more productive. Lucas (1988) argued in a seminal paper that human capital spillovers may be significant enough to account for long-run income differentials across rich and poor countries.

Despite the economic importance and significant policy implications, the empirical evidence on human capital spillovers remains relatively limited. In the literature, several different mechanisms for human capital spillovers have been suggested. Marshall (1890) argued that social interactions among workers within an industry

---

[3] Acemoglu (1996) argue that the existing evidence on socially increasing returns on human capital may be interpreted as social increasing return on capital accumulation. It is beyond the scope of this paper to distinguish between the two effects. See Moretti (2004a) for a discussion.

and same location creates learning opportunities and thereby makes workers more productive. In some models, it is the exchange of ideas through social interactions among workers that gives rise to human capital spillovers (Jovanovic and Rob 1989 and Glasear 1999). Acemoglu (1996) suggests that socially increasing returns to scale may arise without social interaction and learning.

This paper takes a direct approach to estimating the human capital spillover effects by examining if and how human capital spillovers affect firm productivity. If the presence of educated workers creates human capital spillovers, we would expect firms that are located in regions with relatively educated workforces to be more productive than firms that are located in regions with relatively low levels of human capital.

This method was used by Moretti (2004a), who examined the spillover effects for US manufacturing plants. Moretti's main finding is that as the share of college graduates in a city increases by 1%, the productivity increases by 0.5–0.6.[4] This is an economically significant spillover, suggesting that policies that increase the share of educated workers will increase productivity of firms in these cities, ultimately making them more competitive.

Data and Variables

We estimate firm level production functions with micro data obtained from Statistics Sweden. The data has been collected from Statistics Sweden and covers all firms and individuals from 2001 until 2010. In other words, we have more or less the full population of firms in a single location. The data does not include firms with multiple plants in different regions. After removing inactive firms and firms with no employees, the dataset has approximately 500,000 firm-year observations.

We define skilled labor as workers with some sort of post-high school degree. This group includes all individuals with college or university degrees at any level. Unskilled labor is defined as individuals who have not attained a college or university degree.[5] As a measure of the capital stock, we use total assets.

In addition to this information we have information on where firms are located (region and county). There are several possible regional subdivisions. At the finest level, we use municipalities with the smallest possible regional subdivision. There are 290 counties, which are local administrative units. At the next level, we use functional labor market regions. These regions do not have any administrative meaning, but are instead based on commuting and traveling patterns. Work and commuting patterns to and from workplaces define these regions. The counties are

---

[4] Morreti's (2004a) estimates are robust to different assumptions of technology, omitted variables and various other specifications.

[5] Further decomposition is possible; however, this drastically reduces the sample. For empirical reasons, we therefore abstain from further decomposition.

nested in these functional regions. When appropriate, we adjust the variables for inflation with CPI (Monetary values in 2000 prices).

An important caveat is that we must exclude firms that have activities in more than one region, since we are unable to identify productivity at establishment level. This also means that the economically most important firms in Sweden are excluded from the data, because they have multiple plants spread out in different regions, which makes it impossible to estimate production functions which include human capital spillover effects.

Individual Data

For individuals, we have information on their educational attainment. This means that we can identify their number of years of schooling, type of education and highest degree achieved. Since we are interested in assessing the effect of higher education in particular, we identify two types of workers: those with low education which corresponds to no more than a high school degree (a maximum of 12 years of education) and educated workers that have a tertiary education. In most cases, a tertiary education correspond to some kind of university or university college education.

While further decomposition is possible, this will cause empirical problems due to the fact that as the number of factors increase in the production function, the number of observations decrease rapidly. We also use information on industry at the three-digit level.[6]

Regional Units of Analysis

In order to identify and estimate the size of spillovers, it is important to determine the regional level at which the spillovers arise. We use two different regional levels in our analysis: county level and labor market regions. These regions are nested in each other. Sweden has 290 counties. The counties are administrative units and are often smaller than what can be regarded as functional local labor market regions. Based on commuting and employment patterns, Sweden is also divided into 72 local labor market regions. Presumably, the most appropriate unit of any regional economic analysis is the local labor market region.

---

[6]Depending on the analysis, we use either SIC at either the 2 or 3 digit level. When necessary, to economize on the degrees of freedom, we use the SIC2 digit.

Theoretical and Empirical Approach

To estimate the social returns to education, we begin by assuming following Cobb-Douglas production function:

$$Y_{ijr} = A_{ijr} \prod_{k=1}^{N} X_{k,ijr}^{\beta_k} \qquad (1)$$

where Y_{ijr} is output of firm i, belonging to industry j (3 digit), in region r. The term Xk is production factor k. We distinguish between two factors of production: (1) the number of skilled workers with a post-high school education; (2) the number of unskilled workers (no post-high school education) and capital. We assume that the total factor productivity, A_{ijr}, is a function of the share of skilled labor in the region, but not active in same industry as the firm ($i \notin j$). Taking the logarithms on both sides of (1) yields following linear function:

$$\ln Y_{ijr} = \ln A_{ijr} + \sum_{k=1}^{N} \beta_k \ln X_{k,ijr} \qquad (2)$$

Further, by assuming that total factor productivity depends on regional educational attainment, we have:

$$\ln A_{ijr} = \gamma S_{-jr} + \varepsilon_{ijr} \qquad (3)$$

where $\underline{S}_{-jr}$ is the share of skilled labor (tertiary education) among workers in region r with the exception of workers in industry j (the industry in which firm i operates), and ε is an unobserved productivity shock. The index represents the large region in which the firm is located. Note that this approach is functionally equivalent to a multilevel approach. Finally, by substituting (3) into (2) we have the following linear production function:

$$lnY_{ijr} = S_{-jr} + \sum_{k=1}^{N} \beta_k X_{k,ijr} + \varepsilon_{ijr} \qquad (4)$$

One concern with (4) is that any correlation between S_{jr} and any of the error terms will result in biased estimates of γ.

Our basic empirical specification, based on (4), is as follows:

$$lnY_{ijr} = \gamma \underline{S}_{-jr} + \beta_{LH} lnL_{ijr}^{high} + \beta_{LL} lnL_{ijr}^{low} + \beta_K lnK_{ijr} + \varepsilon_{ijr} \qquad (5)$$

We also experiment with additional controls, such as time-specific and regional effects. Further, we also look into other specifications of (4), such as the translog and stochastic frontier models.

Empirical Estimates of Human Capital Spillovers

As a first step in the analysis, we estimate cross-sectional production functions, and this setting allows the technology to vary over time. The results are presented in Table 1. Including industry dummy variables controls for industry specific effects at the three-digit industry level. We estimate regressions both with and without the restriction that the beta-coefficients to sum to one,[7] i.e. assumption of constant returns to scale. To adjust the standard errors for the presence of clustered errors and heteroscedasticity, we have used robust standard errors clustered over regions. We find significant human capital spillover effects both at the metropolitan and county levels. The spillover effects in counties and labor market regions and at county level seem to be similar to each other, which one should expect if the regions accurately reflects the functional labor market region. Thus, we only report results for regions. See appendix for further estimations. The spillover effect appears to be diminishing over time. For the 2001 cross-section, the estimates are in the range 0.7–0.9, whereas for 2010, the estimates are in the range 0.4–0.6. This means that an increase by 1% of the regional share of educated worker corresponded with a 0.7–0.9% increase in firm productivity in the beginning of the period and diminished to 0.4–0.6 at the end of the period. Thus, on average similar to Moretti's results. This can be interpreted as evidence that social return to education is marginally diminishing. In economic terms, this means that the social return on education is about 30–40% lower in 2010 than it was a decade earlier.

As a robustness check, we also estimate translog production functions. The translog estimations do not differ in any substantial way from our Cobb-Douglas specifications. These results are reported in Appendix 1. And these results indicates a somewhat less degree in decline over time. Further, we have estimated the spillover effect at both local labor market level as well as at the county level. To lift some of the restrictions of the Cobb-Douglas production function, we also estimate Eq. 4 as a translog equation (see appendix). However, these estimations are plagued with multicollinearity problems due to the number of parameters and cross-product terms that need to be estimated. We therefore center the variable before we run the regressions. Industry dummies have no significant impact on the estimated coefficients. There are a number of empirical and theoretical challenges that must be addressed when estimating the production function. A residual analysis shows that the residuals do not follow a normal distribution. Instead, the residuals appear to be composed of two components, which makes conventional panel data estimation inappropriate. Further, from a more theoretical perspective, there is reason to expect technological changes over time, and we cannot expect all firms to be consistently operating at the efficiency frontier. A more realistic assumption is that firms may occasionally be producing below maximum output. This is actually a reasonable explanation for the non-normal distribution of the residuals. Failing to take these

---

[7]Adding this constraint does not significantly alter the results. We therefore only report results without constraints on the coefficients. For further results see appendix.

stochastic shifts in production into account may lead to biased estimates of the social return to human capital. Further, we see that the spillover coefficient is diminishing over time. For these reasons we choose not to generate any longitudinal estimates.

Stochastic Frontier Production Functions

In the models above, it is implicitly assumed that firms operate at the technological frontier and at full capacity. A more realistic assumption is that firms operate at or below the technical frontier and full capacity, which can be modeled using a stochastic frontier production function. The stochastic frontier models allow us to let firms operate at or below the technical efficiency frontier (TEi). For efficient firms, TE = 1, whereas for firms that are operating below maximum output, TE < 1. To this effect, we add a stochastic component that captures random shocks to the production function $\left(e^{v_i}\right)$. The stochastic frontier production function can therefore be written as:

$$Y_{it} = f\left(x_i;\beta\right) * \omega_i * expexp\{v_i\}, \tag{6}$$

where $\omega_{it} = TE_i$.

Assuming Cobb-Douglas technology, taking the natural logarithm of each side in (6) and letting $u_i = - \ln(\omega_i)$, we have:

$$\ln Y_i = lnA + \sum_h^k \beta_h \ln X_{h,i} - u_i + v_i \tag{7}$$

When estimating this function, it is necessary to assume a functional from for ui. We use the most common form by assuming that ui follows a half-normal distribution.

In Tables 2a and 2b below, we report the cross-sectional estimates using stochastic production functions, without and with the assumption of constant returns to scale.

Naturally, there may be many factors that influence regional competitiveness and firm productivity that are also correlated with Sij. Feldman (1994), for example, identifies four different complementary sources of knowledge: university based R&D, private R&D, knowledge in adjacent sectors and specialized business services. See also Acs et al. (1992). Unfortunately, we are unable to control for private R&D[8] and investments in intangible capital, which may be positively be correlated

---

[8] Most R&D reported is conducted at a relatively small number of large firms, and of these investments, about 75% takes place in one of the three largest regions in Sweden (Stockholm, Malmö and Gothenburg). These three regions also have significantly higher shares of the educated workforce compared to the rest of Sweden.

Table 2a Stochastic frontier production functions with human capital spillovers in local labor market regions

	2001	2002	2003	2004	2005	2006	2007	2008	2009	2010
Sij	0.985 (0.044)	0.822 (0.041)	0.726 (0.045)	0.607 (0.040)	0.587 (0.038)	0.544 (0.037)	0.465 (0.037)	0.447 (0.036)	0.430 (0.038)	0.368 (0.034)
L_low	0.507 (0.003)	0.508 (0.003)	0.525 (0.003)	0.501 (0.003)	0.506 (0.003)	0.500 (0.003)	0.511 (0.003)	0.496 (0.003)	0.498 (0.003)	0.505 (0.003)
L_high	0.466 (0.003)	0.471 (0.003)	0.465 (0.004)	0.495 (0.003)	0.502 (0.003)	0.510 (0.003)	0.523 (0.003)	0.528 (0.003)	0.539 (0.003)	0.540 (0.003)
K	0.169 (0.002)	0.162 (0.001)	0.151 (0.002)	0.162 (0.001)	0.154 (0.001)	0.150 (0.001)	0.137 (0.001)	0.133 (0.001)	0.126 (0.001)	0.118 (0.001)
σ_u^2	0.384	0.383	0.366	0.418	0.410	0.422	0.423	0.423	0.424	0.418
σ_v^2	0.463	0.456	0.548	0.477	0.488	0.496	0.519	0.512	0.514	0.513
γ	0.830	0.842	0.669	0.876	0.839	0.850	0.815	0.827	0.824	0.814
No. obs.	44630	46802	47639	51338	53245	56763	56763	56365	54770	57453
Rest: $\beta_L + \beta_H + \beta_K = 1$	No	No	No	No	No	No	No	No	No	No

The technical inefficiency (u) is assumed to follow an exponential distribution. Standard errors are reported within brackets. Output elasticities have been estimated without constraints

Table 2b Stochastic frontier production functions with human capital spillovers in local labor market regions

	2001	2002	2003	2004	2005	2006	2007	2008	2009	2010
Sij	1.125 (0.045)	0.952 (0.042)	0.848 (0.046)	0.744 (0.040)	0.718 (0.039)	0.677 (0.037)	0.605 (0.038)	0.555 (0.037)	0.546 (0.037)	0.467 (0.035)
L_low	0.468 (0.003)	0.469 (0.003)	0.484 (0.003)	0.453 (0.003)	0.455 (0.003)	0.448 (0.003)	0.455 (0.003)	0.440 (0.003)	0.439 (0.003)	0.445 (0.002)
L_high	0.355 (0.002)	0.362 (0.002)	0.356 (0.003)	0.377 (0.002)	0.383 (0.002)	0.394 (0.002)	0.401 (0.002)	0.417 (0.002)	0.427 (0.002)	0.428 (0.002)
K	0.177 (0.002)	0.170 (0.001)	0.159 (0.002)	0.171 (0.001)	0.162 (0.001)	0.158 (0.001)	0.144 (0.001)	0.143 (0.001)	0.135 (0.001)	0.126 (0.001)
σ_u^2	0.398	0.397	0.379	0.437	0.431	0.442	0.445	0.444	0.446	0.439
σ_v^2	0.467	0.462	0.553	0.482	0.493	0.500	0.525	0.517	0.518	0.518
γ	0.849	0.858	0.686	0.906	0.873	0.885	0.848	0.859	0.860	0.847
No. obs.	44630	46802	47639	51338	53245	55150	56763	56365	54770	57453
Rest: $\beta_L + \beta_H + \beta_K = 1$	Yes	Yes	Yes	Yes	Yes	Yes	Yes	Yes	Yes	Yes

The technical inefficiency (u) is assumed to follow an exponential distribution. Standard errors are reported within brackets. Output elasticities have been constrained to one with regional educational attainment. However, we are able to control for public investments in R&D at universities and at research institutes. The correlation between public/university R&D and the regional share of educated workforce is 0.7, which is a fairly high correlation. We therefore include regional R&D as a control variable. The results are reported in Table 3. We measure regional R&D as the public spending on university-based R&D in the region. We also add a proxy for specialized business services in the region (we proxy this by using the share of self-employed individuals in the region) (Table 4).

In Fig. 2 below the estimated spillover effects, $\hat{S}_{-jr}$, from the reported estimation above are reported. This clearly illustrated the rapidly diminishing social return to education.

A concerned reader may note that we do not control for additional sources of knowledge such as private R&D. This however we expect would only still further reduce our estimates.

Conclusions and Summary

Human capital spillovers arise through social interactions between individuals, which make them more productive. If higher education is associated with positive human capital spillovers, social returns to investments in education are generated. In this article, we estimate the productivity effects on firms when regional educational attainment increases. We use firm-level production functions to estimate these human capital spillovers. We examine human capital spillovers between firms active in different industries, which are sometimes referred to as Jacobs spillovers. We do this since we are primarily interested in measuring the social return to education and how this has evolved over time. To this end, we use a sample of more than 50,000 Swedish firms over the period from 2001–2010. Our estimates are the same magnitude as those estimated by Moretti (2004a), who found the spillovers to be in the range of 0.5–0.6. In the beginning of the period, we find the spillover effect to be 0.75–1.13, but this has declined to 0.0–0.48. This decline is robust and economically significant. When including other measures of knowledge investments (public university-based R&D spending and a proxy for specialized business services) our estimates of the spillover effects further decline. From this, we conclude that not only are the spillover effects declining over time, which we interpret as marginally diminishing social returns on higher education, but they even become insignificant at the end of the 2001–2010 period.

To sum-up, our human capital spillover effects can be interpreted as social returns to education, which implies that we can interpret our results as a rapidly diminishing social return to education over the 10 year period we examined. This result also has implications for educational policy and whether a further, publicly funded, qualitative investigation of higher education in Sweden should be pursued. Further research is necessary to fully understand whether there are industry or educational

Table 3 Stochastic frontier production functions with human capital spillovers in local labor market regions and public spending on R&D

	2001	2002	2003	2004	2005	2006	2007	2008	2009	2010
Sij	1.012	0.816	0.620	0.553	0.501	0.448	0.442	0.286	0.351	0.218
	(0.083)	(0.078)	(0.086)	(0.074)	(0.069)	(0.067)	(0.067)	(0.054)	(0.065)	(0.061)
University R&D	−0.001	0.000	0.005	0.003	0.004	0.005	0.001	0.008	0.004	0.008
	(0.003)	(0.003)	(0.003)	(0.003)	(0.003)	(0.003)	(0.003)	(0.002)	(0.003)	(0.003)
L_low	0.507	0.509	0.525	0.501	0.506	0.500	0.511	0.497	0.499	0.505
	(0.003)	(0.003)	(0.003)	(0.003)	(0.003)	(0.003)	(0.003)	(0.003)	(0.003)	(0.003)
L_high	0.466	0.471	0.465	0.495	0.502	0.510	0.523	0.527	0.539	0.540
	(0.003)	(0.003)	(0.004)	(0.003)	(0.003)	(0.003)	(0.003)	(0.003)	(0.003)	(0.003)
K	0.169	0.162	0.151	0.162	0.150	0.150	0.137	0.134	0.126	0.118
	(0.002)	(0.001)	(0.002)	(0.001)	(0.001)	(0.001)	(0.001)	(0.001)	(0.001)	(0.001)
σ_u^2	0.384	0.383	0.366	0.418	0.422	0.422	0.423	0.423	0.424	0.418
σ_v^2	0.463	0.456	0.548	0.477	0.496	0.496	0.519	0.512	0.514	0.513
γ	0.831	0.842	0.669	0.876	0.850	0.850	0.815	0.827	0.824	0.814
No. obs.	44630	46802	47639	51338	53245	55150	56763	56365	54770	57453
Rest: $\beta_L + \beta_H + \beta_K = 1$	No	No	No	No	No	No	No	No	No	No

Table 4 Stochastic frontier production function with human capital spillovers in local labor market regions including R&D and business services

	2001	2002	2003	2004	2005	2006	2007	2008	2009	2010
Sij	0.746 (0.102)	0.807 (0.087)	0.625 (0.091)	0.472 (0.082)	0.367 (0.081)	0.318 (0.079)	0.281 (0.077)	0.059 (0.067)	0.087 (0.075)	−0.100 (0.076)
University R&D	−0.002 (0.003)	0.000 (0.003)	0.005 (0.003)	0.002 (0.003)	0.003 (0.003)	0.004 (0.003)	−0.001 (0.003)	0.004 (0.002)	0.002 (0.003)	0.006 (0.003)
L_low	0.508 (0.003)	0.509 (0.003)	0.525 (0.003)	0.501 (0.003)	0.506 (0.003)	0.500 (0.003)	0.511 (0.003)	0.498 (0.003)	0.500 (0.003)	0.507 (0.003)
L_high	0.465 (0.003)	0.471 (0.003)	0.465 (0.004)	0.495 (0.003)	0.502 (0.003)	0.510 (0.003)	0.522 (0.003)	0.526 (0.003)	0.538 (0.003)	0.538 (0.003)
K	0.169 (0.002)	0.162 (0.001)	0.151 (0.002)	0.162 (0.001)	0.155 (0.001)	0.151 (0.001)	0.138 (0.001)	0.134 (0.001)	0.126 (0.001)	0.118 (0.001)
Business services	1.209 (0.267)	0.056 (0.246)	−0.043 (0.245)	0.549 (0.245)	0.778 (0.249)	0.806 (0.253)	1.149 (0.271)	1.671 (0.293)	1.887 (0.276)	1.826 (0.255)
σ_u^2	0.384	0.383	0.366	0.418	0.410	0.422	0.423	0.423	0.423	0.417
σ_v^2	0.462	0.456	0.548	0.476	0.488	0.496	0.519	0.512	0.514	0.513
γ	0.831	0.842	0.669	0.876	0.839	0.850	0.815	0.826	0.824	0.814
Industry	No	No	No	No	No	No	No	No	No	No
No. obs.	44630	46802	47639	51338	53245	55150	56736	56365	54770	57453
Rest: $\sum \beta_i = 1$	No	No	No	No	No	No	No	No	No	No

The technical inefficiency (u) is assumed to follow an exponential distribution. Standard errors are reported within brackets. Output elasticities have been estimated without constraints

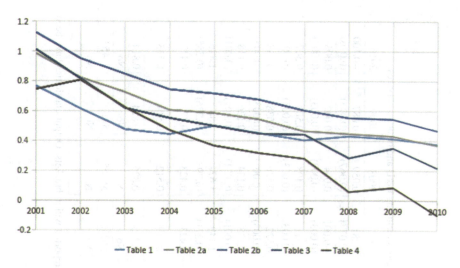

Fig. 2 The rapidly diminishing social return to education. (Source: estimated spillover effects, $\hat{S}_{-jr}$, from the reported estimation above)

differences. Our main conclusion is that our results reduce the argument for indiscriminate subsidization of higher education based on social returns arguments.

Appendix 1

Translog production function
 We also estimate following translog production function:

$$\ln Y = A + \sum_{i}^{n} \beta_i \ln X_i + \frac{1}{2} \sum_{i}^{n} \sum_{j}^{n} \beta_{ij} \ln X_i \ln X_j$$

Where Xi denotes production factors. The total factor productivity, A, is modeled as in the Cobb-Douglas case, and we include the same effects as above. The translog model is estimated under the standard assumptions: $\sum_i \beta_i = 1$ and $\sum_i \beta_{ij} = \sum_i \beta_{ji} = 0$.

Appendix 2

As a robustness check, we estimate the spillover effects at county level. There are 290 counties in Sweden, compared to 72 local labor market regions.

Table A1 Translog function with spillovers in local labor markets

	Translog, Sij per local labor market region									
	2001	2002	2003	2004	2005	2006	2007	2008	2009	2010
Sij	0.865	0.724	0.546	0.547	0.608	0.588	0.530	0.558	0.552	0.531
	(0.043)	(0.044)	(0.076)	(0.060)	(0.039)	(0.047)	(0.042)	(0.040)	(0.040)	(0.041)
L_Low	0.456	0.462	0.471	0.468	0.473	0.469	0.461	0.463	0.471	0.477
	(0.007)	(0.006)	(0.007)	(0.003)	(0.004)	(0.006)	(0.002)	(0.005)	(0.003)	(0.002)
L_High	0.426	0.431	0.426	0.422	0.424	0.435	0.447	0.453	0.454	0.451
	(0.005)	(0.004)	(0.007)	(0.004)	(0.004)	(0.007)	(0.003)	(0.006)	(0.004)	(0.003)
K	0.118	0.107	0.103	0.110	0.104	0.096	0.093	0.084	0.076	0.073
	(0.003)	(0.003)	(0.002)	(0.002)	(0.002)	(0.002)	(0.003)	(0.004)	(0.002)	(0.002)
K2	0.013	0.013	0.013	0.012	0.011	0.014	0.014	0.012	0.013	0.013
	(0.001)	(0.001)	(0.001)	(0.001)	(0.001)	(0.001)	(0.001)	(0.001)	(0.001)	(0.000)
L_High2	0.115	0.118	0.128	0.135	0.134	0.138	0.136	0.137	0.140	0.136
	(0.006)	(0.006)	(0.005)	(0.008)	(0.008)	(0.008)	(0.009)	(0.007)	(0.007)	(0.009)
L_Low2	0.090	0.092	0.090	0.099	0.102	0.102	0.104	0.104	0.109	0.106
	(0.003)	(0.004)	(0.005)	(0.004)	(0.004)9	(0.004)	(0.003)	(0.003)	(0.002)	(0.003)
L_Low* L_High	−0.200	−0.202	−0.213	−0.233	−0.234	−0.235	−0.232	−0.234	−0.243	−0.235
	(0.006)	(0.008)	(0.007)	(0.010)	(0.010)	(0.008)	(0.009)	(0.008)	(0.006)	(0.009)
K*L_High	−0.018	−0.021	−0.018	−0.013	−0.013	−0.019	−0.021	−0.019	−0.019	−0.020
	(0.002)	(0.002)	(0.003)	(0.002)	(0.002)	(0.004)	(0.002)	(0.002)	(0.003)	(0.002)
L_Low*K	−	−	−	−	−	−	−	−	−	−
Industry dummies	Yes	Yes	Yes	Yes	Yes	Yes	Yes	Yes	Yes	Yes
No. obs.	44630	46802	47639	51338	53245	55150	56763	56365	54770	57453
Restrictions: $\sum_i \beta_i = 1$ and $\sum_i \beta_{ij} = \sum_j \beta_{ji} = 0$	Yes	Yes	Yes	Yes	Yes	Yes	Yes	Yes	Yes	Yes

The cross product between L_Low and K has been omitted because of collinearity with the cross product with K and L_High

Table A2 Translog function with spillovers at the county level

	Translog, Sij per county									
	2001	2002	2003	2004	2005	2006	2007	2008	2009	2010
Sij	0.740	0.640	0.561	0.566	0.595	0.591	0.557	0.543	0.526	0.518
	(0.043)	(0.039)	(0.050)	(0.044)	(0.042)	(0.038)	(0.037)	(0.043)	(0.039)	(0.044)
L_Low	0.459	0.465	0.475	0.472	0.477	0.474	0.465	0.467	0.475	0.481
	(0.007)	(0.007)	(0.007)	(0.005)	(0.006)	(0.005)	(0.004)	(0.005)	(0.004)	(0.004)
L_High	0.423	0.427	0.421	0.418	0.418	0.429	0.441	0.448	0.448	0.446
	(0.006)	(0.006)	(0.007)	(0.005)	(0.006)	(0.006)	(0.005)	(0.006)	(0.004)	(0.004)
K	0.118	0.108	0.104	0.111	0.104	0.097	0.093	0.084	0.077	0.074
	(0.003)	(0.002)	(0.002)	(0.002)	(0.002)	(0.002)	(0.003)	(0.004)	(0.002)	(0.002)
K2	0.013	0.013	0.013	0.012	0.011	0.014	0.014	0.012	0.013	0.013
	(0.001)	(0.001)	(0.001)	(0.001)	(0.001)	(0.001)	(0.001)	(0.001)	(0.001)	(0.001)
L_High2	0.113	0.117	0.127	0.134	0.133	0.136	0.134	0.135	0.139	0.135
	(0.005)	(0.006)	(0.006)	(0.007)	(0.007)	(0.006)	(0.007)	(0.006)	(0.006)	(0.007)
L_Low2	0.090	0.091	0.089	0.098	0.100	0.101	0.103	0.103	0.107	0.105
	(0.003)	(0.004)	(0.004)	(0.004)	(0.004)	(0.003)	(0.002)	(0.003)	(0.002)	(0.002)
L_Low*L_High	−0.197	−0.200	−0.221	−0.230	−0.231	−0.232	−0.229	−0.231	−0.240	−0.232
	(0.007)	(0.008)	(0.007)	(0.009)	(0.009)	(0.006)	(0.008)	(0.007)	(0.005)	(0.007)
K*L_High	−0.019	−0.021	−0.019	−0.014	−0.014	−0.019	−0.021	−0.019	−0.019	−0.021
	(0.003)	(0.003)	(0.003)	(0.002)	(0.002)	(0.003)	(0.002)	(0.002)	(0.003)	(0.002)
L_Low*K	–	–	–	–	–	–	–	–	–	–
Industry dummies	Yes	Yes	Yes	Yes	Yes	Yes	Yes	Yes	Yes	Yes
No. obs.	44657	46831	47639	51361	53245	55171	56782	56365	54770	57467
Restrictions: $\sum_i \beta_i = 1$ and $\sum_i \beta_{ij} = \sum_i \beta_{ji} = 0$	Yes	Yes	Yes	Yes	Yes	Yes	Yes	Yes	Yes	Yes

The cross product between L_Low and K has been omitted because of collinearity with the cross product with K and L_High. Robust standard errors clustered over counties in brackets

Table B1 Cross-sectional estimates for human capital spillovers at the county level

	Cobb-Douglas, Sij per county									
	2001	2002	2003	2004	2005	2006	2007	2008	2009	2010
Sij	0.660	0.562	0.506	0.484	0.515	0.501	0.473	0.467	0.436	0.428
	(0.048)	(0.049)	(0.063)	(0.060)	(0.051)	(0.042)	(0.049)	(0.052)	(0.054)	(0.044)
L_Low	0.580	0.587	0.589	0.598	0.605	0.596	0.595	0.592	0.602	0.609
	(0.014)	(0.013)	(0.015)	(0.014)	(0.015)	(0.016)	(0.014)	(0.016)	(0.016)	(0.018)
L_High	0.388	0.391	0.396	0.412	0.416	0.428	0.441	0.447	0.457	0.455
	(0.022)	(0.022)	(0.026)	(0.029)	(0.029)	(0.030)	(0.032)	(0.033)	(0.030)	(0.028)
K	0.151	0.141	0.136	0.139	0.131	0.128	0.119	0.111	0.103	0.096
	(0.003)	(0.003)	(0.002)	(0.003)	(0.003)	(0.003)	(0.004)	(0.004)	(0.003)	(0.003)
Industry dummy	Yes	Yes	Yes	Yes	Yes	Yes	Yes	Yes	Yes	Yes
No. obs.	44657	46831	47668	51361	53245	55171	56782	56378	54770	57467
R2	0.79	0.79	0.77	0.78	0.78	0.77	0.77	0.77	0.76	0.76
Restrictions: ($\beta_L + \beta_H + \beta_K = 1$)	No	No	No	No	No	No	No	No	No	No

Robust standard errors clustered over counties in brackets

References

Audretsch, D. B., & Feldman, M. P. (1996). R&D spillover and the geography if innovation and production. *American Economic Review, 86*(3), 630–640.

Audretsch, D. B., & Feldman, M. P. (2004). Knowledge spillover and the geography of innovation. *Handbook of Regional and Urban Economics, 4*, 2713–2739.

Acs, Z. J., Audretsch, D. B., & Feldman, M. P. (1992). Real effects of academic research: Comment. *American Economic Review, 82*(1), 363–367.

Acemoglu, D. (1996). A micro foundation for social increasing returns in human capital accumulation. *Quarterly Journal of Economics, 111*(3), 779–804.

Acemoglu, D., & Angrist, J. (2000). How large are human capital externalities? Evidence from compulsory schooling laws. In B. S. Bernanke & K. Rogoff (Eds.), *NBER macroeconomic annual* (Vol. 15, pp. 9–59). Cambridge, MA: MIT Press.

Anderson, R., Quigley, J. M., & Wilhelmson, M. (2004). University decentralization as regional policy: The Swedish experiment. *Journal of Economic Geography, 4*, 371–388.

Barro, R. (1991). Economic growth in a cross section of countries. *Quarterly Journal of Economics, 61*, 363–394.

Benhabib, J., & Spiegel, M. M. (1994). The role of human capital in economics development: Evidence from cross-country data. *Journal of Monetary Economics, 28*, 143–173.

Becker, G. S. (1964). *Human capital: A theoretical and empirical analysis with special reference to education.* Chicago: Chicago University Press.

Bhagwati, J., & Rodriguez, C. A. (1975). Welfare-theoretical analyses of the brain-drain. *Journal of Development Economics, 2*, 195–221.

Borjas, G. J., Bronars, S. G. & Trejo, S. J. (1992). Self-selection and internal migration in the United States. NBER Working Paper, No. 4002.

Ciccone, A., & Hall, R. (1996). Productivity and the density of economic activity. *American Economic Review, 86*(1), 54–70.

Ciccone, A., & Peri, G. (2002). Identifying human capital externalities: Theory with an application to US cities. IZA Working paper, No. 488.

Eklund, J. E., & Petersson, L. (2019). *Tertiary education, productivity and economic growth: Evidence from Sweden.* Swedish Entrepreneurship Forum, Working paper, No. 2019: 58.

Feldman, M. (1994). Knowledge complementarity and innovation. *Small Business Economics, 6*(5), 363–372.

Glaeser, E. L., Kallal, D. H., Scheinkman, J., & Shleifer, A. (1992). Growth in cities. *Journal of Political Economy, 100*, 1126–1152.

Glasear, E. (1999). Learning in cities. *Journal of Urban Economics, 46*(2), 254–277.

Henderson, V. (2003). The urbanization process and economic growth: The so-what question. *Journal of Economic Growth, 8*(1), 47–71.

Jacobs, J. (1970). *The economy of cities.* New York: Random House.

Jovanovic, B., & Rob, R. (1989). The growth and diffusion of knowledge. *Review of Economic Studies, 56*(4), 569–582.

Lucas, R. E., Jr. (1988). On the mechanism of economic development. *Journal of Monetary Economics, 22*(1), 3–42.

Mankiw, G., Romer, D., & Weil, D. N. (1992). A contribution to the empirics of economic growth. *Quarterly Journal of Economics, 107*(2), 407–437.

Marshall, A. (1890). *Principles of economics.* New York: MacMillan.

Moretti, E. (2004a). Workers' education, spillovers, and Productivity: Evidence from plant-level production functions. *American Economic Review, 94*(3), 656–690.

Moretti, E. (2004b). Estimating the social returns to higher education: Evidence from longitudinal data and repeated cross-sectional data. *Journal of Economctrics, 121*, 175–212.

Nelson, R. R., & Phelps, E. S. (1966). Investment in humans, technological diffusion, and economic growth. *The American Economic Review, 56*, 69–75.

Rauch, J. (1993). Productivity gains from geographic concentration of human capital: Evidence from the cities. *Journal of Urban Economics, 34*(3), 380–400.

Romer, P. M. (1990). Endogenous technological change. *Journal of Political Economy, 98*(5), 71–102.

Part III
Creating a Community

With the field of entrepreneurship firmly established going into this century, David seemed secure that his efforts had indeed born fruition and he could enjoy the now surging research area that only a few years ago had remained so elusive. However, there seemed to be one challenge that was holding back not just the impact of his own research but the entire research field – each particular research trajectory was subsumed by a broader research area and discipline, rendering entrepreneurship to be limited as a subfield in existing academic disciplines, such as psychology, sociology, economics, geography, finance and strategy. While it was gratifying to see the inroads being made by entrepreneurship within the traditional disciplines, the inability to integrate across those research areas to coalesce into a unique and singular research field stunted entrepreneurship from attaining its potential.

Creating a community is a seemingly daunting concept. Where does one start? A community suggests scale and a focus on the macro, the group over the individual. However, for David, it started exactly the opposite, with individual colleagues where the connection and shared interest in a research topic and approach was natural, energizing and self-evident. For example, he met Georg Licht as a doctoral student at the University of Augsburg. When Georg became the department head of the Zentrum für Europäische Wirtschaftsforschung (ZEW), or Centre for European Economic Research in Mannheim, David quickly teamed up to work with the newly founded research institute and provide focus for its research. Especially in its early years, the research focus on small and medium-sized enterprises and innovation was prominent at the ZEW. His presence was sufficiently important that he became a member of the Scientific Advisory Board or Wissenschaftliche Beirat of the ZEW for a decade. David similarly served as a key member of the Scientific Advisory Board or Wissenschaftliche Beirat of a different research institute, the HWWA in Hamburg for over 5 years. Just as his tenure with the ZEW was ending, he was asked to serve on the Scientific Advisory Board or Wissenschaftliche Beirat of the German Institute for Economic Research, or DIW Berlin. He not only served for over a decade, but actually became the Chair of the Wissenschaftliche Beirat of the DIW for many years. Helping navigate the DIW through its ups and downs during this period, he started working closely with the Vice President, Alexander Kritikos.

Not only did their friendship blossom, but they became highly productive research partners as well. David similarly served for many years on the scientific advisory board of the Basque Institute of Competitiveness in San Sebastian, where he helped oversee the research department focusing on entrepreneurship. For David, creating a community was not a concept or theory, but simply an openness to relationships of colleagues interested in similar research themes and ideas. That a community actually coalesced was more the unintended consequence of those relationships rather than a well-thought out plan or strategy.

When David was offered the position of Director of the third research division at the Max Planck Institute of Economics in Jena, Germany, the President of the Max Planck Society, Professor Dr. Peter Gruss, assumed that his focus would be in the area of his doctoral studies and early research, industrial organization. He was not the only one who was startled when David instead boldly suggested naming the new research division Entrepreneurship, Growth and Public Policy. David clearly viewed the opportunity presented by the Max Planck Society as a unique platform to move entrepreneurship from being a collection of sub-fields within the existing academic disciplines to a broad, inclusive cross-disciplinary research field. To accomplish this would require the new research division to reflect this inclusivity and cross-disciplinarily.

The first thing that occurred to David in taking on the new challenge of creating and growing the Entrepreneurship, Growth and Public Policy research division of the Max Planck Institute of Economics, was to find the right person to serve as the Associate Director. He did not have to look far. In fact, he only had to look to the adjacent office at the Institute of Development Strategies, which was occupied by Erik Lehmann, who was visiting for a year to finish his Habilitation.

David was introduced to Erik, who was a Ph.D. student, at the University of Nuremberg, during the late 1990s, when he was still working in Berlin. When Erik subsequently visited the Institute of Development Strategies at Indiana University for a year, they embarked on what would ultimately be a rich research partnership but an even richer friendship. The relief and gratitude that David felt when Erik accepted his offer to serve as the Associate Director of the new research department was palpable. The other key appointment was Max Keilbach as Senior Research Fellow. David and Max met at the Zentrum für Europäische Wirtschaftsforschung (Center for European Economic Research) in Mannheim, Germany in the late 1990s and had undertaken a series of research projects. Max's sense of adventure and openness resonated with David. When David proposed that Max join the research team in Jena in a senior leadership position, he accepted on the spot. Teamed up with Erik and Max, David dedicated the mission of the new research department to fostering the creation or emergence of an entrepreneurship research field that is integrated across multiple academic disciplines to coalesce into a bona fide field of research. Erik and Max were instrumental in recruiting thoughtful, energetic and creative young scholars from a multitude of disciplinary backgrounds, cultures and nationalities, including Werner Boente, Iris Beckmann, Robin Buerger, T. Taylor Aldridge, Samee Desai, Devrium Goektepc, Stephan Heblich, Anja Klaukien, Stefan Krabel, Prashanth Mahagaonhkar, Erik Monsen, Holger Patzelt, Jagannadha

Pawan Tamvada, Stephpan Schuetze, Viktor Slavtchev, Diemo Urbig, Isabelle M. Welpe, Joerg Zimmermann, Marcus Perry, Siri Terjessen, and Iris Beckmann. All of these bright scholars teamed up with David for a series of studies linking entrepreneurship to economic performance and growth, resulting in the book, Innovation and Economic Growth, published by Cambridge University Press in 2006.

The challenge for the new research department at the Max Planck Institute was not just to contribute to scholarly thinking about entrepreneurship but rather to foster the development of a community of scholars that transcended the boundaries of the traditional academic disciplines. This meant appointing a broad spectrum of diverse young scholars spanning a wide range of academic disciplines, ranging from economics to sociology, political science, regional studies, finance and psychology. The support of external scholars and supporters proved invaluable, such as Simon Parker, Rui Baptista, Sharon Alvarez, Zoltan Acs, Roy Thurik, and Steven Klepper.

Still, obstacles remained. Faced with doubts about the lack of a common methodology and theoretical approach in the new emerging field, David asked two colleagues, a physicist and a chemist at the annual meeting of Directors of the Max Planck society, "What actually constitutes a bona fide research field?" The answer was both swift and resolute," Money and interest." The interest was fueled by not just students but also thought leaders in business and public policy. The financial support came from a vast array of private and public sources, such as the Ewing Marion Kauffman Foundation. In fact, David was appointed as a Visiting Research Scholar at the Kauffman Foundation over a 5 year period, which proved to be a crucial link for both him and the Max Planck Institute of Economics.

This link was more than a formality. It was the basis for creating and coalescing a community of entrepreneurship scholars. Joining forces with the Kauffman Foundation, David and the Max Planck Institute of Economics hosted a series of conferences focusing on entrepreneurship research and scholarship at the Max Planck Society Conference Center at Schloss Ringberg, which is a castle located at Tegernsee in the foothills of the Alps. These conferences brought together the oldest generation of scholars, including the Nobel Prize winners, Robert Mundell and Ned Phelps, along with William Baumol and Richard R. Nelson, and the young generation of scholars committed to serious scholarship and research in the field of entrepreneurship.

The entrepreneurship community was similarly forged through a series of summer school workshops, bringing together some of the most established scholars of entrepreneurship, such as Simon Parker, Steve Klepper, Sharon Alvarez, Dean Shepherd, Mike Wright and Don Siegel and doctoral students and post-doctoral researchers. Both the conferences and workshop made it clear that the emerging community of entrepreneurship was not specific or restricted to a singular academic discipline but rather span a broad spectrum of research disciplines and fields.

Productivity Slowdown, Innovation and Industry Dynamics

Johannes Bersch, Josefine Diekhof, Bastian Krieger, Georg Licht, and Simona Murmann

Abstract Germany, in common with other industrial nations, has in recent years witnessed a decline in productivity growth despite sustained economic growth, falling unemployment and strong technological dynamics. The decline in productivity growth is not a measurement problem. However, the difficulty in measuring productivity has increased as digitalisation has spread and dynamic innovation activities have shifted into the services sector. In many sectors of the economy, the gap between highly productive and less productive firms is now widening more sharply than at the start of the millennium. More and more firms are no longer able to keep pace with the productivity growth achieved by leading firms. At the same time, there are differences between individual sectors when observing the development of intra-industry productivity divergences. The levels of innovation spending by large firms on the one hand and by small and mediumsized enterprises (SMEs) on the other have been diverging for years. As digitalisation has spread, many firms – especially SMEs – are facing considerable problems in adopting new technology. Both the public and private sectors in Germany are laggards compared with other countries when it comes to investing in these technologies. The number of business start-ups has been falling for years. This slowing entrepreneurial activity is both a symptom and a cause of the fact that financial and human resources are tied up for too long in established firms with low (productivity) growth.

Economic and innovation policies are facing three major challenges: stimulating the adaptation of new technologies by investing in research and development (R&D) to foster firm innovation; promoting digitalisation; and improving the digital infrastructure. Tax incentives for R&D, indirect specific programmes to stimulate the diffusion of digital innovations, and adjustments to the regulation of markets for goods, services and factors of production would be sensible options to address these challenges.

J. Bersch (✉) · J. Diekhof · B. Krieger · G. Licht · S. Murmann
Economics of Innovation and Industrial Dynamics, ZEW – Leibniz Centre for European Economic Research, L7 1, Mannheim, Germany
e-mail: johannes.bersch@zew.de; bastian.krieger@zew.de; georg.licht@zew.de; simona.murmann@zew.de; josefine.diekhof@zew.de

© Springer Nature Switzerland AG 2019
E. E. Lehmann, M. Keilbach (eds.), *From Industrial Organization to Entrepreneurship*, https://doi.org/10.1007/978-3-030-25237-3_21

Introduction[1]

For many years, numerous Western industrial countries have been witnessing falling growth rates in their productivity. The exact beginning, evolution and magnitude of this decline vary from country to country. In the aftermath of the financial and economic crisis declining productivity growth rates becomes more visible and were blamed as an obstacle to recovery. . The reasons for the decline have been intensively debated around the world then (Andrews et al. 2015, 2016; Bloom et al. 2017). However, Germany's productivity growth rate is also falling despite its strong economic performance and the significant increase of R&D spending.

The productivity of a country's economy over time is one of the key factors determining its economic growth and prosperity. It is a precondition for rising incomes and improving living standards. Or as Paul Krugman (1997, p. 11) put it: "Productivity isn't everything, but in the long run it is almost everything".

Despite the huge role productivity plays for economic growth, attempts to fully understand the recent productivity slowdown are still at an initial stage. Hence, this paper places productivity growth trends within an international context, discusses various possible explanations and illustrates these with data for the German economy. The paper starts by highlighting empirical evidence on the growth of macroeconomic productivity and analysing parallels between the relevant trends in Germany and other countries. It then focuses on approaches that are often used to explain this phenomenon at an international level. Here, it looks closely at the extent to which these approaches can help to explain the trends observed in Germany. The paper concludes by outlining potential policy options in the fields of research and technology.

The Decline in Productivity Growth

Jones (2017, p. 313) describes the slowdown in productivity growth as "perhaps the most remarkable fact about economic growth in recent decades [...] that occurred around the year 2000. This slowdown is global in nature, featuring in many countries throughout the world." Data from the OECD on the levels of macroeconomic productivity over time illustrate the slowdown in productivity growth. Figure 1 outlines the levels of growth in labour productivity in six selected countries based on individual annual figures and their trend growth. If we look at the relevant trends

---

[1] David Audretsch's publications focussed on research and innovation in SMEs, on growth and the survival of young, small firms as well as on public policies to stimulate technological competencies of regions. Since the beginning of ZEW in 1992 his thinking was always a constant source of inspiration. Hence, we focus especially on those drivers of productivity mirroring David's thinking. Surely, the usual caveats apply and all shortcomings of this review are the responsibility of the authors. An early version of the paper has appeared as "Falling Productivity Growth, Widening Productivity Gaps", ZEW policy brief NO. 4 I APRIL 2018.

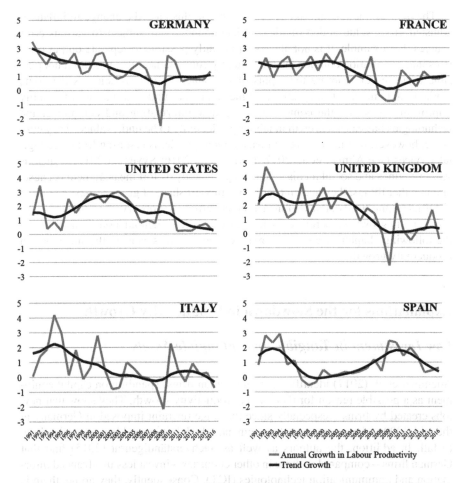

Fig. 1 Growth rates for real labour productivity 1991–2016 (percentage growth). Notes: (1) Trend growth calculated by using the Hodrick-Prescott filter to smooth the original data (2) Recession years of the financial and economic crisis: GE/FR 2009, UK/US 2008/2009, IT 2008–2013. SP 2009–2013. Sources: OECD (2018), calculations by ZEW

since the year 2000, we can clearly see a slowdown in productivity growth in all countries except for Spain. The financial and economic crisis had a severe short-term impact on productivity growth. Whereas Germany and France managed to raise their productivity growth marginally subsequent to the crisis, the relevant growth rates in the United States, the United Kingdom and, to an even greater extent, Italy settled at a low level close to zero. Productivity growth today is much lower than it was in the first half of the 2000s and well below where it was in the 1990s. The crisis had a long-term effect on productivity growth in Spain and Italy, of which the consequences are still visible in present years. The trends shown for Italy and Spain underline the enormous challenges which these countries will face over the next few years.

The measurement of productivity growth – in this case the change in inflation-adjusted gross value added divided by labour input – is subject to various error sources. For example, it is not always sufficiently possible to separate output price rises into an inflation component and a quality component. Also, it is often not possible to accurately capture the inputs of a production process, such as the hours worked. Ademmer et al. (2017) argue that the underestimation of quality improvements within the context of using new information and communication technologies has caused growth in labour productivity to be undervalued. They conclude, however, that the discussed measurement problems resulting from free digital services (see Ahmad et al. 2017; Byrne et al. 2016; Syverson 2017) – such as search engines and social media – do not significantly distort measurement because, among other things, they account for only a modest share of gross domestic product (GDP). Despite the existence of measurement errors, the observed decline in labour productivity growth is therefore not merely a statistical phenomenon. Consequently, the following chapter discusses the real-economy factors causing the slowdown in productivity growth.

Explanations for the Slowdown in Productivity Growth

Low Investment in Tangible and Intangible Assets

Ademmer et al. (2017) identify a gap in German firms' spending on capital equipment as a possible reason for their weak productivity growth. They show that new jobs created by firms – especially since the wage restraint imposed in Germany in the mid-2000s – have less capital equipment, which has caused labour productivity to fall. In addition, the authors as well as Sachverständigenrat (2015) find that German firms – compared to those in other countries – invest less in advanced information and communication technologies (ICT). Consequently, they argue, there is less stimulation of productivity growth by digitalisation. The authors suggest two potential reasons for the lower amount of investment in digitalisation technologies: first, the relatively strong regulation of Germany's markets for goods and labour, which reduces the pressure to compete and innovate; and, second, the large number of small and medium-sized enterprises (SMEs), which are potentially less able than large firms to make effective use of new digital technologies owing to the high implementation costs involved.

Complementary Investment to Exploit the Productivity Potential of Digitalisation

Innovations in ICT caused the prices of ICT hardware to fall in the 1990s and early 2000s. Adjustments to the methodology used to calculate price indices for ICT goods enabled the effects of this price decline to be fairly adequately captured in productivity statistics. These prices have no longer been falling since about 2008. Nowadays, innovations in ICT take place primarily in the service sector. This poses a challenge to our ability to adequately capture the potential of new digitalisation technologies (such as the Internet of Things, Industry 4.0). Brynjolffsson and McAfee (2014) argue that the actual digital revolution has yet to happen and that productivity growth will not start to accelerate until this revolution takes place. They point to necessary complementary investment in new business processes and human capital as well as the opportunities for new business models. A related analogy is the era of the electrification of industry at the end of the nineteenth century when productivity effects did not fully materialise up until four decades later when industrial manufacturing processes had been redesigned (see David 1990). Back then, the productivity potential of electrification was initially underestimated, and the slow diffusion of this new technology and missing organisational co-innovations brought about delayed productivity gains in manufacturing. Hence, shifts in technological paradigms require a certain amount of time until their potential is recognised and technological innovations become widely established, so that productivity gains can subsequently be achieved.

In Germany there are adoption problems with exploiting the opportunities of digitalisation, too. In that line Bertschek et al. (2018) see room for improvement in manufacturing and service sectors such as mechanical engineering, logistics, and healthcare. Hence, the potential to cut costs and tap into new customer groups and markets through product innovation remains unutilised. Looking at the mechanical engineering sector, Rammer et al. (2018a; b) identify further obstacles such as the inability to charge higher prices for quality improvements, given a yet remaining low willingness to pay for the added benefit of digital modules as well as difficulties in implementing Industry 4.0 technologies. The issue at the heart of this argument is therefore once again that the productivity-enhancing effects of digitalisation will not materialise for another few years.

Digitalisation also raises the question of whether it is becoming increasingly difficult to identify productivity growth on the basis of typically used indicators. Varian (2017) illustrates this point by giving the example of smartphones. Only cameras, film and photo development are included in the photography price index, even though the vast majority of the $1.6*10^{18}$ photos nowadays created each year are taken, stored, and distributed using smartphones. The same applies to pocket calculators, GPS and so on. This technological value added is not adequately reflected in price indices and so does not show up in the latest productivity statistics either (see Schmalensee 2018).

Technological Potential Exhausted

A further key hypothesis used to explain the fall in productivity growth is a decline in research productivity. This hypothesis is based on the assumption that technological potential has increasingly been exhausted. Consequently, more and more time and effort are needed to devise new ideas and to turn them into innovative products, processes and business models. A few prominent publications such as those by Bloom et al. (2017) and Gordon (2012) provide evidence of a decline in research productivity. Malerba and Orsenigo (1997) point to the differences between individual sectors. Their investigation of the pharmaceutical industry highlights the fact that although the number of newly approved drugs has remained almost constant since the early 1980s, R&D spending has risen by a factor of 30 over the same period. We can therefore say that in this case there has been a fall in research productivity. On the other hand, Peters et al. (2018) see no convincing evidence of a systematic decline in the rate of return on research and development (R&D) across industries and countries since the 1960s. Consequently, there is no compelling evidence of an across-the-board decrease in research productivity as an explanation for the declining growth in multi-factor and labour productivity.

Growing Productivity Differential Between Firms

Although most countries report positive growth rates in R&D spending, over time this is increasingly being driven by large firms. Germany too reveals a significant widening of the gap in innovation spending between SMEs and large firms since 1995 (Fig. 2). The findings of Rammer et al. (2018a; b) also imply that, overall, growing numbers of SMEs in Germany are withdrawing from innovation activities, whereas a small number of successful SMEs ('hidden champions') are stepping up their innovation activities. Consequently, the divergence in productivity levels within the SME segment itself is also increasing. Possible reasons for this trend are the relatively low returns on innovation activities combined with the significant cost of expanding and permanently maintaining innovation capacities of SMEs.

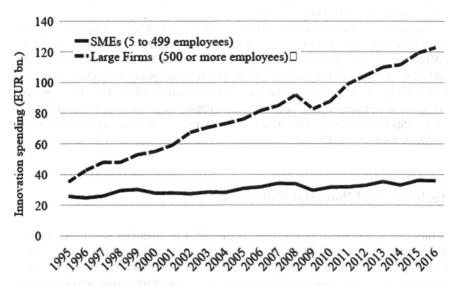

Fig. 2 Innovation spending over time. Source: Mannheim Innovation Panel (MIP), calculations by ZEW

Widening productivity gaps are illustrated by data from other countries as well. The persistence of firms belonging either to the group of productivity leaders or to the group of productivity laggards has also increased over time (see Andrews et al. 2015, 2016). It is furthermore becoming increasingly difficult for laggards to catch up with the most productive firms. This trend is said to have two potential causes. First, the growing complexity of new technologies leads to a decline in the diffusion of innovations from leaders to laggards or, because only the most productive firms can make efficient use of such complex technologies within a short time frame. And, second, the economies of scale and scope offered by new digital technologies are providing productivity leaders with a monopoly-like market position that is hampering the laggards' development.

However, the differentials between productivity leaders and productivity laggards are not increasing to the same extent in all sectors. Although evaluations across all sectors reveal that there are generally growing divergences in German labour productivity as well, Fig. 3 shows that this trend differs considerably in selected sectors. It presents five sectors of the R&D-intensive manufacturing industry in which Germany is a traditional leader. Whereas these intra-industry differentials are widening in the chemical, electrical engineering and mechanical engineering sectors, they remain largely constant in the automotive sector. Productivity gaps are narrowing in the optics, measurement & control technology and medical equipment sectors. The reasons for this divergence in productivity within individual industries are still largely unknown. One explanation, however, could incorporate significant

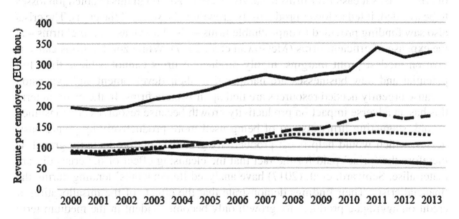

Fig. 3 Changes in intra-industry productivity differentials between highly productive and less productive firms. Notes: Changes in the differential between the 75% and 25% percentiles of the revenue-per-employee ratio in selected R&D-intensive sectors. Explanation: In the chemical industry the productivity differential between the 75% and 15% percentiles of the revenue-per-employee rose from EUR 200,000 to roughly EUR 350,000 per employee between 2000 and 2013. Sources: Mannheim Enterprise Panel (MUP), calculations by ZEW

differences in the intra-industry diffusion of innovative products, processes, and business models. In the chemical industry, for example, there are ordinarily strong firm-specific economies of scale and scope that make it more difficult to transfer innovations to other firms in the industry. By contrast, it is easier for firms in the measurement & control technology and medical equipment sectors to benefit from their competitors' innovations.

Productivity Development in the Aftermath of the Great Economic Crisis

The development of productivity growth in Italy and Spain over time (Fig. 1) illustrates the negative impact of the financial and economic crisis on productivity growth. Productivity has hardly grown in either country in recent years. Gopinath et al. (2017) and Andrews et al. (2015, 2016) provide evidence to show that the productivity growth of the most productive and less productive firms in southern European countries has increasingly diverged since the economic crisis. This trend was intensified by the expansionary monetary policies pursued during the post-crisis years, because loans were provided even to firms with below-average productivity which, without this injection of fresh funds, would have gone out of business. Gropp et al. (2018) demonstrate that less restrictive banking regulation during times of crisis makes it easier for firms to survive a crisis. Although this enabled job losses to be avoided, it led to lower productivity growth in the wake of the crisis. The crisis also saw funding provided to unprofitable firms – also known as 'zombie' firms – at the expense of efficient firms (McGowan et al. 2017). While zombie firms can survive on modest profit margins, highly productive firms cannot achieve their full potential and new businesses are hampered in their development and expansion because urgently needed resources are tied up in zombie firms. In the medium term this has an adverse impact on productivity growth because resources are consumed by old, stagnating firms instead of being used more productively by young businesses, which would help boost productivity growth. Low productivity growth is therefore the 'price' paid for the fact that the cleansing effect of the crisis did not materialise. Schivardi et al. (2017) have analysed Italian banks' lending during the financial crisis. Their findings demonstrate that the effects of the misallocation of credit on aggregate productivity growth only become evident in the medium term and only occur when a large proportion of zombie firms impact on economic growth.

An additional factor is that the economic crisis affected firms' productivity growth to varying degrees. For example, firms that had invested more heavily in information and communication technologies proved to be more resilient to crises. Bertschek et al. (2017) have analysed the innovativeness of firms before and during the financial and economic crisis based on a sample of seven industries from twelve European countries. ICT-intensive firms in particular managed during the crisis to implement process innovations and, consequently, to achieve higher productivity growth and greater resilience to crises. These positive effects of ICT investment were especially evident in service sectors.

Dynamics in the Corporate Landscape

Vibrant economies reallocate resources from unproductive firms to productive ones through market entries and exits. This reallocation stimulates productivity growth both directly through the economic activity of the new businesses and indirectly through their competitive effect on the productivity growth of established firms. Foster et al. (2018) argue that innovation spurts are accompanied by increasing start-up activity and widening productivity differentials and that only as a consequence of this does rising productivity growth occur. They back up their arguments with data from the US dotcom boom. By contrast, the process of dynamic selection in the corporate sector of Western industrial nations has been weakening for years now (Decker et al. 2016).

Audretsch and Keilbach (2008) argue that high investments into innovation might not automatically generate growth and stimulate competitiveness of a region or an economy. Risk-taking individuals and firms are needed to fully translate investments into innovation and subsequently into economic outcomes. New firms pose an advantage to recombine knowledge and develop new business models based on investments in new technologies and new knowledge. Audretsch et al. (2008) and Erken et al. (2016) present evidence of entrepreneurship as a translational channel of innovation. Hence, slow-down in the number of technology-based start-ups will result in a reduction of technology-based (productivity) growth.

Business Demographics in Aging Societies

Germany too has been witnessing a declining number of business start-ups for years now. In 2016, for example, Germany saw 30% fewer high-tech firms and 43% fewer ICT firms being set up than in 2003. Figure 4 shows the changes in the numbers of business start-ups as a proportion of existing firms. Whereas eight new enterprises per 100 existing firms were set up in 2002, this figure had fallen to only five start-ups by 2016. In the Manufacturing Sector, this figure is now down to only four new firms. The competitive pressure of business start-ups has therefore declined significantly in Germany as well.

One possible explanation for the falling numbers of business start-ups is the demographic trend in many industrial nations. Karahan et al. (2016), for example, attribute the declining start-up rates in the US to the slowing growth in the working-age population. There is evidence that the same applies to Germany. The age group of 35-to-45-year-olds, which has the highest start-up rate in Germany, has been contracting for years. And the age group of 45-to-55-year-olds, which is the cohort with the second-highest start-up propensity, has also been shrinking for some years now. As these groups become smaller, then – assuming that individuals' start-up propensity remains unchanged and the institutional framework remains the same – the absolute number of business start-ups will fall. At the same time, the opportunity cost of setting up a business is rising in the age cohorts with the highest start-up rates. Figure 5 shows the relationship between start-up activity and the age structure

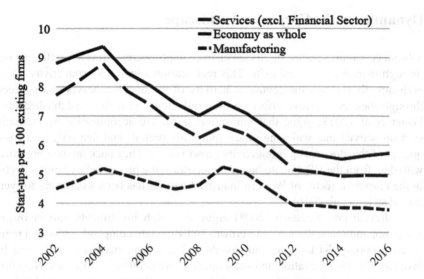

Fig. 4 Number of business start-ups as a proportion of existing firms. Sources: Mannheim Enterprise Panel (MUP), calculations by ZEW

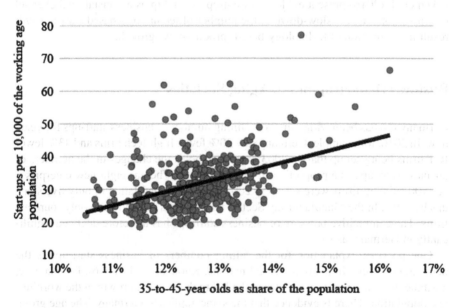

Fig. 5 Start-up activity and age structure as a cross-section of urban and rural districts in Germany, 2010–2015. Notes: Each dot represents an urban or rural district. Sources: Mannheim Enterprise Panel, calculations by ZEW

of the population. It demonstrates that regions with a higher proportion of their population in the cohort with the highest start-up rate – i.e. the 35-to-45-year-olds – also have a comparatively higher level of start-up activity. In addition, Alon et al.

(2017) indicate that the productivity effects of the falling number of start-ups are not solely attributable to the consequent weakening of the selection effect. A declining proportion of young firms as a share of the total firm population also reduces the direct effect of fast-growing, productive young firms on aggregate productivity growth. Given the empirical evidence available, we conclude that demographic trends – in terms of both the human and firm populations – are one factor that explains the slowdown in productivity growth.

Innovation Policies to Stimulate Productivity Growth

The global long-term decline in productivity growth strongly contrasted the current debate on the huge technological potential of digitalisation and the discussion on the impact of digitalisation on jobs. Solely looking at the productivity impact of digitalisation, however, oversimplifies the current situation. The productivity growth debate uncovered a broad spectrum of insights into the multifaceted web of productivity drivers. Public policies on research, technology and innovation need to be proactive in the face of the current trend of declining productivity growth. This literature review is by no means exhaustive and any policy option should be certainly viewed with care. Nonetheless, some challenges and options for innovation policy are shortly touched below.

Integrating the technological potential of digitalisation into new products, processes and business models as well as ensuring their rapid diffusion provides opportunities to reverse the adverse productivity growth trend of recent years. Significant investment in the expansion of broadband network infrastructure is a necessary precondition for exploiting these opportunities, although, on its own far from being sufficient (see Weber et al. (2018) for statistical evidence). It is equally important to constantly review and, where necessary, adjust the rules governing markets for goods, services and factors of production. As it is impossible to know in advance what kind of regulatory framework will yield the best results, experimental clauses should be adjusted so that instruments, such as living labs and pilot schemes, can be used to conduct ex-ante evaluations of different available reform options.

Innovation policy should stimulate the diffusion of digitalisation. The diffusion of new forms of digitalisation requires firms to invest large amounts in equipment, expertise and skills. The situation today is similar to the integration of information technology and automation into manufacturing processes in the late 1980s or early 1990s. Diffusion-based support programmes were often used back then. In the current situation we should build on this experience when launching new programmes.

In the light of the increasing gap between SME and large corporations, R&D tax incentives for SMEs can be employed to provide additional stimuli for knowledge generation. Given that many firms are withdrawing from innovation activities, a R&D tax could further provide a key stimulus for SMEs to continue and increase investments in innovation.

The significant decline in the number of business start-ups in the last 15 years represents a complex issue. Instead of tying up resources (such as financial and human capital) in fairly unproductive firms in order to protect jobs in the short term, these resources should be channelled into new, potentially more productive firms. An expansion of venture capital or other means of equity financing for starting and growing firms as well as further measures to promote the scalability of new business models could support this adverse redistribution process. In order to revitalise business start-up activity effectively, however, it is not sufficient to improve the financing facilities available. Given that the number of start-ups has been declining for years, existing approaches to promote the start of new businesses should be reconsidered and experiments with new approaches should be devised.

These are only a few ideas to revitalise the German economy in the light of current challenges. In the recent past, David Audretsch (2015) published an insightful framework for policies to improve the economic prosperity. His book *"Everything in Its Place"* is a rich source of ideas and concepts which can be used by business managers and innovation policy makers. It convincingly demonstrates theoretical concepts, empirical findings and case studies which provide evidence that carefully designed and implemented public policies can support the economic performance of businesses, regions and countries.

References

Ademmer, M., Bickenbach, F., Bode, E., Boysen-Hogrefe, J., Fiedler, S., Gern, K.-J., Görg, H., Groll, D., Hornok, C., Jannsen, N., Kooths, S., & Krieger-Boden, C. (2017). Produktivität in Deutschland – Messbarkeit und Entwicklung, Kieler Beiträge zur Wirtschaftspolitik Nr. 12.

Ahmad, N., Ribarsky, J., & Reinsdorf, M. (2017). *Can Potential Mismeasurement of the Digital Economy Explain the Post-Crisis Slowdown in GDP and Productivity Growth?* OECD Statistics Working Papers No. 2017/09.

Alon, T. Berger, D. Dent, R., & Pugsley, B. (2017). *Older and slower: The startup deficit's lasting effects on aggregate productivity growth*. NBER Working Paper 23875. Cambridge, MA.

Andrews, D., Criscuolo, C., & Gal, P. N. (2015). *Frontier Firms, Technology Diffusion and Public Policy: Micro Evidence from OECD Countries*. OECD Productivity Working Papers No. 2.

Andrews, D., Criscuolo, C., & Gal, P. N. (2016). *The best versus the rest: The global productivity slowdown, divergence across firms and the role of public policy*. OECD Productivity Working Papers No. 5.

Audretsch, D. B. (2015). *Everything in its place. Entrepreneurship and the strategic management of cities, regions, and states*. New York: Oxford University Press.

Audretsch, D. B., & Keilbach, M. (2008). Resolving the knowledge paradox: Knowledge-spillover entrepreneurship and economic growth. *Research Policy, 37*, 1697–1705.

Audretsch, D. B., Boente, W., & Keilbach, M. (2008). Entrepreneurship capital and its impact on knowledge diffusion and economic performance. *Journal of Business Venturing, 23*, 687–698.

Bertschek, I., Polder, M., & Schulte, P. (2017). *ICT and resilience in times of crisis: Evidence from cross-country micro moments data*. ZEW Discussion Paper No. 17–030. Mannheim.

Bloom, N., Jones, C.J., Van Reenen, J., & Webb, M. (2017). *Are ideas getting harder to find*. NBER Working Paper 23782.

Brynjolfsson, E., & McAfee, A. (2014). *The second machine age: Work, progress, and prosperity in a time of brilliant technologies*. New York: WW Norton & Company.

Byrne, D. M., Fernald, J. G., & Reinsdorf, M. B. (2016). Does the United States have a productivity slowdown or a measurement problem? *Brookings Papers on Economic Activity, Spring 2016*, 109–182.

David, P. (1990). The dynamo and the computer: An historical perspective on the modern productivity paradox. *The American Economic Review, 80*(2), 355–361.

Decker, R. A., Haltiwanger, J., Jarmin, R. S., & Miranda, J. (2016). Declining business dynamism: What we know and the way forward. *American Economic Review, 106*(5), 203–207.

Erken, H., Donselaar, P., & Thurik, R. (2016). Total factor productivity and the role of entrepreneurship. *Journal of Technology Transfer*, 1–29. https://doi.org/10.1007/s10961-016-9504-5.

Foster, L., Grim, C., Haltiwanger, J., & Wolf, Z. (2018). *Innovation, productivity dispersion, and productivity growth.* Center for Economics Studies Working Paper 18–08, US Bureau of Census.

Gopinath, G., Kalemli-Ozcan, S., Karabarbounis, L., & Villegas-Sanchez, C. (2017). Capital allocation and productivity in South Europe. *Quarterly Journal of Economics, 132*, 1915–1967.

Gordon, R. J. (2012). *Is U.S. economic growth over? Faltering innovation confronts the six headwinds.* NBER Working Paper 18315.

Gropp, R., Rocholl, J., & Saadi V. (2018). The cleansing effect of banking crises, Background Paper, BIS-IMF-OECD Joint Conference "Weak productivity: The role of financial factors and policies". 18 Jan 2018, Paris.

Jones, C. I. (2017). The productivity growth slowdown in advanced economies. In European Central Bank (Ed.), *Investment and growth in advanced economies, conference proceedings* (pp. 313–323). Sintra: ECB Forum on Central Banking, 26–28 Juni 2017.

Karahan, F., Pugsley, B., & Sahin, A. (2016). Demographic origins of the startup deficit, Federal Reserve Bank of New York, Technical Report, mimeo.

Krugman, P. (1997). The age of diminished expectations: U.S. economic policy in the 1990s, third edition. Cambridge, England: MIT Press.

Malerba, F., & Orsenigo, L. (1997). Technological regimes and sectoral patterns of innovative activities. *Industrial & Corporate Change, 6*, 83–117.

McGowan, M. A., Andrews, D., & Millot, V. (2017). *The walking dead? Zombie firms and productivity performance in OECD countries.* OECD Working Papers No. 1372.

OECD (2018). Labour productivity and utilisation (indicator). (doi: https://doi.org/10.1787/02c02f63-en, downloaded at Februar 13).

Peters, B., Mohnen, P., Saam, M., Blandinieres, F., Hud, M., Krieger, B., & Niebel, T. (2018). Langfristentwicklung von Innovationen und Produktivität – Säkulare Stagnation? Literaturübersicht zum Productivity Slowdown unter Berücksichtigung von Innovationsaktivitäten (Studien zum deutschen Innovationssystem Nr. 10–2018, Available from www.e-fi.de.

Rammer, C., Jäger, A., Krieger, B., Lerch, C., Licht, G., Peters, B., & Spielkamp, A. (2018a). Produktivitätsparadoxon im Maschinenbau; Studie für VDMA-IMPULS-Stiftung, Available from www.impuls-stiftung.de.

Rammer, C., Riaz, A., & Behrens, V. (2018b). Lange Datenreihen zu Innovatorenquoten (Studien zum deutschen Innovationssystems 2018, mimeo).

Sachverständigenrat (2015). Jahresgutachten 2015/16 "Zukunftsfähigkeit in den Mittelpunkt", Wiesbaden (available at: www.sachverstaendigenrat-wirtschaft.de).

Schivardi, F., Sette, E., & Tabellini, G. (2017). *Credit misallocation during the European financial crisis.* CEPR Discussion Papers 11901.

Schmalensee, R. (2018). *The collapse of labor productivity growth in U.S. manufacturing after 2010.* Available at SSRN: https://ssrn.com/abstract=3121771.

Syverson, C. (2017). Challenges to mismeasurement explanations for the US productivity slowdown. *Journal of Economic Perspectives, 31*(2), 165–186.

Varian, H. (2017). Technology, innovation and industrial organization. In European Central Bank (Ed.), *Investment and growth in advanced economies, conference proceedings, ECB forum on central banking, 26–28 Juni 2017, Sintra Portugal* (pp. 241–244).

Weber, T., Bertschek, I., Ohnemus, J., & Ebert, M. (2018). Monitoring Report. Wirtschaft DIGITAL, Report to German Ministry of Economy and Energy. Available from www.bmwi.de.

Dr. Audretsch: or How I Learned to Stop Worrying and Love Doing Small Business Research

Julie Ann Elston

Abstract Chapter author Julie Ann Elston describes how she met David in Germany as a young researcher herself. Throughout her narrative, she tells how David fought to establish the study of entrepreneurship and small business as legitimate fields of academic inquiry. This chapter clearly depicts David as an academic pioneer – an entrepreneur in his own right.

Dr. Audretsch: or How I Learned to Stop Worrying and Love Doing Small Business Research

I first met David in August of 1992 at the Wissenschaftszentrum Berlin (WZB). I had just completed my Ph.D. in economics and my advisor suggested I accept a research fellowship at a German think tank rather than attempt to build a research portfolio while juggling teaching as a tenure track faculty in the US. During my first week there I was introduced to David in the WZB cafeteria where he presided over a large table of social scientists discussing the importance of research on small business development. I remember being struck by the intensity of the conversation between diverse researchers from around the world, then lunch lead to coffee, which led to long walks in the neighboring *Tiergarden* as we argued and explored points of view all day. Many days, weeks, and years later, David still sparks and leads dynamic dialogues of academic inquiry with other researchers around the world on various issues in entrepreneurship. In my opinion he has single handedly established the acceptance of entrepreneurship as an academic field of study within economics and the social sciences. A daunting statement which I believe is true.

Actually, it took me years to appreciate the importance of small firm studies, as I had been studying the liquidity constraints of large firms in the US and Germany, and the contextual institutional environment which impacted the way that firms financed investment. That's when David and I talked about the fact that even all

J. A. Elston (✉)
Oregon State University, Bend, OR, USA
e-mail: julie.elston@osucascades.edu

© Springer Nature Switzerland AG 2019
E. E. Lehmann, M. Keilbach (eds.), *From Industrial Organization to Entrepreneurship*, https://doi.org/10.1007/978-3-030-25237-3_22

large firms are not the same size, that is that the presence of size effects might exist within the spectrum of traditional or large firms. And if large firms have problems getting funding, think about the tough time that smaller firms might have getting access to resources! And what about differences in corporate financing (and governance) between the US and Germany? Our discussions on the critical role of differences in financial institutions and markets in Germany's economic development, started a series of research studies that examined how country specific institutions were important both during Germany's *Wirstschaftswunder* years and in the 2000's tech boom. Education is important yes, but we also know that Germany has also different financial institutions which have led to the ability of the *Mittelstand* to grow and there is evidence of this in the literature. Financial market innovation, ie... the creation of the *Neuer Markt* also fed young technology firms during the more recent high-technology boom.

The system of finance in Germany is clearly different from its counterpart found in either the United States or Great Britain. A complex system of financial intermediaries may actually have provided more liquidity to the *Mittelstand* in Germany, compared to their small- and medium-sized counterparts under their respective financial systems in the United States and Great Britain.

Certainly the evidence suggests that during the postwar period, the *Mittelstand* in Germany contributed much more to the competitiveness of its country than did small- and medium-sized enterprises in most other developed industrialized countries. Still, even under the German system of finance there is at least some evidence that the relationship between access to finance and firm size has been a positive one. This would suggest that small- and medium-sized enterprises have been subjected to liquidity constraints, as in most other developed countries.

The existence of these financial intermediaries channeling funds into the German *Mittelstand* resulted in the emergence of mechanisms providing smaller firms with access to long-term, fixed rate funds (Vitols 1994). There were also numerous government policies directed towards providing finance for the German *Mittelstand*. For example, the *Kreditanstalt für Wiederaufbau*, which was originally established following the Second World War to facilitate reconstruction, is devoted towards providing finance to develop the technological competence of the German *Mittelstand (Bundesminister for Forschung und Technologie* 1985). Firms with annual sales of less than \$590 million are eligible for grants covering up to 40 percent of the costs of developing and implementing state-of-the-art technology. In addition, small- and medium-sized enterprises are exempt from many of the antimonopoly laws in Germany (*Gesetz gegen Wettbewerbsbeschränkungen*), which helps to facilitate joint marketing, purchasing, and R&D facilities (*Bundesministerium*).

The challenge confronting the German system of finance in the late 1980s was more urgent –how to modify the financial system in order to facilitate finance for new firms in new industries. While the incumbent system of finance may have been highly efficient in channeling funds to *mittelständische* and large firms alike in traditional industries, it was not at all conducive to financing new ideas that lay beyond the boundaries of traditional industries and enterprises.

In Audretsch and Elston (1997, 2001) we found evidence that the German model of finance was largely able to avoid financing constraints on German enterprises prior to the mid-1970s. A particularly striking feature of this era in West Germany was a relative abundance of cheap credit. This time frame seems to coincide with the *Wirtschaftswunder*, or economic miracle, in Germany. Since the mid-1970s there is no evidence that German firms, and in particular the smaller enterprises, have been able to avoid finance constraints.

To facilitate the transformation of the German economy from the traditional manufacturing industries towards emerging new technologies a new segment of the Frankfurt exchange was introduced in 1997—the *Neuer Markt*. To examine whether the Neuer Markt was successful, one need only compare the relationship between firm size and growth for firms listed on the *Neuer Markt* and contrast the results with two benchmarks: (1) for German firms prior to the 1990s (to reflect the older traditional manufacturing sector) and (2) for the stylized results for the US. Audretsch and Elston (2006) provides evidence that not only did many new firms obtain funding from the *Neuer Markt,* but that for the first time in recent history, Germany succeeded in enabling smaller firms to grow faster than larger firms. This suggested that the new policies were not only successful in promoting a new type of firm that otherwise might not exist, but in transforming the sources of growth and innovation within the German economy. I found this research really exciting in terms of the potential for influencing national policy on growth.

At the end of the day, what I appreciate most about David is not his influence on the development of entrepreneurship, but his kind mentoring. With remarkable intellectual generosity and good humor he made every inquiry and research study an academic adventure. To say he was wonderful to work with is an understatement. He is the rarest of intellectuals who is able to bring out the best in others without compromising the intellectual quality of the research process or diminish his own contribution. His vision and breadth of knowledge in entrepreneurship will persevere for decades to come.

References

Audretsch, D., & Elston, J. A. (2006). Can institutional change impact high-technology firm growth? Evidence from Germany's Neuer Markt. *Journal of Productivity Analysis: Special Olympic Issue, 25*(1/2), 9–2.

Audretsch, D., & Elston, J. A. (2001). Does firm size matter? Evidence on the impacts of liquidity constraints on firm investment behavior in Germany, (2001). *International Journal of Industrial Organization, 20,* 1–17.

Audretsch, D., & Elston, J. A. (1997). Financing the German Mittelstand. *Small Business Economics, 9,* 97–110.

Vitols, S. I. (1994). *German banks and the modernization of the small firm sector: Long-term finance in comparative perspective, unpublished manuscript*. Berlin: Wissenschaftszentrum Berlin für Sozialforschung.

"I Want to, But I Also Need to": Start-Ups Resulting from Opportunity and Necessity

Marco Caliendo and Alexander S. Kritikos

Abstract When unemployed persons start businesses, they are often characterized as necessity entrepreneurs because push motives, namely their unemployment, likely prompted their decision. Based on a panel data set of more than 2600 start-ups by unemployed persons, we show that not only push but also pull motives can be observed among previously unemployed business founders. Moreover, a third type of entrepreneur emerges, motivated by a combination of both push and pull factors. When analysing the entrepreneurial performance of these three motivational types over a period of nearly 5 years, we reveal that motivation matters even in the long term: pull type entrepreneurs have higher survival rates and do create more jobs than push type entrepreneurs. Entrepreneurs being motivated by a combination of both, i.e. the start-ups resulting from opportunity and necessity fall between the two extremes.

Introduction

The Global Entrepreneurship Monitor (GEM) has established the opportunity-necessity dichotomy with nascent entrepreneurs being distinguished in two simple categories: opportunity entrepreneurs starting entrepreneurial careers voluntarily usually out of an employed position, and necessity entrepreneurs opting for less voluntary reasons to become entrepreneur, i.e. to end their unemployment situation (Bosma and Harding 2007). This dichotomy has resulted in the perception that the relation holds also the other way around, i.e. that every individual starting out of an employed position is an opportunity entrepreneur while every individual starting

---

M. Caliendo · A. S. Kritikos (✉)
University of Potsdam, Potsdam, Germany

Institute for the Study of Labor (IZA), Bonn, Germany

German Institute for Economic Research (DIW Berlin), Berlin, Germany

IAB, Nuremberg, Germany
e-mail: caliendo@uni-potsdam.de; akritikos@diw.de

© Springer Nature Switzerland AG 2019
E. E. Lehmann, M. Keilbach (eds.), *From Industrial Organization to Entrepreneurship*, https://doi.org/10.1007/978-3-030-25237-3_23

out of unemployment is a necessity entrepreneur (see e.g. Fairlie and Fossen 2018). As necessity entrepreneurs are expected to have low aspiration levels with little potential for innovation, they might only marginally contribute to the economic development of a country (Andersson and Wadensjö 2007). Therefore, several economists argue that public policy should not support any entrepreneurial activities with tax money if entrepreneurs are starting for reasons of necessity, thus basically out of unemployment (see Shane 2009; Roman et al. 2013).

Yet, this picture does not find unanimous support. Other scholars argue that the distinction between necessity and opportunity entrepreneurs may not just be artificial but also harmful, claiming that necessity-driven entrepreneurs, as they depend on incomes out of their business, are not necessarily less ambitious (see Hessels et al. 2008). Valliere and Peterson (2009) point to the fact that necessity entrepreneurs may in particular in developing economies do better than opportunity entrepreneurs. Moreover, and most importantly, David, the jubilar of this scholary collection, and co-authors (Welter et al. 2017) call for more open- mindedness in dealing with motivations of entrepreneurs and the way motivations are classified. As they argue, the "tendency in the entrepreneurship field to dichotomize various categories of entrepreneurship in ways that marginalize research on some types by in effect casting them as 'other' [...] may obscure the dynamics of entrepreneurship". It "keeps us from seeing all of the rich and heterogeneous motivations that actually drive entrepreneurs to create new venture" (Welter et al. 2017, pp. 312 and 316).

In this contribution, we focus on one crucial aspect of this discussion, one of the 'other types', namely those entrepreneurs who start out of unemployment. We investigate to what extent the motivations that actually drive entrepreneurs to create new ventures out of unemployment are more heterogeneous than usually assumed. Therefore, the first aim of this contribution is to explore the extent to which these entrepreneurs are motivated by necessity, i.e. by push motives such as the termination of unemployment, or also by opportunity, i.e. by pull motives such as the perception of a market opportunity, or the desire to be their own boss. Moreover, as we look more deeply into the motivations of entrepreneurs coming out of unemployment, our second aim is to reveal how their initial start-up motivations relate to the subsequent development of their businesses in the long term. To do so, we examine the economic performance of a large number of more than 2600 business founders from Germany who had been registered as unemployed before they began their entrepreneurial activities. We have access to panel data that combines administrative and survey data over a period of nearly 5 years after businesses were ventured. The survey data contain information about personal, business-related, and motivational characteristics allowing us to conduct a differentiated analysis.

The rest of this contribution is organized as follows. Section "Motivations for Becoming an Entrepreneur and their Links to Entrepreneurial Output" shortly describes how motivations may vary among those who are becoming entrepreneurs, and how these motivations may affect later entrepreneurial development. Based on these concise reviews, we derive our research questions. Section "Data Set and

"I Want to, But I Also Need to": Start-Ups Resulting from Opportunity and Necessity 249

Descriptives" contains our description of the data set, as well as descriptive results revealing the varying motivations of entrepreneurs coming out of unemployment. In section "Empirical Analysis", we analyze how these motives influence their entrepreneurial performance in the long term. In section "Discussion, Conclusion and Future Research", we briefly discuss the results and conclude.

Motivations for Becoming an Entrepreneur and their Links to Entrepreneurial Output

Prior research has investigated why people decide to run their own business. Using a questionnaire with 23 different items, Shane et al. (1991) extracted four factors, labeled recognition, independence, learning, and roles. Birley and Westhead (1994) instead identify seven factors: need for approval, need for independence, need for personal development, welfare considerations, perceived instrumentality of wealth, tax reduction, and following role models. On the basis of these findings, Carter et al. (2003) have developed five categories of entrepreneurship reasons, namely, innovation, independence, recognition, roles, and financial success, with self-realization added as a sixth factor.[1]

A more parsimonious approach, inspired by the General Entrepreneurship Monitor (see Bosma and Harding 2007) differentiates between only two classes of motivation: those who initiate entrepreneurial activities voluntarily and those who are pushed into such activities to address their unemployment. Reviewing the existing categories of motivation reveals that much less information pertains to push motives than to pull motives. In this section, we therefore provide a brief overview of these two classes of motivations as well as their influence on entrepreneurial performance.

Entrepreneurial Motives

Characteristic pull motivations include the perception of a market opportunity or an innovative idea, such that the entrepreneur searches for new or better solutions than those given in the actual (market) environment (see McClelland 1961; Shane et al. 1991; Birley and Westhead 1994). An entrepreneur also might recognize an existing network that he or she could try to exploit. Such networks might contain initial customers or provide production capabilities, both of which help ensure market orders. According to the taxonomy suggested by Carter et al. (2003), other pull

---

[1] Other discussions relate to which motivational factors are crucial for starting a business when comparing entrepreneurs with non-entrepreneurs (see, e.g., Carter et al. 2003), or how to model the intentional process between motivations and entrepreneurial development (see, e.g., Krueger et al. 2000, who proposed two competing models of such entrepreneurial intentions).

motivations relate to categories such as independence, recognition, self-realization, or financial incentives. Independence involves the willingness to be free of any external control or to become one's own boss.

Less research considers why necessity entrepreneurs choose to get into business. Prevailing opinion in entrepreneurship research suggests that necessity entrepreneurs lack other or better alternatives to unemployment (see for instance Storey 1991, or Clark and Drinkwater 2000). Unemployed persons who face the termination of their unemployment benefits may also feel a sense of necessity to become self-employed if they have no other income options. A third reason -in contrast to the previous ones- is that external agents advise the unemployed persons to try self-employment as an alternative option (see Caliendo and Kritikos 2010). In all cases, the opportunity cost of deciding to become an entrepreneur is significantly lower than the opportunity cost for those who make this decision while they are employed. Previous research rarely considers the question to what extent entrepreneurs are motivated exclusively by either pull or push motives, or by a combination of both. Potential reasoning why such a mixture of motives may evolve, relates motivational factors with occupational choices. Occupational choice models assert that persons choose entrepreneurship over their current employment position if they are able to increase their utility from doing so. Within our setting, there might be individuals who consider themselves to be latent entrepreneurs while being employed. However, they might have perceived the utility from entrepreneurial activities as lower than the utility from their employment which is why they remain employed. There is a large number of such latent entrepreneurs, as many countries show huge differences between the number of latent entrepreneurs and those who really start (see, Bosma and Harding 2007). Should these individuals lose their job and become unemployed, the calculus of their utility changes. Given their opportunity driven motives in combination with their unemployment position (which makes the opportunity cost of a transition into self-employment lower), the utility of starting an own business may now become greater than the utility of staying unemployed or of hoping for a future salaried job. As a consequence these individuals may become entrepreneurs out of opportunity and necessity.

The Influence of Motivational Factors on Entrepreneurial Development

A common understanding in entrepreneurship research is that opportunity entrepreneurs raise positive and necessity entrepreneurs raise negative expectations. Entrepreneurial activities appear as crucial for economic development for three main reasons. First, entrepreneurs create their own jobs in terms of self-employment (e.g., Evans and Leigthon 1989). Second, entrepreneurs likely invest substantial amounts of capital and create further job opportunities as they build their growing company (e.g., Parker and Johnson 1996). Third and maybe most importantly, entrepreneurs are expected to be innovative (see, e.g., Arrighetti and Vivarelli 1999), which may make them the essence of future economic growth (see, e.g., Audretsch 2007).

By combining expectations about entrepreneurial activities with the motivations of the two classes of entrepreneurs, it is reasonable to expect that opportunity entrepreneurs seem preferable to those that start a company out of necessity. According to the various pull motives opportunity entrepreneurs should not only establish their own jobs, they may also invest significant sums of capital into their entrepreneurial activities, create new and further jobs, and in the best case be innovative. In contrast it seems reasonable to expect that necessity entrepreneurs simply employ themselves. Their lack of pull motives implies that they will create neither further jobs nor innovative ideas. Because they are pushed into running a business by their lack of alternative wage employment opportunities, these entrepreneurs may not really be prepared to launch a business. If this reasoning holds, we should further expect mixed type entrepreneurs who combine pull motives, e.g. like being their own boss and push motives like ending their unemployment situation, to perform worse than pure pull types, but better than pure push types.

However, little empirical analysis considers the motivational characteristics of previously unemployed business founders.[2] Therefore, we will use in this contribution a panel data set which asks unemployed respondents why they decided to get into business at the initial stage of their start-up process. In doing so we investigate the following research questions:

(i) To what extent are individuals who start their entrepreneurial activities out of unemployment driven by only push or only pull motives? And to what extent do we observe a combination of both kind of motives?

(ii) Do the three motivational types, pure pull, pure push and mixed types, differ with respect to their individual background?

(iii) Do entrepreneurial motivations influence the performance of this group of start-ups, i.e. do entrepreneurs out of unemployment who offer only pull motives realize a better performance in terms of survival rates and job creation than entrepreneurs driven only by push motives?

(iv) Do entrepreneurs who are motivated by a combination of pull and push factors perform more like pure pull type or more like pure push type entrepreneurs?

Data Set and Descriptives

Sample

Labor market reforms in Germany in 2003 (the "Hartz reforms") substantially expanded support for business start-ups by unemployed. As a consequence, between 2003 and 2006, more than one million persons -virtually all individuals being in

---

[2] For more general evidence on start-ups out of unemployment in various countries, see Storey and Jones (1987), Evans and Leighton (1990), Storey (1991), Audretsch and Vivarelli (1995), Hinz and Jungbauer Gans (1999), Pfeiffer and Reize (2000), Andersson and Wadensjö (2007), Caliendo and Kritikos (2010), and Caliendo et al. (2012).

transition from unemployment to self-employment- made use of public support schemes to became self-employed. Simultaneously, an evaluation project was launched to collect a unique data set that is representative with respect to start-ups out of unemployment. We use this data set, which consists of a random sample of more than 2600 participants. They became self-employed in Germany during the third quarter of 2003, at which point Germany offered two different public support programs, the bridging allowance (BA, *Überbrückungsgeld*) and the start-up subsidy (SUS, *Existenzgründungszuschuss*). The observed individuals received support from either one of the two programs.[3] Both programs aimed to cover the basic costs of living and social security contributions during the initial stage of self-employment, when businesses might not be able to yield adequate income.[4]

The data set combines administrative information from the Federal Employment Agency (FEA) with survey data, collected at three points in time. In the first interview after approximately 1.3 years, the respondents indicated the reasons why they decided to start their business, and reported basic characteristics about their businesses (start-up capital, industry, previous work experience, etc.). In a second interview, approximately 2.5 years after business formation, they reported on the development of their businesses, such as their employment status and direct job creation. In a third interview, approximately 5 years after business formation, these individuals again reported their status and answered the same questions concerning business development between the second and third interview. In the main regression analysis we will concentrate on the long-term influence of start-up motivations on their entrepreneurial performance.

Motivation to Become an Entrepreneur

To determine their motivation, respondents were asked during the first interview the following question: "Which motivations were crucial for your decision to start your own business?" Multiple answers (with a scale measurement "apply" or "does not apply" for each motive) were allowed. Possible answers were closely linked to the classification presented in section "Motivations for Becoming an Entrepreneur and their Links to Entrepreneurial Output", where we discuss the motivational factors for entrepreneurial activities. Three of the six answers are associated with pull motives: "being my own boss" relates to the independence motive, "had first customers" relates to the recognition of existing networks, and "perceived a market opportunity" relates to having an innovative idea. The other three answers are associated with push motives: "ending unemployment" relates to the motive of having

---

[3] Simultaneous use of both programs was not allowed.

[4] For more details on the two programs and on business development, see Caliendo and Kritikos (2010); for an impact analysis of the support programs, see Caliendo and Künn (2011).

"I Want to, But I Also Need to": Start-Ups Resulting from Opportunity and Necessity 253

Table 1 Motivation to become self-employed

	All	Only Pull	Push and Pull	Only Push
Observations	2615	384	1880	351
Share		0.147	0.718	0.134
1. I always wanted to be my own chef	0.51	0.685	0.572	0.000
		(0.465)	(0.495)	(0.000)
2. Termination of unemployment	0.83	0.000	0.969	0.969
		(0.000)	(0.174)	(0.174)
3. Exhaustion of unemployment benefit entitlement	0.34	0.000	0.404	0.386
		(0.000)	(0.491)	(0.488)
4. Advice from the labor agency	0.15	0.000	0.186	0.131
		(0.000)	(0.389)	(0.338)
5. I already had first customers	0.62	0.633	0.735	0.000
		(0.483)	(0.442)	(0.000)
6. I spotted a market gap	0.33	0.391	0.377	0.000
		(0.489)	(0.485)	(0.000)

Note: Numbers are shares unless stated otherwise; standard deviations are in brackets. Multiple answers were allowed. Those who identify one (or more) of reasons 1/5/6 but not 2/3/4 were assigned to the "Only Pull" group, those stating one (or more) of 2/3/4 but not 1/5/6 the "Only Push" group. Other respondents were assigned to the "Push and Pull" group

no better choice to avoid unemployment, "exhaustion of unemployment benefits" relates to the income motive, and "advice from the labor agency" relates to external party advice.

In Table 1, we report the share of respondents for each variable. Around 83% of all persons were driven by the central push motive, "ending unemployment", 62% of the business founders stated that they already had "first customers", 51% were guided by the main independence motive of "being their own boss". The pull motive with the lowest share is the identification of a market gap (with 33%). The other push motives are similarly less important, including the exhaustion of unemployment benefit entitlements at 34% and advice from the labor agency at 15%. According to these motives, we divided the entrepreneurs into three categories: those who answer that they were driven only by one or more pull but no push motive (i.e. pull types), those for whom only push motives were the reason to become self-employed (push types), and a third category of entrepreneurs who chose a combination of push and pull factors as motivational drivers (mixed types). Our data reveal that less than 30% of this population is driven by clearly delimitable factors. That means, there is a certain, even if relatively small share of pull type entrepreneurs coming out of unemployment. Most entrepreneurs out of unemployment are, however, motivated by a combination of pull and push motives. Table 1 shows which reasons are critical for the three categories and a further distribution of push and pull motives among the mixed types.

Overall, we state as **Observation 1**: 13.4% of all start-ups by unemployed persons are driven by push motives, 14.7% are guided merely by pull motives. A majority of 71.8% of all unemployed persons starting their own business, are guided by both pull and push motives.

Who Are the Three Start-up Types?

In this section we examine the three types in greater depth, in particular to which pure type the mixed types resemble more closely. For this analysis we can rely on the questionnaire that surveyed a further set of explanatory variables. Tables 2 and 3 provide the sample means of selected variables that describe the characteristics of the three types of business founders. We add results from a t-test of mean equality to reveal differences among these types.

We start by inspecting the educational background of these entrepreneurs as well as their working and unemployment experiences. The comparison shows that pull type entrepreneurs are better educated than push type entrepreneurs, as the share of respondents with an upper school degree is highest among pull types (50%), followed by mixed types (39%) and push types (33%). Differences are significant between all three types. For the share of individuals with a low-level school degree, the ranking almost reverses with push type and mixed type entrepreneurs having nearly the same shares. Similar findings hold for tertiary education, where the latter two types have such graduation only in less than 20 percent of all cases.

Having gained working experience in the sector in which founders aim to start their business is another crucial prerequisite for entrepreneurial success (c.f., e.g., Cressy 2006). Among pull types, as we show in Table 3, there is the highest share of respondents with working experience from regular employment in the same industry (74%), followed by mixed types (66%), whereas only 56% of all push types claim to have such experience. Of those with no previous relevant working experience, the ranking reverses. The same picture occurs when comparing previous durations of unemployment, which is known to be the most crucial variable for human and working capital depreciation. While pull types on average have been unemployed for less than 5 months, it takes both mixed and push types around 8 months of unemployment before they decide to become self-employed. With respect to start-up capital, we observe differences between the three types in a similar direction. Among those who invested more than 10,000 Euros, pull types rank first with 38 percent. Among the other two types around 20 percent invested that much while establishing their business. The share of individuals having more than 90 percent in form of own capital is again highest among pull type entrepreneurs. Our analysis of the three start-up types focuses also on other personal characteristics. Starting with age, pull types are, on average, significantly younger (36.4 years) than push types (41.9 years), while mixed types are similar to push types (40.4 years). Interestingly, the typical inverse u-shaped relationship between age and the probability for starting an own business holds for all three groups, however,

"I Want to, But I Also Need to": Start-Ups Resulting from Opportunity and Necessity   255

Table 2 Selected socio-demographic characteristics and labor market history

	Only Pull	Only Push	p	Push and Pull	Only Push	p	Only Pull	Push and Pull	p
N	384	351		1880	351		384	1880	
Age (in years)	36.38	41.91	0.000	40.45	41.90	0.005	36.38	40.45	0.000
18–29	0.232	0.085	0.000	0.122	0.085	0.048	0.232	0.122	0.000
30–39	0.440	0.328	0.002	0.343	0.328	0.575	0.440	0.343	0.000
40–49	0.255	0.365	0.001	0.357	0.365	0.781	0.255	0.357	0.000
50–64	0.073	0.222	0.000	0.178	0.222	0.048	0.073	0.178	0.000
Non-German	0.201	0.276	0.016	0.277	0.276	0.976	0.201	0.277	0.002
Married	0.536	0.652	0.001	0.607	0.652	0.108	0.536	0.607	0.010
School degree									
No degree	0.003	0.014	0.080	0.013	0.014	0.888	0.003	0.013	0.073
Lower secondary schooling	0.146	0.236	0.002	0.249	0.236	0.619	0.146	0.249	0.000
Middle secondary degree	0.352	0.422	0.051	0.343	0.422	0.005	0.352	0.343	0.750
Upper secondary schooling	0.500	0.328	0.000	0.395	0.328	0.018	0.500	0.395	0.000
Months in unemployment	4.52	8.16	0.000	8.65	8.16	0.324	4.52	8.65	0.000
< 3 months	0.500	0.279	0.000	0.236	0.279	0.081	0.500	0.236	0.000
3 months – < 6 months	0.208	0.211	0.934	0.204	0.211	0.780	0.208	0.204	0.857
6 months – < 1 year	0.242	0.299	0.082	0.358	0.299	0.034	0.242	0.358	0.000
1 year – < 2 years	0.049	0.211	0.000	0.202	0.211	0.710	0.049	0.202	0.000
Unemployment benefits (in e/day)	31.43	28.79	0.028	27.07	28.79	0.039	31.43	27.07	0.000
Remaining benefit entitlement (in months)	7.95	5.86	0.000	5.09	5.86	0.031	7.95	5.09	0.000
Qualification:									
Unskilled workers	0.102	0.145	0.071	0.177	0.145	0.154	0.102	0.177	0.000
Tertiary education	0.247	0.191	0.065	0.220	0.191	0.228	0.247	0.220	0.236
Technical college education	0.052	0.085	0.073	0.072	0.085	0.370	0.052	0.072	0.163
Skilled workers	0.599	0.578	0.571	0.532	0.578	0.109	0.599	0.532	0.016

Note: Numbers are shares unless stated otherwise. The p-values refer to t- tests of mean equality in the variables between the groups

with differing peaks in the three groups. It is also important to know more about the personality of entrepreneurs. For one crucial personality characteristics, risk attitudes (Caliendo et al. 2014), we observe that the risk-taking behavior of the three types of business founders differs significantly. On an 11-point scale ranging from "0" (completely un- willing) to "10" (completely willing), pull types are signifi-

Table 3 Business and founders' characteristics

	Only Pull	Only Push	p	Push and Pull	Only Push	p	Only Pull	Push and Pull	p
N	384	351		1880	351		384	1880	
Experience before self-employment									
Yes, from regular work	0.737	0.558	0.000	0.667	0.558	0.000	0.737	0.667	0.007
Yes, from secondary work	0.234	0.128	0.000	0.263	0.128	0.000	0.234	0.263	0.238
Yes, from leisure time	0.258	0.225	0.301	0.311	0.225	0.001	0.258	0.311	0.038
No	0.081	0.256	0.000	0.129	0.256	0.000	0.081	0.129	0.008
Preparation before start-up									
Self-consulted potential customers	0.451	0.353	0.007	0.523	0.353	0.000	0.451	0.523	0.010
Attendance of informative meetings	0.549	0.459	0.014	0.528	0.459	0.017	0.549	0.528	0.446
Use of coaching and consulting offerings	0.352	0.322	0.397	0.374	0.322	0.063	0.352	0.374	0.408
Support by others	0.513	0.436	0.037	0.528	0.436	0.002	0.513	0.528	0.601
Miscellaneous	0.258	0.171	0.004	0.260	0.171	0.000	0.258	0.260	0.926
No certain preparation	0.076	0.165	0.000	0.084	0.165	0.000	0.076	0.084	0.581
Industry/sector of start-up									
Services	0.461	0.527	0.073	0.469	0.527	0.046	0.461	0.469	0.769
Craft	0.070	0.063	0.679	0.086	0.063	0.150	0.070	0.086	0.322
Construction	0.068	0.066	0.906	0.090	0.066	0.128	0.068	0.090	0.149
Retail	0.115	0.108	0.786	0.096	0.108	0.469	0.115	0.096	0.260
IT	0.094	0.051	0.028	0.061	0.051	0.473	0.094	0.061	0.020
Other	0.193	0.185	0.795	0.198	0.185	0.583	0.193	0.198	0.817
Start-up capital:									
0 EUR	0.333	0.507	0.000	0.444	0.507	0.030	0.333	0.444	0.000
Up to 2500 EUR	0.099	0.108	0.680	0.131	0.108	0.244	0.099	0.131	0.086
2500–10,000 EUR	0.193	0.199	0.819	0.221	0.199	0.363	0.193	0.221	0.216
More than 10,000 EUR	0.375	0.185	0.000	0.204	0.185	0.426	0.375	0.204	0.000
Share of own capital:									
No, or < 10%	0.404	0.564	0.000	0.510	0.564	0.061	0.404	0.510	0.000
10–50%	0.154	0.100	0.029	0.104	0.100	0.821	0.154	0.104	0.005
50–90%	0.070	0.034	0.029	0.034	0.034	0.989	0.070	0.034	0.001
>90%	0.372	0.302	0.044	0.353	0.302	0.067	0.372	0.353	0.462

(continued)

"I Want to, But I Also Need to": Start-Ups Resulting from Opportunity and Necessity 257

Table 3 (continued)

	Only Pull	Only Push	p	Push and Pull	Only Push	p	Only Pull	Push and Pull	p
Willingness to take risk (scale from 0–10)	6.141	5.379	0.000	5.648	5.379	0.026	6.141	5.648	0.000
Low (0–3)	0.115	0.177	0.017	0.153	0.177	0.268	0.115	0.153	0.051
Medium (4–6)	0.378	0.504	0.001	0.484	0.504	0.475	0.378	0.484	0.000
High (7–10)	0.508	0.319	0.000	0.363	0.319	0.112	0.508	0.363	0.000

Note: Numbers are shares unless stated otherwise. The p-values refer to t- tests of mean equality in the variables between the groups

cantly more willing to take risks (6.14 points) than both mixed types (5.64 points) and push types (5.38 points).

A final difference across all three types to be highlighted becomes obvious, when we focus on business preparation. This information mirrors the efforts individuals put into their ventures and reveals the degree of goal orientation among them. Table 3 reports two striking differences: The share of individuals not preparing for the venturing of the business was highest among push types. Among them 16 percent claimed to have done no certain preparation while this was true only for around 8 percent among the other two groups. In contrast to this pull types and even to higher degree mixed types were able to rely on support from their networks like friends, family, or other firm owners (both in more than 50 percent of the cases) or used significantly more often coaches and consultants (more than 30% of the cases). Overall, it appears that the three types differ in many individual characteristics like their demographic, educational or employment background, their personality in terms of risk attitudes and in their efforts in preparing the venture of the business.

We conclude with **Observation 2**: Pull type individuals, compared to push type individuals, tend to have more favorable characteristics for entrepreneurial activities in terms of human and financial capital, as well as in terms of demographic characteristics or relevant work experience. Entrepreneurs with mixed motives tend to be in some characteristics more similar to push type entrepreneurs, while with respect to their efforts in preparing their businesses mixed type individuals tend to be more similar to pull type entrepreneurs.Thus entrepreneurs coming out of unemployment are not only very heterogeneous in their motivations to venture an own business, they are also as heterogeneous in what they did earlier in their work lives, with some important similarities between push types and mixed types. Having revealed a deeper understanding of their past, may allow us in a next step to better understand why some of these ventures being started out of unemployment will survive more often and grow better in the future than others.

Empirical Analysis

Descriptives: Survival and Job Creation

We start by showing the Kaplan-Meier survival function for the three types of business founders in Fig. 1 over 5 years. During the first 6 months the development of all three types is quite similar. After this first period we observe for the following 2 years an increasing spread, with survival rates being highest for the pull types with 81%, and lowest for push types at 60%. The mixed types fall in between, with a rate of 70%. During the third period, another 2.5 years, survival rates decrease almost parallel, with differences remaining at around 10% between the three types. After 5 years, at the end of the observation period, about 51% of the push types are in self-employment, while among the pull types 73% and among the mixed types 62% of start- ups are in the market.[5]

We summarize the outcomes of our observation period in Table 4. We need to emphasize that some of the business founders who failed with their business idea take second chances; within the first 5 years for all three types about 5% of the business founders failed and tried self-employment another time. When analyzing return to unemployment as a proxy for business failure,[6] we find after 2.5 years an unam-

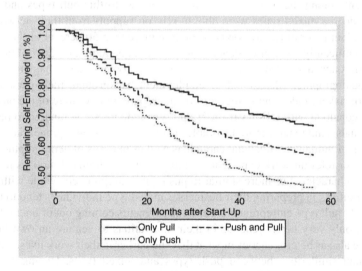

Fig. 1 Kaplan Meier Survival Function (Long-Term). Note: Number of total failures: 1122. Likelihood-ratio test statistic of homogeneity for the three groups: $\chi2(2) = 47.52$, $p = 0.0000$

---

[5] A likelihood ratio test of homogeneity in the survival rates for the three groups is clearly rejected ($\chi2(2) = 47.52$, $p = 0.000$).

[6] For a discussion of the difference between business failure and closure, see Headd (2003).

"I Want to, But I Also Need to": Start-Ups Resulting from Opportunity and Necessity 259

Table 4 Labor market status and share with employees at interview

	Only Pull	Only Push	p	Push and Pull	Only Push	p	Only Pull	Push and Pull	p
N	384	351		1880	351		384	1880	
Employment status (t + 28)									
Self-employed	0.802	0.619	0.000	0.725	0.619	0.000	0.802	0.725	0.002
Regular employed	0.102	0.165	0.011	0.097	0.165	0.000	0.102	0.097	0.773
Unemployed	0.052	0.125	0.000	0.108	0.125	0.349	0.052	0.108	0.001
Other	0.044	0.091	0.011	0.070	0.091	0.171	0.044	0.070	0.062
Business failed	0.214	0.389	0.000	0.294	0.389	0.000	0.214	0.294	0.001
At least one employee(a)	0.271	0.091	0.000	0.120	0.091	0.115	0.271	0.120	0.000
Employment status (t + 56)									
Self-employed	0.727	0.514	0.000	0.621	0.514	0.000	0.727	0.621	0.000
Regular employed	0.167	0.295	0.000	0.184	0.295	0.000	0.167	0.184	0.423
Unemployed	0.034	0.080	0.007	0.088	0.080	0.617	0.034	0.088	0.000
Other	0.073	0.111	0.075	0.107	0.111	0.827	0.073	0.107	0.044
Business failed	0.328	0.537	0.000	0.429	0.537	0.000	0.328	0.429	0.000
At least one employee(b)	0.262	0.087	0.000	0.112	0.087	0.186	0.262	0.112	0.000

Note: Numbers are shares unless stated otherwise. The p-values refer to t- tests of mean equality in the variables between the groups. (a) Measured for those who are still running a business at the time of the interview. The business founders who have at least one employee, employ on average 4.2 employees (Only Pull: 103), .3 (Push and Pull: 224) and 2.7 (Only Push: 32). (b) Measured for those who are still running a business at the time of the interview. The business founders who have at least one employee, employ on average 5.2 employees (Only Pull: 113), 4.9 (Push and Pull: 312) and 3.5 (Only Push: 38)

biguous connection between types and unemployment rates; returning to unemployment is lowest among pull (5.2%) and highest among push types (12.5%), whereas 10.8% of the mixed types are again unemployed. After 5 years the picture is more moderate. Unemployment rates vary between 3% for pull and around 8% to 9% for the two other types. From the group of push types even 30% of all business founders returned back to an employed position.

Table 4 also contains information about the share of businesses with at least one employee after 2.5 and 5 years. Differences are substantial. After 5 years 26% of all pull types (or 36% of those who remained in business) create further jobs. Among pure push and mixed types the shares are much lower with 9% and 11% (or 17–18% for those who remained in business). Pull types who employ further individuals at the end of our observation period created on average 5.2 additional jobs, mixed types 4.9 and push type business founders create 3.5 jobs.

Result 1: (1) Among entrepreneurs out of unemployment, pull type entrepreneurs have higher survival rates, enjoy lower failure and closure rates, and create larger businesses in terms of additional jobs than do push type entrepreneurs.

Entrepreneurs guided by both kind of motives are in-between push and pull types in terms of business survival and of the average size of the created business. (2) Diverging performance in terms of business survival among the three types of entrepreneurs is observed over the first 2.5 years following the launch. Beyond that period the survival rates run in a parallel way.

Regression Analysis: Business Failure and Job Creation

We now aim to find out to what extent the motivation for starting the business has an influence on these two important dimensions of entrepreneurial success business survival and job creation in the first 5 years after business start-up. In our first regression, the outcome variable equals '1' if the person exited self- employment during our observation period (business exit) and '0' if the person is still self-employed. Thus, we use a binary logit model for the estimation and employ the set of explanatory variables described in section "Who Are the Three Start-up Types" which were shown in earlier research to have significant influence on entrepreneurial development. We thus aim to determine whether pull and push motives have a long-term influence on entrepreneurial performance even 5 year after the launch, while controlling for other important characteristics. We provide the results in columns (1) and (2) of Table 5.

The mixed types serve as the base category for this regression. The marginal effects in column (2) can be directly interpreted in relation to the overall exit rate: pull types have a significantly lower exit probability by 6.3%-points. For push types though, we find a significantly higher exit probability of 8.1%-points in comparison to the baseline category. Moreover, we note several influences of other variables on entrepreneurial development which are in line with prior research. With respect to age, we find that middle-aged respondents between 30 and 49 years have a significantly lower exit probability. Formal education is essential to self-employment success, and we find that exit rates decrease with school educational level. Similarly, the availability of financial resources unfolds the expected influence. The share of own capital and the amount of the invested capital have a significant influence on survival rates: respondents who invested 25,000 € and less exit more often. When the share of own capital is higher than 90%, the exit probability decreases. In accordance with prior entrepreneurship research, we find another decisive variable for survival: the entrepreneur's work experience. When having gained experience from regular or secondary work in the specific business segment in which the individuals conduct their start-up activities, exit probabilities decrease, while a change of the business segment increases the exit probability. Overall, we should emphasize that the influence of motivational variables on survival remains relatively strong even in the long run and even if we control for a large number of variables that are known to affect entrepreneurial development.

In our second regression we analyze another success dimension of entrepreneurs, i.e. whether they decided to create further jobs for others. Therefore, we construct an outcome variable that takes the value of '1' if the entrepreneur has at

"I Want to, But I Also Need to": Start-Ups Resulting from Opportunity and Necessity   261

Table 5 Logit estimation results: Failure probability and share with employees (in t + 56)

| | Failure Probability – At least one Employee | | | |
	Coeff. Eff.	Marg. Eff.	Coeff.	Marg.
	(1)	(2)(3)(4)		
Push and pull motives (Reference)				
Only pull motives	−0.262**	−0.063**	0.302*	0.059*
Only push motives	0.326***	0.081***	−0.406*	−0.069**
East Germany	0.058	0.014	0.11	0.021
Women	−0.161	−0.039	−0.251	−0.045
Married	0.018	0.004	0.051	0.009
Health restrictions	0.227	0.056	0.188	0.036
Non-German	0.267***	0.066***	0.013	0.002
Children (yes/no)	0.057	0.014	0.197	0.037
Age in years: 18–29 (Reference)				
30–39	−0.386***	−0.093***	−0.502***	−0.090***
40–49	−0.264*	−0.064*	−0.1749***	−0.130***
50–64	0.058	0.014	−1.099***	−0.164***
School degree – low				
Middle	−0.121	−0.029	−0.237	−0.043
Upper	−0.215	−0.052*	−0.518***	−0.094***
Qualification: Unskilled workers (Reference)				
Skilled workers	−0.083	−0.020	−0.298	−0.055
Technical college education	−0.257	−0.061	−0.237	−0.041
Tertiary education	−0.147	−0.035	−0.228	−0.041
Months in unemployment	0.005	0.001	−0.024**	−0.004**
Unemployment benefits	0.002	0.0004	0.014***	0.003***
Remaining benefit entitlement	−0.009	−0.002	0.021*	0.004*
Start-up capital: 0 EUR (Reference)				
Up to 2500 EUR	0.461**	0.114**	−0.204	−0.036
2500–10,000 EUR	−0.067	−0.016	0.404	0.079
More than 10,000 EUR	−0.250	−0.060	0.952***	0.193***
Share of own capital: No, or < 10%				
10–50%	−0.259	−0.062	0.311	0.061
50–90%	−0.299	−0.071	−0.295	−0.051
>90%	−0.349*	−0.084*	−0.077	−0.014
Industry/sector of start-up: Services				
Craft	−0.752***	−0.169***	−0.053	−0.010
Construction	−0.662***	−0.151***	0.149	0.028
Retail	0.053	0.013	−0.231	−0.041
IT	0.293	0.072	−0.664**	−0.104**
Other	−0.369**	−0.088**	0.164	0.031
Experience before self-employment				

(continued)

Table 5 (continued)

| | Failure Probability – At least one Employee | | | |
	Coeff. Eff.	Marg. Eff.	Coeff.	Marg.
Yes, from regular work	−0.319***	−0.078***	0.098	0.018
Yes, from secondary work	−0.318***	−0.076***	0.012	0.002
Yes, from leisure time	−0.122	−0.030	−0.334**	−0.060**
No	0.192	0.047	0.247	0.048
Preparation before start-up				
Self-consulted potential customers	0.131	0.032	−0.191	−0.035
Attendance of informative meetings	0.134	0.033	−0.057	−0.011
Use of coaching and consulting offerings	−0.048	−0.012	0.148	0.028
Support by others	−0.085	−0.021	0.159	0.029
Readiness to take risks (low: 0–3)				
Medium (4–6)	−0.049	−0.012	−0.115	−0.021
High (7–10)	−0.174	−0.042	0.289	0.054
Obs.	2615	2615	1690	1690
R2	0.063	0.063	0.115	0.115
Log-likelihood	−1.673.517	−1.673.517	−878.501	−878.501

Note: Logit estimation results for the dependent variable "Y = 1 if failure" in columns 1 (coefficients) and 2 (marginal effects). Logit estimation results for the dependent variable "Y = 1 if at least one employee in t + 56" in columns 3 (coefficients) and 4 (marginal effects)
***/**/* indicate significance at the 1%/5%/10% levels

least one employee at the end time of the interview and '0' otherwise. We again use a binary logit model for the estimation; the results are in columns (3) and (4) in Table 5 for the 5 year period. Starting again with the long term impact of motivations on the probability to hire others and, thus, to grow the business, we find that individuals being motivated by a combination of push and pull motives have a 6.9%-points higher probability of creating further jobs than pure push types. The probability of hiring at least one person is another 5.9%-points higher for pull types when compared to the mixed types. Moreover, the probability of employing others decreases with the age of the entrepreneurs and unemployment duration, as well as for people who have earned previous experience through leisure time, or specialize in the IT sector.

It increases with start- up capital. These observations lead to: **Result 2**: The analysis shows that controlling for a large set of characteristics that are relevant for entrepreneurial outcomes, pull types have a lower and push types a higher exit probability than do mixed types. Moreover, pull types do not only survive more often, they have also a higher probability of creating additional jobs in their venture while push types have a lower probability to create jobs than do mixed types.

Discussion, Conclusion and Future Research

In this longitudinal study, we first analyze what motivates individuals coming out of unemployment to start an entrepreneurial career. We show that not only push type but also pull type motivations can be observed among start-ups by previously unemployed persons. A small share of around 15% of them are merely motivated by pull motives. More importantly, we identify a mixed type that accounts for as much as 70% of all entrepreneurs coming out of unemployment: they are start- ups resulting from opportunity and necessity. Hence, a large share of unemployed individuals who go into business instead of looking for another employed position, both want to, but they also need to become an entrepreneur. They might have been latent entrepreneurs in their previous working life, who did not dare starting their businesses while being employed. The second main insight of our analysis is that motivational factors for starting an own business unfold a long- term influence on the subsequent performance of these entrepreneurs coming out of unemployment even if we control for a large number of variables. The outcome variables that we employ in our empirical approach, reveal a clear ranking: throughout the observation period, pull type entrepreneurs have higher survival (lower failure) rates and create more jobs than push types, with individuals being motivated by a combination of push and pull motives always falling between the two extremes. These findings are important for two reasons. On the one hand, the motivation of previously unemployed individuals to become an entrepreneur matters for the subsequent survival and job creation, even in the long run. This means that controlling for a large number of relevant variables, such as education levels or the previous unemployment duration does not capture the information which can be extracted from initial start- up motivations. On the other hand, disclosing a third type of entrepreneur beyond this dichotomy adds important information with regard to the theoretical and the practitioners' debate. Although the individuals who are motivated by a combination of push and pull factors are more similar to push type entrepreneurs with respect to several individual characteristics such as their age, educational background or their unemployment experience, the pull type part of the motivational factors among these mixed types of entrepreneurs makes an important difference. They survive more often than individuals who are only pushed into entrepreneurship and they create more jobs. Overall, it seems that the deterministic association of previous unemployed business founders with pure necessity entrepreneurs needs to be critically evaluated. Our results have important implications for future research. As we were interested in this contribution in examining the motivational background of a certain group of 'other' entrepreneurs, namely those coming out of unemployment, our analysis is explicitly restricted to individuals with an unemployment background. What is left for future research is to make a direct comparison of start-ups coming out of unemployment with individuals with a more favorable employment history, i.e. who have been previously employed or self-employed and who also aim to become entrepreneurs. It will be important to investigate to what extent the two classes of motives exist among these groups as well, and whether the different motivational variables have the same influence on entrepreneurial outcomes as observed in our approach over all business founders irrespective of their employment background. From a policy perspective, it will then also be crucial to analyze to what extent the previous employment status is a valuable proxy for motivations of becoming an entrepreneur, i.e. to show whether (or not) the commonly used dichotomy between opportunity entrepreneurs (from employment) and necessity entrepreneurs (from unemployment) can be uphold.

References

Andersson, P., & Wadensjö, E. (2007). Do the unemployed become successful entrepreneurs? A comparison between the unemployed, inactive and wage-earners. *International Journal of Manpower, 28,* 604–626.

Arrighetti, A., & Vivarelli, M. (1999). The role of innovation in the post entry performance of new small firms: Evidence from Italy. *Southern Economic Journal, 65*(4), 927–939.

Audretsch, D. (2007). Entrepreneurship capital and economic growth. *Oxford Review of Economic Policy, 23,* 63–78.

Audretsch, D., & Vivarelli, M. (1995). New firm formation in Italy. *Economics Letters, 48,* 77–81.

Birley, S., & Westhead, P. (1994). A taxonomy of business start-up reasons and their impact on firm growth and size. *Journal of Business Venturing, 9,* 7–31.

Bosma, N. & R. Harding. (2007). *Global entrepreneurship monitor, summary results 2006. Technical report,* Global Entrepreneurship Research Association.

Caliendo, M., Fossen, F., & Kritikos, A. (2014). Personality characteristics and the decisions to become and stay self-employed. *Small Business Economics, 42*(4), 787–814.

Caliendo, M., Hogenacker, J., Künn, S., & Wießner, F. (2012). Alte Idee, neues Programm: Der Gründungszuschuss als Nachfolger von Überbrückungsgeld und Ich-AG. *Journal for Labour Market Research., 45*(2), 99–123.

Caliendo, M., & Kritikos, A. (2010). Start-ups by the unemployed: Characteristics, survival and direct employment effects. *Small Business Economics, 35*(1), 71–92.

Caliendo, M. & Künn S. (2011). Start-up subsidies for the unemployed: Long-term evidence and effect heterogeneity. *Journal of Public Economics, 95*(3–4), 311–331.

Carter, N., Gartner, W., Shaver, K., & Gatewood, E. (2003). The career reasons of nascent entrepreneurs. *Journal of Business Venturing, 18,* 13–39.

Clark, K., & Drinkwater, S. (2000). Pushed out or pulled in? Self-employment among ethnic minorities in England and Wales. *Labour Economics, 7,* 603–628.

Cressy, R. (2006). Why do most firms die young? *Small Business Economics, 26,* 103–116.

Evans, D., & Leigthon, L. (1989). Some empirical aspects of entrepreneurship. *American Economic Review, 79,* 519–535.

Evans, L., & Leighton, L. (1990). Small business formation by unemployed and employed workers. *Small Business Economics, 2,* 319–330.

Fairlie, R., & Fossen, F. (2018). *Opportunity versus necessity entrepreneurship: Two components of business creation.* Discussion Paper 11258. Bonn: IZA.

Headd, B. (2003). Redefining business success: Distinguishing between closure and failure. *Small Business Economics, 21,* 51–61.

Hessels, J., Gelderen, M. v., & Thurik, R. (2008). Entrepreneurial aspirations, motivations, and their drivers. *Small Business Economics, 31,* 323–339.

Hinz, T., & Jungbauer-Gans, M. (1999). Starting a business after unemployment: Characteristics and chances of success (empirical evidence from a regional German labour market). *Entrepreneurship and Regional Development, 11,* 317–333.

Krueger, N., Reilly, M., & Carsrud, A. (2000). Competing models of entrepreneurial intentions. *Journal of Business Venturing, 15*, 411–432.

McClelland, D. (1961). The achievement motive in economic growth. *American Economic Review, 51*, 179–189.

Parker, S., & Johnson, P. (1996). Spatial variations in the determinants and effects of firm births and deaths. *Regional Studies, 30*(7), 679–688.

Pfeiffer, F., & Reize, F. (2000). Business start-ups by the unemployed – an econometric analysis based on firm data. *Labour Economics, 7*, 629–663.

Roman, C., Congregado, E., & Millan, J. (2013). Start-up incentives: Entrepreneur- ship policy or active labour market programme? *Journal of Business Venturing, 28*, 151–175.

Shane, S. (2009). Why encouraging more people to become entrepreneurs is bad public policy. *Small Business Economics, 33*, 141–149.

Shane, S., Kolvereid, L., & Westhead, P. (1991). An exploratory examination of the reasons leading to new firm formation across country and gender. *Journal of Business Venturing, 6*, 431–446.

Storey, D. (1991). The birth of new firms – does unemployment matter? A review of the evidence. *Small Business Economics, 3*, 167–178.

Storey, D., & Jones, A. (1987). New firm formation – a labor market approach to industrial entry. *Scottish Journal of Political Economy, 34*(3), 7–51.

Valliere, D., & Peterson, R. (2009). Entrepreneurship and economic growth: Evidence from emerging and developed countries. *Entrepreneurship and Regional Development, 21*(5–6), 459–480.

Welter, F., Baker, T., Audretsch, D., & Gartner, W. (2017). Everyday entrepreneurship? A call for entrepreneurship research to embrace entrepreneurial diversity. *Entrepreneurship Theory and Practice, 41*(3), 311–321.

Working with David on Both Sides of the Atlantic

Adam Lederer

Abstract Adam Lederer, author of the following essay, considers David one of the chief mentors in his life. Through his experiences working with David in Germany and the US, Lederer explains how David's natural interest in multidisciplinary studies led him to pursue the creation of entrepreneurship as a recognized academic field. What follows is a tribute from Lederer to one of the most influential people in his life.

Begin

This Festschrift is dedicated to David B. Audretsch, one of the three greatest teacher-mentors to influence my life. I have always wished for an opportunity to thank the other two publicly – Karen Roads and Gregg Cawley – but an appropriate opportunity has never crossed my path.

So, with that, let me get to the core of the matter, as far as I am concerned: David, as a teacher and a mentor, is there whenever I need him. Most big decisions in my life typically involve asking him for sage council. Thus, I am thankful that he has singlehandedly prevented me from making stupid decisions, whether professionally or personally.

Working with David on Both Sides of the Atlantic

Now that I have gotten the obvious and easy out of the way, let me take a step back and say that, as a keen observer of academia since 1992, I can honestly say that David is, hands down, one of the most impressive academics that I have ever met and had the privilege to work with.

A. Lederer (✉)
DIW Berlin, Berlin, Germany

© Springer Nature Switzerland AG 2019
E. E. Lehmann, M. Keilbach (eds.), *From Industrial Organization to Entrepreneurship*, https://doi.org/10.1007/978-3-030-25237-3_24

This is rooted in the fact that David's primary academic interest evolved into studying entrepreneurship. Inherently unable to confine himself to one traditional, narrow, academic silo – because entrepreneurship struggles to be confined – his knowledge reflects the plethora of traditional academic fields that all jointly contribute to the study of entrepreneurship. As a "field," entrepreneurship has clear antecedents in the obvious and the not-so-obvious. The obvious includes economics, management, and business. The not so obvious easily incorporates scholarship from policy, education, psychology, and genetics; just to name the tip of the iceberg. Yet, within each silo, research methodologies, opinions about the usage of statistics, and perspectives of the world, are vastly different. This, for example, makes it a significant challenge for experts from economics to communicate effectively with experts from education. David built his understanding of each silo's knowledge and language, thus not only understanding how each silo fundamentally contributes to the field of entrepreneurship, but also able to unite the traditionally separate traditions that academia otherwise loves to keep apart.

Further, David is exceptionally perceptive about the world around him, remembering everything and, as a result, makes connections between the people he works with, putting people together in ways that spark new ideas and advances the creation of new knowledge. With his unique ability to bridge academic silos, he brings together researchers who work on similar ideas from different disciplinary backgrounds.

In other words, he creates synergy: bringing together two or more things that combined produce a larger result. In David's world, 1 + 1 really equals 3.

Working with David on both sides of the Atlantic, at the Institute for Development Strategies of Indiana University Bloomington and at the Entrepreneurship, Growth and Public Policy Group of the Max Planck Institute of Economics, in Jena, Germany, gave me a front seat to this craft. Expert guests regularly make the trek to work with David, always coming away with far more than they had planned: widened horizons, new ideas, new co-authors, new friends, and the best Hoosier or German Hospitality that one could experience.

One can meet pretty impressive people in his realm: brilliant thinkers, wildly successful business leaders, and top scholars, some even decorated with a Nobel Prize. The two most famous guest speakers (at least from my perspective), are Richard Florida, author of *The Rise of the Creative Class*, and Jack Harding, President and CEO of eSilicon. However, David does not limit himself to the already successful and already famous. He supports and collaborates with doctoral students and other young researchers, sharing his experience and knowledge without a hint of conceit or arrogance. At his core, David is a man who generously provides opportunities. His 2015 Mentor Award from the Entrepreneurship Division of the Academy of Management reflects that and is well deserved. As a long-term career service award, it "recognizes extraordinary contributions in the area of mentoring."

Another way in which David is exceptional is his memory: show me something once and a minute later I have forgotten it; show the same thing to David and he remembers it a decade later as clearly as if it was the second you first showed it to him. What is more remarkable is that this happens even when you are not sure it has.

There was one occasion when David was sitting in an overstuffed seminar room at Indiana University Bloomington's College of Education; it must have been the early 2000s – when one of his German guests gave a talk. The College of Education had seemed like an appropriate venue and the subject of the talk attracted many education scholars, even though these were people who generally did not explicitly contemplate entrepreneurship research. The guest's presentation sparked an unusually lively and diverse Q&A session – which is where my memory is most vivid.

At some point, a question was asked and the guest could not answer it. Flummoxed, there was a brief verbal stumble. Almost immediately, David piped up and said, "Go back to slide 7." She did. The answer to the question was right there on slide 7. Despite the myriad of distractions: the crowded seminar room, the 25 or so slides, and an extensive discussion, David had remembered, thus guiding the conversation forward.

David also guides conversations forward in realms outside of traditional academic circles. In American academic parlance, this falls into the service category: empirical application of knowledge. All too often, academics stay on campus, not necessarily understanding how their work applies to real world situations. For as long as I have known David, he strives to explore the world and to take students along for the ride. At SPEA there was a seminar class that involved taking students on a day-long field trip to Elkhart, Indiana, in order to talk about redevelopment strategies for the city: at the time, a major employer was pulling out and the local chamber of commerce needed outsiders to help spark conversations and ideas. Another trip took a visiting class of Dutch students from Erasmus University Rotterdam to the Crane Naval Research Center in southern Indiana. There the students learned about the US Federal government's Small Business Innovation Research (SBIR) grants, which not only help the US military develop cutting edge technologies, but also help entrepreneurs to get off the ground, in some cases, literally – one entrepreneur had contributed to NASA and the Space Shuttle. Thus, understanding the practical application of his research (or, in some cases, empirical data collection) is another way that David is special.

Since meeting David in 1998, my path has taken me to a new home across the Atlantic Ocean. I have met people and traveled places that I never could have imagined. On the academic side of my life, off the top of my head, I have had the privilege of meeting Rui Baptista, Pontus Braunerhjelm, Magnus Henrekson, Alexander Kritikos, Erik Lehmann, Roy Thurik, and Susanne Warning. However, to try to enumerate the list of everybody I have met as a direct result of working with David Audretsch is impossible, I will never be able to provide the full list of friends and colleagues who I have met as a direct result of David. These include many amazing people I have met outside of academia, including fantastic people at Cambridge University Press, Edward Elgar Publishing, Oxford University Press, and Springer Nature, several of whom I remain friends with, even though they are no longer active in publishing.

The story of David, with respect to me and my life is simple. The larger story of David, looking at what he has done for entrepreneurship research, for building pathways to create new knowledge, and, ultimately, for science, is much more complicated. Having watched him work his magic, I can say that David is not just one of the greatest teacher-mentors to influence my life, he is one of the greatest teacher-mentors to influence the lives of many.

Acknowledgements I must thank several friends (all a result of knowing David) for their advice and help in writing this chapter. Gratitude is due to Alexander Kritikos, Erik Lehmann, Stephan Shütze, Leon Schjoedt, and Susanne Warning. Any errors are clearly my own – the usual disclaimer applies.

Festschrift to David B. Audretsch

J. L. González-Pernía and Iñaki Peña-Legazkue

Abstract The authors, two scholars from the Basque region of Spain, use their chapter to highlight David's career, his contribution to the founding of the entrepreneurial research field, and his impact upon their own careers. Particularly noting David's influence in convincing them to work more closely with local economic development actors, the authors highlight the importance that David has placed on linking theory with practice. This theme flows throughout the chapter.

Introduction

It is difficult to write a Festschrift, especially when one is doing so for the first time and when the short essay is dedicated to a person whom one respects, admires and loves very much. Although we do not know how exactly to approach this unusual task, with this Festschrift, we first want to highlight David B. Audretsch's brilliant scholarly career and, second, to deeply thank him for his outstanding academic contributions to the field of entrepreneurship and for his kind mentoring relationship with us. Since we first contacted David Audretsch from the Basque Institute of Competitiveness approximately 10 years ago, his guidance has been fundamental advancing our research work on entrepreneurship and local development. Moreover, his continuous advice to improve our conditions of local context for entrepreneurship has instrumentally inspired us to humbly serve from our *ivory tower* of the Institute to the wide array of agents in our local entrepreneurial ecosystem of the Basque region. Truly, we feel very honored and proud to be David's academic

---

J. L. González-Pernía (✉)
University of Deusto | DEUSTO (Deusto Business School), Bilbao, Spain
e-mail: gonzalez-pernia@deusto.es

I. Peña-Legazkue
University of Deusto | DEUSTO, Faculty of Economics and Business Administration (Deusto Business School), Bilbao, Spain
e-mail: ipena@deusto.es

© Springer Nature Switzerland AG 2019
E. E. Lehmann, M. Keilbach (eds.), *From Industrial Organization to Entrepreneurship*, https://doi.org/10.1007/978-3-030-25237-3_25

colleagues. We feel blessed to be the friends of such a brilliantly minded person, full of gentleness and generosity. In the following sections, we will explain why we feel so privileged.

David Audretsch's Impact in our Academic Work: Grasping the Beauty of Smallness and *Newness*

Although David Audretsch's work had inspired us in many ways for at least two decades, it was not until 2008 that we started meeting him sporadically in the Basque Institute of Competitiveness and collaborating on different projects linked to entrepreneurship. Indeed, a large bulk of our research work (i.e., publications, research projects and supervision of doctoral theses) draws upon his significant contribution to the field of entrepreneurship, knowledge generation and innovation. In the past 30 years, a major lesson that we have learned from David Audretsch is that *David can beat Goliath*.

Our first encounter with David Audretsch's work occurred in the nineties, when one of us was pursuing a doctorate degree. Like most regions of Europe and North America, the Basque region suffered a severe recession in the early nineties. Companies in the sectors of steel, iron, ship-building, machinery tool, textile, etc. diminished their capacity to successfully compete globally, and the resulting high unemployment became a major problem of the region. To recuperate the wealth of past periods, the Basque region needed to rejuvenate its industrial fabric quickly. New innovative firms were needed to transform the industry, the territory and society.

In that unstable period of the nineties, we were acquainted for the first time with the distinction of two technological regimes: entrepreneurial regimes and routinized regimes (Audretsch 1991). Whereas traditional industrial organization economists continued centering their attention on the analysis of routinized regimes, in which innovation is promoted by the controlling power of large companies in oligopolistic markets, Audretsch's work surfaced the transforming role that, under an entrepreneurial regime, new small firms could play in many industry sectors through innovation. Challenging conventional wisdom, Audretsch, together with Acs, held that innovation is not exclusive to large firms and showed under what circumstances small firms are more innovative than their large counterparts (Acs and Audretsch 1987, 1988). We learned that disrupting entrepreneurs are more likely to commercialize innovative products in highly innovative industries that rely on skilled labor, and new (usually small) entrants tend not only to survive and grow but also to displace other incumbent (usually large) firms from the marketplace.

Audretsch's work (with the coauthorship of Zoltan Acs) on entrepreneurial regimes, learning, and industry turbulence illuminated our minds during the nineties and helped us in understanding how small firms could surmount the *liability of newness* against incumbent firms and contribute to the transformation of industries and territories. Audretsch and his colleague Acs found that small firm turbulence was particularly high in capital-intensive industries and that entrant firms faced market exit quite rapidly in industries with evident *revolving door* effects. Accordingly, their findings suggested that new firms were needed to recover from economic downturn, but entrants had to learn and adapt quickly or face extinction (Audretsch and Acs 1990).

Entrepreneurs depend on new economic knowledge to be innovative. Along these lines, Audretsch (with Feldman) stressed the idea that new knowledge derived from industry R&D, university research and skilled labor concentrated in proximate locations would generate positive externalities, leading to innovation and greater competitiveness in turbulent markets (Audretsch and Feldman 1996).

These lessons learned from David Audretsch and his colleagues were particularly important for our local context of the Basque region. During the late nineties, Basque policy makers, being aware of the magnitude of the economic downturn and admitting that the region lacked adequate conditions for the emergence of innovative new firms, decided to design an ambitious policy agenda to promote entrepreneurship and innovation. An important action implemented by Basque government authorities was the creation of business incubation centers with the twofold goal of creating jobs and fostering innovation.

We examined the extent to which business incubation centers were supportive enough in surmounting barriers to grow, rather than barriers to entry, in the Basque region. Audretsch's path-breaking insights of the nineties were important for us in understanding the need of *entrepreneurial regimes* to leave behind a contracting business cycle. New and small firms were needed, and policy makers were responding to that call from academia. Audretsch opened our eyes, and we learned that entrepreneurship policy actions have to be evaluated and, in most cases, policies have to be correctly (re)implemented to create economic and social value (Peña 2004).

With the arrival of the New Economy in the early twenty-first century, David Audretsch (with Roy Thurik) opened a new research avenue by differentiating the *Managed Economy* (i.e., of the twentieth century) from the more promising *Entrepreneurial Economy* (i.e., of the 21st century). Both authors called for more analytical contributions to better explain the role played by new and small enterprises in the ongoing shift towards a knowledge-based Entrepreneurial Economy (Audretsch and Thurik 2001). It is worth mentioning that during this period, the Basque Government under the Presidency of Lehendakari Ibarretxe, disseminated a message recommending a systemic transition from the old Industrial Era towards a new Knowledge Era. The two calls (i.e., the *academic call* from Audretsch and Thurik and the *institutional call* from the Basque Government) motivated us to continue investigating the subject of knowledge-based entrepreneurship.

While scholars and policy makers seemed to be synchronized in the assessment of the changing context, David Audretsch argued that the transition desired by the leaders of advanced economies required the implementation of a new set of policies. Entrepreneurship policy was at an incipient stage in the US. With the emergence of entrepreneurship policy, David Audretsch, coauthored with Gilbert et al. (2004, p. 321), provided a new vision of regional competitiveness and noted that *"Globalization and the shift towards knowledge as the source of competitiveness rendered the traditional policy instruments less effective. These instruments alone could no longer guarantee high growth and employment, certainly not for all regions and locations, ... As globalization resulted in the loss of jobs and stagnation to local and regional economies, policy makers specifically at the state and local level responded by developing new policy instruments to help them implement the strategic management of regions. These new policy instruments have generally focused on entrepreneurship as an engine of economic development".*

In the early twenty-first century, David Audretsch, with Keilbach (2008), concerned with the Knowledge Paradox, explained why high levels of investment in new knowledge in advanced countries did not necessarily generate the expected levels of economic growth. Further, the authors showed that entrepreneurship served as a conduit of knowledge spillovers and contributed to economic growth. We learned from David Audretsch's work that the entrepreneurial capital of a territory plays a prominent role in the knowledge-spillover process. Regarding the Knowledge Paradox, he instilled a more optimistic view to us through a new Post-Schumpeterian message of "Creative Construction" by which wealth could be enhanced without *displacement effects* and *zero-sum* games (Agarwal et al. 2007).

Motivated by these cutting-edge ideas, we embarked on the analysis of innovation, entrepreneurial activity and competitiveness, but with a special focus on innovation-driven entrepreneurship at a subnational level. Indeed, we published our results with Gonzalez-Pernia et al. (2012), confirming the past findings by Audretsch and Keilbach that investment in innovation alone did not suffice to improve the level of competitiveness of regions and that regions with both a higher capacity to generate new knowledge and to create new firms experienced a higher economic growth. We organized several research workshops on these relevant issues and invited David Audretsch as a keynote speaker to one of the workshops. In view of the interest of the subjects and the findings presented in the workshop, he kindly invited us to collaborate in a special issue on *Entrepreneurial Activity and Regional Competitiveness* published in the journal *Small Business Economics* (Audretsch and Peña-Legazkue 2012).

Audretsch's work on public policy to promote entrepreneurship is ongoing. One of his most recent papers stresses the relevance of externalities and market failures that deter the creation of new businesses as main motivations to encourage entrepreneurship policy (Acs et al. 2016). Market failures abound and are more profound in developing economies. Moreover, externalities, especially knowledge externalities, spread more slowly and weakly in economically less advanced contexts. Acknowledging the relevance of externalities and inspired by Audretsch's work (with Acs et al. 2009) on the knowledge spillover theory of entrepreneurship (KSTE), we tested main notions of KSTE in less developed contexts where market failures and knowledge filters are broader and stronger. According to our results, the KSTE seemed to fall short in explaining the factors triggering the formation of innovative new firms in developing economies (González-Pernía et al. 2015b).

In a study on entrepreneurship and economic development in cities, David Audretsch (with Belitski and Desai, 2015) found that entrepreneurship positively affects the economic development of cities; however, large urban areas are the ones

Festschrift to David B. Audretsch 275

that seem to benefit most from entrepreneurship (i.e., although a broader indirect impact is manifested in the long run and only in urban areas with a size of more than 250,000 inhabitants). Briefly, these results suggest that the relationship between entrepreneurship and economic growth and development varies across subnational territories. Based on this idea, we conducted a study to investigate whether the relationship between economic recession and entrepreneurship differs across regions at a subnational level (González-Pernía et al. 2018). We found that, in a recession, an increase in unemployment negatively affects business creation in low-income regions but not in high-income regions, providing evidence that the relationship between entrepreneurship and economic development differs across subnational locations, as suggested by the work of Audretsch and his coauthors. Their findings motivated us to continue examining and testing how entrepreneurship affects prosperity in local communities and subnational regions.

Put together, Audretsch made several influential intellectual moves that guided our scholarly career and inspired our research work. We learned from him and followed his thoughts on subjects related to small business, innovation, firm creation, knowledge generation, and entrepreneurship policy. These subjects comprise a central theme of Audretsch's work that we have tried to enrich with our modest contributions.

David Audretsch's Impact in the Basque Entrepreneurial Ecosystem: Harvesting the Fruit

In the late 2000s, the Basque Institute of Competitiveness (i.e., a foundation where we worked for several years) invited David Audretsch to participate in the Advisory Board. His major task was to advise on critical issues affecting the local entrepreneurial ecosystem. An important goal was to recover the entrepreneurial values present some centuries ago in the local community (González-Pernía et al. 2015a) and to invigorate the almost nonexisting high-growth entrepreneurial activity. Working for the Institute meant not only conducting research but also interacting with other actors of the local community engaged in entrepreneurship with the aim of generating economic and social value. Our task was to connect the Institute to different actors who could contribute to spurring high-growth entrepreneurship.

We collaborated with David Audretsch mainly on two fronts: (1) building a culture of smart-capital for start-up investment and (2) interacting with local government authorities for policy making. For the first task, we created a business angel network named "Crecer +" (i.e., the English translation would be "Grow More"). Under the advice of David Audretsch, we created a business angel network (BAN) of almost 40 investor members, we trained them on the basics for angel investing, we organized pitching sessions, and most importantly, we created a community of enthusiastic business angels. After four years of hard work, we reached an unparalleled local record of eleven deals for 3.6 million euros. Following the recommendations of David Audretsch, we helped entrepreneurs with potential for growth in expanding the business internationally and closed deals with international business angels (i.e., our BAN was a member of the European BAN network). Further, we invited local institutions to match the amount invested by our BAN members to accelerate the growth of promising ventures. Some years later, new BANs emerged in the Basque community and the access to smart-capital became much easier. None of us imagined before that the guidance we received from David Audretsch would result in such economic and social impact of the BAN.

For the second task, we contacted local policy makers to share the results of our results projects (i.e., we released reports periodically on the projects where we participated: GEM and PSED). From these meetings, we established an enduring relationship with Basque Government authorities and other smaller scale local government authorities. Our reports have been used to inform and provide recommendations for policy makers. For example, GEM reports were extensively used to write the first Law of Entrepreneurship in Spain in year 2013. The same Law was passed in the Basque Parliament 1 year before. Apart from that, the Basque government and local authorities have relied on our reports as one of the sources for the elaboration of their joint policy plans to promote entrepreneurship during the periods of 2013–2016 and 2017–2020.

The contact of these two actors (private investors and public institutions) from the Institute under the advice of David Audretsch was crucial to effectively manage a public-private relationship aimed at increasing the number of high-growth ventures, thereby enhancing the economic and social wealth of the Basque region under an entrepreneurial ecosystem approach. One of the most recent publications of David Audretsch precisely underlines the importance of entrepreneurial ecosystems for regional development (Acs et al. 2017). Learning from outside our ivory tower and harvesting these non-academic outputs have been as gratifying as publishing our research work in highly cited journals.

Conclusions

David Audretsch's abundant and inspiring work has pointed us towards the benefits of entrepreneurship for people, firms and regions, beyond what is usually discussed in debates regarding macroeconomic indicators and globalization. Metaphorically, while acknowledging the strength of Goliath, David has schooled us like no one on the beauty of smallness and newness.

In addition to being one of the most influential and brightest scholars that we have ever met, David Audretsch has demonstrated a distinct ability to listen to our personal stories and to share his thoughts openly. In all these years, we have witnessed how he wanted to see others rise and grow and how he helped in facilitating positive change for others (including us). All of these personal qualities have made David Audretsch a brilliant academic leader who is empathic, caring, trustworthy and very passionate about his and others' work. This is why we feel so privileged to be his colleagues and why we want to provide a well-deserved tribute to a great friend.

References

Acs, Z., Åstebro, T., Audretsch, D. B., & Robinson, D. T. (2016). Public policy to promote entrepreneurship: A call to arms. *Small Business Economics, 47*(1), 35–51.

Acs, Z. J., & Audretsch, D. B. (1987). Innovation, market structure, and firm size. *Review of Economics and Statistics, 69*(4), 567–574.

Acs, Z. J., & Audretsch, D. B. (1988). Innovation in large and small firms: An empirical analysis. *American Economic Review, 77*(4), 678–690.

Acs, Z. J., Braunerhjelm, P., Audretsch, D. B., & Carlsson, B. (2009). The knowledge spillover theory of entrepreneurship. *Small Business Economics, 32*(1), 15–30.

Acs, Z. J., Stam, E., Audretsch, D. B., & O'Connor, A. (2017). The lineages of the entrepreneurial ecosystem approach. *Small Business Economics, 49*(1), 1–10.

Agarwal, R., Audretsch, D. B., & Sarkar, M. B. (2007). The process of creative construction: Knowledge spillovers, entrepreneurship and economic growth. *Strategic Entrepreneurship Journal, 1*(3–4), 263–286.

Audretsch, D. B. (1991). New firm survival and the technological regime. *The Review of Economics and Statistics, 73*(3), 441–450.

Audretsch, D. B., & Acs, Z. J. (1990). The entrepreneurial regime, learning and industry turbulence. *Small Business Economics, 2*(2), 119–128.

Audretsch, D. B., Belitski, M., & Desai, S. (2015). Entrepreneurship and economic development in cities. *The Annals of Regional Science, 55*(1), 33–60.

Audretsch, D. B., & Feldman, M. P. (1996). R&D spillovers and the geography of innovation and production. *American Economic Review, 86*(3), 630–640.

Audretsch, D. B., & Keilbach, M. (2008). Resolving the knowledge paradox: Knolwedge-spillover entrepreneurship and economic growth. *Research Policy, 37*(10), 1697–1705.

Audretsch, D. B., & Peña-Legazkue, I. (2012). Entrepreneurial activity and regional competitiveness: An introduction to the special issue. *Small Business Economics, 39*(3), 531–537.

Audretsch, D. B., & Thurik, A. R. (2001). What's new about the new economy? Sources of growth in the managed and entrepreneurial economies. *Industrial and Corporate Change, 10*(1), 267–315.

Gilbert, B. A., Audretsch, D. B., & McDougall, P. P. (2004). The emergence of entrepreneurship policy. *Small Business Economics, 22*(3), 313–323.

González-Pernía, J. L., Guerrero, M., Jung, A., & Peña-Legazkue, I. (2018). Economic recession shake-out and entrepreneurship: Evidence from Spain. *Business Research Quarterly, 21*(3), 153–167.

González-Pernía, J. L., Guerrero, M., & Peña-Legazkue, I. (2015a). Entrepreneurship and sustainable development: The relevance of shaping intertemporal local intangible conditions. In D. B. Audretsch, A. N. Link, & M. L. Walshok (Eds.), *The Oxford handbook of local competitiveness* (pp. 355–372). Oxford: Oxford University Press.

González-Pernía, J. L., Jung, A., & Peña-Legazkue, I. (2015b). Innovation-driven entrepreneurship in developing economies. *Entrepreneurship and Regional Development, 27*(9–10), 555–573.

González-Pernía, J. L., Peña-Legazkue, I., & Vendrell-Herrero, F. (2012). Innovation, entrepreneurial activity and competitiveness at a sub-national level. *Small Business Economics, 39*(3), 561–574.

Peña, I. (2004). Business incubation centers and new firm growth in the Basque Country. *Small Business Economics, 22*(3–4), 223–236.

An Overview of the Economics of Entrepreneurship and Small Business: The Legacy of David Audretsch

David Urbano and Sebastian Aparicio

Abstract Few scholars can be considered beacons who guide interested (and often disoriented) researchers. David Audretsch is one such scholar, who has shed light on entrepreneurship in a broad sense as well as on the economics of entrepreneurship and small business as a distinct field. Given his noteworthy and abundant contributions, a synthesis is required in order to understand the evolution of entrepreneurial thought from an economics perspective. Based on searches using Google Scholar and Web of Science (WoS), we therefore aim to quantitatively and analytically examine Audretsch's contributions to the economics of entrepreneurship and small business. We employ bibliometric indicators to identify his seminal and most cited articles. We also use keywords analysis and co-occurrence to identify his key concepts over the years. Complementing this general view, we analyze the content of numerous publications that highlight the ways in which the economics of entrepreneurship and small firms has evolved. Suggestions for future research are also provided, which may prove useful for economists and specialists in related areas in order that the field may continue to advance.

David Urbano acknowledges the financial support from the Spanish Ministry of Economy & Competitiveness [project ECO2017-87885-P], the Economy & Knowledge Department—Catalan Government [project 2017-SGR-1056] and ICREA under the ICREA Academia Programme. Additionally, Sebastian Aparicio acknowledges Durham University Business School for constant help and support.

D. Urbano (✉)
Universitat Autònoma de Barcelona, Department of Business and Centre for Entrepreneurship and Social Innovation Research (CREIS), Barcelona, Spain
e-mail: david.urbano@uab.cat

S. Aparicio
Durham University, Durham University Business School, Durham, UK
e-mail: sebastian.aparicio@durham.ac.uk

© Springer Nature Switzerland AG 2019
E. E. Lehmann, M. Keilbach (eds.), *From Industrial Organization to Entrepreneurship*, https://doi.org/10.1007/978-3-030-25237-3_26

Introduction

The field of entrepreneurship and small business research is young but rapidly growing. Carlsson et al. (2013) and Landstrom (1999) have commented on the discipline's fortunes since its origins, as entrepreneurship and small business studies have been viewed and analyzed from various scientific perspectives. Indeed, fields including (but by no means limited to) economics, sociology, geography, anthropology, management, and psychology have contributed to the expansion of entrepreneurship as a research field. Within each science, outstanding scholars have emerged through their devotion and hard work. As an example, every year the Swedish Entrepreneurship Forum (Entreprenörskapsforum), the Research Institute of Industrial Economics (IFN), VINNOVA, and the Stockholms Köpmansklubb offer an award to scholars who have particularly contributed to the development of entrepreneurship and small business research.

In 2001, David Audretsch and Zoltan Acs received the Global Award for Entrepreneurship Research. From an economics perspective, these researchers have shaped our understanding of the creation of new ventures and their importance for economic development. The career of David Audretsch has demonstrated his considerable impact, not only in entrepreneurship and small business research, but also in economics as a whole. For instance, Linß (2014) has highlighted Audretsch's academic influence by analyzing the 60 most important economists from Aristotle to Paul Romer. Accordingly, Audretsch has explored related topics such as innovation in large and small companies, industry development, entrepreneurship and firm growth, competitiveness, economic growth and development, and public policy. As an example, an important concept emerged thanks to Audretsch and Keilbach (2004), in which entrepreneurship is considered an additional capital that spurs economic growth. As such, his contributions span a broad spectrum of areas that have helped consolidate entrepreneurship and small business research in terms of theory, practice and policy.

Therefore, we aim to quantitatively and analytically examine his contributions to the economics of entrepreneurship and small business from 2007 until 2018 (July). To this end, our research combines different tools to gather and analyze his papers in several journals, as well as his books and chapters written with coauthors. First, an overview is provided via bibliometric analysis. This consists of capturing quantitative trends through analyzing his publications, most representative works, citations, co-citations and so forth. According to Landström et al. (2012), such techniques can uncover connections between scholars and their research agendas. It is also argued that through bibliometrics it is possible to obtain an overview of any discipline (Broadus 1987). In this regard, in order to shed light on recent advances in economics entrepreneurship and small business research, bibliometric indicators including the number of publications, number of citations, keywords and connections are analyzed, facilitating the development of conclusions according to the specific parameters studied (Merigó et al. 2016). Second, the bibliometric results are combined with content analysis in order to understand concept development, scope

An Overview of the Economics of Entrepreneurship and Small Business: The Legacy... 281

and future research derived from Audretsch's contributions. The most cited papers and recently published works of an author may help define the research field and the salient agenda that continues to advance the knowledge frontier. In this regard, Landström et al. (2012) have demonstrated how Audretsch joined other scholars in building knowledge, especially after 2000. Here the importance of Audretsch and his peers' works is recognized as a basis to entrepreneurship and small business theory.

This chapter is based on searches using Google Scholar and Web of Science (WoS), which are widely regarded as the most influential databases because they only index well-recognized academic journals and editorials (Harzing and Alakangas 2016). By using the keyword "Audretsch, D∗" in the author profile (Google Scholar) or author search option (WoS), we obtained information regarding his academic production. We opted to consider articles (especially those pertaining to research, editorial notes and book reviews), books, book chapters, and ocassionally working papers. Based on this information, we analyzed the most representative papers that can be considered seminal works and mark significant trends in different areas of the field. From Google Scholar we attained information regarding 153 publications and analyzed their content. We used the title, abstract and introduction to identify how each document may explain different questions related to the economics of entrepreneurship and small business. Overall, the results enabled us to understand the emergence and evolution of economics of entrepreneurship and small business research as a discipline, increasing our understanding of competitiveness and industrial development (first), and institutions and economic development at national and regional levels (second). Innovations in small versus large firms represented a key component of Audretsch's analysis (cf. Acs and Audretsch 1988), providing the basis for small business and entrepreneurship (as a capital input) (Audretsch and Keilbach 2004), knowledge spillover theory of entrepreneurship (Acs et al. 2013), entrepreneurial society (Audretsch 2007a, 2009a, c), and other widely used concepts and theories.

The remainder of this chapter proceeds as follows. Section 2 explores the concept of the economics of entrepreneurship, including the definitions and approaches discussed by different authors. Section 3 presents the results of the bibliometrics and content analysis. Finally, Section 4 concludes and discusses future research directions.

The Economics of Entrepreneurship and Small Business

It has been suggested that the research basis of entrepreneurship stems from Schumpeterian analysis of economic development (Carlsson et al. 2013; Urbano et al. 2019). Indeed, Schumpeter (1911) placed entrepreneurs at the center of economic activity. Although his analysis started from a general equilibrium perspective, he went beyond by suggesting that entrepreneurs create shocks to push up the steady state. The rationale behind Schumpeter's coining of the concept of "entrepreneurs" was that such individuals bring innovations to the market, simultaneously stimulating different cycles in the economy. Since then, entrepreneurs (individuals) and entrepreneurship (actions) have gained considerable relevance in academia and have become significant subjects of study.

Various outstanding economists have considered Schumpeter's ideas, which were published in the *Journal of Evolutionary Economics*. For instance, Samuelson (2015, p. 34) has stated that "what will ever be remembered was his [Schumpeter] now century old emphasis on entrepreneurial innovation as a cardinal catalyst for economic progress". In essence, economists have recognized that entrepreneurship and entrepreneurs are fundamental agents within economic analysis. Although Schumpeter's ideas scarcely seemed sufficient to explaining economic development, Audretsch (2015a, p. 213) has suggested that "in the end, though, it is Schumpeter's scholarship, and certainly his analysis of innovation, entrepreneurship and creative destruction, that has stood the test of time."

In spite of this recognition, Audretsch et al. (2016a, p. 1) have claimed that even though entrepreneurship is studied from different disciplines, economists have been less tempted than scholars from management, sociology and finance to further explore entrepreneurial activity. Baumol (1968) has discussed the absence of entrepreneurs even from the theory of the firm, which was dedicated to understanding the profit maximization process. Based on Schumpeter's ideas, Baumol (1968) has suggested that the analysis of entrepreneurship serves to comprehend why some shifts occur. He has adduced these changes not to external shocks, but to the ability and leadership of entrepreneurs, who are capable of introducing innovations. Minniti (2016) has developed these ideas by asking Baumol to expand upon how entrepreneurs are important agents in the economy, and therefore worthy of attention from economists. Based on their microeconomic behavior, entrepreneurs are innovative, enabling firms to improve their performance, whereas the aggregated outcome leads to greater economic growth. Minniti (2016) has also highlighted Baumol's ideas regarding the importance of institutions to foster entrepreneurship, connected with economic development. Accordingly, from institutional economics (North 1990, 2005) it is possible to understand the environment in which entrepreneurs behave to spur the aggregated output (Urbano et al. 2018).

Entrepreneurs and entrepreneurship are subjects that might fall into the analysis of traditional streams in economics, namely micro- and macro-economics. In this regard, Parker (2004, 2018) has offered a thorough perspective regarding the so-called economics of entrepreneurship. Parker (2018, p. 2) perceives this as a research field and explains that "the economics of entrepreneurship literature continues to develop rapidly, generating numerous insights about how entrepreneurship interacts with the economy." As numerous other authors have argued (cf. Audretsch et al. 2015a), entrepreneurship is marked by a lack of definition and all-embracing theory. Acs and Audretsch (1990a) and Parker (2004, 2018) have sought to provide a rigorous theoretical model that understands economic factors regarding entrepreneurial and firm activity while highlighting how the economic perspective remains meaningful for entrepreneurship and SMEs. Other scholars have been encouraged by this call, and have provided further comment on this research field. For instance, Minniti

An Overview of the Economics of Entrepreneurship and Small Business: The Legacy... 283

and Lévesque (2008) and Audretsch et al. (2016a) have organized different special journal issues gathering outstanding pieces of research, all aimed at comprehending economic antecedents and the consequences of entrepreneurship and small firms.

One may argue that Audretsch's research agenda is aligned with the perspective of the economics of entrepreneurship and small business, given that many of his contributions tackle questions pertaining to economic development, within which entrepreneurs and small firms are fundamental gears. In order to understand different aspects of the economics of entrepreneurship and small business, Parker (2005, pp. 5–6) has suggested different questions that frame how economists can contribute (or have contributed) to the field. These are as follows:

[1.] How many jobs do entrepreneurs create?
[2.] Are small entrepreneurial firms more innovative than large corporations?
[3.] Do tax cuts stimulate entrepreneurship?
[4.] Why are blacks and females (minority groups) less likely to be entrepreneurs in Britain and America?
[5.] Do banks ration credit to new enterprises, and do capital constraints significantly impede entry into entrepreneurship?
[6.] How successful are loan guarantee schemes in providing credit to new enterprises?
[7.] Which entrepreneurial ventures are most likely to survive and grow?
[8.] Why do entrepreneurs work so hard for such little pay?
[9.] Does entrepreneurship cause economic growth?
[10.] Should governments encourage or discourage entrepreneurship?

Main Results

Bibliometric Findings

In one way or another, David Audretsch (alongside his co-authors) has provided insightful answers to the questions listed above. Part of his ability to offer impactful ideas is due to his readiness to share knowledge via different publications regarding small firms, entrepreneurship, innovation and economic development. Such contributions have been acknowledged highly by other academics, who continue to conduct research based on his ideas. For instance, Fig. 1 shows that between 2007 and 2018 (until July), Audretsch produced 153 documents (articles, books, chapters, etc.), and received 61,915 citations on Google Scholar.

In considering these widely cited works, it is possible to recognize that Audretsch initially approached entrepreneurship by exploring small firms' performance. Audretsch and Lehmann (2016c) explained that an initial motivation came from reviewing statistics concerning large companies in both the United States of America (USA) and Germany. They realized that SMEs' performance was increasing whereas larger enterprises' productivity was declining. Innovation capacity constituted one of Audretsch and colleagues' hypotheses. Indeed, Audretsch suggested that SMEs are capable of introducing new processes and adapting to new environ-

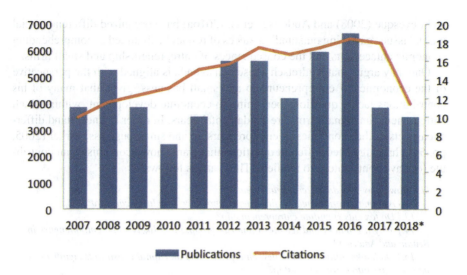

Fig. 1 Number of publications and citations of David Audretsch (2007–2018). * Until July 2018

ments, at least faster than their large counterparts. This idea was entirely aligned with Schumpeter's claims regarding innovation and entrepreneurship as a mechanism to turn new processes and ideas into new market products. Having undertaken SME and innovation analysis, the next topic explored by Audretsch comprised entrepreneurial activity and its backward (e.g., innovation capacity, knowledge, and geography) and forward links (e.g. productivity, economic growth, and competitiveness). This evolution of thought has been recognized by academics from around the world, who have cited Audretsch's publications. Table 1 displays the top 30 works, ranked according to citations on WoS and Google Scholar.

In terms of Audretsch's academic production, it is possible to observe the ways in which different concepts were embraced (or even developed). Figure 2 displays the keywords used in Audretsch's publications. The y-axis is merely informative and enables us to identify the total number of keywords (119) across publications over the years (x-axis). Particularly striking is how the analysis of entrepreneurship and small firms has evolved into understanding the institutions that affect entrepreneurial activity, thus producing socio-economic outcomes (e.g., entrepreneurial society, entrepreneurial university, entrepreneurship capital, entrepreneurship policy, and entrepreneurial choice).

Figure 3 in turn displays the connections between keywords. In this case, we used co-occurrence networks through VOSviewer software. This technique enabled us to appreciate the ways in which keywords co-occur in at least two different publications written by David Audretsch and colleagues. Li et al. (2017) have explained that this method permits exploration of the most commonly used keywords in

Table 1 Top 30 publications by David Audretsch

WoS					Google Scholar				
Authors (year)	Title	Journal/ Editorial	Citations	Type		Authors (year)	Title	Journal/ Editorial	Citations	Type
1	Audretsch and Feldman (1996b)	R&D spillovers and the geography of innovation and production	AER	1785	A	1	Audretsch and Feldman (1996a, b)	R&D spillovers and the geography of innovation and production	AER	6434	A
2	Acs and Audretsch (1988)	Innovation in large and small firms: an empirical analysis	AER	764	A	2	Acs and Audretsch (1990a, b)	Innovation and small firms	MIT	2885	B
3	Feldman and Audretsch (1999)	Innovation in cities: Science-based diversity, specialization and localized competition	EER	612	A	3	Audretsch (1995a)	Innovation and industry evolution	MIT	2690	B
4	Audretsch and Stephan (1996)	Company-scientist locational links: The case of biotechnology	AER	493	A	4	Acs and Audretsch (1988)	Innovation in large and small firms: an empirical analysis	AER	2675	A
5	Ács et al. (2009a, b)	The knowledge spillover theory of entrepreneurship	SBE	384	A	5	Feldman and Audretsch (1999)	Innovation in cities: Science-based diversity, specialization and localized competition	EER	2381	A
6	Audretsch (1998)	Agglomeration and the location of innovative activity	OREP	369	A	6	Audretsch (1998)	Agglomeration and the location of innovative activity	OREP	1599	A
7	Acs et al. (1994)	R&D spillovers and recipient firm size	RES	347	A	7	Audretsch and Stephan (1996)	Company-scientist locational links: The case of biotechnology	AER	1524	A
8	Acs and Audretsch (1987)	Innovation, market structure, and firm size	RES	339	A	8	Acs and Audretsch (1987)	Innovation, market structure, and firm size	RES	1444	A

(continued)

Table 1 (continued)

WoS					Google Scholar				
	Authors (year)	Title	Journal/ Editorial	Citations	Type	Authors (year)	Title	Journal/ Editorial	Citations	Type
9	Audretsch and Mahmood (1995)	New firm survival: new results using a hazard function	RES	324	A	9 Audretsch et al. (2006)	Entrepreneurship and economic growth	Oxford	1351	B
10	Audretsch and Keilbach (2004)	Entrepreneurship capital and economic performance	RS	298	A	10 Audretsch and Feldman (2004)	Knowledge spillovers and the geography of innovation	HRUE	1262	C
11	Audretsch (1991)	New-firm survival and the technological regime	RES	288	A	11 Acs et al. (1994)	R&D spillovers and recipient firm size	RES	1207	A
12	Acs et al. (1992)	Real effects of academic research: Comment	AER	282	A	12 Audretsch and Thurik (2001)	What's new about the new economy? Sources of growth in the managed and entrepreneurial economies	ICC	1190	A
13	Audretsch (1995)	Innovation, growth and survival	IJIO	276	A	13 Audretsch and Mahmood (1995)	New firm survival: new results using a hazard function	RES	1139	A
14	Audretsch and Feldman (1996a, b)	Innovative clusters and the industry life cycle	RIO	259	A	14 Acs et al. (1992)	Real effects of academic research: Comment	AER	1117	A
15	Audretsch and Lehmann (2005)	Does the knowledge spillover theory of entrepreneurship hold for regions?	RP	235	A	15 Audretsch (1991)	New-firm survival and the technological regime	RES	1097	A
16	Gilbert et al. (2006)	New venture growth: A review and extension	JOM	215	A	16 Audretsch (1995)	Innovation, growth and survival	IJIO	991	A

An Overview of the Economics of Entrepreneurship and Small Business: The Legacy,... 287

No	Author	Title	Journal	Cites	Grade
17	Audretsch and Fritsch (2002)	Growth regimes over time and space	RS	203	A
18	Audretsch and Thurik (2000)	Capitalism and democracy in the twenty-first century: from the managed to the entrepreneurial economy	JEE	193	A
19	Acs and Audretsch (1989)	Patents as a measure of innovative activity	Kyklos	178	A
20	Audretsch et al. (2005)	University spillovers and new firm location	RP	178	A
21	Audretsch and Fritsch (1994)	The geography of firm births in Germany	RS	176	A
22	Thurik et al. (2008)	Does self-employment reduce unemployment?	JBV	157	C
23	Agarwal and Audretsch (2001)	Does entry size matter? The impact of the life cycle and technology on firm survival	JIE	157	A
24	Audretsch et al. (1999)	Start-up size and industrial dynamics: some evidence from Italian manufacturing	IJIO	144	A

No	Author	Title	Journal	Cites	Grade
17	Audretsch and Feldman (1996a, b)	Innovative clusters and the industry life cycle	RIO	926	A
18	Audretsch and Keilbach (2004)	Entrepreneurship capital and economic performance	RS	922	A
19	Audretsch and Thurik (2000)	Capitalism and democracy in the twenty-first century: from the managed to the entrepreneurial economy	JEE	758	A
20	Verheul et al. (2002)	An eclectic theory of entrepreneurship: policies, institutions and culture	Ent	721	C
21	Audretsch (2007a, b)	The entrepreneurial society	Oxford	691	B
22	Audretsch and Fritsch (2002)	Growth regimes over time and space	RS	661	A
23	Audretsch and Lehmann (2005)	Does the knowledge spillover theory of entrepreneurship hold for regions?	RP	621	A
24	Agarwal and Audretsch (2001)	Does entry size matter? The impact of the life cycle and technology on firm survival	JIE	620	A

(continued)

Table 1 (continued)

WoS						Google Scholar					
	Authors (year)	Title	Journal/Editorial	Citations	Type		Authors (year)	Title	Journal/Editorial	Citations	Type
25	Audretsch and Keilbach (2007a)	The theory of knowledge spillover entrepreneurship	JMS	134	A	25	Gilbert et al. (2006)	New venture growth: A review and extension	JOM	610	A
26	Braunerhjelm et al. (2010)	The missing link: knowledge diffusion and entrepreneurship in endogenous growth	SBE	129	A	26	Thurik et al. (2008)	Does self-employment reduce unemployment?	JBV	570	A
27	Agarwal et al. (2007)	The process of creative construction: Knowledge spillovers, entrepreneurship, and economic growth	SEJ	128	A	27	Acs and Audretsch (1989)	Patents as a measure of innovative activity	Kyklos	554	A
28	Gilbert et al. (2008)	Clusters, knowledge spillovers and new venture performance: An empirical examination	JBV	124	A	28	Audretsch and Fritsch (1994)	The geography of firm births in Germany	RS	542	A
29	Audretsch et al. (2004)	Gibrat's Law: Are the services different?	RIO	123	A	29	Audretsch et al. (2005)	University spillovers and new firm location	RP	507	A
30	Audretsch (2007b)	Entrepreneurship capital and economic growth	OREP	118	A	30	Audretsch (2007b)	Entrepreneurship capital and economic growth	OREP	497	A

Type A: Article; B: Book; C: Book Chapter. Journal/Editorial. Journals in order of appearance: AER: American Economic Review; EER: European Economic Review; SBE: Small Business Economics; OREP: Oxford Review of Economic Policy; RES: Review of Economics and Statistics; RS: Regional Studies; IJIO: International Journal of Industrial Organization; RIO: Review of Industrial Organization; RP: Research Policy; JOM: Journal of Management; JEE: Journal of Evolutionary Economics; JBV: Journal of Business Venturing; JIE: Journal of Industrial Economics; JMS: Journal of Management Studies; SEJ: Strategic Entrepreneurship Journal; MIT: MIT Press; HRUE: Handbook of Regional and Urban Economics; ICC: Industrial and Corporate Change

An Overview of the Economics of Entrepreneurship and Small Business: The Legacy... 289

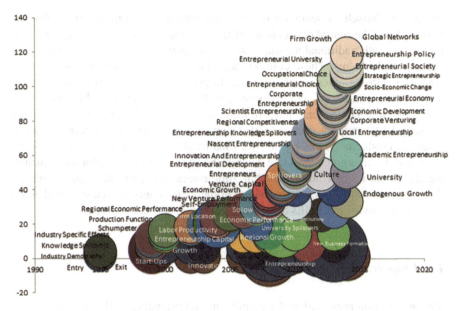

Fig. 2 The keywords used in David Audretsch's publications

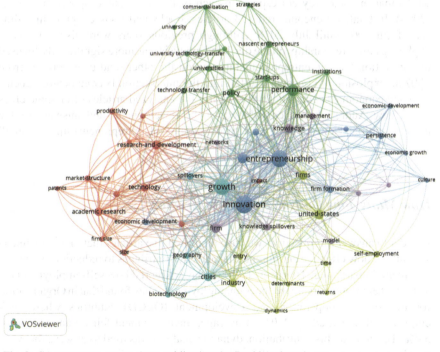

Fig. 3 Co-ocurrences among those publications by David Audretsch

articles. Audretsch's orientation in analyzing entrepreneurship and small firms is thus evident. The central cluster (dark blue) connects entrepreneurship (capital) and innovation with traditional measures in economics (i.e., economic growth and economic development). These concepts are also connected with the upper cluster (green), regarding other variables related to public policy (i.e., university technology transfer, institutions, and performance). The cluster on the left-hand side (red) indicates those components that are close to innovation but that are additionally connected to entrepreneurial activity (such as R&D, market structure, academic research, productivity, among others). Finally, the cluster at the bottom (yellow) reveals some emerging topics that Audretsch leaves for further exploration (including the dynamics of entrepreneurship, time issues, and entry decisions). Overall, these connections facilitate appreciation of the varied concepts that surround entrepreneurial activity and SMEs in terms of both antecedents and consequences.

Findings from Content Analysis

The information presented so far permits an understanding of the landscape upon which Audretsch draws when analyzing entrepreneurship and small firms. However, the questions explored in Section 2 cannot be answered by only taking into consideration bibliometric information. Therefore, we used content analysis to identify works that in some way correspond to each of the questions proposed by Parker (2005). In total, we encountered 153 articles, books and book chapters in a time span from 2007 until July 2018. Although previous years were also devoted to exploring entrepreneurship, on the one hand analysis was more significantly focused on innovation than on entrepreneurship, and on the other (and using Fig. 2) from 2007 an explosion of concepts that fall into the intersection between entrepreneurship and economics occurred. In this regard, the analyzed articles offer some clues about how Audretsch has contributed to the development and answers of the above mentioned questions related to economics of entrepreneurship and small firms.

How Many Jobs Do Entrepreneurs Create?

In order to answer this question, we have identified five articles that facilitate understanding of how effective entrepreneurial activity contributes to reductions in unemployment. In particular, Thurik et al. (2008) have explored how self-employment (as a proxy of entrepreneurship) reduces unemployment. They found that in Organisation for Economic Co-operation and Development (OECD) countries where self-employment increased by 2.7% on average, unemployment fell by an average of 3.4%. Throughout this contribution, dynamic analysis was used to observe the ways in which entrepreneurship can bring long term-benefits. Similarly, Stuetzer et al.

(2016) predicted a significant correlation between entrepreneurship and employment share, even when historical analysis is introduced. In this regard, we might state that entrepreneurs do create jobs, and therefore labor policies should consider entrepreneurship as a mechanism when defining regional and national objectives.

Are Small Entrepreneurial Firms More Innovative Than Large Corporations?

Other sorts of policies that must be considered by regional and national governments are those related to the promotion of innovation within small firms. To answer this particular question, we have identified 25 publications that continue Audretsch's initial research agenda. Current studies compare the importance of SMEs for the economy, especially considering that they create a larger number of employees than their bigger counterparts (cf. Acs and Audretsch 2013). Audretsch (2007b) has explained that the evolution of the economic system is in fact supported by the creative destruction process (Schumpeter 1911), in which incumbent firms as well as entrepreneurs must renovate and innovate to survive. This may imply the diffusion and absorption of knowledge – which is typically easier for SMEs than for big companies (Audretsch and Keilbach 2008b) – appropriate corporate governance (Audretsch and Lehmann 2011), and a national system of innovation (Acs et al. 2017a), where universities play an important role in providing bridging education programmes focused on innovation with market needs (Alshumaimri et al. 2010).

Do Tax Cuts Stimulate Entrepreneurship?

National systems of innovation and entrepreneurship require governments to align their purposes with the productive sector. This implies that certain barriers should be removed in order to generate a continuous flow of ideas, new businesses and products (Audretsch and Aldridge 2009). Although we only identified one article related to this question (Chowdhury et al. 2015a), other areas within the economics of entrepreneurship and small firms can facilitate an understanding of how governments may become enemies of entrepreneurship. The first aspect explored by economists who analyze governmental distortion is related to fiscal policy. Indeed, the national treasury of each country is aware of its limited budget, and so businesses become an easy target for taxation. Chowdhury et al. (2015a) have demonstrated that these sorts of initiatives discourage entry decision. Another reason found in the literature deals with the correlation between taxes and corruption. Indeed, higher taxes may imply an inefficient use of public expenditure. In this regard, Aparicio et al. (2016) have demonstrated that entrepreneurial activity may increase if corruption is reduced.

Why Are Minority Groups Less Likely to Be Entrepreneurs in Britain and America?

Governments not only affect entrepreneurial activity through fiscal issues, but also via policies that favor some communities more than others. We have found that seven publications involving Audretsch's collaboration have analyzed how cultural diversity and specific laws can explain differences in entrepreneurship among countries. For example, Audretsch et al. (2010) have explored the influence of some religions (supported by governments) on entrepreneurial activity and SMEs' performance. Cultural practices in which women are only valued for specific household activities demonstrate lower levels of entrepreneurship and quality (e.g., those that are necessity- driven). Welter et al. (2017) have suggested that policies should guarantee the equality of genders and communities, as well as other social aspects. Effectively, these authors argue that institutional and cultural differences exist not only at the macro level, but also at the individual level. In this sense, such differences should be identified so that the strategies implemented provide equal benefits for the entire community, regardless of the type of motivation.

Do Banks Ration Credit to New Enterprises, and Do Capital Constraints Significantly Impede Entry into Entrepreneurship?

Some strategies that may create egalitarian results are focused on providing capital for those potential entrepreneurs that manifest intention, but for some reason cannot afford the current loan schemes. In order to answer this question, we found six articles that (although not precisely related to the subject) offer some clue regarding how long-term policies support a stable financial system. Audretsch and Aldridge (2012) have emphasized the importance of education in increasing salaries through gaining human capital. For those involved in academia, the experience obtained may enable them to apply for different loan mechanisms that leverage entrepreneurial initiatives. Audretsch et al. (2012a) have found that innovative nascent ventures demonstrate interest in accessing funding for their initiatives. In this regard, if the financial system creates barriers to access, small firms are unable to undertake new product or service development.

How Successful Are Loan Guarantee Schemes in Providing Credit to New Enterprises?

It is critical for entrepreneurship and SMEs to rely on the support of commercial banks, investors and public funds. This question leads us towards the understanding of entrepreneurial finance, which facilitates understanding of the strategic movement of entrepreneurs to attain and manage funding. We can note four articles that explain different means of obtaining funding and surviving in aggressive markets. For instance, Audretsch and Lehmann (2007, 2008) have demonstrated how mergers and acquisitions help the business system to grow, while providing funds for entrepreneurs involved in the inception of the project. In particular, Audretsch and Lehmann (2008) have demonstrated the important role of the financial system (with accessible loans) in the formation and survival of small businesses.

Which Entrepreneurial Ventures Are Most Likely to Survive and Grow?

Public and private strategies can present opportunities to engage in entrepreneurship with growth aspirations, as entrepreneurs can undertake their work without worrying about financial pressures. Nonetheless, Audretsch (2012b) has explained that the adaptation process should also be considered. In this case, small and nascent firms tend to adapt more easily to either the process, product or service than large companies. This may imply that firms must have entrepreneurial spirit and motivation, as the market can change abruptly, causing chaos within the firm (Audretsch and Link 2012a). These entrepreneurial firms are typically characterized by aspects that differentiate them from others. For example, they take greater risks such as by exploring international markets (Audretsch et al. 2018b) and connections with other companies (Gilbert et al. 2008). Overall, these firms work hard, aware that the payments they receive may appreciate after five years or more.

Why Do Entrepreneurs Work So Hard for Such Little Pay?

Entrepreneurial characteristics, intentions and motivations are key components during the entrepreneurial process. Although the 24 works classified under this question do not compare workers' salaries with the benefits obtained by entrepreneurs, Audretsch has increased understandings of why people remain interested in entrepreneurship as a career choice. One of the main reasons is based on the idea that entrepreneurs are constantly innovating. Audretsch (2015c), while synthesizing Shaker Zahra's contribution to entrepreneurship research, has explained that entrepreneurial activity may be manifested through different ways (corporate entrepreneurship and international entrepreneurship), suggesting that everyone can be (and in fact is) an entrepreneur. Audretsch et al. (2015a) have shown how entrepreneurship, by definition, involves elements of organization, psychology and economics that support an understanding of intention, behavior and performance.

Does Entrepreneurship Cause Economic Growth?

Acs et al. (2012) have noted that if we as individuals are part of the entrepreneurial system in one way or another, then better results can be obtained for the economy as a whole. Akin to the first question regarding the importance of entrepreneurship for job creation, Audretsch has demonstrated that entrepreneurial activity matters for economic growth. For example, 32 works have explained the contributions of entrepreneurship to the economy. Audretsch and Keilbach (2008a) have developed the idea that innovative entrepreneurs, who are contained within the concept of entrepreneurship capital, may create superior results in terms of economic growth. Entrepreneurship capital (Audretsch and Keilbach 2004), therefore, represents the endowment that each society has in terms of innovation, coordination and orientation towards entrepreneurship. Again, following the Schumpeterian (1911) notion, Audretsch and Lehmann (2017) have assumed that the key component in entrepreneurship is innovation. Combining these two elements, new ideas can be developed, with some information remaining in the market to be easily absorbed by other entrepreneurs. According to Braunerhjelm et al. (2010), knowledge flows through the economy, new entrepreneurs emerge, and greater economic growth is facilitated.

Should Governments Encourage or Discourage Entrepreneurship?

Part of the challenge of increasing economic performance is to create an environment in which people feel encouraged to engage in entrepreneurial activities that bring social and economic benefit (Audretsch and Keilbach 2008a; Aparicio et al. 2016). As mentioned, the role of different agents is crucial in the development of an entrepreneurial society (Audretsch 2007a, b). Governments represent one such agent, providing mechanisms that help people to overcome different social circumstances, such as poverty and exclusion). In this regard, entrepreneurship is deemed a vehicle that helps individuals to be included into the labor market. According to Audretsch and Thurik (2007) and Audretsch and Lehmann (2016c), part of the success of countries such as Germany is due to the special attention they afford entrepreneurs and SMEs, viewing them as drivers of social and economic transformation. Thus, governments should consider consolidating an amenable financial system (Audretsch and Link 2017a) and form clusters (Audretsch and Lehmann 2016b) and infrastructure at the local level (Audretsch et al. 2015g). Table 2 summarizes the works analyzed from the economics of entrepreneurship and small business perspective.

An Overview of the Economics of Entrepreneurship and Small Business: The Legacy... 295

Table 2 Works that contribute to the field of economics of entrepreneurship and small business

	Question	Works	Total
1	How many jobs do entrepreneurs create?	Audretsch et al. (2008c, 2015b); Stuetzer et al. (2016); Thurik et al. (2008); Welfens et al. (2012).	5
2	Are small entrepreneurial firms more innovative than large corporations?	Acs and Audretsch (2013); Acs et al. (2017a); Alshumaimri et al. (2010); Amoroso et al. (2018); Audretsch (2007b, 2018); Audretsch and Aldridge (2009); Audretsch and Keilbach (2008b); Audretsch and Lehmann (2011); Audretsch et al. (2008b, 2009a, 2011a, e, 2014a, c); Audretsch et al. (2014d); Audretsch and Caiazza (2016); Audretsch et al. (2016b, 2018c); De Massis et al. (2018); Demircioglu and Audretsch (2017); Gulbranson and Audretsch (2008); Huang et al. (2013); Audretsch and Tamvada (2008); Zhang et al. (2015).	25
3	Do tax cuts stimulate entrepreneurship?	Chowdhury et al. (2015a).	1
4	Why are minority groups less likely to be entrepreneurs in Britain and America?	Audretsch et al. (2010, 2016a, 2017a); Chowdhury and Audretsch (2014); Lyons et al. (2012); Obschonka et al. (2016); Welter et al. (2017).	7
5	Do banks ration credit to new enterprises, and do capital constraints significantly impede entry into entrepreneurship?	Audretsch and Aldridge (2012); Audretsch et al. (2011b, c, d, 2012a); Elston and Audretsch (2010); Guerzoni et al. (2014); Patzelt and Audretsch (2008).	6
6	How successful are loan guarantee schemes in providing credit to new enterprises?	Audretsch and Lehmann (2007, 2008); Audretsch et al. (2016c); Elston and Audretsch (2011).	4
7	Which entrepreneurial ventures are most likely to survive and grow?	Audretsch et al. (2012b); Audretsch and Dohse (2007); Audretsch and Link (2012a); Audretsch et al. (2009c, 2013b, 2014b). Firm growth and innovation; Audretsch et al. (2016b, 2017b); Audretsch et al. (2018b); Gilbert et al. (2008).	10
8	Why do entrepreneurs work so hard for such a little pay?	Acs and Audretsch (2009); Acs et al. (2010); Agarwal et al. (2010); Aldridge et al. (2014); Alshumaimri et al. (2012); Alvarez et al. (2016); Audretsch (2012a); Audretsch (2014c); Audretsch et al. (2015c, e); Aldridge and Audretsch (2011); Audretsch and Lehmann (2016a); Audretsch et al. (2013a, 2015a, d, 2016d); Caiazza and Audretsch (2013); Chowdhury et al. (2015b); Kuratko and Audretsch (2009); Kuratko and Audretsch (2013); Rocha et al. (2013); Stam et al. (2008); Welpe et al. (2012); Wiklund et al. (2011).	24

(continued)

Table 2 (continued)

	Question	Works	Total
9	Does entrepreneurship cause economic growth?	Acs et al. (2012, 2013); Aparicio et al. (2016); Audretsch (2007b, 2014a, b); Audretsch and Aldridge (2008); Audretsch and Belitski (2013); Audretsch and Fornielles (2007); Audretsch and Keilbach (2007a, b); Audretsch and Keilbach (2008a); Audretsch and Peña-Legazkue (2012); Audretsch and Monsen (2008); Audretsch and Walshok (2013); Audretsch and Welfens (2013); Audretsch et al. (2008a, 2011b, c, d, 2012b, c, 2013c, d, 2015c, 2016f); Audretsch and Lehmann (2017); Braunerhjelm et al. (2010); Caiazza et al. (2015); Carlsson et al. (2009); Obschonka et al. (2015); Stuetzer et al. (2018); Urbano et al. (2018); Thurik et al. (2013).	32
10	Should governments encourage or discourage entrepreneurship?	Ács et al. (2009, 2016a, b, 2017b); Aldridge and Audretsch (2010); Amable et al. (2008); Audretsch (2007a, 2009b, 2013a, b, 2015b, d); Audretsch (2017); Audretsch and Beckmann (2007); Audretsch and Lehmann (2014, 2016b); Audretsch and Link (2012b); Audretsch and Thurik (2007); Audretsch et al. (2007, 2009b, 2011b, c, d, 2012d, e, 2015e, f, g); Audretsch and Lehmann (2016c); Audretsch et al. (2016a, e); Audretsch and Belitski (2017); Audretsch and Link (2016); Audretsch and Link (2017a, b); Audretsch et al. (2018a); Bischoff et al. (2018); Caiazza and Audretsch (2015); Caiazza et al. (2014); Chowdhury et al. (2018); Tanas and Audretsch (2011).	39

Conclusions and Discussion Regarding Future Research Avenues

In this chapter, we quantitatively and analytically examined Audretsch's contributions to the economics of entrepreneurship and small business, from 2007 until the present day (July 2018). Based on searches using Google Scholar and Web of Science (WoS), we relied upon bibliometrics and content analyses to explore production indexes (number of publications, top articles, citations, keywords and networks) and to show the evolution of the research field.

We have noted that Audretsch is a remarkable scholar, publishing an average of 13 articles, books or chapters per year. Such productivity has been recognized by researchers from all over the world, with Audretsch receiving an average of 5960 citations each year. In reviewing his seminal works, it is possible to identify an evolution in his research agenda, beginning with the examination of innovation in SMEs relative to large companies, and later exploring industrial structure in terms of its actors, such as incumbent firms, governments and entrepreneurs. Thus, entrepreneurship, innovation and SMEs have become key units of analysis, which can be seen as leveraging economic growth. Such findings are corroborated by analysis of keywords and co-occurrence.

An Overview of the Economics of Entrepreneurship and Small Business: The Legacy... 297

David Audretsch has been a key scholar in advancing understandings of entrepreneurship from an economics perspective. By revising the content of 153 articles on Google Scholar, published between 2007 and July 2018, we found that different questions regarding the economics of entrepreneurship and small business (cf. Parker 2005) were completely answered. Audretsch's contributions present general overviews and specific evidence that demonstrate the pertinence of entrepreneurship within the economics of science.

Although we would have liked to embrace all of Audretsch's publications, we are confident that our time period is pertinent to understanding advances in entrepreneurship research. Nevertheless, we believe that future research avenues may create further insights not only regarding entrepreneurial activity as a field of inquiry, but also in terms of the identification and conceptualization of other subfields within the economics of entrepreneurship and small business. These may stimulate further analysis concerning the complexity behind economic development, in which institutions guide entrepreneurs to produce social solutions and outcomes (Audretsch and Keilbach 2008a; Braunerhjelm et al. 2010; Urbano et al. 2018). Here, institutional economics could be applied to the analysis of diversity in entrepreneurship and small firms, as these elements also contribute to the development of markets, places, industries and so forth (Urbano et al. 2018; Welter et al. 2017). In addition, further analysis of Audretsch's publications may help connect social and economic policies aimed at the promotion of an entrepreneurial society, characterized by different types of entrepreneurs, from different communities and contexts.

References

Acs, Z. J., & Audretsch, D. B. (1987). Innovation, market structure, and firm size. *The Review of Economics and Statistics, 59*(4), 567–574.

Acs, Z. J., & Audretsch, D. B. (1988). Innovation in large and small firms: an empirical analysis. *The American Economic Review, 78*(4), 678–690.

Acs, Z. J., & Audretsch, D. B. (1989). Patents as a measure of innovative activity. *Kyklos, 42*(2), 171–180.

Acs, Z. J., & Audretsch, D. B. (1990a). *Innovation and small firms.* Cambridge: MIT Press.

Acs, Z. J., & Audretsch, D. B. (Eds.). (1990b). *The Economics of Small Firms: A European Challenge.* Berlin: Springer Science & Business Media.

Acs, Z., & Audretsch, D. B. (2009). In Partnership with the Global Award for Entrepreneurship Research. *Small Business Economics, 33*(2), 129–130.

Acs, Z. J., Audretsch, D. B., & Feldman, M. P. (1992). Real effects of academic research: comment. *The American Economic Review, 82*(1), 363–367.

Acs, Z. J., Audretsch, D. B., & Feldman, M. P. (1994). R&D spillovers and recipient firm size. *The Review of Economics and Statistics, 76*(2), 336–340.

Ács, Z. J., Braunerhjelm, B., Audretsch, D. B., & Carlsson, B. (2009a). The knowledge spillover theory of entrepreneurship. *Small Business Economics, 32*(1), 15–30.

Ács, Z. J., Audretsch, D. B., & Strom, R. J. (Eds.). (2009b). *Entrepreneurship, growth, and public policy.* Cambridge: Cambridge University Press.

Acs, Z., Audretsch, D., Desai, S., & Welpe, I. (2010). On experiments in entrepreneurship research. *Journal of Economic Behavior and Organization, 1*(76), 1–2.

Acs, Z. J., Audretsch, D. B., Braunerhjelm, P., & Carlsson, B. (2012). Growth and entrepreneurship. *Small Business Economics, 39*(2), 289–300.

Acs, Z. J., Audretsch, D. B., & Lehmann, E. E. (2013). The knowledge spillover theory of entrepreneurship. *Small Business Economics, 41*(4), 757–774.

Acs, Z., Åstebro, T., Audretsch, D., & Robinson, D. T. (2016a). Public policy to promote entrepreneurship: a call to arms. *Small Business Economics, 47*(1), 35–51.

Acs, Z. J., Audretsch, D. B., Lehmann, E. E., & Licht, G. (2016b). National systems of entrepreneurship. *Small Business Economics, 46*(4), 527–535.

Acs, Z. J., Audretsch, D. B., Lehmann, E. E., & Licht, G. (2017a). National systems of innovation. *The Journal of Technology Transfer, 42*(5), 997–1008.

Acs, Z. J., Stam, E., Audretsch, D. B., & O'Connor, A. (2017b). The lineages of the entrepreneurial ecosystem approach. *Small Business Economics, 49*(1), 1–10.

Agarwal, R., & Audretsch, D. B. (2001). Does entry size matter? The impact of the life cycle and technology on firm survival. *The Journal of Industrial Economics, 49*(1), 21–43.

Agarwal, R., Audretsch, D., & Sarkar, M. B. (2007). The process of creative construction: Knowledge spillovers, entrepreneurship, and economic growth. *Strategic Entrepreneurship Journal, 1*(3–4), 263–286.

Agarwal, R., Audretsch, D., & Sarkar, M. B. (2010). Knowledge spillovers and strategic entrepreneurship. *Strategic Entrepreneurship Journal, 4*(4), 271–283.

Aldridge, T., & Audretsch, D. B. (2010). Does policy influence the commercialization route? Evidence from National Institutes of Health funded scientists. *Research Policy, 39*(5), 583–588.

Aldridge, T. T., & Audretsch, D. (2011). The Bayh-Dole act and scientist entrepreneurship. *Research Policy, 40*(8), 1058–1067.

Aldridge, T. T., Audretsch, D., Desai, S., & Nadella, V. (2014). Scientist entrepreneurship across scientific fields. *The Journal of Technology Transfer, 39*(6), 819–835.

Alshumaimri, A., Aldridge, T., & Audretsch, D. B. (2010). The university technology transfer revolution in Saudi Arabia. *The Journal of Technology Transfer, 35*(6), 585–596.

Alshumaimri, A., Aldridge, T., & Audretsch, D. B. (2012). Scientist entrepreneurship in Saudi Arabia. *The Journal of Technology Transfer, 37*(5), 648–657.

Alvarez, S. A., Audretsch, D., & Link, A. N. (2016). Advancing our understanding of theory in entrepreneurship. *Strategic Entrepreneurship Journal, 10*(1), 3–4.

Amable, B., Audretsch, D. B., & Dore, R. (2008). Richard Whitley Business Systems and Organizational Capabilities. The Institutional Structuring of Competitive Competences. Oxford, Oxford University Press, 2007. *Socio-Economic Review, 6*(4), 771–784.

Amoroso, S., Audretsch, D. B., & Link, A. N. (2018). Sources of knowledge used by entrepreneurial firms in the European high-tech sector. *Eurasian Business Review, 8*(1), 55–70.

Aparicio, S., Urbano, D., & Audretsch, D. (2016). Institutional factors, opportunity entrepreneurship and economic growth: Panel data evidence. *Technological Forecasting and Social Change, 102*, 45–61.

Audretsch, D. B. (1991). New-firm survival and the technological regime. *The Review of Economics and Statistics, 73*(3), 441–450.

Audretsch, D. B. (1995a). *Innovation and industry evolution.* Cambridge: MIT Press.

Audretsch, D. B. (1995b). Innovation, growth and survival. *International Journal of Industrial Organization, 13*(4), 441–457.

Audretsch, B. (1998). Agglomeration and the location of innovative activity. *Oxford Review of Economic Policy, 14*(2), 18–29.

Audretsch, D. B. (2007a). *The entrepreneurial society.* Oxford University Press.

Audretsch, D. B. (2007b). Entrepreneurship capital and economic growth. *Oxford Review of Economic Policy, 23*(1), 63–78.

Audretsch, D. B. (2009a). Emergence of the entrepreneurial society. *Business Horizons, 52*(5), 505–511.

Audretsch, D. B. (2009b). The entrepreneurial society. In *New Frontiers in Entrepreneurship* (pp. 95–105). New York, NY: Springer.

An Overview of the Economics of Entrepreneurship and Small Business: The Legacy... 299

Audretsch, D. B. (2009c). The entrepreneurial society. *The Journal of Technology Transfer, 34*(3), 245–254.

Audretsch, D. B. (2012a). Adapt: Why Success Always Starts with Failure. *Journal of Economic Literature, 50*(1), 183–183.

Audretsch, D. B. (2012b). Entrepreneurship research. *Management Decision, 50*(5), 755–764.

Audretsch, D. B. (2013a). *Public policy in the entrepreneurial society.* London: Edward Elgar Publishing.

Audretsch, D. B. (2013b). *Entrepreneurship and competition policy. The International Handbook of Competition* (pp. 88–107).

Audretsch, D. B. (2014a). From the entrepreneurial university to the university for the entrepreneurial society. *The Journal of Technology Transfer, 39*(3), 313–321.

Audretsch, D. B. (2014b). The entrepreneurial society and the role of the University. *Economia Marche-Journal of Applied Economics, 32*(2).

Audretsch, D. B. (2014c). Small Business and Entrepreneurship: The Emergence of a Scholarly Field. 20 years of Entrepreneurship Research, 49.

Audretsch, D. B. (2015a). Joseph Schumpeter and John Kenneth Galbraith: two sides of the same coin? *Journal of Evolutionary Economics, 25*(1), 197–214.

Audretsch, D. B. (2015b). The strategic management of place. In *The Oxford handbook of local competitiveness* (pp. 13–33). Oxford: Oxford University Press.

Audretsch, D. B. (2015c). Shaker A. Zahra: Pioneering entrepreneurship scholar. *Small Business Economics, 44*(4), 721–725.

Audretsch, D. B. (2015d). *Everything in its place: Entrepreneurship and the strategic management of cities, regions, and states.* Oxford University Press.

Audretsch, D. B. (2017). Entrepreneurship and universities. *International Journal of Entrepreneurship and Small Business, 31*(1), 4–11.

Audretsch, D. B. (2018). Industrial organization and the organization of industries: Linking industry structure to economic performance. *Review of Industrial Organization, 52*(4), 603–620.

Audretsch, D. B., & Aldridge, T. T. (2008). The knowledge spillover theory of entrepreneurship and spatial clusters. In C. Karlsson (Ed.), *Handbook of research on cluster theory* (pp. 67–77). London: Edward Elgar Publishing.

Audretsch, D. B., & Aldridge, T. T. (2009). Scientist commercialization as conduit of knowledge spillovers. *The Annals of Regional Science, 43*(4), 897–905.

Audretsch, D., & Aldridge, T. (2012). Transnational social capital and scientist entrepreneurship. *Journal of Management and Governance, 16*(3), 369–376.

Acs, Z. J., & Audretsch, D. B. (2013). Small firms in the 1990s. In S. J. Ackerman & D. B. Audretsch (Eds.), *The economics of small firms: A European challenge* (pp. 1–22). Amsterdam: Springer International Publishing.

Audretsch, D. B., & Beckmann, I. A. (2007). From small business to entrepreneurship policy. In D. B. Audretsch, I. Grilo, & R. Thurik (Eds.), *Handbook of research on entrepreneurship policy* (pp. 36–53). London: Edward Elgar Publishing.

Audretsch, D. B., & Belitski, M. (2013). The missing pillar: The creativity theory of knowledge spillover entrepreneurship. *Small Business Economics, 41*(4), 819–836.

Audretsch, D. B., & Belitski, M. (2017). Entrepreneurial ecosystems in cities: establishing the framework conditions. *The Journal of Technology Transfer, 42*(5), 1030–1051.

Audretsch, D., & Caiazza, R. (2016). Technology transfer and entrepreneurship: cross-national analysis. *The Journal of Technology Transfer, 41*(6), 1247–1259.

Audretsch, D. B., & Dohse, D. (2007). Location: A neglected determinant of firm growth. *Review of World Economics, 143*(1), 79–107.

Audretsch, D. B., & Feldman, M. P. (1996a). Innovative clusters and the industry life cycle. *Review of Industrial Organization, 11*(2), 253–273.

Audretsch, D. B., & Feldman, M. P. (1996b). R&D spillovers and the geography of innovation and production. *The American Economic Review, 86*(3), 630–640.

Audretsch, D. B., & Feldman, M. P. (2004). Knowledge spillovers and the geography of innovation. In J. V. Henderson & J.-F. Thisse (Eds.), *Handbook of regional and urban economics* (pp. 2713–2739). Amsterdam: Elsevier.

Audretsch, D. B., & Fornielles, M. R. C. (2007). La política industrial actual: conocimiento e innovación empresarial. *Economía Industrial, 363*, 33–46.

Audretsch, D. B., & Fritsch, M. (1994). The geography of firm births in Germany. *Regional Studies, 28*(4), 359–365.

Audretsch, D. B., & Fritsch, M. (2002). Growth regimes over time and space. *Regional Studies, 36*(2), 113–124.

Audretsch, D., & Keilbach, M. (2004). Entrepreneurship capital and economic performance. *Regional Studies, 38*(8), 949–959.

Audretsch, D. B., & Keilbach, M. (2007a). The theory of knowledge spillover entrepreneurship. *Journal of Management Studies, 44*(7), 1242–1254.

Audretsch, D. B., & Keilbach, M. (2007b). The localisation of entrepreneurship capital: Evidence from Germany. *Papers in Regional Science, 86*(3), 351–365.

Audretsch, D. B., & Keilbach, M. (2008a). Resolving the knowledge paradox: Knowledge-spillover entrepreneurship and economic growth. *Research Policy, 37*(10), 1697–1705.

Audretsch, D. B., & Keilbach, M. (2008b). Knowledge spillover entrepreneurship and innovation in large and small firms. In J. B. Davis & W. Dolfsma (Eds.), *The Elgar companion to social economics* (pp. 326–347). London: Edward Elgar Publishing.

Audretsch, D. B., & Lehmann, E. E. (2005). Does the knowledge spillover theory of entrepreneurship hold for regions? *Research Policy, 34*(8), 1191–1202.

Audretsch, D. B., & Lehmann, E. E. (2007). Mergers and acquisitions in IPO markets: Evidence from Germany. In G. N. Gregoriou & L. Renneboog (Eds.), *International mergers and acquisitions activity since 1990* (pp. 169–179). Amsterdam: Elsevier.

Audretsch, D. B., & Lehmann, E. E. (2008). The Neuer Markt as an institution of creation and destruction. *International Entrepreneurship and Management Journal, 4*(4), 419.

Audretsch, D., & Lehmann, E. (2011). *Corporate governance in small and medium-sized firms*. London: Edward Elgar Publishing.

Audretsch, D. B., & Lehmann, E. E. (2014). Corporate governance and entrepreneurial firms. *Foundations and Trends in Entrepreneurship, 10*(1–2), 1–160.

Audretsch, D. B., & Lehmann, E. E. (Eds.). (2016a). *The Routledge Companion to the Makers of Modern Entrepreneurship*. Taylor & Francis.

Audretsch, D. B., & Lehmann, E. E. (2016b). Industrial policy in Italy and Germany: yet another look. *Economia e Politica Industriale, 43*(3), 291–304.

Audretsch, D. B., & Lehmann, E. (2016c). *The seven secrets of Germany: Economic resilience in an era of global turbulence*. Oxford University Press.

Audretsch, D. B., & Lehmann, E. E. (2017). Economic performance and the knowledge spillover theory of entrepreneurship: a comment. *The Journal of Technology Transfer, 42*(5), 1234–1235.

Audretsch, D. B., & Link, A. N. (Eds.). (2016). *Essays in public sector entrepreneurship*. Switzerland: Springer International Publishing.

Audretsch, D. B., & Link, A. N. (2012a). Valuing an entrepreneurial enterprise. *Small Business Economics, 38*(2), 139–145.

Audretsch, D. B., & Link, A. N. (2012b). Entrepreneurship and innovation: Public policy frameworks. *The Journal of Technology Transfer, 37*(1), 1–17.

Audretsch, D. B., & Link, A. N. (2017a). Embracing an entrepreneurial ecosystem: An analysis of the governance of research joint ventures. *Small Business Economics*, 1–8. https://doi.org/10.1007/s11187-017-9953-8.

Audretsch, D. B., & Link, A. N. (Eds.). (2017b). *Universities and the entrepreneurial ecosystem*. Edward Elgar Publishing.

Audretsch, D. B., & Mahmood, T. (1995). New firm survival: new results using a hazard function. *The Review of Economics and Statistics, 77*(1), 97–103.

An Overview of the Economics of Entrepreneurship and Small Business: The Legacy...   301

Audretsch, D., & Monsen, E. (2008). Entrepreneurship capital: A regional, organizational, team and individual phenomenon. In R. Barrett & S. Mayson (Eds.), *International handbook of entrepreneurship and HRM* (pp. 47–70). London: Edward Elgar Publishing.

Audretsch, D. B., & Peña-Legazkue, I. (2012). Entrepreneurial activity and regional competitiveness: an introduction to the special issue. *Small Business Economics, 39*(3), 531–537.

Audretsch, D. B., & Stephan, P. E. (1996). Company-scientist locational links: The case of biotechnology. *The American Economic Review, 86*(3), 641–652.

Audretsch, D. B., & Tamvada, J. P. (2008). The distribution of firm start-up size across geographic space. CEPR Discussion paper no. DP6846. [Online], available at SSRN: https://ssrn.com/abstract=1146772

Audretsch, D. B., & Thurik, A. R. (2000). Capitalism and democracy in the 21st century: from the managed to the entrepreneurial economy. *Journal of Evolutionary Economics, 10*(1–2), 17–34.

Audretsch, D. B., & Thurik, A. R. (2001). What's new about the new economy? Sources of growth in the managed and entrepreneurial economies. *Industrial and Corporate Change, 10*(1), 267–315.

Audretsch, D., & Thurik, R. (2007). The models of the managed and entrepreneurial economies. In H. Hanusch & A. Pyka (Eds.), *Elgar companion to neo-Schumpeterian economics* (pp. 211–231). London: Edward Elgar Publishing.

Audretsch, D. B., & Walshok, M. (Eds.). (2013). *Creating competitiveness: Entrepreneurship and innovation policies for growth*. Edward Elgar Publishing.

Audretsch, D. B., & Welfens, P. J. (Eds.). (2013). *The new economy and economic growth in Europe and the US*. Switzerland: Springer International Publishing.

Audretsch, D. B., Santarelli, E., & Vivarelli, M. (1999). Start-up size and industrial dynamics: some evidence from Italian manufacturing. *International Journal of Industrial Organization, 17*(7), 965–983.

Audretsch, D. B., Klomp, L., Santarelli, E., & Thurik, A. R. (2004). Gibrat's Law: Are the services different? *Review of Industrial Organization, 24*(3), 301–324.

Audretsch, D. B., Lehmann, E. E., & Warning, S. (2005). University spillovers and new firm location. *Research Policy, 34*(7), 1113–1122.

Audretsch, D. B., Keilbach, M. C., & Lehmann, E. E. (2006). *Entrepreneurship and economic growth*. Oxford: Oxford University Press.

Audretsch, D. B., Grilo, I., & Thurik, A. R. (Eds.). (2007). *Handbook of research on entrepreneurship policy*. London: Edward Elgar Publishing.

Audretsch, D. B., Bönte, W., & Keilbach, M. (2008a). Entrepreneurship capital and its impact on knowledge diffusion and economic performance. *Journal of Business Venturing, 23*(6), 687–698.

Audretsch, D. B., Aldridge, T. T., & Perry, M. (2008b). *A survey review of university biotechnology and entrepreneurship commercialization* (In Handbook of bioentrepreneurship (pp. 179–191)). New York, NY: Springer.

Audretsch, D., Callejon, M., & Aranguren, M. J. (2008c). Entrepreneurship, small firms and self-employment. In *High technology, productivity and networks* (pp. 117–137). London: Palgrave Macmillan.

Audretsch, D. B., Falck, O., & Heblich, S. (2009a). *Innovation and entrepreneurship*. Edward Elgar Publishing.

Audretsch, D. B., Grimm, H. M., & Schuetze, S. (2009b). Local strategies within a European policy framework. *European Planning Studies, 17*(3), 463–486.

Audretsch, D. B., Litan, R., & Strom, R. J. (Eds.). (2009c). *Entrepreneurship and openness: Theory and evidence*. London: Edward Elgar Publishing.

Audretsch, D., Dohse, D., & Niebuhr, A. (2010). Cultural diversity and entrepreneurship: a regional analysis for Germany. *The Annals of Regional Science, 45*(1), 55–85.

Audretsch, D. B., Martínez-Fuentes, C., & Pardo-del-Val, M. (2011a). Incremental innovation in services through continuous improvement. *The Service Industries Journal, 31*(12), 1921–1930.

Audretsch, D. B., Aldridge, T. T., & Sanders, M. (2011b). Social capital building and new business formation: A case study in Silicon Valley. *International Small Business Journal, 29*(2), 152–169.

Audretsch, D. B., Bönte, W., & Keilbach, M. (2011c). Determinants and impact of entrepreneurship capital: The spatial dimension and a comparison of different econometric approaches. In *New directions in regional economic development* (The role of entrepreneurship theory and methods, practice and policy) (pp. 41–59).

Audretsch, D., Falck, O., & Heblich, S. (2011d). Who's got the aces up his sleeve? Functional specialization of cities and entrepreneurship. *The Annals of Regional Science, 46*(3), 621–636.

Audretsch, D. B., Falck, O., & Heblich, S. (Eds.). (2011e). *Handbook of research on innovation and entrepreneurship*. London: Edward Elgar Publishing.

Audretsch, D. B., Bönte, W., & Mahagaonkar, P. (2012a). Financial signaling by innovative nascent ventures: The relevance of patents and prototypes. *Research Policy, 41*(8), 1407–1421.

Audretsch, D. B., Hülsbeck, M., & Lehmann, E. E. (2012b). Regional competitiveness, university spillovers, and entrepreneurial activity. *Small Business Economics, 39*(3), 587–601.

Audretsch, D. B., Link, A. N., & Peña, I. (2012c). Academic entrepreneurship and economic competitiveness: introduction to the special issue. *Economics of Innovation and New Technology, 21*(5–6), 427–428.

Audretsch, D. B., Leyden, D. P., & Link, A. N. (2012d). Universities as research partners in publicly supported entrepreneurial firms. *Economics of Innovation and New Technology, 21*(5–6), 529–545.

Audretsch, D. B., Falck, O., Feldman, M. P., & Heblich, S. (2012e). Local entrepreneurship in context. *Regional Studies, 46*(3), 379–389.

Audretsch, D. B., Boente, W., & Tamvada, J. P. (2013a). Religion, social class, and entrepreneurial choice. *Journal of Business Venturing, 28*(6), 774–789.

Audretsch, D. B., Hülsbeck, M., & Lehmann, E. E. (2013b). Families as active monitors of firm performance. *Journal of Family Business Strategy, 4*(2), 118–130.

Audretsch, D. B., Link, A. N., & Peña-Legazkue, I. (2013c). Academic entrepreneurship and regional economic development: Introduction to the special issue. *Economic Development Quarterly, 27*(1), 3–5.

Audretsch, D. B., Leyden, D. P., & Link, A. N. (2013d). Regional appropriation of university-based knowledge and technology for economic development. *Economic Development Quarterly, 27*(1), 56–61.

Audretsch, D. B., Lehmann, E. E., & Hinger, J. (2014a). From knowledge to innovation. In A. N. Link & C. Antonelli (Eds.), *Routledge handbook of the economics of knowledge* (pp. 20–28). New York: Routledge Taylor & Francis Group.

Audretsch, D. B., Coad, A., & Segarra, A. (2014b). Firm growth and innovation. *Small Business Economics, 43*(4), 743–749.

Audretsch, D. B., Lehmann, E. E., & Wright, M. (2014c). Technology transfer in a global economy. *The Journal of Technology Transfer, 39*(3), 301–312.

Audretsch, D. B., Segarra, A., & Teruel, M. (2014d). Why don't all young firms invest in R&D? *Small Business Economics, 43*(4), 751–766.

Audretsch, D. B., Kuratko, D. F., & Link, A. N. (2015a). Making sense of the elusive paradigm of entrepreneurship. *Small Business Economics, 45*(4), 703–712.

Audretsch, D. B., Dohse, D., & Niebuhr, A. (2015b). Regional unemployment structure and new firm formation. *Papers in Regional Science, 94*, S115–S138.

Audretsch, D. B., Belitski, M., & Desai, S. (2015c). Entrepreneurship and economic development in cities. *The Annals of Regional Science, 55*(1), 33–60.

Audretsch, D. B., Hayter, C. S., & Link, A. N. (Eds.). (2015d). *Concise guide to entrepreneurship, technology and innovation*. London: Edward Elgar Publishing.

Audretsch, D., Lehmann, E., Richardson, A., & Vismara, S. (2015e). *Globalization and public policy*. Switzerland: Springer International Publishing.

Audretsch, D. B., Lehmann, E. E., & Paleari, S. (2015f). Academic policy and entrepreneurship: A European perspective. *The Journal of Technology Transfer, 40*(3), 363–368.

Audretsch, D. B., Heger, D., & Veith, T. (2015g). Infrastructure and entrepreneurship. *Small Business Economics, 44*(2), 219–230.

Audretsch, D. B., Link, A. N., Sauer, R. M., & Siegel, D. S. (2016a). Advancing the economics of entrepreneurship. *European Economic Review, 86*, 1–3.

Audretsch, D. B., Lehmann, E. E., & Menter, M. (2016b). Public cluster policy and new venture creation. *Economia e Politica Industriale, 43*(4), 357–381.

Audretsch, D. B., Lehmann, E. E., & Wirsching, K. (2016c). Female immigrant entrepreneurship in Germany. In A. Link (Ed.), *Gender and entrepreneurial activity* (pp. 46–68). London: Edward Elgar Publishing.

Audretsch, D. B., Kuratko, D. F., & Link, A. N. (2016d). Dynamic entrepreneurship and technology-based innovation. *Journal of Evolutionary Economics, 26*(3), 603–620.

Audretsch, D., Guo, X., Hepfer, A., Menendez, H., & Xiao, X. (2016e). Ownership, productivity and firm survival in China. *Economia e Politica Industriale, 43*(1), 67–83.

Audretsch, D. B., Lehmann, E. E., Paleari, S., & Vismara, S. (2016f). Entrepreneurial finance and technology transfer. *The Journal of Technology Transfer, 41*(1), 1–9.

Audretsch, D. B., Mamtora, A., & Menendez, H. (2016g). Creating an entrepreneurial society in Europe. *The Journal of Technology Transfer*, 1–12. https://doi.org/10.1007/s10961-016-9471-x.

Audretsch, D., Lehmann, E., Meoli, M., & Vismara, S. (Eds.). (2016h). *University evolution, entrepreneurial activity and regional competitiveness*. Switzerland: Springer International Publishing.

Audretsch, D. B., Obschonka, M., Gosling, S. D., & Potter, J. (2017a). A new perspective on entrepreneurial regions: linking cultural identity with latent and manifest entrepreneurship. *Small Business Economics, 48*(3), 681–697.

Audretsch, D., Sanders, M., & Zhang, L. (2017b). International product life cycles, trade and development stages. *The Journal of Technology Transfer*, 1–44. https://doi.org/10.1007/s10961-017-9588-6.

Audretsch, D. B., Belitski, M., & Desai, S. (2018a). National Business Regulations and City Entrepreneurship in Europe: A Multilevel Nested Analysis. *Entrepreneurship Theory and Practice*. https://doi.org/10.1177/1042258718774916.

Audretsch, D. B., Lehmann, E. E., & Schenkenhofer, J. (2018b). Internationalization strategies of hidden champions: lessons from Germany. *Multinational Business Review, 26*(1), 2–24.

Audretsch, D. B., Seitz, N., & Rouch, K. M. (2018c). Tolerance and innovation: the role of institutional and social trust. *Eurasian Business Review, 8*(1), 71–92.

Baumol, W. J. (1968). Entrepreneurship in economic theory. *The American Economic Review, 58*(2), 64–71.

Bischoff, K., Volkmann, C. K., & Audretsch, D. B. (2018). Stakeholder collaboration in entrepreneurship education: an analysis of the entrepreneurial ecosystems of European higher educational institutions. *The Journal of Technology Transfer, 43*(1), 20–46.

Braunerhjelm, P., Acs, Z. J., Audretsch, D. B., & Carlsson, B. (2010). The missing link: knowledge diffusion and entrepreneurship in endogenous growth. *Small Business Economics, 34*(2), 105–125.

Broadus, R. N. (1987). Toward a definition of "bibliometrics". *Scientometrics, 12*(5–6), 373–379.

Caiazza, R., & Audretsch, D. (2013). A general framework for classifying spin-offs. *International Review of Entrepreneurship, 11*, 1.

Caiazza, R., & Audretsch, D. (2015). Can a sport mega-event support hosting city's economic, socio-cultural and political development? *Tourism Management Perspectives, 14*(1–2).

Caiazza, R., Audretsch, D., Volpe, T., & Debra Singer, J. (2014). Policy and institutions facilitating entrepreneurial spin-offs: USA, Asia and Europe. *Journal of Entrepreneurship and Public Policy, 3*(2), 186–196.

Caiazza, R., Richardson, A., & Audretsch, D. (2015). Knowledge effects on competitiveness: From firms to regional advantage. *The Journal of Technology Transfer, 40*(6), 899–909.

Carlsson, B., Acs, Z. J., Audretsch, D. B., & Braunerhjelm, P. (2009). Knowledge creation, entrepreneurship, and economic growth: A historical review. *Industrial and Corporate Change, 18*(6), 1193–1229.

Carlsson, B., Braunerhjelm, P., McKelvey, M., Olofsson, C., Persson, L., & Ylinenpää, H. (2013). The evolving domain of entrepreneurship research. *Small Business Economics, 41*(4), 913–930.

Chowdhury, F., & Audretsch, D. B. (2014). Institution as looting apparatus: Impact of gender equality and institutions on female entrepreneurship. *Eurasian Business Review, 4*(2), 207–225.

Chowdhury, F., Audretsch, D. B., & Belitski, M. (2015a). Does corruption matter for international entrepreneurship? *International Entrepreneurship and Management Journal, 11*(4), 959–980.

Chowdhury, F., Terjesen, S., & Audretsch, D. (2015b). Varieties of entrepreneurship: Institutional drivers across entrepreneurial activity and country. *European Journal of Law and Economics, 40*(1), 121–148.

Chowdhury, F., Desai, S., & Audretsch, D. B. (2018). *Corruption, entrepreneurship, and social welfare: A global perspective*. Switzerland: Springer International Publishing.

De Massis, A., Audretsch, D., Uhlaner, L., & Kammerlander, N. (2018). Innovation with limited resources: Management lessons from the German Mittelstand. *Journal of Product Innovation Management, 35*(1), 125–146.

Demircioglu, M. A., & Audretsch, D. B. (2017). Conditions for innovation in public sector organizations. *Research Policy, 46*(9), 1681–1691.

Elston, J. A., & Audretsch, D. B. (2010). Risk attitudes, wealth and sources of entrepreneurial start-up capital. *Journal of Economic Behavior & Organization, 76*(1), 82–89.

Elston, J. A., & Audretsch, D. B. (2011). Financing the entrepreneurial decision: an empirical approach using experimental data on risk attitudes. *Small Business Economics, 36*(2), 209–222.

Feldman, M. P., & Audretsch, D. B. (1999). Innovation in cities: Science-based diversity, specialization and localized competition. *European Economic Review, 43*(2), 409–429.

Gilbert, B. A., McDougall, P. P., & Audretsch, D. B. (2006). New venture growth: A review and extension. *Journal of Management, 32*(6), 926–950.

Gilbert, B. A., McDougall, P. P., & Audretsch, D. B. (2008). Clusters, knowledge spillovers and new venture performance: An empirical examination. *Journal of Business Venturing, 23*(4), 405–422.

Guerzoni, M., Aldridge, T. T., Audretsch, D. B., & Desai, S. (2014). A new industry creation and originality: Insight from the funding sources of university patents. *Research Policy, 43*(10), 1697–1706.

Gulbranson, C. A., & Audretsch, D. B. (2008). Proof of concept centers: Accelerating the commercialization of university innovation. *The Journal of Technology Transfer, 33*(3), 249–258.

Harzing, A. W., & Alakangas, S. (2016). Google Scholar, Scopus and the Web of Science: A longitudinal and cross-disciplinary comparison. *Scientometrics, 106*(2), 787–804.

Huang, Y., Audretsch, D. B., & Hewitt, M. (2013). Chinese technology transfer policy: The case of the national independent innovation demonstration zone of East Lake. *The Journal of Technology Transfer, 38*(6), 828–835.

Kuratko, D. F., & Audretsch, D. B. (2009). Strategic entrepreneurship: Exploring different perspectives of an emerging concept. *Entrepreneurship Theory and Practice, 33*(1), 1–17.

Kuratko, D. F., & Audretsch, D. B. (2013). Clarifying the domains of corporate entrepreneurship. *International Entrepreneurship and Management Journal, 9*(3), 323–335.

Landstrom, H. (1999). The roots of entrepreneurship research. *New England Journal of Entrepreneurship, 2*(2), 9–20.

Landström, H., Harirchi, G., & Åström, F. (2012). Entrepreneurship: Exploring the knowledge base. *Research Policy, 41*(7), 1154–1181.

Li, X., Wu, P., Shen, G. Q., Wang, X., & Teng, Y. (2017). Mapping the knowledge domains of Building Information Modeling (BIM): A bibliometric approach. *Automation in Construction, 84*, 195–206.

An Overview of the Economics of Entrepreneurship and Small Business: The Legacy... 305

Linß, V. (2014). *Die wichtigsten Wirtschaftsdenker*. Wiesbaden: Marix Verlag GmbH.

Lyons, T. S., Alter, T. R., Audretsch, D., & Augustine, D. (2012). Entrepreneurship and community: The next frontier of entrepreneurship inquiry. *Entrepreneurship Research Journal, 2*(1), 1–24.

Merigó, J. M., Cancino, C. A., Coronado, F., & Urbano, D. (2016). Academic research in innovation: a country analysis. *Scientometrics, 108*(2), 559–593.

Minniti, M. (2016). The Foundational Contribution to Entrepreneurship Research of William J. Baumol. *Strategic Entrepreneurship Journal, 10*(2), 214–228.

Minniti, M., & Lévesque, M. (2008). Recent developments in the economics of entrepreneurship. *Journal of Business Venturing, 23*(6), 603–612.

North, D. C. (1990). *Institutions, institutional change and economic performance*. Cambridge: Cambridge University Press.

North, D. C. (2005). *Understanding the process of economic change*. Princeton: Princeton University Press.

Obschonka, M., Stuetzer, M., Gosling, S. D., Rentfrow, P. J., Lamb, M. E., Potter, J., & Audretsch, D. B. (2015). Entrepreneurial regions: do macro-psychological cultural characteristics of regions help solve the "knowledge paradox" of economics? *PLoS ONE, 10*(6), e0129332.

Obschonka, M., Stuetzer, M., Audretsch, D. B., Rentfrow, P. J., Potter, J., & Gosling, S. D. (2016). Macropsychological factors predict regional economic resilience during a major economic crisis. *Social Psychological and Personality Science, 7*(2), 95–104.

Parker, S. C. (2004). *The economics of self-employment and entrepreneurship*. Cambridge: Cambridge University Press.

Parker, S. C. (2005). The Economics of Entrepreneurship: What we know and what we don't. *Foundations and Trends in Entrepreneurship, 1*(1), 1–54.

Parker, S. C. (2018). *The economics of entrepreneurship*. Cambridge: Cambridge University Press.

Patzelt, H., & Audretsch, D. B. (2008). The evolution of biotechnology in hostile financing environments. *Journal of Organizational Change Management, 21*(6), 773–785.

Rocha, H., Audretsch, D. B., & Birkinshaw, J. M. (Eds.). (2013). *Concepts of entrepreneurship*. London: Edward Elgar Publishing.

Samuelson, P. A. (2015). The Harvard-Circle. *Journal of Evolutionary Economics, 25*(1), 31–36.

Schumpeter, J. A. (1911). *The theory of economic development: An inquiry into profits, capital, credit, interest, and the business cycle*. New Jersey: Transaction Books.

Stam, E., Audretsch, D., & Meijaard, J. (2008). Renascent entrepreneurship. *Journal of Evolutionary Economics, 18*(3–4), 493–507.

Stuetzer, M., Obschonka, M., Audretsch, D. B., Wyrwich, M., Rentfrow, P. J., Coombes, M., et al. (2016). Industry structure, entrepreneurship, and culture: An empirical analysis using historical coalfields. *European Economic Review, 86*, 52–72.

Stuetzer, M., Audretsch, D. B., Obschonka, M., Gosling, S. D., Rentfrow, P. J., & Potter, J. (2018). Entrepreneurship culture, knowledge spillovers and the growth of regions. *Regional Studies, 52*(5), 608–618.

Tanas, J. K., & Audretsch, D. B. (2011). Entrepreneurship in transitional economy. *International Entrepreneurship and Management Journal, 7*(4), 431–442.

Thurik, A. R., Carree, M. A., van Stel, A., & Audretsch, D. B. (2008). Does self-employment reduce unemployment? *Journal of Business Venturing, 23*(6), 673–686.

Thurik, A. R., Stam, E., & Audretsch, D. B. (2013). The rise of the entrepreneurial economy and the future of dynamic capitalism. *Technovation, 33*(8–9), 302–310.

Urbano, D., Aparicio, S., & Audretsch, D. (2018). Twenty-five years of research on institutions, entrepreneurship, and economic growth: What has been learned? Small Business Economics. In Press. https://doi.org/10.1007/s11187-018-0038-0.

Urbano, D., Aparicio, S., & Audretsch, D. B. (2019). *Institutions, Entrepreneurship, and Economic Performance*. Switzerland, Springer International Publishing.

Verheul, I., Wennekers, S., Audretsch, D., & Thurik, R. (2002). An eclectic theory of entrepreneurship: policies, institutions and culture. In *Entrepreneurship: Determinants and policy in a European-US comparison* (pp. 11–81). Boston, MA: Springer.

Welfens, P. J., Audretsch, D. B., Addison, J. T., & Grupp, H. (2012). *Technological competition, employment and innovation policies in OECD countries*. Switzerland: Springer International Publishing.

Welpe, I. M., Spörrle, M., Grichnik, D., Michl, T., & Audretsch, D. B. (2012). Emotions and opportunities: The interplay of opportunity evaluation, fear, joy, and anger as antecedent of entrepreneurial exploitation. *Entrepreneurship Theory and Practice, 36*(1), 69–96.

Welter, F., Baker, T., Audretsch, D. B., & Gartner, W. B. (2017). Everyday entrepreneurship—a call for entrepreneurship research to embrace entrepreneurial diversity. *Entrepreneurship Theory and Practice, 41*(3), 311–321.

Wiklund, J., Davidsson, P., Audretsch, D. B., & Karlsson, C. (2011). The future of entrepreneurship research. *Entrepreneurship Theory and Practice, 35*(1), 1–9.

Zhang, Z., Hinger, J., Audretsch, D. B., & Song, G. (2015). Environmental technology transfer and emission standards for industry in China. *The Journal of Technology Transfer, 40*(5), 743–759.

Location and Firm Performance

Dirk Dohse and Johanna Schnier

Abstract David Audretsch has made several important contributions to the literature in Economics: He is well-known for his contributions to the study of innovation and firm size, for his highly influential book *Innovation and Industry Evolution*, for the (co-) development of the Knowledge Spillover Theory of Entrepreneurship and as a co-founder and co-editor of the renowned entrepreneurship journal *Small Business Economics*. Apart from this, David has significantly contributed to a better understanding of the role of location as a determinant of firm performance. This chapter deals with two joint papers by David Audretsch and Dirk Dohse (one also co-authored by Annekatrin Niebuhr) that established a direct link between locational characteristics and firm performance, their reception in the scientific community and impact on subsequent literature, and the current state of research in the field.

Introduction

The first paper, entitled "Location: A neglected determinant of firm growth" and referred to as Audretsch and Dohse (2007), links the performance of new technology firms, measured in terms of employment growth, to geographic location. The authors introduce a model of firm growth that is specific to characteristics of the location as well as the firm and industry. The main finding is that regions abundant in knowledge resources provide a particularly fertile soil for the growth of young, technology-oriented firms. Moreover, it is shown that in the case of Germany the impact of location on firm growth is greater in industries that are more knowledge intensive.

The second paper, entitled "Cultural diversity and entrepreneurship: a regional analysis for Germany" and referred to as Audretsch et al. (2010) was the first paper that systematically investigated the impact of cultural diversity on regional start-up

D. Dohse (✉) · J. Schnier
Kiel Institute for the World Economy, Kiel, Germany
e-mail: dirk.dohse@ifw-kiel.de

© Springer Nature Switzerland AG 2019
E. E. Lehmann, M. Keilbach (eds.), *From Industrial Organization to Entrepreneurship*, https://doi.org/10.1007/978-3-030-25237-3_27

activity. The authors combined ideas from Jane Jacobs (1969) pathbreaking book with elements of the Knowledge Spillover Theory of Entrepreneurship, arguing that that for knowledge spillovers to occur, it takes more than localized investments in new knowledge. "Rather, economic agents with the capabilities to access, absorb and commercialize that knowledge through the spillover conduit of entrepreneurship are also essential for generating knowledge spillovers. Diversity will enhance such entrepreneurial activity because diverse economic agents will value new ideas differently, leading them to respond to different ideas in a different way. It is this diversity in economic agents that triggers divergences in the evaluation of new ideas that is the basis for knowledge spillover entrepreneurship." (Audretsch et al. 2010: 58) The main empirical finding is that cultural diversity has a positive and highly significant impact on technology oriented start-ups in general, technology oriented services and high tech start-ups. Moreover, the paper innovated on methodological grounds too by proposing an entropy-based measure of cultural diversity that has been widely adopted in the pertinent literature.

The authors concluded the second paper with a call for more research on this important subject: "The research presented in this paper may be viewed as a modest first step towards a more comprehensive research program. The issue of cultural diversity and entrepreneurship is of high political relevance in modern societies and deserves more attention." (Audretsch et al. 2010: 78).

In fact, both papers have triggered off numerous follow-up studies that have substantially enhanced our knowledge on the links between location and firm growth and the impact of cultural diversity and new firm formation.

Location and Firm Growth

Audretsch and Dohse (2007) identified the relationship between location and firm growth – rather than growth at more aggregated levels – as underexamined issue, which initiated a surge in papers on precisely this issue in the years after 2007. The contributions made in this field were threefold: First, several studies investigated how the effect of location on firm growth varies across firm and industry characteristics. Second, subsequent papers took a closer look at what constitutes localized knowledge resources. While Audretsch and Dohse (2007) viewed localized knowledge resources primarily in terms of human capital, other researchers suggested a broader concepts of localized knowledge resources. Finally, one of the greatest challenges with respect to location and firm growth remains to find a suitable identification strategy. As Stephan (2011) puts it, to identify the effect of location on firm performance, one would ideally put a firm in one location and then put it in another location and the difference in performance could be attributed to locational factors. Since this is practically impossible, developing adequate measures of locational attributes is essential.

Which Kinds of Firms/Industries Benefit from Localized Knowledge Resources?

Prior to 2007, several empirical papers had already argued that knowledge activities tend to benefit more from agglomeration than non-knowledge activities (e.g. Audretsch and Feldman 1996; Zucker et al. 1998; Maurel and Sedillot 1999). Similarly, Audretsch and Dohse (2007) found regional-level evidence for Germany that knowledge-intensive industries benefit more from the proximity to knowledge resources than less knowledge-intensive industries. They argue that this is a plausible result as less knowledge-intensive industries rely to a lesser extent on localized knowledge resources and knowledge spillovers.

One major contribution of the recent economic literature on location and firm performance lies in examining more closely how the effect of location on firm growth varies with the knowledge-intensity of firms. Contrary to the argument outlined above, Grillitsch and Nilsson (2017) questioned whether low-knowledge firms indeed benefit less from localized knowledge resources than their more knowledge intensive counterparts. While it may be true that knowledge-intensive firms have a greater ability to absorb knowledge produced elsewhere, they may, on the other hand, disproportionately be threatened by negative knowledge externalities. Put differently, knowledge-intensive firms may much more be a source than a receiver of knowledge spillovers such that the net effect of being located in proximity to knowledge resources may be negative. Even more, knowledge-intensive firms may have greater capabilities to source knowledge from non-local sources, making them less dependent on localized knowledge resources.

The recent empirical evidence on the relationship between location and firm performance in dependence of firms' knowledge-intensity appears indeed ambiguous. Using Swedish micro-data from 2005–2011, Grillitsch and Nilsson (2017) find evidence in support of their hypothesis that low-knowledge rather than knowledge-intensive firms benefit from localized knowledge resources. They find that knowledge-intensive firms in Sweden do not grow faster in knowledge-intensive regions while firms with weak internal knowledge grow faster when located in knowledge-intensive regions.

Schimke et al. (2013) analyze the impact of location on nanotechnology firms in Germany. They find that firms belonging to knowledge-intensive sectors have a higher employment growth in regions with a high share of highly qualified employees while this is not the case for firms belonging to low-knowledge sectors – a result that is very much in line with Audretsch and Dohse (2007). However, they also find that the outcome is not independent of the way how localized knowledge resources are measured. When Schimke et al. (2013) use a second measure of localized knowledge resources, namely the absolute number of employees in R&D in a region, the effect on employment growth is significantly negative for firms in knowledge-intensive sectors, i.e. firm-level employment growth in knowledge-intensive sectors tends to decline with a higher absolute number of R&D employees in a region. Dohse and Vaona (2014) find that regional human capital density and

R&D density have a particularly strong effect on the regional intensity of highly complex start-ups, where start-up complexity implies – among others – high sophistication of firm activities such as R&D. Although the dependent variable is start-up intensity rather than firm growth, this finding suggests that knowledge-intensive firms are the primary beneficiaries of localized knowledge resources.

What Constitutes Localized Knowledge Resources?

The second contribution of the more recent research on firm location and firm growth lies in a conceptual refinement of localized knowledge resources. Audretsch and Dohse (2007) thought of localized knowledge resources primarily in terms of human capital, which is reflected in their choice of measures for localized knowledge resources. Other researchers suggest to go beyond human capital and additionally consider technological capital as component of localized knowledge resources (Raspe and van Oort 2008). While human capital constitutes an integral part of localized knowledge resources, it leaves out technical- and production-oriented factors. The human and technological capital in a region may be correlated but, still, certain firms may benefit to a greater extent from one than from the other. Raspe and van Oort (2008) propose a more comprehensive concept of localized knowledge resources. They understand localized knowledge resources as regional "Knowledge workers", "R&D" and "Innovativeness", where "Knowledge workers" captures human capital and "R&D" and "Innovativeness" capture technological capital. Using employment data for manufacturing and business services firms in the Netherlands for the period 2001–2006, Raspe and van Oort (2008) find significantly positive effects of regional "R&D" and "Innovativeness" on firm growth, i.e. firms experience higher growth rates in regions with a high intensity of successful innovative firms and with a high intensity of R&D activities. The variable "knowledge workers", by contrast, has no significant effect on firm growth when looking at the entire sample of firms but does have a positive effect on firm growth for the subsample of business services firms. Similarly, Raspe and van Oort (2011) use a variety of indicators (e.g. the R&D employee share in total employment, the regional presence of research organizations, or the introduction of new products and processes in a region) to capture both the human capital and the technological capital of a region. Here, too, the effect of localized knowledge resources on firm growth varies strongly, depending on the explanatory variable used and the industries considered. These results underline the importance of carefully distinguishing between different localized knowledge resources: while certain localized knowledge resources may be conducive to firm growth in certain industries, other resources may have no effect.

Location and Firm Performance

How to Measure Proximity to Localized Knowledge Resources?

One major methodological problem lies in the construction of meaningful location-specific variables. Most authors (Audretsch and Dohse 2007; Raspe and Van Oort 2008; Raspe and Van Oort 2011; Grillitsch and Nilsson 2017) define location-specific variables using data aggregated at a given regional level (typically administrative or functional regions). However, the higher the aggregation level, the more imprecise will be the measure of proximity to knowledge resources. Whether a firm is allocated to one region or another may become arbitrary in the presence of high aggregation levels and this arbitrariness can affect the empirical results in substantial ways. To mitigate this kind of problem, Duschl et al. (2015) calculate location-specific variables using distance-based methods, without any reference to given (administrative) regions. Based on the geolocation of firms and localized knowledge resources, they model the proximity of firms to these resources using travel-time distances and distance-decay functions. Duschl et al. (2015) find that proximity to employees of the same industry reduces firms' growth prospects, which they explain with increased competition for employees and hence higher wages. In contrast, the effect of nearby scientific publications on a firm's growth prospects is significantly positive for knowledge-intensive industries, which is more in line with the findings by Audretsch and Dohse (2007).

Location and Firm Growth: State of the Art

While the more recent literature on location and firm growth confirmed that location is a key determinant of firm performance, there are important differences in detail that need to be considered: Most studies have found that the effect of location on firm performance varies across industries, firm characteristics and knowledge intensity. Still, no systematic picture has evolved as to which industries and firms are the primary beneficiaries of localized knowledge resources. The objective of future research should thus be to analyze the relationship between location and firm performance more systematically and in a larger variety of countries to better understand the conditions that must be satisfied for firms to take advantage of localized knowledge resources.

Cultural Diversity and Entrepreneurship

When Audretsch et al. (2010) published their paper "Cultural diversity and entrepreneurship: a regional analysis for Germany", the relationship between cultural diversity and economic outcomes had high policy relevance already then. In the decades prior to 2010, Germany and other Western societies had become dramatically more culturally diverse and, accordingly, the question how cultural diversity – especially cultural diversity in the labor force – affects economic outcomes was on policymakers' agenda already in 2010. Yet, its policy relevance has even increased in light of the recent migration waves to Europe. Significant parts of the public seem to fear the labor market effects of migration, which is reflected in the rise of populist parties across Europe. Against this background, empirical evidence on the effect of cultural diversity on economic outcomes is much needed. From a theoretical point of view, the effect of cultural diversity seems ambiguous prima facie. On the one hand, cultural diversity in the labor force may positively affect economic performance at the firm and regional level as workers with different cultural backgrounds complement each other's skills (Ottaviano and Peri 2006) and look at a given set of information differently. The difference in perspectives may be particularly beneficial for entrepreneurship, which rests on the different evaluation of knowledge (Audretsch et al. 2010). On the other hand, cultural diversity involves costs arising from communication difficulties due to different languages and cultures, slowing down processes (Niebuhr 2010) and increasing costs in the provision of public goods (Alesina et al. 1999).

Following the paper by Audretsch et al. (2010), various attempts have been undertaken to examine empirically whether the benefits of cultural diversity in the labor force outweigh the associated costs. First, following the call by Audretsch et al. (2010), the relationship between cultural diversity and entrepreneurship has been examined for countries other than Germany (Sobel et al. 2010; Nathan and Lee 2013). Second, researchers examined the effect of cultural diversity on economic variables other than entrepreneurship, providing a broader picture of the economic consequences of cultural diversity. Third and finally, weighing the benefits against the costs of cultural diversity requires a comprehensive concept of cultural diversity. Accordingly, an important contribution of the more recent literature lies in a more differentiated look at the various aspects of cultural diversity.

The Effect of Cultural Diversity on Entrepreneurship: Empirical Evidence from Different Countries

Sobel et al. (2010) examine whether higher levels of cultural diversity in the U.S. increase the rate of entrepreneurship. According to them, the sign of the effect of cultural diversity on economic outcomes hinges on a country's institutions. In a country with good institutions, i.e. protection of property, free markets, rule of law and free media, ethnic subgroups can work together to choose the best local knowledge for entrepreneurship. Where these institutions are missing, cultural diversity cannot be translated into successful entrepreneurship. In contrast to Audretsch et al. (2010) who consider the variety in perspectives associated with cultural diversity as driving force behind entrepreneurship, the focus of Sobel et al. (2010) lies on institutions as moderating the effect of cultural diversity on entrepreneurship. To test the hypothesis that cultural diversity boosts entrepreneurship in countries with good institutions they use US state level data on entrepreneurial activity and cultural diversity. The prediction is that – with the US having relatively good institutions – those states with high levels of cultural diversity should have higher rates of entrepreneurship. Indeed, across various specifications Sobel et al. (2010) find robust evidence for their prediction. While the focus on institutions is a good starting point for the identification of systematic, cross-country differences in the effect of cultural diversity, the research design by Sobel et al. (2010) still lacks cross-country variation in institutions to test the hypothesis that institutions determine the sign of the effect of cultural diversity.

Nathan and Lee (2013) investigate whether migrant status raises the probability of firm formation in London. Their paper is related to the work by Audretsch et al. (2010) and Sobel et al. (2010) but differs in two respects: First, Nathan and Lee (2013) do not consider cultural diversity at the firm or regional level but migrant status of the respective entrepreneur. Second, they restrict their analysis to London – an exceptionally culturally diverse city – and hence cannot provide any evidence on cross-regional variation of the relationship between migrant status and entrepreneurship. Nathan and Lee (2013) find that migrant status in fact raises the probability of (proactive but not reactive) firm formation.

Marino et al. (2012) examine whether a diversified workforce facilitates knowledge transfers and, thereby, entrepreneurship, using a sample of Danish individuals for the period 1996–2002. They find that high degrees of cultural and educational heterogeneity foster the exchange of ideas and ultimately entrepreneurship while demographic diversity, i.e. differences in age, hinder entrepreneurship. The study by Marino et al. (2012) hence supports once more the view that there is a positive relationship between cultural diversity and entrepreneurship.

Linking Cultural Diversity to Economic Variables Other Than Entrepreneurship

A further important contribution of the recent regional economics literature has been to examine the relationship between cultural diversity and economic variables other than entrepreneurship. Trax et al. (2015) examine the effect of cultural diversity at the plant and the regional level on plant-level productivity. They find that the sheer number of foreign employees at the plant as well as at the regional level has no impact on productivity but that the diversification of the foreign employees with respect to their nationalities – both at the plant and at the regional level – has a significantly positive effect on productivity. Trax et al. (2015) conclude that the cost associated with cultural diversity are outweighed by the benefits from synergies arising from different skills and abilities. Niebuhr (2010) investigates how cultural diversity affects regional R&D. She finds that various measures of cultural diversity have a significantly positive effect on patents per capita in a region, suggesting that the difference in knowledge and capabilities associated with a culturally diverse R&D labor force outweighs the negative effects. However, Niebuhr (2010) notes that this positive net effect of cultural diversity may be specific to R&D activities, where employees have above average communication skills and cultural diversity implies only little communication disadvantages. Hence, these results cannot be generalized to activities beyond R&D. There is vast empirical evidence for a positive correlation between migration, diversity, and innovation, both on the regional (Ozgen et al. 2012; Kerr and Lincoln 2010; Niebuhr 2010; Chellaray et al. 2008) as well as on the firm level (Ozgen et al. 2013; Parotta et al. 2014). Nevertheless, there is also some contradictory evidence, indicating 'non-effects' and even negative effects (e.g. Bratti and Conti 2013; Qian 2013; Nathan and Lee 2013). Specifically, Borjas and Doran (2012) point out that increasing immigration of high-skilled researchers might crowd out incumbents' productivity. Overall, there seems to be a link between immigration, cultural diversity and innovation—but the channel through which migration affects innovation are not yet entirely understood.

In an attempt to determine the effect of cultural diversity on regional economies in Europe, Dohse and Gold (2014) regress cultural diversity on GDP per capita at the regional level. Overall, they find a fairly robust significantly positive effect of a region's cultural diversity on its GDP per capita but the strength of this effect varies across European regions. Primary beneficiaries of cultural diversity are long-term EU members, densely-populated areas and states in Central and Western Europe while the effect of cultural diversity is much weaker or even slightly negative in Southern and Eastern Europe.

How to Measure Cultural Diversity

Most researchers have used singular definitions of cultural diversity in the past, with ethnicity as the most commonly used dimension (Audretsch et al. 2010; Trax et al. 2015; Sobel et al. 2010; Niebuhr 2010). However, according to Rodriguez-Pose and Hardy (2015) this one-dimensionality abstracts from reality where many factors such as ethnicity, language, religion and nationality interact to shape cultural diversity. Rodriguez-Pose and Hardy (2015) hypothesize that the effect of cultural diversity on entrepreneurship varies with the measure of cultural diversity used. They consider two related but distinct measures of cultural diversity, namely birthplace diversity and ethnic diversity. They predict that birthplace diversity promotes entrepreneurship to a greater extent than does ethnic diversity because the knowledge stocks of foreign-born migrants differ more radically from the knowledge stock of the native population than does the knowledge stock of second, third or subsequent generations of migrants. In line with Audretsch et al. (2010), Rodriguez-Pose and Hardy (2015) construct Theil indices to capture cultural diversity in terms of birthplace and ethnic diversity. They find that both types of cultural diversity matter and are linked but that birthplace diversity matters more for knowledge-intensive entrepreneurship.

Cultural Diversity and Entrepreneurship: State of the Art

The majority of empirical studies suggests that entrepreneurship – and economic performance in general – benefit from cultural diversity. More specifically, it seems that – more than the size of the share of foreign nationals – the diversity of these foreign nationals raises economic performance. Further, cultural diversity seems to benefit knowledge-intensive sectors more than other sectors.

Despite the advances in the field of cultural diversity and economic performance, several questions raised by Audretsch et al. (2010) have remained unanswered and new research questions have moved on the agenda. First and foremost, Audretsch et al. (2010) had called for cross-country studies to analyze whether the effect of cultural diversity on economic outcomes differs across countries (e.g. between classic immigration countries such as Canada and the US and highly developed countries with a much shorter immigration tradition). To our knowledge such cross-country studies have still not been carried out, although Sobel et al. (2010) have identified country-specific institutions as important moderator between cultural diversity and economic outcomes. Second, the research by Rodriguez-Pose and Hardy (2015) shows that the distinction between different aspects of cultural diversity is essential to better understand the effect of cultural diversity on entrepreneurship. Recognizing the multi-dimensionality of cultural diversity and accounting for it through various measures of cultural diversity is a key challenge of future research.

Conclusion and Outlook

It is by now widely accepted that location is a key determinant of firm performance. The regional environment shapes existing firms' ability to innovate and grow as well as the opportunities and chances of survival of start-up firms. Audretsch and Dohse (2007) were able to show that technology-oriented firms had higher employment growth rates when they were located in regions rich in knowledge resources, whereas Audretsch et al. (2010) were the first to show that cultural diversity at the regional level fosters regional start-up activity. The subsequent literature has by and large confirmed their main findings, although there are interesting differences in detail that need to be considered. The effect of location on firm performance varies across industries, firm characteristics and knowledge intensity, and there is currently an interesting debate going on whether high knowledge firms or low knowledge firms are the main beneficiaries (or losers) of knowledge spillovers. More research for a broader set of countries and industries is necessary to answer this question.

The fact that location matters for firm performance brings location on policy makers' agenda. To the degree that locational attributes – in particular the proximity to knowledge resources – can be modified, policy makers can affect firm performance. In designing policies, two things should be kept in mind. First, policies should account for the fact that only selected localized resources can promote the performance of only selected firms. Put differently, the effect of location on firm performance is highly context dependent and, accordingly, policies targeted at raising firm performance should take firm- and industry-specific needs into account. Second, if it is indeed the case that knowledge-intensive firms are the primary beneficiaries of localized knowledge resources and policies support these firms through the provision of localized knowledge resources, one risks a widening performance gap between knowledge-intensive firms in the centers and low-knowledge firms in the periphery.

Concerning the effects of regional-level cultural diversity, the empirical evidence clearly underlines that entrepreneurship and other economic performance measures such as innovation tend to benefit from cultural diversity. There is, however, little reason to assume that the relationship between cultural diversity and innovation is linear. Against the background that Europe (and Germany, in particular) have seen unprecedented levels of immigration and a rapid increase in ethnic and cultural diversity in recent years, an update of older studies would be highly desirable in order to find out whether the relationship still holds for the current (and much higher) levels of cultural diversity in European regions. In this context, distinguishing between the share of immigrants in a given population versus the diversity of these immigrants is essential. A high share of immigrants is unlikely to foster entrepreneurship and have positive effects on economic performance more generally if this share of immigrants consists of only one ethnic group in the extreme.

Moreover, there is a need for further research to investigate which kinds of entrepreneurship are triggered by cultural diversity, which industries benefit most and how much value to society (in terms of employment and income) is created.

References

Alesina, A., Baqir, R., & Easterly, W. (1999). Public goods and ethnic divisions. *Quarterly Journal of Economics, 114*(4), 1243–1284.

Audretsch, D. B., & Feldman, M. P. (1996). R/D spillovers and the geography of innovation and production. *The American Economic Review, 86*(3), 630–640.

Audretsch, D. B., & Dohse, D. (2007). Location: A neglected determinant of firm growth. *Review of World Economics, 143*(1), 79–107.

Audretsch, D. B., Dohse, D., & Niebuhr, A. (2010). Cultural diversity and entrepreneurship: A regional analysis for Germany. *Annals of Regional Science, 45*, 55–85.

Borjas, G. J., & Doran, K. B. (2012). The collapse of the Soviet Union and the productivity of American mathematicians. *The Quarterly Journal of Economics, 127*, 1143–1203.

Bratti, M., & Conti, C. (2013). *Immigration, population diversity and innovation of Italian regions.* Mimeo. University of Milan, Milan, Italy.

Chellaray, G. C., Maskus, K. E., & Mattoo, A. (2008). The contribution of international graduate students to US innovation. *Review of International Economics, 163*, 444–462.

Dohse, D., & Gold, R. (2014). *Determining the impact of cultural diversity on regional economies in Europe* (WWWforEurope working paper, no. 58). Vienna: WWWforEurope.

Dohse, D., & Vaona, A. (2014). Start-up complexity and the thickness of regional input markets. *Economics Letters, 124*(3), 424–427.

Duschl, M., Scholl, T., Brenner, T., Luxen, D., & Raschke, F. (2015). Industry-specific firm growth and agglomeration. *Regional Studies, 49*(11), 1822–1839.

Grillitsch, M., & Nilsson, M. (2017). Firm performance in the periphery: On the relation between firm-internal knowledge and local knowledge spillovers. *Regional Studies, 51*(8), 1219–1231.

Jacobs, J. (1969). *The economy of cities*. New York: Vintage Books.

Kerr, W. R., & Lincoln, W. F. (2010). The supply side of innovation: H-1B visa reforms and U.S. ethnic invention. *Journal of Labor Economics, 28*, 473–508.

Maurel, F., & Sedillot, B. (1999). A measure of the geographic concentration in French manufacturing industries. *Regional Science and Urban Economics, 29*(5), 575–604.

Marino, M., Parotta, P., & Pozzoli, D. (2012). Does labor diversity promote entrepreneurship? *Economic Letters, 116*, 15–19.

Nathan, M., & Lee, N. (2013). Cultural diversity, innovation, and entrepreneurship: Firm-level evidence from London. *Economic Geography, 89*(4), 367–394.

Niebuhr, A. (2010). Migration and innovation: Does cultural diversity matter for regional R/D activity? *Papers in Regional Science, 89*(3), 563–586.

Ottaviano, G. I. P., & Peri, G. 2006. *Rethinking the effects of immigration on wages*, National Bureau of Economic Research. Cambridge, MA: NBER Working Paper No. 12497.

Ozgen, C., Nijkamp, P./Poot, J. 2013. The impact of cultural diversity on innovation: Evidence from Dutch firm-level data. IZA Journal of Migration, 2:18.

Ozgen, C., Nijkamp, P., & Poot, J. (2012). Immigration and innovation in European regions. In P. Nijkamp, J. Poot, & M. Sahin (Eds.), *Migration impact assessment*. New Horizons, Cheltenham: Edward Elgar.

Parotta, P., Pozzoli, D., & Pytlikova, M. (2014). The Nexus between labor diversity and firms' innovation. *Journal of Population Economics, 27*, 303–364.

Qian, H. (2013). Diversity versus tolerance: The social drivers of innovation and entrepreneurship in US cities. *Urban Studies, 50*, 2718–2735.

Raspe, O., & Van Oort, F. (2008). Firm growth and localized knowledge externalities. *Regional Analysis/Policy, 38*(2), 100–116.

Raspe, O., & Van Oort, F. (2011). Growth of new firms and spatially bounded knowledge externalities. *Annual Regional Science, 46*, 495–518.

Rodriguez-Pose, A., & Hardy, D. (2015). Cultural diversity and entrepreneurship in England and Wales. *Environment and Planning A: Economy and Space., 47*(2), 392–411.

Schimke, A., Teichert, N., & Ott, I. (2013). Impact of local knowledge endowment on employment growth in nanotechnology. *Industrial and Corporate Change, 22*(6), 1525–1555.

Sobel, R. S., Dutta, N., & Roy, S. (2010). Does cultural diversity increase the rate of entrepreneurship? *Review of Austrian Economics, 23*, 269–286.

Stephan, A. (2011). Locational conditions and firm performance: Introduction to the special issue. *Annual Regional Science, 46*, 487–494.

Trax, M., Brunow, S., & Suedekum, J. (2015). Cultural diversity and plant-level productivity. *Regional Science and Urban Economics, 53*, 85–96.

Zucker, L., Darby, M., & Armstrong, J. (1998). Geographically localized knowledge: Spillovers or markets? *Economic Inquiry, 36*(1), 65–86.

The Inclusive Vision

Maria Minniti

Abstract At the end of February 2019, Google Scholar reports more than 85,000 citations to David's work. There is no question that his contribution to scholarship has been enormous, and his influence on the field of entrepreneurship research transformative. No matter what one's theoretical lens and background are, we all benefited from David's work. The number of citations and articles, quality of the outlets, and a long list of prizes and recognitions illustrate the many facets of his impressive career. Yet, they do not tell the whole story. In the following chapter, the author strives to tell that story.

The Inclusive Vision

In my view, one of David's main contribution to the profession cannot be counted in published pages and cites. Yet, it is as tangible and important as written words. Perhaps more so. Interestingly enough, the contribution I am referring to has to do with a sort of "spillover" effect which, of course, fits David's profile very well. I like to call it the "inclusive vision."

David has a cogent and broad vision for entrepreneurship research that goes well beyond making connections in the literature. David's vision of entrepreneurship research is one where real-world challenges are studied rigorously by many different thinkers with different backgrounds and views, where newcomers are particularly welcome because they may bring a novel perspective. David's vision is about bringing in new voices and enabling them to be heard, so that we all can learn and benefit. David tries always to cast the broadest net possible. This is what I call his inclusive vision. The goal of this short piece is to provide an affectionate and personal written account of something that all of us who know David have witnessed but, maybe, never thanked him for.

M. Minniti (✉)
Institute for an Entrepreneurial Society (IES), Whitman School of Management – Syracuse University, Syracuse, NY, USA
e-mail: mminniti@syr.edu

© Springer Nature Switzerland AG 2019
E. E. Lehmann, M. Keilbach (eds.), *From Industrial Organization to Entrepreneurship*, https://doi.org/10.1007/978-3-030-25237-3_28

My first exposure to David's work came when I was still a PhD student in economics at New York University. I was interested in agglomeration effects and path dependency, and his paper with Maryann Feldman was, of course, a must read (Audretsch and Feldman, 1996). As a PhD student, I was significantly influenced by Kirzner's broad view of entrepreneurship as a universal aspect of human action (Kirzner 1972, 1997). I found people's ability to identify new means-ends patterns and solve problems appealing and intriguing at the same time. As Baumol explained in his classic paper on productive and unproductive entrepreneurship, it was also clear that entrepreneurship manifested itself in very different ways (Baumol, 1990). Entrepreneurship is not the outcome of some innate trait. Entrepreneurs are made, not born. Institutions and the context for entrepreneurship mattered. Yet, having grown up in Italy, and having witnessed wide economic disparities across regions, I questioned what caused entrepreneurship to flourish in some areas and not others, in spite of very similar institutional settings. A significant portion of the answer to my puzzle came from reading the knowledge spillover theory of entrepreneurship (KSTE) (Audretsch and Keilbach 2007; Audretsch et al. 2006; Acs et al. 2009).

According to the KSTE, an environment richer in knowledge will produce more entrepreneurial opportunities than a knowledge poor environment. This is the case because entrepreneurial opportunities do not come out of the blue. Instead, they emerge organically and systematically from the investments in knowledge of existing organizations. Entrepreneurs recognize and act upon those opportunities by creating new ventures. By commercializing knowledge that would otherwise remain idle, entrepreneurship produce spillovers and serves as a vehicle for the diffusion of knowledge. While a comprehensive review of the KSTE is clearly beyond the scope of this short appreciation of David's career, I want to emphasize how it informed and influenced my thinking about the role of institutions, and about the presence and importance of non-linearities in agglomeration effects. Traditionally, economies of scale and scope, and the resulting reduction in transaction costs, were identified as the main reasons for these agglomerations. And yet, economic variables had been shown to account for only a portion of the variance in entrepreneurial activity across regions. Thus, actual or potential economic conditions could not be the entire story. The work conducted by David and his co-authors made me appreciate the importance of spillover effects and the self-reinforcing nature of many social phenomena, including entrepreneurship.

At that time, I was particularly interested in the self-reinforcing effects of social conditions. Thus, in my work, I suggested that, when making decisions, individuals follow social cues and are influenced by what others have chosen, especially when facing ambiguous situations (Minniti 2004, 2005). Such influence may be described as a non-pecuniary network externality. I then used a non-linear path-dependent stochastic process to build a model of entrepreneurial dynamics capable of showing why communities with initially similar economic characteristics may end up with different levels of entrepreneurial activity (Minniti 2005). Over the years, I have revisited often the spillover theory of entrepreneurship and grown to appreciate even further its important insights for entrepreneurship and for the diffusion of knowledge. After more than 20 years from the first publications on the topic, the KSTE continues providing fertile grounds for further research opportunities. For example, a particularly important aspect of the KSTE consists in its ability to explain one of the main mechanisms through which entrepreneurs convert knowledge into societal utility (Acs et al. 2009) without resorting to exogenous ad hoc assumptions. At a time when the social role of entrepreneurship is called into questions by some, and emphasized positively by others, the KSTE provides an important framework to show how entrepreneurship can contribute organically to social well being and progress.

Although David's work influenced my thinking already while working on my dissertation, I did not know him personally yet. Thus, after graduating, I took the initiative and reached out to him via email. He graciously responded and encouraged me to expand my work. Then, in 2005, he invited me to spend a few weeks at the Max Planck Institute of Economics in Jena, Germany. It was a great experience that I would gladly repeat in the following years, both in Jena and Berlin. During those periods, most of the time I was not the only visitor. David used his tenure at the Max Planck Institute as an opportunity to invite simultaneously a number of researchers and encourage them to talk to each other. People came from different countries, and from a variety of disciplines and backgrounds, from established researchers to PhD students. David let an intellectual community emerge. The Max Planck Institute in Jena became a place for learning, for exchanging and developing ideas, and, importantly, created a community of entrepreneurship scholars. Jena is where I first met Steve Klepper and Howard Aldrich, who were already world class scholars, but also Alejandro Amezcua, Sami Desai, Larry Plummer, and Rob Wuebker, who were still PhD students at the time. Rui Batista, Julie Elston, Max Keilbach, and many others were there as well. After so many years, they are not only my colleagues, they are my friends. A lot of this is due to David's inclusive vision.

While I have not heard him articulate it explicitly, it is clear that David values people and their ideas greatly. As mentioned earlier, his vision of a community of scholars is one in which a variety of people exchange thoughts and ideas and bring different things to the table. Very few people have David's capacity to see linkages, create bridges, and expand frameworks. When you start talking about something with David he becomes pensive and fixes his eyes on something. Then, after a while, he says: "Ok, so what you are saying is that…." and then explains back to you what you have just said, only, well, better. You go "Exactly!" and he continues: "That's really great! You know, so and so is also doing …" and proceeds to provide you with the names of at least ten other people you should talk to, papers you should read, things to check out and, most importantly, tells you how all of it fits well with what is going on in the profession. You were doing all this! But, if it weren't for David, you wouldn't even know it. David is an intellectual enabler in the best sense of the word.

Over the years, I have got to know David in a variety of roles, including that of Editor in Chief, together with Zoltan Acs, for Small Business Economics. Even in this role, David's vision of inclusiveness comes across clearly. In many occasions I have heard him emphasize that it is important to encourage and develop authors from non-English speaking countries and, in particular, from countries that tend to be under-represented in academic outlets. This is clearly in line with his enabling role in the profession, and his inclusive view where all voices are valued. I am happy I may somehow fit into that vision. David made a difference in my career. I am pleased and honored to celebrate him for his impressive professional achievements but, especially, for being a good friend.

References

Audretsch, D. B., & Keilbach, M. (2007). The theory of knowledge spillover entrepreneurship. *Journal of Management Studies, 44*, 1242–1254.

Acs, Z. J., Audretsch, D. B., Pontus, B., & Carlsson, B. (2009). The knowledge spillover theory of entrepreneurship. *Small Business Economics, 32*(1), 15–30.

Audretsch, D. B., & Feldman, M. P. (1996). R&D spillovers and the geography of innovation and production. *American Economic Review, 86*, 630–640.

Audretsch, D. B., Keilbach, M., & Lehmann, E. (2006). *Entrepreneurship and economic growth*. New York: Oxford University Press.

Baumol, W. J. (1990). Entrepreneurship: Productive, unproductive, and destructive. *Journal of Political Economy, 98*, 893–919.

Kirzner, I. M. (1972). *Competition and entrepreneurship*. Chicago: University of Chicago Press.

Kirzner, I. M. (1997). Entrepreneurial discovery and the competitive market process: An Austrian approach. *Journal of Economic Literature, 35*(1), 60–85.

Minniti, M. (2005). Entrepreneurship and network externalities. *Journal of Economic Behavior and Organization., 57*(1), 1–27.

Minniti, M. (2004). Organization alertness and asymmetric information in a spin-glass model. *Journal of Business Venturing., 19*(5), 637–658.

You Made it the Best of Times

Sharon Alvarez

Abstract Longtime mentee Sharon Alvarez describes how David cultivated an entrepreneurship research community by always offering to help and mentor researchers who sought him out. By never shying away from an opportunity to lend a helping hand, David endeared himself to essentially everyone in the field. Further, his efforts in this regard have inspired those he helped to do the same for others, continuing the sense of community built on the foundation he laid.

You Made it the Best of Times

It is a testimonial to David Audretsch that so many people want to participate in honoring him by celebrating David's 65 birthday. David has been an anchor in the field of entrepreneurship and has mentored so many of us over several decades. David has supported my career from my earliest days as an assistant professor to the present, 2000 to 2018. David wrote one of the letters supporting my tenure decision from assistant to associate professor and he wrote one of the letters supporting my appointment to full professor with a chair. I can't remember a time when David wasn't a part of my academic career.

I first met David at a conference on entrepreneurship policy in Indiana. This was right before he started a new research group at the Max Planck Institute of Economics in Jena and he made me a Max Planck Scholar. Entrepreneurship research, and in particular theoretical work in entrepreneurship was in its infancy and I am extremely grateful for David's support and insights during the early stages of my career. Receiving tenure at an institution such as Ohio State University is not easy, but it was particularly complicated for me by the fact that I was the first person in entrepreneurship ever tenured at Ohio State University. I could not have made it without the support of David and others.

S. Alvarez (✉)
University of Pittsburgh, Joseph M. Katz, Graduate School of Business and College of Business Administration, Pittsburgh, PA, USA
e-mail: salvarez@katz.pitt.edu

© Springer Nature Switzerland AG 2019
E. E. Lehmann, M. Keilbach (eds.), *From Industrial Organization to Entrepreneurship*, https://doi.org/10.1007/978-3-030-25237-3_29

At the Max Planck Institute of Economics I gave many talks and made many new connections that could not have happened without David's assistance. David's excellence in research and his vast network enabled many researchers visit the MPI in Jena. This was a great opportunity for all the junior faculty to get in touch with other researchers in the field. David connects people, particularly junior scholars, introduces them to other colleagues, and fosters their careers.

David personally supported my work in a very committed manner and always made time for me to meet with him to discuss immediate questions. I know that he did this for many other young scholars. The Max Planck Institute and especially David's group, Entrepreneurship, Growth and Public Policy, was a fantastic place to get in touch with many researchers interested in entrepreneurship. Indeed, I edited a special issue of Organization Studies because of the connections and work that I did at Max Planck with David. I learned a lot from my colleagues at Max Planck and always returned energized from my visits there. I remember once arriving at 1:00 a.m. and finding several people still awake talking about ideas and research. It was a magical place and it was David that made the magic happen.

I continue to marvel at David's commitment to the scholars that he works with and really it is impossible to measure all that David has meant to so many people. It is unsurprising that David received the Entrepreneurship Division Mentor Award in 2012. The mentor award was a great way to honor David's engagement and support of colleagues in the field of entrepreneurship.

However, no special times would be complete if there were no funny memories to share. My memory of David will also include his professor disheveled look. As brilliant of a man as David is, as considerate and sweet as he is, it is good that he did not choose modeling for a career. David's lovely, lovely wife Joanne deserves much acknowledgement as David's fashionista. Whatever fashion sense David has, I am sure he owes it to Joanne.

However, Joanne was more than just David's fashion advisor. Joanne was always there as an important part of the team and she supported all of the junior scholars in her own way. I can remember having many a career discussion with Joanne over pizza and salad in Weimer, Germany. She always gave such good advice, about changing jobs, finding new homes, and settling in. Joanne made all of us feel like a community. Joanne – it would not have been as good without you.

David, and Joanne, we all admire you and your dedication to your colleagues, particularly the junior colleagues. David, you always knew how to transform your colleagues to be the very best they could be. The profession is lucky to have you, and we, all the scholars you have natured are blessed to have you in their lives.

Happy Birthday David and may you have many, many more.

Sharon Alvarez

On Regional Innovator Networks as Hubs for Innovative Ventures

Uwe Cantner and Tina Wolf

Abstract At least since Schumpeter published his work 'The Theory of Economic Development' (1912), a wide body of literature has focused on the evolutionary process behind firm growth and survival. Recently a growing interest is devoted to the variable 'location' as a critical factor, shaping firm performance. However, less attention has been paid to the region-specific characteristics that may play a relevant role in determining the growth and survival of a firm. Some works see university-based knowledge spillovers as one such factor (Audretsch and Lehmann 2005, Cassia et al. 2009). This paper extends this approach to the regional innovator network, promoting region-specific knowledge spillovers. Two data bases are applied. First, patent data delivers the innovator network for Thuringia. The second data base contains firm specific information on innovative ventures founded in Thuringia in the period between 1990 and 2006. The results show that the firm's individual probability to be innovative and connected to the innovator network positively influences the chances of this firm to survive.

Introduction

Innovation can be defined as "a process that begins with an idea, proceeds with the development of an invention, and results in the introduction of a new product, process or service to the marketplace" (Edwards and Gordon 1984, p.1). Both, (i) the founding of a new firm and (ii) the survival of existing firms are substantially affected by this complex construct. As to (i), innovation is considered to be one of three important characteristics entailed by entrepreneurship (OECD 1998). This view stems from Schumpeter's (1912) suggestion that innovation is a creative

U. Cantner (✉)
Friedrich Schiller University, Jena, Germany

University of Southern Denmark, Odense, Denmark
e-mail: uwe.cantner@uni-jena.de

T. Wolf
Friedrich Schiller University, Jena, Germany

© Springer Nature Switzerland AG 2019
E. E. Lehmann, M. Keilbach (eds.), *From Industrial Organization to Entrepreneurship*, https://doi.org/10.1007/978-3-030-25237-3_30

modus operandi of an entrepreneur (Nijkamp 2009). And, rather prominently, Audretsch and Lehmann (2005, p. 1192) formulate the relationship as follows: "... entrepreneurship is an endogenous response to the potential for commercializing knowledge that has not been adequately commercialized by the incumbent firms". Thus, entrepreneurs discover an opportunity to exploit a new technology (Shane 2000) and implement this by founding a firm. As to (ii) by creating new variations, new innovative firms compete with incumbent firms, which force the latter to improve or change their production processes or product portfolios. Under these conditions, incumbent firms must be innovative if they are to survive (Brown and Eisenhardt 1997). Non-innovators will fall behind, while first movers respectively firms with an entrepreneurial orientation secure a position of competitive advantage (Lumpkin and Dess 1996, Pyka 1999).

Before World War II, and thus also in Schumpeter's theory, the linear model of innovation was the generally accepted one (Kline and Rosenberg 1986). In this model, events flow smoothly in a one-way street. First, one does research, after that follows development which is followed by production which itself is followed by marketing. Looking more closely on how new ideas are created and innovations come up, according to the definition of Edwards and Gordon (1984), a more complex process as compared to the linear model is going on. Kline and Rosenberg (1986) tried to formalize this complex process and proposed the 'chain-linked model' which entails five different paths of activity and considers feedbacks between the different stages of innovation. This model however does not recover, where feedbacks and information flows are coming from. Over the last decades the concept of collective invention and innovation, brought up by Allen (1983) and von Hippel (1987), has been developed which answers this question. This concept has been said to form the basis for the systemic view of innovative activities and the innovation process (Cantner 2000). Innovations are considered as new combinations that are brought to the market (Schumpeter 1912). Consequently, they require recombining different pieces of existing knowledge (Cantner and Meder 2007). These pieces of knowledge, necessary to successfully innovate, may not be in the immediate reach of an actor or firm but may rather lay outside (Cowan et al. 2006). Thus, access to external knowledge may be an important prerequisite for innovative success. At this point, collectivity comes into play. No single individual or firm can solve all problems (Ejermo and Karlsson 2006) since it does not hold all knowledge available in the world. Especially invention processes are based on the combination of various pieces of knowledge which are possessed by various economic actors. With this perspective in mind, we can argue that invention and innovation activities rely on processes of collective or social learning and exchange of knowledge between actors (Lundvall 1992; Doloreux and Parto 2005), whereas learning is the process whereby existing knowledge is selected and combined based upon a new perspective (Ejermo and Karlsson 2006). Consequently the creation of innovation requires knowledge spillover-producing interaction. These knowledge spillovers can happen deliberately, for example in the context of research collaborations, or involuntary and unintended.

In this research paper, the approach of the innovator network (IN) is used in order to explain if knowledge spillovers that are distributed via connections among inventors influence the success of a new venture if this venture has been founded by a person which is connected to this network. INs can be defined as networks that are built up by actors which cooperatively engage in the creation of new ideas and then economize the results (Cantner and Graf 2007). This economization can be realized within an existing firm or by the formation of a new venture. It is assumed that if a new venture is connected to a well-functioning IN, knowledge spillovers may result in new ideas, promoting firm's success.

Two data bases are used. First, patent data delivers the innovator network for Thuringia. The second data base contains information on innovative ventures founded in the period between 1990 and 2006, drawn from the register for commercial and private companies in Thuringia. Both data sources were merged by the names of inventors and founders.

The analysis is conducted in three steps. First survival analysis explains the relation between a firm's innovativeness and its survival. In a second step, the connection to the innovator network and its influence on a firm's innovativeness is analysed. In the third and last step the differences in chances to survive between innovative and connected firms as compared to innovative and non-connected firms are investigated.

The remainder of the paper will proceed as follows. Section 2 provides an overview on the mechanisms that are connecting innovator networks with entrepreneurial success and presents hypotheses based on these considerations. Section 3 is devoted to the description of the database and methods used. In section 4, results are presented. Section 5 discusses the paper's results and concludes.

Innovation, New Ventures and the Innovator Network

In evolutionary economics the emergence and diffusion of innovation is seen as the most important driver of economic change (Pyka 1999). Economic change in this context is driven by a selection process where firms having competitive advantages as compared to average of an industry over time gain market shares while other firms with below average competitiveness lose. The resource based view of the firm considers specific individual characteristics of a firm as most important resources to gain competitive advantages (Penrose 1959). One kind of such individual characteristic is a firm's knowledge base which is an important prerequisite for innovation. Therefore, the knowledge base of a firm enabling it to generate innovation is generally seen as a key driver for economic success of firms. This relation has been empirically detected by several authors. Jaffe (1986) was one of the first to empirically show that there is a systematic relationship between firms' patents, profits and market value to the technological position of firms' research programs. In a more recent study, Hall and Bagchi-Senb (2002) show for firms in the Canadian biotech industry that R&D intensity correlates with patent measures, while innovation measured in terms of new product introductions is associated with business performance. To mention one more, Thornhill (2006) has shown that innovative firms are likely to enjoy revenue growth, irrespective of the industry in which they operate and that firm knowledge, industry dynamism and innovation interact in the way they influence firm performance. Based on this reasoning, the first hypothesis is formulated as follows:

Hypothesis 1 *Innovation and survival: Innovative firms have better chances to survive the selection process of the market than non-innovative ones.*

As it has been pointed out in the introduction, innovation requires a recombination of different pieces of already existing knowledge (Cantner and Meder 2007) which creates new knowledge. Since these pieces may not be in the immediate reach of a firm (Cowan et al. 2006), access to external knowledge may be an important prerequisite for innovative success. Therefore, the creation of innovation requires knowledge spillover-producing interaction.

Cassia et al. (2009), as well as Audretsch and Lehmann (2005), see university-based knowledge spillovers as the most important form of knowledge spillovers. They argue that knowledge from universities flows in the economic system and affects firms' propensity to create new market opportunities and introduce new ideas in the market. Both studies have shown that a university's knowledge spillovers have a positive influence on firm's growth (measured as sales respectively as number of employees). Besides university-based knowledge spillovers, also spillovers from firm-researchers and employees of research institutes may play an important role since this knowledge may be more applied and ready for the market.

As stated above, knowledge spillovers are an important device for the generation of innovations and they are mainly transferred via personal contacts. In their seminal works, Breschi and Lissoni (2006) comprehensively elaborated this process. They argue that pure spillovers can only take place by trade-unrelated personal communication or through reverse engineering (Breschi and Lissoni 2006). However, when tacitness of knowledge plays a role, knowledge spillovers are not possible anymore without active participation of the inventor. As to the question why inventors should accept to pass information deliberately, Breschi and Lissoni (2006) find the answer in 'social obligations'. University researchers for example obey to the principles of open science and dedicate themselves to the production of public goods. Also corporate researchers may be willing to provide their colleagues with free advice as long as it happens reciprocally. In this sense and regarding tacitness as an important characteristic of newly generated knowledge, one could think of knowledge as a club good. Outsiders of such a club, defined as actors that are not connected to the social network of innovators, can be excluded from consuming the knowledge while insiders, defined as actors that are connected to the social network of innovators, profit from accessibility and non-rivalry in the consumption of the shared knowledge.

Such a social network can be defined as innovator network (IN) that is built up by actors which cooperatively engage in the creation of new ideas and then economize the results in the market - either within an existing firm or by the formation of a new venture (Cantner and Graf 2007; Balconi et al. 2004). Innovative actors building the IN are employees of firms, of research institutes or of universities, students or self-employed individuals who actively conduct research. These research oriented relationships indicate knowledge transfers and exchanges respectively knowledge spillovers which form the basis for new ideas facilitated by the recombination of existing knowledge (Edwards and Gordon 1984). However, its not just their innovative effort which brings them together. Moreover, they get into contact by different means. They may of cause be partners in formal research cooperations between several firms. Additionally, they may be former colleagues, thus innovator mobility may play a role. It can also not be excluded that they may know each other from playing tennis in the same sports club, eating in the same restaurant or from bringing their little ones to the same nursery.

For a firm that employs an actor who is socially connected to the innovator network, the connection to the IN promotes the expansion of its knowledge base and its potential to innovate. Consequently an actor who is connected to the IN can provide an important prerequisite for the generation of innovations and therefore it may serve as an important facilitating device for long term firm survival of a firm (Thornhill 2006).

Hypotheses 2 and 3 are summing up these considerations:

Hypothesis 2 *Innovator network and innovative output: Firms that are connected to an innovator network are more innovative than non-connected ones.*

Hypothesis 3 *Innovator network and survival: Innovative firms survive longer than non-innovative firms and this effect is driven by the connection to an innovator network.*

In order to test hypotheses 1 to 3, a biographical firm database has been created which will be presented in the following section.

Database and Variables

Database

The analysis in this paper aims at finding out whether the social connection to the innovator network influences firms' survival. To answer this question a biographical firm dataset has been constructed based upon two data bases. The first one is data on incorporations of enterprises in Thuringia which is based on the commercial register and the second one is patent data comprising all German patents applied for at the German Patent Office in the time period between 1993 and 2004.

Incorporations

Information on new ventures was collected by the Thuringian Founder Study.[1] The data base was drawn from the commercial register for commercial and private companies in Thuringia and contains information on the founders (date of birth, name, surname, academic title, address, gender) and on the firms (date of founding, date of closing, trade name, location, legal form, spin-off or not, industry). The survey population consists of 12,505 founders whose 7016 companies were founded between 1990 and 2006 and are either active or have failed meanwhile. After cleaning the data (exclusion of firms founded before 1993 since the German reunification came with a phase of many management buyouts of former state combines, exclusion of firms where the founding date was missing, extraction of only those firms that are active in innovative industries following the classification of Grupp and Legler (2000)) a population of 4568 companies is left for investigation.

Innovator Network

Per definition, the innovator network comprises persons who cooperatively engage in the creation of new ideas and then economize the results (Cantner and Graf 2007). Both aspects have to be elaborated further. First, to be cooperatively engaged in the creation of new ideas does not necessarily mean being involved in active research cooperation. Rather it means that people may also be in the same sports club, meet each other in the same bars or restaurants, are former colleagues, have met on a conference/trade fair or take their little ones to the same nursery. The pivotal role in this respect comes to the fact that people are in contact. Also in a bar or in a sports club people talk about their jobs. Besides private information, they exchange information on what they are working on, what some colleagues of them are doing, what they have read about or what projects they are working on. This information must not be specifically related to innovative activities but at least these contacts lead to know-who respectively knowledge of who may be able to help you solving a certain problem. The underlying assumption of our approach is that a firm which is founded by one or more persons has access to the social capital of exactly these contacts they bring with. If it's not new influences for innovative activities, then this social capital at least helps to find an appropriate contact person for solving (also technical) problems. Of course, it would also be possible to find appropriate contact persons at the internet but face-to-face contacts and personal acquaintances are an important feature since members of social networks who personally know each other tend to exchange more information, help or advice (Breschi and Lissoni 2006). Measuring these kinds of relationships of cause is impossible. In order to picture the innovator

---

[1] Note that this data base was just the starting point for the Thuringian Founder Study Questionnaire. It is therefore not identical to the questionnaire data collected by the Thuringian Founder Study.

network, at least in the form of linkages that arise from the participation in a common team of inventors, we use patent data. In the same line of reasoning as Breschi and Lissoni (2006), we assume that inventors who worked together on the same patent know each other well enough to be willing to exchange information and to tolerate that this information may be passed on to somebody else than the receiver. Since those networks include members of various companies, circulation of knowledge across companies can be expected.

Second, there is the aspect of economization. This aspect restricts the network to those persons who develop new products or processes for their own firm or for their employer. They may be researchers, technologists or engineers whose aim is to create marketable ideas respectively innovations. Of course, if we measure patent networks, we do not know whether these patents will end in a new product or process and there is no information available about how the invention has been pursued. However, since a patent application protects the knowledge from usage by other actors, it signals an intention to further use it in order to generate an innovation which per definition is the economization new ideas.

For this study, the inventor network of Thuringia has been constructed by including all patent applications to the German Patent Office between 1993 and 2004 on which at least one Thuringian inventor (the assignment was made by postal codes of inventors' address) was listed. The resulting data base contains information on 6969 inventors (name, surname, address) and 5381 patent applications (IPC-Code, name and address of the applicant, application date and year). The number of inventors results after checking raw data for misspelling of personal names. Using this data set, the one-mode affiliation network of inventors, where the connection is based upon co-inventions, could be constructed. The information resulting from an analysis of the network of inventors can be effectively combined with other sources of information (Balconi et al. 2004) - in this case with the firm database.

Combination of both

The combination of information gained from the innovator network with the firm database has been conducted by matching names of firm founders with names of inventors in the innovator network. It must be pointed out that this approach does not come without bias. However, the authors checked for addresses and birth dates in order to make the matches as accurate as possible. If one or more founders of a firm are listed as inventor on a patent with an application date later than the date of firm founding, then in a first step, this firm was counted to be innovative. Certainly, this assumes something that cannot observed, namely that the founder intends to economically exploit his invention within his own firm rather than selling licences or leaving the exploitation to the applicant.

If a firm is identified as being innovative in the sense of having patents, it need not necessarily be connected to the (regional) innovator network. Therefore, in a second step, an attribute dataset has been created, identifying inventors which at the same time have incorporated a firm. Subsequently network analysis has been applied in order to distinguish between connected and isolated inventor-founders. Of course, if a firm was founded by more than one inventor-founder it is counted to be connected as soon as at least one founder is not isolated.

The information received from the analysis of the innovator network is used in order to create the core variables of the analysis. The variables will be presented in more detail in the following subsection.

Variables

Table 1 reports descriptive statistics for the data base created. Tables 6a and 6b in the appendix show the correlations of the variables on a significance level of 5%.

Table 1 Descriptive Statistics

	Variable	Description	Obs	Mean	Std. Dev.	Min	Max
H1	Innovative	Binary variable, indicating whether the founders of the respective firm have applied for patents (1) or not (0).	4568	0.11	0.32	0	1
H2	No.Patents	Count variable, indicating the number of patents the founders of the respective firm have applied for.	4568	0.21	1.48	0	47
	Connected	Binary variable, measuring for those firms of founders who have applied for patents, whether they are connected to the innovator network or isolated from it.	516	0.37	0.48	0	1
	PatExperience	Count variable, indicating the number of patents the founders of the respective firm have applied for before the firm has been founded.	516	1.83	3.24	0	26
H3	InnoConn	Binary variable indicating that an innovative firm is connected to the network (1) or isolated from it (0).	516	0.37	0.48	0	1
	Prob(InnoConn)	Probability for a firm to be innovative and connected to the network at the same time, dependent on certain individual characteristics.	4494	0.04	0.12	0	0.97

(continued)

On Regional Innovator Networks as Hubs for Innovative Ventures

Table 1 (continued)

	Variable	Description	Obs	Mean	Std. Dev.	Min	Max
Regional Differences	ABG	Dummy for Altenburg.	3508	0.03	0.18	0	1
	GGrz	Dummy for Gera/Greiz.	3508	0.07	0.26	0	1
	JShk	Dummy for Jena/ Saale-Holzland-Kreis.	3508	0.12	0.33	0	1
	SOK	Dummy for Saale-Orla-Kreis.	3508	0.02	0.15	0	1
	SaalRud	Dummy for Saalfeld/ Rudolstadt.	3508	0.04	0.21	0	1
	Central	Dummy for Central Thuringia (Sömmerda, Erfurt, Weimar, Weimarer Land, Ilm-Kreis, Gotha).	3508	0.33	0.47	0	1
	Sonne	Dummy for Sonneberg.	3508	0.03	0.18	0	1
	Schmalle	Dummy for Schmalkalden/ Meiningen.	3508	0.14	0.35	0	1
	EAWak	Dummy for Eisenach/ Wartburgkreis.	3508	0.08	0.26	0	1
	UHK	Dummy for Unstrut-Hainich-Kreis.	3508	0.03	0.17	0	1
	Eichs	Dummy for Eichsfeld.	3508	0.04	0.19	0	1
Controls	ShareStudents	Share of students in the whole population of the region the firm is located at.	3508	0.02	0.04	0	0.12
	Meanturb	Mean of industry turbulence in the time span of three years before the firm has been founded and the three years afterwards.	2900	3.96	6.64	−4,87	23.24
	Capcomp	Binary variable indicating whether the firm is a incorporated company (1) or a private company (0).	4568	0.93	0.26	0	1
	Academics	Number of founding-team members that hold an academic degree.	4560	0.12	0.39	0	9
	Spinoff	Binary variable identifying academic spin-offs (1).	4568	0.02	0.15	0	1
	No. Founders	Team size by the number of individuals that have founded the firm.	4560	1.39	0.77	0	16

Dependent Variables

The survival of a firm is its life span from the year of founding on up to the year of closing in the case the firm failed. Since firms are only observable here until the year 2006, for those firms that lived longer, failure cannot be observed after 2006. The Cox-proportional hazards model which will be described in more detail in chapter "Perhaps David Audretsch Is Not a Good Man", accounts for this truncation problem of survival data.

The variable *No.Patents* counts the number of patents the firm's founder(s) applied for during the life span of the firm. This number ranges between 0 and 47 while the majority of firms (4267 out of 4568) count a zero.

InnoConn is a binary variable indicating whether the founders of innovative firms are connected to the innovator network (*InnoConn* = 1; 192 out of 516 firms with innovative founders either before or after founding the firm) or whether they are isolated notes of the net (*InnoConn* = 0; 324 out of 516 firms with innovative founders either before or after founding the firm). As argued above, the analysis in this paper assumes for young and small firms, that social scientific capital of the founders can be directly translated into social scientific capital of the firm. Since social relations usually do not break up from 1 year to the other, also the connection of the founder(s) to the network in the years before firm founding as part of the scientific social capital of the firm has been encountered.

Control for Regional Differences

Of course, regions differ in regards to their economic environment, the structure of the regional network and other factors which cannot be analysed within this paper. However, in order to cope with this problem and to control for pure regional differences, dummies for the 12 travel to work areas of Thuringia as defined by Granato and Farhauer (2007) have been included.

Independent Variables

The variable *Innovative* is a binary variable, which measures whether the founders of the firm have applied for patents (*Innovative* = 1; 516 out of 4568) or not (*Innovative* = 0; 4052 out of 4568) before and after the firm has been founded. This variable indicates whether one can consider the firm to be innovative or not.

Connected is a binary variable indicating whether the founders of a firm are connected to the innovator network (*Connected* = 1; 192 out of 516 innovative firms) or whether they are isolated notes of the net (*Connected* =0; 324 out of 516 innovative firms). As has been argued above, the authors assume for young and small firms,

On Regional Innovator Networks as Hubs for Innovative Ventures

that social scientific capital of the founders can be directly translated into social scientific capital of the firm. Since social relations usually do not break up from one year to the other, also the connection of the founder(s) to the network in the years before firm founding as part of the scientific social capital of the firm has been encountered.

PatExperience is a count variable, indicating how many patents the founders of a respective firm have applied for before founding it. For the 516 innovative firms in the sample, this variable ranges between 0 and 26. For 213 firms one finds a 0 which means that they have no patenting experience. The founder(s) of the other 303 firms bring along experience in patenting.

Prob(InnoConn) measures the probability of a firm to be connected to the innovator network and at the same time to be innovative (which means that the founders have applied for patents before or after the firms has been founded). This variable gets zero for all firms that have no connection to innovative activities that might be measurable through patent information. For all the other firms where the founders have shown patenting activities, even before the firm has been founded, it takes a value between 0 and 1.

Control Variables

In order to control for regional differences, dummies for the 12 Thuringian travel-to-work areas as defined by Granato and Farhauer (2007) were created. Figure 1 in the appendix illustrates these areas.

The probability to be an innovative firm might differ dependent on whether a region is a so called student-region or not. Therefore, the variable *ShareStudents* measures the share of students in a travel-to-work area compared to the whole population in this area.

The firms in the sample are active in different industrial sectors and of cause the sector plays an important role to for the survivability of a firm. Since this paper is analyzing young firms, it is not only controled for sectors but to also for the economic environment/stage of the sector they are active in. For this purpose, data from the IAB (Institut für Arbeitsmarkt- und Berufsforschung) has been used, which contains the number of firm founding and closing for each industry (Nace 2-digit level) for the years 1976 to 2010. Based on this data, the variable named *Meanturb* has been constructed, which is measuring the turbulence in the sector the firm is active in for a time span of 6 years, 3 years before the firm has been founded and 3 years afterwards. The turbulence is measured as number of firm founding in a certain sector in the specific years minus the number of firm close downs in the same sector in the same years. From this value, the mean over the 6 years around the firm founding is estimated and used for analysis.

The variable *Capcomp* (1 of it is a capital company, 0 otherwise) controls whether the firm is a private company. *Academics* measures the number of team member that is holding an academic degree. *Spinoff* measures whether the firm is an academic

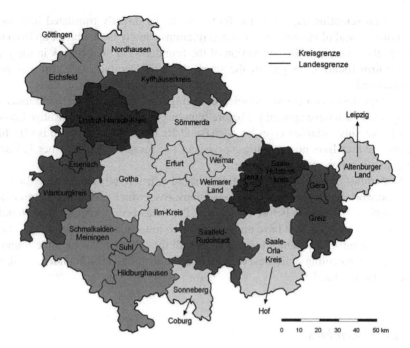

Fig. 1 Thuringia and its Travel-to-work areas. Thuringian travel to work areas according to the estimations of Granato and Farhauer (2007). TTWA(i), (i = 1..., 12): Altenburger Land (1), Gera/Greiz (2), Jena/Saale-Holzland-Kreis (3), Saale-Orla-Kreis (4), Saalfeld-Rudolstadt (5), Central Thuringia (6), Sonneberg (7), Schmalkalden-Meiningen/Suhl/Hildburghausen (8), Eisenach/Wartburgkreis (9), Unstrut-Hainich-Kreis (10), Eichsfeld (11), Nordhausen/Kyffhäuser-Kreis (12)

spin-off, which means a spin-off from a university or research institute ($Spinoff = 1$) or not. *No.Founders* measures the founding team's size.

Method

Innovation and Survival

In order to analyze the role an innovator network plays for the survivability of a young and innovative firm, the analysis in this paper proceeds in three steps. The first step is to identify the relation between innovativeness and survival of a firm. Since in this first step success is measured in terms of survival, Cox's proportional hazards model (1972) is applied. It has been widely recognized that survival as an outcome variable does not come without bias. The problem arises due to non-complete measurements on all 'members' or entities of a random sample (Kaplan and Meier 1958). For example in medical follow-up studies, contact to some of the individuals will be lost before their death and others will die due to other reasons.

Similarly the observation of the lifetime may be ended at a certain point in time, due to the need to get out a report within a reasonable time. In many applications, and this holds also for our investigation, survival may be a subject to right censoring and left truncation (Tsai et al. 1987). Right-censored cases are study objects whose failure event is not observed. The term "right-censored" implies that the event of interest is to the right of our data point (Kaplan and Meier 1958). In other words, if the units were to keep on operating, the failure would occur at some time after our data point. Truncation is a source of bias in survival analysis, in which certain objects are ignored and not sampled (Tsai et al. 1987). Left-truncation occurs when some subjects are registered at a delayed time. The present database contains firms founded at several points in time. Thus, there is a problem with left-truncation. Also, the event of interest (closure) is not observed for some of our observations, thus the data is right-censored. Cox proportional hazards model (1972) is used since it gives a valid estimate of the survival rate for data sets including right-censored and left truncated cases.

Innovator Network and Innovative Output

After having identified the relation between innovativeness and survival, the analysis is, in a second step, devoted to the relation between the connection to the innovator network and innovativeness. This means that it is asked whether in the group of innovative firms those with connection to the innovator network are more successful in innovating than the isolated ones. Since the number of patents applied for as our outcome variable is highly skewed to the left with a high number of zeros, negative binomial regression as proposed by Greene (2003) as well as Cameron and Trivedi (1998) is applied.

Innovator Network and Survival

The third step of the analysis aims at bringing together the first two steps. The authors want to see whether the combination of being innovative and connected to the network influences firm survival. In order to do this, first the factors that explain this aforementioned combination are analysed. This means that special characteristics are regressed on the binary variable *InnoConn*. Since the outcome variable is binary, logistic regression is applied. The individual coefficient of this regression (the fitted value), reveals for each firm that is at least innovative, the probability to be innovative and connected at the same time based on certain characteristics. This value is stored and in the next step and used as explanatory variable (*Prob(InnoConn)*) for the survivability of the firm in a cox regression.

Empirical Results

Innovation and Survival

Table 2 shows the results for the first step of analysis which is devoted to hypothesis 1 stating that innovative firms have better chances to survive the selection process of the market than non-innovative ones. As to the controls, being a incorporated company (*Capcom*) reduces the exit hazard whereas being in an industry with higher market turbulences (*Meanturb*) increases the hazard rate.

Models 1–3 differ in the inclusion of regional control variables. Considering all three models, we find that the coefficient for the dummy variable *Innovative* ranges between 0.64 and 0.76 on a 1–10% significance level. This means that innovative firms have a risk to die in the upcoming period which is only about 70% of the risk for non-innovative firms. Therefore, hypothesis 1 cannot be rejected.

Innovator Network and Innovative Output

The second step of analysis is devoted to the second hypothesis which is assuming that innovative firms that are connected to the innovator network show a higher innovation output than isolated ones. The causality, however, appears to remain unclear. It might be the case that firms apply for more patents since they are connected to the innovator network. But it might as well be that the highly innovative firms are connected since they have more patents. The authors do not claim to have an answer to this point here. The models just aim at revealing the connection in the data. The question which direction is the correct one remains unsolved. Table 3 shows the results of the negative binomial regression on the number of patents a firm applied for in four models which differ with respect to the inclusion of control variables.

Over all models, the relationship between the connection to the innovator network and the number of patents a firm applies for is significant and positive. Interpreting model 4, one can say that, all the other variables considered being constant, being connected to the innovator network goes hand in hand with a higher difference in the logs of the patent count. Therefore, hypothesis 2 cannot be rejected and it can be assumed that the innovator network has a positive influence on the degree of innovativeness in the group of innovative firms. As to the controls, having a higher share of academics (Academics) in the founding team increases the number of patents.

On Regional Innovator Networks as Hubs for Innovative Ventures

Table 2 Cox proportional hazards model– regression on the influence of innovativeness on the hazard of a firm to be closed in the next period

Method	Cox regression - Breslow Method for ties		
Dep. Var.	Survival		
Population	All firms		
	Model 1	Model 2	Model 3
Innovative	0.7568*	0.7015**	0.6433***
	(−1.66)	(−2.09)	(−2.59)
ABG			6.0795***
			(4.53)
GGrz			5.3627***
			(4.59)
JShk		1.4725***	4.7279***
		(2.85)	(4.39)
SOK			4.7730***
			(3.60)
SaalRud			6.2421
			(4.79)
Central		0.4627***	1.4790
		(−5.61)	(1.10)
Sonne			3.1264***
			(2.76)
Schmalle			4.1954***
			(4.06)
EAWak			0.5847
			(−1.02)
UHK			1.3157
			(0.49)
Eichs			1.0088
			(0.02)
Capcomp	0.7404*	0.7105**	0.7113**
	(−1.75)	(−1.98)	(−1.97)
Meanturb	1.0351***	1.0387***	1.0340***
	(5.00)	(5.52)	(4.77)
No. of Obs.	2199	2199	2199
No. of failures	367	367	367
Prob>Chi2	0.000	0.000	0.000
Robust z statistics in parentheses			

*Significant at 10%
**Significant at 5%
***Significant at 1%

Table 3 Negative binomial regression-the influence of being connected to the innovator network on the number of patents an innovative firm applies for

Method	Negative binomial regression			
Dep. Var.	No. Patents			
Population	All firms			
	Model 1	Model 2	Model 3	Model 4
Connected	0.5164***	0.5013***	0.5543***	0.5955***
	(3.23)	(3.16)	(3.15)	(3.31)
PatExperience		0.0434**	0.0377*	0.0302
		(2.09)	(1.81)	(1.45)
ABG				2.6978**
				(2.25)
GGrz				0.8015
				(1.52)
JShk			6.2492	−24.3060*
			(1.55)	(−1.89)
SOK				2.1660
				(1.63)
SaalRud				2.6545**
				(2.32)
Central			−0.1042	1.7021**
			(−0.53)	(2.13)
Sonne				2.8368**
				(2.41)
Schmalle				2.9570***
				(2.90)
EAWak				1.5311**
				(2.01)
UHK				2.2234*
				(1.78)
Eichs				Omitted
Academics	0.4409***	0.4130***	0.4576***	0.4617***
	(3.48)	(3.27)	(3.54)	(3.54)
Spinoff	−0.1214	−0.2315	−0.1827	−0.1730
	(−0.47)	(−0.88)	(−0.68)	(−0.66)
No.Founders	0.1024	0.1115	0.0978	0.0900
	(1.05)	(1.15)	(1.01)	(0.93)
ShareStudents	1.0681	1.6061	−51.9694	225.9738*
	(0.71)	(1.06)	(−1.51)	(1.94)
Constant	−0.0089	−0.1106	0.0695	−2.7225**
	(−0.05)	(−0.59)	(0.32)	(−2.43)
No. of Obs.	442	442	442	442
Pseudo R2	0.0266	0.0295	0.0312	0.0412
Robust z statistics in parentheses				

*Significant at 10%
**Significant at 5%
***Significant at 1%

Innovator Network and Survival

In order to test hypothesis 3, the authors start by calculating the individual probability of a firm to be innovative and connected to the innovator network at the same time (*Prob(InnoConn)*). Table 4 shows the logistic regression for this.

The probability to be connected and innovative depends on the firm's experience in patenting (*PatExperience*), the number of academics in the team (*Academics*), whether the firm is a spin-off (Spinoff) and the share of students among the whole population in the region (*ShareStudents*). For all firms where, *InnoConn* is 0, the authors set *Prob(InnoConn)* to 0 which means that not the fitted but the real value is used in order to explain whether the connection to the innovator network is positively linked to the survivability of firms. Cox proportional hazards model is applied to explain survival with the probability to be connected to the innovator network and innovative as well as some control variables. Table 5 shows the results.

Again, models 1–3 differ simply in the inclusion of control variables. Looking at the main variable of interest, *Prob(InnoConn)*, one can see that a high probability to be innovative and connected to the innovator network reduces the hazard ratio to about 48%.

Table 4 Logistic regression – Variables that are determining the probability for a firm to be innovative and connected to the innovator network at the same time

Method	Logistic regression
Dep. Var.	InnoConn
Population	All firms
	Model 1
PatExperience	0.1560***
	(4.19)
Academics	0.5708***
	(3.04)
Spinoff	0.8551**
	(2.42)
No.Founders	0.1113
	(0.8)
ShareStudents	−7.2862***
	(−3.11)
Constant	−1.1191***
	(−4.20)
No. of Obs.	442
Pseudo R2	0.0851
Robust z statistics in parentheses	

*Significant at 10%
**Significant at 5%
***Significant at 1%

Table 5 Cox proportional hazards model – influence of the probability to be innovative and connected to the innovator network on the hazard of a firm to be closed in the next period

Method	Cox regression – Breslow Method for ties		
Dep. Var.	Survival		
Population	All firms		
	Model 1	Model 2	Model 3
Prob(InnoConn)	0.4851*	0.4784*	0.3796***
	(−1.68)	(−1.65)	(−2.14)
ABG			6.0375***
			(4.51)
GGrz			5.3268***
			(4.57)
JShk		1.4329***	4.5649***
		(2.67)	(4.30)
SOK			4.7659***
			(3.60)
SaalRud			6.1765***
			(4.76)
Central		0.4646***	1.4817
		(−5.58)	(1.11)
Sonne			3.1189***
			(2.76)
Schmalle			4.1853***
			(4.05)
EAWak			0.5820
			(−1.03)
UHK			1.3085
			(0.48)
Eichs			1.0124
			(0.02)
Capcomp	0.7402*	0.7098**	0.7105**
	(−1.75)	(−1.99)	(−1.98)
Meanturb	1.0351***	1.0390***	1.0343***
	(5.00)	(5.56)	(4.81)
No. of Obs.	2199	2199	2199
No. of failures	367	367	367
Prob > Chi2	0.000	0.000	0.000
Robust z statistics in parentheses			

*Significant at 10%
**Significant at 5%
***Significant at 1%

On Regional Innovator Networks as Hubs for Innovative Ventures 343

Therefore, hypothesis 3 cannot be rejected and it can be assumed that the connection to the innovator network plays an important role in the explanation of differences in the survival of firms. As to the controls for *Capcom* and *Meanturb* the coefficients show up to be equivalent to the ones in Table 1.

Discussion and Conclusions

The aim of this paper was to show for young firms in innovative industries in how far the connection to the innovator network or in other words, the amount of scientific social capital the firm can make use of, is a hub for its chances to survive the economic or market selection process. An analysis of 4568 newly founded companies in innovative industries in the German state of Thuringia between 1993 and 2006 was pursued to shed light on these relationships.

In a first step of the analysis the authors found that innovative firms have a lower exit hazard than non-innovative ones. Being an incorporated firms lowers the hazard additionally whereas being active in a turbulent market increases the hazard.

In a second step, the authors looked at the factors that are influencing innovativeness and find the connection to the innovator network to be one of the main ones. However also experience in patenting positively influences whether the founders of the respective firm go on with their patenting activities. Additionally the number of founders with academic background positively influence tendency of a firm to apply for patents.

In the third step, the authors addressed the connection between innovativeness, the innovator network and the survivability of firms. The theoretical framework suggested that this relation is positive and that an innovative firm which is connected to the innovator network has more success in gaining competitive advantages through innovation and therefore has better chances to survive. The results indicate that the probability of a firm to be innovative and connected to the innovator network at the same time is positively related to its probability to survive.

Besides the connection to the innovator network, three further factors turn out to be influential for the viability of a young company. First, it was found that incorportated companies have a reduced hazard ratio as compared to private companies.

Secondly, the mean turbulence of the industry the firm is active in for the time span three years before and three years after firm founding is negatively related to the hazard ratio. A high value of turbulence indicates a recently growing sector where there are more company founding's than closings. According to Gort and Klepper's (1982) theory on the diffusion of product innovations (Industry Life Cycle), this industry is in phase II which is the interval from the take-off point of the net entry until the net entry starts to decline drastically. This explains the negative connection which we find for the survival of firms. If a firm is founded in phase II it has to go through phase IV which is a phase of shake out where the net entry becomes negative and where many firms are closed until the market stabilizes. The probability that a firm does not survive this stage is quite high which goes in line with what has been found in the present data.

Third, the authors also find that survival differs regionally. This showed up in various significant regional dummies.

This regional dimenions opens up further avenues of research. With respect to firm's survival and success, location has been identified in the literature as one among many critical factors (Heckmann and Schnabel 2005; Storey 1994). However, locations differ with respect to their organizations like universities, research institutes, firms or public agencies, as well as with respect to institutional factors like norms and regulations, a qualified labour force or business taxes. Besides these, but related, an important locational factor is the regional innovation system as defined by Cooke et al. (1997). The network of innovators (IN) can be seen as one core element of such an innovation system. However, it may not be irrelevant to which IN a firm is connected. On these terms, various researches have shown that innovative activities are spatially not evenly spread but a rather regionally bounded phenomenon (Asheim and Isaksen 2002). Already by this unequal distribution innovative performance differs among regional innovation systems (e.g. Porter 1990; Jaffe et al. 1993). Moreover, regions differ with respect to the success of their respective firms or with respect to founding rates (e.g. Storey 1994). The success of incumbent firms as well as their founding rate is driven by innovation (Nijkamp 2009; Audretsch and Lehmann 2005; Brown and Eisenhardt 1997; Lumpkin and Dess 1996) which in turn is driven by the IN. If regions differ with respect to innovative and firm performance, this may be due to different characteristics of the respective regional innovator networks (RINs). Among those characteristics may be network properties like a high degree of connectedness, a high centrality of single actors or the existence of structural holes. Additionally, one might expect differences occurring due to the characteristics of the knowledge that is flowing in the network. Some regions are highly specialized, thus concentrated on a small number of industries. In these regions, the knowledge flowing through the RIN will also be very specialized and therefore the knowledge bases of the network-actors will have a high degree of overlap. Other regions are more diverse with respect to industries. Consequently, the knowledge flowing through the network is rather diverse and the actors' knowledge bases show a low degree of overlap. These considerations leave lots of space for further research on the connection between network characteristics and firm's success.

Appendix

Table 6a Correlations – full sample (2199 Observations; Estimations in Tables 2 and 5)

	1	2	3	4	5	6	7	8	9	10	11	12	13	14	15	16
1 Innovative	1.0000															
2 Prob(InnoConn)	0.9094*	1.0000														
3 ABG	−0.0097	−0.0158	1.0000													
4 GGrz	−0.0225	−0.0188	−0.0503*	1.0000												
5 JShk	0.1256*	0.0457*	−0.0680*	−0.1047*	1.0000											
6 SOK	−0.0263	−0.0288	−0.0285	−0.0438*	−0.0593*	1.0000										
7 SaalRud	0.0348*	0.0350*	−0.0390*	−0.0600*	−0.0812*	−0.0340*	1.0000									
8 Central	−0.0069	0.0387*	−0.1268*	−0.1952*	−0.2639*	−0.1105*	−0.1513*	1.0000								
9 Sonne	0.0025	0.0050	−0.0333*	−0.0512*	−0.0693*	−0.0290	−0.0397*	−0.1292*	1.0000							
10 Schmalle	−0.0332*	−0.0283	−0.0726*	−0.1117*	−0.1511*	−0.0633*	−0.0866*	−0.2817*	−0.0739*	1.0000						
11 EAWak	−0.0309	−0.0380*	−0.0518*	−0.0797*	−0.1078*	0.0451*	−0.0618*	−0.2009*	−0.0527*	−0.1150*	1.0000					
12 UHK	−0.0229	−0.0206	−0.0322	−0.0496*	−0.0671*	−0.0281	−0.0384*	−0.1250*	−0.0328	−0.0716*	−0.0511*	1.0000				
13 Eichs	−0.0372*	−0.0260	−0.0352*	−0.0541*	−0.0732*	−0.0307	−0.0420*	−0.1365*	−0.0358*	−0.0781*	−0.0557*	−0.0347*	1.0000			
14 ShareStudents	0.1250*	0.0457*	−0.0813*	−0.0748*	0.9978*	−0.0709*	−0.0971*	−0.2613*	−0.0828*	−0.1703*	−0.0993*	−0.0802*	−0.0876*	1.0000		
15 Meanturb	−0.0645*	−0.0732*	0.0432*	0.0566*	−0.0056	0.0022	−0.0385	0.0728*	0.0193	−0.0504*	−0.0691*	−0.0431*	−0.0478*	−0.0024	1.0000	
16 Capcomp	0.0195	0.0129	0.0027	0.0058	0.0281	−0.0050	−0.0183	0.0122	−0.0183	−0.0074	−0.0051	0.0130	−0.0386*	0.0292	0.0454*	1.0000

*Significant at 10%

Table 6b Correlations Sub sample (442 Observations; Estimations in Tables 3 and 4))

	1	2	3	4	5	6	7	8	9	10	11	12	13	14	15	16	17	18	19
1 No. Patents	1.0000																		
2 Connected	0.1920*	1.0000																	
3 PatExperience	0.1457*	0.2275*	1.0000																
4 InnoConn	0.1920*	1.0000*	0.2275*	1.0000															
5 ABG	−0.0096	0.0174	−0.0465	0.0174	1.0000														
6 GGrz	−0.0193	0.0780	−0.0208	0.0780	−0.0503*	1.0000													
7 JShk	0.0540*	−0.1194*	−0.0240	−0.1194*	−0.0680*	−0.1047*	1.0000												
8 SOK	−0.0187	−0.0892	−0.0386	−0.0892	−0.0285	−0.0438*	−0.0593*	1.0000											
9 SaalRud	0.0059	−0.0629	0.0034	−0.0629	−0.0390*	−0.0600*	−0.0812*	−0.0340*	1.0000										
10 Central	0.0220	0.3816*	0.0854	0.3816*	−0.1268*	−0.1952*	−0.2639*	−0.1105*	−0.1513*	1.0000									
11 Sonne	−0.0024	−0.0648	0.0347	−0.0648	−0.0333*	−0.0512*	−0.0693*	−0.0290	−0.0397*	−0.1292*	1.0000								
12 Schmalle	0.0000	−0.1599*	−0.0510	−0.1599*	−0.0726*	−0.1117*	−0.1511*	−0.0633*	−0.0866*	−0.2817*	−0.0739*	1.0000							
13 EAWak	−0.0250	−0.0579	−0.0517	−0.0579	−0.0518*	−0.0797*	−0.1078*	−0.0451*	−0.0618*	−0.2009*	−0.0527*	−0.1150*	1.0000						
14 UHK	−0.0192	−0.1097*	−0.0208	−0.1097*	−0.0322	−0.0496*	−0.0671*	−0.0281	−0.0384*	−0.1250*	−0.0328	−0.0716*	−0.0511*	1.0000					
15 Eichs	−0.0279	−0.0328	0.0751	−0.0328	−0.0352*	−0.0541*	−0.0732*	−0.0307	−0.0420*	−0.1365*	−0.0358*	−0.0781*	−0.0557*	−0.0347*	1.0000				
16 ShareStudents	0.0533*	−0.1166*	−0.0240	−0.1166*	−0.0813*	−0.0748*	0.9978*	−0.0709*	−0.0971*	−0.2613*	−0.0828*	−0.1703*	−0.0993*	−0.0802*	−0.0876*	1.0000			
17 Academics	0.1793*	0.1290*	0.1008*	0.1290*	−0.0350*	−0.0174	0.1590*	−0.0432*	−0.0433*	0.0451*	−0.0154	−0.0522*	−0.0593*	−0.0207	−0.0172	0.1603*	1.0000		
18 Spinoff	0.0559*	0.1000*	0.0575	0.1000*	−0.0106	−0.0402*	0.0842*	−0.0266	−0.0364*	0.0814*	−0.0310	−0.0174	−0.0483*	−0.0301	−0.0328	0.0841*	0.0722*	1.0000	
19 No. Founders	0.0841*	0.0620	0.0427	0.0620	0.0141	−0.0086	0.1168*	−0.0078	−0.0254	0.0209	−0.0305	−0.0339*	−0.0345*	−0.0408*	−0.0274	0.1175*	0.3006*	0.0934*	1.0000

*Significant at 10%

References

Allen, R. (1983). Collective invention. *Journal of Economic Behavior and Organization, 4*, 1–24. https://doi.org/10.1016/0167-2681(83)90023-9.

Asheim, B., & Isaksen, A. (2002). Regional innovation systems: The integration of local sticky and global ubiquitous knowledge. *Journal of Technology Transfer, 27*, 77–86. https://doi.org/10.1023/A:1013100704794.

Audretsch, D. B., & Lehmann, E. E. (2005). Does the knowledge spillover theory of entrepreneurship hold for regions? *Research Policy, 34*, 1191–1202. https://doi.org/10.1016/j.respol.2005.03.012.

Balconi, M., Breschi, S., & Lissoni, F. (2004). Networks of inventors and the role of academia: An exploration of Italian patent data. *Research Policy, 33*, 127–145. https://doi.org/10.1016/S0048-7333(03)00108-2.

Breschi, S., & Lissoni, F. (2006). Cross-firm inventors and social networks: Localized knowledge spillovers revisited. *Annales d'Economie et Statistique, 79–78*. http://www.jstor.org/stable/20777575.

Brown, S. L., & Eisenhardt, K. M. (1997). The art of continuous change: Linking complexity theory and time-paced evolution in relentlessly shifting organizations. *Administrative Science Quarterly, 42*, 1–34. https://doi.org/10.2307/2393807.

Cameron, A. C., & Trivedi, P. K. (1998). *Regression analysis of count data*. Cambridge, UK: Cambridge Univ. Press. ISBN: 0 521 63567 5.

Cantner, U. (2000). Die Bedeutung von Innovationssystemen für die internationale Wettbewerbsfähigkeit. In U. Staroske, M. Wiegand-Kottisch, & K. Wohlmuth (Eds.), *Innovation als Schlüsselfaktor eines erfolgreichen Wirtschaftsstandortes*. Lit Verlag Wien-Zürich-Berlin. ISBN: 3825850188, 9783825850180.

Cantner, U., & Graf, H. (2007). Growth, development and structural change of innovator networks – The case of Jena. *Jena Economic Research Papers*, #2007-090. http://zs.thulb.uni-jena.de/servlets/MCRFileNodeServlet/jportal_derivate_00085907/wp_2007_090.pdf

Cantner, U., & Meder, A. (2007). Technological proximity and the choice of cooperation partner. *Journal of Economic Interaction and Coordination, 2*, 45–65. https://doi.org/10.1007/s11403-007-0018-y.

Cassia, L., Colombelli, A., & Pelari, S. (2009). Firm's growth: Does the innovation system matter? *Structural Change and Economic Dynamics, 20*, 211–220. https://doi.org/10.1016/j.strueco.2009.01.001.

Cooke, P., Uranga, M. G., & Etxebarria, G. (1997). Regional innovation systems: Institutional and organisational dimensions. *Research Policy, 26*, 475–492. https://doi.org/10.1016/S0048-7333(97)00025-5.

Cowan, R., Jonard, N., & Zimmermann, J. B. (2006). Evolving networks of inventors. *Journal of Evolutionary Economics, 16*, 155–174. https://doi.org/10.1007/s00191-005-0013-1.

Cox, D. R. (1972). Regression models and life-tables. *Journal of the Royal Statistical Society B, 34*(2), 187–220. http://www.jstor.org/stable/2985181.

Doloreux, D., & Parto, S. (2005). Regional innovation systems: Current discourse and unresolved issues. *Technology in Society, 27*, 133–153.

Edwards, K. L., & Gordon, T. J. (1984). Characterization of innovations introduced on the U.S. market in 1982. The Futures Group, prepared for the U.S. Small Business Administration under contract no. SBA-6050-0A-82.

Ejermo, O., & Karlsson, C. (2006). Interregional inventor networks as studied by patent coinventorships. *Research Policy, 35*, 412–430. https://doi.org/10.1016/j.respol.2006.01.001.

Gort, M., & Klepper, S. (1982). Time paths in the diffusion of product innovations. *The Economic Journal, 92*, 630–653. https://doi.org/10.2307/2232554.

Granato, N., & Farhauer, O. (2007). *Die Abgrenzung von Arbeitsmarktregionen: Gütekriterien und Maßzahlen*. Wirtschaftswissenschaftliche Dokumentation der TU Berlin, 2007/2. http://econstor.eu/bitstream/10419/36434/1/526619074.pdf

Greene, W. H. (2003). *Econometric analysis* (5th ed.). New York: Prentice Hall.

Grupp, H., & Legler, H. (2000). *Hochtechnologie 2000 – Neudefinition der Hochtechnologie für die Berichterstattung zur technologischen Leistungsfähigkeit Deutschlands*. Karlsruhe/ Hannover. http://publica.fraunhofer.de/eprints/urn_nbn_de_0011-n-36794.pdf.

Hall, L. A., & Bagchi-Senb, S. (2002). A study of R&D, innovation, and business performance in the Canadian biotechnology industry. *Technovation, 22*, 231–244. https://doi.org/10.1016/S0166-4972(01)00016-5.

Heckmann, M., & Schnabel, C, (2005). *Überleben und Beschäftigungsentwicklung neu gegründeter Betriebe*. Discussion paper no. 39. Friedrich-Alexander-Universität Erlangen-Nürnberg. http://doku.iab.de/externe/2005/k051230f14.pdf

Jaffe, A. B. (1986). Technological opportunity and spillovers of R&D: Evidence from firms' patents, profits, and market value. *The American Economic Review, 76*, 984–1001. http://www.jstor.org/stable/1816464.

Jaffe, A., Trajtenberg, M., & Henderson, R. (1993). Geographic localization of knowledge spillovers as evidenced by patent citations. *The Quarterly Journal of Economics, 108*, 577–598. http://www.jstor.org/stable/2118401.

Kaplan, E. L., & Meier, P. (1958). Nonparametric estimation from incomplete observations. *Journal of the American Statistical Association, 53*(282), 457–481. http://www.jstor.org/stable/2281868.

Kline, S. J., & Rosenberg, N. (1986). An overview of innovation. In R. Landau & N. Rosenberg (Eds.), *The positive sum strategy* (pp. 275–305). Washington, DC: National Academy Press.

Lumpkin, G. T., & Dess, G. G. (1996). Clarifying the entrepreneurial orientation construct and linking it to performance. *Academy of Management Review, 21*, 135–172. http://www.jstor.org/stable/258632.

Lundvall, B. A. (1992). National systems of innovation: An analytical framework, London: Pinter.

Nijkamp, P. (2009). Entrepreneurship, development and the spatial context. In *Studies in development economics and policy, entrepreneurship and economic development*. https://doi.org/10.1057/9780230295155_13.

OECD. (1998). *Fostering entrepreneurship*. Paris: OECD. https://doi.org/10.1787/9789264163713-en.

Penrose, E. (1959). *The theory of the growth of the firm*. New York: Wiley.

Porter, M. (1990). The competitive advantage of nations. *Harvard Business Review, 68*(2), 73–93.

Pyka, A. (1999). *Der kollektive Innovationsprozess, Eine theoretische Analyse informeller Netzwerke und absorptiver Fähigkeiten*. Berlin: Duncker und Humblot.

Schumpeter, J. (1912). *Theorie der wirtschaftlichen Entwicklung. Eine Untersuchung über Unternehmergewinn, Kapital, Kredit, Zins und den Konjunkturzyklus*. Berlin: Duncker & Humblot.

Shane, S. (2000). Prior knowledge and the discovery of entrepreneurial opportunities. *Organization Science, 11*, 448–469. https://doi.org/10.1287/orsc.11.4.448.14602.

Storey, D. J. (1994). *Understanding the small business sector*. Thomson Learning.

Thornhill, S. (2006). Knowledge, innovation and firms performance in high- and low-technology regimes. *Journal of Business Venturing, 21*, 687–703. https://doi.org/10.1016/j.jbusvent.2005.06.001.

Tsai, W., Jewell, N. P., & Wang, M. (1987). A note on the product-limit estimator under right censoring and left truncation. *Biometrica, 74*(4), 883–886. https://doi.org/10.1093/biomet/74.4.88.

von Hippel, E. (1987). Cooperation between rivals: Informal know-how trading. *Research Policy, 16*, 291–302. https://doi.org/10.1016/0048-7333(87)90015-1.

The Emergence of Parental Entrepreneurship: Some Thoughts About Family Life, Professional Careers and Entrepreneurship

Iris Kunadt

Abstract Chapter author Iris Kunadt discusses the emergence of parental entrepreneurship. She classifies parental entrepreneurship as a new socio-economic phenomenon that concerns men and women alike. The most important drivers to become a parental entrepreneur are professional opportunities while avoiding typical parent-related barriers in the job market. Another strong incentive is the improvement of the personal work-life balance. Altogether, parental entrepreneurs can have an important impact on the economy and society. The phenomenon should receive more attention from policy-makers and research.

Introduction

It was one of the best coincidences in my life when I met David at a conference in September 2003. He, then, became my PhD. supervisor. In German a very special word exists for PhD supervisor: *Doktorvater*! I like the expression – "PhD Father", because it describes the importance of the relationship between the supervisor and the doctoral student. It implies a role model function, closeness, responsibility, sympathy and support. In fact, there are some parallels between real family life and the research family.

About Turning Points in Life

The relationship between a *Doktorvater* and its doctoral student is key to success for the doctoral thesis and the future career of the student. If it is a good supporting relationship, the personal and professional career accelerates. If it is a bad one that builds on ignorance or even exploitation, it can have great destructive effects. Very

---

I. Kunadt (✉)
Founder karuu – Karriere unter Umständen, Vienna, Austria
e-mail: iris@karuu.eu; http://www.karuu.eu/

© Springer Nature Switzerland AG 2019
E. E. Lehmann, M. Keilbach (eds.), *From Industrial Organization to Entrepreneurship*, https://doi.org/10.1007/978-3-030-25237-3_31

often it is rather a coincidence whether one gets a great *Doktorvater* or not, because on the student's side a lack of knowledge and transparency exists concerning the success factors for a PhD thesis. Hence, finding the right *Doktorvater* can be a turning point in life.

When Private Issues Become Professionally Relevant

Without doubt, there are many more turning points in life that shape a professional career and these are often related to family issues. For most people, becoming a parent is one of the biggest turning points in life. Being a father or a mother can change your "world view", your personal plans and very often your professional ones. Children do influence and even change parental careers.

Why is this so? Because balancing family responsibilities and career challenges in the right way can be a quadrature of the circle. Often, the new (family) life does not fit to the old job. This is true for a couple of reasons: Long working hours, business trips or meetings in the evening hours collide with opening hours of Kindergartens and schools. Parents cannot compete in a business culture where the maxim "the one who leaves office last, is the best" dominates.

At the same time people's attitudes regarding their work-life-balance are changing! Mothers and fathers want to care for their families at an equal share. Women who are very well educated and successful in their career don't want to go back home. Men want to spent time with their families just like women do. Altogether, parents don't want to be left behind in their professional career because of family responsibilities.

Although, for historical reasons, mothers are more often in the position to step back from work, things are changing fast. Role models of the 1950s when women were responsible for family and household and men working-full time as the family's sole wage earner are outdated. The increased labor force participation of women has a strong impact on men when children are born. Women require from their spouses to share family work and to have equal professional opportunities.

How parents – mothers and fathers – react to the new challenge of integrating family and work responsibilities depends very much on the cultural and social environment and background. How long fathers or mothers opt-out of work – the full-time/part-time question – is an individual decision, but very much shaped by social norms, role models of the working environment and parental leave policies. As a consequence, one can see great differences across countries (Koslowski et al. 2016).

Since 2011 I have been living in Vienna, Austria, and have exchanged personal views and ideas with many parents who juggle with the family-work interface in their daily life. During this time, I have been diving deeply into this subject that is influenced by personal experiences, social norms, the working environment and policies.

Let's take a look at the current state of the job market for parents who want to opt-out of work for family reasons. In many countries in Europe, for example in Germany and Austria, policy schemes are in place that allow mothers and fathers to opt-out from work for a certain time to care for their young children after birth.

Dearing (2016) compares parental leave policies of 27 European countries to an ideal leave model that best supports gender equality in the division of labor. In these countries, taking parental leave, is widely accepted, but more for mothers than for fathers. However – slowly changing – more and more fathers opt-out of work for some months. These family policies are really of great help for both parents and support re-entering the job market.

Yet, there are challenges when parents go back to work. What happens when mothers go back to their old job, most often part-time, after parental leave? And when fathers ask for the same right to step back from work and spent time with their children at an equal share? Parents are confronted with an extremely inflexible "job market" that has not adapted fast enough to ease the work-family interface, especially when children are still very young. Weisshaar (2018) concludes:

> We know from existing literature that mothers are "pushed out" of work when workplaces are inflexible and intensely demanding (e.g. Stone 2008). My research shows that, after being pushed out, they are kept out and have reduced job opportunities when attempting to regain employment. When fathers opt out—challenging the normative gendered division of labor—they too face penalties, and in some contexts greater penalties than opt out mothers. (p.55)

The new attitudes towards family life of today's mothers and fathers do collide with the still traditional job market that functions well for the old role model, fathers working full-time and mothers, for the most, working part-time. Zimmerman and Clark (2016) provide a great detailed overview of women's opting-out and opting-in decisions and the evolvement over time. Research in this field has increased. Yet, with regard to the changing demographics and an increased participation of women in the workforce as well as women's career values, they call for more research on women's career breaks.

An interesting remaining question is why parents fail in a working environment where they were very successful before they became parents? What kind of penalties do women and men experience when opting-out from work for family reasons? While there is only little research on this specific question, anecdotal evidence gives a hint on what happens in this phase of parental life. In talks with parents in Austria and Germany I have often experienced that parents face career breaks when they return to their old job. Very often, women are degraded and cannot continue in the same position with the same responsibilities when returning to their old job, because they work part-time. In fact, the Austrian Wiedereinstiegsmonitor (Riesenfelder and Danzer 2017) shows that within a five-year period after reentering the job market one third of the women have changed their employer (p.58). This is interpreted as an indicator for women being pushed out of the old job. Furthermore, women have to fight against a stigma that they lack the ability to be a "good" mother and a "good" professional or a "good" scientist, for example. In fact, this stigma fires back already when women get married. Because married women might potentially get children soon, they are not considered for a job promotion.

For fathers, however, persistent social norms kick in even before they go on parental leave. Colleagues warn them that they will experience a career break. Employers tell them that they don't have to come back when they take their right for parental leave.

Needless to say, that not all companies insert penalties for their workforce who take family responsibilities seriously. Some have established a supportive culture for parents where careers even accelerate after parental leave. For example, the head of HR of A1, a huge telecom company in Austria, soon after coming back from parental leave now leads a team that works mostly part-time. At Ikea Vienna, two women share a leading position and work part-time. This has a great signaling effect! Yet, the number of enterprises with meaningful HR policies that both motivate and take advantage of the potentials that parent employees have for their businesses is still limited, and more progressive examples are needed.

Nowadays, more and more parents do not accept penalties in their job anymore, because they take family responsibilities seriously. They look for alternatives that allow them to combine both, family time and a professional career that matches their competences and professional background. For many parents, the family factor is gaining importance. Greenhaus and Powell (2012) find:

> Due to global trends such as the increased labor force participation of women, the growing presence of dual-earner couples and single parents in the labor force, and changing values regarding the importance of life balance, individuals' work decisions are being increasingly influenced by family considerations. (p.246)

And this is not just true for women. Lysova et al. (2015) show that companies should be aware of the importance of family issues for their workforce, male and female alike. There findings reveal the "influential role of family-career salience, parent role identification, and the role of spousal career support in shaping the involvement of family considerations in the managers' career sensemaking." (p.516). They find that career decisions by managers, male and female alike, are "family related (i.e. intended to foster a positive outcome for the family) rather than being purely career focused" (p.505).

When career development is important for both, partners need to find a way to integrate their private and professional life. The next career step competes with family responsibilities and the spouses career path. Companies have to keep this in mind.

In addition, the new generation is challenging established role models and social norms, on the one hand, and insists on a new role for family in society (Scholz 2018). One can observe great social changes in Europe and elsewhere. Changes in the working environment go hand in hand with great changes in social attitudes and a new importance of family life, especially when we take a look at the *Generation Z*.

Parents' Strategies and Solutions: The Emergence of Parental Entrepreneurship

When both parents want to follow their professional career and care for their family, parents face a challenge that can be described as the quadrature of the circle. And when they even experience penalties at their workplace for taking family responsibilities seriously, they start to look for alternatives and solutions.

The Emergence of Parental Entrepreneurship: Some Thoughts About Family Life... 353

One solution how to overcome this challenge is parental entrepreneurship. Looking at parental entrepreneurship tells us a lot about opportunities and, at the same time, the lack of opportunities in the working environment for parents. On the other hand, it's a story about how turning points in life like a child birth inspire and empower people to realize their dreams and to start new projects.

The experience of parenthood motivates and inspires parental entrepreneurs. The new family life becomes the initial phase for entrepreneurship and a turning point in life for their professional career. Without this new family role these people might have not even considered to become entrepreneurs. Rather than framing this as necessity entrepreneurship, one should focus on the parents' personal motivation and the desire to spent time with the family, to have a well needed flexibility, plus a window of opportunity to realize a professional dream. Focusing on the emergence of parental entrepreneurship, I like to tell a (future) story about a new work-family interface, about changing working environments and a new gender equality regarding professional careers. We can find some indications in current research for the emergence of this new phenomenon.

So far, research has been dominated by work on female entrepreneurship. Some researchers look at the performance of women's entrepreneurial businesses (for example Bögenhold and Klinglmair (2015), Andersson Joona (2018), Bullini Orlandi (2017) researches on women's self-perception as entrepreneurs and the impact of social roles on women's perception as entrepreneurs. Mari et al. (2016) focuses on women's motives to become entrepreneurs and highlights the importance of family factors. And Rønsen (2014) finds that whereas children do not hinder female self-employment, the partner's working hours have a great impact on women's entrepreneurial activities.

In fact, the search for a better balance between work and family is considered as one of the strongest motivations leading women to start and run their own business (Poggesi et al. 2016). Furthermore, women's businesses growth strategies are influenced by family factors and the family life cycle has a strong impact on female entrepreneurs. In their overview article on female entrepreneurship Poggesi et al. (2016) show that the perception of family as a factor for entrepreneurial activities is also changing in the literature.

> First, family is no longer analyzed as only a liability for women but is always considered more as an important asset (Powell and Eddleston 2013). Second, a more dynamic outlook is used to investigate the female entrepreneurs' experience; thus, by means of the life cycle model, some pioneer scholars are starting to shed light on how, using a life course perspective, the centrality of career, the sense of self-efficacy, and personal work values change over the years. As far as future research directions are concerned, time has come to better define the meaning of "family". Indeed, as Aldrich and Cliff (2003) claim, the nature of families is evolving and a broader definition of what is meant by family seems appropriate to date. (p.756)

Guo and Werner (2016) take a look at the family-entrepreneurship interface and find a lot of positive impacts of family factors on entrepreneurship, true for men and women.

Family-to-business enrichment theory suggests that family can serve as an "oxygen tank" that feeds the fire of entrepreneurship (Eddleston and Powell, 2008, 2012; Rogoff and Heck, 2003). Business can benefit from family in two ways: positive spillover (Hanson et al., 2006) and facilitation (Tompson and Werner, 1997; Wayne et al., 2007). Married individuals can transfer their positive mood or happiness from family domain to work domain; they can also transfer the skills (e.g. ability to multitask) and behavior (e.g. being supportive) nurtured from family to business (Eddleston and Powell, 2008, 2012). Carr (1996) found that marital status had a positive impact on starting a business. Similarly, multiple studies found that having young children at home had a positive impact on women starting a business (Boden, 1996, 1999; Carr, 1996; Heilman and Chen, 2003; Noseleit, 2014; Patrick et al., 2016). Past research has found a positive effect for spouse or family supportiveness on starting a business for both men and women (Hisrich and Brush, 1985; Baron, 2002; Jennings and McDougald, 2007). (p.376)

It is worth looking at the family as a system and the parents as an entrepreneurial team that can have a great supportive effect on entrepreneurship. Family can empower people to be entrepreneurial!

This is not only true in theory, but we can see a community of entrepreneurial parents emerging. The platform *Parentpreneur.com*, founded in 2015 and based in the UK, supports parents in starting up their businesses through consulting and podcasts. Parentpreneur.com shows exactly what parents with entrepreneurial intentions look for: They want to build a successful business whilst having time with the people they love. The founder, a parent and entrepreneur himself, explains why parental businesses are very successful (The Guardian, June 10 2016). First, parents' definition of success changes. Instead of aiming at a billion-dollar enterprise, goals shift to a good income, financial independence and time to spent with the family. Second, there is an age and experience factor. And third, the social circle widens when one gets in touch with other parents and these new networks should not be underestimated. Similarly, the network *mompreneur.de*, founded in 2014 based in Germany, is a network for self-employed mothers that offers exchange, consulting and visibility. The founder states that moms are probably the most underestimated resource in the economy. One can find entrepreneurial parents all over the globe. Around this, businesses and initiatives have evolved that specifically address parents and support them in growing their own business and make their career flying. Start-ups like *chairmanmom.com* and *startuppregnant.com* focus on empowering and "redefining working motherhood as an edgy, aspirational brand, not something women should feel guilt or shame over" (Peck 2018).

Some prerequisites support the emergence of parental entrepreneurship. First, the ICT revolution. Because of digital opportunities parental businesses can grow from home. Furthermore, the world wide web is a great inspiration for all parents being in the same situation. Role models help to risk and realize professional changes. Nowadays, through the web, no one is left alone and without inspiration. Second, the change of working environments. Today, people are experts and work in projects rather than in the same position with the same job profile for all their working life.

When keeping in mind the barriers in the job market with which parents are confronted, on the one hand, and the increasing importance of family issues for mothers and fathers, on the other, I am convinced that we will see more parental entrepreneurship not just by women, but by men in the future. When not just mums, but also dads are confronted with the challenge of managing the work-family interference, men will regard entrepreneurship as a very attractive alternative for the same reasons women are. Although there are probably still more mompreneurs compared to dadpreneurs, I argue that this will change in the future. Men will take family responsibilities more serious in the future as women work full time and don't want to skip their career because of a child birth. Furthermore, when partners don't want to live at two different sides of the globe because of their career opportunities, starting a business could be a very good alternative. In fact, parents and their specific professional situation can be one of the strongest drivers shaping the future of work.

Parental Entrepreneurship: The Importance of the Phenomenon

At first sight, from an economic perspective, parental entrepreneurship seems to be a niche phenomenon with very small businesses at most that were started out of the blue. However, parental entrepreneurship as an emerging phenomenon tells us a lot about changing attitudes in society regarding work-life-balance, the current state of the job market, its inflexibility and opportunities, and the lack of opportunities for parents and their professional careers respectively. Taken from this perspective, the emergence of parental entrepreneurship is an indicator for a great challenge that societies and the businesses face. The society has to say good-bye to role models that have their origin in the 1950s when moms stayed home and dads were the only breadwinners. The economy, on the other hand, is under global pressure and desperately in need of high-qualified people. With regard to demographic changes, this is even more difficult. As a consequence, working environments will have to change. The future of work will have to be more family-friendly in order to integrate not just men with family responsibilities, but also high-qualified women into the job market. This is true not just for the economy, but for science as well.

Baker and Welter (2017) strongly argue to change research perspective from a focus on entrepreneurship that is "only valuable in terms of its economic functions" (p.172) and away from a "handful of rapid-growth gazelles" (p.172) towards niche research fields that, however, are of far greater importance for the society and economy.

> As we question the dominance of an economistic paradigm, we argue instead that research in the twenty-first century should and will increasingly recognize the diversity of entrepreneurship by building on a deepened understanding of the diversity of stakeholders, of their distinctive life courses and interpretations of why entrepreneurship is worth pursuing, and of the contexts that shape and are shaped by entrepreneurial activity. Entrepreneurship plays a variety of roles for people and for the economies and societies in which they live. We view entrepreneurship as a general purpose social technology, as an organizing tool through which individuals and groups of people across many different contexts create ventures aimed at bringing some change to the world and to their own lives. (p.177)

356 I. Kunadt

There is the need for more scientific work on this. At the same time, policy-makers should take a closer look at the emergence of parental entrepreneurship since they could help to make parents' businesses more successful and growing by designing special policy programs for parental entrepreneurs, keeping in mind the contextual socioeconomic factors. Finally, parents should consider parental entrepreneurship as a chance for their professional career and family situation at the same time.

Conclusion

Parental entrepreneurship is a reinforcing power and a source of opportunity for mothers and fathers who want to reorganize their family and professional life and find new ways of work. This paper suggests that research should not be on women and "all other" entrepreneurs separately, but on parents as an entrepreneurial team, as well as the context they are acting in.

Of course, entrepreneurship is not the easiest way one can take! Entrepreneurial moms or dads face very special challenges. A paper from the vocational behavior and career development literature, for example, is dealing with parenting stress that entrepreneurs face (Semerci and Volery 2018). Hence, it would be worth further elaborating on the family factor and its impact on entrepreneurship, i.e. family as a system and a source of innovation that shapes parents acting entrepreneurially.

With this in mind, however, it is great to see very successful parental entrepreneurs all over the world! Great business ideas very often emerged out of the clash of two worlds, the private and the professional one. In fact, being a parent can set free creativity and innovation, because children teach us to change perspective and to see the world with their eyes. This experience can change our world view and the priorities of our (professional) life.

Acknowledgments When I met David and he offered me to become my *Doktorvater*, my life as a doctoral student accelerated. His continued support, his willingness to be a sparring partner with whom I could discuss my research ideas, his encouragement and belief that I would succeed was the best that can happen to a doctoral student. Even when there seemed to be a dead end and no way out he knew how to encourage a young and inexperienced doctoral student. We were talking about the great changes taking place because of globalization and the digital revolution and I remember David saying: "People don't have to work more, but smarter!" This is what parental entrepreneurs try to do.

References

Andersson Joona, P. (2018). How does motherhood affect self-employment performance? *Small Business Economics, 50*, 29–54.

Baker, T., & Welter, F. (2017). Come on out of the ghetto, please! – Building the future of entrepreneurship research. *International Journal of Entrepreneurial Behavior & Research, 23*(2), 170–184.

The Emergence of Parental Entrepreneurship: Some Thoughts About Family Life... 357

Bögenhold, D., & Klinglmair, A. (2015). Female solo self-employment – Features of gendered entrepreneurship. *International Review of Entrepreneurship Article 1504, 13*(1), 47–58.

Bullini Orlandi, L. (2017). Am I an entrepreneur? Identity struggle in the contemporary women entrepreneurship discourse. *Contemporary Economics, 11*(4), 487–498.

Dearing, H. (2016). Gender equality in the division of work: How to assess European leave policies regarding their compliance with an ideal leave model. *Journal of European Social Policy, 26*(3), 234–247.

Greenhaus, J., & Powell, G. N. (2012). The family-relatedness of work decisions: A framework and agenda for theory and research. *Journal of Vocational Behavior, 80*, 246–255.

Guo, X., & Werner, J. M. (2016). Gender, family and business: An empirical study of incorporated self-employed individuals in the US. *International Journal of Gender and Entrepreneurship, 8*(4), 373–401.

Koslowski, A., Blum, S., & Moss, P. International review of leave policies and research 2016. Available at: http://www.leavenetwork.org/lp_and_r_reports/

Lysova, E. I., Korotov, K., Khapova, S. N., & Jansen, P. G. W. (2015). The role of the spouse in managers' family-related career sensemaking. *Career Development International, 20*(5), 503–524.

Mari, M., Poggesi, S., & De Vita, L. (2016). Family embeddedness and business performance: Evidences from women-owned firms. *Management Decision, 54*(2), 476–500.

Peck, S. K. (2018, March 8). These 8 entrepreneurs are changing what it looks like to be a working parent. https://www.forbes.com/sites/sarahkathleenpeck/2018/03/08/8-entrepreneurs-changing-vision-working-parent/#3dce51dc924d

Poggesi, S., Mari, M., & De Vita, L. (2016). What's new in female entrepreneurship research? Answers from the literature. *International Entrepreneurship Management Journal, 12*, 735–764.

Riesenfelder, A., & Danzer, L. (2017). Wiedereinstiegsmonitoring. Ein Überblick über die Ergebnisse der dritten Fassung des Wiedereinstiegsmonitoring zu den Kohorten 2006 bis 2014 in Österreich und in den Bundesländern. Veröffentlicht durch die Kammer für Arbeiter und Angestellte Wien.

Rønsen, M. (2014). Children and family: A barrier or an incentive to female self-employment in Norway? *International Labour Review, 153*(2), 337–349.

Scholz, L. (2018). Zusammenleben. Über Kinder und Politik Hanser Verlag, Berlin.

Semerci, A. B., & Volery, T. (2018). Entrepreneurs as parents: The antecedents and consequence of parenting stress. *International Journal of Entrepreneurial Behavior & Research, 24*(1), 41–58.

The Guardian. (2016, June 10). How being a parent and an entrepreneur can be good for business. https://www.theguardian.com/small-business-network/2016/jun/10/parent-entrepreneur-good-for-business

Weisshaar, K. (2018). From opt out to blocked out: The challenges for labor market re-entry after family-related employment lapses. *American Sociological Review, 83*(1), 34–60.

Zimmerman, L. M., & Clark, M. A. (2016). Opting-out and opting-in: A review and agenda for future research. *Career Development International, 21*(6), 603–633.

Financial and Institutional Reforms for an Entrepreneurial Society

Mark Sanders

> We need to imagine things to make them happen. If you don't imagine, it will never happen.
> – Muhammed Yunus, Nobel Peace Prize Laureate

Abstract Mark Sanders, chapter author, discusses David's key role in the advancement in academic thought regarding the creation, promotion, and maintenance of an entrepreneurial society. Highlighting key contributions that David made to the entrepreneurship literature, Sanders details the manner in which this concept has developed. Again, David accounts for much of the inspiration that many researchers cite as they advance this academic cause.

Introduction

In May of 2018 we concluded the Financial and Institutional Reforms for an Entrepreneurial Society (FIRES) project (www.projectfires.eu) in Brussels. David Audretsch was one of the great inspirators for this project and helped us all enormously in making it a success. When he wrote his book about the rise of the Entrepreneurial Society in 2007 (Audretsch, 2007), the term (coined in 1985 by Peter Drucker) stuck with me and ultimately became the major inspiration for this project. At the time it was not immediately clear to me why this concept appealed to me, but in the end it dawned on me. There is a clear relationship between David's concept of the entrepreneurial and Popper's (1945) idea of an open society. In Popper's work the status quo in an open society should always be contestable. Freedom of speech and democracy guarantee an open exchange of ideas. And Popper argued that if we bring all ideas to the debate and weigh them on merit,

---

M. Sanders (✉)
Utrecht School of Economics (USE), Utrecht University, Utrecht, The Netherlands
e-mail: m.w.j.l.sanders@uu.nl

© Springer Nature Switzerland AG 2019
E. E. Lehmann, M. Keilbach (eds.), *From Industrial Organization to Entrepreneurship*, https://doi.org/10.1007/978-3-030-25237-3_32

progress is the result. Popper's Open Society has been the rallying cry for liberal democrats around the world to fight the big historicist, closed society ideologies of the twentieth century: Communism and Fascism. Fukuyama (1992) in his End of History and the Last Man declared victory for liberal democracy and the capitalist market economy after the fall of the Berlin Wall. But by his own admission, he cried victory too soon. Perhaps the closed society ideologies of the day had to admit defeat, but it proves more difficult to create and maintain a truly open society. As in politics, so in economics. The entrepreneurial society too, has its enemies. Many of them from within.

The idea of an entrepreneurial economy, first formulated by Schumpeter (1934), underpins the entrepreneurial society that the FIRES project aimed to promote in Europe. Schumpeter (1934) argued that entrepreneurship drives progress in capitalist societies, when everybody can propose an idea, enter a market, challenge the status quo and compete on a level playing field for the favor of the client. But once the entrepreneur becomes the incumbent, his interest no longer lies with maintaining an open system in which his position in turn, can be challenged. As we cannot trust the voters to protect democracy, so we cannot trust the entrepreneurs to maintain an entrepreneurial society. Instead it has to be entrenched in the institutions we build. Like Popper (1945), in FIRES we then asked ourselves: What institutional framework would best support a more open, entrepreneurial society in Europe?

And there are two ways to go about this. One can try to tailor very detailed reform strategies to the heterogeneous local contexts to do justice to Europe's diversity. Or one can focus on what all entrepreneurs need and propose more general and simple solutions. The FIRES-consortium has gone the former route and we developed well-received tailored strategies for three European member states. Tailoring the strategy to local conditions allows you to prioritize and address the bottlenecks in specific entrepreneurial ecosystems to achieve maximum impact for given reform efforts. In this essay, however, I will explore the latter route. And in the spirit of the quote from Yunus above, I will here present three reforms that, although perhaps unconventional, I believe will promote entrepreneurial activity, more or less across the board.

The enemies of the open society are those that stick to tradition, wish to keep people in their position and believe history has a higher purpose that men need to realize. To them, society is closed and there is no doubt or uncertainty about the way ahead. Similarly, the enemies of the entrepreneurial society are those that wish to maintain the economic status quo and suggest that in the end, we can decide the way forward by looking back using algorithms that are essentially closed. The most powerful weapon of these enemies is our collective fear of the unknown. By claiming that the institutions that history has left us with are somehow in accordance with some natural or divine order, they offer stability and predictability. But in the process, these voices close up society and the economy. And there is no room (or need) for entrepreneurship in a closed society.

Popper (1945) instead teaches us that the institutions we have in place are not God given but man-made. They are inherently flawed and should therefore be rethought and improved and in fact, according to Popper (1945), it is our responsi-

Financial and Institutional Reforms for an Entrepreneurial Society 361

bility to do so. Not only as politically active members of society, but also as scientists. Modern scholars hesitate to engage in that debate, as one cannot deduce normative statements from purely positive analysis. There is no regression model or dataset I can offer in support of the reforms I will propose below. Still I firmly believe academics should get engaged in imagining the future. To leave this only to (populist) politicians and pundits is to leave the future in the hands of the enemies of the entrepreneurial society.

What Entrepreneurs need

I will not get entangled in the academic debate on what defines "the" entrepreneur. Scholars have given many definitions and depending on the data they have available will define it as they like. For me, an entrepreneur must be defined by what she does. All agents performing the entrepreneurial function in the economy qualify. And this function is, in essence, to challenge the status quo. A firm owner or self-employed person that does not challenge the status quo, is not an entrepreneur. An employee or unemployed person who does, is. For Kirzner (1973) challenging the status quo meant acting on existing arbitrage opportunities and making a profit by bringing the economy back to short run equilibrium. Say the George Soros type. For Schumpeter (1934) it meant introducing new products, services and methods to capture the profits of incumbent firms or even create entirely new markets, upsetting short run equilibrium. Think of Steve Jobs. Whatever your definition of choice, it is clear that for a person or firm to challenge the status quo, she needs access to resources that often the beneficiaries of that status quo will seek to keep from their challengers. Wherever they succeed in doing so, the entrepreneurial society is dead or dying. In this essay I will therefore zoom in on what I consider three key resources to any entrepreneurial venture: Finance, Labor and Knowledge. The access to these key resources in society is governed by institutions. And I believe these institutions should be reformed to promote entrepreneurial activity.

Entrepreneurs need:

- a secure payment system that allows you to transact, store value and smooth consumption;
- an efficient financial system that allocates sufficient (equity) capital to high-risk experimental early stage activity and allows proven concepts to scale to global markets rapidly;
- a form of social protection that ensures that the basic needs of life for everybody at some minimum level;
- a redistribution system that closes the system by stimulating the creation of wealth but also provides mechanisms to prevent its unproductive accumulation and instead promotes its productive reconstitution:

- that starts with universal access to education and health care;
- culminates in an academic environment that fosters excellent basic research and broad access to knowledge;
- and is completed with an intellectual property system that rewards individuals for the fruits of their effort and creativity but does not exclude others from building on that knowledge or challenging it.

With these basics firmly in place, entrepreneurial talents in any specific cultural context will have every opportunity to succeed. And then I have every confidence that they will, giving shape to a more prosperous and Open, Entrepreneurial Society.

Imagine better finance...

For finance I propose a transition to a system of full reserve banking or alternatively a (return to a) fully publicly backed system of payment and savings services to individuals and companies using modern technology. This will take deposits and transaction money off private banks' balance sheets, effectively decreasing their leverage. More equity in banks, required by both regulation and the market, will then increase their risk absorbing capacity and justifies deregulating them on the asset side of the balance sheet. This would allow banks to return to a role of intermediation (borrow to lend out, originate to hold) with more equity and hence shareholders' skin in the game. Good banks will thrive and attract investors. Bad banks go bust without endangering the system or requiring taxpayer bailouts. This separation of functions will allow and incentivize banks to take more of the right risks, financing real, innovative economic activity, not toxic mortgage backed securities, exotic derivatives and boring government debt.

For the long run one might consider reforming the current monetary system, that has commercial, private banks issue debt obligations serving as the public medium of exchange. As long as private debt circulates as money in society, that debt on the liability side of the banks' balance sheets is subsidized. Banks can thus finance their assets too cheap. To tackle the ensuing moral hazard problem, regulators are forced to monitor and interfere heavily in the capital allocation decisions banks make on the asset side of their balance sheet. And this regulation, by prioritizing security and limiting downside risk, works against a more Entrepreneurial Society. There are many ways in which such a transition can be shaped (Lainà 2015) and the debate in the academic literature is still ongoing (Fontana and Sawyer 2016; Dyson et al. 2016). The FIRES-project did not research this option in great detail, but the appealing feature of such a system is that the money in circulation again becomes a claim on the central bank, whereas commercial banks only intermediate the savings they attract before they can be invested. In the modern economy, however, banks will also be competing against alternative intermediation mechanisms. To survive that competition, banks will have to return to building long term relationships in specialised niches. A more diverse landscape of such smaller, better capitalized and more specialized banks is likely to cater better to the heterogeneous needs of the

Entrepreneurial Society (DeYoung et al. 2015). At the same time as a system it is more resilient to exteral and internal financial shocks. More diversity in the banking sector should then be coupled with more diversity in the financial system at large.

By clearly separating public from private functions, I believe banks can take a bigger role in financing new ventures and SMEs, as they have in the past. The financial crisis has shown the devastating effects of the toxic mix of public guarantees, failing regulation and strong private profit motives. By requiring more equity in banking and investing, we can responsibly allow traditional financial intermediaries to take on more risk and uncertainty, without having to fear they will offload such risks onto tax payers in case things turn bad. When the core of our financial system has been reformed in that way, this will also create a level playing field for the many innovative FinTech ideas. Because some offer innovative solutions in the public infrastructure of payments and savings, whereas others complement the more traditional forms of intermediation, tapping and providing more and more diverse sources and forms of direct and indirect, debt and equity finance. Currently the regulation and supervision of our financial system drives us to a monoculture that fails to serve the entrepreneurial society (Haldane and May 2011; Polzin et al. 2017). More diversity is key. Separating the public infrastructure from private risk taking in intermediation is the way forward for the Entrepreneurial Society in a bank based European financial landscape.

Imagine more secure livelihoods...

For all the heterogeneity that exists among people and countries, there are some things all of us need secured before any other projects can be considered. In the age of abundance most Western societies find themselves in, we can collectively afford these basics many times over. Still, we have organized our labor markets in accordance with Genesis 3:19: "By the sweat of thy brow shalt thou eat". For labor markets a system of universal basic income (UBI) or negative income taxes (NIT) could ensure that all legal residents attain a minimum standard of living that is unconditional. That standard of living can be agreed upon in real terms. That is, it needs to be cost of living adjusted and indexed. A NIT system ensures all individuals above 18 can be sure their basic needs: Health insurance, a decent home, clothes and food, are met. If you earn less than the amount needed to acquire such basics, the tax you pay on that low income should be a negative amount. In other words: the tax authorities pay out a supplement. The effective marginal tax rate on earnings should then be set such that when you earn the minimum wage, the net tax you pay is 0. Above that you start paying positive taxes.

An initiative to put a universal basic income on the European agenda was supported by over 200.000 citizens and in a briefing to the European Parliament support among EU-citizens was reported to be 60+%. Still, the evidence base to support such a radical reform is (naturally) thin. The FIRES-consortium discussed the proposal only considering the proposed transition to a more Entrepreneurial Society. We agree with some critics (e.g. Kay 2017) that the basic income is unlikely to deliver on all the promises its most ardent supporters make. As Kay (2017) puts it: "Either the level of basic income is unacceptably low, or the cost of providing it is unacceptably high". To finance such a scheme the tax burden should be shifted from labor to consumption. This has many additional advantages. To drive the economy in the right direction on energy transition and more circular economy we should consider carbon, energy and virgin resource taxes in addition to an across the board increase in value added taxation. Such taxes do not distort the level playing field among entrepreneurs and drives them to compete on addressing the important challenges the world faces on energy, decarbonization and reducing its dependencies and ecological footprint. In fact, it may well give the many entrepreneurs dying to show the world their innovative solutions to these global challenges the edge they need to compete with the ecologically outdated industrial heritage of the twentieth century. Note that an NIT-system can be tailored to local conditions by setting the parameters of the system to reflect local cultural attitudes and costs of living. What people consider the social minimum and a fair tax schedule differs from place to place. What is common to all around the world is that challenging the status quo should not imply you risk falling below that minimum.

A UBI or NIT scheme, however low, would eliminate (some) necessity entrepreneurship (and employment) and release talent to engage in more fulfilling lifestyle or more productive opportunity driven entrepreneurship. It is an empirical fact that people are willing, all else equal and on average, to accept much lower incomes when self-employed and receiving an inheritance increases the probability of being self-employed substantially (Blanchflower and Oswald 1998). Currently this is partially explained by the fact that self-employed do and employed workers do not compete on wage and labor conditions. Self-employed are therefore forced to accept lower pay and higher risk. But their willingness to do so also suggests that formal employment carries a penalty. Putting a floor in the income distribution for all will then affect formal employment more than it does entrepreneurship. And as an unconditional basic income reduces income volatility and risks that especially more marginal entrepreneurs face, the predicted effect on entrepreneurial activity would be positive (Nooteboom 1987). Scarce empirical evidence on win-for-life lottery winners in Belgium (Peeters and Marx 2006) has shown that even substantial levels of basic income do not significantly affect people's propensity to become entrepreneurs themselves. But the positive effect may well be indirect. Evidence on how this would affect the willingness of employees to join less secure jobs in start-up firms is absent and well-designed field experiments should urgently fill this gap.

The main benefit of a basic income scheme would be to reduce the need to reform current, highly conditional and complex welfare state arrangements to create access for the hard to classify self-employed and freelance workers that are making up a growing share of the modern labor force. When some basic level for a decent living is taken care of as a collective responsibility, unemployment benefits, disability and illness insurance and pension systems go from being essential to being nice-to-have and can arguably be left (more) to private initiative or self-insurance. With some basic income to fall back on, even a(n income) risk averse entrepreneur may not need expensive insurance for temporary involuntary unemployment or illness and compete on merit rather than risk appetite.

Financial and Institutional Reforms for an Entrepreneurial Society 365

Imagine smarter IPR...

For knowledge institutions I propose we reform the system of intellectual property rights protection. The problem with the current system is that legal ownership to knowledge is awarded exclusively to the creator of the knowledge. This ignores the crucial importance of actually making the knowledge useful in practice. That is, it denies the importance of entrepreneurship and favors the inventor over the innovator. That is not a problem if inventors also innovate. But the modern innovation model rarely operates in that way. From entrepreneurship research we know that the best, most creative inventors are rarely the best and most successful entrepreneurs. A few super-entrepreneurs make the headlines and catch the spotlight. But most successful innovation is a team effort where many people play small but essential parts. In addition, also established firms increasingly choose to spin out and repurchase to develop risky projects at arms length and off the mother company balance sheet. Trying to incentivize knowledge creation by first creating a temporary monopoly and then having the rents from that monopoly reward the inventor fits the "geek tinkering in the garage" model of innovation, but is a roundabout and inefficient way to try and internalize the positive externalities of knowledge creation. Moreover, by entitling the knowledge owner to claim realized profits from commercial products that embody (part of) his knowledge ex post, we put a risk on entrepreneurship and commercialization that should not be there. Direct subsidization of knowledge creation combined with an open source patent that needs to be cited but need not be bought, would come closest to truly internalizing the positive externalities at hand. The marginal social costs of using knowledge that already exists are zero. Efficient allocation then requires that such knowledge is used up to the point where private marginal benefits are zero. Hence the use of knowledge should be priced at 0. It fits the European model to then compensate the knowledge creators with a decent reward from public sources. We do this for arts, where the benefits are much harder to quantify and our largely public universities are perfectly positioned to take on that role. Alternatively, if we want the users/beneficiaries of the knowledge and not the general public to pay for the creation of the knowledge, intellectual property should be priced and marketed as any other good. That is, the creator of the knowledge should be required to not only disclose the knowledge (so others can build on it), but also the price he/she charges for the use of that knowledge ex ante. And maintaining the monopoly rights to the use of some piece of knowledge should be made costly in proportion to the price that is charged. Then if an inventor wants to price a patent or license high, the fee he pays for getting that right awarded should also be high. That way inventors can charge a price that covers their costs and includes a reasonable and healthy return on their investment, whereas potential users (entrepreneurs) can evaluate if the knowledge offers value for money. They then remain full and complete residual claimant to the profits of their venture. As they should be.

With patent registration and holding fees depending on this pre-set licence fee, inventors can charge a fair reward to recover the costs of generating knowledge, while innovators need not worry about unexpected claims on their profits. After paying a fair price for the invention, the residual rents to innovation accrue to the entrepreneur for coming up with a commercial application of the idea. Taking a more extreme position on the issue, some have argued that IPR is simply not the right tool to mobilize resources for knowledge generation and allocation in a knowledge intensive, entrepreneurial economy. They have gone as far as to suggest we abandon the system of patent protection and intellectual property altogether (e.g. Boldrin and Levine 2013; Lobel 2013), as it simply fails to deliver the desired results. Patent protection historically emerged in Medieval Italy and only gradually evolved into the instrument for incentivizing knowledge creation for commercial purposes it is (perceived to be) today. Consequently: "What one is faced with is the mixture or intended and unintended consequences of an undirected historical process on which the varied interests of different parties (some widely separated in time and space) have left an enduring mark." (David 1993, p. 21). Boldrin and Levine (2013) present empirical evidence to support their case, showing strong patent protection is not promoting innovation. In the absence of patents, knowledge generation could alternatively be funded through patronage or procurement (David 1993) and commercialization would be motivated by profit but not by legally enforceable monopoly rents. Such drastic reforms, however, would involve backing out of complex and encompassing treaties and implies withdrawing for example from the WTO altogether. Obviously, such drastic steps would cause large collateral damage. Moreover, due to historical co-evolution and complementarities among interacting institutions, radical institutional reform inevitably spills over in other domains. Patents, and IPR in general are for example also deemed important for entrepreneurs as signals of quality and potential financiers look for IPR in new ventures (e.g. Hsu and Ziedonis 2008) as patents serve as a proxy for innovativeness, quality and give some collateral, where uncertainty reigns. The patent registry serves as a repository of knowledge that tracks the origin of ideas and can be consulted for commercial and policy purposes. And finally, the role of and therefore total abolishment of patent protection would work out very differently in different sectors. In some there is no problem achieving the same results with trade secrets (e.g. software), whereas in others (e.g. medicines), mandatory and highly uncertain certification procedures make it difficult to conceive of efficient alternatives. Given the legal complexities and institutional complementarities I propose a cautious approach of experiments that retain the system's benefits while increasing the free flow of knowledge because the monopoly rents that patent holders can now extract ex post reduce the ex ante private incentives to commercialize and serve as a tax on consumers (Acs and Sanders 2012). Because everybody, not only the buyers of the patented good or service, benefits from the knowledge spillovers that widely diffused knowledge generates (Acs et al. 2012; Braunerhjelm et al. 2010), it is more efficient to incentivize and finance knowledge generation (and documentation) out of general tax revenue. And I would agree with Verspagen (2007) that policy makers in this area must be entrepreneurs themselves. Ready to implement reforms in this general direction, take the risk of failure and learn from their mistakes when that happens.

…it's easy if you try

With the above reforms, entrepreneurs have access to a reliable payment system, fairly priced capital, relevant knowledge at known costs, a skilled labor force and are ensured of the basics in life. That provides a firm foundation for new ventures, allowing them to take economic risks by challenging the status quo in capitalist markets. In open market-capitalism such challenges will then be judged in globalizing markets in fair and open competition. Some will hit the jackpot, many more will fail. But that is how an economy at the global frontier progresses. If entrepreneurs create value to their (global) customers, they will thrive and pay a fair share of their gains to the knowledge creators that enabled them (but who did not do the hard work of finding and bringing the knowledge to the markets at their own risk). If the venture fails, they can easily rebound and try something else without creating large negative externalities on their employees and financiers. Financiers, in turn, are true intermediaries that will charge a fair price for the risks their investees take. And such intermediation may come from traditional banking, innovative forms of finance, including traditional US style venture capital and private equity as well as more novel platform based intermediation methods. Employees are ensured the basic minimum level and can sort into risky, early stage ventures or more established mature employers according to risk preferences and appetites while entrepreneurs and their employees need not fear destitution or stigma from business failure.

The proposed reforms above are particularly suited for European countries. In Europe's bank based financial systems and deeply entrenched social-democratic traditions of well developed welfare states, these reform respect the need and desire to provide for a basic quality of life to all while keeping open the opportunity to rise above the mean. Europe owes it to its history and traditions to try and combine social justice and inclusive security with fair and open competition that rewards real value creation and true merit.

I congratulate David on his 65th birthday and wish he sees his vision realized. To do so we, academics, need to help policy makers to align our institutions across the board to entrench contestability and defeat the enemies of the Entrepreneurial Society in the twenty-first century.

References

Acs, Z. J., & Sanders, M. W. J. L. (2012). Patents, knowledge spillovers, and entrepreneurship. *Small Business Economics, 39*(4), 801–817.

Acs, Z. J., Audretsch, D. B., Braunerhjelm, P., & Carlsson, B. (2012). Growth and entrepreneurship. *Small Business Economics, 39*(2), 289–300.

Audretsch, D. B. (2007). *The entrepreneurial society*. Oxford: Oxford University Press.

Blanchflower, D. G., & Oswald, A. J. (1998). What makes an entrepreneur? *Journal of Labor Economics, 16*(1), 26–60.

Boldrin, M., & Levine, D. K. (2013). The case against patents. *Journal of Economic Perspectives, 27*(1), 3–22.

Braunerhjelm, P., Acs, Z. J., Audretsch, D. B., & Carlsson, B. (2010). The missing link: Knowledge diffusion and entrepreneurship in endogenous growth. *Small Business Economics, 34*(2), 105–125.

David, P. A. (1993). Intellectual property institutions and the panda's thumb: Patents, copyrights, and trade secrets in economic theory and history. National Academy.

DeYoung, R., Gron, A., Torna, G., & Winton, A. (2015). Risk overhang and loan portfolio decisions: Small business loan supply before and during the financial crisis. *The Journal of Finance, 70*(6), 2451–2488.

Drucker, P. F. (1985). The entrepreneurial society. *Industry Week, 224*(4), 52–55.

Dyson, B., Hodgson, G., & van Lerven, F. (2016). A response to critiques of 'full reserve banking'. *Cambridge Journal of Economics, 40*(5), 1351–1361.

Fontana, G., & Sawyer, M. (2016). Full reserve banking: More 'cranks' than 'brave heretics'. *Cambridge Journal of Economics, 40*(5), 1333–1350.

Fukuyama, F. (1992). *The end of history and the last man*. New York: Free Press.

Haldane, A. G., & May, R. M. (2011). Systemic risk in banking ecosystems. *Nature, 469*(7330), 351–355.

Hsu, D. and R. Ziedonis (2008), Patents as quality signals for entrepreneurial ventures, Academy of Management Best Paper Proceedings, 1, 6, 2008.

Kay, J. (2017). The basics of basic income. *Intereconomics, 52*(2), 69–74.

Kirzner, I. M. (1973). *Competition and entrepreneurship*. Chicago: Chicago University Press.

Lainà, P. (2015). Proposals for full-reserve banking: A historical survey from David Ricardo to Martin wolf. *Economic Thought, 4*(2), 1–19.

Lobel, O. (2013). *Talent wants to be free: Why we should learn to love leaks, raids, and free riding*. New Haven: Yale University Press.

Nooteboom, B. (1987). Basic income as a basis for small business. *International Small Business Journal, 5*(3), 10–18.

Peeters, H., & Marx, A. (2006). Lottery games as a tool for empirical basic income research. *Basic Income Studies, 1*(2), 1.

Polzin, F., Sanders, M., & Täube, F. (2017). A diverse and resilient financial system for investments in the energy transition. *Current Opinion in Environmental Sustainability, 28*, 24–32.

Popper, K. R. (1945). *The open society and its enemies. Vol. I and II*. New York: Routledge Classics.

Schumpeter, J. A. (1934). *The theory of economic development: An inquiry into profits, capital, credit, interest and the business cycle*. Cambridge: Harvard University Press.

Verspagen, B. (2007). University research, intellectual property rights and European innovation systems. In M. McAleer & L. Oxley (Eds.), *Economic and legal issues in intellectual property*. London: Blackwell Publishers.

Entrepreneurship in Public Policy Education: The Willy Brandt School as a Case

Heike M. Grimm

Abstract This contribution discusses entrepreneurship as an important asset and feature of policy making and education. Attention is drawn to the increasing role of entrepreneurship in public policy education for the training of innovative professionals in public and non-profit organizations. The paper highlights the rising prominence of policy entrepreneurship and social entrepreneurship that have taken on particular importance for the curriculum of the first Master of PublicPolicy program, which has been offered at a public university in Germany since 2002. The Willy Brandt School of Public Policy at the University of Erfurt is selected as a case to describe the shift from a traditional public policy program to integrating new disciplines beyond just political, social, and administrative sciences, including an emphasis on entrepreneurship education. This paper is dedicated to David B. Audretsch whose unique, innovative, transformative, multidisciplinary approach to entrepreneurship research has had a very significant impact not only on academia, but also on public policy making and teaching, influencing, among others, the program development of the Brandt School.

Introduction

Reflecting on the last two decades of extraordinary global changes worldwide, we face pressing new challenges in policy making, which also affect the content and methods of teaching in the fields of public policy and political sciences. Due to new political parameters, threats to liberal democracies, the renaissance of populist parties and actors, financial crises, increased migration, climate changes, digitalization, and many more issues, the demand for interdisciplinary, transformative, application-oriented teaching has increased tremendously within a short time frame, generating the need for applying new technologies in the classroom, as well as modern pedagogical insights. This paper describes the transformations of a public policy

---

H. M. Grimm (✉)
Willy Brandt School of Public Policy, University of Erfurt, Erfurt, Germany
e-mail: heike.grimm@uni-erfurt.de

© Springer Nature Switzerland AG 2019
E. E. Lehmann, M. Keilbach (eds.), *From Industrial Organization to Entrepreneurship*, https://doi.org/10.1007/978-3-030-25237-3_33

program which started-off in 2002 as the first graduate program of its kind in Germany. It looks specifically at the shift from a traditional public policy program incorporating methodologies, theories, and thoughts of the Anglo-American, but also continental Western European, model to integrating new disciplines beyond political, social, and administrative realities that have not been regarded as classic in the context of public policy education (Lasswell 1951, 1956). Attention is drawn to the importance of entrepreneurship as an essential asset and feature of innovative public policy making and entrepreneurship education, with the goal of promoting policy entrepreneurship, as well as the development and implementation of new solutions for local-global problems (Hynes 1996; Lackeus 2015; Volkmann and Audretsch 2017). The paper aims at filling a research gap, because knowledge about the interrelationships between entrepreneurship and public administrations, on one hand, and policy makers and entrepreneurs, on the other, is still rare, though essential to better understand the key challenges of societies and to design innovative policies for sustainable and inclusive development.

The classic term entrepreneurship has predominantly been used in an economic sense, referring to start-up activities in the private sector, and, therefore, has rarely been of any importance for public policy programs at higher educational institutions in the twentieth century. Meanwhile, the term has been defined in different ways across disciplines and applied to the public, social, and non-profit sectors. Audretsch et al. (2015) underline that constricting the field and meaning of entrepreneurship may be the wrong approach for future research and identify an emerging, eclectic view of entrepreneurship across disciplines. Following these thoughts, this paper will distinguish between economic, social, and policy entrepreneurship, which have taken on particular importance for the curriculum of the Master of Public Policy program (MPP) of the Willy Brandt School of Public Policy (Brandt School) at the University of Erfurt in Germany in recent years.

Although the activities of policy entrepreneurs have received some attention in several studies (Bernie and Hafsi 2007; Roberts and King 1996, 1998), the concept of policy entrepreneurship is currently only vaguely defined and, therefore, hardly integrated within analyses of change, problem solving, development, and, above all, education (Grimm 2019a). Silander (2016) points out that entrepreneurship research has focused on economic entrepreneurs, but is lacking in research on entrepreneurial activity in the public and political sector, which would contribute to the definition and theoretical grounding of policy entrepreneurship. To facilitate more integration of the concept, this paper offers a brief theoretical discussion of the typological classification of policy entrepreneurship with the goal of answering the question: Why should this concept be taken into consideration in a public policy program? In that context, what training do policy entrepreneurs need to promote change and innovation in public sector as well as non-profit organizations?

These questions are related to a research agenda presented by Audretsch et al. (2015, p. 709) who foresee "(...) the development of a dynamic theory of entrepreneurship to apply to decision making and behavior within the context of the public sector". This paper presents a case study for further investigating what educational program and curriculum is suitable for future policy entrepreneurs. It is hypothesized that young academics with multifaceted learning experiences have a high potential for policy and institutional entrepreneurship but also for social entrepreneurship to promote development at various levels in bureaucracies and societies.

The interest in entrepreneurship education has increased significantly in recent years (Volkmann and Audretsch 2017). Young people and academics see the need to learn and adopt entrepreneurial skills and develop creative mindsets to cope with challenges, design new policies and solutions, and promote transformations in the public sector. Future policy entrepreneurs have the potential to support attitudes and activities for developing and implementing creative, innovative ideas, and solutions for overcoming social and institutional challenges. Public entrepreneurs are motivated by diverse interests, including improving services to their own communities and increasing the level and quality of public goods – e.g. peace, safety, health etc. – available to citizens (Ostrom 2005; Mintrom and Norman 2009). Furthermore, economic and social entrepreneurship are regarded as alternatives to complement or even substitute traditional tools of development policy making, and as a trigger for promoting self-initiated, bottom-up development in lower and less developed countries (Koltai and Muspratt 2017).

Therefore, I hypothesize that it is crucial for future professionals in public bureaucracies to be familiar with the concepts of entrepreneurship and the tools and techniques to develop entrepreneurial ideas and innovations for sustainable growth. This paper will explain why the importance of incorporating entrepreneurship in the core curriculum of a public policy program has increased. In section "Entrepreneurship as a Core Element of a Public Policy Curriculum", the concept of entrepreneurship will be explained with a conceptual differentiation between social and policy entrepreneurship, because both concepts play a crucial role for a public policy program. In section "Profile of the Willy Brandt School of Public Policy at the University of Erfurt", the profile of the Brandt School will be presented. In the following, the concept of entrepreneurship education at the Brandt School will be introduced. The last Section wraps up the arguments why entrepreneurship is crucial for public policy education and provides an outlook.

Entrepreneurship as a Core Element of a Public Policy Curriculum

The reasons for the emerging role of entrepreneurship in a public policy program are manifold. First, entrepreneurship is important at the individual level with regard to certain skills and attitudes, including creativity and innovativeness, and a specific mindset characterized by a positive understanding of risk, action, and failure (Schumpeter 1934, 2008; Drucker 1985; Shane and Venkataraman 2000). Entrepreneurs perceive opportunities and exploit them. They contribute to transformations at all levels and contribute not only to economic, but also social and institutional development. The term entrepreneurship refers to professional independence, on one hand, and to the "discovery and exploitation of profitable opportunities" (Shane and Venkataraman 2000, p. 217), on the other. The many definitions of the term highlight very significant aspects, including personality aspects, such as innovativeness, the willingness to take risks, the urge for action, the creative development of ideas and entrepreneurial implementation; furthermore, the functions and actions of entrepreneurial individuals, firms, or other organizations, traits and behaviors. Audretsch et al. (2015, p. 708) provide an extensive overview of the literature referring to variety of meanings of entrepreneurship and distinguish between status, behavior, and performance as main elements of an eclectic paradigm of entrepreneurship.

From the 1980s onwards, researchers put strong emphasis on investigating the relationship between businesses and economic growth in highly industrialized countries, as well as in this context, the role of size (small, medium, or big) and status (new or old) of firms with reference to their role in creating new jobs, promoting innovation, and economic development (Birch 1981). David Audretsch was one of the prominent scholars emphasizing the role of small companies for development, not only from an economic, but also a more comprehensive point of view. When I started writing my doctoral thesis about "Existenzgründungen in den neuen Bundesländern" (start-ups in the new German states) at the beginning of the 1990s, the Discussion Papers written by David Audretsch during his research period at the Wissenschaftszentrum Berlin (WZB) were a major source of inspiration. At that time, hardly any policies were developed for small firms in Germany, policy makers frequently spoke about the importance of the Mittelstand, but a strong policy to support the development of so-called small and medium-sized companies was rather lacking. David Audretsch further pursued his research by highlighting the importance of new firms and start-ups for regional development from the early 1990s onwards, emphasizing that entrepreneurship contributes to economic development, which is reflected by an abundant amount of literature and research about the role of new businesses for development and job creation (Audretsch et al. 2005b; Audretsch et al. 2015; GEM 2017).

The geographic focus of entrepreneurship research shifted slowly from industrialized countries to places in transition (such as the new German states) and to lower developed countries, envinced by the increasing interest of scholars, students and policy makers (Audretsch et al. 2005a; Mwasalwiba 2010). The emergence of entrepreneurship education and programs in developing countries and emerging markets is a recent consequence, which has also influenced the program development of the Brandt School in Erfurt, due to the high number of students from the Global South.

From a management perspective, Peter Drucker, economist and pioneer of a modern management theory, specified that entrepreneurs do not only act in private-sector organizations and start-ups, but also in public and non-profit organizations. Drucker focused his perspective on social organizations, such as schools, hospitals, churches, theatres, and others, and transferred instruments of innovative management to the third sector with the mission to improve inefficient administration (Drucker 1985). He associated entrepreneurship with the creation and implementation of new forms of management. In line with Schumpeter, he stressed that innovation and creativity are definitely correlated with entrepreneurship and a precondition for professionally managing public and non-profit organizations. He underlined that entrepreneurship is a mindset that produces certain kinds of behavior. These include grasping opportunities, transferring and implementing new ideas, and the ability to change: "(...) the entrepreneur always searches for change, responds to it, and exploits it as an opportunity" (Drucker 1985, p. 28).

The urge for individual creativity and innovativeness is mainly determined by the inner motivation of an actor such, for example, his or her desire for self-realization and for improving the personal status quo (Shane and Venkataraman 2000, p. 138), but also by the micro- and macro-social environment which explains the growing focus on entrepreneurship ecosystems in the last years (Audretsch and Belitski 2016; O'Connor et al. 2018; Cohen 2006). David Audretsch emphasized already in the early 1990s that new firms play a crucial role for the strategic management of places and presented recommendations to promote entrepreneurial activity (Audretsch et al. 2005a, Audretsch 2015).

All these factors contributed to the rising importance of entrepreneurship as a specialization in academic study programs. Before specifying features and forms of entrepreneurship education and discussing them in the context of the classroom experience, I will first explain the terms policy entrepreneurship and social entrepreneurship more thoroughly.

Policy Entrepreneurship

Entrepreneurs contribute not only to economic progress, but also overall societal change through entrepreneurial activity. Policy entrepreneurs focus on political change and learning processes (Grimm 2019a). Such processes are driven by a type of actor who develops innovative and creative ideas for the solution of socio-political challenges, as well as tools and instruments to transfer and implement them in order to promote political and policy change. Policy entrepreneurs are frequently, in the Schumpeterian sense, visionaries who think the unthinkable (*Undenkbares denken*) and set in motion rather unimaginable ideas and political processes by mobilizing the public, forming new coalitions, and accepting, if necessary, considerable costs in the form of time or money to reach their mission (Mintrom and Norman 2009). "Policy entrepreneurs represent actors that are capable of bringing about the implementation of their political ideas, even if material distribution conflicts have gained the upper hand in the political process and lead to the organization of powerful oppositional interests" (Kingdon 1995, p. 5). The policy entrepreneur overcomes political stagnation and inertia caused by short-term, instrumentally rational, and even egoistic thinking of political actors who seek to maximize their own benefit in the political process. Consequently, the policy entrepreneur does not act according to routine (maximizing short-term interests), which would lead to political stagnation. He (or she) acts as a promoter of political change processes. He enters new paths, recognizes new political possibilities (windows of opportunities), and is not afraid of any resistance in the implementation of innovative ideas. "In public policy a new technology, a new service, a new administrative process or procedure might be examples of such innovation" (Roberts and King 1996, p. 5). Osborne and Gaebler (1993) provide a wealth of examples on how it is possible for policy entrepreneurs to overcome bureaucratic red tape, promote civil society involvement, and convince government actors to pursue innovative actions. The result is the further development of an efficient and effective bureaucracy and the promotion of an innovative civil society that is subject to constant change and must adjust to a rapidly changing, globalized knowledge economy.

Link and Link (2007) regard government as entrepreneurial and dynamic in terms of the ability to act in new and innovative ways, and its willingness to undertake policy actions that have uncertain outcomes. They discuss various policy actions and programs (such as the U.S. Small Business Innovation Program) that contributed successfully to development.

In their research on the role of policy entrepreneurs in political change processes, Roberts and King (1998, p. 117) have created a typology of their activities, which can be divided into four categories: Creative/intellectual activities (such as developing and disseminating new policy ideas), strategic activities (such as formulating visions and developing political strategies and action plans), mobilization activities (such as building up lobby groups and media support and obtaining support from politicians), and administrative/evaluative activities (such as program evaluation).

Policy and social entrepreneurship often go hand in hand. One example is Wilhelm von Humboldt, who aligned the innovative ability of a policy and social entrepreneur and made a revolutionary contribution to reforming the education system in Germany (Grimm 2010, p. 446; Audretsch 2017).

Social Entrepreneurship

Social entrepreneurship describes an old phenomenon with a new label (Grimm 2010, p. 449ff). The reasons for the renaissance in social entrepreneurship – in the broadest sense defined as social engagement or involvement – are diverse. Certainly, a permanent and lasting disappointment with governmental and philanthropic efforts that had only moderate or no success in decreasing socio-economic drawbacks played a crucial role. New, innovative ideas and initiatives for the solution of social and other problems were required. A growing number of actors accepted the challenge of developing and implementing creative solutions for urgent problems.

From the Brandt School's perspective, the interest in social entrepreneurship increased significantly over the last few years. The reason is predominantly a dissatisfaction and exhaustion with traditional approaches to development in so-called developing countries that have not been successful after many years of governmental involvement, driven by both national and external actors. The desire to learn more about new tools, strategies, and approaches to promote bottom-up development is high, which explains the rising interest in social entrepreneurship as an alternative to traditional development policy making. For implementing new social entrepreneurial ideas and policies, policy entrepreneurship as an attitude and mindset is needed. Both forms of entrepreneurship (policy and social) go hand in hand in practice when it comes to policy change. But what makes social entrepreneurship different from other forms of entrepreneurship?

"Social entrepreneurs are one species in the genus entrepreneur. They are entrepreneurs with a social mission", stressed J. Gregory Dees in his treatise, which is still groundbreaking for research in this field (2001, p. 2). The clear, explicit formulation of a social mission as the purpose of action is central for social entrepreneurs. The primary goal of the social entrepreneur is not the generation of profits or prosperity, but rather the fulfillment of a social mission. Conversely, this does not mean that the social entrepreneur considers the generating of income to be a *quantité négligeable*. On the contrary, the social entrepreneur differs fundamentally from the traditional, purely altruistically-acting philanthropist because the generating of income for the financial security of a socially motivated project is recognized as an important means to an end. The financial security of his or her project may be critical for the success of a social entrepreneur who is interested in the sustainable fulfillment of his mission. "In this perspective, social entrepreneurs have used business skills and knowledge to create enterprises that accomplish social purposes in addition to being commercially viable" (Emerson and Twersky 1996).

It should be emphasized that social entrepreneurship is not synonymous with philanthropy. It is characterized by all kinds of activities and is, above all, replacing the antiquated image of selfless altruists as the main social actor with an excellently organized, assertive entrepreneurial type: "It combines the passion of a social mission with an image of business-like discipline, innovation, and determination commonly associated with, for instance, the high-tech pioneers of Silicon Valley" (Dees 2001, p. 1).

Dees provided an idealized characterization of the social entrepreneur (Dees 2001, p. 4). He emphasized that the specific mission, to create and primarily maintain social (and not individualistic or private) values, is the decisive criterion for social entrepreneurship. The social entrepreneur is – like Schumpeter's entrepreneur – a reformer and innovator accomplishing something revolutionary in the social sector. "Making a profit, creating wealth, or serving the desires of customers may be part of the model, but these are means to a social end, not the end of itself" (Dees 2001). The social entrepreneur pursues his mission sustainably and systematically. Reaching a goal has a long-term perspective.

Furthermore, social entrepreneurs identify and seize innovative ideas and opportunities in order to achieving a social mission. The social entrepreneur is driven by a vision that there is a feasible solution for a certain socio-societal problem. Due to the complexity of socio-societal problems, however, it is assumed that there is no ideal solution for the achievement of the mission, but rather a creative and innovative process of experimenting, learning, and adjusting. There is a high probability that social entrepreneurs may fail which explains that social entrepreneurs are characterized by an above-average risk-taking attitude (Dees 2001, p. 5).

But what differentiates social and economic entrepreneurship in practice? "Social entrepreneurship is best understood as a multi-dimensional and dynamic construct moving across various intersecting points between the public, private and social sectors" explains Nicholls Alex from the Skoll Centre for Entrepreneurship at Oxford University. He defines it as "(...) the practice of responding to market failures with transformative, financially sustainable innovations aimed at solving social problems" (Nicholls 2006, p. 12).

The social entrepreneur is interested in the sustainable success of his engagement. "Instead of maximizing profits (...), the first premise is the maximizing of the social profit under the ancillary condition of economic sustainability" (Nicholls 2006). The social entrepreneur fulfills his mission (1) if he dissolves existing, inefficient structures through social innovation and replaces them with more efficient and effective ones; (2) if he implements new tools for problem-solving over the long term; and (3) generates change through social engagement. A successful social entrepreneur generates "positive results in all three dimensions" (Harbrecht 2010, p. 49).

Profile of the Willy Brandt School of Public Policy at the University of Erfurt

The Brandt School – founded as Erfurt School of Public Policy (ESPP) in 2002, and re-named in 2009 – was Germany's first public institution to offer a two-year international graduate course of study in public policy. David Audretsch started serving as Director of a Max Planck research group in Jena two years later. Until today, I regard this coincidence as one of the greatest in my life. I received the privilege and honor to cooperate with Professor Audretsch and his team, and my knowledge about entrepreneurship advanced tremendously. Thanks to David Audretsch and his brilliant global network of experts in the field we have had a very inspiring and successful time; because of his excellent leadership skills and his creative and entrepreneurial mindset, we learned to think out of the box and to act as innovatively as possible. This period has certainly inspired me to believe in the professional school project, which has boldly been launched by Professor Dietmar Herz. The MPP, taught entirely in English, places students in a unique international and intercultural environment. Around 120 young people from more than 50 countries studied at the school in 2015, for example. Such a diverse setting offers the opportunity to experience and address the challenges and peculiarities of globalization at a comparatively small German university. Over the course of two years, students are given the opportunity to specialize in European public policy, international affairs, public and non-profit management, international political economy, or conflict studies and management.[1] The specialization on European public policy seemed obvious for the

---

[1] See www.brandtschool.de for more information.

founding members due to the setting of the Brandt School in one of the former East German states (Thuringia), the school's proximity to Central and East Europe (CEE) states, the high demand for education by young people from former socialist and communist countries, and the strong ties that still existed between the university and partners from those regions. Furthermore, the experience of living and studying in a state that finds itself in transition in economic, administrative, bureaucratic, social, and democratic terms, seemed highly attractive for applied learning and teaching. Next to students from CEE, students from fragile, emerging, and developing countries enrolled in the Brandt School. As a consequence, the program was complemented by a specialization in conflict management, incorporating theories and practical issues of transition, but also peace keeping. The aim of the program was and is to prepare students with international backgrounds to take on governmental and administrative leadership roles, as well as positions within non-government organizations in their respective home countries.

Furthermore, the Brandt School has developed a research profile over the past few years. In addition to addressing issues of good governance, the school's strategic and analytical expertise in conflict management in so-called fragile states has contributed to a remarkable reputation among decision makers in the realms of politics and administration. Moreover, the research area of entrepreneurship has flourished steadily. No longer merely defined by its significance for economic development, the study of entrepreneurship has also been acknowledged for acquiring practical and methodological competencies necessary for the promotion of transformative, progressive processes within public administrations and other organizations. Entrepreneurial, innovative, creative, and independent thinking and acting has become increasingly important for professionals in an innovation and knowledge society (Grimm 2009; Audretsch 2007; Karlsson et al. 2016). New forms of governance demand high social skills and the development of social capital to professionally and successfully act in polycentric systems (Ostrom 2005). As such, the focus on entrepreneurship in a public policy program – both in terms of teaching and research – has been a logical consequence for meeting high standards in education.

Transferring Entrepreneurship Education into a Public Policy Program

With the majority of students coming from countries of the Global South, the traditional approach in teaching public bureaucrats turned out to have severe limitations in the context of accelerated globalization. The concepts, methods, and tools in policy making known and applied in the Western hemisphere turned out to have shortcomings when transferred to developing or fragile contexts. The Independent Commission on International Development Issues chaired by Willy Brandt in 1980 pinpointed to the limitations of just transferring large-scale resources from North to

South, because only a restructuring of the global economy will allow developing countries to facilitate and walk own ways of economic and further development. "The courage to act" (Quilligan 2002, p. 62) is one of the main themes of the Brandt Report; and taking action is by definition linked to entrepreneurship. "The best way to predict the future is to create it". This quote by Willy Brandt, the former German chancellor and Nobel peace prize laureate, along with his global perspectives in solving complex issues, became the leading theme of the Brandt School named after him. The vision was to create the future by developing, implementing, and assessing innovative policies rather than transferring policies without prior efforts in lesson learning and geographic, cultural, or political contextualization (Rose 1993). How can the future be created? How can local, national, and global problems be analyzed, addressed and solved? How can decision makers in policy making and politics be trained and supported in reaching goals while sticking to Willy Brandt's vision? (Grimm 2019b).

Public policy tries to examine and answer these questions with the goal to consult and inform governments and political decision makers using scientific insights, and to help formulate a decision that is ideally suited to the needs of all interest groups involved. An academic discipline striving to master this challenge and develop consensus must inevitably build bridges between politics, administration, citizens, social groups, and science (Lasswell 1951, 1956; Ostrom 2005).

In the context of a public policy making, entrepreneurship serves as a driving force for a better quality and delivery of public goods and services, social change, and development. The policy entrepreneur is a type of actor who not only develops ideas for solutions to political and social challenges, but also designs measures and instruments for implementing and promoting change (Grimm 2010). The complexity and extent of political action taken by decision makers, as well as the demands they face, have increased drastically due to globalization and digitalization over the past two decades. This also explains the rapid emergence of new academic courses in public policy and governance and the incorporation of a specialization in entrepreneurship.

In the early years, the Brandt School focused on research and teaching in the context of entrepreneurship in a rather narrow, economic sense, and largely examined the role of entrepreneurship and start-up activity for regional growth, specifically concentrating on the transformation processes in the new German states (Grimm 2006; Audretsch et al. 2009). Due to the aforementioned reasons, entrepreneurship education was adapted in various ways to fit into a public policy program that aims to educate future professionals in the public and non-profit sector.

Entrepreneurship Education

Valerio et al. (2014) provide an overview about entrepreneurship education and training (EET) worldwide, therefore, only major characteristics will be highlighted in the following, with reference to the case presented in the paper. Although entrepreneurship education became a pillar of business and management studies, there is an ongoing debate whether entrepreneurship can be learned, and which content and aspects should be taught (Lackeus 2015; Pittaway and Cope 2007). Traditionally, EET aimed at preparing future entrepreneurs to develop a new business idea or product and to exploit it in an entrepreneurial and profitable way. Akola and Heinonen (2006) underline that business and management skills which are, among others, regarded as the `science´ of entrepreneurship that can be learned. In this context, tools, such as writing a business plan or business canvas, are applied. Other entrepreneurial skills and competences are regarded as the `art´ of entrepreneurship and as difficult to be learned, including creative and innovative thinking, but also soft skills, such as negotiation, resilience, risk propensity, leadership, persistence, and ways of facing critical stages of development (Fayolle and Gailly 2015; World Bank 2010; Rauch and Frese 2007). The World Bank defines EET as an "(…) academic education or formal training interventions that share the broad objective of providing individuals with the entrepreneurial mindsets and skills to support participation and performance in a range of entrepreneurial activities" (Valerio et al. 2014, p. 21). Fayolle's definition of EET is similar and also useful for further analysis in context of policy entrepreneurship: "(…) any (short or long term) pedagogical program or process of education for entrepreneurial attitudes and skills which involves developing certain personal qualities" (Fayolle et al. 2006, p. 702). Erkkilä (2000) has proposed a unitizing term for defining EET that incorporates business and entrepreneurship education.

Lackeus (2015) developed and applied three categories of EET that are useful for a better understanding on how to teach policy entrepreneurship: education for, about and through entrepreneurship. Whereas the first category highlights a very practical understanding and learning, the second category includes theoretical aspects and awareness education, and the third category goes beyond both other aspects by reflecting on entrepreneurial values and skills, problem-solving, conflict management, communication etc. and is, therefore, also important for the education of future policy entrepreneurs. By turning to practical and real-life experiences, including role plays, participation in business idea competitions, and interaction with real world practitioners, the processes and challenges of entrepreneurial activity, as well as a capability for overcoming obstacles and reaching high goals, can be taught, and the entrepreneurial mindset of the participants will be strengthened (Ramirez-Gonzalez 2017, p. 18). This form of entrepreneurship education is, therefore, most important for the education of policy entrepreneurs.

Teaching Policy Entrepreneurship

The role of entrepreneurship for policy making is not evident at first glance, but when reconsidering the shift from traditional public administration to new public management (NPM) reforms that evolved into new forms of governance, the role of entrepreneurship within a public sector context appears to have evolved slowly.

With their path seminal volume on re-inventing government, Osborne and Gaebler (1993) offered a variety of ideas on how to make bureaucracies more entrepreneurial without following the ideas of the NPM or the new steering model. Entrepreneurship is rather seen as an attitude and mindset promoting action to make bureaucracies more efficient, innovative, and attractive. Policy entrepreneurs are crucial to paving new paths for designing and implementing public policy. Examples and ideas from good practice approaches are integrated in lectures while drawing on experiences of diverse countries and places. Teaching public policy in a globalized world means to consider and carefully weigh to what context and in what way policies can and should be transferred across contexts. Future policy makers need competences to draw lessons, understand context, align bottom up and top down approaches, communicate professionally, build up trust, and engage with an entrepreneurial attitude, rather than to apply a one size fits all approach (Rose 1993).

Teaching Social Entrepreneurship

The Brandt School has been offering courses on social entrepreneurship since 2014. The approach has been a mix of theory and practice. The application-oriented part includes developing a social business idea, working with a business canvas, collaborating with practitioners and successful entrepreneurs, receiving support and advice from local start-up public and non-profit consultancies, and participating in competitions. These are all elements of a public policy program today that aim to enhance entrepreneurial skills. The success of this teaching approach has been impressive after a short time of application; several teams won start-up and business idea competitions at the local level and turned them into valuable social business ideas.

In this context, the Commitment Award Ceremony is a format specifically developed by the Brandt School to promote creative social ideas and turn knowledge into practice. The *Engagementpreis* Foundation has been sponsoring the Commitment Award at the Brandt School since 2012. It seeks to give students the opportunity to apply what they have learned at the Brandt School and to initiate new social initiatives in Erfurt and around the world. A jury of experts carefully evaluates the applications while considering the following questions: How charitable is the project? How much potential and sustainability is incorporated into the project? Will the prize money be used responsibly and effectively? Is the project likely to be actualized?

The successful cases highlighted above demonstrate that entrepreneurship capital defined as a type of social capital is conducive to entrepreneurship and that "diversity enhances entrepreneurship capital by injecting heterogeneity in both thinking and backgrounds into a place, which has been shown to fuel entrepreneurship" (Audretsch 2017, p. 9). This statement by David Audretsch materialized especially in context of the Brandt School, whose profile is coined by the diversity, heterogeneity, and entrepreneurial spirit of the student body. The examples further

Entrepreneurship in Public Policy Education: The Willy Brandt School as a Case

show that (social) innovations emerge if creative people interact in a certain, supportive, open-minded context.

These are just a few examples that show that the transfer of ideas and knowledge plays an important role in the MPP curriculum. Willy Brandt himself put emphasis on the transfer of expertise and knowledge to bring about political and social change which is reflected by his social and political reform steps and policies that made his leadership unique in Germany's post war period. He believed that policies need a clear objective and focus and a strong will to be realized and put into practice; if policy makers do not have a specific goal and vision in mind when creating policies, there will be no effective policy outcome.

Conclusion and Outlook

This paper focuses on the role and importance of entrepreneurship as an important asset and feature of the Willy Brandt School's public policy program and curriculum at the University of Erfurt in Germany which is selected as a case study. In a knowledge-based society, entrepreneurial, innovative, creative, and independent thinking and action are crucial for the sustainable development, effectiveness, and efficiency not only of private, but also public and non-profit organizations. Future professionals in public administrations and governments need entrepreneurial, personal, organizational, and social skills to solve complex and multifaceted problems. Therefore, the integration of theories, methods and good practice cases in teaching economic, policy, and social entrepreneurship have become of major importance for a public policy program that started in a traditional manner.

The case study incorporates a reconsideration of the meaning and increasing importance of policy entrepreneurs for professional policy making in the context of local-global challenges. It can be assumed that the role of policy entrepreneurship will increase. The policy entrepreneur tends to operate at the intersection of the three classical sectors and takes action in areas where the government, private, and non-profit sectors are not yet active or effective. Due to financial limitations of state and municipal budgets, but also government failure, for example, in the areas of protecting global common goods or human rights, the engagement of policy entrepreneurs will rise. In this context, policy entrepreneurs can uphold an important role, since they create a balance between state and social-entrepreneurial action and make an important contribution to social change. The clear accentuation and support of transparent and effective social entrepreneurial projects could enable policy entrepreneurs to build a bridge across politics and society and serve as an important driver, but also control element, in the policy process. The potentials of policy, but also social entrepreneurs, lie in experimenting, developing, and implementing creative and innovative ideas and solutions for overcoming social (and also political) challenges, which is why he or she works as a provider of ideas to the government. Neither governments nor politicians have room for experiments; both can, however, benefit from the creativity and innovativeness of policy entrepreneurs. Additionally, both have an interest in identifying efficient, sustainable solutions for social challenges. In this regard, the policy entrepreneur has the potential to serve as an important mediator and communicator promoting and impacting change sustainably.

References

Akola, E., & Heinonen, J. (2006). How to support learning of entrepreneurs. A study of training programmes for entrepreneurs in five European countries. Paper presented at the RENT XX Conference, Research in Entrepreneurship and Small Business.

Audretsch, D. B. (2007). *The entrepreneurial society*. New York: Oxford University Press.

Audretsch, D. B. (2015). *Everything in its place. Entrepreneurship and the strategic management of cities, regions, and states*. Oxford: Oxford University Press.

Audretsch, D. B. (2017). Entrepreneurship and universities. *International Journal of Entrepreneurship and Small Business, 31*(1), 4–11.

Audretsch, D. B., & Belitski, M. J. (2016). Entrepreneurial ecosystems in cities: establishing the framework conditions. *The Journal of Technology Transfer, 41*, 1–22.

Audretsch, D. B., Grimm, H. M., & Wessner, C. (2005a). *Local heroes in the global village. Globalization and the new entrepreneurship policies*. New York: Springer.

Audretsch, D. B., Keilbach, M., & Lehmann, E. (2005b). *Entrepreneurship and economic growth*. New York: Oxford University Press.

Audretsch, D. B., Grimm, H., & Schuetze, S. (2009). Local strategies within a European policy framework. *European Planning Studies, 17*(3), 463–486.

Audretsch, D. B., Kuratko, D. F., & Link, A. N. (2015). Making sense of the elusive paradigm of entrepreneurship. *Small Business Economics, 45*, 703–712.

Bernie, L., & Hafsi, T. (2007). The changing nature of public entrepreneurship. *Public Administration Review, 67*, 488–503.

Birch, D. L. (1981). Who creates jobs? *The Public Interest, 65*, 3–14.

Cohen, B. (2006). Sustainable valley entrepreneurial ecosystems. *Business Strategy and the Environment, 15*(1), 1–14.

Dees, J. G. (2001). *The meaning of "social entrepreneurship"*. Durham: Centre for Advancement of Social Entrepreneurship (CASE), Fuqua School of Business, Duke University.

Drucker, P. (1985). *Innovation and entrepreneurship. Practice and principles*. New York: Harper & Row Publishers.

Emerson, J., & Twersky, F. (1996). *New social entrepreneurs: The success, challenge and lessons of non-profit enterprise creation*. San Francisco: The Roberts Foundation, Homeless Economic Development Fund.

Erkkilä, K. (2000). *Entrepreneurial education: Mapping the debates in the United States, the United Kingdom and Finland*. Abingdon: Taylor & Francis.

Fayolle, A., & Gailly, B. (2015). The impact of entrepreneurship education in entrepreneurial attitudes and intention: Hysteresis and persistence. *Journal of Small Business Management, 53*(1), 75–93.

Fayolle, A., Gailly, B., & Lassas-Clerc, N. (2006). Assessing the impact of entrepreneurship education programmes: A new methodology. *Journal of European Industrial Training, 30*(9), 701–720.

Global Entrepreneurship Monitor (GEM). (2017). Global Report 2016/117. Global Entrepreneurship Research Association (GERA), Babson Park: Babson College.

Grimm, H. (2006). Do public information and subsidies contribute to the entrepreneurial environment? An exploratory transatlantic study with local-global perspectives. *International Journal of Public Administration, 39*(13), 1167–1193.

Grimm, H. (2009). Creating an entrepreneurial economy: The role of public policy. In D. B. Audretsch & R. Strom (Eds.), *Entrepreneurship, growth, and public policy* (pp. 299–318). Cambridge: Cambridge University Press.

Grimm, H. (2010). Entrepreneur – Social Entrepreneur – Policy Entrepreneur. Typologische Merkmale und Perspektiven. *Zeitschrift für Politikberatung, 3*(3–4), 441–456.

Grimm (2019a). Chapter 7: Public and policy entrepreneurship research: A synthesis of the literature and future perspectives. In D.B. Audretsch, E. Lehmann and A. Link. A research agenda for entrepreneurship and innovation. Cheltenham: Edward Elgar.

Grimm. (2019b). *Public policy research in the global south. Public policy research in the global south. A cross-country perspective* (Vol. 1). Cham, Switzerland: Springer Nature.

Harbrecht, A. (2010). *Social Entrepreneurship – Gewinn ist Mittel, nicht Zweck. Eine Untersuchung über Entstehung, Erscheinungsweisen und Umsetzung.* Karlsruhe: Karlsruher Institut für Technologie.

Hynes, B. (1996). Entrepreneurship education and training – Introducing entrepreneurship in non-business disciplines. *Journal of European Industrial Training, 20*(8), 10–17.

Karlsson, C., Silander, C., & Silander, D. (2016). *Political entrepreneurship. Regional growth and entrepreneurial diversity in Sweden.* Cheltenham: Edward Elgar Publishing Limited.

Kingdon, J. W. (1995). *Agendas, alternatives, and public policies* (2nd ed.). Boston: Little, Brown & Company.

Koltai, S., & Muspratt, M. (2017). *Peace through entrepreneurship: Investing in startup culture for security and development.* Washington, D.C.: Brookings Institute Press.

Lackeus, M. (2015). *Entrepreneurship in education. What, why, when, how. Entrepreneurship360. Background Paper.* Paris: OECD.

Lasswell, H. D. (1951). The policy orientation. In D. Lerner & H. D. Lasswell (Eds.), *The policy sciences* (pp. 3–15). Palo Alto: Stanford University Press.

Lasswell, H. D. (1956). *The decision process: Seven categories of functional analysis.* College Park: University of Maryland Press.

Link, A. N., & Link, J. R. (2007). *Government as entrepreneur.* New York: Oxford Press.

Mintrom, M., & Norman, P. (2009). Policy entrepreneurship and policy change. *Policy Studies Journal, 37*(4), 649–667.

Mwasalwiba, E. S. (2010). Entrepreneurship education: A review of its objectives, teaching methods, and impact indicators. *Education + Training, 52*(1), 20–47.

Nicholls, A. (Ed.). (2006). *Social entrepreneurship: New paradigms of sustainable social change.* Oxford: Oxford University Press.

O'Connor, A., Stam, E., Sussan, F., & Audretsch, D. (2018). Entrepreneurial ecosystems: The foundations of place-based renewal. In A. O'Connor, E. Stam, F. Sussan, & D. B. Audretsch (Eds.), *Entrepreneurial ecosystems. Place-based transformations and transitions* (pp. 1–22). New York: Springer.

Osborne, D., & Gaebler, T. (1993). *Reinventing government. How the entrepreneurial spirit is transforming the public sector.* New York: Penguin Books.

Ostrom, E. (2005). Unlocking public entrepreneurship and public economies. Working Paper DP2005/01, World Institute for Development Economic Research (UNU-WIDER).

Pittaway, L., & Cope, J. (2007). Entrepreneurship education: A systematic review of the evidence. *International Small Business Journal, 25*(5), 479–510.

Quilligan, J. B. (2002). *The Brandt equation. Century blueprint for the new global economy.* Philadelphia: Brandt 21 Forum.

Ramirez-Gonzalez, F. L. (2017). Entrepreneurship education and the promotion of small business. The case of Pilar, Paraguay. Master Thesis Submitted to the Willy Brandt School of Public Policy, University of Erfurt.

Rauch, A., & Frese, M. (2007). Let's put the person back into entrepreneurship research: A meta-analysis on the relationship between business owners' personality traits, business creation and success. *European Journal of Work and Organizational Psychology, 16*(4), 353–385.

Roberts, N., & King, P. J. (1996). *Transforming public policy.* San Francisco: Jossey-Bass Publishers.

Roberts, N., & King, P. J. (1998). Policy entrepreneurs: Their activity structure and function in the policy process. *Journal of Public Administration Research and Theory, 1*, 147–175.

Rose, R. (1993). *Lesson drawing in public policy: A guide to learning across time and space.* Chatham: Chatham House.

Schumpeter, J. A. (2008). *The theory of economic development: An inquiry into profits, capital, credit, interest, and the business cycle* (16th ed.). New Brunswick: Transaction Publishers. 1934.

Shane, S., & Venkataraman, S. (2000). The promise of entrepreneurship as a field of research. *The Academy of Management Review, 25*(1), 217–226.

Silander, D. (2016). The political entrepreneur. In C. Karlsson, C. Silander, & D. Silander (Eds.), *Political entrepreneurship. Regional growth and entrepreneurial diversity in Sweden* (pp. 7–20). Cheltenham: Edward Elgar Publishing Limited.

Valerio, A., Parton, B., & Robb, A. (2014). *Entrepreneurship education and training programs around the world: Dimensions for success. Directions in development-human development.* Washington, DC: World Bank.

Volkmann, C. K., & Audretsch, D. B. (2017). *Entrepreneurship education at universities – Learning from twenty European cases.* Berlin: Springer.

World Bank. (2010). *Stepping up skills: For more jobs and higher productivity.* Washington, D.C.: World Bank.

Connecting People and Knowledge: Knowledge Spillovers, Cognitive Biases, and Entrepreneurship

Werner Bönte and Diemo Urbig

Abstract Having served under David at the Max Planck Institute in Jena, the authors witnessed first hand as he worked to build up entrepreneurship as an academic discipline. While he was building this community in the field writ-large, he was also building a strong network of entrepreneurship scholars within the team itself. While reflecting upon the benefits of cognitive biases such as optimism for entrepreneurial knowledge spillovers and demonstrating context-dependency of the benefits and drawbacks of cognitive biases, the authors also connect this to how they have experienced David's way of developing a research network.

Introduction

When the two authors of this paper started working at the Max Planck Institute (MPI) of Economics in Jena a long time ago, they each had very different scientific backgrounds. While one was a postdoctoral economist working in the field of industrial organization and innovation, researching the link between *knowledge spillovers* and productivity, the other author had just completed his Master's in both business administration and computer science and was going to work on *cognitive biases* of entrepreneurs in his doctoral dissertation. Meanwhile their research agendas converged and they regularly collaborate in various research projects. They started, for instance, researching links between biology and

---

W. Bönte (✉)
Jackstädt Center of Entrepreneurship and Innovation Research, University of Wuppertal, Wuppertal, Germany
e-mail: boente@wiwi.uni-wuppertal.de

D. Urbig
Jackstädt Center of Entrepreneurship and Innovation Research, University of Wuppertal, Wuppertal, Germany

School of Business and Economics, Vrije Universiteit Amsterdam, The Netherlands, The Netherlands

© Springer Nature Switzerland AG 2019
E. E. Lehmann, M. Keilbach (eds.), *From Industrial Organization to Entrepreneurship*, https://doi.org/10.1007/978-3-030-25237-3_34

entrepreneurship (Bönte et al. 2016), something neither had considered prior to starting at the MPI. This leap was possible because David Audretsch established an open and creative atmosphere in his "Entrepreneurship, Growth, and Public Policy Group" at the MPI of Economics, encouraging scholars to look at the entrepreneurial process from very different angles, to test limits, and to end up combining very different strands of research. The two authors of this paper, along with other former members of the EGP group, benefited greatly from David's support, even after leaving Jena, since he continues to wholeheartedly foster their research and personal development. While this paper's title in its first part is meant to describe and honor how we have experienced David Audretsch, the second part shows that that although the authors' research agendas look unrelated at first glance, but actually are related and jointly also relate to how the authors have experienced David Audretsch.

This paper links two strands of literature that focus on different aspects of the entrepreneurial process. First, we refer to the literature linking entrepreneurship to knowledge spillovers. On the one hand, the Knowledge Spillover Theory of Entrepreneurship suggests that knowledge created endogenously by other agents, like incumbent firms, results in knowledge spillovers that allow entrepreneurs to identify and exploit opportunities (Audretsch and Keilbach 2007; Audretsch et al. 2008). While endogenous growth theory suggests that profit-maximizing firms' R&D activities are an important driver of economic growth (Romer 1990), the essential role of the entrepreneur is emphasized by Acs et al. (2009) arguing that new ventures exploit intra-temporal knowledge spillovers that are not appropriated by incumbent firms. On the other hand, new ventures started by entrepreneurs may not just be an *outcome* of knowledge spillovers, but may also be a *source* of knowledge spillovers (De Clercq et al. 2008), which tends to be especially true for new technology-based firms where founders' human capital is essential for firm growth (Colombo and Grilli 2010). Moreover, Acs et al. (2016) state that new ventures may generate externalities because they demonstrate that entrepreneurship is rewarding and viable, requiring certain capabilities and competencies (demonstration externalities) and because even when businesses fail, other firms may benefit from the information generated by the failed entrepreneurial firms (failure externalities). Consequently, different types of market failures associated with knowledge and information creation may lead to an underinvestment in entrepreneurship. Some justifications of entrepreneurship policies are driven by efforts to overcome this underinvestment and to generate related positive knowledge spillovers.

Second, we refer to a strand of entrepreneurship literature suggesting that the decision to enter entrepreneurial activities may not only be driven by expected profits but also by individual differences in perceptions of activities associated with entrepreneurship. Unrealistic optimism regarding the risk associated with entrepreneurship (Palich and Bagby 1995; Busenitz and Barney 1997; Chen et al. 1998; Forbes 2005) and regarding chances of winning entrepreneurial competitions (cf., Camerer and Lovallo 1999) might, in fact, trigger a tendency to excessively enter entrepreneurship and, thus, might lead to an overinvestment into entrepreneurial activities. Cognitive biases may be so strong that they eventually reduce entrepreneurs' performances, with empirical evidence suggesting that unsuccessful entrepreneurs might be those who excessively exhibit specific biases (Baron 1998). In accord with this view, Koellinger et al. (2007) find that in countries characterized by more confident and possibly overconfident entrepreneurs, failure rates are also relatively higher. At the firm level, Hmieleski and Baron (2009) report a possibly negative relationship between entrepreneurs' optimism and their new venture's revenues and employment growths. Consequently, some scholars argue that policy makers should discourage biased entrepreneurs from becoming entrepreneurs (see, e.g., Parker 2007). Similarly, Kahneman and Riepe (1998) argue that the 'potent brew' of overconfidence and unrealistic optimism should be avoided and investors should be trained to suffer less from these biases. We even observe efforts to debias people through law (Jolls and Sunstein 2006). In line with these efforts, business and entrepreneurship education often also seeks to provide future managers and potential entrepreneurs more realistic beliefs about their ventures (e.g., Fischhoff 1982; Soll et al. 2015). However, there is also literature suggesting that these individual cognitive biases may, in fact, create information externalities that benefit an entrepreneurial ecosystem, such that the overinvestment due to cognitive biases might counterbalance the underinvestment due to information externalities (Bernardo and Welch 2001).

We take this observation as starting point to explore the relationship between cognitive biases and information externalities created by entrepreneurship. We briefly discuss an analysis provided by Bernardo and Welch (2001), which demonstrates the information externalities and the resulting social benefits of individuals being overconfident in their private evaluations of business opportunities. We discuss the model's limitations in the context of entrepreneurship research and explore extensions of it. We eventually link these analyses back to the discussion of entrepreneurship policy either stimulating entrepreneurship or related investments into education de-biasing entrepreneurs.

Cognitive Biases Revealing Ex Ante Knowledge

Some researchers argue that cognitive biases may trigger socially beneficial information externalities, thereby suggesting that deviations from expected payoff maximization may actually create positive knowledge externalities (Bernardo and Welch 2001; Kariv 2005; Urbig 2010). Building on such information diffusion arguments, in general, and the model by Bikhchandani et al. (1992), in particular, Bernardo and Welch (2001) theoretically show that potential entrepreneurs who exaggerate their own ability to evaluate business opportunities are beneficial for society. The information externality is created through individuals observing other individuals' decisions to either exploit or not exploit a business opportunity. Without any public information, individuals might base their decisions purely on their private evaluations of the opportunity and their decisions, hence, through their decisions reveal private information. Since potential entrepreneurs may recognize an opportunity at different points in time and typically no two share the exact same information set at the exact same time (Shane and Venkataraman 2000), other entrepreneurs' private evaluations as revealed by their decision can be informative to a potential entrepreneurs. If a sufficient number of individuals have decided to either exploit or not exploit an opportunity, the public information becomes so dominant that individuals just join the crowd. By exaggerating the precision of their individual ex ante evaluations of business opportunities, however, overconfident individuals are less likely to follow fads and fashions. If these private ex ante evaluations drive their observable decisions, their individual evaluations become additional public information, such that an ex ante information externality is triggered by the overconfidence bias. Extending this discussion and also building upon the model introduced by Bikhchandani et al. (1992), Urbig (2010) analyzes the effects of another cognitive bias: the base rate neglect (Kahneman and Tversky 2000). He demonstrates that in a society of interacting individuals, neglecting the base rate enables social learning processes even in situations where due to an unfavorable base rate no single individual would even consider evaluating that opportunity; that is, even if private ex ante information might indicate a favorable business opportunity, the base rate is so negative such that individuals do not act upon that opportunity. Hence, through their decisions, individuals neglecting the base rate reveal their private information to the public and, thus, benefit society.

While Bernardo and Welch (2001) describe their overconfident individuals as entrepreneurial, their model does not capture essential entrepreneurship elements. Information that can be gained by individuals before these individuals actually engage in any entrepreneurial action related to an emerging opportunity does not need entrepreneurial action to be explored. Instead, a publicly funded large-scale market research and distributing the aggregated information to potential entrepreneurs could be more efficient than any support of entrepreneurship. Such publicly supported research would avoid inefficiencies resulting from parallel, private, and competitive information searches. Hence, the revelation of ex ante available knowledge is not what most entrepreneurship researchers would consider the core exploratory function of entrepreneurship. As Candida Brush (2014) succinctly formulates it in a Forbes mini-blog, *"Entrepreneurship is, by definition, about experimenting – trying something, seeing what the results are, learning from the results, and then trying it again."* Kerr et al. (2014, p. 25) referring to Hayek (1948) emphasize that *"the solution of the economic problem of society is... always a voyage of exploration into the unknown"* and summarize that, *"for entrepreneurs, it can be virtually impossible to know whether a particular technology or product or business model will be successful, until one has actually invested in it."* Hence, the unique knowledge created by entrepreneurs results from acting and doing and cannot otherwise be created, such as by merely passively observing and analyzing markets (Brush 2014; Kerr et al. 2014). Thus, further developments of social learning models focusing on the exploratory and knowledge-generating function of entrepreneurship should not focus on the revelation of *ex ante* available knowledge (such as in models by Bernardo and Welch 2001, and Urbig 2010), but on knowledge generated through the exploitation of opportunities.

Cognitive Biases Revealing Knowledge from Entrepreneurial Action

While in Bernardo and Welch's (2001) model, entrepreneurs collected information about the value of an opportunity before exploitation and, hence, any related information externality is about ex ante available information, related subsequent entrepreneurial action will ex post either validate or invalidate the *ex ante* knowledge. As Shane and Venkataraman (2000, p. 221) emphasize, *"[a]s opportunities are exploited, information diffuses to other members of a society who can imitate the innovator and appropriate some of the innovator's entrepreneurial profit."* While knowledge about successful exploitations is emphasized by Shane and Venkataraman, knowledge about failure can also be helpful. Future entrepreneurs can then avoid replicating the same strategy, following different routes if not exploiting other business opportunities, thereby, saving costs and increasing their success probabilities. At first glance, one might argue that observable outcomes perfectly reveal the characteristics of an opportunity in the real economy, however, there are substantial idiosyncratic risks and chances that make an observed success just an imperfect signal. These idiosyncrasies may make individuals fail although most others would succeed or vice versa.

Cao and Hirshleifer (2000) extend the original model of Bikhchandani et al. (1992) to include observable outcomes as well as idiosyncratic risks. Although Cao and Hirshleifer only investigate rational decision-making, Urbig and Weitzel (2009) note that the inclusion of idiosyncratic risks allows an additional analysis of cognitive biases related to this type of risk; e.g. ignorance of idiosyncratic risks as reported by Moskowitz and Vissing-Jørgensen (2002) and Wu and Knott (2006). Cao and Hirshleifer (2000) emphasize that their model brings together two different mechanisms: the diffusion of private information revealed through decisions and acquired before the actual decision, but also the revelation of new previously completely unknown information through observation of actual exploitations of opportunities. We believe this combination is particularly promising for the analysis of entrepreneurial dynamics.

We now briefly and informally explore the interdependencies of cognitive biases and information externalities resulting from entrepreneurial action itself rather than from revealed decisions to act entrepreneurially. A simple initial implication is that, since the action is the source of externalities, any cognitive bias that favors action is likely to trigger related information externalities. However, the two biases explored in the context of the model by Bikhchandani et al. (1992) – overconfidence in one's own evaluation of an opportunity (Bernardo and Welch 2001) and base rate neglect

(Urbig 2010) – only trigger action-related information externalities under very specific conditions and may suppress information in others. Overconfident individuals will only become more optimistic and, thus, become more likely to act entrepreneurially than others, if the opportunity is *ex ante* positively evaluated. The resulting information externality would be particularly strong and, in fact, be a combination of ex ante and action-related information, if the odds associated with an opportunity are very low (e.g. low base rate for succeeding) and individual ex ante evaluations are not very informative (e.g. very disruptive technologies that are difficult to evaluate ex ante). Under such conditions, rational individuals who positively evaluate an opportunity would nevertheless not exploit the opportunity. The base rate neglect would also have its strongest positive effect on triggering entrepreneurial action just under the same conditions. While both overconfidence and base rate neglect might not be unambiguously in favor of action, it seems that the scenario where they are able to trigger entrepreneurial action and, hence, generate information externalities, very much coincide with how entrepreneurial contexts are described and where innovation – even disruptive innovations – are important, that is, for low odds of succeeding and often difficult to evaluate opportunities.

The existence of two types of information externalities, that is, information gained through pre-exploitation activities (ex ante information) and information gained through exploitation activities themselves (action-based information), can lead to situations where biases may reduce the likelihood of one information externality while increasing the likelihood of the other. Consider, for example, that an individual faces very positive public information, e.g. through some people already starting to exploit an opportunity and perhaps already observing initial successes, but her own evaluation still indicates that the opportunity is not a sustainably good one. An unbiased individual would perhaps, nevertheless, engage in entrepreneurial activities, thereby not revealing the ex ante knowledge but generating additional information from action. An individual overconfident in her private evaluation might not be as entrepreneurial, thereby revealing her unfavorable private evaluation to the public, but not generate the action-based information. Whether or not the overconfidence is beneficial in this setting obviously depends on the relative strengths of the two types of information externalities. The less success of one individual implies success of another one (weak action-based knowledge externality) and the better a business can be evaluated ex ante (strong ex ante knowledge externality), the more beneficial overconfidence would be. Note that this trade-off only appears for negative private evaluations in face of positive public information, but not in the opposite case. If public information would suggest to not exploit an opportunity, but private evaluation turns out to be more favorable, then not being overconfident would not trigger entrepreneurial action and, hence, not reveal any action-related information. Hence, for unfavorable public information and favorable private information, overconfidence would nevertheless be beneficial and it would, because it increases the likelihood of entrepreneurial action, trigger additional action-based information externalities. This asymmetry with respect to the presence of favorable public and private information only shows up in the model once outcomes of actions can be observed in addition to observed decision to act and this feature affects the social benefits of overconfidence. Hence, it is important to revisit the analysis by Bernardo and Welch (2001) and to augment their model such that observable outcomes and, more generally, information externalities resulting from entrepreneurial action itself are included in the model (cf., Cao and Hirshleifer 2000).

Overconfidence in own evaluations and base rate neglect, however, are not the only cognitive biases that are discussed in the context of entrepreneurship. Optimism and an underestimation of the idiosyncratic risks are also attributed to entrepreneurs (Moskowitz and Vissing-Jørgensen 2002; Wu and Knott 2006). Further, lower loss and risk aversion are attributed to entrepreneurs (e.g., Caliendo et al. 2009; Wu and Knott 2006). Any distortion of beliefs and decisions that directly and unconditionally leads to more exploitation will also lead to more action-based information externalities. Hence, even unrealistic optimism that is independent of one's privately available evaluation and independent of the general base rate can trigger positive information externalities. As for overconfidence in private evaluations, also the effects of unrealistic optimism are subject to trade-offs. Individuals with negative private evaluation facing moderately positive public evaluations might still abstain from exploitation, thereby, revealing their negative information. If such an individual is unrealistically optimistic, she may exploit regardless, hence, suppressing the revelation of the ex ante available information but, due to exploiting, create an action-based information externality. In such situations, unrealistic optimism can increase the likelihood of one at the expense of the likelihood of the other information externality. However, for individuals with positive private information facing very negative public evaluations, who without being biased would not engage in entrepreneurial actions, unrealistic optimism unambiguously generates more information externalities. They might follow their private information, which generates an ex ante information externality and their action generates an action-based information externality.

In sum, cognitive biases can create substantial information externalities and the existence of different types of information externalities, i.e. ex ante available information and action-based information, renders related analyses of social effects rather complex. Furthermore, the interplay between the different biases implies that bundles of cognitive biases may eventually maximize a society's welfare. Our preliminary discussion seems to suggest that under certain conditions Kahneman and Riepe's 'potent brew' of both overconfidence and unrealistic optimism may indeed have substantial socially beneficial effects and related de-biasing efforts may possibly hurt an entrepreneurial ecosystem more than it helps. The conditions seem to be characterized by very negative public evaluations, that is, when ex ante evaluations of success rates are rather negative. Furthermore, the combination might be especially beneficial if action-based information externalities are stronger than ex ante information externalities. Such conditions seem to be rather consistent with evaluations of disruptive innovations before they have been successfully exploited.

Policy Implications for Schumpeterian and Kirznerian Entrepreneurship

While many politicians see policies fostering entrepreneurship as a promising way to increase social welfare, entrepreneurship scholars tend to be less optimistic, pointing to the downsides of such policies, even providing arguments why it could be a good idea to discourage new start-ups and to educate entrepreneurs in ways that reduce the cognitive biases causing unrealistic optimism (Acs et al. 2016; Parker 2007; Shane 2009). The observation that most startups are non-innovative makes it unlikely that the majority of entrepreneurial investments exhibit high social rates of return. This is a major argument put forward against entrepreneurship policies generally fostering the creation of new ventures (Acs et al. 2016). Even worse, empirical evidence suggests that the average private rate of return is also relatively low since individuals who become self-employed are, on average, worse off than employees in terms of income, as the typical "entrepreneurial discount" is between 5 and 15% per year (Åstebro 2012; Åstebro and Chen 2014). Nevertheless, many people start new ventures and our previous discussion suggests that market entry could be induced by cognitive biases that may have negative or positive effects on social welfare depending on contextual conditions. We argue that cognitive biases can lead to overinvestment in entrepreneurship if it is not associated with positive externalities whereas the same cognitive biases due to the same mechanism can counteract underinvestment in entrepreneurship in the case of and resulting from strong information externalities. Contextual conditions tend to influence whether ex ante or action-based information spillovers are generated and what combinations of biases are beneficial for an entrepreneurial ecosystem. Thus, from a policy perspective, entrepreneurship policies fostering start-up activities or discouraging entrepreneurs should account for different types of externalities and cognitive biases as well as the specific contexts.

Ex ante and *action-based* information externalities are related to two different types of entrepreneurship, as described by Kirzner (1973) and Schumpeter (1934). Kirznerian and Schumpeterian entrepreneurship not only differ with respect to their function within an economic system, but also with respect to the type of information externalities they may generate. Ex ante information externalities arise when entrepreneurs identify market disequilibria, enter markets, and these decisions reveal information about their ex ante identified opportunities to other entrepreneurs. According to Acs et al. (2016, p. 37), Kirznerian entrepreneurship can be described as *routine entrepreneurship* based on the assumption "that there are always agents that are ready to enter an industry if profits are above equilibrium" and that "while some uncertainty remains, no new knowledge is being applied in the process." This type of entrepreneurship refers to "competition in the market" where no new products or processes are introduced. Routine (Kirznerian) entrepreneurship, hence, mostly reveals *ex ante* knowledge about market disequilibria rather than technological or market uncertainties. In contrast, Acs et al. (2016, p. 37) describe Schumpeterian entrepreneurship as *novel entrepreneurship*, which means "activities necessary to create or carry on an enterprise where not all the markets are well established or clearly defined." Novel (Schumpeterian) entrepreneurship is characterized by a general uncertainty about markets and the potential of technologies, an uncertainty that requires testing through actual entrepreneurial action. Knowledge about new markets and technologies generated by actual entrepreneurial action is what other entrepreneurs can learn from the Schumpeterian entrepreneur. Hence, the Schumpeterian entrepreneurs generate action-based knowledge externalities.

Linking Kirznerian and Schumpeterian entrepreneurship to our discussion of externalities and cognitive biases, we can conclude that the benefits of certain cognitive biases promoting action-based knowledge spillovers are most beneficial for Schumpeterian entrepreneurship. They are most beneficial in contexts where ex ante knowledge is weak and substantial uncertainties are present, which can only be resolved by acting rather than thinking. As discussed above, if uncertainties are as large as to make even rational entrepreneurs who hold weak but favorable private evaluations of business opportunities to not engage in entrepreneurial action, then the 'potent brew' of overconfidence and unrealistic optimism might actually be the key to letting society explore such opportunities. High uncertainty and difficulties to predict outcomes seem to match with characteristics associated with disruptive innovations. In contrast, benefits of cognitive biases triggering the revelation of ex ante information is most likely to be particularly beneficial in contexts characterized by Kirznerian entrepreneurship, when the key is to spot market disequilibria rather than developing and testing new products and services. While cognitive biases may counteract potential underinvestment in both, Kirznerian entrepreneurship, characterized by arbitrage, as well as in Schumpeterian entrepreneurship, characterized by innovation, it can be expected that the social rate of return to Schumpeterian entrepreneurship is much higher than the social rate of return to Kirznerian entrepreneurship. This is likely to be the case, because Schumpeterian entrepreneurship is associated with stronger uncertainty that requires action to be resolved, while such action-based externalities are less important for Kirznerian entrepreneurship. On the one hand, this implies that debiasing potential entrepreneurs, e.g. by forcing the development and systematic analysis of business plans, thereby, reducing their inappropriately high tendency to engage in entrepreneurship, might be the right entrepreneurship policy for Kirznerian-type of entrepreneurship. Such an entrepreneurship policy might prevent potential entrepreneurs with cognitive biases, like unrealistically optimistic individuals, from entering "into highly contested markets, with products and services that are typically already offered, and where there is already a large supply present" (Acs et al. 2016, p. 46). On the other hand, de-biasing might not be the right and possibly a welfare-reducing entrepreneurship policy when it comes to Schumpeterian entrepreneurship. In the latter case, cognitive biases may counteract underinvestment in entrepreneurship and might, therefore, be beneficial for the society as they motivate Schumpeterian entrepreneurs to enter market and to generate knowledge externalities, even if their true private returns are low. Without cognitive biases, like unrealistic optimism, market entry of information externality generating Schumpeterian entrepreneurs would have to be motivated by extrinsic incentives, like governments' financial support to Schumpeterian start-ups, with all the disadvantages of potential crowding out of intrinsic motivation and resulting effects on entrepreneurs' motivation and perseverance. Consequently, entrepreneurship policy, including education and training related to de-biasing, needs to take into account different types of entrepreneurs and entrepreneurial contexts.

These thoughts are just the beginning of a deeper analysis and we leave open a large set of questions and aspects that deserve much more attention. The models of Bikhchandani et al. (1992) and, building on it, of Bernardo and Welch (2001) are based on many critical assumptions and relaxing these assumptions and enriching their analyses of knowledge externalities is likely to provide new insights on the social benefits of cognitive biases. One of these assumptions relate to how information externalities can be exploited. Social learning models assume that each potential entrepreneur can benefit from the information externality. Shane and Venkataraman (2000, p. 221) emphasize that *"[a]s opportunities are exploited, information diffuses to other members of a society who can imitate the innovator and appropriate some of the innovator's entrepreneurial profit.* "This implies that the benefits of the information externality are strategically related to other entrepreneurs' benefits and that the benefits may fall the more other people learn. We suggest future research should more deeply investigate the role of such strategic interaction for social learning processes.

Furthermore, we observe increased competition between entrepreneurial ecosystems of different regions or countries. The learning within each of these ecosystems and the externalities between these systems are likely to create different dynamics. While the learning within an entrepreneurial ecosystem may generate many positive externalities, competition between ecosystems may limit how individual ecosystems may organize their learning. If, for instance, a slower exploitation would generate more reliable public information within an entrepreneurial ecosystem in the long run, by exploiting faster, a competing ecosystem might simply take over markets and reduce the benefits that the former ecosystem can generate from their learning. In fact, such competition creates endogenous windows of opportunities for the exploitation of entrepreneurial opportunities. Hence, while studies like those by Bernardo and Welch (2001) and Urbig (2010) might be interesting for the sake of creating awareness for fundamental social learning processes, the strategic management of places introduces an aspect that should be acknowledged in these models, that is, the possibly endogenous creation of windows of opportunities (Audretsch and Lehmann 2017).

Conclusion

Our discussion shows that in the context of entrepreneurship, cognitive biases, like unrealistic optimism or overconfidence, might not necessarily be bad for the society as a whole if they trigger market entry by innovative Schumpeterian entrepreneurs engaging in entrepreneurial activities resulting in positive knowledge externalities.

Connecting People and Knowledge: Knowledge Spillovers, Cognitive Biases... 395

However, this effect of cognitive biases might not only be relevant for entrepreneurship, but may also apply to science and the decisions of scientists. Often scientists tend to be unrealistically optimistic and may also be overconfident when starting new research projects. This implies that such cognitive biases may trigger engagement in new research, even though the "private return" to scientific research is often low and chances of failing high. Nevertheless, such research, possibly driven by the highly idiosyncratic judgments of scientists, may result in remarkable knowledge, while these externalities snowball through communication among scientists. By establishing an open, creative, and diversity-welcoming atmosphere in his "Entrepreneurship, Growth, and Public Policy Group" at the MPI of Economics, David Audretsch created an environment that allowed senior scientists as well as young scientists to engage in new research of their own, possibly biased, choices and to share knowledge with other members of the group and research fellows, thereby generating knowledge spillovers. By focusing on people rather than research topics, by encouraging exploration and accepting a wide range of research and research outcomes, David Audretsch reveals his focus on generating action-based knowledge externalities. With respect to this paper's contribution to this book, we may conclude that, after all, this paper is merely a rational justification for the long-standing entrepreneurial research management that David Audretsch is well known and appreciated for, with very positive externalities.

References

Acs, Z., Braunerhjelm, P., Audretsch, D. B., & Carlsson, B. (2009). The knowledge spillover theory of entrepreneurship. *Small Business Economics, 32*(1), 15–30.

Acs, Z., Astebro, T., Audretsch, D. B., & Robinson, D. T. (2016). Public policy to promote entrepreneurship: A call to arms. *Small Business Economics, 47*(1), 35–51.

Åstebro, T. (2012). Returns to entrepreneurship. *Handbook of entrepreneurial finance, 45*, 108.

Åstebro, T., & Chen, J. (2014). The entrepreneurial earnings puzzle: Mismeasurement or real? *Journal of Business Venturing, 29*(1), 88–105.

Audretsch, D. B., & Keilbach, M. (2007). The theory of knowledge spillover entrepreneurship. *Journal of Management Studies, 44*(7), 1242–1254.

Audretsch, D. B., & Lehmann, E. E. (2017). The knowledge spillover theory of entrepreneurship and the strategic management of places. In *The Wiley handbook of entrepreneurship*. London: John Wiley (pp. 349–377).

Audretsch, D. B., Bönte, W., & Keilbach, M. (2008). Entrepreneurship capital and its impact on knowledge diffusion and economic performance. *Journal of Business Venturing, 23*(6), 687–698.

Baron, R. A. (1998). Cognitive mechanisms in entrepreneurship: Why and when entrepreneurs think differently than other people. *Journal of Business Venturing, 13*, 275–294.

Bernardo, A. E., & Welch, I. (2001). On the evolution of overconfidence and entrepreneurs. *Journal of Economics & Management Strategy, 10*, 301–330.

Bikhchandani, S., Hirshleifer, D., & Welch, I. (1992). A theory of fads, fashion, custom, and cultural change as informational cascades. *Journal of Political Economy, 100*(5), 992–1026.

Bönte, W., Procher, V., & Urbig, D. (2016). Biology and selection into entrepreneurship: The relevance of prenatal testosterone exposure. *Entrepreneurship, Theory & Practice, 40*(5), 1121–1148.

Brush, C. G. 2014. *Practicing entrepreneurship: Experimentation*. Babson Mini-Blog: Forbes. com. https://www.forbes.com/sites/babson/2014/11/09/practicing-entrepreneurship-experime ntation/#64ebed3a52f3

Busenitz, L. W., & Barney, J. B. (1997). Differences between entrepreneurs and managers in large organizations: Biases and heuristics in strategic decision-making. *Journal of Business Venturing, 12*, 9–30.

Caliendo, M., Fossen, F. M., & Kritikos, A. S. (2009). Risk attitudes of nascent entrepreneurs–new evidence from an experimentally validated survey. *Small Business Economics, 32*(2), 153–167.

Camerer, C. F., & Lovallo, D. (1999). Overconfidence and excess entry: An experimental approach. *The American Economic Review, 89*, 306–318.

Cao, H. H. & Hirshleifer, D. A., (2000). Conversation, observational learning, and informational cascades. Dice center working paper. London: John Wiley. no. 2001–5 https://doi.org/10.2139/ ssrn.267770.

Chen, C. C., Greene, P. G., & Crick, A. (1998). Does entrepreneurial self-efficacy distinguish entrepreneurs from managers? *Journal of Business Venturing, 13*, 295–316.

Colombo, M. G., & Grilli, L. (2010). On growth drivers of high-tech start-ups: Exploring the role of founders' human capital and venture capital. *Journal of Business Venturing, 25*(6), 610–626.

De Clercq, D., Hessels, J., & van Stel, A. (2008). Knowledge spill-overs and new ventures' export orientation. *Small Business Economics, 31*(3), 283–303.

Fischhoff, B. (1982). Chapter 31. Debiasing. In D. Kahneman, P. Slovic, & A. Tversky (Eds.), *Judgement under uncertainty: Heuristics and biases* (pp. 422–444). Cambridge, New York, Melbourne, Port Chester, Sydney: Cambridge University Press.

Forbes, D. P. (2005). Are some entrepreneurs more overconfident than others? *Journal of Business Venturing, 20*, 623–640.

Hayek, F. A. (1948). *Individualism and economic order*. Chicago: University of Chicago Press.

Hmieleski, K. M., & Baron, R. A. (2009). Entrepreneurs' optimism and new venture performance: A social cognitive perspective. *Academy of Management Journal, 52*(3), 473–488.

Jolls, C., & Sunstein, C. R. (2006). Debiasing through law. *The Journal of Legal Studies, 35*(1), 199–242.

Kahneman, D., & Riepe, M. W. (1998). Aspects of investor psychology. *Journal of Portfolio Management, 24*(4), 52–65.

Kahneman, D., & Tversky, A. (2000). Conflict resolution: A cognitive perspective. In D. Kahneman & A. Tversky (Eds.), *Choices, values, and frames* (pp. 473–487). Cambridge, New York, Melbourne, Madrid, Cape Town: Cambridge University Press.

Kariv, S. (2005). Overconfidence and informational cascades. unpublished working paper.

Kerr, W. R., Nanda, R., & Rhodes-Kropf, M. (2014). Entrepreneurship as experimentation. *Journal of Economic Perspectives, 28*(3), 25–48.

Kirzner, I. (1973). *Competition and entrepreneurship*. Chicago, IL: University of Chicago Press.

Koellinger, P., Minniti, M., & Schade, C. (2007). "I think I can, I think I can": Overconfidence and entrepreneurial behavior. *Journal of Economic Psychology, 28*(4), 502–527.

Moskowitz, T. J., & Vissing-Jørgensen, A. (2002). The returns to entrepreneurial investment: A private equity premium puzzle? *The American Economic Review, 92*, 745–778.

Palich, L. E., & Bagby, D. R. (1995). Using cognitive theory to explain entrepreneurial risk-taking: Challenging conventional wisdom. *Journal of Business Venturing, 10*(6), 425–438.

Parker, S. C. (2007). Policymakers beware! In D. B. Audretsch, I. Grilo, & A. R. Thurik (Eds.), *Handbook of research on entrepreneurship policy* (pp. 54–63).

Romer, P. M. (1990). Endogenous technological change. *The Journal of Political Economy, 98*, 71–102.

Schumpeter, J. A. (1934). *The theory of economic development*. Cambridge, MA: Harvard University Press.

Shane, S. (2009). Why encouraging more people to become entrepreneurs is bad public policy. *Small Business Economics, 33*(2), 141–149.

Shane, S., & Venkataraman, S. (2000). The promise of entrepreneurship as a field of research. *The Academy of Management Review, 25*, 217–226.

Soll, J. B., Milkman, K. L., & Payne, J. W. (2015). A user's guide to debiasing. In *The Wiley Blackwell handbook of judgment and decision making*. London: John Wiley (Vol. 2, pp. 924–951).

Urbig, D. (2010). Base rate neglect for the wealth of interacting people. *Advances in Complex Systems, 13*(05), 607–619.

Urbig, D., & Weitzel, U. (2009). A plea for individually 'irrational' entrepreneurship: How entrepreneurial overconfidence affects payoffs of an entrepreneurial population. *Frontiers of Entrepreneurship Research, 29*(6), 300.

Wu, B., & Knott, A. M. (2006). Entrepreneurial risk and market entry. *Management Science, 52*(9), 1315–1330.

Where Would I Be If My 25 Year-Old Self Was Aware of the Gravitas of Dr. David Audretsch?

Brett Anitra Gilbert

Abstract Using their relationship and years of academic discussions as a backdrop, chapter author Brett Anitra Gilbert outlines David's career, interests, and impact, highlighting the last two decades. Noting David's long-standing high profile in academia, Gilbert discusses David's humility and willingness to grant opportunities to others. Gilbert includes comments on David's famous ability to recall journal articles and to organize his thoughts on the fly.

The Gravitas of Dr. David Audretsch

It is not often that you have the privilege of meeting someone who would so profoundly shape the course of your life destiny. But this is precisely what happened to me as a 25 year-old, first year PhD student who took a seminar with Dr. David Audretsch. The seminar was on Globalization, Entrepreneurship and Economic Development. It was a second semester course for me, but also a requirement for my entrepreneurship major. I knew the topic would be of interest to me, but never did I imagine that it would shape my research trajectory for nearly two decades and counting.

David structured the course such that one of the topics introduced to us was on Silicon Valley - one of the most preeminent geographic cluster regions. We learned about how successful this region had been in producing innovative firms and generating economic development for the region, but also on the negative effects that the success had created. We learned that cluster regions were being used as policy tools in many other countries to promote economic development. As a native of Detroit, Michigan, I was drawn to the way that entrepreneurship had revolutionized Silicon Valley to its level of success. I was curious to know what could be learned from such regions that could be transferred to economically repressed regions in inner cities

---

B. A. Gilbert (✉)
American University, Washington, DC, USA

Kelley School of Business, Indiana University, Bloomington, IN, USA
e-mail: bgilbert@american.edu

© Springer Nature Switzerland AG 2019
E. E. Lehmann, M. Keilbach (eds.), *From Industrial Organization to Entrepreneurship*, https://doi.org/10.1007/978-3-030-25237-3_35

like Detroit, where I was from, but also to developing countries where the entire nation could benefit from economic development. The more I learned from David, the more I wanted to know.

One day after class, I approached David with my interest in learning more about how cluster policy was being used to promote entrepreneurship. Unbeknownst to me at the time, David's research had largely focused on entrepreneurship, innovation and geography, policy, and knowledge. In the years leading up to 2001 when I was his student, he was engaged in extensive independent and collaborative research around industry, innovation and geography with esteemed scholars such as Drs. Maryann Feldman and Roy Thurik. He was also engaged in a variety of research on the policy side.

On the geography track, his work leading up to 2001 had explored interesting questions such as the relationship between geography and innovation, and its influence on international advantage (Audretsch 1998); how economic activities are organized within regions and how the composition of regional economic activity influences innovation (Feldman and Audretsch 1999) and production (Audretsch and Feldman 1996). His policy work was exploring the content (e.g. Audretsch 2000a, 2001) and impact (e.g. Audretsch 2000, 2000b,) of policy.

My interest in more thoroughly exploring how clusters contribute to the success of regions naturally struck a cord with David's work. Through weekly meetings, we began to develop the paper that eventually evolved into our publication entitled, "The Emergence of Entrepreneurship Policy" (Gilbert et al. 2004). As David's work had long centered on understanding various aspects of firm characteristics on innovation or performance, it is no surprise that our conversations led to my dissertation topic which explored how cluster regions affect new venture performance. David served as a key committee member on my dissertation, which received a Kauffman Dissertation Grant and was also nominated for the Heizer Award for best dissertations by the Entrepreneurship division of the Academy of Management. We later published two other manuscripts with my dissertation chair – Dr. Patricia McDougall-Covin – one of which was from my dissertation; the other an article a review of the literature on new venture growth (Gilbert et al. 2008).

Writing the manuscript, "The Emergence of Entrepreneurship Policy," gave me unique insights into the way David's mind works. At each meeting, we sat down at the computer and typed as our discussion on the topic unfolded. I recall being amazed at the ease with which David recalled articles and was able to structure his thoughts into a coherent framework as we talked. I rarely left his office without a book or article that I used to read up on the topic. Oftentimes these books came directly from David's shelves (I can only hope I remembered to return them all!).

This experience not only produced a manuscript, but also a very rewarding mentorship.

David often invited his graduate students to the many dinner parties that he and his equally wonderful wife, Joanne, hosted at their home. It is because of David that I have met many great scholars in the field, and made great friends through functions he hosted at Indiana University as well as at the Max Planck Institute in Germany. While I loved both settings, the visits to Germany were particularly special memories for me as someone who had studied in Germany as an undergraduate and truly doubted I would actually use the language after I graduated! The visits that David's office often funded, were amazing memories from my doctoral program.

From writing letters of recommendation, to introducing me to prominent scholars, and selecting me to serve as an Editor for *Small Business Journal: An Entrepreneurship Journal*, David has been a mentor who has gone above and beyond to create opportunities for me. As an African-American woman who has achieved a level of success in academia, I am acutely aware of how far one can go when given the opportunity. I am grateful to have had David as one of several mentors to do this on my behalf, and also to continue to enjoy his support to this very day! It is always a pleasure to see David annually at the Academy of Management Conference each August, where if I am not breaking bread with him over a meal, I am seeing him in a meeting we are both attending. He is always one of my favorite people to catch up with at the conference.

As I conclude my reflections, I recall the awe I experienced as I looked back over David's CV to prepare this manuscript. And when I specifically examined the publications that David had prior to 2001 when I took his PhD seminar, I was shocked by the sheer number of publications he already had accumulated 20 years ago. I and am convinced that if the Internet of today had existed back then, and my 25 year old self had looked up his CV, I would have been entirely too intimidated to approach him with my idea. This is truly one time in my life that I was grateful for my ignorance!

Thank you, David, for being a wonderful mentor, co-author and importantly friend throughout the years. Your significant impact on our field is forever imprinted in the books. I hope you now also know how significantly you have impacted my life as well!

References

Audretsch, D. B. (2000a). *Small business problems: The policy response in the U.S. Wirtschaftspolitische Blaetter 47*, 155–164.

Audretsch, D.B. (2000b). Statistical Analysis of the National Academy of Sciences Survey of SBIR Awardees: Analyzing the Influence of the Fast Track Program. In C. Wessner (ed.), The Small Business Innovation Research Program. National Academy Press.

Audretsch, D. B. (2001). *Programs to support innovation and the development of small business in Finland and the United States: A review of current policy and research*, Otaniemi International Innovation Centre. *Small business problems: The policy response in the U.S. Wirtschaftspolitische Blaetter 47*, 155–164.

Audretsch, D. B. (1998). Agglomeration and the location of innovative activity. *Oxford Review of Economic Policy, 14*(2), 18–29.

Audretsch, D. B., & Feldman, M. (1996). R&D spillovers and the geography of innovation and production. *American Economic Review, 86*(3).

Audretsch, D.B., Weigand, J., & Weigand, C. (2000). Does the small business innovation research program Foster entrepreneurial behavior? Evidence from Indiana. In C. Wessner (ed.), The small business innovation research program. National Academy Press, 160–193.

Feldman, M. P., & Audretsch, D. B. (1999). Innovation in cities: Science-based diversity, specialization and localized monopoly. *European Economic Review, 43*, 409–429.

Gilbert, B. A., Audretsch, D. B., & McDougall, P. P. (2004). The emergence of entrepreneurship policy. *Small Business Economics, 22*(3–4), 313–323.

Gilbert, B. A., McDougall, P. P., & Audretsch, D. B. (2006). New venture growth: A review and extension. *Journal of Management, 32*(6), 926–950.

Gilbert, B. A., McDougall, P. P., & Audretsch, D. B. (2008). Clusters, knowledge spillovers and new venture performance: An empirical examination. *Journal of Business Venturing, 23*(4), 405–422.

The Multidisciplinary Entrepreneurship Scholar

Erik Stam

Abstract A scholar is a person who studies an academic subject and knows a lot about it. A great scholar in the academic subject of small business economics is David B. Audretsch. He even co-created small business economics as an academic subject! But David has also had an impact on a broad range of academic disciplines. A look at David's most highly cited publications (in Google Scholar and Web of Science) shows the broad disciplinary range of his high-impact publications. It is first and foremost economics (including the journals American Economic Review, European Economic Review, Review of Economics and Statistics). He is even the 20th most cited economist of the world according to Google Scholar. But his high-impact work can also be found in geography (Regional Studies, Annals of Regional Science), management (Journal of Management, Journal of Management Studies), entrepreneurship (Journal of Business Venturing, Entrepreneurship Theory and Practice), and innovation journals (Research Policy, Industry and Innovation, Journal of Technology Transfer). In his recent research he also endeavours into psychology (Welpe et al., Entrepreneurship Theory and Practice 36:69–96, 2012); (Obschonka et al., Social Psychological and Personality Science 7:95–104, 2016). The Small Business Economics Journal, just like David's research, is first and foremost economics, but is also very much a multidisciplinary endeavour. It is an endeavour to achieve a better understanding of entrepreneurship, firms and the economy at large, informing and improving public policy to stimulate entrepreneurship and economic growth, not by coincidence the name of the unit David founded and led at the Max Planck Institute of Economics in Jena. In this essay I will discuss the value of multidisciplinary scholarship, in general and in particular for economics, and use David as an exemplar scholar in that respect.

E. Stam (✉)
Utrecht University School of Economics, Utrecht, Netherlands
e-mail: e.stam@uu.nl

© Springer Nature Switzerland AG 2019
E. E. Lehmann, M. Keilbach (eds.), *From Industrial Organization to Entrepreneurship*, https://doi.org/10.1007/978-3-030-25237-3_36

Multidisciplinary Scholarship

Academic disciplines can be defined as academic studies that focus on a self-imposed limited field of knowledge. Academic disciplines as the primary unit of internal differentiation of science is a nineteenth century invention: before the rise of academic disciplines there was no such thing as disciplinary scholarship. Disciplines can be demarcated based on three criteria: the phenomena of interest, their research methods, and their theories (epistemologies). The good thing is that academic disciplines provide a means for the accumulation of knowledge (theories and tools) about particular phenomena: expertise of one community, build up over time. The bad thing is that a disciplinary view on the world, tends to be reductionistic (focusing on one aspect). Sticking to one discipline has at least two drawbacks. First, research that limits its scope to one disciplinary silo is likely to be inferior to research drawing from the fields of knowledge beyond any one disciplinary silo. Second, solving the world's problems requires knowledge from multiple disciplines (Terjesen and Politis 2015). Even though there are great benefits in having academic disciplines, most scientific and societal progress is likely to be realized with multidisciplinary scholarship. David's work is an excellent example of the power of multidisciplinary scholarship: producing superior research starting with economics, but enriched with other disciplines, in order to better understand this multifaceted phenomenon called entrepreneurship. Starting with economics, can his research be qualified as multidisciplinary economics?

Multidisciplinary Economics?

Multidisciplinary economics is an odd term. Can one discipline be multidisciplinary? This seems to be a linguistic impossibility. From a historical point of view, however, economics has always been multidisciplinary. Economics largely emerged out of (moral) philosophy, and initially evolved as political economy, considered as a branch of the science of the legislator (Smith), combining what we would now call economics, law and political science. Economics has been created as a separate discipline in the nineteenth century. The disciplines it teamed up with have changed. Initially, history and sociology were its companions, with the German historical school (Schmoller, Sombart), and the 'sociological' studies of capitalism by Marx and Weber. But later on mathematics and physics became the preferred partners, going back to Cournot, Von Thunen, Walras, Fisher, combined into the 'invention' of econometrics (Frisch, Tinbergen), and creating the dominance of general equilibrium theory (Arrow, Debreu). More recently we see combinations with psychology in behavioral economics (Kahneman, Tversky), with history, law, sociology and political science in institutional economics (North, Williamson, Ostrom), and with history and geography in evolutionary economics (Arthur, Boschma). So economics has always been in the company of other disciplines. One may say that combining economics with other disciplines is a good thing. Friedrich Hayek even claimed that an economist who is only an economist cannot be a good economist. The question is what makes a good economist? I suggest that the answer is that a good economist is someone who develops and disseminates scientifically rigorous and societally relevant economics knowledge. The rigor and relevance can be improved with enriching economics with other disciplines. Teaming up with physics and mathematics made economics more rigorous, while teaming up with the other social sciences and humanities made economics more relevant.

Rigor and Relevance: Small Business Economics for the Real World

A good economist is someone who develops and disseminates scientifically rigorous and societally relevant economics knowledge: economics for the real world. This is in contrast to irrelevant economics that is disengaged, ivory tower science. It is also in contrast to economics that has turned into a belief, not setting itself up for discussion. This happens when economist say that they "believe in the market", or "believe in entrepreneurship". The latter has frequently been stated by policy economists, advocating entrepreneurship policy. A situation in which policy runs ahead of theory. David is an excellent example of "small business economics for the real world". Leading the small business economics field, while standing on the shoulders of (scientific) giants before him (Schumpeter, Galbraith, Solow, Arrow), and using the tools and theory of economics to better understand the antecedents and consequences of entrepreneurship. It is a scientific approach for better understanding entrepreneurship, but also engaging with public policy to improve the real world.

David is a great multidisciplinary scholar, who combines economics with other disciplines, combines rigor and relevance, and in this way created a "small business economics for the real world".

References

Obschonka, M., Stuetzer, M., Audretsch, D. B., Rentfrow, P. J., Potter, J., & Gosling, S. D. (2016). Macropsychological factors predict regional economic resilience during a major economic crisis. *Social Psychological and Personality Science, 7*(2), 95–104.

Terjesen, S., & Politis, D. (2015). From the editors: In praise of multidisciplinary scholarship and the polymath. *Academy of Management Learning & Education, 14*(2), 151–157.

Welpe, I. M., Sporrle, M., Grichnik, D., Michl, T., & Audretsch, D. B. (2012). Emotions and opportunities: The interplay of opportunity evaluation, fear, joy, and anger as antecedent of entrepreneurial exploitation. *Entrepreneurship Theory and Practice, 36*(1), 69–96.

Thoughts About David

Sameeksha Desai

Abstract David has been a strong and consistent influence on the career of Prof. Sameeksha Desai for more than a decade, being an advisor, colleague, mentor, coauthor and collaborator, and friend. In this chapter the author considers how she has gained a great deal, professional and personally, from his wisdom, mentoring, generosity, and friendship for so many years. Having met David in 2005, when he became the external member on her dissertation committee, Prof. Desai went on to become a research fellow in his group at the Max Planck Institute of Economics in Germany. In 2010, the author joined the faculty at Indiana University, where she occupied the office next door to him and became his colleague.

David has been a strong and consistent influence on my career for more than a decade, and I have been fortunate to know him in many formulations – as an advisor, colleague, mentor, coauthor and collaborator, and friend. I have gained a great deal, professional and personally, from his wisdom, mentoring, generosity, and friendship for so many years.

I met David in 2005, when he became the external member on my dissertation committee. Later, I was a research fellow in his group at the Max Planck Institute of Economics in Germany. In 2010, I joined the faculty at Indiana University, where I occupied the office next door to him and became his faculty colleague.

The nature of my relationship with David has changed many times. His sincerity and his advice, however, have not changed over the years. As a PhD student working on what some might have considered a risky topic, David reminded me that if I cared about it, I should do it. As a junior researcher unsure about how to navigate publishing, conferences, and the job market, David spent many hours helping me think through my decisions. He encouraged creativity and collaboration. As a faculty colleague at Indiana, David has been my collaborator and friend. I am very grateful for the proximity that allows me to pop my head into his office for a quick chat. Those chats continue to contribute meaningfully to my career, and are a highlight and a perk of coming to work.

S. Desai (✉)
Indiana University Bloomington, Bloomington, IN, USA
e-mail: desai@indiana.edu

© Springer Nature Switzerland AG 2019
E. E. Lehmann, M. Keilbach (eds.), *From Industrial Organization to Entrepreneurship*, https://doi.org/10.1007/978-3-030-25237-3_37

It is difficult to sum up the impact of David's influence on my career and on my personal intellectual development, so I instead will share a few observations and memories about David over the years.

I first met David when he came to a workshop at my university when I was a PhD student. I lived near the airport and offered to drop him off for his flight, but then I remembered that my muddy dog had been in the front seat earlier that morning. I apologized for the mess and offered to call a taxi for him. David sat on the muddy seat, told me a little mud wasn't going to hurt his clothes, and we had a great conversation about research all the way to the airport.

David has made a few simple suggestions that come up again and again. When I asked him for advice about a new work environment, he said to do good work, ask interesting questions, and get along with people. When I asked him an almost identical question several years later, he said something very similar. He's right – good researchers should do work they can be proud of, should be asking interesting questions to stay passionate and curious, and – of course – should be easy to get along with, so you enjoy having them as colleagues. Sitting in the office next door gave me the opportunity to observe that he embodies these three things himself. He has been working on entrepreneurship for decades, and he continues to be enthusiastic about new questions. His passion and his curiosity are obvious, and he enjoys the intellectual challenge of dealing with complicated problems. He is also easy to work with, provides value, and enthusiastic about collaborating on projects. I have collaborated on several projects and coauthored many papers with David, which has been meaningful for my career.

Another noteworthy thing about David is that he has never been too busy to make time. I have been struck, again and again, by his willingness to talk about ideas and problems, and to help me think through hard decisions. But this is just who he is, and how he is. I have seen him do this with colleagues and with students, and his sincerity in wanting to help is remarkable. I remember a PhD student, who was going through some difficult personal circumstances, stopping by my office after speaking with David to tell me that he felt much more clear about his plan and how he would get through the next year. I was not surprised to hear this, and his experience was not unique. David is genuinely interested in the well-being of the people around him – his colleagues, friends, and students - and he makes the time to share advice and to help when he can.

David is particularly supportive of junior researchers, and he is generous with his time, his networks, and his advice. When I was preparing my tenure dossier at Indiana, David gave me great advice on some of the challenges of going up for tenure in an interdisciplinary program, where there are no clear or unified disciplinary lists. He talked to me about the importance of describing and demonstrating the value of my research. His advice made me consider things I had not previously thought about, and it ultimately helped me shape my tenure dossier.

I have also benefited from David's advice about the trajectory of my career when presented with unusual and tempting opportunities. David has always encouraged me to pursue what is interesting, meaningful, and what I really want to do. When I have been given opportunities to do meaningful and interesting work, David wholeheartedly supported my interest and helped me realize that some risks are absolutely worth taking. I have not regretted any of these decisions.

David's influence on my career spans more than a decade, and I look forward to the next several decades. It is a pleasure to work with him and to know him, and to be able to walk down the hall and knock on his door. He is a bright light in my career and professional development, and I am grateful for his time, expertise, advice, and mentoring.

Part IV
Creating the Future

As the community of entrepreneurship scholars solidified into a bona fide research field, David turned increasingly to impact. David is well known for citing Johann Wolfgang von Goethe, and in particular the insight that, "Es ist nicht genug zu wissen, man muss es auch anwenden; es ist nicht genug zu wollen, man muss es auch tun," or "Knowledge alone does not suffice, it must also be applied: wanting is not enough, one actually has to do it."

In particular, David strove to influence thought-leaders in business and policy. This resulted in the 2007 book, *The Entrepreneurial Society*, published by Oxford University Press, where David explained how and why entrepreneurship matters not just to the entrepreneurs and their firms, but to a much broader constituency spanning the far reaches of society. As the founder and CEO of the Silicon Valley company, e-Silicon, Jack Harding described, "David Audretsch understands entrepreneurship. In *The Entrepreneurial Society* he rationalizes the history, causes, and significance of entrepreneurship as the current driving force behind America's successful return to global financial leadership. He also outlines the threats we face from abroad, again, if we fail to recognize the world is reshaping itself to compete on our knowledge turf. Once only a punchline to describe the maverick behavior of Silicon Valley, Audretsch has brought entrepreneurship permanently into the shared spotlight of academic research, public policy, and most important, global corporate strategy. His book is a first."

A second book followed, *Everything in its Place: Entrepreneurship and the Strategic Management of Cities, Regions and States*, published by Oxford University Press in 2015. From his time living and working Germany, David had been deeply impressed by *Standortpolitik*. Translated literally, it means place-based policies. David felt deeply that the deeply rooted mandate in Germany at the local, regional and state levels, resulted in enhanced competitiveness and higher levels of economic well-being along with social cohesion. His more liberal interpretation of *Standortpolitik* is the strategic management of place, which he explains in considerable detail in the book with applications throughout the developed countries.

Just as that book was being published, David and Erik were driving from Augsburg, Germany through the alps, *en route* to Bergamo, Italy. They marveled at the obvious prosperity of the Bavarian towns they passed through, and much of the rest of Germany that had seemingly proven to be resilient and untouched by the global economic crisis just a few years earlier. While the rest of Europe struggled, Germany was thriving. Yet, Germany's singular path to economic success remained virtually unmentioned both by the popular press as well as by the more analytic analyses of researchers and scholars. During their eight-hour drive they not only determined to write a book explaining what Germany was doing right when much of the rest of the world seemed bogged down by globalization, but they even drafted chapter titles. The result was *The Seven Secrets of Germany: Economic Resilience in an Era of Global Turbulence*, published by Oxford University Press in 2016. As Richard Baldwin, Professor of International Economics at the Graduate Institute in Geneva and Director of the Center for Economic Policy and Research (CEPR) shared, "Just when so many are asking 'How did Germany do it? A new book appears with some answers. In an enormously well-informed, erudite, and accessible manner, the authors point to seven features that help Germany thrive in the face of globalization, demographic challenges, the Eurozone crisis, and much more. The seven 'secrets', or features – which range from the small-is-beautiful Mittelstand to the growing comfort zone that Germans feel about being German citizens of the EU – allow Germany to foster the central drivers of economic prosperity: innovation, labor skills, and entrepreneurship."

While David's intellectual and early career roots may have been in the United States, his ideas, thinking and career was launched in the old world, and in particular first in Berlin at the Wissenschaftszentrum fuer Sozialforschung and later in Jena at the Max Planck Institute of Economics. As another of David's favorite quotes from Goethe, "The greatest thing that a father can give his son is roots, so he knows where he comes from. The second greatest thing is wings to escapes those roots." Just as economics and the field of industrial organization provided the intellectual roots for David, entrepreneurship research served as the wings to move beyond the roots.

In the twilight of his career, David prioritizes enabling the next generation to experience the joys and benefits accruing from both the roots and the wings. He is particularly passionate about the course he created, together with Erik and Silvio, which brings together students from the United States, Germany and Italy to work together to understand policies to ignite entrepreneurship at the local and regional levels. The course divides its time between Augsburg and Bergamo and has the students working in small, international teams. Even in an era when globalization and trans-national commonalities are on the defensive, David, together with his close colleagues and friends, remains busy with the relaunch: providing the next generation with the gift of wings to escape the roots.

Building Stronger Research Communities and Collaboration Between Established and Young Scholars

Maksim Belitski

Abstract Chapter author Maksim Belitski describes his life experiences with David and the broad impact that David has had in the area of the knowledge spillover theory of entrepreneurship. Citing personal stories and observations, Belitski details how David has always been a willing partner for academic collaboration and also provides insights on the secrets to David's success. This chapter thus forms an example of how David has ensured the future of entrepreneurship research by helping and inspiring up-and-coming scholars.

Introduction

This is the first time I have participated in the great academic exercise known as festschrift. Although at first I was not entirely sure how to approach the task of writing it, I decided to put together some ideas, experiences, thoughts, and future plans with a person who has been my advisor, mentor, friend and a significant person in my life. Indeed as one of my heroes as well as a highly-influential individual and scholar in the field of entrepreneurship, public policy, regional development and science research, David Audretsch has built strong communities among established, young and mid-career scholars. His ability to collect evidence and knowledge and then to engage scholars in a constant search for new ideas and evidence while remaining open to collaboration has produced many strong and robust ideas, co-creating and co-developing new scientific products in the spirit of the knowledge spillover theory of entrepreneurship (KSTE) (Audretsch and Lehmann 2005; Audretsch 2007; Audretsch et al. 2006; Acs et al. 2013). Having developed the KSTE, David himself has become a conduit of new ideas from from large established academic communities to newer communities with and young and mid-career scholars. He has sparked creativity and novelty in their visions of the world, creating small and innovative communities of new entrepreneurial scholars.

M. Belitski (✉)
Henley Business School, University of Reading, Whiteknights, Reading, UK
e-mail: m.belitski@reading.ac.uk

© Springer Nature Switzerland AG 2019
E. E. Lehmann, M. Keilbach (eds.), *From Industrial Organization to Entrepreneurship*, https://doi.org/10.1007/978-3-030-25237-3_38

Three Secrets of David Audretsch

What is the secret to David's successful implementation of the KSTE? The answer is collaboration and an ability to bring leading scholars together. Each scholar David introduced me to has to a greater or lesser extent contributed into my professional development as an entrepreneurship scholar.

David as a conduit of new ideas to both the established and newer academic communities. This is an important task, as many academic communities often remains blocked off within their professional and geographical boundaries with knowledge exchange being weak and rare. There are three factors which can help us understand why this happens and how to leverage a challenge of collaboration between academic communities.

The factor is that young academics usually lack funds to travel, participate in conferences or go on international trips to leading universities, so they are unable to integrate and make themselves visible to established communities of scholars. David is able to pick up talent and most importantly offer opportunities to engage with the community. He can help fledgling academics to become part of the wider community. Having secured the Fullbright scholarship, I started looking for a partner university in the United States to host me. I came across four world-leading scholars in entrepreneurship and regional development with whom I wanted to collaborate during the scholarship period. I emailed all of them a copy of my paper and a request to collaborate. Each of the four scholars was located in a different part of the USA: North Carolina, California, New England and the Midwest (David). Two of them never replied, while the Californian scholar put it on hold with the Dean. Meanwhile I will never forget David's response: he replied within ten minutes asking me what do I need to go to Indiana University's Institute for Development Strategies.

I was surprised and grateful to David and inspired by the trip to Indiana University, where I later enjoyed the best of the Hoosier's Midwest hospitality. This is how I learned about Indiana and the Midwest. At the time I worked part-time at the peripheral Brunel University in West London and studied at the University of Leicester where I was finishing my PhD. Ever since then I have continued to return to Indiana and work with David. Visiting Indiana University granted further opportunities to meet really talented people at the School of Public Economics and Environmental Affairs (such as Monika Herzig, Maureen A. Pirog, Marah Cohen, Chemain Nanney, Robert Kravchuk and John Graham) as well as at Indiana University's Kelley Business School (including Siri Terjesen, Don Kuratko and Jeffery McMullen). Building emotional connections requires time, commitment and most importantly hard work – reading, writing, putting puzzle pieces, travelling and reaching out to your stakeholders and building a relationship within your community.

The second factor why academic communities may experience difficulties in collaboration and delivering academic outputs is that academic researchers generally assume that the diversity of external collaboration partners increases the likelihood of complementarities in academic outputs. This may not be the case and leads many young scholars to fall into the "collaboration diversity trap". Young scholars often work hard on writing papers or a book while aiming to outreach as many different academic partners and communities locally, nationally and internationally as they can. They become a victim of the exploratory search and still may not know which academic communities are first and second best. Working with David I have come to realise the scope of collaboration and understand the importance of complementarities as well as "smart" research specialization. Smart specialization does not mean specialization within a narrow area or diversification; rather, it refers to working on two or three theories which are based on common grounds across various fields of science. David explained this very well using the example of academics and universities who successfully commercialize their research within the entrepreneurial university context (Audretsch 2014). These complementarities have sprouted in our collaboration with industrial, economic and geographic experts (such as Prof. Michael Fritsch and Erik Lehmann), family business and Mittelstand experts (Prof. Christina Guenther), public and entrepreneurship policy experts (Prof. Sameeksha Desai and Dr. Farzana Chowdhury) as well as talented scholars from side disciplines such as the music (in collaboration with Monika Herzig, talented musician and the author of Sheroes) and supporting entrepreneurship ecosystems in South Tyrol (in collaboration with PhD student Georg Eichler). The breadth and depth of collaboration is vast, although always focused within the area of entrepreneurship, innovation management, strategic management of places and the creativity perspective of the KSTE. While I deviate from smart academic specialization occasionally due to new exciting opportunities and work commitments, this has embellished the importance of the core field.

Although complementarities and the successful absorption of knowledge from the scholars I have met thanks to David has been extremely important and has profoundly facilitated my productivity and skills (Cohen and Levinthal 1989), I deeply enjoy working and writing with David, much more than with any of the other scholars in my community. Yes, much in our business relates to knowledge transfer and tapping into the world of ideas. However, it is also vital to have someone to challenge you across different areas. David's personal charisma, intelligence, wisdom and ability to fulfil his promises and never betray or compromise his relationships with the people who trust and collaborate with him has been one of his strongest assets in collaboration. This is possibly the most important virtue of both a man and an academic. Sometimes issues of funding can affect decision-making. People do compromise and go for "who pays more", while David is after long-term collaboration and strong professional relationships. For example, in 2013 one of my projects on "Externalities from investment in training for the UK innovative firms", which was sponsored by the UK government, was stolen from me by the host institution (not sponsor). For confidentiality reasons I will not disclose the name of the institution. I had two co-investigators on the project, one of which was David. Having realised the project was stolen from me he immediately left this project and never collaborated with that community again. I highly appreciated this decision, while the second collaborator chose to take the funding and continue with the project.

So far David and I, supported by various external collaborators and fellows, have successfully implemented two collaborative projects on "Knowledge transfers and knowledge boundaries for the New UK". We have delivered two exceptional workshops jointly with Professor Erik Lehman, Dr. Samee Desai and Dr. Rosa Caiazza. We are now starting work on an ambitious project on the application of the Newtonian laws of motion as a new scaling up model for entrepreneurs.

The third factor why established academic communities may be hard to enter is the reciprocal exchange of commitments and responsibilities, an ability to offer "blood, toil, tears and sweat" to community. I explain this using the resource-based view (Teece 1986) which suggests that collaborations are established to enhance a community's dynamic capabilities, and that established scholars are also required to contribute with resources. The engagement between new and established communities is likely to be more beneficial for young scholars, as it allows them to accumulate skills and exploit both internal and external knowledge sources within the community. Balancing the costs and benefits of such collaboration and building on the ideas of established scholars would require time and coordination costs. This may be a challenge, as many young and mid-career scholars would be reluctant to invest time working on the "ideas of others". In my experience, I have enjoyed working with David and following up and building on his ideas, in particular entrepreneurial society (Audretsch 2007), entrepreneurial university (Audretsch 2014) and the KSTE (Acs et al. 2013). Over time, I have made an important realisation – you cannot do all the work yourself, and need to let other scholars build on your ideas. I also started hiring younger scholars, usually part-time (to minimize costs and increase motivation) to collect data which could later be used to test research ideas. Collaborating across communities is not only a matter of skills; also important are how well collaborators get along and the extent to which their personalities match.

Towards a Successful Integration of New and Established Communities of Scholars

The effective integration of the skills and capabilities of young scholars with those of more established academic communities entails four obstacles to knowledge exchange. David's personality and reputation serves as a conduit of new ideas to produce new knowledge.

The first obstacle is that reaching out to different academic communities increases the time and transaction costs of collaboration, and may limit the returns on collaboration as it takes longer to return to the paper and do it again (coordination challenge). Workshops, research visits and communication with David via email has always helped me to keep track on what we have done and what we are developing, following the approach "If you do not send it to the journal – it will never be published". This wisdom has been a call to action to myself and many young scholars within David's academic community. I know people who have built their professional academic careers following David's principles.

The second obstacle is the incorporation challenge. How can you identify the best strategy to push your work forward? While sending our works to reviewers in the leading per review journals has not always been a success, the feedback we received in response has sometimes greatly facilitated further paper development. David motivated me by explaining the best ways to integrate knowledge from editors and reviewers and communication with other scholars into my daily research routines, which facilitated the successful acceptance of my papers and shortened the paper development process. We have never had the attitude that letters from editors and reviewers represent an implicit "indictment" of our own knowledge, as many scientists may feel when someone else tries to teach them how to do research and will resist to it (Veugelers 1997).

Thirdly is the valuation challenge. How much is your paper worth? I discovered with David that there are two answers to this question. Firstly, you will never know how many citations, reads and downloads it is worth unless you get it published, whether independently as a working paper, report or blog, or as a final academic paper. You need to get it out there – that's the rule. As the number of research questions increases exponentially, we are required to differentiate and publish some results as a blog (Belitski and Audretsch 2018). Secondly, you will never know how much your paper is worth if you do not apply for funding, adapting the paper to the project call. We have been successful in securing Newton's Fund grants from the British Council as well as the British Academy for the project "Tackling the UK's international challenges", and found out how much the paper we worked on was worth. Involving David as a co-investigator has without a doubt increased my chances of funding due to the high quality of all the grant applications we made together. David's leadership has increased the likelihood of success and getting our work out to potential stakeholders. Our collaboration has helped to distribute the time and emotional costs associated with innovating and commercializing research ideas while reducing the paper development life-cycle. I also received a promotion last year at the University of Reading to the post of Associate Professor in Entrepreneurship and Innovation.

Fourth is the knowledge appropriation challenge. Young scholars are very careful about sharing their ideas, as they are made to believe that ideas are very radical and intangible so it is easy to copy them. When collaborating the knowledge may indeed flow away and leak to other scholars (Cassiman and Veugelers 2002; Cassiman and Valentini 2016). Preventing this would require a monitoring cost, which young scholars are unable to afford, or knowledge protection, which is again not an option at the exploratory stage of research. While David is always very calm, he is also thrilled by knowledge inflows and outflows between scholars. I have learnt from him to appreciate opportunities to share ideas and blend them with other people's knowledge and inspiration. "You cannot fully protect your business ideas", David says; "you play as in jazz and you learn on the go... what is important is the knowledge spillover. As the result of idea creation new knowledge is produced, which always happens when you share knowledge. You give it away, but you also benefit by sharing ideas with others". The net effect of collaboration is always positive, which is the key as new ideas are generated. "We dedicated our life to the world of ideas", says David. Of course the knowledge collaboration pays off, and we acknowledge it has both costs and benefits.

Talking to David while development of new projects is itself the principal strategic resource, the knowledge which is difficult to access at the conferences and workshops, its intangible knowledge.

Conclusion and Future Plans

Over the last 9 years I have collaborated with Professor David Audretsch on many different projects, and I respect him for his power of thought and action to the highest degree. He is talented in the way that he sends messages across, and has made a decisive historical impact in the field of entrepreneurship and regional economic development. I also respect him as a friend, since I share his ideas about the world and life. I also very much enjoy talking to David about movies and the importance of films in explaining the most complex phenomenon in entrepreneurship and economics research. I believe the examples found in movies could be easily integrated into academic work as well as the teaching curricular of universities across the world.

Another useful skill I have learnt from David is working while I am travelling. This has become a very useful habit, and as long as I have my laptop and a socket to plug it into I can work anywhere. Many laptops can be used while travelling long distances by plane. I can almost picture David with his laptop in the airports of Amsterdam, Indianapolis, Charlotte, and even Paris! I wish to bring him to England in the near future as there are so many places, people and facts to be discovered. Working and travelling makes you more productive and replying to emails within 24 hours, as David does, gives a good picture of you.

One of the most crucial skills is being open and ready to go wherever research and partnerships will take you. The mix and match of new ideas and giving back to young scholars and international communities in the United States and Europe further enriches David's role as a conduit between scholars and different academic communities.

David's enthusiasm and openness to new ideas and people always strategically pays off to Indiana University and the global community of entrepreneurial scholars. His impact across disciplines and communities is a role model for young and mature scholars. Many of those who would prefer to stay locked in their office "bubble" or occasionally attending a national-level conference will struggle to scale up and enable knowledge spillover within or across scientific communities.

While knowledge is becoming increasingly more complex, be this entrepreneurship cognition, changes in labour market regulation or the knowledge spillover of entrepreneurship in a company, such s SAP, David's ability to explain complex issues with examples, stories and even anecdotal evidence is so valuable and important.

David's sense of humour unites, sparks and energizes people around him. The humour is always instructive and thought-provoking, and is also about asking hard questions about hard questions. Humour enters our life from the TV, cinema, travelling, speaking to friends and also scholars who share amusing stories about situations they have encountered. The ability to bring an audience's attention to important issues which are nonetheless usually overlooked with attention to details is one of David's skills. Telling stories which derive from movies, life situations, the experiences of friends and other events make theories and hypotheses more appealing and easier to comprehend and explain.

David's future research along with his interdisciplinary communities will bring new perspectives to the knowledge spillover theory of entrepreneurship, strategic management of places, collaboration and exogenous growth theories. We need David to further guide and inspire young and mid-career scholars on the theoretical, empirical and methodological aspects of our research.

On his anniversary, I would like to wish him many more years of productive and novel work as well as limitless health and ambition. David, thank you for your humour, knowledge and wisdom, and for being an exceptional collaborator and a friend! This has meant so much to me.

References

Acs, Z. J., Audretsch, D. B., & Lehmann, E. E. (2013). The knowledge spillover theory of entrepreneurship. *Small Business Economics, 41*(4), 757–774.

Audretsch, D. B. (2007). *The entrepreneurial society*. New York: Oxford University Press.

Audretsch, D. B. (2014). From the entrepreneurial university to the university for the entrepreneurial society. *The Journal of Technology Transfer, 39*(3), 313–321.

Audretsch, D. B., & Lehmann, E. E. (2005). Does the knowledge spillover theory of entrepreneurship hold for regions? *Research Policy, 34*(8), 1191–1202.

Audretsch, D. B., Keilbach, M., & Lehmann, E. (2006). *Entrepreneurship and economic growth*. New York: Oxford University Press.

Belitski, M., & Audretsch, D. (2018). What do cities want? Blog of the International Network for Small and Medium Sized Enterprises (INSME). Published 17 September 2018. Available from: https://insme.wordpress.com/2018/09/17/what-do-cities-want/

Cassiman, B., & Valentini, G. (2016). Open innovation: Are inbound and outbound knowledge flows really complementary? *Strategic Management Journal, 37*, 1034–1046.

Cassiman, B., & Veugelers, R. (2002). R&D cooperation and spillovers: Some empirical evidence from Belgium. *American Economic Review, 92*(4), 1169–1184.

Cohen, W. M., & Levinthal, D. A. (1989). Innovation and learning: The two faces of R&D. *The Economic Journal, 99*(3), 569–596.

Teece, D. J. (1986). Profiting from technological innovation: Implications for integration, collaboration, licensing and public policy. *Research Policy, 15*(6), 285–305.

Veugelers, R. (1997). Internal R&D expenditures and external technology sourcing. *Research Policy, 26*(3), 303–315.

"Lessons from David Audretsch" in Festschrift for David Audretsch

Siri Terjesen

Abstract It is an honor to covey best wishes to David Audretsch on his "Festschrift." It is my great privilege to have known David for more than 15 years. This essay conveys ten of the personal lessons I have learned, often quite tacitly, from David during our shared time at the Max Planck Institute of Economics and Indiana University, as well as our many interactions through Small Business Economics, Academy of Management, and other conferences.

Lessons from David Audretsch

While I've had the opportunity to publish interviews with terrific economists and thinkers such as Nobel Laureates Vernon Smith and the late Ronald Coase (Economics) and Muhammad Yunus (Peace) as well as the late Bill Baumol, I only spent a few hours one-on-one talking with these individuals. With David, I benefited from sustained and frequent interactions on many topics, and am deeply grateful to David for conveying wisdom which I seek to pass on to the next generation of scholars. Thank you, David, for all your lessons which I can't possibly distill and convey as eloquently as you have, but let me offer a top ten list.

Create a network of scholars with complementary skillsets: Like the many other young scholars who spent summers and sometimes years at the Max Planck Institute of Economics, I was first introduced to David's outstanding ability to bring together scholars from varying disciplines—a propensity that continues on with David's network of scholars in SPEA's Institute for Development Strategies and other endeavors. David created the backdrop for so many wonderful "collisions" of researchers, young and experienced, across a breadth of disciplines. While we built terrific and long-standing professional networks and often co-authorships, we also gained a true sense of belonging to a community. More than a decade later, I count my Max

---

S. Terjesen (✉)
Florida Atlantic University, Boca Raton, FL, USA

Norwegian School of Economics, Bergen, Norway
e-mail: sterjesen@fau.edu

© Springer Nature Switzerland AG 2019
E. E. Lehmann, M. Keilbach (eds.), *From Industrial Organization to Entrepreneurship*, https://doi.org/10.1007/978-3-030-25237-3_39

Planck colleagues among my closest friends and collaborators, and am so grateful for this warm welcome into what can sometimes be a harsh field.

Put others in the path of opportunity: David's legacy also includes his willingness to put others in the path of opportunity, whether nominating young scholars to serve as reviewers at *Small Business Economics*, to present or discuss at conferences, or to run for office in the Academy of Management's Entrepreneurship Division. Once again, these "early collisions" with the leading institutions in our field provided tremendous leadership experience, and an opportunity to interact with a wider network. In doing so, David often delegated and allowed these young scholars to really rise to the occasions and flourish.

Take time to mentor junior scholars: Although David was infinitely busy with a number of projects, I was among many junior scholars to benefit from his close mentoring on research papers and general topics in academia, as well as how to manage three young children. David has always been so focused on helping others, often sharing his own trials and tribulations as a lesson. I'm particularly grateful that David often took a devil's advocate approach, really digging in and testing the underlying assumptions so that I might make more informed decisions.

Exercise and take care of oneself: During our shared Bloomington years, one could often find David (and his awesome wife Joanne) at the local YMCA "Y" gym, working out. I admire how again an infinitely busy David could still find time to get to the "Y" for stair-climbing, tread-milling, and track-walking. In the earliest years of my career, when it was hard to justify getting away from my research to go for a run or a bike ride, I thought of David and Joanne, and how this "off" time really gave me better "on" time later.

Throw a great party every once in a while: Again, during our Bloomington years, I was so fortunate to join some terrific Thanksgiving and other parties that David and Joanne hosted. These parties were always welcome to families (the children often clustered around the ping pong table and other activities in the basement) and brought together an eclectic and merry bunch for hours on end.

Create a guest bedroom called the "The Famous Economist Room" and host scholar friends often: David and Joanne hosted many a "famous economist" in their guest bedroom downstairs for visits. We quickly instituted the same tradition at our house, and have enjoyed many terrific stays over the years.

Make time for adventures: At Max Planck, I witnessed how David and Joanne brought their (then young) sons Alex, James, and Christopher to Jena for summers and the chance to really live in another country. Back in the US, they took a 2006 Honda Odyssey minivan for many adventures around the city, state, and country. When my twins Britt and Finn were born in 2012 and the Audretsch boys were nearly all in college, we bought the "Audretsch Adventure" van, and have subsequently driven it through many states and up to 120,000 miles.

Choose your battles wisely: As a distinguished professor at Indiana and an honorary professor at several other universities, David could have sought to exert an influence on all matters of the school and university. I watched as David was extremely gracious and frankly seemingly not bothered by most administrative matters. He selectively pursued only a few "battles" which were really critical to him and his colleagues and students.

Treat all colleagues as equals: David is gracious to all colleagues across the universities and institutions that he interacts with, treating them with respect and compassion. This egalitarian nature extends from secretarial staff to undergraduates, graduates, and faculty. I believe that this culture also inspired undergraduate students to work on research projects with faculty, with some students going on to their own PhD studies.

Pursue new ideas and a unique path: David often shared the story of how Nobel Laureate Elinor "Lin" Ostrom came to Indiana University and followed a quite unusual path of teaching at undesirable hours, and working outside traditional departments to develop her scholarship. David has frequently given me the advice to try something new, and that this "new thing" might then lead to other new and exciting options.

I am indebted to David for these and other life lessons, and look forward to many lessons to come.

Off to New Shores: Knowledge Spillovers Between Economics and Psychology or How I Published with David Audretsch in PLOS One

Martin Obschonka

Abstract It is probably correct to say that David Audretsch's impressive research oeuvre demonstrates a strong interest in the question of where new ideas and knowledge come from, and why and how they matter for the modern economy and society as a whole. This obviously concerns research on patents, universities and scientists, industry structure, finance, public policy, and knowledge spillover processes. This chapter describes how David was always willing to stretch a hand across the academic aisle, constantly willing to embrace a true multidisciplinary mindset.

Knowledge Spillovers Between Economics and Psychology

For people like me, a psychologist by training with a strong interest in economics and management research, this, at first glance, does not seem to be a research question where a lot of psychology and psychological processes are involved. Typically, psychologists care about psychological factors and processes associated with thinking, feeling, and actual behavior. So how did I end up working and publishing with THE David Audretsch – something that turned out to be one of the most rewarding and enriching experiences in my academic career (although our probably most important and best paper ended up in an open access journal that, I assume, very few economists would consider a "fancy" outlet for economic research).

First, and I guess the reader gets a very direct impression of this when trying to follow my long, awkwardly structured sentences in this essay, I am German. David Audretsch has many links to Germany and I guess this helped a bit. We both spend considerable time in our academic career in the city of Jena, he in one of the highest positions the German academic system has to offer, as a director of a Max Planck Institute, and me in one of the lowest positions – a PhD student and then Postdoc. Jena is widely known as a prime example of successful knowledge spillover from

---

M. Obschonka (✉)
Australian Centre for Entrepreneurship Research, QUT Business School, QUT, Brisbane, QLD, Australia
e-mail: martin.obschonka@qut.edu.au

© Springer Nature Switzerland AG 2019
E. E. Lehmann, M. Keilbach (eds.), *From Industrial Organization to Entrepreneurship*, https://doi.org/10.1007/978-3-030-25237-3_40

university to society. The lens maker Carl Zeiss, for example, would have never become a worldwide leading producer of optical systems if Ernst Abbe, a research professor at the local university, would not have helped with his research findings around 150 years ago. Just another example of a fruitful collaboration of two worlds, in this case manufacturing and basic university research. And of an interaction between knowledge and entrepreneurial people (what is exactly the topic of the PLOS One paper that I am going to describe later).

Second, David Audretsch is of course very interested in entrepreneurship research. Entrepreneurial processes are crucial in knowledge spillover processes, when new ideas and knowledge get transformed into actual economic outputs, like Ernst Abbe's research helped Zeiss to produce groundbreaking new microscopes that, in turn, helped Nobel Prize laureate Robert Koch to set the foundations of modern bacteriology. Although a psychologist, which means a Diploma in Psychology in Germany, I did my Phd and Postdoc in Jena in the field of entrepreneurship research, in an interdisciplinary project with economists. It was a longer way and required a lot of sweating until I became the new Director of the Australian Centre for Entrepreneurship Research (ACE) at QUT in Brisbane, Australia, my current position, but this focus on entrepreneurship as a fascinating research field seems to be another common feature between David Audretsch and me.

Third, in my Postdoc time I had published a paper on something that nobody ever did before, but that seems so close to David Audretsch's work and that could potentially be considered a knowledge spillover from psychology to economics: Linking regional differences in the Big Five personality traits within a country to entrepreneurship outcomes such as startup rates of a region (Obschonka et al. 2013). In fact, the paper looked at an entrepreneurial constellation of the Big Five traits, measured by means of large-scale psychological datasets, and replicated the regional link between this local entrepreneurial personality structure and hard entrepreneurial outcomes in the US, the UK, and Germany. Or in other words, it established that regions and regional populations differ in their entrepreneurial personality structure and that this has implications for actual economic outcomes and trajectories of regions – and of course also for knowledge spillover processes. Indeed, when I asked him if he wants to collaborate on a new paper that takes this research agenda linking the geography of psychology to hard economic outcomes to the next level he immediately agreed. I think this was at an Academy of Management Conference in Orlando, Florida or so. I am still very grateful that I got this unbelievable chance.

So what did we do in the project, which also involved Michal Stuetzer, an economist – a highly talented colleague and my counterpart since the Jena PhD period, and Sam Gosling and Jason Rentfrow, two internationally renowned psychologists and leading in the field of geographical psychology? Together with David Audretsch, we developed a research agenda that, supported by a grant from the German Fritz Thyssen Foundation, would examine the interplay between the psychological infrastructure, so to speak, and central economic features of places. This time we would not examine large spatial units like in my 2013 JPSP paper, but smaller units such as MSA's in the USA, metropolitan areas where economic activity, new knowledge, and people really cluster and interact. David Audretsch came up with the idea to

Off to New Shores: Knowledge Spillovers Between Economics and Psychology or How... 427

look at the knowledge paradox – namely that a pure focus on knowledge production (e.g., investments in universities and research labs, and human capital in general) did not lead to economic growth per se, although leading economists and policy makers assumed for a long time that knowledge production is the via regia to a successful modern economy – where new ideas and knowledge is really everything. Something was missing. And we believed this something could be the local culture and the psychological infrastructure of a region. It might require both the production of new ideas and knowledge in a region, but also a certain local psychological climate and entrepreneurial people and mindsets to stimulate entrepreneurial activity and thus local growth and prosperity in the modern economy.

We therefore tested statistical interactions between the regional prevalence in the entrepreneurial personality profile, measured from almost 1 million US residents via an internet project, and local knowledge production, measured via human capital (local population share with a college degree) and also industry structure (assuming that a diverse mix in the local industry facilitates knowledge creation and spillover processes). We could not only replicate the earlier US state-level correlation between regional entrepreneurial personality and entrepreneurial activity at this smaller and more fine-grained spatial level, but, more importantly, we also found the expected interaction between the knowledge recourses and the psychology of places. In other words, the data was consistent with one potential but so far only hypothetical solution of the knowledge paradox, that regional knowledge per se might not lead to particularly strong and productive economic activity, but that it also requires a certain psychological infrastructure that might turn this local and other knowledge into entrepreneurial activity and thus actual economic outputs that can be measured empirically. This was a great finding, in our view – probably a breakthrough. Particularly since we could replicate it in a completely independent study in the UK (analyzing regional personality differences collected from more than 400 thousand people). We added this replication to the paper – so we had a major two-study paper on our desk.

So we had to decide which journal could be interested in such truly interdisciplinary work combining economics and psychology with such interesting, replicated results. Well, what can I say, in the end we decided to try SCIENCE and PNAS, something like holy grails for such interdisciplinary work. Since these journals want shorter but highly sophisticated papers, we were confronted with a set of new challenges and we really invested some energy in writing such a SCIENCE-like paper. I must say I learnt a lot in this process and David Audretsch really helped us in many ways. And he was always open for feedback and comments and this was truly special, given that he is such a high caliber researcher and economist that could have easily dominated the whole process. We were all full of passion for the project, and on something very important, at least we thought so. Anyway, long story short, we were rejected from SCIENCE and PNAS (something very common, of course, for many papers submitted there), mostly for the typical criticism in economic research, namely causality issues. For some reasons, we then thought it might be a good idea to stick to interdisciplinary journals – probably also because the paper was really written from an interdisciplinary point of view, which might make it hard to publish in a specialized journal like an economic geography journal. So we came up with the idea of trying PLOS One, and I remember that this was the idea of the psychologists in the team, but David Audretsch agreed. PLOS One was considered, and I think it still is, an innovative outlet for interdisciplinary work as it follows a very different model than the standard journals. It would make all papers open access (authors have to pay for this though) and it would only judge the scientific rigor in the paper to determine whether this paper can be published. So in the end we were successful and published our paper in PLOS One (Obschonka et al. 2013). I like the journal and I think PLOS One really paved the way for further positive developments in the publication business. However, today I also often wonder whether we should have stopped when getting negative feedback from SCIENCE and PNAS and thought about other major outlets that economists and policy makers obviously take more seriously. But this would have involved a lot of effort and time, and when one is younger in the academic career, like Michael Stuetzer and me at that time, without tenure and under considerable publication pressure, one cannot always find this time and patience. Today I, and also Michael, have tenure and we can reflect on this, but in this earlier phase we wanted to get the interesting paper published, rather sooner than later. So this is the story why I published with David Audretsch in PLOS One (Obschonka et al. 2015), and also why the main paper is actually so short (it still reflects the SCIENCE style of writing papers). On the one hand, I still think that it makes a lot of sense to submit one's best research to such an open access journal because many people can actually read it. On the other hand, and maybe David Audretsch would agree, we sold the study a little bit under value. C'est la vie.

Nevertheless, at the end of the day, and also in the eyes of the funder, the collaboration with David Audretsch was a unique success with a number of additional papers published in this project, for example also one that links regional personality to actual economic growth of regions. I am very grateful for this. I also think that particularly the PLOS One paper, but also the following publications in this project, played an important role for my personal career progress – although I cannot really say how. While writing these lines, I am sitting in the basement of MIT Sloan, one of the world's powerhouses in economic and management research. I am fortunate to be working here as International Faculty Fellow in this semester and I am literately sitting on a new project that continues the fruitful combination between psychology and economics, and that also builds on the PLOS One paper and the intellectual input by David Audretsch. But this new project is a different story and I have to come to an end.

I wish David Audretsch all the best for his future and I hope this short essay could express my gratefulness and excitement associated with every second of our collaboration. I will go home now, the day is over, and on my way home I will probably think a little bit about the fascinating question of what makes Boston so unique as a place and one of the entrepreneurial hotspots of the world. This will probably, and I am in fact quite sure about this, involve something that David Audretsch has said, written about, or maybe even thought. Who knows.

References

Obschonka, M., Schmitt-Rodermund, E., Silbereisen, R. K., Gosling, S. D., & Potter, J. (2013). The regional distribution and correlates of an entrepreneurship-prone personality profile in the United States, Germany, and the United Kingdom: A socioecological perspective. *Journal of Personality and Social Psychology, 105*(1), 104–122.

Obschonka, M., Stuetzer, M., Gosling, S. D., Rentfrow, P. J., Lamb, M. E., Potter, J., & Audretsch, D. B. (2015). Entrepreneurial regions: do macro-psychological cultural characteristics of regions help solve the "knowledge paradox" of economics? *PLoS One, 10*(6), e0129332.

A Brief Case Study of the Audretsch Form of Davidial Entrepreneurship Research Ecosystems

Allan O'Connor

Abstract The concept of an ecosystem has been adapted to human societies through the lens of human ecologies. However, to date there has been no research conducted on the unique context of the Davidial Entrepreneurship Research Ecosystem (DERE) particularly in its Audretsch form. In this article, we examine the ideas of boundary influences of a DERE through a specific case study of the Audretsch Davidial ecosystem. We conclude that a specific David of the Audretsch type, is an essential part of the dynamics of entrepreneurship research and in a DERE analysis neither the David nor his writings are an appropriate unit of analysis to comprehend the scale of influence. Rather, it is the dominant entrepreneurship research ecosystem that becomes focal, and within that, we find the Audretsch Davidial influence is a powerful force of change that transcends any possible specification of boundaries.

Introduction

Most of the entrepreneurship literature has analysed entrepreneurship as an isolated phenomenon shaped by the influences of the individual herself or the firm itself but with little acknowledgment of outside external influences. However, since the late twentieth Century the analysis of ecosystems has become more prominent. Recently a wave of important studies has specifically linked context to entrepreneurship research (Autio et al. 2014; Malerba and McKelvey 2018; Spigel 2017; Shepherd 2015) but none to date have considered the Davidial influence. However, such questions as, what exactly is meant by a Davidial entrepreneurship research ecosystem, and how a Davidial entrepreneurship research ecosystem emerges, are yet to be revealed. Here we examine how the Davidial entrepreneurship research ecosystem influences and is influenced by boundary effects that apply across various levels.

A. O'Connor (✉)
University of South Australia, Adelaide, SA, Australia
e-mail: Allan.OConnor@unisa.edu.au

© Springer Nature Switzerland AG 2019
E. E. Lehmann, M. Keilbach (eds.), *From Industrial Organization to Entrepreneurship*, https://doi.org/10.1007/978-3-030-25237-3_41

Boundaries of Place and Space

I approach the topic of a Davidial entrepreneurship research ecosystem (DERE) by questioning how boundaries have evolved around the presence of a David in a particular place. Place is generally considered as 'bounded and specific to a location, and is a materialization of social forms and practices as well as affective experience' (Gieseking et al. 2014, p. xx). I approach the analysis of the DERE by borrowing from a branch of the biological sciences that deals with the relations between organisms and their environment (Aldrich 1990) and hence the reference to environment induces or suggests the concept of place. Therefore, I argue a DERE is strongly related to a physical place that renders an environment hosting social relationships that shape and influence where and how people interact in various ways and over time. While this may be the case, it does not diminish the challenge of 'how to figure out where an ecosystem starts and where it ends' (Ahokangas et al. 2018, p. 399) and this is particularly the case of the Audretsch Davidial entrepreneurship research kind. Nevertheless, the DERE is implicitly connected to the ideas of place and our case study of the Audretsch DERE for instance is more specifically responsible for producing books that focus on issues such as the strategic management of place.

Space is something distinct to place. Space is defined as 'abstract, unlimited, universalizing, and continuous' and concerned with the 'ether of flows and travel, or the metaphorical space one needs to think' (Gieseking et al. 2014, p. xx). Considering the DERE from this perspective suggests distinct dimensions of place and space. For instance, the DERE fits well with multi-level studies that engage different geographical boundaries with flows between and across micro-, meso-, and macro-levels of analysis. In our case, the Audretsch DERE nurtured in Detroit (the micro-level), commenced studies at a university located in a state some 600 miles away, e.g. Drew University (meso-level), and later contributed significantly to the United Nations, the World Bank, the OECD, the EU Commission, and the U.S. Department of State affecting national and international levels (macro-level). Consider also social networks and social capital dimensions encountered by the Audtrestch DERE, freely mixing with different ethnicities and races or various learning institutions such as the Max Planck Institute, and one can understand how relationships and networks span the globe exploding any inference of boundary. It quickly becomes apparent that the DERE in these terms may stretch across countries with flows of ideas, articles, books and friendships forming part of the ecosystem construct for any particular DERE (Neumeyer et al. 2018). When thinking about a Davidial ecosystem, avoiding fixation on a geographic place, opens up countless possibilities of interactions across unbounded and abstract dimensions of space.

The reach of a DERE, I argue, is strongly influenced by a David's Bachelor degree education. For instance, the Audretsch type of David of our case, studied at a University in the forest, Drew University, Madison, New Jersey, which initiated the early development of the DERE. A forest, in general terms, is a terrestrial eco-

A Brief Case Study of the Audretsch Form of Davidial Entrepreneurship Research...   433

system within which the inter-relational processes between communities of organisms and their environment are supported by a dominant system of trees (Kimmins 2004). Systems of trees vary according to temperature, longitude and latitude (Vogt et al. 1995). The species of trees between those zones can also vary and furthermore not all forests within the same zone will have exactly the same species of trees. Influenced by this education in the forest, the Audretsch type of David learned early that forests differed according to their climatic and spatial positioning and in composition of flora, fauna and inanimate objects. I argue this background education influenced the evolution of the Audretsch DERE, inspiring a persistent quest to engage with various universities around the globe to forge new links with forests of all forms. In so doing, the influence of the Audretsch DERE steadily expanded.

The distances between boundaries of a DERE may also be deceptive when considered through various lenses of geography, industry, journals, articles, co-authors and farmers. Hence, credence is given to the claim that ecosystem boundaries are inherently fluid and difficult to identify (Jansson et al. 2014; Ahokangas et al. 2018). In these terms, a DERE may transcend a geographical identity of place whereby global or national flows of knowledge and resources, transitory stakeholders and dissociated farmers extend beyond the bounds of a specific place from within which the affective Davidial activity has taken place. To illustrate, through our case, consider the distinguished Audretsch David on his way to an important meeting at Purdue University. This David transcends locality, buzzing around the country and while at the margins of the ecosystem influence, he becomes disoriented and frustrated by seemingly contradictory directional choices. Stopping at frequent forks in the road, with unfathomable equidistant choices to the same destination, the Audretsch David persistently calls upon the assistance of hard working farmers to ask directions. Sweaty and dusty, invariably the farmers provide a consistent response and take no responsibility or interest in the frustrated Audretsch David's choice of road to travel. While the Audretsch DERE has extraordinary national and international reach, the envelope of boundaries for the Audretsch David can mean nothing to farmers lurking at the edges of a DERE or between DEREs and this is particularly so for those farmers in the rural heart of the USA.

Appreciating the difference between place and space therefore has significant implications for the way we think about and treat of DEREs. This is so as definitions of entrepreneurship ecosystems contain specific reference to the interactions among the actors and elements (Acs et al. 2014; Audretsch and Belitski 2016; Regele and Neck 2012; Roundy et al. 2018) and this is no less so for the Davidial form of entrepreneurship research ecosystem. If we are to examine the interactions then it would seem necessary to know within which boundary definition to examine such interactions. However, a place-based view suggests or imposes a set of conditions within which the interactions take place and interactions outside of or crossing the boundary of place are contextualised with the specific definition of a place centric DERE. By contrast, a space-based view of the same concept opens up all manner of interactions so much so that a bounded DERE becomes almost meaningless because the interactions are beyond any empirical specification. Taken to the absurd, the DERE of a small community on a remote island called Australia is the equivalent to

434 A. O'Connor

the best performance of the DERE in Berlin as the dimensions of space in abstract terms are universal and continuous with all things, in some way, sitting within a series of interactions. The remote island of Australia is part of the space of Berlin and vice versa and while it may invite the theoretical lens of chaos theory for its analysis, it does not serve our purpose well in understanding more specifically the relevance of boundary to a DERE.

In practice, we argue neither a pure place nor space definition of boundary for a DERE can reliably be scrutinised to reveal the essence of a DERE. For example, in an era of rapid global movement among people, ideas, and capital, our case illustrates that the Sydney School for Entrepreneurs in Australia interacts with Indiana University, USA at some level through transportations of an Audretsch David (reminiscent of the early penal colonies of Australia). At the same time, the interactions within Sydney will be influenced by the Audretsch DERE differently to the nature and manner of interactions within Indiana. Both in theorising and practice terms, simply put, context matters for DERE theorising.

The changing contexts of Davids of all types, risks concealing issues that influence the range and mix of Davidial activity that may occur within any place specification. If we are concerned with what is 'Davidial' in the ecosystem, then we must determine both the underpinnings that support the dominant entrepreneurship research pattern and then the change effect of Davidial influence both within and outside of the boundaries embracing both place and space dimensions. We need to acknowledge the dominant entrepreneurship research pattern of the place specification and how it is influenced by global trends and cycles. Within the place specification, the pattern of micro distinctive areas of entrepreneurship research need to be identified within that dominant macro pattern. The distinctive areas that contrast to the dominant activity are where a DERE is most likely to assert some influence, changing and bringing about subsequent growth of new areas of entrepreneurship research. For instance, at one time Detroit was considered a strong ecosystem of secondary industry but its diversity was arguably severely diminished by the loss of the Audretsch David, leaving the ecosystem vulnerable and less resilient during times of change and declining global trends. The study of DEREs needs to acknowledge first the dominant dispersion of entrepreneurship research to identify the effect the DERE causes and this is especially so, our case reveals, when it is of an Audretsch Davidial form.

Conclusion

In conclusion, returning briefly to the forest ecological roots of the Audretsch David, we find that forests are defined by the specific characteristics of five terrestrial ecology attributes, namely: structure, function, interconnectedness, complexity and change over time (Kimmins 2004). A definition of a DERE therefore, should account for the specific characteristics of the entrepreneurship research attributes that drives and encourages Davidial activity. Thereafter, governance can focus on planning specific interactions that alter the characteristics of the entrepreneurship research to, preferentially, attain increasing levels of Davidial influence, however defined. Therefore, the primary unit of analysis is not the 'species' of activity (e.g. the Audretsch David) but what function the Audretsch Davidial activity performs within a place and how that function is supported or otherwise. Our discussion therefore concludes that the structural issues of entrepreneurship research is to a large extent affected by Davidial activity, as the Audretsch case illustrates. DEREs have the capacity to change the course of entrepreneurship research. When that Davidial influence is of a particular Audretsch type, whether it be the mid-west of the USA, or in diverse countries in Europe such as Spain or Germany, or in remote parts of Australia, like Adelaide, the Audretsch Davidial influence is immense and invariably manages to transcend any notion of boundaries.

References

Acs, Z., Autio, E., & Szerb, L. (2014). National systems of entrepreneurship; measurement issues and policy implications. *Research Policy, 43*(3), 465–622. https://doi.org/10.2139/ssrn.2008160.

Ahokangas, P., Boter, H., & Iivari, M. (2018). Ecosystems perspective on entrepreneurship. In R. V. Turcan & N. M. Fraser (Eds.), *The Palgrave handbook of multidisciplinary perspectives on entrepreneurship* (p. 387). Cham: Palgrave Macmillan.

Aldrich, H. E. (1990). Using an ecological perspective to study organizational founding rates. *Entrepreneurship Theory and Practice, 14*(3), 7–24.

Audretsch, D. B., & Belitski, M. (2016). Entrepreneurial ecosystems in cities: Establishing the framework conditions. *Journal of Technology Transfer.* https://doi.org/10.1007/s10961-016-9473-8. Accessed Dec 2016.

Autio, E., Kenney, M., Mustar, P., Siegele, D., & Wright, M. (2014). Entrepreneurial innovation: The importance of context. *Research Policy, 43*, 1097–1108.

Gieseking, J. J., Mangold, W., Katz, C., Low, S., & Saegert, S. (2014). In J. J. Gieseking, W. Mangold, C. Katz, S. Low, & S. Saegert (Eds.), *The people, place, and space reader* (p. xx). New York, USA: Routledge.

Jansson, N., Ahokangas, P., Iivari, M., Perälä-Heapeh, M., & Salo, S. (2014). The competitive advantage of an ecosystemic business model: The case of OuluHealth. *Interdisciplinary Studies Journal, 3*(4), 282–295.

Kimmins, J. P. (2004). Forest ecology. In T. G. Northcote & G. F. Hartman (Eds.), *Fishes and forestry: Worldwide watershed interactions and management* (pp. 19–43). Oxford, UK: Blackwell Publishing Company.

Malerba, F., & McKelvey, M. (2018). Knowledge-intensive innovative entrepreneurship integrating Schumpeter, evolutionary economics, and innovation systems. *Small Business Economics.* https://doi.org/10.1007/s11187-018-0060-2.

Neumeyer, X., Santos, S. C., & Morris, M. H. (2018). Who is left out: Exploring social boundaries in entrepreneurial ecosystems. *The Journal of Technology Transfer, 44*, 462–484. https://doi.org/10.1007/s10961-018-9694-0.

Regele, M. D., & Neck, H. M. (2012). The entrepreneurship education sub-ecosystem in the United States: Opportunities to increase the entrepreneurial activity. *Journal of Business and Entrepreneurship, Winter, 25*.

Roundy, P. T., Bradshaw, M., & Brockman, B. K. (2018). The emergence of entrepreneurial ecosystems: A complex adaptive systems approach. *Journal of Business Research, 86*, 1–10.

Shepherd, D. A. (2015). Party on! A call for entrepreneurship research that is more interactive, activity based, cognitively hot, compassionate, and prosocial. *Journal of Business Venturing, 30*(4), 489–507. https://doi.org/10.1016/j.jbusvent.2015.02.001.

Spigel, B. (2017). The relational organization of entrepreneurial ecosystems. *Entrepreneurship Theory and Practice, 41*(1), 49–72.

Vogt, K. A., Vogt, D. J., Brown, S., Tilley, J. P., Edmonds, R. L., Silver, W. L., & Siccama, T. G. (1995). Dynamics of forest floor and soil organic matter accumulation in boreal, temperate and tropical forests. In J. M. Kimble, E. R. Levine, & B. A. Stewart (Eds.), *Soil management and greenhouse effect* (p. 159). Boca Raton: CRC Press.

David Audretsch Has Impacted My Academic Life in Many Ways and I Would Like to Use This Opportunity to Thank Him for His Tremendous Support

Kathrin Bischoff

Abstract Kathrin Bischoff, who authored the following chapter, tells of how David is an excellent mentor and promoter of the development of young scholars on both sides of the Atlantic. With David on her dissertation committee, Bischoff was able to receive his guidance on multiple occasions and also benefitted from his invitation to come from Germany to spend a summer researching with him in Indiana. Always thinking of ways that he could be a resource to the future generation of research, David's mentorship of the author is typical of his generous personality.

I first met David in 2015 when I was enrolled as a Ph.D. student at the University of Wuppertal, Germany. My supervisor, Prof. Christine Volkmann, has crossed parts with David beforehand and has enabled me a three-month stay with David as visiting scholar at the Institute for Development Strategies of Indiana University. I was very thankful for this opportunity. During my visit to Bloomington, I had the opportunity to discuss my research with David. Not only did David provide me with valuable feedback on my papers but he also used his network to introduce me to fellow researchers and lecturers in the field of entrepreneurship. I felt very well supported during my time at Indiana University by David and his team. Moreover, David invited me to become a junior research fellow at the Institute of Development Strategies which I am very grateful about. David has allowed me to step into new networks of experts related to entrepreneurship. After my stay in Bloomington, I was invited to participate in three different conferences twice in Berlin (physically) and once in Bloomington (virtually via Skype) in order to present the findings of my research. This feedback has been highly valuable in order to sharpen my papers for publication.

After my second thesis supervisor passed away, David agreed to step in as a second supervisor. I am very flattered and honored that David wrote an evaluation of my PhD thesis and was part of my oral defense committee. Throughout my thesis

---

K. Bischoff (✉)
Entrepreneurship and Intercultural Management Schumpeter School of Business and Economics University of Wuppertal, Wuppertal, Germany
e-mail: Kathrin.bischoff@mwide.nrw.de

© Springer Nature Switzerland AG 2019
E. E. Lehmann, M. Keilbach (eds.), *From Industrial Organization to Entrepreneurship*, https://doi.org/10.1007/978-3-030-25237-3_42

process David has strengthened the development of my papers and has helped me prepare my work for submission and publication. Based on David's feedback I was able to submit to and ultimately publish a co-authored paper in a leading journal which has helped my academic career significantly.

Overall, I believe that David is an excellent mentor and promoter of the development of young scholars. I am extremely thankful for all his support throughout the years.

David Audretsch: A Great Mind, An Outstanding Researcher, and A Humble Individual

Mehmet Akif Demircioglu

Abstract If somebody asked me to define David Audretsch in a few words, I would define him as the following: a great mind, an outstanding researcher, and a humble individual. Few people possess these three characteristics at the same time. His characteristics have entirely shaped my career, and David became my academic role model.

The first time I met Prof. Audretsch was when I was offered a position as his research assistant for a project on the economic performance of cities in the spring of 2010. Although I used to hear his name mentioned as the most productive scholar at the School of Public and Environmental Affairs (SPEA) at Indiana University-Bloomington, I had not found a chance to meet him. Two other research assistants and I worked hard to finish the project; we spent close to 3 months preparing a report while receiving regular feedback from Prof. Audretsch. After we submitted the project to him, he worked on it for only a few days, and we realized that he had completely updated what we wrote. I was really impressed by what he accomplished in a few days, as his version was a much better and more highly-developed paper compared to the version that three research assistants prepared over 3 months. However, he appreciated our efforts and told us that our product was very good.

The next time I interacted with Prof. Audretsch is when I went for an overseas study at the Hertie School of Governance in Berlin (Germany) in May 2010, which was organized by SPEA. When I saw the course advertisement, I found that Prof. Audretsch was leading the program, and I did not want to miss this opportunity. I wanted to learn useful information from him, hear his stories (since he is a great storyteller with outstanding experiences of the Cold War in Berlin), visit high quality German institutions with him and other classmates, motivate myself to work harder (as he is also a great motivator), and start writing my papers on organizational change and innovation in public organizations.

M. A. Demircioglu (✉)
Lee Kuan Yew School of Public Policy, National University of Singapore, Singapore, Singapore
e-mail: mehmet@nus.edu.sg; https://lkyspp.nus.edu.sg/our-people/faculty/demircioglu-mehmet-akif

© Springer Nature Switzerland AG 2019
E. E. Lehmann, M. Keilbach (eds.), *From Industrial Organization to Entrepreneurship*, https://doi.org/10.1007/978-3-030-25237-3_43

When the overseas program started at the Hertie School, he gave us a lecture on how and why institutions matter. At first glance, his lecture did not seem well organized; he was talking about Germany, other European Union countries, the United States, Turkey, then moved on to his early experience in Berlin, Turkish doner kebaps, eventually returning to the topic again, providing an example from a movie, then moving to another topic, drawing something on the blackboard, and so on. Although all these examples seemed unrelated, however, he was able to connect all the dots at the end of the lecture. For me, it was one of the best lectures I had ever attended in my entire life. The lecture was highly original, creative, and effective in connecting seemingly unrelated examples with one another. I can never forget the satisfaction I felt about his lecture and the joy of learning. I wished to interact with him more often to gain more knowledge, to look at the same issues from different angles and become more creative.

Because the program in Germany was 2 weeks long and David and the students used the same metro to go from the hotel to the school, I talked with him and learned a lot on these shared trips, and he was very patient with my questions. In addition, we visited many public organizations in Berlin together. Overall, his guidance made this summer program highly productive and a great experience.

Life passed smoothly after that and I was enjoying my first year of the doctoral program. It was during this time that I tried visiting his office once a month to learn something, exchange ideas, seek his advice, and talk about how to write good papers. However, I postponed visiting his office for a while due to my qualifying exams. When I finally passed my exams, I started visiting his office again (after 2014). It was during my final year of the doctoral program (the 2016–2017 academic year) that I submitted my first article on "Conditions For Innovation in Public Organizations" to the Journal *Research Policy*. I was asked to revise and resubmit this work. But I became somewhat stuck in the revision, so I asked if I could collaborate with him for this piece. I still remember that when he agreed, it was a great moment for me. We worked on the paper together and after multiple revisions, the paper was finally accepted. Thus, it became my first major publication (Demircioglu and Audretsch 2017). And while this paper was in the process of being published, we started working on a new paper that analyzed the effects of universities on the benefits of innovation. We were able to publish this piece in the *Journal of Technology Transfer* (Demircioglu and Audretsch 2019). I was also interested in complex innovations in the public sector, so I asked him whether he could collaborate with me on this project. After working on the manuscript for a year with multiple changes and many iterations, our third piece, "Conditions for Complex Innovations," was recently published by the *Journal of Technology Transfer* (Demircioglu and Audretsch 2018). We have also worked on a project on sources and types of innovation using original data from the United States, and another joint paper was published in *Industrial and Corporate Change* (Demircioglu et al. 2019). Meanwhile, we have continued to work on many different projects, including two book proposals. Our collaboration makes my academic writing more efficient and effective.

David Audretsch: A Great Mind, An Outstanding Researcher, and A Humble Individual 441

Another milestone for me was when David Audretsch visited the Lee Kuan Yew School of Public Policy, at the National University of Singapore, as a distinguished professor. Despite his busy schedule, I was privileged to host him at our school for a week in April 2018. During this visit, we worked together for at least 2 hours every day, and this allowed us to not just start our work on a new project but also to have deep conversations about life outside academia. We walked to the Botanic Gardens and many other places, and all of these moment provided opportunities for great conversation. In addition, my colleagues at the LKY School found his visit to be very helpful. He was generous in giving us two different lectures, and one of them was on how to write and publish. His presentations, his meetings with several administrators, faculty members, and students clearly showed everyone that he was not just an outstanding researcher with a great mind, but also a very humble and generous individual.

Collaboration between the two of us did not just bring about publications, but the process of collaborating with him helped me shape my career. I have witnessed and observed how he writes his papers, and I have learned a lot about crafting a paper from him. In addition, he has encouraged me and my work on many occasions. I have witnessed that he is supportive and encouraging of all his students. He cares about his students, and he writes strong reference letters for his outstanding students. Even though he is always busy, he still finds time to meet with his students. He is humble and always open to suggestions. My experiences have shown me that he is original, creative, smart, and he is always committed to what he does.

Upon reading my observations about Prof. Audretsch, one might think that he was my advisor, but he was not; he was not even a member of my dissertation committee. Readers may imagine the legacy and influence of Prof. Audretsch on his students. For me, he has been an inspiration, a mentor, and an academic role model. Sometimes I wish I could spend more time with him and just observe how he does his research. Apart from being a wonderful human, he is a great researcher and an important academic figure. He will be remembered not only because of his outstanding work on innovation and entrepreneurship but also because of his warm personality, advising, and mentoring of students. I am honored to know him, delighted to talk with him, privileged to collaborate with him on several publications, and I look forward to writing more papers with him.

Finally, since not everyone is lucky enough to work with Prof. Audretsch, I would like to share some of the advice that I have received from him, which may be useful to other readers in their work.

Some lessons that I learned from Prof. Audretsch:
- Your work should have quality and it should not have "obvious mistakes." Prof. Audretsch defines them as important mistakes, especially when they consist of important missing information in the literature, method, results, or the discussion part. However, he asks one not to be a perfectionist since a paper will never be perfect.
- Try to finish a project, but don't give up. If you cannot publish the paper in the best journal, send it to another journal.

- Even when you make just one contribution to a paper, do it well. Be clear and explicit about your contribution; keep emphasizing it. It is about both efficiency and effectiveness. Trying to make a bigger contribution may challenge you from the standpoint of your reviewers. Also, you may save your other ideas or contributions for your next project.
- "The key to getting a paper published is not to explain 'Everything.' It is to explain 'One Thing' that has not yet been (adequately) analyzed. Keep your focus on the donut and not the hole."
- "Journals these days don't just want a good paper. They want a paper that is good for their literature and community."
- "It's much better to be as general and universal as possible. No need to explain the measurement, data or methods in the title, unless they are really the contribution."
- "Think of common sense in trying to explain and justify each hypothesis. You (we) should be able to explain this without any literature. Then insert the literature to support and/or change your arguments as they evolve. The most important thing is the story. No one is going to quibble if you interpret or apply a study broadly and with anticipation. First story. Then support from the literature."

References

Demircioglu, M. A., & Audretsch, D. (2017). Conditions for innovation in public sector organizations. *Research Policy, 46*(9), 1681–1691. https://doi.org/10.1016/j.respol.2017.08.004.

Demircioglu, M. A. & Audretsch, D. (2019). Public Sector Innovation: The Effect of Universities. *The Journal of Technology Transfer, 44*(2), 596–614.

Demircioglu, M. A., & Audretsch, D. (2018). Conditions for complex innovations: evidence from public organizations. *Journal of Technology Transfer.* https://link.springer.com/article/10.100 7%2Fs10961-018-9701-5.

Demircioglu, M. A., Audretsch, D. B., & Slaper, T. F. (2019). The effects of sources of innovation on innovation type: Firm-level evidence from the United States. *Industrial and Corporate Change.* https://doi.org/10.1093/icc/dtz010.

Happy Birthday, David Audretsch: And All That Jazz

Monika Herzig

Abstract Being honored to contribute to this special Festschrift and express gratitude to David, chapter author Monika Herzig refers to David as, "my brilliant, generous, funny, and inspirational colleague at Indiana University." Herzig chose to write a personal salute to David and a celebration of community, as her expertise is the collaborative and improvisatory art form of jazz music.

All That Jazz

The School of Public and Environmental Affairs at Indiana University fosters an interdisciplinary community and with David's inspiration I was able to integrate the artistic practice of jazz as a model for the creative aspect of entrepreneurship. David Audretsch's support and encouragement played a major role in combining the fields and building bridges amongst the disciplines. Being a facilitator and building bridges is the trademark of a great visionary like David – this is my example, the transformational story from the entrepreneurial artist to the artistic entrepreneur.

More than 30 years ago, I arrived in Tuscaloosa at the University of Alabama with a one-year scholarship on a one-way ticket from Germany. I was determined to create a career as a musician and composer and tour the world. I quickly realized that besides putting in many hours of practice I also needed to hone my business and entrepreneurial skills finding places to play, producing recordings, running a record label, running non-profit organizations, marketing and advertising, branding, creating business plans and itineraries and so much more. Most of these skills were acquired by trial and error and many detours. Hence, after finishing my Doctorate at the Indiana University Jacobs School of Music and teaching about any music class possible I decided to create a course that would help future generations of musicians and music professionals avoid the detours and move quickly towards their goals.

M. Herzig (✉)
O'Neill School of Public and Environmental Affairs, Indiana University, Bloomington, IN, USA
e-mail: mherzig@indiana.edu

© Springer Nature Switzerland AG 2019
E. E. Lehmann, M. Keilbach (eds.), *From Industrial Organization to Entrepreneurship*, https://doi.org/10.1007/978-3-030-25237-3_44

The Music Industry courses that I designed eventually became popular ingredients of a new Arts Administration program, the vision of Chuck Bonser, former Dean of the School of Public and Environmental Affairs (SPEA) at Indiana University.

The breadth of fields and degree offerings in SPEA is quite broad, and I found myself working next to experts in governance, law, chemistry, biology, non-profit management, business, entrepreneurship and so much more – initially quite confusing and the cause of a bit of an identity crisis. In my quest of finding role models, I put a book together on legendary jazz educator and one of my biggest mentors David Baker and worked with him on an analysis of the unique dynamics of jazz jam sessions. As a result of our research, we were able to extract seven essential factors of jam sessions that facilitated creative group interaction.

Former Dean Bonser sensed my need to find my niche and like-minded individuals and one day walked me into David Audretsch's office to meet this brilliant individual and share about my work on group creativity. David showed a genuine interest in the model and we laughed and chatted for hours about jazz and Germany and entrepreneurship and so much more. He loved the idea and of course immediately had stories to exemplify the concepts. My favorite one is how he gets his students to realize that it's ok to come up with different solutions for the same problem. He will play Julie Andrews singing "My Favorite Things" for his students and then put on the famous jazz version by John Coltrane. Even though the recordings have very little in common in terms of style, performance, or concept, it's still the same song just different interpretations – both are different solutions to the same problem. Little did David know how important this message and his encouragement was for me in my academic identity crisis.

A few weeks later, a dynamic young man with a British/Russian accent knocked on my door and told me that David had sent him over to learn about my jam session model. Maksim Belitski is an Entrepreneurship expert from the Henley School of Business in Reading, UK. David thought we should collaborate and boy was he right. Maks helped me translate the model into his field, we published together and I even got to spend several weeks in Reading teaching his students and creating an Arts Entrepreneurship course. In the meantime, David invited me to write a chapter on group creativity for a book on Entrepreneurship, facilitated the publication of our article, and extended an invitation to a Berlin conference with his colleagues. Just by opening the doors to all of these opportunities he transformed me into the academic with the necessary credentials and confidence that integrated me into the SPEA community and solved my identity crisis. He believed in me to the extent of making me a co-author for one of his many book projects when others dismissed me as a homeless jazz musician among real academics. He built bridges by facilitating connections, providing encouragement, telling stories – and he always made me laugh.

Oh – and do ask me sometimes about the evening when the international gathering of Entrepreneurship professors decided to go to the Yorckschlößchen in Berlin, Kreuzberg to witness a live jazz jam session. Neither the professors nor the musicians were quite sure what to expect from each other. I joined the group of musicians on stage and soon had everyone cheering and snapping fingers, witnessing the unique and immediate interaction during a jazz jam session. A picture is worth a thousand words, they say, and no scientific paper presentation and discussion could have clarified the principles of the jam session model as clearly as this evening's live demonstration. But it took someone to facilitate the conference and the communal evening activity in order to make the connection between the fields and experts, and that someone was sitting at the back table sipping a beer and observing the process with a big smile. Another Entrepreneurship mission accomplished –

Thank you from the bottom of my heart for believing in this jazz musician, helping me connect the dots, building my confidence and research skills, writing countless letters of recommendations, and guiding me towards finding the ideal balance of creativity and research. And of course, you have permission to single me out in every meeting and use me as the odd example to make everyone laugh. I'm hoping on many more years of fascinating collaborations, travels, jam sessions, dinners, and most of all laughter.

A Simple Behavioral Model of Stochastic Knowledge Accumulation

Torben Klarl and Matthias Menter

Abstract This short paper highlights selected achievements of David B. Audretsch, outlines the special role David played in shaping our academic careers and introduces a simple behavioral model of stochastic knowledge accumulation with a link to David's work. Compared to the rational economy, this model assumes that behavioral agents do not fully acknowledge a change of the knowledge production due to aggregated knowledge stock changes. One explanation for this behavior is that behavioral agents cognitively discount future events more, the more distant such events are in the future.

Introduction

David B. Audretsch is without any doubts one of the most renowned scholars in the field of innovation economics, small business and entrepreneurship. We are very honored to contribute to this *Festschrift* with an essay, having the opportunity to both outline David's enormous impact on small business and entrepreneurship research and our academic careers as well as compose a very short research paper with a link to David's work, which we hope, he feels comfortable with.

David shaped our careers early on and helped us to develop our independent research profiles in the fields of entrepreneurship, innovation, regional development

---

T. Klarl (✉)
Research Fellow at SPEA, Institute for Development Strategies, Indiana University, Bloomington, Bloomington, IN, USA

University of Bremen, Faculty of Business Studies and Economics, Bremen, Germany
e-mail: tklarl@uni-bremen.de

M. Menter
Research Fellow at SPEA, Institute for Development Strategies, Indiana University, Bloomington, Bloomington, IN, USA

Friedrich Schiller University Jena, Faculty of Economics and Business Administration, Jena, Germany
e-mail: matthias.menter@uni-jena.de

© Springer Nature Switzerland AG 2019
E. E. Lehmann, M. Keilbach (eds.), *From Industrial Organization to Entrepreneurship*, https://doi.org/10.1007/978-3-030-25237-3_45

and macroeconomics respectively. He continuously supported us through his ongoing advice with regard to research and beyond, resulting in multiple joint publications, the invitation to come to his institution as visiting scholars, and the admission to the *Institute for Development Strategies* at the School of Public and Environmental Affairs at Indiana University Bloomington as research fellows. David has served us as a role model throughout our entire careers for various reasons. First, his irrepressible urge to question existing perspectives and come up with valuable and relevant new research questions. His seminal research on innovation in small and large firms, the integration of (R&D) spillovers and local/regional dimensions, or the conceptualization of the knowledge spillover theory of entrepreneurship are thereby just some highlights of his outstanding track record. Second, his engagement beyond the scientific community, serving as a consultant for the World Bank, the European Commission and the United States Small Business Administration. Hence, David can be metaphorized as the incarnation of university's 'third mission', prompting academia to give something back to society. Third, his down-to-earth attitude despite his overwhelming successes such as establishing the journal *Small Business Management: An Entrepreneurship Journal*, which serves as a prominent outlet for cutting-edge research in the field of innovation economics, small business and entrepreneurship, winning the *Global Award for Entrepreneurship Research by the Swedish Entrepreneurship Forum*, or being mentioned in the same breath as Adam Smith, Alfred Marshall, Joseph Schumpeter, Kenneth Joseph Arrow, Robert Solow, or Paul Romer by being listed among the 60 most influential economists of all time. Despite these enormous achievements, David still stayed hungry and curious which is just amazing and deserves our utmost respect.

Inspired by David's work on innovation economics, we want to take the opportunity and combine his work with the field of applied macroeconomics to add something new, at least for the macroeconomics community, namely, some ingredients from the psychological and behavioral economics literature. In what follows, we will present a starting point for future research on the macroeconomic impact of innovation and entrepreneurship, given agents do not fully understand the entire complexity of our world.

Particularly for non-economists, or even for some economists, the imagination of a perfectly foresight looking agent, who computes the whole equilibrium and the optimal path towards this equilibrium, seems to be a somehow strict assumption. In one of our first econ classes, we have learned that the purpose setting up a model is to reduce the world's complexity to an appropriate degree. By doing this, we also admit that we, as economists, are not fully rational in the sense that we understand the entire complexity of the world. Hence, the question that pops up is the following: Why do we model fully rational people in our model, where at the same time, we as economists, admit that we are not fully rational? Recently, there has been made great success tackling this counter-intuitive observation. The prospect theory, hyperbolic discounting or overconfidence of people among others are some prominent examples showing how behavioral economics is nowadays an accepted way dealing with some deviations from classic assumptions by keeping the assumption of rationality. Tackling the holy grail of rationality, however, it seems that there is no common and generally accepted alternative theory. In this short contribution, we will relegate to some recently published papers by Xavier Gabaix, who proposes a compromise between the rational approach and the behavioral approach, with a focus on inattention and simplification. In particular, this theory assumes that the world's agents are bounded-rational in the way that it is assumed that they only acknowledge a subset of components in their optimization problem. For example, if an agent does not pay attention to interest rate changes, but fully reacts to income changes, the consumption policy has to replicate this realistic fact as well. Typically, this behavioral agent ends up with a much simpler policy rule compared to the fully rational agent.

The next section introduces the simple model of stochastic knowledge accumulation, which can be seen as a starting point for richer models dealing with endogenous growth due the knowledge accumulation or entrepreneurship, a topic David contributed to a lot (among many others see Audretsch and Keilbach (2008) or Audretsch et al. (2006)). The arguments we will use closely follow Gabaix (2016) and the reader is invited to consult this paper gaining more background information regarding computational issues and further applications. The key insight of this model is that people react more to their own variables, such as private stock of knowledge compared to economy-wide aggregates.

A Simple Example of Stochastic Knowledge Accumulation with Bounded Rationality

In what follows, is an intuitive argument why behavioral agents react less to aggregate-knowledge shocks compared to fully rational agents. We will not afflict you with all the formal details normally used to introduce such a model. Instead, what we will present is a snap-shot of a fully fledged out model.

Assume that, in the aggregate, the knowledge stock K_t evolves as

$$K_{t+1} = Y_t + (1-\delta)K_t, \tag{1}$$

with $\delta \in (0, 1)$ as the depreciation rate of knowledge. $Y_t = \omega_t F(K_t, L)$ shows the production function of knowledge, using existing knowledge as well as labor $L = 1$ which, is, for simplicity, assumed to be constant over time. ω_t represents the level of technology. We assume that the deviation from the mean level of technology, $\hat{\omega}_t$, is stochastic. For simplicity, we assume that $\hat{\omega}_t = \varepsilon_t$ where ε_t is an independently and identically distributed (i.i.d.) random variable with mean-zero and constant variance σ_K^2.

If there are no shocks, i.e. $\varepsilon_t = 0$, the economy would be at a steady-state with a knowledge stock K^*. If we now consider the deviation of the knowledge stock K_t from its steady-state level, K^*, i.e. $\hat{K}_t \equiv K_t - K^*$, we can rewrite Eq. (1) as:

$$\hat{K}_{t+1} = F_K\left(K_t, L\right)\hat{K}_t + \left(1 - \delta\right)\hat{K}_t + \varepsilon_t, \tag{2}$$

with $F_K(K_t, L)$ as the partial derivative of the knowledge production function with respect to knowledge K_t. Assume for a moment that $\varepsilon_t = 0$. Let us further write $\xi \equiv F_K(K_t, L)$. Hence, we obtain

$$\hat{K}_{t+1} = \left(\xi + 1 - \delta\right)\hat{K}_t, \tag{3}$$

where the term $\rho^r \equiv \delta - \xi > 0$[1] can be interpreted as the speed of mean-reversion.

Now assume that the behavioral firm[2] react less attentive than a rational firm to changes of the aggregate stock of knowledge, i.e. $\xi^b < \xi^r$, where the superscript $r(b)$ stands for the rational (behavioral) firm. Hence

$$0 < \xi^b < \xi^r. \tag{4}$$

It is easy to see that the speed of mean-reversion ρ^b in the behavioral world will be, anything else equal, larger than in the rational world:

$$\rho^b > \rho^r \Leftrightarrow \xi^b < \xi^r. \tag{5}$$

Next, assume that $\varepsilon_t > 0$. Directly applying the variance operator to equation (2) using further $\xi \equiv F_K(K_t, L)$ and $\rho \equiv \delta - \xi$, evaluated at the steady-state $\left(Var\left(\hat{K}_{t+1}\right) = Var\left(\hat{K}_t\right)\right)$ we arrive at

$$Var\left(\hat{K}_{t+1}\right) = \left(1 - \rho\right)^2 Var\left(\hat{K}_t\right) + \sigma_K^2 \tag{6}$$

$$\Rightarrow Var\left(\hat{K}_t\right) = \frac{\sigma_K^2}{1 - \left(1 - \rho\right)^2}, \tag{7}$$

which holds for the behavioral as well as for the rational economy. Summing up, this simple model shows the following:

Fluctuations mean-revert less quickly in the rational economy as the speed of mean-reversion for rational firms is lower compared to behavioral firms.

As fluctuations mean-revert less quickly in the rational economy, the variance of shocks given in equation (7) will be higher in the rational economy as $\rho^b > \rho^r$. Thus, the rational economy produces larger fluctuations of the knowledge stock compared to the behavioral economy.

---

[1] For simplicity, we assume that $\delta > \xi$. Saying this, we know that the derived results below crucially depend on this assumption.

[2] We assume that all rational (behavioral) firms are symmetric.

Discussion

The fact that behavioral firms react less to shocks of the aggregate knowledge stock is the key assumption in this model and drives its results. How can we link this result to evidence? One idea is that behavioral firms discount future changes of the knowledge stock the more the more distant these events are in the future. This can be seen from the following: Taking expectations of equation (2) at time t, iterating forward to time k, we find a relationship between the expectations of the rational and the behavioral agent as follows:

$$E_t^b\left[K_{t+k}\right] = \theta^k E_t^r\left[K_{t+k}\right], \tag{8}$$

with $\left(\dfrac{1-\rho^b}{1-\rho^r}\right) < \theta \leq 1$ as $\rho^b > \rho^r$. Thus, in contrast to rational agents, behavioral agents have a very imprecise imagination of future events. Hence, $\theta \in [0, 1]$ can be interpreted as a cognitive discount factor measuring attention to the future. Only for the limit case of $\theta = 1 \iff \rho^r = \rho^b = \rho$, the behavioral agent acts like the rational. There is also evidence for cognitive discounting in the literature. For instance, the findings made by Coibon and Gorodnichenko (2015) might be associated with cognitive discounting. Moreover, Gabaix and Laibson (2017) argue that the vast literature on hyperbolic discounting is a closely related to cognitive discounting as well.

But what exactly are the irrationalities behavioral agents face and what are potential explanations for this behavior? The general assumption why individuals pursue entrepreneurship relates to the expected high future returns to entrepreneurship. Although this is true for a very limited set of entrepreneurial ventures such as AirBnB, Uber, WhatsApp or Facebook, a growing body of literature affirms that the vast majority of entrepreneurs earn on average low risk-adjusted returns. Hall and Woodward (2010) even suggest that the expected utility of entrepreneurial ventures is negative, meaning that engagement in entrepreneurship is not preferable. Hence, why do individuals still enter and persist in entrepreneurship? Research in behavioral economics offers multiple explanatory approaches for this phenomenon, ranging from differences in risk aversion and the resulting utility to take on risks, overconfidence and overoptimism, i.e. potential biases and misperceptions of probability distributions, to non-pecuniary rewards derived from being self-determined and rather independent (see Åstebro et al. 2014).

Especially overconfidence is often used as an explanation for entrepreneurial engagement, e.g. Shane (2008) refers to a Global Entrepreneurship Monitor survey that recorded the perceptions of US entrepreneurs who overestimated their yearly sales potential by more than five times in comparison to the empirical base. Moore and Healy (2008) distinguish between three forms of overconfidence: overestimation, overplacement, and overprecision. Overconfidence thereby refers to the misjudgment of an individual's abilities or performance and is therefore often associated with overoptimism, i.e. the belief that one's abilities automatically lead to higher risk-adjusted returns. Overplacement relates to a wrong assessment of one's skills in comparison to others, e.g. direct competitors. Overprecision concerns the underestimation of the variance of own information, i.e. a misinterpretation of the available scope of action. A holistic stochastic knowledge accumulation model should take these and further characteristics of entrepreneurs into account that consciously or unconsciously influence their decision-making processes and entrepreneurial endeavors.

Conclusion

This short paper introduces a simple behavioral model of stochastic knowledge accumulation. The model assumes that compared to the rational economy, behavioral agents do not fully acknowledge a change of the knowledge production due to aggregated knowledge stock changes. One explanation for that behavior is that behavioral agents cognitively discount future events the larger the more distant such events are in the future. This simple model can be easily extended to model overconfidence of entrepreneurs in the form of overestimation, overplacement, and overprecision. In a nutshell, including behavioral aspects in the economics of innovation economics sphere will certainly enrich our understanding of entrepreneurial behavior.

References

Åstebro, T., Herz, H., Nanda, R., & Weber, R. A. (2014). Seeking the roots of entrepreneurship: Insights from behavioral economics. *Journal of Economic Perspectives, 28*(3), 49–70.
Audretsch, D. B., & Keilbach, M. C. (2008). Resolving the knowledge paradox: Knowledge-spillover entrepreneurship and economic growth. *Research Policy, 37*(10), 1697–1705.
Audretsch, D. B., Keilbach, M. C., & Lehmann, E. E. (2006). *Entrepreneurship and economic growth.* Oxford/Toronto: Oxford University Press.
Coibon, O., & Gorodnichenko, Y. (2015). Information rigidity and the expectations formation process: A simple framework and new facts. *The American Economic Review, 105*(8), 2644–2678.
Gabaix, X. (2016). Behavioral macroeconomics via sparse dynamic programming. NBER Working Paper No. 21848.
Gabaix, X., & Laibson, D. (2017). Myopia and discounting. NBER Working Paper No. 23254.
Hall, R. E., & Woodward, S. E. (2010). The burden of the nondiversifiable risk of entrepreneurship. *American Economic Review, 100*(3), 1163–1194.
Moore, D. A., & Healy, P. J. (2008). The trouble with overconfidence. *Psychological Review, 115*(2), 502–517.
Shane, S. (2008). *Fool's gold?: The truth behind angel investing in America.* Oxford: Oxford University Press.

David Audretsch: A Literary Steckbrief

Sandra Schillo

Abstract The purpose of a Festschrift may be to celebrate and perhaps roast the object of the Festschrift, Prof. Audretsch in this case. However, special circumstances dictated that we instead present the findings from a very serious academic study (Note to readers: This sentence is entirely untrue and in fact this article is anything but a serious academic study. If you do not enjoy our sense of humour, please skip this article and only read the following sentence: "This paper is a heartfelt tribute to the work of David Audretsch and written with the greatest admiration of his character and community engagement."). Specifically, we conducted an initial text analysis of Prof. Audretsch's work, which revealed that neither the words humor, joke, nor fun were mentioned even a single time in any of the documents we were able to download.

Introduction

Prof. Audretsch is an extremely prolific and impactful author, his Google Scholar profile lists 1004 entries (Nov 7, 2018) and over 82,000 citations. This body of work is rather intimidating and for sure, it seems close to impossible to do justice and summarize such an impressive body of work. Therefore, in this paper we do what all quantitative researchers tend to do when reality seems too deep and complex to grasp within a couple of hours of consideration: We develop and apply a set of measures and analyses to provide insights into Prof. Audretsch's work. True to established academic traditions, the insights presented here are entirely novel and original, and have been derived using leading-edge research methods. Surely, this approach guarantees that the work is of high academy quality publishable in a reputable academic outlet.

S. Schillo (✉)
University of Ottawa, Telfer School of Management, Ottawa, ON, Canada
e-mail: schillo@telfer.uottawa.ca

© Springer Nature Switzerland AG 2019
E. E. Lehmann, M. Keilbach (eds.), *From Industrial Organization to Entrepreneurship*, https://doi.org/10.1007/978-3-030-25237-3_46

Data and Methods

Starting with Prof. Audretsch's CV, we were able to download 215 publications[1]; in most cases we obtained the full-text version, in a few cases we only were able to retrieve abstracts. These 215 publications included 191 journal articles (including editorials for special issues), the remainder consisting of edited books and other documents. The analyses below are based only on the journal articles, in order to not capture content authored by other authors, as would be the case in edited books.

We completed a series of natural language processing (NLP) analyses. Simple keyword searches were performed using the Acrobat search function, more complex analyses we completed using the analysis platform KNIME. Originally developed in computer and information science, NLP is increasingly finding applications in the entrepreneurship literature. In fact, many PhD students entering the field apply versions of it in their literature work – of course never as a substitute of careful reading of the ever increasing number of publications, and of course with the most rigorously researched, validated and interpreted outcomes. Prof. Audretsch can surely be considered to be a key driver of this trend – the number of his publications alone leaves the students no choice but to resort to automated knowledge acquisition methods.

Common to all NLP methods is the requirement of carefully preparing (preprocessing) the text, in order to then extract relevant pieces of information. In the study presented here, we have taken great care to rigorously preprocess the texts obtained. Note that it took considerable experimentation, googling, expletives in several languages, serious amounts of coffee, and eventually thorough validation to achieve the results presented. As with many methods applying quantitative methods to qualitative phenomena, the validation process for text analysis offers ample opportunities to reinforce pre-conceived notions, to distort subject matter, and to selectively acknowledge research results. For the purposes of this paper, we made sure to exploit such opportunities to the greatest extent possible.

Results and Discussion

We present results first from keyword analyses, and then from a small set of more complex analyses. The results of the keyword analyses are presented in the form of a 'Literary Steckbrief', summarized in Table 1.

---

[1] I would like to acknowledge the generous contributions of Mohammad Seifollahi, Hassan Ebrahimi, Yuqing He, and Chen Li in this effort. I would also like to thank Hassan Ebrahimi for his assistance with the keyword analysis.

David Audretsch: A Literary Steckbrief   455

Table 1 Literary Steckbrief Prof. Audretsch

Favourite colour:	Not decisive on this matter. Green, white, black and red are very commonly mentioned. Particular interest in black boxes and red tape or lines.
Favourite day of the week:	Tuesday
Food or drinks:	Clear preference for a good meal over drinks (food: 171 instances, drink: 2 instances, beverages: 9 instances, beer: 4 instances, wine: 0 instances)
Work or play:	Plays hard (391 instances) but works harder (1451 instances)
Movies or theatre:	Slight preference for theatre (4 vs 2 instances)
Sport or transport:	Demonstrates some interest in sports (13 instances), but clearly more interested in transport (32 instances)
Global or local:	Immense interest in both (1365 and 1300 instances respectively), presumably related to the strong interest in transport.
Plant or animal:	Clear preference of plants over animals (177 vs 21 instances)
Summary:	Prof. Audretsch likes to travel, works a lot, is not interested in pets or animals, but very interested in plants. We suggest a nice houseplant might make a great gift for Prof. Audretsch. Use a black box and red tape to package. NB: Do not serve wine to Prof. Audretsch.

Keyword Analyses

Table 1 presents the "Steckbrief" of Prof. Audretsch's preferences, as derived from a keyword analysis of his literary work. Clearly, the keyword-based text analysis provides deep insights into his preferences, which we will discuss in the following paragraphs.

The most important question on a Steckbrief is the one about a favourite colour. Unfortunately, Prof. Audretsch does not seem to have made up his mind on this matter yet. We noticed many mentions of green, white, black, and also red. Among those mentions, co-occurrence analysis shows that Prof. Audretsch does display an obsession with black boxes of all kinds, as well as red tape or red lines.

With regards to days of the week, Prof. Audretsch has a clear preference for Tuesdays, none of the other days were mentioned at all.

Prof. Audretsch extensively covers food in his work, mostly using the general term "food" (mentioned 171 times), but also making reference to bread and butter. Cheese, on the other hand is not mentioned at all, so it is unlikely bread and butter refers to either sandwiches or German Butterbrote. Rather, we conclude he refers to fine meals, served with bread and butter on the side. As for accompanying drinks, his work reflects very limited interest in either drinks or beverages in general (2 and 9 mentions, respectively) and even very little interest in alcoholic beverages. Beer was only mentioned 4 times, and wine not at all: Prof. Audretsch clearly appears entirely uninterested in wine.

We complemented these traditional Steckbrief questions with several choice questions, the first one juxtaposes work and play. Play is among the more frequently mentioned terms in this Steckbrief with 391 mentions, but pales in comparison to work, mentioned 1451 times. Thus, our results indicate Prof. Audretsch plays hard, but works even harder. Of course, the fact that he has 1004 publications listed on Google Scholar, leaves no room for doubt that Prof. Audretsch works extremely hard, and clearly corroborates the validity of our methods and results.

With the tremendous emphasis on work over play, it is not surprising that Prof. Audretsch's work makes little mention of cultural activities, such as theatre (4 instances) and movies (2 instances). However, considered from a different perspective, this is rather concerning, as the introduction to the book "The Entrepreneurial Society" includes many cultural references and in fact starts with the mention of a movie in the second sentence. Unfortunately, our methods cannot provide deeper answers, for example whether we should suspect a deep insecurity over the like for movies, resulting in a lack of mention of movies in academic work of a more subconscious suppression of a personal interest in movies.

Finally, for the last set of keyword analyses we investigated some additional leisure activities. Prof. Audretsch shows some interest in sports (13 instances), but clearly favours other transportation (32 instances) means. We investigated this preference further and found that Prof. Audretsch shows a tremendous interest in global considerations (1365 instances) and local (1300) characteristics. Clearly this suggest a deep interest in travel, in engaging with people all over the world and the local fauna and flora. Thus as a last keyword analysis, we drilled deeper down on this interest and found that he is much more interested in plants (presumably from interesting global locations; perhaps locally native plants) than in animals.

Additional Analyses

For the topic extraction, we used Latent Dirichlet allocation (LDA), setting a target of 10 topics with seven words per topic, and an emphasis on extracting more rather than fewer topics per document (alpha = 1), and fewer words per topic (beta = 0.001).

We expected the results of the topic analyses to provide additional insights into what makes Prof. Audretsch's work unique. However, the results were rather disappointing in that topics covered by Prof. Audretsch proved rather closely aligned with many of the over 82,000 academic articles that quoted him – essentially the mainstream literature of entrepreneurship:

- Firm and industry growth through innovation
- The role of governments and institutions in industrial and technological change
- Knowledge spillover theory
- Measurement of industrial innovation and small firms
- Entrepreneurial processes and theories
- Financing of entrepreneurial firms
- Unemployment and growth of cities and regions
- Trade, exports and stages of growth

- Resource management and strategy of innovative ventures
- Technological innovation and knowledge transfer

While the lack of unique research topics that have not been deeply discussed in subsequent articles cannot be explained through topic analyses, we can make two conjectures about reasons why this might be the case. The first reason may be that Prof. Audretsch has an uncanny ability to anticipate and shape the main topics of entrepreneurship research. Given that there are no quantitative methods that might confirm this hypothesis, we will discard it.

The second reason might be that his work exhibits a level of contagious positivity that compels other researchers to engage in the conversations of his main topics. Sentiment analysis allows us to explore this hypothesis. We use a standard sentiment dictionary, the MPQA dictionary, and analyse the body of his work. This dictionary is not particularly suited to business studies, so if Prof Audretsch's work achieves even slightly positive scores using this method, it must be considered overwhelmingly positive. Indeed, the analysis of every single word in Prof. Audretsch's articles results in a positive versus negative score of 102 versus 88. We thus conclude that his work is overwhelmingly and contagiously positive. Obviously, in the dry and boring world of economics and entrepreneurship, Prof. Audretsch's positivity must have attracted much interest and many followers, meaning few of his topics have remained marginal and unique.

Conclusion

Like all worthwhile academic papers do, we would like to acknowledge that all academic papers have limitations, and that ours is no exception. Of course this study has more limitations and methodological issues than most, which is why we would like to defend our findings with particular vigour.

Firstly, the authors for this present study are not to blame for any shortcomings, as we did not write any of the work produced by Prof. Audretsch. Any methodological shortcuts were made necessary by the prolific nature of his work.

Secondly, it was the intent of this work to apply NLP methods in creative ways to an excellent body of work. We hope our article made it obvious that these methods can successfully be applied in literature work, and that it is easy to derive interesting-looking results (in the eye of the beholder). We hope we have further demonstrated that analyses that do not build on in-depth content matter expertise may be entertaining, but not typically insightful with regards to the actual content matter.

The work presented in this paper also points to several areas that should urgently be addressed by future research projects.

From a methods perspective, our expert application of text analysis should be further refined and made available to all aspiring entrepreneurship students, in order to improve the quality of their work.

458   S. Schillo

Most importantly, however, the theoretical literature analysis presented here should be followed up with extensive empirical work. To this end, we encourage all readers to gift Prof. Audretsch with house plants and nice meals (remember not to include wine), preferably packaged in a black box with a red ribbon or tape, and report the resulting responses to the authors of this study.

Given the positive sentiments in Prof. Audretsch's work, we hypothesize that the responses will be significant and extremely positive.

Wings to Escape the Roots

Alexander Starnecker

Abstract The greatest thing a father can give to his son is roots. The second greatest thing is wings to escape those roots. In their book "The Seven Secrets of Germany" David and Erik E. Lehmann cite this famous quote from Johann W. von Goethe (Audretsch & Lehmann, The seven secrets of Germany. Economic resilience in an era of global turbulence. Oxford University Press, Oxford, 2016). While roots keep us from falling and are our source of energy, they tend to keep us from moving on. Only wings can help us to free ourselves from this rigor. During a career, our character is shaped by experience and a large number of people. Only a few people, however, really contribute to the growth of our wings. Wings provide the possibility to look beyond the boundaries of roots. In the case of this chapter's author, Alexander Starnecker, David helped him to spread his wings.

The Technology Transfer Society

David not only accompanied my scientific development. He also guided me outside the ivory tower. I am pretty sure, that I can remember most of my meeting with him, at least the personal ones. On the one hand, this is because all of those meetings were really impressive. On the other hand, we all now, meeting David is quite a rare event. My first personal contact with David was when he received his doctorate of honor at my home institution, the University of Augsburg, Germany. It basically came down to a handshake. Our second meeting, and this one describes David at his best, was at my first international conference, the Technology Transfer Conference in Greensboro, North Carolina. I presented a natural experiment developed together with Erik E. Lehmann and Marcel Hülsbeck, analyzing the changes in inventor's compensation at university due to the reunification of Germany (Hülsbeck et al. 2009). Not knowing anybody, Erik, my later Phd thesis supervisor and meanwhile, very close friend, told me to look for David. In the evening reception, I found David surrounded by numerous peoples and introduced myself. David, not feeling

---

A. Starnecker (✉)
Weisser Spulenkörper, Neresheim, Germany

© Springer Nature Switzerland AG 2019
E. E. Lehmann, M. Keilbach (eds.), *From Industrial Organization to Entrepreneurship*, https://doi.org/10.1007/978-3-030-25237-3_47

bothered at all, welcomed and connected me to several people, making me feel as a part of the Technology Transfer Society (T²S) right away. This is David as we know him - always happy to share and help, even if it is only a scientific rookie from Germany.

Our contact intensified when Erik and David decided to host the first T²S Conference outside the United States in Augsburg in September 2011. David supported with his unbelievable network and his judgement on the scientific contributions. Nevertheless, we were all quite nervous when we had sent out our Call for Papers. That is why we still know who our first registration was: Mary Walshok, UC San Diego. From this moment on, we were confident of organizing a successful conference. What we did! The results of this great conference could not be better summarized as in Audretsch et al. (2014). We even managed to bring all the participants back home from the Oktoberfest in Munich. To be honest, losing a great scientist in the chaos of the Oktoberfest, was my greatest fear.

Based on the constant exchange with David, our relationship has grown. Not only that we presented our first joint research on the u-shape relationship between economic freedom and innovation performance at the T²S Conference in Augsburg (Audretsch et al. 2011). We also edited a book together with Erik and Al Link (Audretsch et al. 2012) where we also published one of the first research that has been done on the contribution of the unique Universities of Applied Science to technology transfer (Lehmann & Starnecker 2012). I could not be more honored when David invited me as an Assistant Professor at Indiana University in 2012. He, together with his exceptional team and his lovely family, especially warm-hearted and caring Joanne, made this an unforgettable time. After my decision to leave the ivory tower and join the industry, we still stayed in contact and talked about our observations, especially on German family-owned companies.

Spatial Proximity in the German Biopharmaceutical Industry

When I worked for a German biopharmaceutical company, I wrote David (proven biotechnology expert not only from Audretsch & Stephan 1996), that in contrast to his research on spatial proximity, I followed my impression that knowledge spill-over in German biotech clusters are not very intense. Of course, my personal observations is no representative scientific work, since they are only based on informal exchange with company representatives. Nevertheless, I was surprised to hear, that the only positive effect of spatial proximity is found to be the facilitated access to human resources. This brings the war for talents in the boundaries of the cluster and consequently lowers the willingness of intellectual exchange between company leaders. I did not expect to find this in one of most scientific and high tech industries of German economy. Consequently, I had to discuss this with David.

The medical biotech industry in Germany creates revenue of around 10 billion dollars with an annual growth rate of more than 10% (BCG 2018). In Germany, overall biopharmaceuticals have a share of 25% of the pharmaceutical market

(BCG 2018). The most important resource every company in this industry is desperate to get is human capital. To win the war for talents is crucial for the survival of those companies. Consequently, they heavily invest in improving the access to industry expects. Industry clusters like the Munich Biotech Cluster (BioM) in Martinsried are perfect platforms. Founded in 1997, BioM has supported the foundation of more than 150 companies and is part of the European Cluster Excellence Initiative (BMWi 2018). Spatial proximity to the best German universities (Technische Universität München & Ludwig-Maximillian Universität München), most important research institutes and organizations (Max-Planck Institute, Fraunhofer Institute & Helmholtz Institute) and big biotech companies (Amgen, Medigene, MorphoSyS) enhances not only knowledge spillovers. There is also a high exchange of employees moving in all directions between companies, universities and research institutes, which could be a more important contribution for the knowledge transfer than knowledge spillover based on spatial proximity. At least, that is what I found talking to some leaders, of whom one even told me that the only benefit of being located in this cluster is the facilitation of the recruiting of high potentials from other companies. David responded to this observation with an example: this is like moving in close spatial proximity with your girlfriend only because it is easier to meet new people. Company representatives should think twice if this is the only gain they can find. There is a reason why the failure rate in those industries is so high. David further emphasized: "just because one doesn't perceive opportunities doesn't mean they aren't there. It is all about relationship!" We all know, he is right!

Linking David to My Roots

David puts a lot of effort in science and scientific exchange, but he also cares about his students. The first lecture I attended was via a video conference from Erik's office in Augsburg to a lecture room in Bloomington. Today, this is nothing unusual, but 10 years ago, holding a lecture via video from another continent, was quite innovative. However, since David was in Augsburg for the SPEA Summer School, we had to make it work. The Summer School really means a lot to him. Therefore, I was very honored when David asked me to present my parents company, Weisser Spulenkörper, to the Summer School students. A company that is now about to be past to the 4th generation, developing from a paper manufacturer to a high-tech company producing plastic parts for the electronics, automotive and medical industry is not common, even in Germany. Consequently, we decided that talking about the company is not enough, students should get the change to visit it. Their visit has become a tradition, so my parents and myself had the honor to welcome David and his Summer School students for the 5th time this year.

David and I also developed a constant exchange about our company and his economic observations. One example is the hidden champion strategy of investing in close and long-lasting relationships with key clients and developing customer specific solutions, also discussed in "The Seven Secrets of Germany" (Audretsch & Lehmann 2016). The focus on individual customer specifications is the company's innovation strategy. "Customer satisfaction and loyalty is the most important output of our innovation efforts", my father, Manfred Starnecker, is cited. Also our discussion of protecting intellectual property is presented in "The Seven Secrets of Germany". Hidden champions prefer to shield their innovative activities rather than investing in legal protection of intellectual property (Audretsch & Lehmann 2016). This is also supported by my father's quote: "It is important that we are known and respected personally by our customers but remain unknown to our competitors".

We also discussed the fact that numerous family-owned, small and medium sized companies, the German "Mittelstand", tend to be equity financed. The main reason is, that family firms prefer to maintain ultimate control over the company across generations (De Massis et al. 2018). This corresponds also with the long-term perspective of Weisser Spulenkörper and comparable companies. To executives of Mittelstand firms, it is more important to ensure longevity than achieving short-term pay-offs (De Massis et al. 2018). Another interesting finding of De Massis et al. (2018) was discussed prior between David and myself: the employee relationship. Protected by the war for talent in bigger cities, Mittelstand firms grew together with the development of their employees. In those companies, it is common to celebrate 30, 40, even 50 years of job tenure. This is because employees experience a high esteem beyond keeping their jobs. Their experience and knowledge is highly valued. Therefore, they are included in the decision making process across all levels of hierarchy. Vice versa, the discussion with David improved our understanding of the German Mittelstand as well as it helped me to recognize what I experienced as being "normal".

Currently, David, Erik and I discuss another interesting development within the German Mittelstand. Despite their economic success, passing the business on to the next generation has become their most important task. This is because of a circumstance that used to be one of their competitive advantages and has now become their misfortune. The German Mittelstand evolved in rural areas. The German countryside has continuously lost its attractiveness. The "heirs" of the company explore the world, receive the best possible education and are highly attracted either by power and impact of big companies or the freedom and inspiration of startups. Consequently, they find their wings in the bigger German cities, further decreasing the attractiveness of their roots. In my opinion, the German Mittelstand fail to emphasize the appeal of family-controlled firms. They combine the power to generate impact, while they provide the (financial) freedom to follow inspiration on business and corporate development. It is a gift not a burden. Roots get stronger when passed on over generations.

Nevertheless it is of great importance to also develop strong wings. David had a huge impact on the growth of my wings. Not only because of his scientific work where he showed the importance of regional spillovers and technology transfer (i.e. Acs & Audretsch 1988; Acs et al. 2013; Audretsch & Feldman 1996; Audretsch & Lehmann 2005), entrepreneurial theory (i.e. Acs et al. 2016; Audretsch et al. 2016) and impacts on family firms (i.e. Audretsch et al. 2013, Audretsch & Lehmann 2015).

What influenced most were the discussions about those topics and his feedback on my experiences. Out of this, only a few examples are described above. I will always be thankful for your continuous support, David!

References

Acs, Z., & Audretsch, D. (1988). Innovation in large and small firms: An empirical analysis. *The American Economic Review, 78*(4), 678–690.

Acs, Z. J., Audretsch, D. B., & Lehmann, E. E. (2013). The knowledge spillover theory of entrepreneurship. *Small Business Economics, 41*(4), 757–774.

Acs, Z. J., Audretsch, D. B., Lehmann, E. E., & Licht, G. (2016). National systems of entrepreneurship. *Journal of Small Business Economics, 46*, 527–535.

Audretsch, D., & Feldman, M. (1996). R&D spillovers and the geography of innovation and production. *The American Economic Review, 86*(3), 630–640.

Audretsch, D. B., & Lehmann, E. E. (2005). Does the knowledge spillover theory of entrepreneurship hold for regions? *Research Policy, 34*(8), 1191–1202.

Audretsch, D. B., & Lehmann, E. E. (2015). In University of Augsburg (Ed.), *The emergence of the Mittelstand Company: A German perspective.* Working Paper.

Audretsch, D. B., & Lehmann, E. E. (2016). *The seven secrets of Germany. Economic resilience in an era of global turbulence.* Oxford: Oxford University Press.

Audretsch, D., & Stephan, P. (1996). Company-scientist locational links: The case of biotechnology. *The American Economic Review, 86*(3), 641–652.

Audretsch, D., Lehmann, E., Link, A. & Starnecker, A. (2011) Democracy and innovation: A country level perspective presented at technology transfer society conference, Augsburg 2011 (Sept.).

Audretsch, D., Lehmann, E., Link, A., & Starnecker, A. (2012). *Technology transfer in the global economy in international handbook series on entrepreneurship.* New York: Springer.

Audretsch, D. B., Hülsbeck, M., & Lehmann, E. E. (2013). Families as active monitors of firm performance. *Journal of Family Business Strategy, 4*(2), 118–130.

Audretsch, D. B., Lehmann, E. E., & Wright, M. (2014). Technology transfer in a global economy. *Journal of Technology Transfer, 39*, 301–312.

Audretsch, D. B., Lehmann, E. E., Paleari, S., et al. (2016). Entrepreneurial finance and technology transfer. *Journal of Technology Transfer, 41*, 1–9.

Boston Consulting Group (BCG, 2018). Medizinische Biotechnologie in Deutschland 2018.

Bundesministerium für Wirtschaft (BMWi, 2018). BioM – Münchner Biotech Cluster, https://www.clusterplattform.de/CLUSTER/Redaktion/DE/Cluster/go-cluster/munich_biotech_cluster_m4.html.

De Massis, A., Audretsch, D., Uhlaner, L., & Kammerlander, N. (2018). Innovation with limited resources: Management lessons from the German Mittelstand. *Journal of Product Innovation Management, 35*(1), 125–146.

https://www.vfa-bio.de/download/bcg-vfa-bio-biotech-report-2018.pdf

Hülsbeck, M., Lehmann, E.E. & Starnecker, A. (2009). The Bayh-Dole Act: Only an Export Hit to Former Communist Countries. Presented at Technology Transfer Society Conference, Greensboro, NC, USA, 2009 (Sept.).

Lehmann, E., & Starnecker, A. (2012). Introducing the University of Applied Science in the technology transfer process. In D. B. Audretsch, E. E. Lehmann, A. N. Link, & A. Starnecker (Eds.), *Technology transfer in the global economy* (pp. 90–115). New York: Springer.

Professor David Audretsch: My Doktorvater

Jagannadha Pawan Tamvada

Abstract When JP Tamvada wrote an email to David in the summer of 2004, he never expected a quick reply and invitation to come and meet him at the Max Planck Institute. In the 5 years following that first meeting, David taught the author invaluable lessons of life, exemplified ideal leadership, and shaped their scholarship.

My Doktorvater

After my first presentation at the Max Planck Institute based on preliminary thoughts on why the famous U curve of Wennerkers and Thurik might not give a full picture on entrepreneurship and economic development, David called me to his office. I was not sure what his reaction was going to be. At the meeting, I couldn't believe my ears when he spent all of time giving superlatively positive feedback, and wanted to put me in a plane to America to give the presentation at a conference in America. His irresistible optimism left me inspired.

Often, I walked with him to the Jena station to see him off while discussing things we believed were significant for science and society. Most times, he would ask me to hop into the train to continue the conversation. For me, these moments gave me an opportunity to intellectually engage with him on topics beyond my dissertation. Armed with a ticket that he'd buy for me, we used to have lively conversations until he got into a connecting train at Weimar. Sometimes, he'd hijack me into the next train while never once forgetting to give me cash to buy my return ticket to Jena. David, a distinguished professor for the world, remains a loving Doktorvater for me.

My first paper with him taught me the art of science. David's meticulous attention to detail ensured that no stone was left unturned when it came to teaching me the art of writing a scientific paper. Once I learnt this from the master craftsman, I wrote my dissertation on entrepreneurship and economic development that

---

J. P. Tamvada (✉)
Southampton Business School, University of Southampton, Southampton, UK
e-mail: jp.tamvada@soton.ac.uk

© Springer Nature Switzerland AG 2019
E. E. Lehmann, M. Keilbach (eds.), *From Industrial Organization to Entrepreneurship*, https://doi.org/10.1007/978-3-030-25237-3_48

eventually received a best PhD award from DRUID in Denmark and won me the Otto Hahn Medal in Germany. Not just me, but everyone in David's entrepreneurship group brought laurels to the Max Planck Institute. If Jim Collins's bestseller "Good to Great" needed a legendary example of a level five leader, David should be its most compelling choice.

One of the many exciting things we did as a team at Max Planck Institute was go to India to organise two conferences with the Indian Institute of Science. David led from front by being there both times. For the first workshop the Max Planck Society gave us funds. For the second one, it didn't. But David did. He funded it from the Institute's budget. He could have easily closed down the project but he pushed us forward, as he always did. These conferences in Bangalore attracted some of the leading academics and policy makers from within India, Germany and the US. It laid new foundations for entrepreneurship research in developing countries.

David became a unifying force bringing some of the best entrepreneurship scholars from around the world to Max Planck while galvanising young researchers to passionately pursue a diverse range of subfields within the broad areas of entrepreneurship, innovation and public policy. His genius at spotting research opportunities, childlike excitement at new ideas, eagerness to support while trusting people blended together to create a fertile landscape for young scholars and scholarship to thrive. Entrepreneurship research at the Max Planck Institute flourished not because of his toughness but because of his love.

David-ness aspires the very best for everyone who crosses one's path. It is a way of life, and delights in leading by serving. If replicated, this incredible David-ness can transform workplaces, human relationships, and our lives. As I take this delightful walk down my memory lane, I can't help but thank him for being David.

Building Entrepreneurial Societies Through Entrepreneurial Ecosystems and Business Incubators

Based on a Face-to-Face Interview with David B. Audretsch

Christina Theodoraki

Abstract This chapter highlights how David Audretsch shaped my career by articulating key themes on building entrepreneurial societies through entrepreneurial ecosystems and business incubators. It offers insight into a broad view of entrepreneurship and its links to entrepreneurial ecosystems and business incubators. It also provides advices and recommendations for PhD students, and offers a clear view of the research community.

Introduction

During my second year of PhD studies, I had the chance to meet David during the Interdisciplinary European Conference on Entrepreneurship Research – IECER in Montpellier (February 2015). I will never forget the "epic moments" before I talk to David, with hand shaking, cold sweat, legs start shivering, rapid heart rate, generalized anxiety. I must confess that as a "beginner" PhD student, I was afraid to start a discussion with a "prominent" researcher. I couldn't imagine at this moment that I would find the mentor who will show me the research world. David warmly accepted my request to join him in Bloomington for an academic visiting and some months later, the journey to knowledge has begun.

David has been a towering figure in research on entrepreneurship and entrepreneurial societies. His work framed worldwide standards and transformed scholarship in this field. Both his publications and his talks witness how David is engaged in the research community by perfectly connecting the worlds of theory and business.

C. Theodoraki (✉)
TBS Business School, Toulouse, France
e-mail: c.theodoraki@tbs-education.fr

© Springer Nature Switzerland AG 2019
E. E. Lehmann, M. Keilbach (eds.), *From Industrial Organization to Entrepreneurship*, https://doi.org/10.1007/978-3-030-25237-3_49

467

468 C. Theodoraki

Among several discussions on entrepreneurship, David helped me to frame and understand my research topic on entrepreneurial ecosystem and business incubators. Furthermore, he showed me how to connect theory and practice, and conciliate the research and business worlds. Since then, a great friendship was born that shaped my career.

This chapter offers some extracts from a face-to-face interview with David on: the entrepreneurial ecosystem, business incubators and advices for PhD students, and concludes with best wishes to David.

Broad View: Introducing the Entrepreneurial Ecosystem to the Entrepreneurship Research Field

A. What's your favorite topic in entrepreneurship?

My favorite one is the role of entrepreneurship in the strategic management of places. Because one thing we all know is "the place", and this is what impresses me. When I got to the most successful places in the world, Stockholm, Munich, London, San Francisco, San Diego, they're very concerned with how they keep investing in entrepreneurship. And if these places are concerned about that. But what about the rest of the world? I think that's a great topic. Because all places want to be beautiful and healthy places. It's great to be beautiful, but it's even better to be beautiful and talented, which in our analogy means to have knowledge and entrepreneurship, to be innovative. And now I'm back to, so what is it that places need to do to be entrepreneurial? Part of that says to get places to realize this is what matters. No, it's not so easy. That's why there's a great research opportunity.

B. What do you think about the entrepreneurial ecosystem as an emerging topic?

I love that question. I've been in the last year, to ten conferences on entrepreneurial ecosystems (in Australia, in Germany, in America, etc.). Here's my take on it, I find it so interesting. You could say that the North American perspective of academics dominates the world view of the market. And from this view, has really come a sense that firms in markets matter. Governments or policies don't matter at all except in the negative sense. So that we've had, "we" meaning in academics, have had trouble dealing with the role, or seeing the role of governments. For example, Michael Porter had this giant insight with his clusters. Everybody knows the clusters. What's interesting originally, where did the clusters come from? They seemed to be almost self-organized by the firms themselves. And his orientation was to the firms and said if you want better performance, get in a cluster. Now where the cluster comes from, who creates it, he was less clear about but it was more for the firm. We know we've had this cluster approach. I think that the tradition in the United States in the business schools, is the entrepreneur (like Steve Jobs and Mark Zuckerberg). In the business schools it's how do we help these people realize their dreams? I mean I think that's great. How do we help the firms realize their goals? But that's very different than saying, how do we help places become better.

Building Entrepreneurial Societies Through Entrepreneurial Ecosystems and Business... 469

More recently of course the European Union has its Smart Specialization Strategy (3S) which is broader. But now, I think many of us have felt for years, we could see the places that were entrepreneurial were doing better. My take on the entrepreneurial ecosystem is that it adds a framework for a place, and I use the word 'place', the Americans hate the word 'place'. I think that in French you call it the 'territory'. I think that the French are much more comfortable with the word 'territory' than we are with the word 'territory' or 'place'. In German, there's a word 'standort' which means place or territory. Because territory can be a city or it can be a region. And the Americans are always saying what is a place? It's not defined. And I think it's this uncomfortableness that place should play a role rather place exists in individuals and firms, use place. Where I think of the European view, places almost use firms and individuals to do well. It's a different kind of perspective that says the place is going to take itself.

My previous book is called "Everything in its Place, Entrepreneurship and the Strategic Management of Cities, Regions and States". And that's my intent, to look at the key role that entrepreneurship plays in strategies of the territory. It seems to be very important now. Now, what does this have to do with entrepreneurial ecosystems? I think I'm very ambivalent, is the word. Because of course I'd love to see entrepreneurship becoming the center. In some ways, we tried clusters for a long time. And clusters are all about existing firms. The entrepreneurial ecosystem is all about what can a place do, a territory do, to generate entrepreneurship. I think that this is really acknowledgement that entrepreneurship matters to a territory or to a place. In fact, what makes places work, it's a much broader portfolio of strategies, targets, and instruments. Entrepreneurship being an important one, but not the only one.

C. What do you think about the entrepreneurial ecosystem as research topic in entrepreneurship?

I think it is a great topic that now there is a lot of interest and this is the right moment to doing this. It's very clear, the entrepreneurial ecosystems, the word is resonating. Policy makers, the people out there like it, they feel comfortable using it, I would say this, it's a great research opportunity. It seems to sell. There's money and interest, we can publish articles now because the journals are going to want it. I would say that's what makes an applied field like entrepreneurship different from a discipline. If you're going to be in an applied field, it's like being in fashion or popular music versus classical music. Money and interest are going to shape your success. And if you really want knowledge for its own sake, retreat back to the discipline. The good news is that it's a great research question. In fact, the entrepreneurial ecosystems sound like a criticism but it's really saying there's an opportunity, really all we're doing right now is trying to uncover and say that they exist. But that's going to make them better, stronger, then it's got to be linked to performance of the system, and then it's got to be linked to what can they do differently to get a stronger performance?

D. How can we distinguish the entrepreneurial ecosystem from other concepts?

I would say don't look for equilibrium, it almost goes back to what we started, the world of ideas, until much later. You can look back 20 years from now, just like we can look back to classical music, it's been done, it's complete. Right now, what we're seeing is competition. That's why it's all early stage of lots of different ideas and they all go in different directions. Because these are different kind of perspectives on the same thing. And I think in some ways, you know we saw that same thing in a way with networks. And some people said well networks are a geographic, a territory dimension. Other scholars, would say that networks are about the industry, it can be global, in fact it can be both. But it's kind of a question of the perspective. And I would say it seems to me that the territory view won. Because it's policy. People care about territories, they care about places, they want to see their place do well.

Businesses have their own networks, they have their own ecosystems. And I think that's a difference again. Do you care about the business, the organization, or do you care about the territory? It's a different conversation, it moves more and more away from entrepreneurship, why we're not sensitive to the performance of the territory, but we're very sensitive to the performance of firms and individuals. But where entrepreneurship comes in, for the territory to do well, it needs entrepreneurship. That's where entrepreneurship and territory kind of come together, that's where the entrepreneurial ecosystem comes. I think that we're placed to realizing, they have a hard time controlling established large companies. They do what they want to do, they locate where they want, they use territory for their own performance. They outsource, they offshore, they choose. The thing about entrepreneurship is pretty much of a local phenomenon. So that the policy makers know, if you have entrepreneurship there's like little children. I had little children, now I have big boys. Little children stay local, big boys, like here they go any place in the world.

David defends a place-centered perspective of the entrepreneurial ecosystem, recognized as an emerging framework for a place. In this perspective, the main critical point is the differences between clusters and entrepreneurial ecosystems. David clearly distinguishes these concepts by considering the focus of clusters on the existing firms. In contrast, the entrepreneurial ecosystem is focused on the place and the actions to develop entrepreneurship. However, both concepts include entrepreneurial interactions and networks. This perspective of introducing the entrepreneurial ecosystem in the entrepreneurship field inspired me to consider the entrepreneurial ecosystem in broader terms, and better position it in relation to other concepts. Furthermore, I was more confident of defining the entrepreneurial ecosystem and ready to open the *black box* and discuss the connections with business incubators (cf. §2).

Building Entrepreneurial Societies Through Entrepreneurial Ecosystems and Business... 471

Opening the Black Box of Entrepreneurial Ecosystems:
The Role of Business Incubators

A. What's your opinion about the criticism on business incubators?

This criticism is so ignorant, naïve, and misguided because it implies that other strategies and decisions, either private business decisions or decisions by individuals or policy decisions, work all the time and always meet their goal. And we know investments by companies where they were talking about new plants and factories, mergers, research and development especially, that doesn't work all the time. In fact, we know that the more the activity deals with ideas and therefore attempting to innovate, the lower is the likelihood of success. If incubators had 100% success rate, that would mean they're not actually contributing to innovation. Incubators are meant to be all about innovation and so it's inherently uncertain. There's got to be a high rate of failure, but the immediate goals are not met because there's so much uncertainty involved in the innovation process. That's one criticism I have. So, this implicit benchmark of 100% is absurd. We don't see that benchmark attained anyplace else in the economy. So why, whether it's private investments, certainly R&D or public policies in other parts, should we suddenly impose 100% of success, and say all the time that incubators aren't working?

The other criticism is that actual practices, management matters, like in every other aspect of life, either for individuals or for organizations, public, private, that the actual people involved, the actual management practices make a difference. So that we think that R&D's good. Well just because you want to do R&D doesn't mean it's going to work, just because there's entrepreneurship, just because there's venture capital, it doesn't mean it's going to work. It depends on due diligence. And then of course there's always the issue of luck actually, and just random luck. And then you get to the issue of the time arising. Just because something hasn't worked yet, doesn't mean it won't work, there's learning that can take place.

B. Do you think that incubators may be the key strategy of a place?

I remember when Google was started, I don't think that came from an incubator, it did come from a university, but all the smart guys that I read about in the Wall Street Journal and the New York Times, they said this will never work. Same thing with Amazon, they said this will never work, there's not business model. Well, it didn't work, until it did. It took some time. I think many incubators are poorly designed, they're poorly managed, they have the wrong strategy, perhaps they're in the wrong way, just like much investment by companies, R&D by companies is poorly designed etc. This is the real world we live in. But to say don't try, is to really then doom a region to say no, you're not worthy of trying to get better. You should just accept that you're a second-rate region, unless you have some other strategy which is okay too. I don't think every region of the world wants to base its strategy on incubators. I don't think entrepreneurship and innovation are the right strategy for every place. I think that some places may have a different strategy which is based on natural resources, based on my book Entrepreneurship Policy and the Strategic Management of Place. Of course, incubators are about making a place have a better performance, make it more competitive. At which point, the incubators become important. Even if it is difficult and there's no formula for most business practices involving innovation. But to say oh, what the grownups do to incubators in someplace is not worthy of it, I think is very condescending and actually flies in the face of what we've learned in research and empirical evidence. We've seen a lot of places turn around. It's hard to find a place that transformed itself only because of the incubator. Because typically a place will try many different strategies.

C. Do you think of any examples where incubator was an efficient strategy of a place?

I can name so many places that turned around and they all had incubators. Incubators were part of the strategy. Bavaria for example, it's in both of my books now, but certainly in the "Seven Secrets of Germany". A young person like you probably think of Bavaria as being wealthy, successful, prosperous. However, when I was your age, Bavaria was a joke. It was the poor cousin of Germany in Europe. The rest of Germany had to transfer money to Bavaria. It was rural, low GDP per capita, low productivity, didn't seem to have competitive industries. They did one policy, they had an incubator. They did lots and lots of different things, including incubators. They had lots of investments in knowledge, you either could call it technology transfer conduits, mechanisms, or knowledge spill-over mechanisms. Either way you want to think about an incubator. How important was the incubator relative to the others? I would say it's like going back to my book again the "Seven Secrets". It's like looking at Germany's soccer team that won the World Cup and asking, which player was it that was the key to team A? If you take out one of the many things that Bavaria did, would it be the Bavaria of today? I don't know. We know players get hurt and they have substitutes.

But of course, not just Bavaria, closer to home, if I look to Indianapolis. Indianapolis, they used to call "Indiana Nowhere". And its strategy was based on being the crossroads of America. It was based on infrastructure transportation. Then they kind of shifted, evolved, to amateur sports and the college sports. But a decade ago the new strategy emerged which was life sciences and biotechnology. And they've got incubators. They've got lots of knowledge spill-over, conduits, mechanisms, technology transfer mechanisms, and the city's doing pretty well. It's hard to see a successful place that doesn't have an incubator. The problem is you can find places that aren't successful and they have the incubators. But as I recall, in the last World Cup, I don't think the Greeks (team) made it. And you know what, they have a team. Just because you have a team, doesn't mean you're going to make it. And just because you have an incubator doesn't mean that you are going to be a successful place. But if you don't have a team, you're not going to make the World Cup. And if you don't have an incubator, it is more likely that you will not be successful.

Well a lot of places don't have incubators, are they doomed? If they don't have another strategy, tourism, nice natural resources that they can take advantage of … I was just in Nova Scotia, people from Newfoundland they have oil, natural resource. They don't need an incubator, they have a different strategy. But of course, there are many parts of Indiana that don't have an incubator, and they don't have a strategy, and they're struggling. It's not just in Indiana.

The criticism of studied concepts is the major source of frustration for both PhD students and well-established scholars. The optimistic point of view considers that the criticism is necessary to determine the existence of the research topic. This proves that there is a research community that is interested on this topic and their discussions contribute to its progression. David demonstrated how to "*think outside the box*", defend a topic and accept that criticism can be a good thing. Thus, criticism is welcomed and recommended as is meant to push to be better.

Entering the Research Community: Advices and Recommendations to PhD Students

A. What PhD students should do?

The interesting thing of being young is that you have to find your way to the world. And everybody tells you different things. You are a dissertation student and you got to do what your advisor and the community say. That's what you got to do and in a way, it is like parents. In German, we call a dissertation advisor 'a doctoral father'. It's like parents who tell you this is what you have to do but in the end, you have to find your own way. It doesn't matter where you are, you can be at Harvard, everybody tells you what they think it is right to be but you have to find your own way. It is important this point to do what you like but the important thing is that then you are going to fly away.

B. How can we defend innovative research ideas?

I understand it in universities, they want everything to be needed and then you can organize it. The interesting thing about research in the world of ideas is that we are always looking for something new and new comes when something is not done before. That is why they say that we need innovation but not too much. In a way, we really value newness but we cannot know what to value on. Is like you say, please do something new, but do it the way I do. But this is not new.

C. I believe it is the same thing with the innovation of a product. If the market is not ready to accept it, the product fails.

In research, it is the same. People always will have problems. The problem is when people come up with ideas which are not connected to anything. It is always a fight. The gains for entrepreneurship research are constantly to break out to these barriers: is it management, is it sociology, is it strategy? This is people interested in entrepreneurship and to all its different perspectives. Somewhat you can look Europe in the same way. Do you see Greece and Spain and Portugal... do you see the differences or do you see the Europe with a communality? And those people who are pro-Europe want to fight this communality.

Personally, I think for the field of entrepreneurship, I think that all journals think that way, they are happy to take all the different perspectives. I think you can be Swedish and European at the same time. And I think you can have a kind of perspective and have a value and be interesting. But I know that there are traditions at the universities but in some ways, this is what disciplines are.

D. What do you think about the type of research which is more suitable for publications? Quantitative vs. qualitative methods?

Journals are open to high quality papers rather conceptual, qualitative or quantitative papers. Another thing is what people call qualitative and quantitative data. Someone will call it qualitative data but they are going to present it as quantitative data. It is like theory. The point is, this is what you do, this is what you want.

E. Do you think that it may be a problem for publishing when there is not big database on a topic?

This is the opportunity. I see this all the time. If there are big database, like GEM, you can still write papers but everyone can use that database but the fact when we do not have a database you can collect exactly what you need. And people may say that there are not enough data but this is the way that science works or policy works. Because why society would invest millions of euros to create a database unless they are really feel that there is something there? We need those first studies that kind of say that we think that there is something there. And my research has often been on things like that. I was hearing what people are thinking about and you have new ideas. And yes, you will get criticized but the one thing you learn is that you will always be criticized in our business and you have to defend yourself. You have to defend yourself and you have to create what you create and then try to explain it but yes of course if you wait until there is a database, that means that you have waited too long. So, the thing is to motivate the importance of the question that issue and then make sure that you get it out-there by publishing it and then move on to another issue and keep going.

F. How can we defend a criticized topic?

This is the nice thing of being older, you see things come and go. I remember when Paul Reynolds created the Global Entrepreneurship Monitoring, everybody criticized it by saying that you could never publish the data and that there are not good etc. But now what happens for your generation, you see studies all over. Yes, it got better but actually not really. It is just that people get used to it.

And so, what we see with entrepreneurial ecosystems, it is so interesting, we have seen it also with social entrepreneurship, that it is an idea and it is really how our business works in the world of ideas. What it is interesting is that you are attracted to it for whatever reason. But now you have to be as everybody else. You have to fight to get the idea in and then 3 years later, you will see that everybody is doing it.

I do not really support the idea of staying in your office and write the greatest papers. I believe you should fight and work, and try to make a publication and fight again and try to make another and another. And the most thing you are going to get is rejection but this is good because you will get better.

G. PhD students are inspired from the pioneers and previous literature. How can they become autonomous?

PhD students may be related to other researchers and do research but each one has to create its own style in research. The important thing I am looking to see to a PhD student is to see if they are motivating the topic, if they are linking it to the literature, can I see what is unique about what you are doing, do you have hypothesis etc. What I can say is to judge if it is better that the others? As an editor, I am trying to see if it is unique. Then may I be critical, if there are only case studies or if there are not enough data etc. I am somebody that likes these things. That we are trying to discover concepts. Other people, mainly economist people may look more to quantitative data. But you see people in management acting like that too. They want to see what techniques do you use to data, is that what it makes it valuable.

H. What is the danger that we should avoid in research?

I think the danger is when the tendency to create purely academic definitions and concepts of entrepreneurship. We've got colleagues in the field who want to say entrepreneurship is exclusively this behaviorist view. Opportunity creating, and then acting on that. I think that's a good perspective. I think the danger is that's not what the world thinks entrepreneurship is. If you got to anybody out there in the world, nobody says that's what entrepreneurship is. What people in the world say typically entrepreneurship is starting companies, small companies, all renewal income, but everybody knows this. What the danger is, I think when a small group of academics says we know better than you, we're right and you're wrong, guess who wins? It's the world. Just like a small group of academics who would say, probably including me in a way, saying I don't think social entrepreneurship is really a distinct concept. All entrepreneurship is social. I mean I can understand that argument, but it's a dysfunctional argument. The world knows social entrepreneurship exists, so we have to adjust. Because we're an applied, interdisciplinary, solutions-provider field, we have to be sensitive to what the world thinks. It doesn't mean the world's right. But to say you're wrong, you don't understand, we're going to tell you, and then have a definition that isn't useful to people. For example, people say: 'he's acting very entrepreneurial', that doesn't mean somebody who just started a company. That means they're kind of opportunistic. People are very flexible, the world's flexible. I think that's one danger.

I think along with that, and it is true of academics in general, that any time one research trajectory keeps being done, the contributions become increasingly incremental. As they become incremental, the value of the field becomes less interesting.

And what you see is that's the beginning of the demise of the field. I think as I said before, I think that entrepreneurship is ultimately driven by interest from what's going on in the world. I think we have to look at what are the problems and issues of involving entrepreneurship in the world. Part of it is involving so that when we look at issues about access to finance, that's been a popular theme, that reflected a problem people had. In the United States that's less of a problem than it probably was twenty, 30 years ago when we looked at the issue of are entrepreneurs born or made? That was probably an issue, because people thought this twenty, 30 years. People don't really worry about this anymore. It's like asking the question are women as good as men? They used to worry about this but no anymore. You could say we're past that now. I think that for the research field to have value, it's got to have value as research in the world.

These precious advices helped me understand the research world and position myself in this community. David answered all my questions with honesty, openness and transparency. Even the questions that most try to avoid. I believe that these values strengthen his powerful impact and distinguish his leading and mentoring skills. To conclude this chapter, I would present my wishes to David and synthetize some of his mentoring skills.

Best Wishes to David and Highlighted Mentoring Skills

I would like to thank David for this wonderful experience and fruitful journey. During my visiting to Bloomington, I met a mentor who guided me on the right path, an advisor, but mostly a friend. I am grateful to him for the many interviews and discussions, and sharing advices and network information. It would be impossible to count all the ways that he has helped me in my career and shaped my research on entrepreneurial ecosystems and business incubators. His passion, creativity, energy, great insight and openness allowed to inspire and stimulate the research community, design new research paths, provide a powerful impact and remain productive and intellectually vibrant during all these years. I would like to highlight some selective but not exhaustive examples of his distinctive mentoring skills.

A. Optimistic point of view: I still remember the powerful message of David Audretsch to the entrepreneurship community.

Keep linking ideas and research to the most important and crucial challenges and problems in the real world. At research, we have to be innovative but not too much, and insist to make others believe in our research. And for American people, I would say "Stay thirsty my friends!".[1] What makes you thirsty is looking at the world. I think we have to be addressing, adding value to the real world. And I think the opportunity, so stay thirsty says you've got to look out in the world. But you also have to learn the language of the journals.

---

[1] Famous advertising phrase from the American actor Jonathan Goldsmith.

His enthusiasm and captivating talks were always a source of inspiration. I was also impressed by his respectfulness, ability to accept contradiction and listen. His concern to others opinion on different topics was remarkable. He favors smoothly, equal and friendly interactions with people who feel confident, valued and actively participant to the process of knowledge co-construction.

B. "Think outside the box": I still remember the feeling after our fruitful discussions when I enjoyed the benefits of his knowledge and competency. David is a visionary person who believes in creativity, compassion, motivation, optimism, passion, respect and of cause in research on places. I believe these values shape my career and open my horizons in research. I always appreciated his openness to others, simplicity, particularly the way of explaining difficult phenomenon by providing concrete and practical examples rather than making general statements.

C. Leader: David is also active in creating a worldwide community (i.e. Institute for Development Strategies) where people care about research on places, how they perform, and what it needs to be done to make them better. David has made significant and lasting contributions to both research and business worlds. His exceptional qualities attest his ability to gather people around him, inspire and lead them to accomplish things together and build entrepreneurial societies.

Finally, I wish all the best to him and his family as he continues to inspire all of us. I enjoyed every second to talk with David and I can say that he has been my lifetime inspiration.

Acknowledgement This study is sponsored by the LabEx Entreprendre: government-funded through the National Research Agency as part of the "Invest in the Future" program; reference: ANR-10-LABX-11-01.

David B. Audretsch, a Gatekeeper and Globetrotter

Silvio Vismara, Katharine Wirsching, and Jonah Otto

Abstract The authors of this chapter know each other through their connection to their mutual friend, David. They are from Germany, Italy, and the United States. They describe how they got to know David and how he supported them by "opening gates" to research and teaching experiences and much more, always in an international context. Following this, as a paradigmatic example, they focus on a successful international program in which they are all involved, with David.

From Acquaintances, to Colleagues, to Friends (Silvio Vismara)

June 18, 2012. This is when all started. I had met David a few times before, as I attended some of the workshops and conferences where he delivered keynote speeches. However, I organized my first event directly with David on June 2012. The workshop was entitled "Driving innovation. Challenges for US and Europe: Policy, Research and Practices", and we enjoyed the participation of some scholars, policy-makers and practitioners. For the first time in my career, I organized something of interest for the local entrepreneurs, managers, and bank officers. Also, for the first time, I organized a workshop that attracted colleagues from different areas and departments. David was there to "open the gates".

Of course, Erik was there too. Back then, I had known Erik Lehmann for not much more than 1 year. Still, he gave me total trust and invited some of his dearest col-

---

S. Vismara (✉)
University of Bergamo, CCSE – CISAlpino Institute for Comparative Studies in Europe, Bergamo, Italy

Department of Accounting, Corporate Finance and Taxation, University of Ghent (Belgium), Belgium, Italy
e-mail: silvio.vismara@unibg.it

K. Wirsching · J. Otto
University of Augsburg, Chair of Management and Organization, Augsburg, Germany
e-mail: katharine.wirsching@wiwi.uni-augsburg.de; jonah.otto@wiwi.uni-augsburg.de

© Springer Nature Switzerland AG 2019
E. E. Lehmann, M. Keilbach (eds.), *From Industrial Organization to Entrepreneurship*, https://doi.org/10.1007/978-3-030-25237-3_50

leagues and friends from inside and outside academia. This event was the first of many others. Most importantly, it was the beginning of a relationship that would extend in my ways. Soon after the workshop, David and Zoltan Acs invited me to join the editorial board of Small Business Economics: An Entrepreneurship Journal. I was elated. Six years later, I have managed 169 papers submitted to the journal, plus three special issues (one of them is currently open). Later, I was appointed associate editor of two other journals, the Financial Review and the Journal of Technology Transfer, as well as member of the editorial review board of a few other journals. I don't think this would have been possible without David first opening the gates to editorship.

These are only some of the milestones of this journey. Just to give an example, while I am writing, I am in my hotel room in Chicago, back from a dinner with Chiara (my fiancée), David and Joanne (his wife). Zac Rolnik of Now Publishing was there too. Zac is now a friend, like other executives of publishing companies. As editorial team of Small Business Economics, we meet twice each year, one time at the Academy of Management Conference in the United States and one time in a European branch of Springer Nature. David has invited me a couple of times for workshops and seminars in Bloomington, where he works at the School of Public and Environmental Affairs of the Indiana University. These were other opportunities for me to meet colleagues, and I very much look forward to the seminar I will deliver at IU in April, 2019.

It was in these occasions that I met the rest of David's family. My memories go to his sons; Alex picking me up at the Indianapolis airport with his fancy sporty car, to James playing soccer with me on the Venetian walls of Bergamo, to Christopher playing the piano at the gala dinner of a conference in Bloomington. Unfortunately, differently from 4 years ago, this summer we did not really get to watch many soccer matches of the World Cup together. Not a good year for soccer in Italy and in the States. Despite this, like every year, I met David in the States at the Academy and in Bergamo, for the summer school.

Out of the cooperation with Erik, the University of Bergamo and the University of Augsburg established in 2011 the CISAlpino Institute for Comparative Studies in Europe. This has been an important move to formalize and strengthen the cooperation between the two universities. Over the years, we had over one hundred exchange students. Each year, seven students leave Bergamo to study at Augsburg University as Erasmus students, and vice versa. PhD students, young scholars, and colleagues frequently spend a research or a teaching period between the two universities. In a recent institutional visit, the two Rectors agreed on a plan to extend this cooperation to other faculties. Last but not least, together with Indiana University, each year we run a summer school.

David B. Audretsch, a Gatekeeper and Globetrotter 481

How I Grew Up from a Chick to a Pig on His Farm, or: How David Supported My Academic Career (Katharine Wirsching)

I can still remember where and when I first met David Audretsch. Around 10 years ago in 2008, he received an honorary doctoral degree from the University of Augsburg and thus came to visit Augsburg and Erik Lehmann's chair. At this time, I already worked for Erik's chair for 3 years as a scientific student assistant and was involved in the organization of the celebration in honor of David. I want to mention that I cannot write about my relation to David without mentioning and thanking my supervisor and mentor Erik. Without his trust in me and promotion of my abilities, he would have never introduced me to his esteemed colleague and old friend, David. My former colleague Alex Starnecker and I first met Dr. Audretsch in our conference room and Erik introduced us as his chicks – we both planned to start working at Erik's chair as PhD students in 2009. Back then, I was surprised at how open and interested that David was in the two of us. I was expecting a professional expert who had already received several honors and was used to being around only those that were his peers. However, David came with his wife and sons; he talked to us young people and was interested in our ideas and plans for the future. From my perspective today, this interest and openness is typical of David and distinguishes him, but at the time, I just did not expect it.

Some time passed after this first meeting and I think the next time I met David was in 2011, when the T2S Annual Meeting took place in Augsburg. Researchers and practitioners presented their papers and ideas about "Technology Transfer in a Global Economy" and for sure, David as a keynote speaker had a decisive influence on the success of this conference. Our social highlight during this conference was an excursion to the Octoberfest in Munich, where we all enjoyed the Bavarian culture with beer, bratwurst and traditional costumes. As always, David and Joanne were pleasant guests and we had a great time together.

During this time, I worked on my doctoral thesis about family firms, their financial performance and innovation behavior. As David is also active in this field of research, our discussions about this topic have helped me a lot. Not only because David has a good overview of related theories and current empirical studies, but also because his cultural experiences and his knowledge about German curiosities from the perspective of an American who has lived in Germany for a long while, our conversations were inspiring for me. As German family firms are often Mittelstand firms (a special kind of medium-sized companies), we also exchanged views on this topic, which is still today one of the main pillars of our joint Summer School program. One could say that our Summer School program itself is a little bit like a German Mittelstand company, run by a more or less old family, involving several generations of researchers with different backgrounds (some are more economists, some more managers or engineers), and all together are responsible for the success of our sustainable product. Like in smaller companies, we have some experts and everybody has their expertise, but in the end all work together, pull in the same direction and have to be able to trust each other and rely on each other's work. As will be described later, company visits are essential for the program and the transfer of knowledge and thus, we included various types of companies. One company is my husband's employer, Roschmann IDL, a construction and engineering company for individual steel and glass facades all over the world. Especially in the last years, Roschmann's involvement gives multifaceted insights in the German-American trade relations, as they have many customers in the United States and are directly affected by political changes. This collaboration is helpful for the students and I am grateful for the opportunity to use this personal relation, which makes things easier.

Besides my research on family firms, David also influenced my interest for additional topics. As a passionate and field-influencing researcher on entrepreneurship, he aroused my interest in entrepreneurship. I started researching female immigrant entrepreneurship in Germany and during one of our summer school programs, David suggested to write a joint contribution together with Erik (Audretsch, Lehmann & Wirsching 2017). This was my first publication with David Audretsch as a co-author and writing with him was as pleasant as organizing or discussing. This joint work evolved during my summer in Bloomington in 2016. If I had to decide which support from David was most important to my career, his invitation to visit SPEA and work as a visiting scholar and adjunct lecturer will be near the top. As usual in Germany and thanks to Erik, I already taught a lot at Augsburg. However, the opportunity to teach at the School of Public and Environmental Affairs and be part of the academic community there was a wonderful experience. I really enjoyed teaching an undergraduate course in "Public Policy and Economic Development in Europe", having interesting discussions with the students there and having an immersive experience.

Being part of David's Institute for Development Strategies and working together with other research fellows is a delightful opportunity to enlarge my research focus and extend my research network. The fact that David likes to expand his network and always gives impulses for new projects and ideas is very helpful for me and promotes my scientific career. A good example are the workshops at the Indiana University Europe Gateway in Berlin. In 2017 and 2018, a group of around 20 interested researchers from Indiana University and all over Europe met and discussed "Entrepreneurship in Times of Increased Competition" as well as "Entrepreneurship and Reigniting Growth in the European Union". These workshops are valuable because the setting allows for having in-depth discussions, and developing and pushing forward new research ideas. One last thing I would like to mention in this section is that David gave me the chance to work for "Small Business Economics: An Entrepreneurship Journal" as member of the editorial review board as well as a guest editor for a special issue about "Entrepreneurship in Context". I hope that there will be a lot more joint projects in the future; and thus, thanks to all the support and encouragement I have received, I will hopefully be in a position to follow David's spirit and then give something back to a younger generation.

David B. Audretsch, a Gatekeeper and Globetrotter 483

First a Waive, Then the World (Jonah Otto)

I first met David as a graduate student in my early 20's, having no idea who he was, what his academic background was, what classes he taught or who he was collaborating with; nothing. I had already been studying for my Master of Public Affairs (MPA) degree at the School of Public and Environmental Affairs (SPEA) on the Indiana University campus in Bloomington for an entire semester and our paths had never crossed. In fact, even the day I met him it was simply a five second introduction. He was the academic and strategic director of the SPEA International Office, which was where I was interviewing for a placement as a graduate assistant. I had come to SPEA with dreams of 1 day becoming an upper-level administrator in university international relations, and once I realized that the faculty had its own international office, I knew where I wanted to be. After I was granted the position I was quickly ushered past David's office on my "new guy" tour, even though I wouldn't start work there until the next semester. Little did I know that the man I had briefly waived to would drastically alter the course of my life.

It did not take long for me to realize that working with David would not be like any other position I had held before. After 2 weeks of completing random odds-and-ends tasks and projects for the full-time staff, David called me into his office out of the blue. Having never said more than, "hi", to me in passing, his first sentence in our first ever meeting was, "Want to be an author?" Naturally, I was caught off-guard, but recovered quickly enough to stammer, "Uh, sure," and just like that, my research career was born. Unbeknownst to me, David had received positive reports about my early work for his team and subsequently recruited me to edit a chapter of a forthcoming project where he and his colleagues were compiling student reports from a summer study abroad program to form a cohesive book of cases in European public policy and economic development. This would go on to become my first publication and sparked an interest within me for this area of academia.

After completing my MPA degree, a year of which I worked in David's office in conjunction with my studies, I was on the hunt for a position within international relations in the university setting. I had cast my net pretty wide geographically, applying to positions on the east and west coasts of the United States, as well as to everywhere in between and multiple countries abroad. However, David played a key role in keeping me close to home. Under his supervision, the full-time staff of the SPEA International Office had greatly expanded the scope of its international relations responsibilities for the faculty, as well as its corresponding programmatic offerings. To effectively accommodate this growth David supported the creation of a new administrative position, the Assistant Director of International Programs, whose purview was the creation and management of agreements, partnerships and programming for the faculty with institutions, governments and organizations around the globe. With the recommendation of his staff, David vouched for my application and I was quickly brought in to join the team on a permanent basis where I was able to hit the ground running. This incredible opportunity was absolutely foundational to my early professional development. Not only did David help provide the opportunity for me, but he also provided the space for me to make it my own. I was given the freedom, autonomy and respect that I had always desired in a position; where my contributions to strategy were taken seriously while also being held accountable for my decisions. The ability to learn on the fly, be creative and take ownership over projects prepared me for my future in ways that I am still discovering on a continual basis. I owe a great deal of this to David and his staff at SPEA.

Further, David supported my endeavors to expand my responsibilities at SPEA. Having been spurred by my previous experiences in research and supervising student seminar groups with David, I had decided that I wanted to start teaching undergraduate courses. Again, David backed me for the opportunity and I began teaching courses in international economic development and public policy as well as in cultural competency and immersion, which reignited my passion for working with students. During this time the administrative leader of the office, who was also my direct supervisor and a great champion and mentor of mine, became very ill and had to take a substantial period of time away from work. In her absence, David trusted me to operate as an "interim director" of sorts, granting me the chance to take on responsibilities that I wouldn't have normally been in a position to at such a young age. With his confidence, I was representing our office at budget meetings and advocating for our mission to the faculty's top administrators as well as to the alumni advisory council. The experience of teaching and managing international strategy clarified what I wanted for my career; to not only become a international relations officer at a university, but to do so while being an academic that contributes to teaching and research. By putting his faith in me, David helped me to realize my professional aspirations.

The most recent contribution that David has made to my career was to encourage me to leave. He was approached by his close friend and colleague, Prof. Erik Lehmann, to see if it would be ok to gauge my interest in an opportunity with his team at Universität Augsburg in Germany. Having worked on several projects with him during my time at SPEA, Prof. Lehmann wanted me to undertake a PhD program under his supervision back at Augsburg. Having benefitted himself from taking a position in Germany early in his career, as well as understanding that obtaining a PhD was the next step in achieving my professional goals, David encouraged Prof. Lehmann to come to me with the offer. After speaking extensively with David and Prof. Lehmann about pursuing a doctoral degree abroad and about the nuances of moving to a new country, I chose to accept the position; an opportunity which would have never been possible in the first place without David.

In many ways, having the opportunity to get to know David has changed the trajectory not only of my professional career, but also my personal life. Starting by providing me with countless opportunities as a graduate student and young professional, to challenging me to push the boundaries of my comfort zone, David has helped to instill within me a desire to keep learning and growing; to resist settling. Further, his confidence in me has been the source for immeasurable support in my development as an administrator, academic and person as a whole. There is much that I owe to David, but knowing him, I'm sure that he simply wants me to pass it on.

Sharing his Passion for Global Opportunities with Students

For a man that did not even obtain his passport until he was already in his thirties, it is remarkable how much work David has undertaken abroad and how important internationalism has become in many aspects of his professional life. This is very apparent in his prolific amount of research and publications, seemingly all of which have taken a global and comparative tone since his initial posting outside the US as a research fellow and professor at the WZB Berlin Social Science Center in the 1980's. What some might not know is how heavily David has incorporated his interest in internationalization into the student-facing portion of his career. Upon returning to the American Midwest and taking up his current distinguished professorship at the School of Public and Environmental Affairs at Indiana University, he was also appointed as the faculty's Director of Overseas Programs; giving him strategic oversight over study abroad programming for students and members of the faculty. In this capacity, David has collaborated with his close colleagues Erik and Silvio to create what has become a central piece of the international offerings of three institutions: the Summer School.

What started as a dinner and a conversation between friends and colleagues has gone on to become so much more. From its exciting, yet cautious roots, the Summer School program has grown into an expansive endeavor that has brought together two continents, three universities, well over two hundred students and numerous cultures (see Fig. 1).

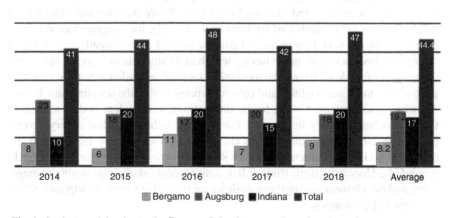

Fig. 1 Student participation to the Summer School program by university and year

With his fellow co-directors, Prof. Silvio Vismara and Prof. Erik Lehmann, the leadership of the program nurtured a formal partnership between Universität Augsburg, Università degli studi di Bergamo and Indiana University that has resulted in an intensive, three-week seminar course that brings together graduate and undergraduate students from all three institutions to work together on group projects that address regional economic development and public policy. The program is designed so that the students not only benefit from hands-on academic training, but they also are able to build invaluable skills in international project management and cross-cultural competence by working in intercultural teams on rigorous research projects. This is ensured by requiring that every group have no more than 50% of its members from just one university.

The Summer School is co-hosted by the Università degli studi di Bergamo and Universität Augsburg, splitting the program duration between the two locations. The content of the seminar is comprised of lectures, guest speakers, site visits and cultural excursions so as to maximize the breadth and depth of experience for the students that attend. Through lectures and talks from various voices and areas of expertise, the students are exposed to the expansive and interdisciplinary nature of economic development and are provided with a theoretical foundation and examples of practical application. By making site visits to smaller, family-run firms as well as large, multinational corporations in the local community, the students learn about the important role of private enterprise in economic development, as well as the benefits of nurturing a diversified regional economy. The cultural excursions teach the valuable, yet often ignored, lesson of context; that the historical and cultural context of a place bears significant implications for regional economies and the public policies that are intended to shape them. At the conclusion of the program, the students formally present their findings to demonstrate what they have learned and show the progress that they have made towards their group papers. They then use the feedback from the presentations to finalize their work.

Aside from the efforts of David and his colleagues, the students of the Summer School have truly been its driving force: providing the demand for such a program, contributing greatly to in-class discussion and giving valuable feedback so that the program can be refined and improved each year. While the Summer School been able to serve a large number of students in total (222), the program has also been popular from the very beginning and has maintained a consistently high level of student interest each year, never having less than 41 students in a given year. While the number of students from each university is significant, what is not shown is that there are far more nationalities and cultures represented in the data than just Italian, American and German. Owing to the internationalized student bodies at each of these universities, every iteration of the Summer School has had a very diverse population. Not only are the students culturally diverse, but they are academically diverse as well. The Indiana University students come from a public affairs background, the Università degli studi di Bergamo students study engineering management, and the Universität Augsburg students are trained in various disciplines within business and economics.

The academic focus of the Summer School revolves around the group projects: consulting-style reports where the students outline an economic development problem within a place (municipality, city, region, etc.) and propose public policy recommendations within the context of strategic management. At the beginning of the course, students arrange themselves into groups of four or five, with the caveat that no more than two group members can come from the same university. This not only ensures that each group has multiple cultural perspectives, but that each group will also have different academic nuances. With the groups being comprised as such, they are instructed to take a multicultural and interdisciplinary approach to their work. Each group selects a place and an issue that is hindering economic development within that place, then they are tasked with combining their own independent research with the lessons learned from the readings, lectures, site visits and cultural excursions to formulate strategic recommendations that policy-makers within that place can use to appropriately manage and improve local economic development. In the first year of the Summer School, the resulting papers were published within a book edited by David and his colleagues: *Globalization and Public Policy: A European Perspective (2015)*.

While typical lectures and assigned readings are essential to providing the students with a theoretical foundation in economic development and the strategic management of places, these methods alone do not sufficiently equip the students to understand best practices, and worst mistakes, that policy makers and economic actors make in regional ecosystems. The best way to be exposed to this type of practical application is to meet local decision makers and see the outcomes of their strategies and policies first-hand. Leveraging the geographic locations of the Summer School and the relationships that have been forged and nurtured by David and his fellow co-directing professors, the students are not only given the opportunity to hear from economic development experts, government officials, corporate executives, socially-minded entrepreneurs and non-governmental organization leaders, but they are often able to visit their work places too. Throughout the years the Summer School has been fortunate to welcome high profile guest speakers (such as the U.S. Consul General of Munich and a former Senior Vice President of American Express Bank) and gain rare access to public sites and private firms (such as KUKA Robotics Corporation, MAN Group, the Bavarian Center for Transatlantic Relations, Roschmann IDL and Weisser Spulenkörper). This wide array of guest speakers and site visits has given the Summer School students an invaluable look at economic development and the strategic management of places in action; living case studies displaying how public-private partnerships and governmental policy and support can lead to economic prosperity. In this manner, the hands-on nature of the Summer School is a crucial component of the student learning process and greatly informs the final products of the student groups.

The final, yet vitally important, components of the Summer School are the cultural excursions. One of the key lessons to be learned in the strategic management of the economic performance of a place is that culture and context matter. It is often the case that a policy solution that works in one place cannot simply be implemented elsewhere without at least some modification, and this is owed to the unique cultural and historical considerations of each place. Cultural excursions are built into the program of the Summer School for this reason; so that students can understand the specific nuances of where they are studying and be able to compare and contrast with the context of their home. This enables the students to dig into the background of a place, identifying root causes of economic and social issues so that they may tailor their policy recommendations in a way that addresses these causes, and doesn't merely put a bandage on the symptoms. The cultural excursions also provide an insight into the preservation, operation, marketing and management of historical and cultural sites, showing how these resources can be included in a local portfolio for economic development.

David and Internationalization: Not Just Programs, but People

As one can see, David has invested a tremendous amount of time and effort into programs such as the Summer School, reflecting the value he sees in internationalization. For David, the Summer School serves as a shining example of his dedication to his students; ensuring that they have affordable access to global experiences that will pay immeasurable dividends to them and those that they come into contact with in the future. However, the students are not the only ones that have been on the receiving end of David's generosity, as is evidenced by the incredible impact that he has had on the lives and careers of the three authors of this chapter. No matter who you are or where you come from, David sees potential and is always willing to lend a hand in your development. He has a way of finding the best in people and maximizing it; not for his own gain, but because he genuinely cares. Having the opportunity to learn and grow in an international context has greatly benefitted David throughout his life and career, and because of the giving person that he is, the opportunities and benefits have not stopped with him but continue to spread.

Reference

Audretsch, D. B., Lehmann, E. E., & Wirsching, K. (2017). Female immigrant entrepreneurship. In A. N. Link (Ed.), *Gender and entrepreneurial activity* (pp. 46–68). Cheltenham: Edward Elgar Publishing.